Survey of Accounting

Custom Seventh Edition

Warren

CENGAGE
Learning·

Australia • Brazil • Japan • Korea • Mexico • Singapore • Spain • United Kingdom • United States

Survey of Accounting, Custom Seventh Edition

Survey of Accounting, 7th Edition
Carl S. Warren

© 2015 Cengage Learning. All rights reserved.

Senior Manager, Student Engagement:

Linda deStefano

Janey Moeller

Manager, Student Engagement:

Julie Dierig

Marketing Manager:

Rachael Kloos

Manager, Production Editorial:

Kim Fry

Manager, Intellectual Property Project Manager:

Brian Methe

Senior Manager, Production and Manufacturing:

Donna M. Brown

Manager, Production:

Terri Daley

For product information and technology assistance, contact us at
Cengage Learning Customer & Sales Support, 1-800-354-9706

For permission to use material from this text or product,
submit all requests online at **cengage.com/permissions**
Further permissions questions can be emailed to
permissionrequest@cengage.com

This book contains select works from existing Cengage Learning resources and was produced by Cengage Learning Custom Solutions for collegiate use. As such, those adopting and/or contributing to this work are responsible for editorial content accuracy, continuity and completeness.

Compilation © 2014 Cengage Learning

ISBN-13: 978-1-305-04659-7

ISBN-10: 1-305-04659-5

WCN: 01-100-101

Cengage Learning

5191 Natorp Boulevard
Mason, Ohio 45040
USA

Cengage Learning is a leading provider of customized learning solutions with office locations around the globe, including Singapore, the United Kingdom, Australia, Mexico, Brazil, and Japan. Locate your local office at:
international.cengage.com/region.

Cengage Learning products are represented in Canada by Nelson Education, Ltd.
For your lifelong learning solutions, visit **www.cengage.com/custom.**
Visit our corporate website at **www.cengage.com.**

Printed in the United States of America

The Start Smart Guide
for students

CENGAGE
Learning™

THE START SMART GUIDE FOR STUDENTS

DIRECTOR OF PROGRAM MANAGEMENT AND
LMS SYSTEMS:
TOM GREGA

PROGRAM MANAGER:
KALLIE SWANSON THOMAS

EXECUTIVE MARKETING MANAGER:
ERIC LA SCOLA

PROJECT MANAGER:
KEN HARLAN

CREATIVE AND INSTRUCTIONAL DESIGNER:
CORE 5

SYSTEM ANALYSTS:
TOM HILT, KEVIN STANEK, ANDREW KIRK

LEAD ENGINEER:
HAROLD HERSEY

ENGINEERING:
CONCENTRIC SKY, EMBEREX, COMPETENTUM

RELEASE MANAGER:
MARK PORTELLI

QUALITY ASSURANCE:
QA INFO TECH

DOCUMENTATION:
CONCENTRIC SKY

SPECIAL THANKS TO:
PAT CALL, WHOSE VISION, SUPPORT, AND
DEDICATION RESULTED IN THE CENGAGENOW
WE HAVE TODAY

For general information about our
products, contact us at:

1-800-423-0563

For permission to use material from
this guide or Cengage Learning
products, submit a request online at:
http://www.cengage.com/
permissions

Any additional questions about
permissions can be submitted by
e-mail to:
permissionrequest@cengage.com

CENGAGE LEARNING
10 DAVIS DRIVE
BELMONT, CA
94002-3098 USA

PDF REV.03 07-28-11

STUDENT QUICK START GUIDE

First Time User Registration

1. Go to
   http://academic.cengage.com/login

2. Under **Students Register Here**, click **Create a new Student Account**.

3. Enter your access code exactly and click **Continue**. (The access code came with your new textbook, or you may have purchased it at the bookstore or online.)

   If redirected to CengageNOW, please follow the instructions you find there instead of this guide.

4. Enter your account information, accept the License Agreement, confirm your age, and click **Continue**. (Be sure to make note of your email and password.)

5. Indicate if your school is U.S. or International, and then use the **Search** tools to list your school.

6. Select your school on the **Search** results list and click **Register**.

   Your **CengageBrain My Home** page opens.

7. To go to CengageNOW, click **Open** under **My Courses & Materials**.

   The CengageNOW **Courses** page opens.

8. If your instructor has provided you with a **Course Key**, enter it in the **Instructor-Led Course** input box and click **Submit**.

Returning User Sign-In

1. Go to
   http://academic.cengage.com/login

2. Under **Returning Users**, enter your email address and password exactly and click **Sign In**.

3. On your **My Home** page, click **Open** under **My Courses & Materials**.

Registering New Materials

1. Sign in to your **CengageBrain My Home** page (if necessary, sign out of CengageNOW to do so).

2. Under **Add another title to your bookshelf**, enter the **Content Access Code** exactly.

3. Click the **Go** button.

4. The **Congratulations!** message indicates your book is registered.

Self-Study

You can use your CengageNOW materials for self-study (outside of a course assignment).

1. Sign in to CengageNOW and click the **Study Tools** tab.

2. Select your book's title from the **Textbook** menu and click **Go**.

3. Next, choose the appropriate course material and click **Go**.

Technical Support

Get FAQs, chat, or email support at
http://academic.cengage.com/
support

CengageNOW System Requirements

To ensure the best experience with CengageNOW and enjoy all of its features, please make sure your computer system and browser settings meet or surpass the specifications and settings on this page. Use the enclosed links to download any of the recommended browser and "plug-in" software you may need.

Windows®

- Microsoft® Windows 2000, Windows XP, Windows Vista, Windows 7
- Intel® or AMD® CPU, 266MHz or better
- 128 MB RAM or more
- Web browsers: Microsoft® Internet Explorer 6.0-8.0; Google Chrome 9.0; Mozilla™ Firefox® 2.0 or higher
- Java JRE 1.5/5.0 or higher recommended (http://java.com)

Macintosh®

- Mac OS® X 10.3–10.x and greater
- Power Mac® G3 or better
- 128 MB of RAM or more
- Web browser: Safari™ 3.0 or higher; Mozilla™ Firefox® 2.0.0.1 or higher

Linux®

- Current Linux distribution (Fedora™, SuSE®, etc.)
- Intel or AMD CPU at 266MHz or better
- 128MB RAM or more
- Web browser: Mozilla™ Firefox® 2.0 or higher
- Java JRE 1.5/5.0 or higher recommended (from http://java.com)

Additional Requirements (All Systems)

- Adobe® Flash® Player (download from http://www.adobe.com/products/flashplayer/)
- Adobe® Reader® (download from http://www.adobe.com/products/acrobat/readstep2.html)
- Screen resolution of 800 x 600 or higher, and color quality of 16-bit or higher
- Internet connection speed of 56k or higher
- Popup-blocking software turned off or configured to allow **http://*.cengagenow.com** to display popup windows
- Browser set to check for newer versions of cached pages and refresh automatically.
- Apple® QuickTime® player, RealPlayer®, and Adobe Shockwave® player (These free browser plug-ins are used to display multimedia components in some products.)
- Sound card for audio content

CONTENTS

As a live, Web-based program, CengageNOW is regularly updated with new features and improvements. Please refer to the CengageNOW online Help for the most current information.

Contents

GETTING STARTED

Welcome to CengageNOW™, the integrated, online learning system that gives you 24/7 access to your course assignments and Study Tools. Working at your own pace, or within a schedule set up by your instructor, you can now do homework, read textbooks, take quizzes and exams, and track your grades. CengageNOW provides an easy-to-use, personalized online environment that you can manage to best suit your needs.

Note: As a live, web-based program, CengageNOW is updated regularly with new features and improvements. Please refer to the CengageNOW online Help for the most current information.

Registering as a New User

Are you new to CengageNOW? If you've never used CengageNOW before, or if you're using it for the first time from a new school, there are two codes you will need to use before accessing your online content.

- ○ The first code is bundled with new textbooks. The CengageNOW **Content Access Code** comes with your new textbook, or you may have purchased it at the bookstore or online. This code allows you to create a user account with Cengage Learning.

- ○ The second code is a **Course Key** that your instructor will provide. With this code you can register into a specific course within CengageNOW.

➢ **To register as a new user**

1. Connect to the Internet and go to:
   http://login.cengagebrain.com

2. Under **Create a New Account**, click the **Create an Account** button.

   The **Enter Code or Course Key** page will open.

---

3. Enter your CengageNOW access code and click the **Continue** button. The **Account Information** page will open.

Entering an Access Code

Note: Some access codes may redirect you to CengageNOW to register. If you are redirected, please follow the instructions, Help, and Start Smart Guide you find there instead of this guide.

---

4. Enter your personal account information, password, time zone, and select a security question/answer.

5. Select **I Agree** for the **License Agreement**, confirm your age, indicate your message preferences.

6. Click the **Continue** button when you have completed the form.

   The **Select Your Institution** page will open.

Note: Be sure to make note of the email address and password you use when creating your account. You will need this information later, when signing in.

---

7. Choose a location from the drop-down menu to indicate if your school is a U.S. or International institution. Your selection will open additional fields to help you find your school.

8. Select the appropriate search criteria and other pertinent information:

   - Select the institution type.

   - Select a distance range to search from the zip code or city nearest your school.

   - Enter either the zip code or state and city where your school is located.

9. Click the **Search** button to list matching institutions.

10. Select your school if it is listed and click **Continue**.

Note: If you do not see your school, you can click **Search Again** to return to the **Select Your Institution** page.

The **CengageBrain Log In** page opens.

11. To continue to your CengageNOW course, enter your email address as your **Username** and your **Password**.

12. Click **Log In** and your CengageBrain **My Home** page will open.

The CengageBrain My Home Page

13. Click the appropriate **Open** button under **My Courses & Materials** and the **New CengageNOW Account** page will open.

14. Verify the correct institution is listed and click **Continue**.

Your CengageNOW **Courses** page will open.

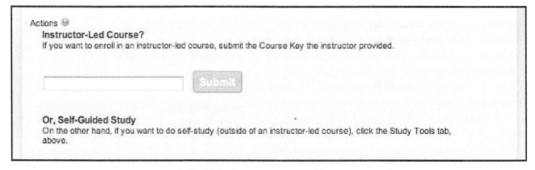

Initial Course Enrollment

15. Enter the **Course Key** provided by your instructor in the **Instructor-Led Course** input box and click **Submit**.

Next you should see a confirmation message, letting you know you have successfully enrolled. Your **Assignments** page should now be displaying test and homework information.

Signing In as a Returning User

Once you've registered for CengageNOW, you can sign in as a returning user from any place you have Internet access.

➤ **To sign in to CengageNOW**

1. Go to http://login.cengage.com/cb/

2. Under **Returning Users**, enter your email address and password exactly as you entered them when you created your account, and then click **Sign In**.

3. On the **CengageBrain My Home** page, click **Open** under **My Courses & Materials** to access your course assignments and Study Tools.

➤ **To use your registered CengageNOW book for self-study**

1. Sign in to CengageNOW.

2. Click the **Study Tools** tab.

3. Find the title of the desired book in the **Textbook** dropdown menu.

4. Select the appropriate title and click **Go**. The page will refresh and display links to the available book resources.

5. Choose the content you would like to access and click the adjacent **Go** button.

> **Note:** Course assignments taken from the **Assignments** page are graded CengageNOW coursework.
>
> Work completed in the **Study Tools** area, however, is typically ungraded practice or self-study.

➤ To register for an additional course

1. Sign in to CengageNOW.

2. On the **Courses** page, click **Register for Another Course**.

3. Enter the **Course Key** provided by your instructor in the input box and click **Use This Course Key**.

System Setup for CengageNOW

Once you are signed in, you can use the **Run System Check** tool to evaluate your browser and plug-in settings in detail. A link to the CengageNOW System Check is located in the **Tools** menu at the top of most pages. If you should need to make any updates, you will be notified. You can then click the help icon (💿) in **Results** to see detailed instructions for downloading browser plug-ins.

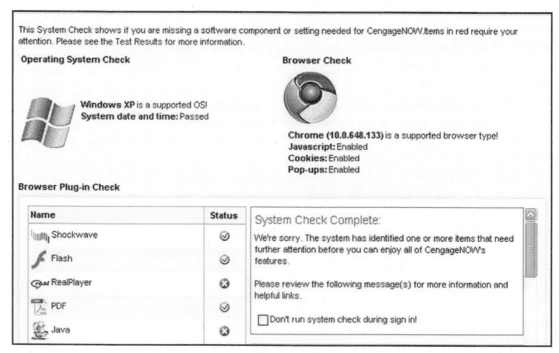

The CengageNOW System Check

Note: You can also refer to the "CengageNOW System Requirements" on page iv for additional information on configuring your computer for CengageNOW.

Using the Header Links and Page Tabs

The header links and page tabs appear at the top of nearly every page in CengageNOW. The header links provide several tools that you may find useful.

Tools

Use this link to access the **System Check** and the **Math/Graphing Tool**.

The **Math/Graphing Tool** contains several helpful utilities you can use, including a scientific calculator, a math glossary, a shapes library, and graphing tools.

The **Run System Check** tool verifies that your system and browser settings conform to the CengageNOW system requirements.

Help

Use this link to open the CengageNOW online help with the table of contents, index, and search functions enabled.

Sign Out

Use this link to sign out of your current CengageNOW session.

Note: For technical support, please use the **Technical Support** link in the page footer.

Click the page tabs below the header links to navigate to the following pages:

Courses

From this page you initially register for your new course. Once you are registered, the Courses page displays your instructor(s) and your overall grade for all of your CengageNOW courses. In the **Go To** column there are buttons which are links to pages where you can view your assignments, grades, and the syllabus specific to each course.

Grades

The **Grades** page allows you easily keep track of your grades, with sorting options for organizing the view of your assignments and courses. These multiple views help you monitor your progress in self-study materials and find specific grades quickly.

Assignments

The **Assignments** page allows you to **Take** an assignment, or **Retake** or **Resume** an assignment (if your instructor permits it). You can list your assignments in several ways, including looking at a particular course or at all your assignments or just those that are available for you to take right now. The page shows the assignment **Date Due**, **Actions** you can perform, **# of Submissions**, **# of Submissions Allowed**, **Time Allowed**, **Notes**, and your **Score** for completed and partially completed assignments such as tests and homework.

Study Tools

The **Study Tools** page displays all of your registered self-study materials in CengageNOW such as eBooks, Tutorial books, and Personalized Study books.

Work that you access and complete on the **Study Tools** page is for ungraded self-study only. Your progress is tracked in your Grades page and your instructor's Gradebook, but your work is separate from your course assignments.

PowerSearch

You may see a **PowerSearch** tab if your school library subscribes to the PowerSearch service. **PowerSearch** allows students and instructors to access a wide range of periodical, reference, and source information over multiple databases.

Signing Out

When you are done accessing your personal CengageNOW pages and assignments, be sure to click the **Sign Out** link in the page header to close the current session properly.

Note: Always use the provided CengageNOW buttons and links to close assignments or go to another page. Do not use your browser's **Close** button or **Back/Forward** buttons; this could cause you to lose unsaved work.

VIEWING YOUR SYLLABUS

Your instructor may have set up a syllabus page or document to relate important information about your class such as the start and end dates, your instructor's office hours, or contact information. A syllabus may also include a short description of the class, its objectives, and any prerequisites.

If there is a syllabus linked to your course, you will see a **Syllabus** button on the **Courses** tab in the **Go To** column. To view the syllabus for that course, you can click either the **Syllabus** button or the course name.

USING THE COURSES PAGE

The **Courses** page, gives you a quick view of all your CengageNOW courses. From here, you can get access to your assignments, syllabus, and grades. You are also able to register for new or additional courses from this page.

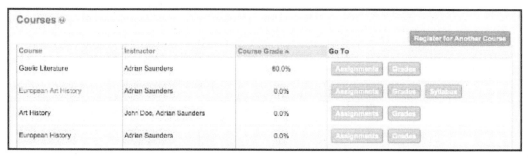

The Courses Page

Sorting

Click a column title (or "header") for **Course**, **Instructor**, or **Course Grade** to sort the table by that column heading. To reverse the list order using that column, click its header again. The arrow icon in the header shows if that column's sort order is ascending (A-Z) or descending (Z-A).

Course Grade

Displays your total percentage score, to date, for your assignments for this class. (This score excludes any assignment results your instructor has chosen not to display, has not yet graded, or is not viewable for other reasons.)

Go To column

From the **Go To** column, you can quickly access current course information and pending tasks in other areas of CengageNOW by using the buttons provided. You can easily go to the **Assignments** page, the **Grades** pages, and the course **Syllabus** (if available).

Register for Another Course

Click **Register for Another Course** to enroll in an additional courses by entering a **Course Key**. Instructor will usually supply this code via email, in the syllabus, or during your first class.

WORKING WITH ASSIGNMENTS

Your instructor creates and assigns activities which you can access from the **Assignments** page. These activities can include all assignment types, from graded tests to practice homework, and from reading to Study Tools to external WebQuizzes.

CengageNOW is able to grade most of your assignments electronically, it tracks your progress, and then reports your scores to your instructor. Assignment content can range from simple lists of multiple-choice questions, to complex equations or multi-entry forms, to reading an eBook chapter or Web page, depending on the course, subject, and textbook content.

Some assignments offer hints or multimedia examples to help guide you in developing your answers. Others may include personalized, interactive learning plans that are determined by diagnostic pre-test results.

Understanding the Assignments Page

Select the **Assignments** tab to open the **Assignments** page where you can take, print, and see the status of your assignments.

Above the columns are two assignment view selectors:

Course or Section

Use this drop-down menu to organize the view for assignments in any of your courses. You can choose between **All My Courses(Merged)**, **All My Courses (Separated)**, or view assignments for a specific course or section only. Once you have selected the view you want, click the adjacent **Go** button.

Show me: All Assignments | Assignments I Can Take Now

Click on the appropriate link to view all of your assignments, or view only those that are currently available for you to take.

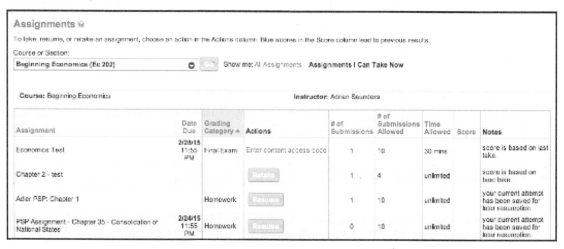

The Assignments Page

The **Assignments** page provides your available assignment actions, and can display your current score and remaining attempts.

Note: The availability of particular actions and information for an assignment depends on the assignment's type, its current status, and the settings chosen by your instructor.

Assignment

The assignment name.

Date Due

The last day you can submit the assignment. You may be able to submit a late assignment, but your instructor can assign a penalty.

Grading Category

Here you can see the grading category for a particular assignment. If an assignment is placed in a grading category, it will determine how much impact your grade in a particular assignment can have on your total grade.

Any grading categories and how they are weighted are established by your instructor. This column will appear only when your instructor uses this feature.

Actions

Use the buttons and links in the **Actions** column to manage and access your assignments. The availability of the particular action or information depends on the assignment's type, its current status, and the settings chosen by your instructor.

Take. [Take] Begin taking an assignment.

Retake. [Retake] Retake a previously completed assignment.

Resume. [Resume] Continue taking an unfinished assignment.

Note: An assignment may no longer be available to **Take**, **Retake**, or **Resume** if its Date Due has passed or you have already taken it the allowed number of times.

Available on: Displays the date when this assignment is first available. You can only see this information if you have selected the option to view **All My Assignments**.

Password. password: [   ] Enter the password your instructor has required to take this assignment.

Print blank assignment. [Print blank assignment] Print the assignment before taking it. This option, when available, allows you to work through the assignment on paper before entering answers online.

Print. [Print] Print the completed assignment. This option allows you to print out your assignment results and related feedback for a completed assignment (if allowed by your instructor).

Enter Content Access Code. |Enter content access code If this link is available, you need to register the Content Access Code while logged into your **CengageBrain** account before you can gain access to the online book content required for your assignment. See "Registering Additional Study Materials" on page 37.

Closed. "Closed" means you can no longer take the assignment. Its unavailable date may have passed, or the instructor may have graded it already, or it may have a late penalty that would lower your current score.

of Submissions

Here you can see how many times you've submitted an assignment for grading. (Not all assignments allow multiple attempts.)

of Submissions Allowed

Here you can see how many more times you can submit an assignment. (Not all assignments allow multiple attempts.)

Time Allowed

Here you can see how much time your instructor is allowing to take an assignment, or if there is unlimited time.

Score

For completed assignments, this column shows your current score as a percentage (if made viewable by the instructor). To see related feedback on a completed assignment click the score to go to the **View Assignment Results** page.

Notes

Here you can see information on the status of your score, any available extra credit, and how your grade is calculated when you have the option for multiple takes.

Taking a Personalized Study Assignment

Personalized Study products are learning tools that evaluate your knowledge and then help you gauge your unique study needs. The **Personalized Study Plan** they provide focuses your study time on the key concepts and problems you most need to learn.

Your work on a Personalized Study assignment is graded only when you access it from the **Assignments** tab (even if you can also access it from the **Study Tools** tab for self-study).

Typically, a Personalized Study assignment consists of a **Pre-Test**, a **Personalized Study Plan**, and a **Post-Test**.

First, you will take a **Pre-Test** and then be provided with an interactive, personalized study plan based on your results. These study plans vary from one discipline to another, but typically include tutorials, interactive exercises, videos, animations, figures, and other on-line learning materials drawn from your text.

After you have worked through the personalized study plan, you can take a **Post-Test**. The Post-Test will assess your progress, and then provide you with additional, revised study materials to help you focus on areas where you need to improve.

When Study Tools are given as an assignment, your instructor may choose to score the **Pre-Test**, exclude the **Pre-Test** or **Post-Test** from the assignment, or allow access to these sections only as graded assignments (so you can't access them from **Study Tools**, in other words).

Caution: Be sure to complete all sections of your Personalized Study assignment before you submit it for grading.

> ➢ **To take a Personalized Study assignment for credit**

1. Click the **Assignments** tab.

   The **Assignments** page opens.

2. Select the appropriate course, if necessary, from the **Course or Section** drop-down menu and click the adjacent **Go** button.

3. Click the **Take** button for the available assignment you want to start. If a password is required, enter it into the **password** field.

   Click the **Retake** button to start an assignment you have taken previously. (Not all assignments allow multiple tries.)

   Click the **Resume** button to continue an assignment that you have previously saved in progress. (Not all assignments can be saved in progress.)

   Note: An assignment may no longer be available to **Take**, **Retake**, or **Resume** if its Date Due has passed or you have already taken it the allowed number of times.

   ---

4. The **Assignment Ready** page opens. (If this try is subject to a late penalty, the penalty will be noted here.)

Your assignment, Adler PSP: Chapter 1, is ready. ⊚

Please Note

- This will be a continuation of your 2nd take of this assignment. You are limited to 10 takes of this assignment.
- The work you completed earlier will reappear when you enter the assignment.
- If your computer loses its connection to the server during this take, you will be able to resume if you return to the assignment within a few minutes.
- Because of an option prescribed by your instructor, when you start this assignment, you will see all correct answers from your previous take carried forward into this new take.

[Cancel] [Resume Assignment Now]

The Assignment Ready Page

5. To exit without starting the assignment, click **Cancel**. If you cancel at this point, the try will not be counted.

To begin taking the assignment, click the **Start Assignment Now** button. (Depending on the status of your assignment, this button can be labeled **Resume Assignment Now** or **Retake Assignment Now**.)

Your Personalized Study assignment loads. It typically includes a **Pre-Test**, a **Personalized Study Plan**, and a **Post-Test**.

6. To start your **Pre-Test**, click the **Pre-Test** link in the middle or on the left side of the screen.

Note: Some books may label these sections differently.

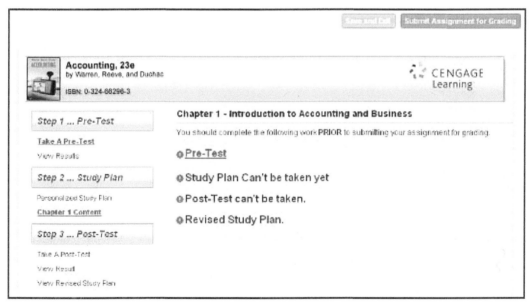

Starting a Personalized Study Assignment

7. Move through the questions with the **<< Previous** and **Next >>** links, or select them by question number from the drop-down list.

8. Select your answer to the question, and then click the **Enter Answer** button. You can return to previous questions and change answers, if needed.

Some questions offer **Hints** or **Show Additional Info** as well. Questions with multiple answers may provide a **Clear All** link to let you start that question over.

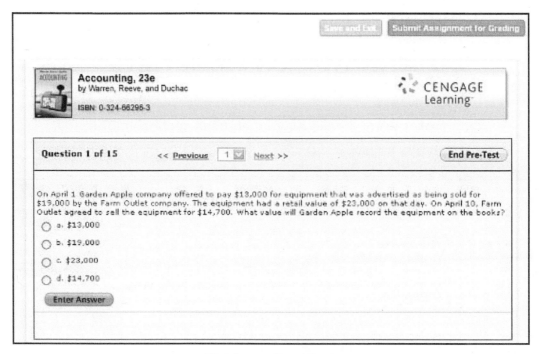

Taking a Pre-Test

9. When you have answered all the questions, finish the **Pre-Test** by clicking the **End Pre-Test** button.

A summary screen appears with your **Pre-Test** results. It highlights your scores on particular topics and selects chapter sections for your further study.

Caution: If you see a **Save & Exit** button, you can save the assignment in progress and resume work on it later as part of the same try. If you don't have this button, however, be sure to complete *all* available sections of the assignment before you click **Submit Assignment for Grading**.

---

10. To access your study plan, click the **Personalized Study Plan** link in the middle or on the left side of the screen, or a **View Results** topic link. Your study plan may link to a variety of learning materials, including videos, textbook PDFs, simulations, web sites, and lecture outlines. As you work through the linked materials and examples, your progress through each section will be checked off.

Personalized Study Plan

11. After you have studied the assigned sections of your Study Plan thoroughly and checked them off, you will take the **Post-Test** to demonstrate your command of the material. Click on the **Post-Test** link in the middle or on the left side of the page.

Your **Post-Test** appears.

12. Navigate between questions with the **<< Previous** and **Next >>** links, or select a question number from the drop-down list.

13. Select your answer to the question, and then click the **Enter Answer** button. You can return to previous questions and change answers, if needed.

WARNING: *Use only the CengageNOW buttons to end the assignment. If you just close your browser window, your assignment will be submitted and graded "as is."*

---

14. When you are finished, click on the **End Post-Test** button to see your score summary.

Your test results appear, showing what you've learned after working through the **Personalized Study Plan**.

15. If your **Post-Test** reveals any areas of the chapter where you could use additional study time, you will receive a **Revised Study Plan**. This is considered part of the assignment. You should complete it before submitting the assignment for grading.

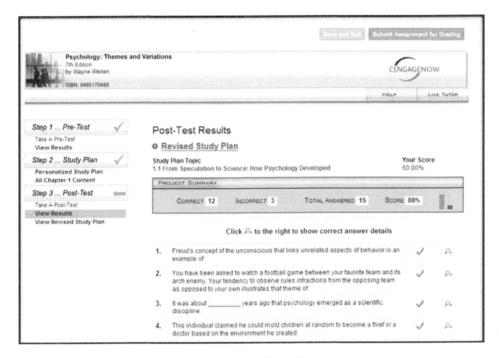

Post-Test Results

16. When you are completely finished with all sections of the assignment, click the **Submit Assignment for Grading** button.

The **Submit Assignment for Grading** message asks you to confirm that you are finished with the assignment and ready to turn it in.

17. To confirm that you want to submit your assignment and exit, click **Submit for Grading**.

Caution: Each time you click **Submit for Grading** to finish the assignment counts as one try.

Taking a WebQuiz

Instructors can set up "external" assignments to track your work on a variety of activities outside of CengageNOW. The most common type of external assignment is the WebQuiz.

A WebQuiz can behave much like a regular assignment when you take it from the **Assignments** page. In some circumstances you can take a WebQuiz without signing into CengageNOW.

Note: If a WebQuiz session is left inactive for more than 60 minutes, the session will expire without saving your answers.

➢ To take a WebQuiz

1. Click **Take** to start it, **Retake** or **Resume** to take it again.

   The **WebQuiz Ready** page opens.

   Note: Alternatively, your instructor may simply provide you with the WebQuiz URL (web address). If so, you can click the WebQuiz link or enter its URL directly into your browser address box to start it.

   ---

2. Click the **Start Assignment Now** button, and then click the **CLICK HERE TO BEGIN** link.

3. If the options are available, choose between the **display all questions on one page** or **one at a time** display options.

   Note: It is recommended that you select to display your questions **one at a time**, otherwise you will not be able to see any available feedback.

   ---

4. Click the **Start Assignment Now** button and your WebQuiz will open in a new browser window.

---

5. Depending on the question display option you selected, you use **Enter Answer** to submit and save your answers. If you want to clear all of your current answers and begin again, you can click **Start over**.

   If you are viewing your questions **one at a time**, you will need to click the **Enter Answer** button to save your work before proceeding to the next question.

   Note: If you initially selected to **display all questions on one page**, clicking **Enter Answer** submits all your answers and takes you a new page with two links:

   Continue working on the quiz. Allows you to resume your WebQuiz with your answers preserved and also displays feedback on the questions you answered.

   End quiz and view summary. Takes you to the **Summary of Results** page and ends the current session.

   ---

6. When you have answered all the questions and you are ready to end the WebQuiz, click the **Review** button or the **End quiz and view summary** link.

   The **Summary of Results** page opens and your WebQuiz will close.

7. Fill in the required fields and click the **Send Email** button to send the test results to your instructor.

8. Close your browser window or tab to return to the previous page. If you started the WebQuiz from the **Assignments** page, you will also need to click the **Submit Assignment** or **Submit Assignment for Grading** button to finalize your assignment and go to the **Assignment Finished** page.

9. Click OK in the confirmation window and the **Assignment Finished** page will open. From this page you can choose to **Take This Assignment Again** or **Go Back to the Assignments Page**.

Taking a Homework, Test, or Reading Assignment

These instructions show you how to go about taking a homework, test, or reading assignment. In summary, you can make sure you get full credit for your work by always doing the following:

○ Complete and submit the assignment before its Date Due and Time Allowed.

○ Read the on-screen instructions carefully.

○ Take advantage of the **Check My Work** link for questions that provide it. This checks your current answer, and will give you helpful feedback that allows you to improve your answer before you are graded.

○ Click the Submit Assignment for Grading button only when you are completely finished with the assignment. Each time you submit an assignment for grading it is counted as one "take" (not all assignments will allow multiple takes).

○ Click the **Save** button every so often, particularly on long, multi-part questions. Your progress is saved each time you move to a new question or use the **Check My Work** link. Even so, saving your work manually ensures you won't lose much work on the current question in the event of a computer problem

---

Note: During an assignment, never close your browser, go to another site, or use your browser's forward and back buttons— you may lose your current work, and the assignment will be counted as a "take." Use only the navigation buttons and links within CengageNOW. Be sure each page loads completely before proceeding.

➤ **To take an assignment**

1. Select the **Assignments** tab.

   The **Assignments** page opens.

2. If necessary, select the appropriate course from the drop-down list and click the **Go** button.

   Note: If you access CengageNOW assignments through eCollege® or Blackboard®, these steps will be different. Please refer to the user guides for those products.

   ---

3. Click on the **Take** button [Take] for the available assignment you want to start taking. If a password is required, enter it into the **password:** field.

   Click on the **Retake** button [Retake] to start an assignment you have taken previously. (Not all assignments allow multiple tries.)

   Click on the **Resume** button [Resume] to continue an assignment that you have previously saved in progress. (Not all assignments can be saved in progress.)

   Note: An assignment may no longer be available to **Take**, **Retake**, or **Resume** if its Date Due has passed or you have already taken it the allowed number of times.

   ---

4. The **Assignment Ready** page opens. This page tells you how many times you have taken this assignment or test, how many "takes" you have available, and the time limit (if any) for completing the take.

   Graded assignments will describe any special scoring conditions or late penalty in effect on this take. Assignments labeled **(Practice)** are not graded.

Your assignment, Chapter 2, is ready.

Please Note

- This will be a continuation of your 1st take of this assignment. You are limted to 6 takes of this assignment.
- This assignment is due at 11:55 PM on Mar 24, 2015.
- Correct responses from your previous take have been copied into this take.
- If your computer loses its connection to the server during this take, you will be able to resume if you return to the assignment within a few minutes.
- Because of an option prescribed by your instructor, when you start this assignment, you will see all correct answers from your previous take carried forward into this new take.

Cancel   Resume Assignment Now

The Assignment Start Page

5. To exit without starting the assignment, click **Cancel**. If you cancel at this point, the try will not be counted.

To begin taking an assignment for the first time, click the **Start Assignment Now** button. If you are continuing an assignment, the button is labeled **Resume Assignment Now**.

Your assignment or test appears. If the assignment has a time limit, the **Time Remaining** is displayed right under the assignment title.

6. Read each question carefully, and answer as directed.

The **Questions** column on the left marks your progress with the following status indicators:

- **Not Answered** ○ . - A question you have not answered or viewed (or the question you are currently viewing).

- **Not Intended for a Grade** ⊘ . - A question that will not have an impact on your assignment score.

- **Visited, Not Yet Judged** ● . - A question you have viewed. This icon will appear whether or not you have provided an answer or saved your work.

You can also mouse over a question number to open a text "tool tip" about that question's status.

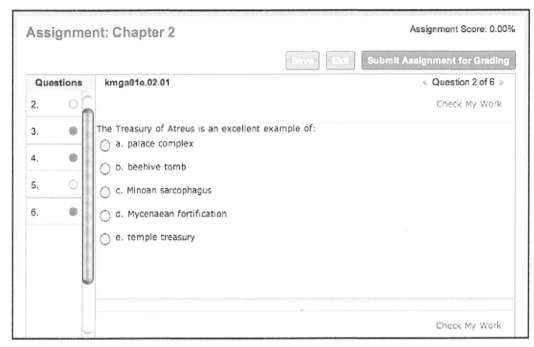

The Take Assignment Page

Questions can appear in a variety of formats. For multiple choice and true/false questions, you select a choice from a list. For other question formats, you may need to enter multiple answers, type short essay responses, use graph or equation editors, or link matching items with your mouse.

Some questions offer links for **Check My Work**, **Hints**, or **Show Additional Info** as well. Questions with multiple answers may provide a **Clear All** link to let you start that question over. You also might have assignments that include no questions, but simply track your reading of your online textbook or other materials.

Note: Assignments that start with a **Pre-Test** are called **Personalized Study** or "study tools" assignments. They work a little differently. See "Taking a Personalized Study Assignment" on page 15 for details.

---

7. Any work on the current question will be saved when you click the **Save** button or go to another question. Be sure to save your progress on long questions, and follow up on partial answers before submitting the assignment.

8. For questions that provide it, be sure to click the Check My Work link to provide feedback and evaluate the correctness of your current answer. This will allow you to improve your answer on that question before you submit the assignment for grading. Standard feedback can include the following:

- **Correct** ⊘.

- **Partially Correct** ⊘. The answer has one or more elements that are incomplete or incorrect.

- **Incorrect** ⊗.

- **Needs Instructor Grading** ❗. The answer you entered must be evaluated by your instructor.

9. If your instructor has enabled it, clicking **Check My Work** can also display a collapsible feedback window. This window tells you if your answer is "correct," "partially correct," or "incorrect" in addition to additional feedback or the solution, as determined by your instructor.

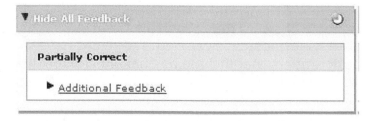

Collapsible Feedback Window

Click the arrow icons to collapse or expand either the entire window or individual feedback sections.

10. To go to a new question, just click its question number on the left, or use the arrow controls in the header to go to the previous question or the next question in the sequence.

You can work through the questions in any order. This makes it easy to answer skipped questions and change your previous answers before submitting the assignment for grading.

Assignments with a time limit will show the **Time Remaining** at the upper left. This indicator turns red to warn you when less than one minute remains.

Assignments that provide a running score will display it in the upper right and will update after each answer.

11. If the assignment allows it, you can click the **Exit** button then select the option to **Save and Exit**. You are able to then finish your work in a later session. You can then **Resume** your assignment as long as you take it before its Date Due.

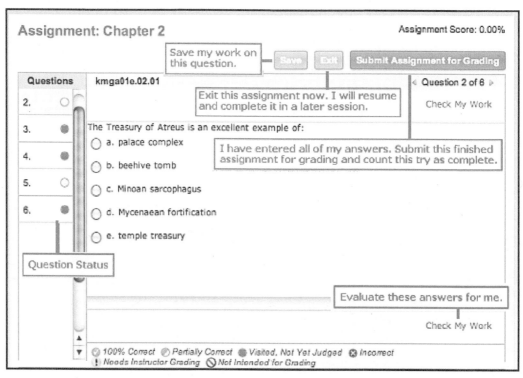

Entering answers, submitting assignments

12. When you are completely finished with all sections of the assignment, click the **Submit Assignment for Grading** button (labeled **Submit Assignment** for Practice work).

The **Submit Assignment for Grading?** message window opens to confirm that you are ready to turn in the assignment. It also will caution you if any answers are still incomplete and give you an option to continue the assignment.

13. To confirm you want to submit your assignment for grading and exit, click the **Submit for Grading** button.

Caution: Each time you click **Submit Assignment for Grading**, you consume one of your available tries. Many assignments are set up to allow only one try.

---

14. The **Assignment Finished** page opens to give you several options for your next step. Depending on the assignment settings, you may be able to click **View Assignment Results** to review your answers, **Take This Assignment Again**, **Go Back to the Assignments List**, or **Print This Take of This Submission** with your answers if allowed by your instructor.

Assignment Finished ☉

Your assignment, Chapter 1, has been submitted to your instructor.

You scored: **0.00%** on this assignment take.

You have taken this assignment **1 time**. You are not limited in the number of times you can take this assignment.

What would you like to do next?

- Take This Assignment Again
- View Assignment Results
- Print Assignment Results
- Go Back to the Assignments List

The Assignment Finished Page

Note: If this submission was subject to a late penalty, you will see the penalty reflected in your score.

TRACKING YOUR GRADES

From the **Grades** page, you can keep track of your grades with a variety of sorting options that help you find specific grade information quickly. In addition to clicking on the **Grades** tab, you can access your grades from the **Courses** page by clicking the **Grades** button for a specific course in the **Go To** column.

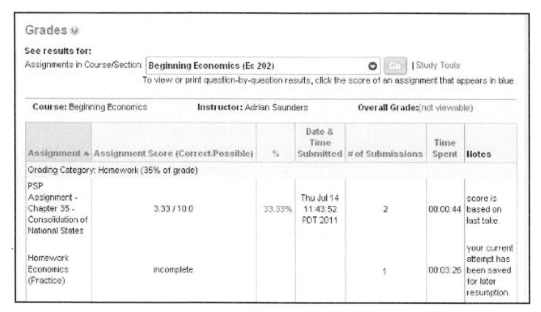

The Grades Page: Assignments in Course/Section

You can change how you view your grades by clicking the **See results for: Assignments in Course/Section** selector just above the **Grades** table. In addition to providing information for your graded assignments, this view allows you to use the drop-down menu to choose how courses and sections are displayed in the Grades list.

All My Courses(Merged)

This view lists your grades for all your CengageNOW courses. Each of the courses and the related assignments are merged into one table. You can use the headings to sort the information in the columns in ascending or descending order.

All My Courses(Separated)

This view lists your grades for all your CengageNOW courses. Each of the courses and the related assignments are listed in their own individual table.

Selecting a specific course or section

Choosing a specific course or section lists your grades for a single course/section only. You can use the drop-down menu again to make a different selection.

The table in the **Assignments in Course/Section** view provides the following information on your graded course assignments:

○ **Course** The name of the course for this assignment.

○ **Instructor** The name of the instructor for the course.

○ **Overall Grade** Your grade displayed both as a percentage of the highest possible score and total points earned/total points possible. If for some reason your grade is not available, you will see the message **(not viewable)**.

Note: Information for **Instructor** and **Overall Grade** are not displayed if you have selected to view your grades as **All My Courses(Merged)**.

○ **Assignment**. The assignment name.

○ **Assignment Score (Correct/Possible)**. The points for your correct answers and the highest possible score for submitted assignments. For assignments that are not yet graded, you can also see your assignment status such as **not taken**, **incomplete**, or **taken(not graded)**.

○ **%**. Your score expressed as a percentage of the highest possible score. (This grade excludes any assignment results your instructor has chosen not to display.) Clicking on a score that is an active link takes you to the **View Assignment Results** page.

Note: The availability of your assignment scores can depend on the status of manual grading or how your instructor set up the assignment options.

- ○ **Date & Time Submitted**. The date and time of your most recent submission.

- ○ **# of Submissions**. The number of times you have submitted the assignment for grading (for assignments that allow multiple attempts).

- ○ **Time Spent**. The time you spent to complete your most recent submission.

- ○ **Notes**. Details on the status of your assignment and how your grade is calculated (if the assignment is currently graded).

Grades ⊚

See results for:
Assignments in Course/Section | Study Tools

The Study Tools gradebook tracks the work you do when you are on the "Study Tools" tab.

Book	Study Tool	Chapter	Score	Date & Time Last Submitted	# of Submissions	Time Spent(Most Recent Submission) ▲
Adler: World Civilizations, 4e	Personalized Study Book	2 Mesopotamia	75.00%	7/14/11 11:59 AM	1	00:03:25
Adler: World Civilizations, 4e	Personalized Study Book	19 The European Middle Ages	0.00%		1	00:01:54

The Grades Page: Study Tools View

Click the See Results for: Study Tools link to open a Grades page that displays details and progress for any content you have worked on while on the Study Tools page. This information includes the type of study tool, dates, number of submissions, time spent, and score.

Selecting the **Study Tools** view for the **Grades** page provides the following information:

○ **Book**. The title of the book from the **Study Tools** tab you accessed.

○ **Study Tool**. Displays whether the Study Tools content you worked on came from an **eBook**, **Personalized Study Book**, or **Tutorial**.

○ **Chapter**. This column identifies what section you accessed while working with your Study Tool book. Generally, this corresponds to the chapter title you clicked in the book's table of contents. In the case where there is no table of contents, this column will display **All**.

○ **Score**. When there is a score to report, your score and the highest possible score. Uncompleted content you can still take are labeled **not yet taken**. Any work that you have done that can not be electronically graded by CengageNOW is labeled **not gradable**. When you have opened an eBook, this column displays **n/a**.

○ **Date & Time Last Submitted**. The date and time of your most recent submission. When this information is for an eBook, it displays the number of times you accessed the chapter.

○ **# of Submissions**. For **Post-Tests** and **Chapter Tests** this is the number of times you have submitted your work for a score. When this information is for an eBook, it displays the number of times you accessed the chapter.

○ **Time Spent (Most Recent Submission)**. The time you spent to complete your most recent submission (does not include time spent on eBooks).

ACCESSING YOUR STUDY TOOLS

The **Study Tools** page displays the self-study products you can access through CengageNOW, such as eBooks, Tutorials, and Personalized Study products. Your products will appear on this page once you have registered them using the **Content Access Code**. See <u>"Registering Additional Study Materials"</u> on page 37.

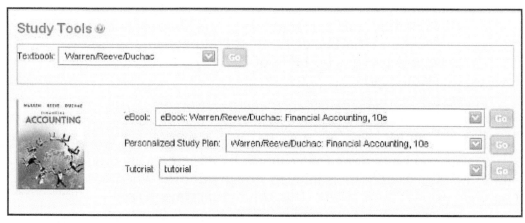

Accessing Study Tools for Self-Study

You do not need to be enrolled in a course to use your **Study Tools** materials for your own practice or self-study. Some tests with the **Study Tools** may not be available to you, however, if your instructor is using them as a graded course assignment.

When you are ready to access your registered Study Tools, click on the **Study Tools** tab to open the page. Next select a book from the **Textbook** menu and click **Go**. You can then select from any of the associated eBook, Tutorial, or Personalized Study material listed on the page. Click the adjacent **Go** button and your Study Tools content will open.

You may see some of the same questions, **Pre-Tests**, chapters, etc. in your course assignments that you do in **Study Tools**, but there is a key difference:

○ Course assignments taken from the **Assignments** page are *graded* CengageNOW coursework.

○ Work accessed from and completed in the **Study Tools** area is *ungraded* practice or self-study.

Note: Instructors may choose to hide a **Pre-Test** or **Post-Test** from your **Study Tools** view if the test has been made part of a graded assignment for your course.

REGISTERING ADDITIONAL STUDY MATERIALS

To register a new book or product, you'll need its **Content Access Code**—a long alphanumeric code that is usually included with your new textbook. This code can also be purchased separately online or in a bookstore.

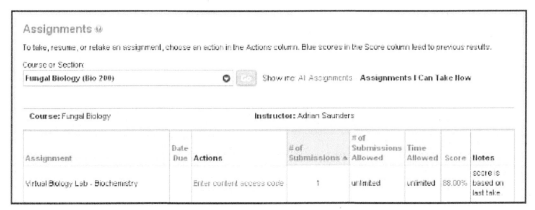

Assignment Requiring a New Content Access Code

Note: Depending on the book edition, the **Content Access Code** is also sometimes called a PIN Code or Passcode.

➤ **To enter a Content Access Code**

1. Sign in to your **My Home** page, if you have not already done so. (If you have already signed in to CengageNOW, sign out to return to **My Home**.)

2. Under **Have Another Product to Register?**, enter the **Content Access Code** exactly as it appears, including dashes and capitalization. This code is case-sensitive.

3. Click the **Register** button.

   If the code is not accepted, try re-entering it, paying close attention to capitalization and differentiating numbers and letters.

4. When you see the **Congratulations!** message, you have registered your product.

Purchasing a New Content Access Code

A **Content Access Code** can typically be used only once and only for a specific period of time. If you purchased your book used, for example, the previous owner may have used your book's code already. If this is the case, you will need to buy a new code before you can access on-line assignments that include questions or other material from that book.

Note: You can purchase a new **Content Access Code** for your textbook through your school bookstore, or you can also go to http://www.cengagebrain.com/shop/index.html to buy it online.

After you receive your new Content Access Code, enter it as described in "To enter a Content Access Code" on page 37. You then will be able to access your course assignments that use that content.

TECHNICAL SUPPORT

If you have trouble signing in or registering for your classes or materials, you can go to the CengageNOW Customer Support page for FAQs and Technical Support.

CengageNOW Phone Support:

1-800-354-9706 Option 5, then Option 2 (toll free)

Monday–Thursday: 8:30 am to 9:00 pm EST

Friday: 8:30 am to 6:00 pm EST

When contacting Technical Support, be prepared to provide the following information:

○ First and last name

○ School (including campus)

○ Operating system

○ Browser

Note: Also be sure to let Technical Support know if you are accessing CengageNOW through an integrated product such as eCollege or Blackboard.

➤ To access online technical support

1. Go to http://academic.cengage.com/support to open the Cengage Customer Support page. (Within CengageNOW, you can click the **Technical Support** link available at the bottom of most pages).

2. Under **Student**, select **CengageNOW** from the dropdown menu and click **Go**.

3. From the support site, you can use the following methods to contact technical support:

   • Click the **Live Student Chat** link to chat with a technical support representative during chat hours.

- Enter key words in the **Search in CengageNOW** function to find specific information in the **Cengage Knowledge Base**.

- View or download documentation which contains specific instructions on registration and taking an assignment.

- View instructional videos that can guide you through the process of creating and accessing your CengageNOW account.

- Click the **questions** link under the **Contact Us** heading to submit your question using an email form.

Note: When using the email form, all fields marked with a red asterisk (*) are required. Email support requests are usually responded to within 48 hours.

INDEX

G

grades, viewing *32*
grading category *12*

H

header links *7*
Help link *7*
homework assignment, taking
  24–31

I

Internet browser requirements *iv*

L

links *7*
Linux, system requirements *iv*
log in *see* sign in

M

Macintosh, system requirements *iv*
managing assignments *11–21*
Math/Graphing Tool *7*

P

password, assignment *13*
personalized study
  options *15*
  taking *15–21*
Personalized Study Assignment

illus. 17
Personalized Study Plan
  illus. 19
personalized study plan *19*
pop-ups, unblocking *iv*
Post-Test Results
  illus. 21
post-test, taking *20*
PowerSearch *9*
pre-test, taking *17*
printing
  blank assignment *13*
  completed assignment *13*

Q

Quick Start guide *iii*

R

registering
  as new user *1–4*
  new materials *37–38*
requirements, system *iv*
returning user sign in *5*
revised study plan *21*
Run System Check *7*
running a system check *6*

S

selectors, assignment view *11*
sign in *5*
sign out *9*
signing out *7*
study plan
  personalized *19*
  revised *21*

*S*urvey of Accounting, Seventh Edition, is designed for a one-term introductory accounting course. Written for students who have no prior knowledge of accounting, this text emphasizes how managers, investors, and other business stakeholders use accounting reports. It provides an overview of the basic topics in financial and managerial accounting, without the extraneous accounting principles topics that must be skipped or otherwise modified to fit into a one-term course.

Hallmark Features

The seventh edition of this text continues to emphasize elements designed to help instructors and enhance the learning experience of students. These features include the following:

- **Integrated Financial Statement Framework** shows how transactions impact each of the three primary financial statements and stresses the integrated nature of accounting.
- **Infographic art** examples help students visualize important accounting concepts within the chapter.

The Operating Cycle

The operations of a merchandising business involve the purchase of merchandise for sale (purchasing), the sale of the products to customers (sales), and the receipt of cash from customers (collection). This overall process is referred to as the operating cycle. Thus, the operating cycle begins with spending cash, and it ends with receiving cash from customers. The operating cycle for a merchandising business is shown to the right. Operating cycles for retailers are usually shorter than they are for manufacturers because retailers purchase goods in a form ready for sale to the customer. Of course, some retailers will have shorter operating cycles than others because of the nature of their products. For example, a jewelry store or an automobile dealer normally has a longer operating cycle than a consumer electronics store or a grocery store. Businesses with longer operating cycles normally have higher profit margins on their products than businesses with shorter operating cycles. For example, it is not unusual for jewelry stores to price their jewelry at 30%–50% above cost. In contrast, grocery stores operate on very small profit margins, often below 5%. Grocery stores make up the difference by selling their products more quickly.

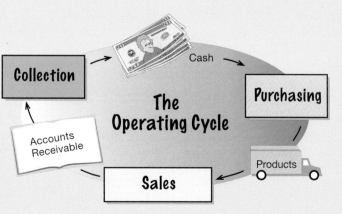

- **Illustrative Problems** help students apply what they learn by walking them through problems that cover the most important concepts addressed within the chapter.

Illustrative Problem

McCollum Company, a furniture wholesaler, acquired new equipment at a cost of $150,000 at the beginning of the fiscal year. The equipment has an estimated life of five years and an estimated residual value of $12,000. Ellen McCollum, the president, has requested information regarding alternative depreciation methods.

Instructions

Determine the annual depreciation for each of the five years of estimated useful life of the equipment, the accumulated depreciation at the end of each year, and the book value of the equipment at the end of each year by (a) the straight-line method and (b) the double-declining-balance method.

Solution

	Year	Depreciation Expense	Accumulated Depreciation, End of Year	Book Value, End of Year
a.	1	$27,600*	$ 27,600	$122,400
	2	27,600	55,200	94,800
	3	27,600	82,800	67,200
	4	27,600	110,400	39,600
	5	27,600	138,000	12,000

*$27,600 = ($150,000 − $12,000) ÷ 5

	Year	Depreciation Expense	Accumulated Depreciation, End of Year	Book Value, End of Year
b.	1	$60,000**	$ 60,000	$ 90,000
	2	36,000	96,000	54,000
	3	21,600	117,600	32,400
	4	12,960	130,560	19,440
	5	7,440***	138,000	12,000

**$60,000 = $150,000 × 40%
***The asset is not depreciated below the estimated residual value of $12,000.

- **"Integrity, Objectivity, and Ethics in Business"** features describe real-world dilemmas, helping students apply accounting concepts within an ethical context, using integrity and objectivity.

Integrity, Objectivity, and Ethics in Business

WHERE'S THE BONUS?

Managers are often given bonuses based on reported earnings numbers. This can create a conflict. LIFO can improve the value of the company through lower taxes. However, in periods of rising costs (prices), LIFO also produces a lower earnings number and therefore lower management bonuses. Ethically, managers should select accounting procedures that will maximize the value of the firm, rather than their own compensation. Compensation specialists can help avoid this ethical dilemma by adjusting the bonus plan for the accounting procedure differences.

- **"How Businesses Make Money"** vignettes emphasize practical ways in which businesses apply accounting concepts when generating profit strategies.

HOW BUSINESSES MAKE MONEY

WHAT IS A PRODUCT?

A product is often thought of in terms beyond just its physical attributes. For example, why a customer buys a product usually impacts how a business markets the product. Other considerations, such as warranty needs, servicing needs, and perceived quality, also affect business strategies.

Consider the four different types of products listed below. For these products, the frequency of purchase, the profit per unit, and the number of retailers differ. As a result, the sales and marketing approach for each product differs.

Product	Type of Product	Frequency of Purchase	Profit per Unit	Number of Retailers	Sales/Marketing Approach
Snickers®	Convenience	Often	Low	Many	Mass advertising
Sony® TV	Shopping	Occasional	Moderate	Many	Mass advertising; personal selling
Diamond ring	Specialty	Seldom	High	Few	Personal selling
Prearranged funeral	Unsought	Rare	High	Few	Aggressive selling

- The **"International Connections"** feature, in select chapters, highlights key differences between international accounting standards and U.S. GAAP.

International Connection

DEVELOPMENT COSTS UNDER IFRS

In the United States, research and development costs must be expensed in the period in which they are incurred. IFRS, however, allow certain development costs to be recorded as an asset if specific criteria are met. Included in the criteria are the technical feasibility of completing the development of the intangible asset and whether the company intends to use or sell the asset. Whether development costs are recorded as an asset or expensed can have a significant impact on the financial statements. For example, **Nokia Corporation** reported €40 million of development costs as an asset on a recent balance sheet. [€ stands for the euro, the common currency of the European Economic Union.]

- **An attractive design** engages students and clearly presents the material. The Integrated Financial Statement Framework benefits from this pedagogically sound use of color, as each statement within the framework is shaded to reinforce the integrated nature of accounting.

Integrated Financial Statement (IFS) Approach

This framework clearly demonstrates the impact of transactions on the balance sheet, income statement, and the statement of cash flows and the corresponding relationship among these financial statements. The IFS framework moves the student from the simple to the complex and explains the how and why of financial statements.

Chapter 1 introduces students to this integration in the form of actual company financials from The Hershey Company, a well-known manufacturer of chocolates.

EXHIBIT 10

Integrated Financial Statements

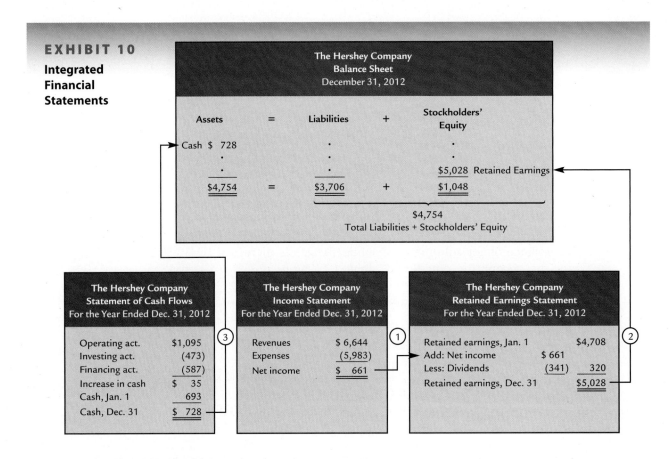

Chapter 2 begins with an example format of the integrated framework used throughout the financial chapters. Early in the course, students will gain a greater understanding of how important trends or events can impact a company's financial statements, which add valuable insight into the financial condition of a business.

Integrated Financial Statement Framework   **EXHIBIT 1**

Statement of Cash Flows	Balance Sheet				Income Statement
	Assets = Liabilities +		Stockholders' Equity		
	Assets = Liabilities +	Capital Stock +	Retained Earnings		
Transactions	XXX	XXX	XXX	XXX	
	XXX	XXX	XXX	XXX	

Statement of Cash Flows		
+/– Operating activities	XXX	
+/– Investing activities	XXX	
+/– Financing activities	XXX	
Increase or decrease in cash	XXX	
Beginning cash	XXX	
Ending cash	XXX	

INTEGRATED FINANCIAL STATEMENT FRAMEWORK

Income Statement	
Revenues	XXX
Expenses	XXX
Net income or loss	XXX

The primary focus in Chapter 2 is on cash transactions, which helps eliminate confusion for students who may have difficulty determining whether an event or transaction should be recorded.

Transaction (d)

During the first month of operations, Family Health Care earned patient fees of $5,500, receiving the fees in cash.

The effects of this transaction on Family Health Care's financial statements are recorded as follows:

1. Under the Statement of Cash Flows column, Cash from Operating activities is increased by $5,500.
2. Under the Balance Sheet column, Cash under Assets is increased by $5,500. To balance the accounting equation, Retained Earnings under Stockholders' Equity is also increased by $5,500.
3. Under the Income Statement column, Fees earned is increased by $5,500.

This transaction illustrates an inflow of cash from operating activities by earning revenues (fees earned) of $5,500. Retained Earnings is increased under Stockholders' Equity by $5,500 because fees earned contribute to net income and net income increases stockholders' equity. Since fees earned are a type of revenue, Fees earned of $5,500 is also entered under the Income Statement column.

The effects of this transaction on Family Health Care's financial statements are shown below.

Statement of Cash Flows	Balance Sheet						Income Statement
	Assets		=	Liabilities +	Stockholders' Equity		
	Cash	+ Land	=	Notes Payable +	Capital Stock +	Retained Earnings	
Balances	4,000	12,000		10,000	6,000		
d. Fees earned	5,500					5,500	d.
Balances	9,500	12,000		10,000	6,000	5,500	

Statement of Cash Flows		Income Statement	
d. Operating	5,500	d. Fees earned	5,500

Seventh Edition Changes and Enhancements

Financial Analysis

- A Financial Analysis section has been added to each of the financial accounting chapters (Chapters 1–8). Each financial analysis section describes common financial ratios and analyses and then uses real world companies to illustrate and interpret the results. For example, in Chapter 1, Apple Inc. and Dell Inc. are used to illustrate the computation and analysis of the rate of return on assets.
- The objective of the financial analysis section is to provide students meaningful insights into how financial statements are used in the real world. This, in turn, emphasizes the importance of understanding financial statements, their integrations, and interpretations.

- A separate end-of-chapter financial analysis section has also been added. This section extends the chapter discussion to a variety of real world companies. For example, in Chapter 1, FA 1-4 asks students to (1) think about how the rate of return on assets might differ for ExxonMobil, Coca-Cola, and Walmart; (2) compute the rate of return on assets for each company using recent financial statements; and (3) analyze the differences.
- New key terms have been added to reflect the additional content in the Financial Analysis sections.

Other Enhancements

- The "Activities" section of previous editions is now renamed "Cases," which better reflects the scenario-based issues presented in these items. The Cases have been updated and refreshed.
- Designed for today's students, the seventh edition's new full-color design enhances the presentation of integrated financial statements, clarity of graphs and illustrations, and invites student engagement.
- This edition uses an innovative, high-impact writing style that emphasizes topics concisely and clearly. Direct sentences, concise paragraphs, numbered lists, and step-by-step calculations provide students with an easy-to-follow structure for learning accounting without sacrificing content or rigor.
- Instead of identifying specific years such as 2014, we have converted most year designations to 20Y1, 20Y2, 20Y3...20Y9. Using a date-neutral approach extends the 7th edition's usefulness over a longer period. One exception is made in the discussion and illustration of Hershey Company's financial statements in Chapter 1. This exception was made so that students and instructors could compare the chapter's adapted illustration with Hershey's actual financial statements, if so desired.
- All real-world company data have been updated including The Hershey Company, Home Depot, Starbucks, and Microsoft. All real-world company names are identified in blue boldface color font as shown in the preceding sentence. All other names, including individuals and companies, are fictitious, and any resemblance to existing individuals or companies is a coincidence.
- Company names, numerical data, and solutions to end-of-chapter exercises and problems have been extensively revised to create unique course content.

Technology

What is CengageNOW?

CengageNOW is an online **teaching and learning resource** that provides **more control in less time** and delivers **better student outcomes** – NOW. CengageNOW provides a more interactive way for students to read, study, and learn online.

What can CengageNOW™ do for me?

Learning accounting is often like learning a new language. Repetition and practice are crucial to the student learning process. CengageNOW allows students to learn concepts when and how they want – *accelerating their success!*

1. **It provides *students*** with a tool that enhances their learning process by supplying them with:
    - Resources that support their understanding of core concepts so they come to class prepared

- The right type and amount of feedback when they need it and resources to help them as they complete their homework
- Assignments to help them go further and make connections between concepts and apply what they've learned to different scenarios

2. **It provides *instructors* with a tool that allows them to:**
   - Easily manage your assignments and students
   - Achieve continuity and time savings term after term
   - Diagnose students' level of comprehension at any given point
   - Help you report on outcomes to accrediting bodies or internally to your institution

CengageNOW for Warren's *Survey of Accounting, 7e* is designed to help students learn more effectively by providing engaging resources at unique points in the learning process:

When to use it?	What to use?	How will it help?
Preparing for Class	Lecture Activities Animated Activities Experience Managerial Accounting Videos	Recall Understand
Completing Homework	Solutions Videos Enhanced Feedback	Apply
Going Further	Mastery Assignments Conceptual Conversions	Analyze Evaluate

Preparing for Class

CengageNOW helps you motivate students and prepare them for class with a host of resources. These resources were developed with visual learners and those that don't like to read textbooks in mind. Available in the Study Tools tab in CengageNOW, students may access these resources on demand. Each resource is fully assignable and gradable – great for **Flipping the Classroom**!

New **Lecture Activities** are available and correlate to each Learning Objective (LO). These Lecture Assignments review the material covered in each LO, giving students a way to review what is covered in each objective in a digestible video activity format so they come to class more prepared and ready to participate.

Animated Activities are available on a chapter-by-chapter basis. Animated Activities are assignable/gradable illustrations that visually explain and guide students through selected core topics. Each activity uses a realistic company example to illustrate how the concepts relate to the everyday activities of a business. After finishing the video, a student is expected to answer questions based on what they've seen. These activities offer excellent resources for students prior to coming to lecture and will especially appeal to visual learners.

For selected Managerial chapters, **Experience Managerial Accounting Videos** are available to show how real-world companies apply managerial topics in a day-to-day business setting.

By using these resources, you have a powerful suite of content to help you ensure students can familiarize themselves with content prior to coming to class – an excellent way to help you flip the classroom!

Completing Homework

Students sometimes struggle with accounting homework. By using CengageNOW's powerful instructor tools you can fine-tune the amount of help that your students

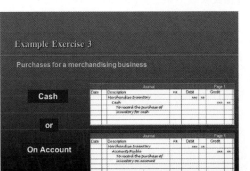

receive as they work on their homework. Help your students succeed by making the right amount of assistance available at the right time!

Solutions Videos are available for the most commonly assigned end-of-chapter assignments. *Linked only to algorithms*, Solutions Videos provide students with both a detailed walk-through of a similar problem and problem-solving strategies.

Enhanced feedback for each homework question! CengageNOW questions provide additional, immediate feedback so your students can learn as they go. In addition to showing students the fields they got correct or incorrect, written guidance is offered when students click on "Check My Work" within an assignment attempt. You have the ability to turn this assistance on or off in the assignment settings options.

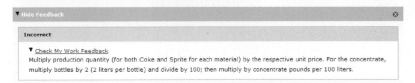

Going Further

Mastering accounting includes making connections between concepts and asking students to apply what they've learned to different scenarios. CengageNOW has the tools that help you assess your students' abilities in these key skill areas!

In CengageNOW, all of the special activities in Warren, *Survey of Accounting, 7th Edition* are available for you to assign to your students. These **Mastery Assignments** do more than test your students' ability to recall, understand and apply. These assignments challenge your students to go further by demonstrating their ability to analyze and evaluate accounting information.

Conceptual Conversions are open-ended requirements from the end-of-chapter homework that have been converted into automatically gradable formats in CengageNOW. Now you can assess your students' understanding of more conceptual, open-ended questions previously not available to assign in an online environment.

To view a demo of CengageNOW, please visit: **www.cengage.com/digital/ cnowdemo**

Supplements for the Instructor

- **Product Companion Site** includes convenient downloads of the instructor supplements, including PowerPoint presentations, Instructor's Manual, Solutions Manual, and Excel® template solutions. Log in at www.cengage.com/login.
- **Test Bank** For each chapter, the Test Bank includes true/false questions, multiple-choice questions, and problems. Each question is marked with a

difficulty level, chapter objective association, and a tie-in to standard course outcomes.
- **Cengage Learning Testing Powered by Cognero** is a flexible, online system that allows you to:
  - author, edit, and manage test bank content from multiple Cengage Learning solutions
  - create multiple test versions in an instant
  - deliver tests from your LMS, your classroom, or wherever you want.
- **PowerPoint® Presentation Slides** Included on the product companion site. Each presentation enhances lectures and simplifies class preparation.
- **Instructor Excel® Templates** This resource provides the solutions for the problems and exercises that have enhanced Excel® templates for students.
- **Instructor's Manual** Each chapter contains a number of resources designed to aid instructors as they prepare lectures, assign homework, and teach in the classroom.
- **Solutions Manual** The Solutions Manual contains answers to all exercises, problems, and cases that appear in the text. As always, the solutions are author-written and verified multiple times for numerical accuracy and consistency with the core text.

Acknowledgments

Many people deserve thanks for their contributions to this text over the past several editions. Kenneth Martin provided a thorough technical review. Jim Emig, Cathy Xanthaky Larson, and ANSR Source were diligent resources in their verification of end-of-chapter materials. The comments from the following reviewers also influenced recent editions of the text:

Sharon Agee, *Rollins College*
Tim Alzheimer, *Montana State University, Bozeman*
Scott R. Berube, *University of New Hampshire, Whittemore School of Business & Economics*
Jekabs Bikis, *Dallas Baptist University*
Jerold Braun, *Daytona State College*
Suzanne Lyn Cercone, *Keystone College*
H. Edward Gallatin, *Indiana State University*
Robert E. Holtfreter, *Central Washington University*
José Luis Hortensi, *Miami Dade College*
Daniel Kerch, *Pennsylvania Highlands Community College*
William J. Lavelle, *Ave Maria University*
Ann E. Martel, *Marquette University*
Edna C. Mitchell, *Polk State College*
Tami Park, *University of Great Falls*
Craig Pence, *Highland Community College*
Patricia G. Roshto, *University of Louisiana at Monroe*
Geeta Shankar, *University of Dayton*
Alice Sineath, *Forsyth Technical Community College*
Hans Sprohge, *Wright State University*
Gary Volk, *Wayne State College*

Your comments and suggestions as you use this text are sincerely appreciated.

Carl S. Warren

Carl S. Warren

Dr. Carl S. Warren is Professor Emeritus of Accounting at the University of Georgia, Athens. For over twenty-five years, Professor Warren has taught all levels of accounting classes. In recent years, Professor Warren has focused his teaching efforts on principles of accounting and auditing courses. Professor Warren has taught classes at the University of Iowa, Michigan State University, and University of Chicago. Professor Warren received his doctorate degree (PhD) from Michigan State University and his undergraduate (BBA) and master's (MA) degrees from the University of Iowa. During his career, Professor Warren published numerous articles in professional journals, including *The Accounting Review, Journal of Accounting Research, Journal of Accountancy, The CPA Journal,* and *Auditing: A Journal of Practice & Theory.* Professor Warren's outside interests include handball, skiing, hiking, fly-fishing, and golf. Professor Warren also spends time backpacking U.S. national parks (Yellowstone and the Grand Canyon), playing with his grandchildren, and riding ATVs and motorcycles.

BRIEF CONTENTS

CONTENTS

Contents

Chapter 7 Fixed Assets and Intangible Assets 253

Chapter 8 Liabilities and Stockholders' Equity 285

Chapter 9 Financial Statement Analysis 325

Contents

CHAPTER 1

The Role of Accounting in Business

LEARNING OBJECTIVES
After studying this chapter, you should be able to:

Obj | 1 Describe the types and forms of businesses, how businesses make money, and business stakeholders.

Obj | 2 Describe the three business activities of financing, investing, and operating.

Obj | 3 Define accounting and describe its role in business.

Obj | 4 Describe and illustrate the basic financial statements and how they interrelate.

Obj | 5 Describe eight accounting concepts underlying financial reporting.

Obj | 6 Financial Analysis: Describe and illustrate how the rate of return on assets can be used to analyze and assess a company's financial performance.

LinkedIn

How much are you willing to pay for stock of a company that has never been traded on a public market? Investors must come up with an answer to this question for companies that offer stock to the public for the first time, which is called an *initial public offering*.

In the United States, before such companies can offer stock for sale, they must file a prospectus (Form S-1) with the Securities and Exchange Commission. The prospectus includes background information on the company, including its business strategy and the range of prices that the stock is expected to sell for in the market. Also included in the prospectus are the company's financial statements for the past three years.

Recently, **LinkedIn Corporation** offered its stock for sale to the public. LinkedIn is the world's largest professional network on the Internet with more than 100 million members in over 200 countries. Members join the network free of cost and are able to create and manage their professional identity online. LinkedIn generates its revenues by offering premium services to its members and by selling services such as hiring and marketing solutions to businesses and professional organizations.

In its prospectus filed with the Securities and Exchange Commission, LinkedIn indicated that it anticipated a price for its stock of between $42.00 and $45.00 per share. On the first day the stock was publicly traded, LinkedIn's stock rose to a high of $122.70, more than two and a half times its highest anticipated price of $45.00.

Is LinkedIn's stock really worth $122.70 per share? To answer this question, investors examined LinkedIn's stock prospectus and will monitor its financial condition and performance over time. LinkedIn's current and future financial statements will be an important input into investors' valuation of LinkedIn.

In this chapter, the nature, types, and activities of businesses, such as LinkedIn, are described and illustrated. In addition, the role of accounting in business, including financial statements, basic accounting concepts, and how to use financial statements to evaluate a business's performance, is also described and illustrated.

Obj | 1

Describe the types and forms of businesses, how businesses make money, and business stakeholders.

Roughly eight out of every ten workers in the United States are service providers.

Nature of Business and Accounting

A **business**[1] is an organization in which basic resources (inputs), such as materials and labor, are assembled and processed to provide goods or services (outputs) to customers. Businesses come in all sizes, from a local coffee house to Starbucks, which sells almost $11 billion of coffee and related products each year.

The objective of most businesses is to earn a profit. **Profit** is the difference between the amounts received from customers for goods or services and the amounts paid for the inputs used to provide the goods or services. In this text, we focus on businesses operating to earn a profit. However, many of the same concepts and principles also apply to not-for-profit organizations such as hospitals, churches, and government agencies.

Types of Businesses

Three types of businesses operated for profit include service, merchandising, and manufacturing businesses. Each type of business and some examples are described below.

Service businesses provide services rather than products to customers.

Delta Air Lines (transportation services)

The Walt Disney Company (entertainment services)

Merchandising businesses sell products they purchase from other businesses to customers.

Walmart (general merchandise)

Amazon.com (books, music, videos)

Manufacturing businesses change basic inputs into products that are sold to customers.

General Motors Corporation (cars, trucks, vans)

Dell Inc. (personal computers)

Forms of Business

A business is normally organized in one of the following four forms:

- proprietorship
- partnership
- corporation
- limited liability company

A **proprietorship** is owned by one individual. More than 70% of the businesses in the United States are organized as proprietorships. The frequency of this form is due to the ease and low cost of organizing. The primary disadvantage of proprietorships is that the financial resources are limited to the individual owner's resources. In addition, the owner has unlimited liability to creditors for the debts of the company.

A **partnership** is owned by two or more individuals. About 10% of the businesses in the United States are organized as partnerships. Like a proprietorship, a partnership may outgrow the financial resources of its owners. Also, the partners have unlimited liability to creditors for the debts of the company.

1. A complete glossary of terms appears at the end of the text.

A **corporation** is organized under state or federal statutes as a separate legal entity. The ownership of a corporation is divided into shares of stock. A corporation issues the stock to individuals or other companies, who then become owners or stockholders of the corporation. A primary advantage of the corporate form is the ability to obtain large amounts of resources by issuing shares of stock. In addition, the stockholders' liability to creditors for the debts of the company is limited to their investment in the corporation.

A **limited liability company (LLC)** combines attributes of a partnership and a corporation. The primary advantage of the limited liability company form is that it operates similar to a partnership, but its owners' (or members') liability for the debts of the company is limited to their investment.

Many professional practices such as lawyers, doctors, and accountants are organized as limited liability companies.

In addition to the ease of formation, ability to raise capital, and liability for the debts of the business, other factors such as taxes and legal life of the business should be considered when forming a business. For example, corporations are taxed as separate legal entities, while the income of sole proprietorships, partnerships, and limited liability companies is passed through to the owners and taxed on the owners' tax returns. As separate legal entities, corporations also continue on, regardless of the lives of the individual owners. In contrast, sole proprietorships, partnerships, and limited liability companies may terminate their existence with the death of an individual owner.

The characteristics of sole proprietorships, partnerships, corporations, and limited liability companies are summarized below.

Organizational Form	Ease of Formation	Legal Liability	Taxation	Limitation on Life of Entity	Access to Capital
Proprietorship	Simple	No limitation	Nontaxable (pass-through) entity	Yes	Limited
Partnership	Simple	No limitation	Nontaxable (pass-through) entity	Yes	Average
Corporation	Complex	Limited liability	Taxable entity	No	Extensive
Limited Liability Company	Moderate	Limited liability	Nontaxable (pass-through) entity by election	Yes	Average

The three types of businesses we discussed earlier—manufacturing, merchandising, and service—may be proprietorships, partnerships, corporations, or limited liability companies. However, businesses that require a large amount of resources, such as many manufacturing businesses, are corporations. Likewise, most large retailers such as Walmart, Sears, and JCPenney are corporations.

Because most large businesses are corporations, they tend to dominate the economic activity in the United States. For this reason, this text focuses on the corporate form of organization. However, many of the concepts and principles discussed also apply to proprietorships, partnerships, and limited liability companies.

How Do Businesses Make Money?

The objective of a business is to earn a profit by providing goods or services to customers. How does a company decide which products or services to offer its customers? Many factors influence this decision. Ultimately, however, the decision is based on how the company plans to gain an advantage over its competitors and, in doing so, maximize its profits.

Companies try to maximize their profits by generating high revenues while maintaining low costs, which results in high profits. However, a company's competitors are also trying to do the same, and thus, a company can only maximize its profits by gaining an advantage over its competitors.

Generally, companies gain an advantage over their competitors by using one of the following two strategies:

- A **low-cost strategy**, where a company designs and produces products or services at a lower cost than its competitors. Such companies often sell no-frills, standardized products and services.
- A **premium-price strategy**, where a company tries to design and produce products or services that serve unique market needs, allowing it to charge premium prices. Such companies often design and market their products so that customers perceive their products or services as having a unique quality, reliability, or image.

Walmart and Southwest Airlines are examples of companies using a low-cost strategy. John Deere, Tommy Hilfiger, and BMW are examples of companies using a premium-price strategy.

Since business is highly competitive, it is difficult for a company to sustain a competitive advantage over time. For example, a competitor of a company using a low-cost strategy may copy the company's low-cost methods or develop new methods that achieve even lower costs. Likewise, a competitor of a company using a premium-price strategy may develop products that are perceived as more desirable by customers.

Examples of companies utilizing low-cost and premium-price strategies include:

- Local pharmacies who develop personalized relationships with their customers. By doing so, they are able to charge premium (higher) prices. In contrast, Walmart's pharmacies use the low-cost emphasis and compete on cost.
- Grocery stores such as Kroger and Safeway develop relationships with their customers by issuing preferred customer cards. These cards allow the stores to track consumer preferences and buying habits for use in purchasing and advertising campaigns.
- Honda promotes the reliability and quality ratings of its automobiles and thus charges premium prices. Similarly, Volvo promotes the safety characteristics of its automobiles. In contrast, Kia uses a low-cost strategy.
- Harley-Davidson emphasizes that its motorcycles are "Made in America" and promotes its "rebel" image as a means of charging higher prices than its competitors Honda, Yamaha, or Suzuki.

Companies sometimes struggle to find a competitive advantage. For example, JCPenney and Sears have difficulty competing on low costs against Walmart, Kohl's, T.J. Maxx, and Target. At the same time, JCPenney and Sears have difficulty charging premium prices against competitors such as The Gap, Eddie Bauer, and Talbot's. Likewise, Delta Air Lines and United Airlines have difficulty competing against low-cost airlines such as Southwest. At the same time, Delta and United don't offer any unique services for which their passengers are willing to pay a premium price.

Exhibit 1 summarizes low-cost and premium-price strategies with common examples of companies that employ each strategy.

EXHIBIT 1

Business Strategies and Industries

Business Strategy	Industry					
	Airline	Freight	Automotive	Retail	Financial Services	Hotel
Low cost	Southwest	Union Pacific	Hyundai	Sam's Club	Ameritrade	Super 8
Premium price	Virgin Atlantic	FedEx	BMW	Talbot's	Morgan Stanley	Ritz-Carlton

Business Stakeholders

A **business stakeholder** is a person or entity with an interest in the economic performance and well-being of a company. For example, owners, suppliers, customers, and employees are all stakeholders in a company.

Business stakeholders can be classified into one of the four categories illustrated in Exhibit 2.

EXHIBIT 2

Business Stakeholders

Business Stakeholder	Interest in the Business	Examples
Capital market stakeholders	Providers of major financing for the business	Banks, owners, stockholders
Product or service market stakeholders	Buyers of products or services and vendors to the business	Customers and suppliers
Government stakeholders	Collect taxes and fees from the business and its employees	Federal, state, and city governments
Internal stakeholders	Individuals employed by the business	Employees and managers

Capital market stakeholders provide the financing for a company to begin and continue its operations. Banks and other long-term creditors have an economic interest in receiving the amount loaned plus interest. Owners want to maximize the economic value of their investments.

Product or service market stakeholders purchase the company's products or services or sell their products or services to the company. Customers have an economic interest in the continued success of the company. For example, customers who purchase advance tickets on Delta Air Lines are depending on Delta continuing in business. Likewise, suppliers depend on continued success of their customers. For example, if a customer fails or cuts back on purchases, the supplier's business will also decline.

Government stakeholders such as federal, state, county, and city governments collect taxes from companies. The better a company does, the more taxes the government collects. In addition, workers who are laid off by a company can file claims for unemployment compensation, which results in a financial burden for the state and federal governments.

Internal stakeholders such as managers and employees depend upon the continued success of the company for keeping their jobs. Managers of companies that perform poorly are often fired by the owners. Likewise, during economic downturns companies often lay off workers. Stakeholders are illustrated in Exhibit 3.

EXHIBIT 3

Business Stakeholders

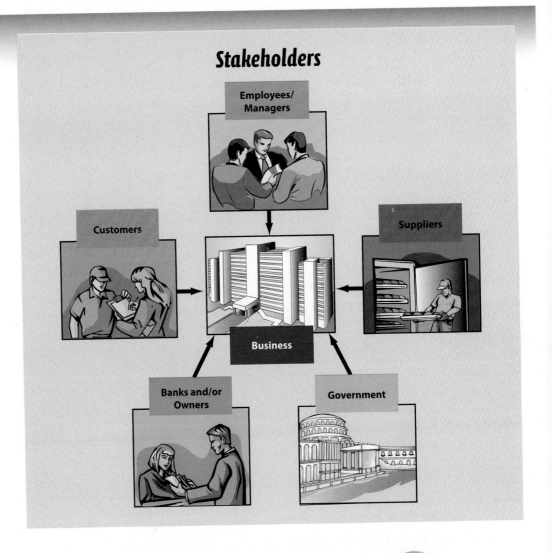

Integrity, Objectivity, and Ethics in Business

THE HERSHEY TRUST COMPANY

Milton Snavely Hershey founded The Hershey Company after serving as a candy apprentice in Philadelphia, running a failing candy shop, and finally succeeding at caramel making. Milton started The Hershey Company in the early 1900s after selling his caramel company.

Milton and his wife, Catherine, couldn't have children, and in 1909, they created the Milton Hershey School. After Catherine's death, Milton willed virtually his entire fortune, including his interest in The Hershey Company, to the School. Today, the School provides free

education, meals, clothing, health care, and a home to almost 2,000 children in financial and social need. The School is run by The Hershey Trust Company, which is the largest shareholder of The Hershey Company.

A public uproar was created in 2002 when the trustees of The Hershey Trust Company tried to sell their controlling stock interest in The Hershey Company. As a result of the public outcry, the majority of the trustees were forced to resign.

Source: Adapted from www.thehersheycompany.com.

Business Activities

Obj **2**

Describe the three business activities of financing, investing, and operating.

All companies engage in the following three business activities:

* **Financing activities** to obtain the necessary funds (monies) to organize and operate the company
* **Investing activities** to obtain assets such as buildings and equipment to begin and operate the company
* **Operating activities** to earn revenues and profits

The preceding business activities are illustrated in Exhibit 4.

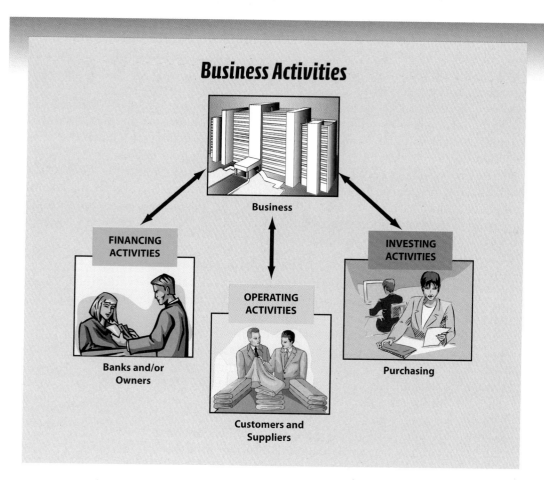

EXHIBIT 4
Business Activities

Financing Activities

Financing activities involve obtaining funds to begin and operate a business. Companies obtain financing through the use of capital markets by:

* borrowing
* issuing shares of ownership

When a company borrows money, it incurs a liability. A **liability** is a legal obligation to repay the amount borrowed according to the terms of the borrowing agreement. When a company borrows from a vendor or supplier, the liability is

On a recent balance sheet **Google** reported total liabilities of $14,429 million, of which $7,148 million were accounts payable.

called an **account payable**. In such cases, the company promises to pay according to the terms set by the vendor or supplier. Most vendors and suppliers require payment within a relatively short time, such as 30 days.

A company may also borrow money by issuing bonds. *Bonds* are sold to investors and require repayment normally with interest. The amount of the bonds, called the *face value*, usually requires repayment several years in the future. Thus, bonds are a form of long-term financing. The interest on the bonds, however, is normally paid semiannually. Bond obligations are reported as **bonds payable**, and any interest that is due is reported as **interest payable**.

Many companies borrow by issuing notes payable. A **note payable** requires payment of the amount borrowed plus interest. Notes payable are similar to bonds except that they may be issued on a short-term or long-term basis.

A company may finance its operations by issuing shares of ownership. For a corporation, shares of ownership are issued in the form of shares of stock. Although corporations may issue a variety of different types of stock, the basic type of stock issued to owners is called **common stock**. The term **capital stock** refers to all the types of stock a corporation may issue.[2] Investors who purchase the stock are referred to as **stockholders**.

Microsoft is currently paying $0.92 per share for dividends on its common stock, which with a market price of $35.00 yields a return of 2.6% ($0.92 ÷ $35.00).

The claims of creditors and stockholders on the assets of a corporation are different. **Assets** are the resources owned by a corporation (company). Creditors have first claim on the company's assets. Only after the creditors' claims are satisfied do the stockholders have a right to the corporate assets.

Creditors normally receive timely payments, which may include interest. In contrast, stockholders are not entitled to regular payments. However, many corporations distribute earnings to stockholders on a regular basis. These distributions of earnings to stockholders are called **dividends**.

Investing Activities

Investing activities involve using the company's assets to obtain additional assets to start and operate the business. Depending upon the nature of the business, a variety of different assets must be acquired.

Most businesses need assets such as machinery, buildings, computers, office furnishings, trucks, and automobiles. These assets have physical characteristics and as such are **tangible assets**. Long-term tangible assets such as machinery, buildings, and land are normally reported separately as "Property, plant, and equipment." Short-term tangible assets such as cash and inventories are reported separately.

On a recent balance sheet, **Apple** reported goodwill and other intangible assets of over $5 billion.

A business may also need **intangible assets**. For example, a business may obtain patent rights to use in manufacturing a product. Long-term assets such as patents, goodwill, and copyrights are reported separately as intangible assets.

A company may also prepay for items such as insurance or rent. Such items, which are assets until they are consumed, are reported as **prepaid expenses**. In addition, rights to payments from customers who purchase merchandise or services on credit are reported as **accounts receivable**.

Operating Activities

Operating activities involve using assets to earn revenues and profits. The management of a company does this by implementing one of the business strategies discussed earlier.

---

2. Types of stock are discussed in Chapter 8, "Liabilities and Stockholders' Equity."

Revenue is the increase in assets from selling products or services. Revenues are normally identified according to their source. For example, revenues received from selling products are called **sales**. Revenues received from providing services are called **fees earned**.

To earn revenue, a business incurs costs, such as wages of employees, salaries of managers, rent, insurance, advertising, freight, and utilities. Costs used to earn revenue are called **expenses**, which may be identified and reported in a variety of ways. For example, the cost of products sold is referred to as the **cost of merchandise sold**, **cost of sales**, or **cost of goods sold**. Other expenses are normally classified as either selling expenses or administrative expenses. **Selling expenses** include those costs directly related to the selling of a product or service. For example, selling expenses include such costs as sales salaries, sales commissions, freight, and advertising costs. **Administrative expenses** include other costs not directly related to the selling, such as officer salaries and other costs of the corporate office.

By comparing the revenues for a period to the related expenses, it can be determined whether the company has earned net income or incurred a net loss. **Net income** results when revenues exceed expenses. A **net loss** results when expenses exceed revenues.

As discussed next, the major role of accounting is to provide stakeholders with information on the financing, investing, and operating activities of businesses. Financial statements are one source of such information.

On a recent income statement, Best Buy Co. Inc. reported revenues of $50,705 million, cost of goods sold of $38,132 million, and selling and administrative expenses of $10,242 million.

What Is Accounting and Its Role in Business?

The *role of accounting* is to provide information about the financing, investing, and operating activities of a company to its stakeholders. For example, accounting provides information for managers to use in operating the business. In addition, accounting provides information to other stakeholders, such as creditors, for assessing the economic performance and condition of the company.

In a general sense, **accounting** is defined as an information system that provides reports to stakeholders about the economic activities and condition of a business. This text focuses on accounting and its role in business. However, many of the concepts discussed also apply to individuals, governments, and not-for-profit organizations. For example, individuals must account for their hours worked, checks written, and bills paid. Stakeholders for individuals include creditors, dependents, and the government. A main interest of the government is making sure that individuals pay the proper taxes.

Accounting is often called the "language of business." This is because accounting is a primary means by which business information is communicated to the stakeholders.

A primary purpose of accounting is to summarize the financial performance of the business for external stakeholders, such as banks and governmental agencies. The branch of accounting that is associated with preparing reports for users external to the business is called **financial accounting**. Accounting also can be used to guide management in making financing, investing, and operations decisions for the company. This branch of accounting is called **managerial accounting**. Financial and managerial accounting may overlap. For example, financial reports for external stakeholders are often used by managers in assessing the potential impact of their decisions on the company.

The chief accountant of a company is called the comptroller or chief financial officer.

The two major objectives of financial accounting are:

- To report the financial condition of a business at a point in time
- To report changes in the financial condition of a business over a period of time

The relationship between these two financial accounting objectives is shown in Exhibit 5.

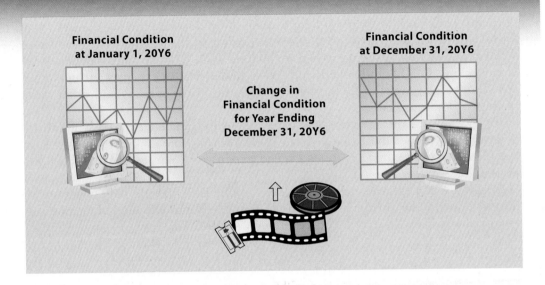

EXHIBIT 5

**Objectives
of Financial
Accounting**

The first objective can be thought of as a still photograph (snapshot) of the company's financial (economic) condition as of a point in time. The second objective can be thought of as a moving picture (video) of the company's financial (economic) performance over time.

The objectives of accounting are achieved by (1) recording the economic events affecting a business and then (2) summarizing the impact of these events on the business in financial reports, called **financial statements**.

Obj | **4**

Describe and illustrate
the basic financial
statements and how they
interrelate.

Financial Statements

Financial statements report the financial condition of a business at a point in time and changes in the financial condition over a period of time. The four basic financial statements and their relationship to the objectives of financial accounting are listed below.

Financial Statement	Financial Accounting Objective
Income Statement	Reports change in financial condition
Retained Earnings Statement	Reports change in financial condition
Balance Sheet	Reports financial condition
Statement of Cash Flows	Reports change in financial condition

The order in which each financial statement is prepared and the nature of each statement is described below.

Order Prepared	Financial Statement	Description of Statement
1	Income Statement	A summary of the revenue and expenses for a specific period of time, such as a month or a year.
2	Retained Earnings Statement	A summary of the changes in the retained earnings in the corporation for a specific period of time, such as a month or a year.
3	Balance Sheet	A list of the assets, liabilities, and stockholders' equity as of a specific date, usually at the close of the last day of a month or a year.
4	Statement of Cash Flows	A summary of the cash receipts and cash payments for a specific period of time, such as a month or a year.

The preceding four financial statements are described and illustrated in Exhibits 6 through 9 using The Hershey Company. These illustrations will introduce you to the financial statements that you will be studying throughout this text. The data for the statements are adapted from a recent annual report of The Hershey Company.[3]

Income Statement

The **income statement** reports the change in financial condition due to the operations of the company. The time period covered by the income statement may vary depending upon the needs of stakeholders. Public corporations are required to file quarterly and annual income statements with the Securities and Exchange Commission (SEC). The income statement shown in Exhibit 6 for The Hershey Company is for the year ended December 31, 2012.

Since the objective of business operations is to generate revenues, the income statement begins by listing the revenues for the period. During 2012, Hershey generated sales of $6,644 million. These sales are listed under "Revenues." The numbers shown in Exhibit 6 are expressed in millions of dollars. It is common

EXHIBIT 6

Income Statement: The Hershey Company

The Hershey Company
Income Statement
For the Year Ended December 31, 2012 (in millions)

Revenues:		
Sales		$6,644
Expenses:		
Cost of sales	$3,784	
Selling and administrative expenses	1,704	
Interest expense	96	
Income taxes expense	354	5,983
Other expense	45	
Net income		$ 661

3. The financial statements for The Hershey Company can be found at http://www.hersheys.com through the Investor Relations Link.

for large companies to express their financial statements in thousands or millions of dollars.

Following the revenues, the expenses used in generating the revenues are listed. For Hershey, these expenses include cost of sales, selling and administrative, interest, income taxes, and other expenses. By reporting the expenses and the related revenues for a period, the expenses are said to be matched against the revenues. This is known in accounting as the *matching concept*, which is discussed later in this chapter.

When revenues exceed expenses for a period, the company has *net income*. If expenses exceed revenues, the company has a *net loss*. Net income means that the business increased its net assets through its operations. That is, the assets created by the revenues exceeded the assets used in generating those revenues.

The objective of most companies is to maximize net income or profit. A net loss means that the business decreased its net assets through its operations. While a business might survive in the short run by reporting net losses, in the long run a business must earn net income to survive.

During 2012, Hershey earned net income of $661 million. Is this good or bad? Certainly, net income is better than a net loss. However, the stakeholders must assess net income according to their objectives. For example, a creditor might be satisfied that the net income is sufficient to ensure that it will be repaid. In contrast, a stockholder might assess the corporation's profitability as less than its competitors' profits and thus be disappointed. Throughout this text, various methods of assessing corporate performance will be described and illustrated.

Retained Earnings Statement

The **retained earnings statement** reports changes in financial condition due to changes in retained earnings for a period. **Retained earnings** are the portion of a corporation's net income that is retained in the business. A corporation may retain all of its net income for expanding operations, or it may pay a portion or all of its net income as dividends. For example, high-growth companies often do not distribute dividends but instead retain profits for future expansion. In contrast, more mature corporations normally pay a regular dividend.

Since retained earnings depend upon net income, the time period covered by the retained earnings statement is the same period as the income statement. Thus, the retained earnings statement for Hershey shown in Exhibit 7 is for the year ended December 31, 2012.

EXHIBIT 7

Retained Earnings Statement: The Hershey Company

The Hershey Company Retained Earnings Statement For the Year Ended December 31, 2012 (in millions)		
Retained earnings, January 1, 2012..		$4,708
Add net income..	$661	
Less dividends	341	
Increase in retained earnings		320
Retained earnings, December 31, 2012..		$5,028

Dividends are reported in the retained earnings statement rather than the income statement. This is because dividends are not an expense but a distribution of net income to stockholders.

During 2012, Hershey distributed (declared) dividends of $341 million and retained $320 million of its net income in the company. Thus, Hershey's retained earnings increased from $4,708 million to $5,028 million during 2012.

Balance Sheet

The balance sheet reports the financial condition *as of a point in time*. This is in contrast to the income statement, retained earnings statement, and statement of cash flows, which report changes in financial condition *for a period of time*. The financial condition of a business as of a point in time is measured by its total assets and claims or rights to those assets. Thus, the financial condition of a business can be represented as:

$$\text{Assets} = \text{Claims (Rights to the Assets)}$$

The claims on a company's assets consist of rights of creditors and stockholders. The rights of creditors are *liabilities*. The rights of stockholders are referred to as **stockholders' equity** or **owners' equity**. Thus, the assets and the claims on those assets can be expressed in equation form as:

$$\text{Assets} = \text{Liabilities} + \text{Stockholders' Equity}$$

This equation is called the **accounting equation**. This equation is the foundation of accounting information systems, which are discussed in later chapters.

The **balance sheet**, sometimes called the **statement of financial condition**, is prepared using the accounting equation. The balance sheet is prepared by listing the accounting equation in vertical rather than horizontal form as follows:

Step 1. Each *asset* is listed and added to arrive at *total assets*.
Step 2. Each *liability* is listed and added to arrive at *total liabilities*.
Step 3. Each *stockholders' equity* item is listed and added to arrive at *total stockholders' equity*.
Step 4. Total liabilities and total stockholders' equity is added to arrive at *total liabilities and stockholders' equity*.
Step 5. Total assets must equal total liabilities and stockholders' equity.

The accounting equation must balance in Step 5; hence, the name balance sheet. The balance sheet for The Hershey Company as of December 31, 2012, is shown in Exhibit 8.

As of December 31, 2012, Hershey's total assets of $4,754 million equal its total liabilities of $3,706 million plus its total stockholders' equity of $1,048 million.

Statement of Cash Flows

The **statement of cash flows** reports the change in financial condition due to the changes in cash during a period. The statement of cash flows is organized around the three business activities of financing, investing, and operating. Any changes in cash must be related to one or more of these activities.

The *net cash flows from operating activities* is reported first. This is because cash flows from operating activities is a primary focus of the company's stakeholders. In the short term, creditors use cash flows from operating activities to

EXHIBIT 8

**Balance Sheet:
The Hershey
Company**

The Hershey Company
Balance Sheet
December 31, 2012 (in millions)

Assets

Cash	$ 728
Accounts receivable	461
Inventories	633
Prepaid expenses	168
Property, plant, and equipment	1,674
Intangibles	803
Other assets	287
Total assets	$4,754

Liabilities

Accounts payable	$ 442
Accrued liabilities	651
Notes and other debt	2,611
Income taxes payable	2
Total liabilities	$3,706

Stockholders' Equity

Capital stock	$ 579
Retained earnings	5,028
Repurchased capital stock and other equity items	(4,559)
Total stockholders' equity	$1,048
Total liabilities and stockholders' equity	$4,754

assess whether the company's operating activities are generating enough cash to repay them. In the long term, a company cannot survive unless it generates positive cash flows from operating activities. Thus, cash flows from operating activities is also a focus of employees, managers, suppliers, customers, and other stakeholders who are interested in the long-term success of the company.

The *net cash flows from investing activities* is reported second. This is because investing activities directly impact the operations of the company. Cash receipts from selling property, plant, and equipment are reported in this section. Likewise, any purchases of property, plant, and equipment are reported as cash payments. Companies that are expanding rapidly, such as start-up companies, normally report negative net cash flows from investing activities. In contrast, companies that are downsizing or selling segments of the business may report positive net cash flows from investing activities.

The *net cash flows from financing activities* is reported third. Any cash receipts from issuing debt or stock are reported in this section as cash receipts. Likewise, cash payments of debt and dividends are reported in this section.

The statement of cash flows is completed by adding the net cash flows from operating, investing, and financing activities to determine the *net increase or decrease in cash* for the period. This net increase or decrease in cash is then added to the *cash at the beginning of the period* to arrive at the *cash at the end of the period.*

The statement of cash flows for The Hershey Company for the year ended December 31, 2012, is shown in Exhibit 9.

EXHIBIT 9

Statement of Cash Flows: The Hershey Company

The Hershey Company Statement of Cash Flows For the Year Ended December 31, 2012 (in millions)	
Net cash flows from operating activities..	$1,095
Cash flows used in investing activities:	
Investments in property, plant, equipment, and other long-term assets....................	$ (473)
Net cash flows used in investing activities...	$ (473)
Cash flows from financing activities:	
Cash receipts from financing activities, including debt......................................	$ 380
Dividends paid to stockholders..	(341)
Repurchase of stock..	(511)
Other, including repayment of debt...	(115)
Net cash flows used in financing activities...	$ (587)
Net increase in cash during 2012...	$ 35
Cash as of January 1, 2012...	693
Cash as of December 31, 2012	$ 728

During 2012, Hershey's *operating activities* generated a positive net cash flow of $1,095 million. Hershey's *investing activities* used $473 million of cash primarily to purchase property, plant, equipment, and other long-term assets. Hershey's *financing activities* used $587 million of cash. This cash was used to pay dividends of $341 million, pay debt of $115 million, and purchase $511 million of its own stock. A company may purchase its own capital stock if the corporate management believes its stock is undervalued or for providing stock to employees or managers as part of an incentive (stock option) plan.[4] Hershey received cash of $380 million primarily by borrowing from creditors.

During 2012, Hershey increased its cash by $35 million. This increase is added to the cash at the beginning of the period of $693 million to arrive at net cash at the end of the period of $728 million.

Overall, Hershey's statement of cash flows indicates that Hershey generated over $1,095 million in cash flows from its operations. It used this cash to expand its operations and pay dividends to stockholders. Thus, Hershey appears to be in a strong operating position.

Integrated Financial Statements

The financial statements are prepared in the following order:

1. income statement
2. retained earnings statement
3. balance sheet
4. statement of cash flows

4. The accounting for a company's purchase of its own stock is discussed in a later chapter.

Preparing the financial statements in the preceding order is important because the financial statements are integrated as follows:[5]

1. The income and retained earnings statements are integrated. The net income or net loss reported on the income statement also appears on the retained earnings statement as either an addition (net income) to or deduction (net loss) from the beginning retained earnings.

2. The retained earnings statement and the balance sheet are integrated. The retained earnings at the end of the period on the retained earnings statement also appears on the balance sheet as a part of stockholders' equity.

3. The balance sheet and statement of cash flows are integrated. The cash on the balance sheet also appears as the end-of-period cash on the statement of cash flows.

To illustrate, The Hershey Company's financial statements in Exhibits 6 through 9 are integrated as follows:

4. *Net income* of $661 million is also reported on the retained earnings statement as an addition to the beginning retained earnings.

5. *Retained earnings* of $5,028 million as of December 31, 2012, is also reported on the balance sheet.

6. *Cash* of $728 million on the December 31, 2012, balance sheet is also reported as the end-of-period cash on the statement of cash flows.

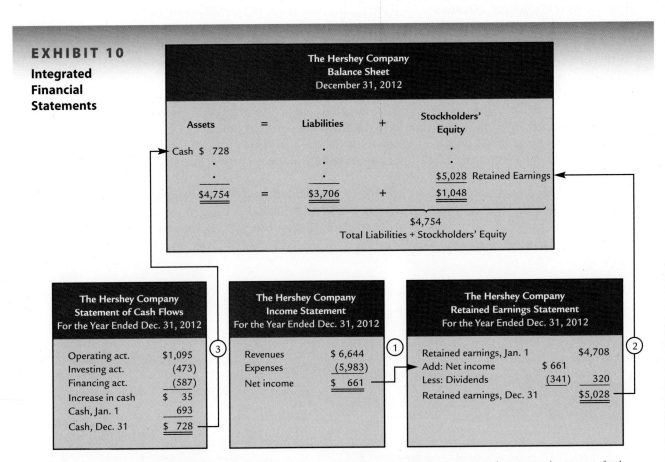

EXHIBIT 10

Integrated Financial Statements

5. Depending upon the method of preparing cash flows from operating activities, net income may also appear on the statement of cash flows. This method of preparing the statement of cash flows is called the indirect method. This link and method are illustrated in a later chapter. In addition, Chapter 2 illustrates how cash flows from operating activities may equal net income.

The preceding integrations are shown in Exhibit 10. These integrations are important in analyzing (1) financial statements and (2) the impact of transactions on the financial statements. In addition, these integrations serve as a check on whether the financial statements have been prepared correctly. For example, if the ending cash on the statement of cash flows doesn't agree with the balance sheet cash, then an error has occurred.

Accounting Concepts

Obj 5

Describe eight accounting concepts underlying financial reporting.

The four corporate financial statements described and illustrated in the preceding section were prepared using accounting "rules," called **generally accepted accounting principles (GAAP)**. Generally accepted accounting principles (GAAP) are necessary so that stakeholders can compare companies across time. If the management of a company could prepare financial statements as they saw fit, the comparability between companies and across time would be impossible.

Accounting principles and concepts develop from research, accepted accounting practices, and pronouncements of regulators. Within the United States, the **Financial Accounting Standards Board (FASB)** has the primary responsibility for developing accounting principles. The FASB publishes *Statements of Financial Accounting Standards* as well as interpretations of these *Standards*.

The **Securities and Exchange Commission (SEC)**, an agency of the U.S. government, also has authority over the accounting and financial disclosures for corporations whose stock is traded and sold to the public. The SEC normally accepts the accounting principles set forth by the FASB. However, the SEC may issue *Staff Accounting Bulletins* on accounting matters that may not have been addressed by the FASB.

Many countries outside the United States use generally accepted accounting principles adopted by the **International Accounting Standards Board (IASB)**. The IASB issues International Financial Reporting Standards (IFRS). Significant differences currently exist between FASB and IASB accounting principles. However, the FASB and IASB are working together to reduce and eliminate these differences towards the goal of developing a single set of accounting principles. Such a set of worldwide accounting principles would help facilitate investment and business in an increasingly global economy.

Generally accepted accounting principles (GAAP) rely upon eight supporting accounting concepts, as shown in Exhibit 11. Throughout this text, emphasis is on accounting principles and concepts. In this way, you will gain an understanding

International Connection

ADOPTION OR CONVERGENCE?

The largest public accounting firms, known as the Big Four, have pushed for the "adoption" of IFRS in the United States within a relatively short period of time. Such a strategy of adoption would generate millions of dollars of consulting and accounting work within the U.S. for the Big Four: Deloitte Touche Tohmatsu, PwC (PriceWaterhouseCoopers), Ernst & Young, and KPMG.

In contrast, others have argued for a strategy of gradual "convergence" to IFRS over time. Currently, it appears that regulators within the United States and the FASB are favoring convergence rather than adoption. For example, since November 2010, the FASB and IASB have completed several projects to converge U.S. and IFRS standards.[1]

1. FASB.org, "Progress Report on IASB-FASB Convergence Work," April 21, 2011.

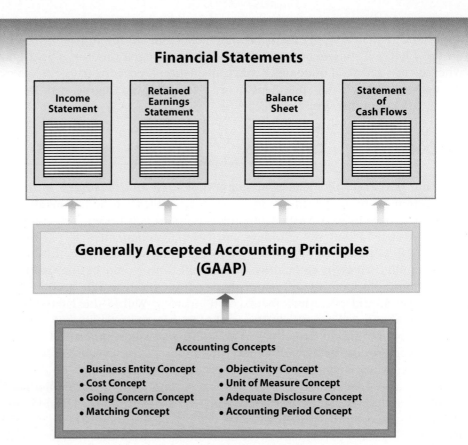

EXHIBIT 11

Accounting Principles and Concepts

of "why" as well as "how" accounting is applied in business. Such an understanding is essential for analyzing and interpreting financial statements.

Business Entity Concept

The **business entity concept** limits the economic data recorded in an accounting system to data related to the activities of that company. In other words, the company is viewed as an entity separate from its owners, creditors, or other companies. For example, a company with one owner records the activities of only that company and does not record the personal activities, property, or debts of the owner. A business entity may take the form of a proprietorship, partnership, corporation, or limited liability company (LLC).

To illustrate, the accounting for The Hershey Company, a corporation, is separate from the accounting for other entities. In other words, the accounting for transactions and events of individual stockholders, creditors, or other Hershey stakeholders is not included in The Hershey Company's financial statements. Only the transactions and events of the corporation are included.

Cost Concept

The **cost concept** initially records assets in the accounting records at their cost or purchase price. To illustrate, assume that Aaron Publishers purchased the following land on August 3, 20Y4, for $150,000:

Price listed by seller on March 1, 20Y4	$160,000
Aaron Publishers' initial offer to buy on January 31, 20Y4	140,000
Estimated selling price on December 31, 20Y8	220,000
Assessed value for property taxes, December 31, 20Y8	190,000

Under the cost concept, Aaron Publishers records the purchase of the land on August 3, 20Y4, at the purchase price of $150,000. The other amounts listed above have no effect on the accounting records.

The fact that the land has an estimated selling price of $220,000 on December 31, 20Y8, indicates that the land has increased in value. However, to use the $220,000 in the accounting records would be to record an illusory or unrealized profit. If Aaron Publishers sells the land on January 9, 20Y9, for $240,000, a profit of $90,000 ($240,000 − $150,000) is then realized and recorded. The new owner would record $240,000 as its cost of the land.

Going Concern Concept

The **going concern concept** assumes that a company will continue in business indefinitely. This assumption is made because the amount of time that a company will continue in business is not known.

The going concern concept justifies the use of the cost concept for recording purchases, such as land. For example, in the preceding illustration Aaron Publishers plans to build a plant on the land. Since Aaron Publishers does not plan to sell the land, reporting changes in the market value of the land is irrelevant. That is, the amount Aaron Publishers could sell the land for if it went out of business is not important. This is because Aaron Publishers plans to continue its operations.

If, however, there is strong evidence that a company is planning on discontinuing its operations, then the accounting records are revised. To illustrate, the assets and liabilities of businesses in receivership or bankruptcy are valued from a quitting concern or liquidation point of view, rather than from the going concern point of view.

Matching Concept

The **matching concept** reports the revenues earned by a company for a period with the expenses incurred in generating the revenues. That is, expenses are *matched* against the revenues they generated.

Revenues are normally recorded at the time a product is sold or a service is rendered, which is referred to as *revenue recognition*. At the point of sale, the sale price has been agreed upon, the buyer acquires ownership of the product or acquires the service, and the seller has a legal claim against the buyer for payment.

The following excerpt from the notes to Hershey's annual report describes when it records sales:

> The Corporation records sales when [a] customer order with a fixed price has been received, . . . the product has been shipped, . . . there is no further obligation to assist in the resale of the product, and collectability (of the account receivable) is reasonably assured.

Objectivity Concept

The **objectivity concept** requires that entries in the accounting records and the data reported on financial statements be based on verifiable or objective evidence. For example, invoices, bank statements, and a physical count of supplies on hand are all objective and verifiable. Thus, they can be used for entering amounts in the accounting system. In some cases, judgments, estimates, and other subjective factors may have to be used in preparing financial statements. In such situations, the most objective evidence available is used.

Unit of Measure Concept

In the United States, the **unit of measure concept** requires that all economic data be recorded in dollars. Other relevant, nonfinancial information may also be recorded, such as terms of contracts. However, it is only through using dollar amounts that the various transactions and activities of a business can be measured, summarized, reported, and compared. Money is common to all business transactions and thus is the unit of measurement for financial reporting.

Adequate Disclosure Concept

The **adequate disclosure concept** requires that the financial statements, including related notes, contain all relevant data a stakeholder needs to understand the financial condition and performance of the company. Nonessential data are excluded to avoid clutter.

Accounting Period Concept

The **accounting period concept** requires that accounting data be recorded and summarized in financial statements for periods of time. For example, transactions are recorded for a period of time such as a month or a year. The accounting records are then summarized and updated before preparing the financial statements.

The financial history of a company may be shown by a series of balance sheets and income statements. If the life of a company is expressed by a line moving from left to right, the financial history of the company may be graphed as shown in Exhibit 12.

EXHIBIT 12   Financial History of a Company

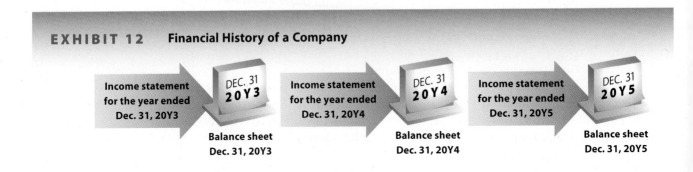

Responsible Reporting

The reliability of the financial reporting system is important to the economy and for the ability of businesses to raise money from investors. That is, stockholders and creditors require accurate financial reporting before they will invest their money. Scandals and financial reporting frauds threaten the confidence of investors. Exhibit 13 is a partial list of financial reporting frauds and abuses.

The companies listed in Exhibit 13 were caught in the midst of ethical lapses that led to fines, firings, and criminal or civil prosecution. The second column of Exhibit 13 identifies the accounting concept that was violated in committing these unethical business practices. For example, the WorldCom fraud involved reporting various expense items as though they were assets. This is a violation of the matching concept and resulted in overstating income and assets. The third

Accounting Frauds   **EXHIBIT 13**

Company	Concept Violated	Result
Adelphia	*Business Entity Concept:* Rigas family treated the company assets as their own.	Bankruptcy. Rigas family members convicted of fraud and lost their investment in the company.
AIG	*Business Entity Concept:* Compensation transactions with an off-shore company that should have been disclosed on AIG's books.	CEO (Chief Executive Officer) resigned. AIG paid out $126 million in fines.
AOL and PurchasePro	*Matching Concept:* Back-dated contracts to inflate revenues.	Civil charges filed against senior executives of both companies. Fined $500 million.
Computer Associates	*Matching Concept:* Fraudulently inflating revenues.	CEO and senior executives indicted. Five executives pled guilty. Fined $225 million.
Enron	*Business Entity Concept:* Treated transactions as revenue, when they should have been treated as debt.	Bankruptcy. Criminal charges against senior executives. Over $60 billion in stock market losses.
Fannie Mae	*Accounting Period Concept:* Managing earnings by shifting expenses between periods.	CEO and CFO fired. $9 billion in restated earnings.
HealthSouth	*Matching Concept:* $4 billion in false entries to overstate revenues.	Senior executives faced regulatory *and* civil charges.
Quest	*Matching Concept:* Improper recognition of $3 billion in revenue.	CEO and six other executives charged with "massive financial fraud." Fined $250 million by SEC.
Tyco	*Adequate Disclosure Concept:* Failure to disclose secret loans to executives that were subsequently forgiven.	CEO forced to resign and was convicted in criminal proceedings.
WorldCom	*Matching Concept:* Improperly treated expenses as assets.	Bankruptcy. Criminal conviction of CEO and CFO. Over $100 billion in stock market losses. Directors fined $18 million.
Xerox	*Matching Concept:* Recognized $3 billion in revenue in periods earlier than should have been recognized.	Fined $10 million by SEC. Six executives fined $22 million.

column of the exhibit identifies some of the results of these events. In most cases, senior and mid-level executives lost their jobs and were sued by upset stakeholders. In some cases, the executives also were criminally prosecuted and are serving prison terms.

Integrity, Objectivity, and Ethics in Business

DOING THE RIGHT THING

Time magazine named three women as "Persons of the Year 2002." Each of these not-so-ordinary women had the courage, determination, and integrity to do the right thing. Each risked their personal careers to expose short-comings in their organizations. Sherron Watkins, an **Enron** vice president, wrote a letter to Enron's chairman, Kenneth Lay, warning him of improper accounting that eventually led to Enron's collapse. Cynthia Cooper, an internal accountant, informed **WorldCom**'s Board of Directors of phony accounting that allowed WorldCom to cover up over $3 billion in losses and forced WorldCom into bankruptcy. Coleen Rowley, an FBI staff attorney, wrote a memo to FBI Director Robert Mueller, exposing how the Bureau brushed off her pleas to investigate Zacarias Moussaoui, who was indicted as a co-conspirator in the September 11 terrorist attacks.

What went wrong for the managers and companies listed in Exhibit 13? The answer normally involved one or both of the following factors:

- *Failure of Individual Character.* Ethical managers and accountants are honest and fair. However, managers and accountants often face pressures from supervisors to meet company and investor expectations. In many of the cases in Exhibit 13, managers and accountants justified small ethical violations to avoid such pressures. However, these small violations became big violations as the company's financial problems became worse.
- *Culture of Greed and Ethical Indifference.* By their behavior and attitude, senior managers set the company culture. In most of the companies listed in Exhibit 13, the senior managers created a culture of greed and indifference to the truth.

In 2008, Bernard Madoff admitted defrauding clients of up to $50 billion in a massive Ponzi scheme that was committed over a number of years.

As a result of accounting and business frauds, the United States Congress passed laws to monitor the behavior of accounting and business. For example, the Sarbanes-Oxley Act of 2002 (SOX) was enacted. SOX established a new oversight body for the accounting profession called the Public Company Accounting Oversight Board (PCAOB). In addition, SOX established standards for independence, corporate responsibility, and disclosure.

How does one behave ethically when faced with financial or other types of pressure? Guidelines for behaving ethically are shown in Exhibit 14.

EXHIBIT 14

Guidelines for Ethical Conduct

1. Identify an ethical decision by using your personal ethical standards of honesty and fairness.
2. Identify the consequences of the decision and its effect on others.
3. Consider your obligations and responsibilities to those that will be affected by your decision.
4. Make a decision that is ethical and fair to those affected by it.

Many companies have ethical standards of conduct for managers and employees. In addition, the Institute of Management Accountants and the American Institute of Certified Public Accountants have professional codes of conduct.

Obj | 6

Describe and illustrate how the rate of return on assets can be used to analyze and assess a company's financial performance.

Financial Analysis: Rate of Return on Assets

Financial statements are often used in analyzing and assessing a company's financial condition and performance. One method is simply to compare financial statements and financial ratios across companies. Such comparisons often are made within an industry and across competing companies within the same industry.

The rate of return on assets is often used to compare a company's performance over time and with competitors. The rate of return on assets is a measure of a company's profitability. Normally, it is expressed as a percent such as 12%. However, it may also be expressed as an amount per dollar invested. For example, a 12% rate of return on assets could also be expressed as $0.12 return per $1 invested. In other words, the company is returning 12 cents per dollar invested.

The **rate of return on assets** is computed as a percentage as follows:

$$\text{Rate of Return on Assets} = \frac{\text{Net Income before Taxes and Interest Expense}}{\text{Average Total Assets}}$$

Taxes and interest are excluded from the numerator. Taxes are excluded to minimize differences among company tax strategies and tax structures. Interest expense is excluded to minimize differences in how companies are financed. For example, some companies finance their operations primarily by debt, while other companies finance their operations primarily by equity.

To illustrate, the rate of return on assets (rounded to one decimal place) is computed for Apple Inc. and Dell Inc. The computations use data (in millions) from recent financial statements.

	Apple Inc.	Dell Inc.
Net income before taxes and interest expense	$ 55,763	$ 4,431
Total assets at beginning of year	$176,064	$44,533
Total assets at end of year	$116,371	$38,599
Average total assets:		
Apple Inc. [($176,064 + $116,371) ÷ 2]	$146,218	
Dell Inc. [($44,533 + $38,599) ÷ 2]		$41,566
Rate of return on assets:		
Apple Inc. ($55,763 ÷ $146,218)	38.1%	
Dell Inc. ($4,431 ÷ $41,566)		10.7%

As shown above, Apple is 3.8 (38.1% ÷ 10.7%) times more profitable as measured by the rate of return on assets than is Dell Inc. Apple's profitability is largely due to its innovative technology, including its iPad, iPhone, iPod, and iMac computers. Whether Apple will be able to continue to innovate since Steve Jobs's death is a continuing question for investors.

Key Points

1. **Describe the types and forms of businesses, how businesses make money, and business stakeholders.**

The three types of businesses operated for profit include manufacturing, merchandising, and service businesses. Such businesses may be organized as proprietorships, partnerships, corporations, and limited liability companies. A business may make money (profits) by gaining an advantage over its competitors using a low-cost or a premium-price emphasis. Under a *low-cost emphasis*, a business designs and produces products or services at a lower cost than its competitors. Under a *premium-price emphasis*, a business tries to design products or services that possess unique attributes or characteristics for which customers are willing to pay more. A business' economic performance is of interest to its stakeholders. Business stakeholders include four categories: capital market stakeholders, product or service market stakeholders, government stakeholders, and internal stakeholders.

2. **Describe the three business activities of financing, investing, and operating.**

All businesses engage in financing, investing, and operating activities. Financing activities involve obtaining funds to begin and operate a business. Investing activities involve obtaining the necessary resources to start and operate the business. Operating activities involve using the business's resources according to its business emphasis.

3. **Define accounting and describe its role in business.**

Accounting is an information system that provides reports to stakeholders about the economic activities and condition of a business. Accounting is the "language of business."

4. **Describe and illustrate the basic financial statements and how they interrelate.**

The principal financial statements of a corporation are the income statement, the retained earnings statement, the balance sheet, and the statement of cash flows. The income statement reports a period's net income or net loss, which also appears on the retained earnings statement. The ending retained earnings reported on the retained earnings statement is also reported on the balance sheet. The ending cash balance is reported on the balance sheet and the statement of cash flows.

5. Describe eight accounting concepts underlying financial reporting.

The eight accounting concepts discussed in this chapter include the business entity, cost, going concern,

matching, objectivity, unit of measure, adequate disclosure, and accounting period concepts.

6. Describe and illustrate how the rate of return on assets can be used to analyze and assess a company's financial performance.

The rate of return on assets is computed by dividing net income before taxes and interest expense by average total assets. It is useful in assessing how much a company is earning for each dollar of invested assets.

Key Terms

Accounting (9)
Accounting equation (13)
Accounting period concept (20)
Accounts payable (8)
Accounts receivable (8)
Adequate disclosure concept (20)
Administrative expenses (9)
Assets (8)
Balance sheet (13)
Bonds payable (8)
Business (2)
Business entity concept (18)
Business stakeholder (5)
Capital stock (8)
Common stock (8)
Corporation (3)
Cost concept (18)
Cost of goods sold (9)

Cost of merchandise sold (9)
Cost of sales (9)
Dividends (8)
Expenses (9)
Fees earned (9)
Financial accounting (9)
Financial Accounting Standards Board (FASB) (17)
Financial statements (10)
Financing activities (7)
Generally accepted accounting principles (GAAP) (17)
Going concern concept (19)
Income statement (11)
Intangible assets (8)
Interest payable (8)
International Accounting Standards Board (IASB) (17)

Investing activities (7)
Liabilities (7)
Limited liability company (LLC) (3)
Low-cost strategy (4)
Managerial accounting (9)
Manufacturing business (2)
Matching concept (19)
Merchandising business (2)
Net income (9)
Net loss (9)
Note payable (8)
Objectivity concept (19)
Operating activities (7)
Owner's equity (13)
Partnership (2)
Premium-price strategy (4)
Prepaid expenses (8)
Profit (2)
Proprietorship (2)

Rate of return on assets (22)
Retained earnings (12)
Retained earnings statement (12)
Revenue (9)
Sales (9)
Securities and Exchange Commission (SEC) (17)
Selling expenses (9)
Service business (2)
Statement of cash flows (13)
Statement of financial condition (13)
Stockholders (8)
Stockholders' equity (13)
Tangible assets (8)
Unit of measure concept (20)

Illustrative Problem

The financial statements at the end of Spratlin Consulting's first month of operations follow.

SPRATLIN CONSULTING
Income Statement
For the Month Ended June 30, 20Y8

Fees earned		$ 36,000
Operating expenses:		
Wages expense	$12,000	
Rent expense	7,640	
Utilities expense	(a)	
Miscellaneous expense	1,320	
Total operating expenses		23,120
Net income		$ (b)

SPRATLIN CONSULTING
Retained Earnings Statement
For the Month Ended June 30, 20Y8

Net income for June..	$ (c)
Less dividends	(d)
Retained earnings, June 30, 20Y8	$ (e)

SPRATLIN CONSULTING
Balance Sheet
June 30, 20Y8

Assets

Cash...	$ 5,600
Land..	50,000
Total assets	$ (f)

Liabilities

Accounts payable	$ 1,920

Stockholders' Equity

Capital stock...	$ (g)
Retained earnings...	(h)
Total stockholders' equity	$ (i)
Total liabilities and stockholders' equity	$ (j)

SPRATLIN CONSULTING
Statement of Cash Flows
For the Month Ended June 30, 20Y8

Cash flows from operating activities:		
Cash received from customers....................................	$36,000	
Deduct cash payments for operating expenses...................	(k)	
Net cash flows from operating activities.........................		$14,800
Cash flows from investing activities:		
Cash payments for acquisition of land		(l)
Cash flows from financing activities:		
Cash received from issuing capital stock	$48,000	
Deduct dividends...	7,200	
Net cash flows from financing activities.........................		(m)
Net cash flow and June 30, 20Y8 cash balance......................		$ (n)

Instructions

By analyzing how the four financial statements are integrated, determine the proper amounts for (a) through (n).

Solution

a. Utilities expense, $2,160 ($23,120 − $12,000 − $7,640 − $1,320)
b. Net income, $12,880 ($36,000 − $23,120)
c. Net income, $12,880 [same as (b)]
d. Dividends, $7,200 (from statement of cash flows)
e. Retained earnings, $5,680 ($12,880 − $7,200)
f. Total assets, $55,600 ($5,600 + $50,000)
g. Capital stock, $48,000 (from the statement of cash flows)
h. Retained earnings, $5,680 [same as (e)]
i. Total stockholders' equity, $53,680 ($48,000 + $5,680)
j. Total liabilities and stockholders' equity, $55,600 ($1,920 + $53,680) [same as (f)]
k. Cash payments for operating expenses, $21,200 ($36,000 − $14,800)
l. Cash payments for acquisition of land, $50,000 (from balance sheet)
m. Net cash flows from financing activities, $40,800 ($48,000 − $7,200)
n. Net cash flow and June 30, 20Y8, cash balance, $5,600 ($14,800 − $50,000 + $40,800)

Self-Examination Questions *(Answers appear at the end of chapter)*

1. A profit-making business operating as a separate legal entity and in which ownership is divided into shares of stock is known as a:
   A. proprietorship.
   B. service business.
   C. partnership.
   D. corporation.

2. The resources owned by a business are called:
   A. assets.
   B. liabilities.
   C. the accounting equation.
   D. stockholders' equity.

3. A listing of a business entity's assets, liabilities, and stockholders' equity as of a specific date is:
   A. a balance sheet.
   B. an income statement.
   C. the retained earnings statement.
   D. a statement of cash flows.

4. If total assets are $20,000 and total liabilities are $12,000, the amount of stockholders' equity is:
   A. $32,000.
   B. ($32,000).
   C. ($8,000).
   D. $8,000.

5. If revenue was $45,000, expenses were $37,500, and dividends were $10,000, the amount of net income or net loss would be:
   A. $45,000 net income.
   B. 7,500 net income.
   C. $37,500 net loss.
   D. $2,500 net loss.

Class Discussion Questions

1. What is the objective of most businesses?

2. What is the difference between a manufacturing business and a merchandising business? Give an example of each type of business.

3. What is the difference between a manufacturing business and a service business? Is a restaurant a manufacturing business, a service business, or both?

4. Why are most large companies like Apple, Pepsi, General Electric, and Intel organized as corporations?

5. Both KIA and BMW produce and sell automobiles. Describe and contrast the business emphasis of KIA and BMW.

6. Assume that a friend of yours operates a family-owned pharmacy. A super Walmart, scheduled to open in the next several months, will also offer pharmacy services. What business emphasis would your friend use to compete with the Super Walmart pharmacy?

7. What services does eBay offer its customers?

8. A business's stakeholders can be classified into capital market, product or service market, government, and internal stakeholders. Will the interests of all the stakeholders within a classification be the same? Use bankers and stockholders of the capital market as an example in answering this question.

9. The three business activities are financing, investing, and operating. Using Southwest Airlines, give an example of a financing, investing, and operating activity.

10. What is the role of accounting in business?

11. Briefly describe the nature of the information provided by each of the following financial statements: the income statement, the retained earnings statement, the balance sheet, and the statement of cash flows. In your descriptions, indicate whether each of the financial statements covers a period of time or is for a specific date.

12. For a recent year ending January 28, Target Corporation had revenues of $69,865 million and total expenses of $66,936 million. Did Target Corporation report a net loss or a net income?

13. What particular item of financial or operating data appears on both the income statement and the retained earnings statement? What item appears on both the balance sheet and the retained earnings statement? What item appears on both the balance sheet and statement of cash flows?

14. Billy Jessop is the owner of Valley Delivery Service. Recently, Billy paid interest of $6,000 on a personal loan of $75,000 that he used to begin the business. Should Valley Delivery Service record the interest payment? Explain.

15. On October 1, Wok Repair Service extended an offer of $100,000 for land that had been priced for sale at $150,000. On December 19, Wok Repair Service accepted the seller's counteroffer of $110,000. Describe how Wok Repair Service should record the land.

16. Land with an assessed value of $500,000 for property tax purposes is acquired by a business for $600,000. Four years later, the plot of land has an assessed value of $750,000 and the business receives an offer of $975,000 for it. Should the monetary amount assigned to the land in the business records now be increased?

Exercises

E1-1 Types of businesses

Obj 1

Indicate whether each of the following companies is primarily a service, merchandise, or manufacturing business. If you are unfamiliar with the company, you may use the Internet to locate the company's home page or use the finance Web site of Yahoo.com.

1. Allstate	9. First BanCorp
2. Best Buy	10. Ford Motor
3. Boeing	11. Goodyear Tire & Rubber
4. Caterpillar	12. Hilton Hotels
5. Citigroup	13. H&R Block Inc.
6. CVS Caremark	14. Pfizer
7. Dow Chemical	15. Sears Roebuck
8. Eli Lilly	

E1-2 Business emphasis

Obj 1

Identify the primary business emphasis of each of the following companies as (a) a low-cost emphasis or (b) a premium-price emphasis. If you are unfamiliar with the company, you may use the Internet to locate the company's home page or use the finance Web site of Yahoo.com.

1. Allegiant Travel Services	7. Lowe's
2. Best Buy	8. Nike
3. BMW	9. Pepsi
4. Dollar Tree	10. Staples
5. E*TRADE	11. Sub-Zero
6. Goldman Sachs Group	12. Trader Joe's

E1-3 Accounting equation

Obj 4

✔ Best Buy, $3,745

The total assets and total liabilities for a recent year of Best Buy and Gamestop are shown below.

	Best Buy (in millions)	Gamestop (in millions)
Assets	$16,005	$4,847
Liabilities	12,260	1,805

Determine the stockholders' equity of each company.

E1-4 Accounting equation

Obj 4

✔ Dell, $8,917

The total assets and total liabilities for a recent year of Apple and Dell are shown here.

	Apple (in millions)	Dell (in millions)
Assets	$176,064	$44,533
Liabilities	57,854	35,616

Determine the stockholders' equity of each company.

Obj 4

✔ a. $160,000

E1-5   Accounting equation

Determine the missing amount for each of the following:

	Assets	=	Liabilities	+	Stockholders' Equity
a.	X	=	$ 70,000	+	$90,000
b.	$ 95,000	=	X	+	$18,000
c.	$675,000	=	$227,000	+	X

Obj 4

✔ a. $12,361

E1-6   Accounting equation

Determine the missing amounts (in millions) for the condensed balance sheets shown below.

	Costco	Target	Walmart
Assets	$27,140	$46,630	$ (c)
Liabilities	14,779	(b)	117,645
Stockholders' equity	(a)	15,821	75,761

Obj 4

E1-7   Net income and dividends

The income statement of a corporation for the month of November indicates a net income of $90,000. During the same period, $100,000 in cash dividends were paid.

Would it be correct to say that the business incurred a net loss of $10,000 during the month? Discuss.

Obj 4

✔ Company Chang:
   Net income,
   $225,000

E1-8   Net income and stockholders' equity for four businesses

Four different companies—Chang, Henry, Nagel, and Wilcox—show the same balance sheet data at the beginning and end of a year. These data, exclusive of the amount of stockholders' equity, are summarized as follows:

	Total Assets	Total Liabilities
Beginning of the year	$775,000	$400,000
End of the year	900,000	300,000

On the basis of the preceding data and the following additional information for the year, determine the net income (or loss) of each company for the year. (*Hint:* First determine the amount of increase or decrease in stockholders' equity during the year.)

Company Chang: No additional capital stock was issued, and no dividends were paid.
Company Henry: No additional capital stock was issued, but dividends of $90,000 were paid.
Company Nagel: Capital stock of $125,000 was issued, but no dividends were paid.
Company Wilcox: Capital stock of $125,000 was issued, and dividends of $90,000 were paid.

Obj 4

✔ a. (1) $6,415,471

E1-9   Accounting equation and income statement

Staples, Inc., is a leading office products distributor, with retail stores in the United States, Canada, Asia, Europe, and South America. The following financial statement data were adapted from recent financial statements of Staples:

	Year 2 (in thousands)	Year 1 (in thousands)
Total assets	$13,430,622	$13,911,667
Total liabilities	(1)	6,967,957
Total stockholders' equity	7,015,151	(2)
Sales	25,022,192	
Cost of goods sold	18,280,364	
Selling and administrative expenses	5,048,492	
Other expense (net)	233,372	
Income tax expense	475,308	

a. Determine the missing data indicated for (1) and (2).

b. Using the income statement data for Year 2, determine the amount of net income or loss.

E1-10 Balance sheet items

Obj 4

From the following list of selected items taken from the records of Flip Flop Sandals Inc. as of a specific date, identify those that would appear on the balance sheet.

1. Accounts Receivable
2. Capital Stock
3. Cash
4. Fees Earned
5. Rent Expense

6. Salaries Expense
7. Salaries Payable
8. Supplies
9. Supplies Expense
10. Utilities Expense

E1-11 Income statement items

Obj 4

Based on the data presented in Exercise 1-10, identify those items that would appear on the income statement.

E1-12 Financial statement items

Obj 4

Identify each of the following items as (a) an asset, (b) a liability, (c) revenue, (d) an expense, or (e) a dividend:

1. Amounts due from customers
2. Amounts owed suppliers
3. Cash on hand
4. Cash paid to stockholders
5. Cash sales

6. Equipment
7. Note payable owed to the bank
8. Rent paid for the month
9. Sales commissions paid to salespersons
10. Wages paid to employees

E1-13 Retained earnings statement

Obj 4

Financial information related to Coil Company for the month ended June 30, 20Y7, is as follows:

Net income for June	$230,000
Dividends during June	45,000
Retained earnings, June 1, 20Y7	615,000

Prepare a retained earnings statement for the month ended June 30, 20Y7.

✔ Retained earnings, June 30, 20--: $800,000

E1-14 Income statement

Obj 4

Moonlight Services was organized on February 1, 20Y5. A summary of the revenue and expense transactions for February follows:

Fees earned	$925,000
Wages expense	400,000
Miscellaneous expense	25,000
Rent expense	92,000
Supplies expense	13,000

Prepare an income statement for the month ended February 28.

✔ Net income: $395,000

Note: The spreadsheet icon indicates an Excel template is available on the student companion site at www.cengagebrain.com.

Obj 4

✔ (a) $90,000

E1-15   Missing amounts from balance sheet and income statement data

One item is omitted in each of the following summaries of balance sheet and income statement data for four different corporations, AL, CO, KS, and MT.

	AL	CO	KS	MT
Beginning of the year:				
Assets	$400,000	$300,000	$550,000	$ (d)
Liabilities	200,000	130,000	325,000	350,000
End of the year:				
Assets	800,000	460,000	660,000	1,200,000
Liabilities	450,000	110,000	360,000	700,000
During the year:				
Additional issue of capital stock	(a)	50,000	100,000	100,000
Dividends	50,000	20,000	(c)	90,000
Revenue	175,000	(b)	115,000	420,000
Expenses	65,000	70,000	130,000	480,000

Determine the missing amounts, identifying them by letter. [*Hint:* First determine the amount of increase or decrease in stockholders' equity during the year.]

Obj 4

✔ b. $53,000

E1-16   Balance sheets, net income

Financial information related to Montana Interiors for October and November 20Y8 is as follows:

	October 31, 20Y8	November 30, 20Y8
Accounts payable	$ 40,000	$ 65,000
Accounts receivable	75,000	118,000
Capital stock	60,000	60,000
Retained earnings	?	?
Cash	110,000	140,000
Supplies	15,000	20,000

a. Prepare balance sheets for Montana Interiors as of October 31 and as of November 30, 20Y8.

b. Determine the amount of net income for November, assuming that no additional capital stock was issued and no dividends were paid during the month.

c. Determine the amount of net income for November, assuming that no additional capital stock was issued but dividends of $20,000 were paid during the month.

Obj 4

E1-17   Financial statements

Each of the following items is shown in the financial statements of ExxonMobil Corporation. Identify the financial statement (balance sheet or income statement) in which each item would appear.

a. Accounts payable
b. Cash equivalents
c. Crude oil inventory
d. Equipment
e. Exploration expenses
f. Income taxes payable
g. Investments
h. Long-term debt
i. Marketable securities
j. Notes and loans payable
k. Operating expenses
l. Prepaid taxes
m. Retained earnings
n. Sales
o. Selling expenses

E1-18   Statement of cash flows

Obj **4**

Indicate whether each of the following cash activities would be reported on the statement of cash flows as (a) an operating activity, (b) an investing activity, or (c) a financing activity.

1. Issued capital stock
2. Paid rent
3. Paid for office equipment
4. Sold services
5. Issued a note payable

6. Sold excess office equipment
7. Paid officers' salaries
8. Paid for advertising
9. Paid insurance
10. Paid dividends

E1-19   Statement of cash flows

Obj **4**

Indicate whether each of the following activities would be reported on the statement of cash flows as (a) an operating activity, (b) an investing activity, or (c) a financing activity.

1. Cash received from investment by stockholders ℭ
2. Cash received from fees earned a
3. Cash paid for expenses a
4. Cash paid for land ♭

E1-20   Statement of cash flows

Obj **4**

Looney Inc. was organized on July 1, Year 1. A summary of cash flows for July follows.

Cash receipts:	
Cash received from customers	$600,000
Cash received from sale of capital stock	200,000
Cash received from note payable	75,000
Cash payments:	
Cash paid out for expenses	$380,000
Cash paid out for purchase of equipment	95,000
Cash paid as dividends	25,000

✔ Net cash flows from operating activities, $220,000

Prepare a statement of cash flows for the month ended July 31, Year 1.

E1-21   Using financial statements

Obj **4**

A company's stakeholders often differ in their financial statement focus. For example, some stakeholders focus primarily on the income statement, while others may focus primarily on the statement of cash flows or the balance sheet. For each of the following situations, indicate which financial statement would be the likely focus for the stakeholder. Choose either the income statement, balance sheet, or statement of cash flows and justify your choice.

Situation 1: Assume that you are considering purchasing a personal computer from Dell.
Situation 2: Assume that you are considering investing in LinkedIn (capital market stakeholder).
Situation 3: Assume that you are employed by Campbell Soup Co. (product market stakeholder) and are considering whether to extend credit for a 60-day period to a new grocery store chain that has recently opened throughout the Midwest.
Situation 4: Assume that you are considering taking a job (internal stakeholder) with either Sears or JCPenney.
Situation 5: Assume that you are a banker for US Bank (capital market stakeholder), and you are considering whether to grant a major credit line (loan) to Target. The credit line will allow Target to borrow up to $400 million for a five-year period at the market rate of interest.

E1-22   Financial statement items

Obj **4**

Amazon.com, Inc., operates as an online retailer in North America and internationally. Both Amazon and third parties, via the Amazon.com Web site, sell products across various product categories.

The following items were adapted from a recent annual report of Amazon.com for the year ending December 31, 20Y1:

	In millions
1. Accounts payable	$14,896
2. Accounts receivable	2,922
3. Cash	5,269
4. Cost of sales	37,288
5. Income tax expense	291
6. Interest expense	65
7. Inventories	4,992
8. Net cash provided by operating activities	3,903
9. Net cash flows used for investing activities	(1,930)
10. Net sales	48,077
11. Other income	125
12. Property, plant, and other long-term assets	7,788
13. Selling, general, and administrative expenses	9,927
14. Retained earnings (Jan. 1, 20Y1)	1,955

Using the following notations, indicate on which financial statement you would find each of the preceding items. (*Note:* An item may appear on more than one statement.)

IS	Income statement
RE	Retained earnings statement
BS	Balance sheet
SCF	Statement of cash flows

Obj **4**

✔ Net income, $631

E1-23 Income statement

Based on the Amazon.com, Inc., financial statement data shown in Exercise 1-22, prepare an income statement for the year ending December 31, 20Y1.

Obj **4**

E1-24 Financial statement items

Though the McDonald's menu of hamburgers, cheeseburgers, the Big Mac®, Quarter Pounder®, Filet-O-Fish®, and Chicken McNuggets® is easily recognized, McDonald's financial statements may not be as familiar. The following items were adapted from a recent annual report of McDonald's Corporation:

1. Accounts payable
2. Accrued interest payable
3. Capital stock outstanding
4. Cash
5. Cash provided by operations
6. Food and packaging costs used in operations
7. Income tax expense
8. Interest expense
9. Inventories
10. Long-term debt payable
11. Net income
12. Net increase in cash
13. Notes payable
14. Notes receivable
15. Occupancy and rent expense
16. Payroll expense
17. Prepaid expenses not yet used in operations
18. Property and equipment
19. Retained earnings
20. Sales

Identify the financial statement on which each of the preceding items would appear. An item may appear on more than one statement. Use the following notations:

IS	Income statement
RE	Retained earnings statement
BS	Balance sheet
SCF	Statement of cash flows

E1-25   Financial statements

Outlaw Realty, organized August 1, Year 1, is owned and operated by Julie Baxter. How many errors can you find in the following financial statements for Outlaw Realty, prepared after its first month of operations? Assume that the cash balance on August 31, Year 1, is $51,600 and that cash flows from operating activities is reported correctly.

Obj **4**

✔ Correct amount of total assets is $200,000

OUTLAW REALTY
Income Statement
August 31, Year 1

Sales commissions		$408,400
Operating expenses:		
Office salaries expense	$272,600	
Rent expense	31,200	
Miscellaneous expense	2,200	
Automobile expense	7,900	
Total operating expenses		313,900
Net income		$134,500

JULIE BAXTER
Retained Earnings Statement
August 31, Year 2

Retained earnings, August 1, Year 1	$ 7,800
Less dividends during August	12,000
	$ 5,800
Net income for the month	134,500
Retained earnings, August 31, Year 1	$ 40,300

Balance Sheet
For the Month Ended August 31, Year 1

Assets

Cash		$ 51,600
Accounts payable		17,500
Land		60,000
Total assets		$129,100

Liabilities

Accounts receivable		$ 81,200
Prepaid expenses		7,200

Stockholders' Equity

Capital stock	$100,000	
Retained earnings	140,300	240,300
Total liabilities and stockholders' equity		$328,700

Statement of Cash Flows
August 31, Year 1

Cash flows from operating activities:		
Cash received from customers..	$327,200	
Cash paid for operating expenses..............................	303,600	
Net cash flow from operating activities		$ 23,600
Cash flows from financing activities:		
Cash received from issuance of capital stock	$100,000	
Dividends paid to stockholders................................	(12,000)	
Net cash flow from financing activities.........................		88,000
Net cash flow and cash balance as of January 31, Year 1..............		$111,600

E1-26   Accounting concepts

Match each of the following statements with the appropriate accounting concept. Some concepts may be used more than once, while others may not be used at all. Use the notations shown to indicate the appropriate accounting concept.

Accounting Concept	Notation
Accounting period concept	P
Adequate disclosure concept	D
Business entity concept	B
Cost concept	C
Going concern concept	G
Matching concept	M
Objectivity concept	O
Unit of measure concept	U

Statements

1. Assume that a business will continue forever.
2. Material litigation involving the corporation is described in a note.
3. Monthly utilities costs are reported as expenses along with the monthly revenues.
4. Personal transactions of owners are kept separate from the business.
5. This concept supports relying on an independent actuary (statistician), rather than the chief operating officer of the corporation, to estimate a pension liability.
6. Changes in the use of accounting methods from one period to the next are described in the notes to the financial statements.
7. Land worth $800,000 is reported at its original purchase price of $220,000.
8. This concept justifies recording only transactions that are expressed in dollars.
9. If this concept was ignored, the confidence of users in the financial statements could not be maintained.
10. The changes in financial condition are reported at the end of the month.

E1-27   Business entity concept

Crazy Mountain Sports sells hunting and fishing equipment and provides guided hunting and fishing trips. Crazy Mountain is owned and operated by Karl Young, a well-known sports enthusiast and hunter. Karl's wife, Mila, owns and operates Mila's Boutique, a women's clothing store. Karl and Mila have established a trust fund to finance their children's college education. The trust fund is maintained by First Bank in the names of their children, Steve and Isabelle.

For each of the following transactions, identify which of the entities listed should record the transaction in its records.

Entities

C	Crazy Mountain Sports
B	First Bank Trust Fund
M	Mila's Boutique
X	None of the above

1. Karl paid a local doctor for a physical, which was required by the workmen's compensation insurance policy carried by Crazy Mountain Sports.

2. Karl received a cash advance from customers for a guided hunting trip.

3. Mila paid her dues to the YWCA.

4. Karl paid a breeder's fee for an English Springer spaniel to be used as a hunting guide dog.

5. Mila deposited a $10,000 personal check in the trust fund at First Bank.

6. Karl paid for an advertisement in a hunters' magazine.

7. Mila authorized the trust fund to purchase mutual fund shares.

8. Mila donated several dresses from the store's inventory to a local charity auction for the benefit of a women's abuse shelter.

9. Karl paid for dinner and a movie to celebrate the couple's fifteenth wedding anniversary.

10. Mila purchased two dozen spring dresses from a Boise designer for a special spring sale.

Problems

P1-1 Income statement, retained earnings statement, and balance sheet

Obj **4**

The amounts of the assets and liabilities of Utah Travel Service as of April 30, 20Y6, the end of the current year, and its revenue and expenses for the year are listed below. The retained earnings were $300,000, and the capital stock was $90,000 as of May 1, 20Y5, the beginning of the current year. Dividends of $75,000 were paid during the current year.

Accounts payable	$ 71,500
Accounts receivable	188,100
Cash	428,300
Fees earned	1,594,200
Miscellaneous expense	16,000
Rent expense	226,800
Supplies	20,100
Supplies expense	42,600
Taxes expense	33,600
Utilities expense	135,000
Wages expense	890,200

✔ 1. Net income: $250,000

Instructions

1. Prepare an income statement for the current year ended April 30, 20Y6.

2. Prepare a retained earnings statement for the current year ended April 30, 20Y6.

3. Prepare a balance sheet as of April 30, 20Y6.

Obj **4**

✔ j. $314,000

P1-2 Missing amounts from financial statements

The financial statements at the end of Paradise Realty's first month of operations are shown below.

PARADISE REALTY
Income Statement
For the Month Ended November 30, 20Y3

Fees earned		$149,300
Operating expenses:		
Wages expense	$ (a)	
Rent expense	14,400	
Supplies expense	12,000	
Utilities expense	8,100	
Miscellaneous expense	4,950	
Total operating expenses		69,300
Net income		$ (b)

PARADISE REALTY
Retained Earnings Statement
For the Month Ended November 30, 20Y3

Net income for November	$ (c)
Less dividends	(d)
Retained earnings, November 30, 20Y3	$ (e)

PARADISE REALTY
Balance Sheet
November 30, 20Y3

Assets

Cash	$ 99,200
Supplies	6,000
Land	(f)
Total assets	$ (g)

Liabilities

Note payable	$ 7,200

Stockholders' Equity

Capital stock	$ (h)	
Retained earnings	(i)	
Total stockholders' equity		(j)
Total liabilities and stockholders' equity		$ (k)

PARADISE REALTY
Statement of Cash Flows
For the Month Ended November 30, 20Y3

Cash flows from operating activities:		
Cash received from customers	$ (l)	
Deduct cash payments for expenses and payments to creditors	68,100	
Net cash flows from operating activities		$ (m)
Cash flows used for investing activities:		
Cash payments for acquisition of land		(216,000)
Cash flows from financing activities:		
Cash received from issuing capital stock	$270,000	
Deduct dividends	36,000	
Net cash flows from financing activities		(n)
Net cash flow and November 30, 20Y3, cash balance		$ (o)

Instructions

1. Would you classify a realty business such as Hamel Realty as a manufacturing, merchandising, or service business?

2. By analyzing the interrelationships among the financial statements, determine the proper amounts for (a) through (o).

P1-3 Income statement, retained earnings statement, and balance sheet

Obj 4

The following financial data were adapted from a recent annual report of Target Corporation for the year ending January 28, 20Y2.

	In millions
Accounts payable	$ 6,857
Capital stock	2,862
Cash	794
Cost of goods sold	47,860
Debt and other borrowings	17,483
Income tax expense	1,527
Interest expense	866
Inventories	7,918
Other assets	2,842
Other expenses	2,577
Other liabilities	6,469
Other credit card revenue	1,399
Property, plant, and equipment	29,149
Receivables	5,927
Sales	68,466
Selling, general, and administrative expenses	14,106

✔ 1. Net income, $2,929

Instructions

1. Prepare Target's income statement for the year ending January 28, 20Y2.

2. Prepare Target's retained earnings statement for the year ending January 29, 20Y2. (*Note:* The retained earnings at January 29, 20Y1, was $12,698. During the year, Target paid dividends and had other reductions in retained earnings of $2,668.)

3. Prepare a balance sheet as of January 28, 20Y2, for Target.

P1-4 Statement of cash flows

Obj 4

The following cash data were adapted from a recent annual report of Google Inc. for the year ended December 31, 20Y1. The cash balance as of January 1, 20Y1, was $13,630 (in millions).

	In millions
Receipts from issuing debt, etc.	$ 829
Purchases of property, plant, and equipment, etc.	67,787
Receipts from sale of investments (net)	48,746
Net cash flows from operating activities	14,565

✔ Net decrease in cash, $3,647

Instructions

Prepare Google's statement of cash flows for the year ended December 31, 20Y1.

Obj 4

✔ 1. Net income,
$230,000

P1-5   Financial statements, including statement of cash flows

Cassandra Corporation began operations on January 1, Year 1, as an online retailer of computer software and hardware. The following financial statement data were taken from Cassandra's records at the end of its first year of operations, December 31, Year 1.

Accounts payable	$ 20,000
Accounts receivable	110,000
Capital stock	252,000
Cash	?
Cash payments for operating activities	657,000
Cash receipts from operating activities	690,000
Cost of sales	435,000
Dividends	30,000
Income tax expense	53,000
Income taxes payable	8,000
Interest expense	2,000
Inventories	115,000
Note payable (due in ten years)	50,000
Property, plant, and equipment	265,000
Retained earnings	?
Sales	800,000
Selling and administrative expenses	80,000

Instructions

1. Prepare an income statement for the year ended December 31, Year 1.
2. Prepare a retained earnings statement for the year ended December 31, Year 1.
3. Prepare a balance sheet as of December 31, Year 1.
4. Prepare a statement of cash flows for the year ended December 31, Year 1.

Financial Analysis

FA1-1   Rate of return on assets

The financial statements of The Hershey Company are shown in Exhibits 6 through 9 of this chapter. Based upon these statements, answer the following questions.

1. What are Hershey's sales (in millions)?
2. What is Hershey's cost of sales (in millions)?
3. What is Hershey's net income (in millions)?
4. What is Hershey's percent of the cost of sales to sales? Round to one decimal place.
5. The percent that a company adds to its cost of sales to determine the selling price is called a markup. What is Hershey's markup percent? Round to one decimal place.
6. What is the percentage of net income to sales for Hershey? Round to one decimal place.
7. Using Exhibit 6, determine income before taxes and interest for Hershey for 2012.
8. Hershey had total assets of $4,412 (million) at the end of 2011. Compute the rate of return on assets for Hershey for 2012.

FA1-2   Rate of return on assets

The following data (in millions) were adapted from recent financial statements of Tootsie Roll Industries Inc.:

Sales	$533
Cost of goods sold	366
Net income	44
Interest expense	0
Tax expense	17
Average total assets	858

1. What is Tootsie Roll's percent of the cost of sales to sales? Round to one decimal place.

2. The percent a company adds to its cost of sales to determine selling price is called a markup. What is Tootsie Roll's markup percent? Round to one decimal place.

3. What is the percentage of net income to sales for Tootsie Roll? Round to one decimal place.

4. Compute the rate of return on assets for Tootsie Roll.

5. Using FA1-1, compare the markup percentages, net income per sales dollar, and rate of return on assets for Hershey and Tootsie Roll.

FA1-3   Rate of return on assets

Obj 6

Pfizer Inc. discovers, produces, and distributes medicines, including Celebrex and Lipitor. **Ford Motor Co.** develops, markets, and produces automobiles and trucks. **Microsoft Corporation** develops, produces, and distributes a variety of computer software and hardware products including Windows, Office, Excel, and the Xbox.

1. Without computing the rates of return on total assets, rank from highest to lowest Pfizer, Ford, and Microsoft in terms of their rates of return on total assets.

2. The following data (in millions) were taken from recent financial statements of each company.

	Pfizer	Ford	Microsoft
Income before taxes and interest	$ 12,762	$ 13,112	$ 22,267
Total assets at the beginning of the year	195,014	164,687	108,704
Total assets at the end of the year	$188,002	$178,348	$121,271

Compute the rate of return for each company using the preceding data, and rank the companies' rates of return from highest to lowest. Round the rates of return to one decimal place.

3. Analyze and explain the rankings in (2).

FA1-4   Rate of return on assets

Obj 6

ExxonMobil Corporation explores, produces, and distributes oil and natural gas. **The Coca-Cola Company** produces and distributes soft drink beverages, including Coke. **Walmart Stores, Inc.,** operates retail stores and supermarkets.

1. Without computing the rates of return on total assets, rank from highest to lowest Exxon-Mobil, Coca-Cola, and Walmart in terms of their rates of return on total assets.

2. The following data (in millions) were taken from recent financial statements of each company.

	ExxonMobil	Coca-Cola	Walmart
Income before taxes and interest	$ 73,504	$11,856	$ 26,720
Total assets at the beginning of the year	302,510	72,921	180,782
Total assets at the end of the year	$ 331,052	$79,974	$193,406

Compute the rates of return for each company using the preceding data, and rank the companies' rates of return from highest to lowest. Round the rates of return to one decimal place.

3. Analyze and explain the rankings in (2).

Obj **6**

FA1-5 Rate of return on assets

Target Corporation is a major competitor of **Walmart**. The following data (in millions) were taken from recent financial statements of Target.

Income before taxes and interest	$ 5,325
Total assets at the beginning of the year	43,705
Total assets at the end of the year	46,630

1. Compute the rate of return for Target using the preceding data. Round to one decimal place.

2. Compare the rate of return for Walmart from FA1-4 to that of Target.

Cases

Case 1-1 Integrity, objectivity, and ethics at The Hershey Company

The management of **The Hershey Company** has asked union workers in two of its highest cost Pennsylvania plants to accept higher health insurance premiums and take a wage cut. The workers' portion of the insurance cost would double from 6% of the premium to 12%. In addition, workers hired after January 2000 would have their hourly wages cut by $4, which would be partially offset by a 2% annual raise. Management says that the plants need to be more cost competitive. Management has indicated that if the workers accept the proposal, the company would invest $30 million to modernize the plants and move future projects to the plants. Management has refused, however, to guarantee more work at the plants even if the workers approve the proposal. If the workers reject the proposal, management implies that it would move future projects to other plants and that layoffs might be forthcoming. Do you consider management's actions ethical?

Source: Susan Govzdas, "Hershey to Cut Jobs or Wages," *Central Penn Business Journal,* September 24, 2004.

GROUP PROJECT

Case 1-2 Ethics and professional conduct in business

Loretta Smith, president and owner of Custom Enterprises, applied for a $250,000 loan from City National Bank. The bank requested financial statements from Custom Enterprises as a basis for granting the loan. Loretta has told her accountant to provide the bank with a balance sheet. Loretta has decided to omit the other financial statements because there was a net loss during the past year.

In groups of three or four, discuss the following questions:

1. Is Loretta behaving in a professional manner by omitting some of the financial statements?

2. a. What types of information about their businesses would owners be willing to provide bankers? What types of information would owners not be willing to provide?

  b. What types of information about a business would bankers want before extending a loan?

  c. What common interests are shared by bankers and business owners?

GROUP PROJECT

Case 1-3 How businesses make money

Assume that you are the chief executive officer for a national poultry producer. The company's operations include hatching chickens through the use of breeder stock and feeding, raising, and processing the mature chicks into finished products. The finished products include breaded chicken nuggets and patties and deboned, skinless, and marinated chicken. The company sells its products to schools, military services, fast-food chains, and grocery stores.

In groups of four or five, discuss the following business emphasis and risk issues:

1. In a commodity business like poultry production, what do you think is the dominant business emphasis? What are the implications in this dominant emphasis for how you would run the company?

2. Identify at least two major business risks for operating the company.

3. How could the company try to differentiate its products?

Case 1-4   Net income versus cash flow

On January 9, 20--, Dr. Susan Tempkin established DocMed, a medical practice organized as a professional corporation. The below conversation took place the following September between Dr. Tempkin and a former medical school classmate, Dr. Phil Anzar, at an American Medical Association convention in London.

Dr. Anzar: Susan, good to see you again. Why didn't you call when you were in Chicago? We could have had dinner together.

Dr. Tempkin: Actually, I never made it to Chicago this year. My husband and kids went to our Wisconsin Dells condo twice, but I got stuck in New York. I opened a new consulting practice this January and haven't had any time for myself since.

Dr. Anzar: I heard about it . . . Doc . . . something . . . right?

Dr. Tempkin: Yes, DocMed. My husband chose the name.

Dr. Anzar: I've thought about doing something like that. Are you making any money? I mean, is it worth your time?

Dr. Tempkin: You wouldn't believe it. I started by opening a bank account with $40,000, and my August bank statement has a balance of $215,000. Not bad for eight months—all pure profit.

Dr. Anzar: Maybe I'll try it in Chicago. Let's have breakfast together tomorrow and you can fill me in on the details.

Comment on Dr. Tempkin's statement that the difference between the opening bank balance ($40,000) and the August statement balance ($215,000) is pure profit.

Case 1-5   The accounting equation

Obtain the annual reports for three well-known companies, such as Ford Motor Co., General Motors, IBM, Microsoft, or Amazon.com. These annual reports can be obtained from the library, the company's Web site under "Investor Relations," **http://www.finance.yahoo.com** (type in the company name for Get Quotes), or the company's 10-K filing with the Securities and Exchange Commission at **http://www.sec.gov/**.

To obtain annual report information under Filings & Forms, click on "Search for Company Filings." Next, click on "Companys or funds, ticker symbol...." Key in the company name. The Electronic Data Gathering, Analysis, and Retrieval system (EDGAR) will list the reports available for the company. Click on the 10-K (or 10-K405) report for the year you want to download. If you wish, you can save the whole 10-K report to a file on your computer.

Examine the balance sheet for each company and determine the total assets, liabilities, and stockholders' equity. Verify that total assets equal the total of the liabilities plus stockholders' equity.

Case 1-6   Financial analysis of Enron Corporation

Enron Corporation, headquartered in Houston, Texas, provided products and services for natural gas, electricity, and communications to wholesale and retail customers. Enron's operations were conducted through a variety of subsidiaries and affiliates that involved transporting gas through pipelines, transmitting electricity, and managing energy commodities. The following data were taken from Enron's December 31, 2000, financial statements:

	In millions
Total revenues	$100,789
Total costs and expenses	98,836
Operating income	1,953
Net income	979
Total assets	65,503
Total liabilities	54,033
Total stockholders' equity	11,470
Net cash flows from operating activities	4,779
Net cash flows from investing activities	(4,264)
Net cash flows from financing activities	571
Net increase in cash	1,086

At the end of 2000, the market price of Enron's stock was approximately $83 per share. Eventually, however, Enron's stock was selling for $0.22 per share.

Review the preceding financial statement data and search the Internet for articles on Enron Corporation. Briefly explain why Enron's stock dropped so dramatically in such a short time.

Answers to Self-Examination Questions

1. **A** A corporation, organized in accordance with state or federal statutes, is a separate legal entity in which ownership is divided into shares of stock (answer D). A proprietorship (answer A) is an unincorporated business owned by one individual. A service business (answer B) provides services to its customers. It can be organized as a proprietorship, partnership, or corporation. A partnership (answer C) is an unincorporated business owned by two or more individuals.

2. **A** The resources owned by a business are called assets (answer A). The debts of the business are called liabilities (answer B), and the equity of the owners is called stockholders' equity (answer D). The relationship among assets, liabilities, and stockholders' equity is expressed as the accounting equation (answer C).

3. **A** The balance sheet is a listing of the assets, liabilities, and stockholders' equity of a business at a specific date (answer A). The income statement (answer B) is a summary of the revenue and expenses of a business for a specific period of time. The retained earnings statement (answer C) summarizes the changes in retained earnings during a specific

period of time. The statement of cash flows (answer D) summarizes the cash receipts and cash payments for a specific period of time.

4. **D** The accounting equation is:

Assets = Liabilities + Stockholders' Equity

Therefore, if assets are $20,000 and liabilities are $12,000, stockholders' equity is $8,000 (answer D), as indicated in the following computation:

Assets	= Liabilities + Stockholders' Equity
+$20,000	= $12,000 + Stockholders' Equity
+$20,000 − $12,000	= Stockholders' Equity
+$8,000	= Stockholders' Equity

5. **B** Net income is the excess of revenue over expenses, or $7,500 (answer B). If expenses exceed revenue, the difference is a net loss. Dividends are the opposite of the stockholders investing in the business and do not affect the amount of net income or net loss.

CHAPTER 2

Basic Accounting Concepts

LEARNING OBJECTIVES
After studying this chapter, you should be able to:

Obj 1   Describe the basic elements of a financial accounting system.

Obj 2   Analyze, record, and summarize transactions for a corporation's first period of operations.

Obj 3   Prepare financial statements for a corporation's first period of operations.

Obj 4   Analyze, record, and summarize transactions for a corporation's second period of operations.

Obj 5   Prepare financial statements for a corporation's second period of operations.

Obj 6   Financial Analysis: Describe and illustrate the use of common-sized income statements in assessing a company's financial performance.

Every day it seems like you get an incredible amount of incoming e-mail messages; you get them from your friends, relatives, subscribed e-mail lists, and even spammers! But how do you organize all of these messages? You might create folders to sort messages by sender, topic, or project. Perhaps you use keyword search utilities. You might even use filters or rules to automatically delete spam or send messages from your best friend to a special folder. In any case, you are organizing information so that it is simple to retrieve and allows you to more easily understand, respond to, or refer to the messages.

In the same way that you organize your e-mail, companies develop an organized method for processing, recording, and summarizing financial transactions. For example, **Twitter** is an information network used by millions to share messages of up to 140 characters. Such messages, called Tweets, are available free to the public. Twitter earns revenue by selling advertisements on the Internet as "Promoted Tweets, "Promoted

Trends," or "Promoted Accounts." In order to analyze revenue by these three sources, Twitter records and summarizes its revenues by each advertising category. In addition, Twitter records and summarizes various metrics for its customers such as Retweets, clicks, replies, mentions, and follows. In doing so, Twitter has an integrated information system that includes an accounting component.

This chapter describes the basic elements of financial accounting systems. Such systems process, record, and summarize financial transactions, allowing for the preparation of financial statements, as discussed in Chapter 1.

The simplest form of an accounting system records and summarizes only transactions involving the receipt and payment of cash. For this reason, this chapter describes and illustrates a cash basis accounting system. This serves as a foundation for later discussions of more complex accounting systems and financial reporting issues.

Obj | **1**

Describe the basic elements of a financial accounting system.

These basic elements are found in all financial accounting systems, including those of **Apple, Ford Motor Company,** and **Twitter.**

Elements of an Accounting System

A financial accounting system is designed to produce financial statements. The financial statements include the income statement, retained earnings statement, balance sheet, and statement of cash flows.

The basic elements of a **financial accounting system** include:

- *Rules* for determining what, when, and the amount that should be recorded
- A *framework* for preparing financial statements
- *Controls* to determine whether errors may have arisen in the recording process

Rules

The rules for determining what, when, and the amount recorded are derived from the eight concepts discussed in Chapter 1. These concepts are the basis of generally accepted accounting principles (GAAP), which require the recording of transactions affecting elements of the financial statements.

A **transaction** is an economic event that under GAAP affects the financial statements. A transaction may affect one, two, or more items within the financial statements. For example, equipment purchased for cash affects only assets. That is, one asset (equipment) increases while another asset (cash) decreases. If, on the other hand, the equipment is purchased on credit, assets (equipment) and liabilities (accounts or notes payable) increase.

Framework

Transactions must be analyzed, recorded, and summarized using a framework. The accounting equation is the basis for all such frameworks. The accounting equation is expressed as follows:

$$\text{Assets} = \text{Liabilities} + \text{Stockholders' Equity}$$

By expanding the accounting equation, as shown in Exhibit 1, an integrated financial statement approach can be designed for analyzing, recording, and summarizing transactions. This is done by including columns for the statement of cash flows, balance sheet, and income statement.

The *left-hand* column in Exhibit 1 shows the effects of transactions on the statement of cash flows. Each cash transaction is recorded and classified as an operating, investing, or financing activity. This serves as a basis for preparing the statement of cash flows.

The cash at the beginning of the period plus or minus the cash flows from operating, investing, and financing activities equals the end-of-period cash. This end-of-period cash amount is reported as an asset on the balance sheet. Thus, the statement of cash flows is integrated with the balance sheet in Exhibit 1.

The *right-hand* column in Exhibit 1 shows the effects of transactions on the income statement. Each revenue and expense transaction is recorded and classified as a revenue or expense. This serves as a basis for preparing the income statement.

Net income for the period (revenues less expenses) is added to beginning retained earnings.[1] Thus, revenue and expense transactions are also recorded under the Retained Earnings column of the balance sheet. By doing so, the balance sheet is integrated with the income statement in Exhibit 1.

---

1. A net loss for the period, which occurs when expenses exceed revenues, is subtracted from beginning retained earnings.

Integrated Financial Statement Framework   **EXHIBIT 1**

Statement of Cash Flows	Balance Sheet				Income Statement
	Assets = Liabilities +		Stockholders' Equity		
	Assets = Liabilities +		Capital Stock +	Retained Earnings	
Transactions	XXX	XXX	XXX		XXX
	XXX	XXX	XXX		XXX

Statement of Cash Flows			Income Statement	
+/– Operating activities	XXX		Revenues	XXX
+/– Investing activities	XXX		Expenses	XXX
+/– Financing activities	XXX		Net income or loss	XXX
Increase or decrease in cash	XXX			
Beginning cash	XXX			
Ending cash	XXX			

INTEGRATED FINANCIAL STATEMENT FRAMEWORK

Exhibit 1 also illustrates the importance of the balance sheet as the connecting link between the statement of cash flows and the income statement.[2] This integrated financial statement approach for analyzing, recording, and summarizing transactions is illustrated later in this chapter.

The integrated financial statement approach shown in Exhibit 1 is an invaluable tool for analyzing transactions and their effects on the financial statements. It is also an aid for analyzing and interpreting a company's financial statements. This is because, without understanding how a company's financial statements are integrated, important trends or events may be missed or misinterpreted.

To illustrate, assume a company reports net income (profits) on its income statement. As a result, it might be mistakenly concluded that the company's operations are doing well and no major changes are necessary. In fact, the company might be experiencing a continuing negative net cash flow from operations and thus be headed towards bankruptcy. This is why it is essential to analyze all the financial statements and their integration.

Controls

The integrated financial statement approach shown in Exhibit 1 has built-in controls to ensure that all transactions are correctly analyzed, recorded, and summarized. These controls include the following:[3]

1. The accounting equation must balance.
2. The ending cash on the statement of cash flows must equal the cash on the balance sheet.
3. The net income on the income statement must equal the net effects of revenues and expenses on retained earnings.

2. In Chapter 3, the use of the balance sheet to reconcile net cash flows from operating activities with net income is described and illustrated.

3. Additional accounting controls are discussed in Chapter 5.

First, the accounting equation requires that total assets equal total liabilities plus total stockholders' equity. If at the end of the period this equality does not hold, an error has occurred.

To illustrate, assume that a cash purchase of equipment for $10,000 is incorrectly recorded as a $10,000 increase in equipment and a $10,000 increase (instead of decrease) in cash. In this case, the total assets exceed the total liabilities plus stockholders' equity by $20,000. Likewise, assume that the equipment was increased by $10,000, but the $10,000 decrease in cash was omitted. In this case, the total assets exceed total liabilities plus stockholders' equity by $10,000. In both cases, the inequality of the equation indicates that an error has occurred.

The equality of the equation doesn't necessarily mean that no errors have occurred. To illustrate, assume that a business purchased $10,000 of equipment on credit and recorded the transaction as an increase in equipment of $10,000. However, instead of increasing the liabilities by $10,000, the transaction was recorded as a $10,000 decrease in cash. In this case, the accounting equation still balances, even though cash and liabilities are understated by $10,000.

Second, the ending Cash shown in the Statement of Cash Flows column must equal the ending cash under Assets in the Balance Sheet column. If these two amounts do not agree, an error has occurred.

To illustrate, assume that a $5,000 cash receipt was recorded as an increase in Cash in the Balance Sheet Column under Assets but was omitted from the Statement of Cash Flows column. In this case, the ending cash shown in the Statement of Cash Flows column would be $5,000 less than the balance of Cash under Assets in the Balance Sheet column.

Third, the net income or loss from the Income Statement column must equal the net effects of revenues and expenses on retained earnings. If these two amounts do not agree, an error has occurred.

To illustrate, assume that a $7,500 payment for rent expense was recorded under Retained Earnings in the Balance Sheet column but was omitted from the Income Statement column. In this case, the Net income in the Income Statement column would be $7,500 more than the net effects of revenues and expenses on retained earnings.

HOW BUSINESSES MAKE MONEY

GOT THE FLU? WHY NOT CHEW SOME GUM?

Facing a slumping market for sugared chewing gum—such as Juicy Fruit™ and Doublemint™—Wm. Wrigley Jr. Company, a subsidiary of Mars Incorporated, is reinventing itself by expanding its product lines and introducing new chewing gum applications. Wrigley's new products include sugarless breath mints and more powerful flavored mint chewing gum, like Extra Polar Ice™. In addition, Wrigley is experimenting with health-care applications of chewing gum. For example, the company founded the Wrigley Science Institute™ with the objective of promoting scientific research on the benefits of chewing gum. Specifically, the Institute sponsors research in such areas as weight reduction, management and stress relief, and cognitive focus. The Institute provides grants to leading researchers who investigate the role of chewing gum in health and wellness.

Source: Wrigley.com and *USA Today*, "Wrigley Wants Science to Prove Gum-Chewing Benefits," by Dave Carpenter, The Associated Press, March 28, 2006.

Recording a Corporation's First Period of Operations

Obj | **2**

Analyze, record, and summarize transactions for a corporation's first period of operations.

The integrated financial statement framework shown in Exhibit 1 is illustrated using the transactions for a corporation's first period of operations. Assume that on September 1, 20Y5, Lee Landry, M.D., organizes a professional corporation to practice general medicine. The business is to be known as Family Health Care, P.C., where P.C. refers to a *professional corporation.*

Each of Family Health Care's transactions during September is described and recorded in this section. These transactions are then summarized into financial statements. The transactions begin with Dr. Landry's investment to establish the business.

Transaction (a)

Dr. Landry deposits $6,000 in a bank account in the name of Family Health Care, P.C., in return for shares of stock in the corporation.

Stock issued to owners (stockholders) such as Lee Landry is referred to as **capital stock**. In recording this transaction, increases are recorded as positive numbers, while decreases are recorded as negative numbers.

The effects of this transaction on Family Health Care's financial statements are recorded as follows:

1. Under the Statement of Cash Flows column, Cash from Financing activities is increased by $6,000.
2. Under the Balance Sheet column, Cash under Assets is increased by $6,000. To balance the accounting equation, Capital Stock under Stockholders' Equity is also increased by $6,000.

Since no revenues or expenses are affected, there are no entries under the Income Statement column. The effects of this transaction on Family Health Care's financial statements are shown below.

Statement of Cash Flows	Balance Sheet			Income Statement
	Assets	= Liabilities +	Stockholders' Equity	
	Cash	=	Capital Stock	
a. Investment by Dr. Landry	6,000		6,000	

Statement of Cash Flows	
a. Financing	6,000

Note that the preceding recording of transaction (a) relates only to the business, Family Health Care, P.C. Dr. Landry's personal assets (such as a home or a personal bank account) and personal liabilities are excluded. This is because under the business entity concept, Family Health Care is treated as a separate entity, with cash of $6,000 and stockholders' equity of $6,000.

Transaction (b)

Family Health Care borrows $10,000 from First National Bank to finance its operations.

To borrow the $10,000, Dr. Landry signs a note payable with First National Bank in the name of Family Health Care. The note payable is a liability that Family Health Care must pay in the future. The note payable also requires the payment of interest of $100 per month until the note of $10,000 is paid on September 30, 20Y9. The interest is to be paid at the end of each month.

The effects of this transaction on Family Health Care's financial statements are recorded as follows:

1. Under the Statement of Cash Flows column, Cash from Financing activities is increased by $10,000.
2. Under the Balance Sheet column, Cash under Assets is increased by $10,000. To balance the accounting equation, Notes Payable under Liabilities is also increased by $10,000.

This transaction changes the mix of assets and liabilities on the balance sheet but does not change Family Health Care's stockholders' equity of $6,000. Since no revenues or expenses are affected, no entries are made under the Income Statement column.

The effects of this transaction on Family Health Care's financial statements are shown below.

Statement of Cash Flows	Balance Sheet			Income Statement
	Assets	=	Liabilities + Stockholders' Equity	
			Notes Capital	
	Cash	=	Payable + Stock	
Balances	6,000		6,000	
b. Loan from bank	10,000		10,000	
Balances	16,000		10,000 6,000	

Statement of Cash Flows	
b. Financing	10,000

Transaction (c)

Family Health Care buys land for $12,000 cash.

The land is located near a new suburban hospital that is under construction. Dr. Landry plans to rent office space and equipment for several months. When the hospital is completed, Family Health Care will build on the land.

The effects of this transaction on Family Health Care's financial statements are recorded as follows:

1. Under the Statement of Cash Flows column, Cash from Investing activities is decreased by $12,000.
2. Under the Balance Sheet column, Cash under Assets is decreased by $12,000. To balance the accounting equation, Land under Assets is increased by $12,000.

This transaction illustrates the use of cash for an investing activity. As a result, $12,000 was entered under the Statement of Cash Flows column. In addition, the mix of assets changes on the balance sheet. Since no revenues or expenses are affected, no entries are made under the Income Statement column.

The effects of this transaction on Family Health Care's financial statements are shown below.

Statement of Cash Flows	Balance Sheet					Income Statement
	Assets		=	Liabilities +	Stockholders' Equity	
	Cash	+ Land	=	Notes Payable	+ Capital Stock	
Balances	16,000			10,000	6,000	
c. Purchase of land	−12,000	12,000				
Balances	4,000	12,000		10,000	6,000	

Statement of Cash Flows	
c. Investing	−12,000

Transaction (d)

During the first month of operations, Family Health Care earned patient fees of $5,500, receiving the fees in cash.

The effects of this transaction on Family Health Care's financial statements are recorded as follows:

1. Under the Statement of Cash Flows column, Cash from Operating activities is increased by $5,500.
2. Under the Balance Sheet column, Cash under Assets is increased by $5,500. To balance the accounting equation, Retained Earnings under Stockholders' Equity is also increased by $5,500.
3. Under the Income Statement column, Fees earned is increased by $5,500.

This transaction illustrates an inflow of cash from operating activities by earning revenues (fees earned) of $5,500. Retained Earnings is increased under Stockholders' Equity by $5,500 because fees earned contribute to net income and net income increases stockholders' equity. Since fees earned are a type of revenue, Fees earned of $5,500 is also entered under the Income Statement column.

The effects of this transaction on Family Health Care's financial statements are shown below.

Statement of Cash Flows	Balance Sheet						Income Statement
	Assets		=	Liabilities +	Stockholders' Equity		
	Cash	+ Land	=	Notes Payable	+ Capital Stock	+ Retained Earnings	
Balances	4,000	12,000		10,000	6,000		
d. Fees earned	5,500					5,500	d.
Balances	9,500	12,000		10,000	6,000	5,500	

Statement of Cash Flows		Income Statement	
d. Operating	5,500	d. Fees earned	5,500

Transaction (e)

Family Health Care paid expenses during September as follows: wages, $1,125; rent, $950; utilities, $450; interest, $100; and miscellaneous, $275.

Miscellaneous expenses include small amounts paid for such items as postage, newspapers, and magazines. The effects of this transaction on Family Health Care's financial statements are recorded as follows:

1. Under the Statement of Cash Flows column, Cash from Operating activities is decreased by $2,900, which is the sum of the expenses ($1,125 + $950 + $450 + $100 + $275).

2. Under the Balance Sheet column, Cash under Assets is decreased by $2,900. To balance the accounting equation, Retained Earnings under Stockholders' Equity is also decreased by $2,900.

3. Under the Income Statement column, each expense is listed as a negative amount.

This transaction illustrates an outflow of cash of $2,900 for operating activities (paying expenses). Thus, $2,900 is entered in the Statement of Cash Flows column as an Operating activity. Expenses have the opposite effect from revenues on net income and retained earnings. As a result, $2,900 is entered for Retained Earnings under Stockholders' Equity. In addition, each expense is listed under the income statement column as a negative amount.

The effects of this transaction on Family Health Care's financial statements are shown below.

Statement of Cash Flows	Balance Sheet					Income Statement
	Assets	=	Liabilities +	Stockholders' Equity		
	Cash +	Land =	Notes Payable +	Capital Stock +	Retained Earnings	
Balances	9,500	12,000	10,000	6,000	5,500	
e. Paid expenses	−2,900				−2,900	e.
Balances	6,600	12,000	10,000	6,000	2,600	

Statement of Cash Flows		Income Statement	
e. Operating	−2,900	e. Wages expense	−1,125
		Rent expense	−950
		Utilities expense	−450
		Interest expense	−100
		Misc. expense	−275

Transaction (f)

Family Health Care paid $1,500 to stockholders (Dr. Lee Landry) as dividends.

Dividends are distributions of a company's earnings to stockholders. Dividends should not be confused with expenses. Dividends do not represent assets consumed or services used in earning revenues. Instead, dividends are a distribution of earnings to the stockholders.

The effects of this transaction on Family Health Care's financial statements are recorded as follows:

1. Under the Statement of Cash Flows column, Cash from Financing activities is decreased by $1,500.

2. Under the Balance Sheet column, Cash under Assets is decreased by $1,500. To balance the accounting equation, Retained Earnings under Stockholders' Equity is also decreased by $1,500.

This transaction illustrates an outflow of cash of $1,500 for financing activities (paying dividends). Thus, $1,500 is entered in the Statement of Cash Flows column as a Financing activity. Dividends decrease retained earnings; thus, $1,500 is entered for Retained Earnings under Stockholders' Equity. Since dividends are not an expense, no entry is made under the Income Statement column.

The effects of this transaction on Family Health Care's financial statements are shown below.

| Statement of Cash Flows | Balance Sheet | | | | | Income Statement |
| | Assets | = | Liabilities + | Stockholders' Equity | | |
	Cash + Land	=	Notes Payable +	Capital Stock +	Retained Earnings	
Balances	6,600 12,000		10,000	6,000	2,600	
f. Paid dividends	–1,500				–1,500	
Balances	5,100 12,000		10,000	6,000	1,100	

Statement of Cash Flows

f. Financing   –1,500

The September transactions of Family Health Care are summarized in Exhibit 2. Each transaction is identified by letter, and the balances are shown as of the end of September.

Exhibit 2 illustrates the three controls that are built into the integrated financial statement approach. These controls are as follows:

1. The accounting equation under the Balance Sheet column balances. That is, total assets of $17,100 ($5,100 + $12,000) equals total liabilities plus stockholders' equity of $17,100 ($10,000 + $6,000 + $1,100).

2. The ending cash under the Statement of Cash Flows column of $5,100 equals the cash balance under the Balance Sheet column of $5,100.

3. The net income under the Income Statement column of $2,600 equals the net effects of revenues of $5,500 and expenses of $2,900 on retained earnings ($5,500 − $2,900).

Integrity, Objectivity, and Ethics in Business

A HISTORY OF ETHICAL CONDUCT

The Wm. Wrigley Jr. Company, which is now a subsidiary of Mars Incorporated, has a long history of integrity, objectivity, and ethical conduct. When pressured to become part of a cartel, known as the Chewing Gum Trust, the company founder, William Wrigley Jr., said, "We prefer to do business by fair and square methods or we prefer not to do business at all." In 1932, Phillip K. Wrigley, called "PK" by his friends, became president of the Wrigley Company after his father, William Wrigley Jr.,

died. PK also was president of the Chicago Cubs, which played in Wrigley Field. He was financially generous to his players and frequently gave them advice on and off the field. However, as a man of integrity and high ethical standards, PK docked (reduced) his salary as president of the Wrigley Company for the time he spent working on Cubs-related activities and business.

Source: St. Louis Post-Dispatch, "Sports—Backpages," January 26, 2003.

EXHIBIT 2   **Family Health Care Summary of Transactions for September**

Statement of Cash Flows	Balance Sheet						Income Statement
	Assets		= Liabilities +	Stockholders' Equity			
	Cash +	Land =	Notes Payable +	Capital Stock +	Retained Earnings		
a. Investment by Dr. Landry	6,000			6,000			
b. Loan from bank	10,000		10,000				
c. Purchase of land	−12,000	12,000					
d. Fees earned	5,500				5,500	d.	
e. Paid expenses	−2,900				−2,900	e.	
f. Paid dividends	−1,500				−1,500		
Balances, Sept. 30	5,100	12,000	10,000	6,000	1,100		

Statement of Cash Flows	
a. Financing	6,000
b. Financing	10,000
c. Investing	−12,000
d. Operating	5,500
e. Operating	−2,900
f. Financing	−1,500
Increase in cash and Sept. 30 cash	5,100

Income Statement	
d. Fees earned	5,500
e. Wages expense	−1,125
Rent expense	−950
Utilities expense	−450
Interest expense	−100
Misc. expense	−275
Net income	2,600

On a recent balance sheet, **Apple** reported (in millions) assets of $176,064, which equals its liabilities of $57,854 plus its stockholders' equity of $118,210.

In reviewing Exhibit 2, you should note that the following apply to all companies:

- The Balance Sheet column reflects the accounting equation (Assets = Liabilities + Stockholders' Equity).
- The two sides of the accounting equation are always equal.
- Every transaction affects (increases or decreases) one or more of the balance sheet elements—assets, liabilities, or stockholders' equity.
- A transaction may or may not affect (increase or decrease) an element of the statement of cash flows or the income statement. Some transactions affect elements of both statements, some transactions affect only one statement and not the other, and some transactions affect neither statement.
- Every cash transaction increases or decreases the asset (cash) on the balance sheet. Every cash transaction also increases or decreases an operating, investing, or financing activity on the statement of cash flows.
- The ending balance of Cash under the Statement of Cash Flows column ($5,100 in Exhibit 2) agrees with the ending cash balance shown on the balance sheet. Since September was Family Health Care's first period of operations, this ending cash balance equals the net increase in cash for the period. In future periods, the net increase (decrease) in cash is added to (or subtracted from) the beginning cash balance to equal the ending cash balance. This ending cash balance is reported in the statement of cash flows and balance sheet.
- The stockholders' equity is increased by amounts invested by stockholders (capital stock).

- Revenues increase stockholders' equity (retained earnings) and expenses decrease stockholders' equity (retained earnings). The effects of revenue and expense transactions are also shown in the Income Statement column.
- Stockholders' equity (retained earnings) is decreased by dividends paid to stockholders.
- The change in retained earnings for the period is the net income minus dividends. For a net loss, the change in retained earnings is the net loss plus dividends.
- The statement of cash flows is linked to the balance sheet through cash.
- The income statement is linked to the balance sheet through revenues and expenses (net income or loss), which affects retained earnings.

Exhibit 3 summarizes the effects of the various transactions affecting stockholders' equity.

Effects of Transactions on Stockholders' Equity   **EXHIBIT 3**

Financial Statements for a Corporation's First Period of Operations

Obj|3 Prepare financial statements for a corporation's first period of operations.

Exhibit 2 lists Family Health Care's September transactions in the order they occurred. Exhibit 2, however, does not group and summarize like transactions together. The accounting reports that provide this summarized information are financial statements.

Family Health Care's September financial statements can be prepared from Exhibit 2. These financial statements are shown in Exhibit 4.

The financial statements shown in Exhibit 4 are prepared from Exhibit 2 as follows:

1. The income statement is prepared using the Income Statement column.
2. The retained earnings statement is prepared next because the ending balance of retained earnings is needed to prepare the balance sheet. The retained earnings statement is prepared using net income from the income statement and the amount recorded for dividends under retained earnings.

3. The balance sheet is prepared next using the balances shown under the Balance Sheet column.
4. The statement of cash flows is normally prepared last using the Statement of Cash Flows column.

Each financial statement is identified by the name of the business, the title of the statement, and the date or period of time.

Income Statement

The income statement for Family Health Care shown in Exhibit 4 reports fees earned of $5,500, total operating expenses of $2,900, and net income of $2,600. The $5,500 of fees earned is taken from the Income Statement column of Exhibit 2. Likewise, the expenses are summarized from the Income Statement column of Exhibit 2. These expenses are reported under the heading "Operating expenses." Operating expenses are normally listed in order of size, beginning with the largest expense. Miscellaneous expense is usually shown as the last item, regardless of amount.

Retained Earnings Statement

Since Family Health Care has been in operation for only one month, it has no retained earnings at the beginning of September. The ending September balance is the change in retained earnings created by net income and dividends. This change, $1,100, is the beginning retained earnings balance for October.

EXHIBIT 4

Family Health Care Financial Statements for September

Family Health Care, P.C. Income Statement For the Month Ended September 30, 20Y5		
Fees earned		$5,500
Operating expenses:		
Wages expense	$1,125	
Rent expense	950	
Utilities expense	450	
Interest expense	100	
Miscellaneous expense	275	
Total operating expenses		2,900
Net income		$2,600

Family Health Care, P.C. Retained Earnings Statement For the Month Ended September 30, 20Y5	
Net income for September	$2,600
Less dividends	1,500
Retained earnings, September 30, 20Y5	$1,100

(Continued)

Family Health Care, P.C.
Balance Sheet
September 30, 20Y5

Assets

Cash		$ 5,100
Land		12,000
Total assets		$17,100

Liabilities

Notes payable		$10,000

Stockholders' Equity

Capital stock	$6,000	
Retained earnings	1,100	
Total stockholders' equity		7,100
Total liabilities and stockholders' equity		$17,100

Family Health Care, P.C.
Statement of Cash Flows
For the Month Ended September 30, 20Y5

Cash flows from operating activities:			
Cash received from customers		$ 5,500	
Deduct cash payments for expenses		2,900	
Net cash flow from operating activities			$ 2,600
Cash flows used in investing activities:			
Cash payments for acquisition of land			(12,000)
Cash flows from financing activities:			
Cash received from sale of capital stock	$ 6,000		
Cash received from notes payable	10,000	$16,000	
Deduct cash dividends		1,500	
Net cash flow from financing activities			14,500
Net increase in cash			$ 5,100
September 1, 20Y5, cash balance			0
September 30, 20Y5, cash balance			$ 5,100

Balance Sheet

Family Health Care's assets, liabilities, and stockholders' equity as of September 30, 20Y5, are taken from the last line of the Balance Sheet column of Exhibit 2. The September 30, 20Y5, balance sheet is shown in Exhibit 4.

In the Assets section of the balance sheet, assets are normally listed in order of liquidity, starting with cash. **Liquidity** refers to the ability to convert an asset to cash. Land is less liquid than cash and thus would be listed second in Family Health Care's balance sheet.

In the Liabilities section of Family Health Care's balance sheet, notes payable is the only liability. When there are two or more categories of liabilities, each should be listed and the total amount reported. Liabilities should be presented in the order that they will be paid in cash. Thus, the notes payable due in 2018 will be listed after the liabilities that are due earlier.

The stockholders' equity for Family Health Care as of September 30, 20Y5, consists of $6,000 of capital stock and retained earnings of $1,100. The retained earnings is the ending retained earnings reported on the retained earnings statement.

Statement of Cash Flows

Family Health Care's statement of cash flows for September is prepared from the Statement of Cash Flows column of Exhibit 2. Cash increased from a zero balance at the beginning of the month to $5,100 at the end of the month.

The $5,100 increase in cash during September was created by:

1. Operating activities that generated $2,600 of cash
2. Investing activities that used $12,000 of cash
3. Financing activities that generated $14,500 of cash

The details of how the operating, investing, and financing activities generated or used cash is reported in the statement of cash flows. For example, financing activities generated $6,000 from the sale of capital stock and $10,000 from borrowing by issuing a note payable. Financing activities used $1,500 for paying dividends.

Integration of Financial Statements

Exhibit 5 shows how Family Health Care's financial statements for September are integrated. As shown in Exhibit 5, these statements are integrated as follows:

1. The ending cash balance of $5,100 on the balance sheet equals the ending cash balance reported on the statement of cash flows.
2. The net income of $2,600 is reported on the income statement and the retained earnings statement.

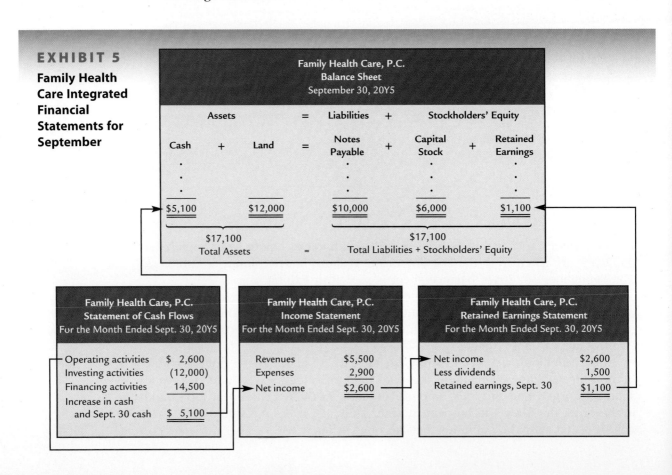

EXHIBIT 5

Family Health Care Integrated Financial Statements for September

3. The ending retained earnings of $1,100 is reported in the retained earnings statement and the balance sheet.

4. The cash flows from operating activities of $2,600 reported on the statement of cash flows equals the net income on the income statement. The relationship between cash flows from operating activities and net income is further described and illustrated in Chapter 3.

Recording a Corporation's Second Period of Operations

Obj 4
Analyze, record, and summarize transactions for a corporation's second period of operations.

During October, Family Health Care entered into the following transactions:

a. Received, in cash, fees of $6,400
b. Paid expenses, in cash, as follows: wages, $1,370; rent, $950; utilities, $540; interest, $100; and miscellaneous, $220
c. Paid cash dividends of $1,000

The October transactions are analyzed and entered into the integrated financial statement framework shown in Exhibit 6.

The Balance Sheet column of Exhibit 6 begins with the ending balances as of September 30, 20Y5, taken from Exhibit 2. This is because the balance sheet is the cumulative total of the entity's assets, liabilities, and stockholders' equity since the company's inception.

As of October 1, 20Y5, Family Health Care has cash of $5,100, land of $12,000, notes payable of $10,000, capital stock of $6,000, and retained earnings of $1,100. In contrast, the statement of cash flows and the income statement report only transactions for a period and are not cumulative.

Family Health Care Summary of Transactions for October   **EXHIBIT 6**

Statement of Cash Flows	Cash +	Land =	Notes Payable	+ Capital Stock +	Retained Earnings	Income Statement
Balances, Oct. 1	5,100	12,000	10,000	6,000	1,100	
a. Fees earned	6,400				6,400	a.
b. Paid expenses	−3,180				−3,180	b.
c. Paid dividends	−1,000				−1,000	
Balances, Oct. 31	7,320	12,000	10,000	6,000	3,320	

Statement of Cash Flows
a. Operating 6,400
b. Operating −3,180
c. Financing −1,000
Increase in cash 2,220

Income Statement
a. Fees earned 6,400
b. Wages expense −1,370
Rent expense −950
Utilities expense −540
Interest expense −100
Misc. expense −220
Net income 3,220

Obj | **5**

Prepare financial statements for a corporation's second period of operations.

Financial Statements for a Corporation's Second Period of Operations

Family Health Care's financial statements for October are shown in Exhibit 7. These statements were prepared from Exhibit 6.

Income Statement

The income statement for October reports net income of $3,220. This is an increase of $620, or 23.8% ($620/$2,600), from September's net income of $2,600. The increase in net income was due to fees increasing from $5,500 to $6,400, a $900, or 16.4% ($900/$5,500), increase from September. At the same time, total operating expenses increased only $280, or 9.7% ($280/$2,900). This suggests that Family Health Care's operations are profitable and expanding.

Retained Earnings Statement

The retained earnings statement is prepared by first listing the retained earnings as of the beginning of the period. This is the ending retained earnings balance of the prior period. As shown in Exhibit 4, Family Health Care's retained earnings statement for the month ending September 30, 20Y5, is $1,100. Thus, retained earnings as of October 1, 20Y5, is reported as $1,100 in Exhibit 7.

EXHIBIT 7

Family Health Care Financial Statements for October

Family Health Care, P.C.
Income Statement
For the Month Ended October 31, 20Y5

Fees earned		$6,400
Operating expenses:		
Wages expense	$1,370	
Rent expense	950	
Utilities expense	540	
Interest expense	100	
Miscellaneous expense	220	
Total operating expenses		3,180
Net income		$3,220

Family Health Care, P.C.
Retained Earnings Statement
For the Month Ended October 31, 20Y5

Retained earnings, October 1, 20Y5		$1,100
Net income for October	$3,220	
Less dividends	1,000	2,220
Retained earnings, October 31, 20Y5		$3,320

(Continued)

EXHIBIT 7

Family Health Care Financial Statements for October (*Concluded*)

Family Health Care, P.C.
Balance Sheet
October 31, 20Y5

Assets

Cash	$ 7,320
Land	12,000
Total assets	$19,320

Liabilities

Notes payable	$10,000

Stockholders' Equity

Capital stock	$6,000	
Retained earnings	3,320	
Total stockholders' equity		9,320
Total liabilities and stockholders' equity		$19,320

Family Health Care, P.C.
Statement of Cash Flows
For the Month Ended October 31, 20Y5

Cash flows from operating activities:		
Cash received from customers	$6,400	
Deduct cash payments for expenses	3,180	
Net cash flow from operating activities		$ 3,220
Cash flows from investing activities		0
Cash flows used for financing activities:		
Cash dividends		(1,000)
Net increase in cash		$ 2,220
October 1, 20Y5, cash balance		5,100
October 31, 20Y5, cash balance		$ 7,320

During October, Family Health Care reported an increase in retained earnings of $2,220. This increase is the result of net income ($3,220) less the dividends ($1,000). The ending retained earnings balance as of October 31, 20Y5, is $3,320.

Balance Sheet

The balance sheet in Exhibit 6 shows that total assets increased from $17,100 on September 30, 20Y5, to $19,320 on October 31. This increase of $2,220 was due to an increase in cash from $5,100 to $7,320. Total liabilities of $10,000 remained the same.

Since total assets increased by $2,220 and total liabilities remained the same, total stockholders' equity must also have increased by $2,220. This is because the accounting equation must always balance. Exhibit 7 shows that total stockholders' equity did increase by $2,220, which is the increase in retained earnings.

Statement of Cash Flows

Family Health Care's statement of cash flows for October indicates that cash increased by $2,220. This increase is cash generated from operating activities of $3,220 less cash used by financing activities to pay dividends of $1,000.

The net increase in cash of $2,220 is added to the beginning cash balance of $5,100 to yield the ending cash balance of $7,320. This ending cash balance of $7,320 also appears on the October 31, 20Y5, balance sheet.

Integration of Financial Statements

Exhibit 8 illustrates that Family Health Care's financial statements for October are integrated as follows:

1. The ending cash balance of $7,320 on the balance sheet equals the ending cash balance reported on the statement of cash flows.
2. The net income of $3,220 is reported on the income statement and the retained earnings statement.
3. The ending retained earnings of $3,320 is reported in the retained earnings statement and the balance sheet.
4. The cash flows from operating activities of $3,220 reported on the statement of cash flows equals the net income on the income statement. The relationship between cash flows from operating activities and net income is further described and illustrated in Chapter 3.

EXHIBIT 8   **Family Health Care Integrated Financial Statements for October**

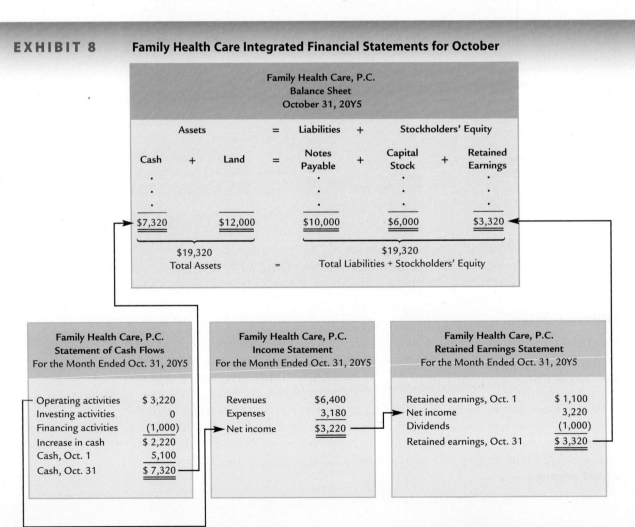

Financial Analysis: Common-Sized Income Statements

Obj 6

Describe and illustrate the use of common-sized income statements in assessing a company's financial performance.

Common-sized financial statements are useful in assessing a company's financial condition and performance over time. Common-sized financial statements are also useful in comparing companies with one another.

Common-sized financial statements are prepared by expressing financial statement amounts as a percent of a base amount. A **common-sized income statement** is prepared by expressing income statement amounts as a percent of sales. A **common-sized balance sheet** is prepared by expressing each asset as a percent of total assets. Each liability and stockholders' equity item is expressed as a percent of total liabilities plus stockholders' equity.[4]

To illustrate common-sized income statements, we use data (in millions) adapted from recent financial statements of The Kroger Co.[5] Kroger operates over 2,400 supermarkets, over 1,000 fueling centers, and over 700 convenience stores. The following are recent income statements (in millions) of Kroger.

	Year 2	Year 1
Sales	$ 90,374	$ 82,049
Cost of sales	(71,494)	(63,803)
Gross profit	$ 18,880	$ 18,246
Operating expenses:		
Selling and administrative	$(15,345)	$(13,823)
Other expenses	(2,257)	(2,241)
Total operating expenses	$(17,602)	$(16,064)
Operating income	$ 1,278	$ 2,182
Other income (expense)		
Interest expense	$ (435)	$ (601)
Tax expense	(247)	(448)
Other income (expense)	6	(17)
Net income	$ 602	$ 1,116

Kroger's common-sized income statements (rounded to one decimal place) for Year 2 and Year 1 are shown below. Each income statement item is expressed as a percent of sales. For example, the cost of sales for Year 2 of 79.1% is computed as $71,494 ÷ $90,374.

	Year 2	Year 1
Sales	100.0%	100.0%
Cost of sales	(79.1)	(77.8)
Gross profit	20.9	22.2
Operating expenses:		
Selling and administrative	(17.0)	(16.9)
Other expenses	(2.5)	(2.7)
Total operating expenses	(19.5)	(19.6)
Operating income	1.4	2.6
Other income (expense)		
Interest expense	(0.5)	(0.7)
Tax expense	(0.2)	(0.5)
Other income (expense)	0.0	(0.0)
Net income	0.7	1.4

4. Since total assets equals total liabilities plus total stockholders' equity, common-sized balance sheets can be prepared simply by expressing each balance sheet item as a percent of total assets.

5. A common-sized balance sheet for Kroger is included as part of the end-of-chapter item FA 2-5.

The common-sized income statements for Kroger indicate that the company's net income declined from 1.4% of sales to 0.7%. One of the primary causes of this decline is the increase cost of sales of 1.3% (79.1% − 77.8%). The total operating expenses changed slightly from Year 1 to Year 2. The other income (expense) changed slightly and is not a significant factor affecting net income. As a result, the main focus of Kroger should be determining the cause of the increase in cost of sales as a percent of sales. The increase may have been caused by an increasing cost of obtaining merchandise (grocery items) for sale. If this is the case, then Kroger should have been more aggressive in passing on the cost to customers through increased selling prices.

When comparing operating performance across companies within the same industry, common-sized income statements are often prepared only through operating income rather than through net income. This is because other income and expense are influenced by a variety of factors that are independent of operations and that can differ significantly across companies. For example, financing and tax strategies can vary significantly across companies and thus, affect the comparability.

Key Points

1. Describe the basic elements of a financial accounting system.

The basic elements of a financial accounting system include (1) a set of rules for determining what, when, and the amount that should be recorded; (2) a framework for preparing financial statements; and (3) one or more controls to determine whether errors may have arisen in the recording process.

2. Analyze, record, and summarize transactions for a corporation's first period of operations.

Using the integrated financial statement framework, September transactions for Family Health Care are recorded and summarized in Exhibit 2.

3. Prepare financial statements for a corporation's first period of operations.

The financial statements for Family Health Care for September, its first period of operations, are shown in Exhibit 4.

4. Analyze, record, and summarize transactions for a corporation's second period of operations.

Using the accounting equation as a basic framework, October transactions for Family Health Care are recorded and summarized in Exhibit 6.

5. Prepare financial statements for a corporation's second period of operations.

The financial statements for Family Health Care for October, its second period of operations, are shown in Exhibit 7.

6. Describe and illustrate the use of common-sized income statements in assessing a company's performance.

A common-sized income statement is prepared by expressing each income statement amount as a percent of sales.

Key Terms

Capital stock (47)
Common-sized balance sheet (61)
Common-sized financial statements (61)
Common-sized income statement (61)

Financial accounting system (44)
Liquidity (55)
Transaction (44)

Illustrative Problem

Beth Sumner established an insurance agency on April 1, 20Y4, and completed the following transactions during April:

a. Opened a business bank account in the name of Sumner Insurance Inc., with a deposit of $15,000 in exchange for capital stock.

b. Borrowed $8,000 by issuing a note payable.

c. Received cash from fees earned, $11,500.

d. Paid rent on office and equipment for the month, $3,500.

e. Paid automobile expenses for the month, $650, and miscellaneous expenses, $300.

f. Paid office salaries, $1,400.

g. Paid interest on the note payable, $60.

h. Purchased land as a future building site, $20,000.

i. Paid dividends, $1,000.

Instructions

1. Indicate the effect of each transaction and the balances after each transaction, using the integrated financial statement framework.

2. Prepare an income statement and retained earnings statement for April.

3. Prepare a balance sheet as of April 30, 20Y4.

4. Prepare a statement of cash flows for April.

Solution

1.

Statement of Cash Flows	Cash	+	Land	=	Notes Payable	+	Capital Stock	+	Retained Earnings	Income Statement
a. Investment	15,000						15,000			
b. Issued note payable	8,000				8,000					
Balances	23,000				8,000		15,000			
c. Fees earned	11,500								11,500	c.
Balances	34,500				8,000		15,000		11,500	
d. Rent expense	–3,500								–3,500	d.
Balances	31,000				8,000		15,000		8,000	
e. Paid expenses	–950								–950	e.
Balances	30,050				8,000		15,000		7,050	
f. Paid salary expense	–1,400								–1,400	f.
Balances	28,650				8,000		15,000		5,650	
g. Paid interest expense	–60								–60	g.
Balances	28,590				8,000		15,000		5,590	
h. Purchased land	–20,000		20,000							
Balances	8,590		20,000		8,000		15,000		5,590	
i. Paid dividends	–1,000								–1,000	
Balances, April 30	7,590		20,000		8,000		15,000		4,590	

Balance Sheet — Assets = Liabilities + Stockholders' Equity

Statement of Cash Flows	
a. Financing	15,000
b. Financing	8,000
c. Operating	11,500
d. Operating	–3,500
e. Operating	–950
f. Operating	–1,400
g. Operating	–60
h. Investing	–20,000
i. Financing	–1,000
Increase in cash and April 30 cash	7,590

Income Statement	
c. Fees earned	11,500
d. Rent expense	–3,500
e. Auto expense	–650
e. Misc. expense	–300
f. Salary expense	–1,400
g. Interest expense	–60
Net income	5,590

2.

SUMNER INSURANCE, INC.
Income Statement
For the Month Ended April 30, 20Y4

Revenues:		
Fees earned...		$11,500
Expenses:		
Rent expense..	$3,500	
Salaries expense...	1,400	
Automotive expense	650	
Interest expense...	60	
Miscellaneous expense	300	
Total expenses..		5,910
Net income		$ 5,590

SUMNER INSURANCE, INC.
Retained Earnings Statement
For the Month Ended April 30, 20Y4

Net income	$5,590
Less dividends	1,000
Retained earnings, April 30, 20Y4	$4,590

3.

SUMNER INSURANCE, INC.
Balance Sheet
April 30, 20Y4

Assets

Cash		$ 7,590
Land		20,000
Total assets...		$27,590

Liabilities

Note payable...		$ 8,000

Stockholders' Equity

Capital stock	$15,000	
Retained earnings	4,590	
Total stockholders' equity		19,590
Total liabilities and tockholders' equity............................		$27,590

4.

SUMNER INSURANCE, INC.
Statement of Cash Flows
For the Month Ended April 30, 20Y4

Cash flows from operating activities:		
Cash receipts from operating activities	$11,500	
Deduct cash payments for operating activities	5,910	
Net cash flows from operating activities		$ 5,590
Cash flows used for investing activities:		
Cash payments for land...		(20,000)
Cash flows from financing activities:		
Cash receipts from issuing capital stock	$15,000	
Cash receipts from issuing note payable..........................	8,000	
Cash payments for dividends	(1,000)	
Net cash flows from financing activities................................		22,000
Net increase in cash during April		$ 7,590
Cash as of April 1, 20Y4...		0
Cash as of April 30, 20Y4		$ 7,590

Self-Examination Questions *(Answers appear at the end of chapter)*

1. The purchase of land for $50,000 cash was incorrectly recorded as an increase in land and an increase in notes payable. Which of the following statements is correct?

   A. The accounting equation will not balance because cash is overstated by $50,000.

   B. The accounting equation will not balance because notes payable are overstated by $50,000.

   C. The accounting equation will not balance because assets will exceed liabilities by $50,000.

   D. Even though a recording error has been made, the accounting equation will balance.

2. The receipt of $8,000 cash for fees earned was recorded by Langley Consulting as an increase in cash of $8,000 and a decrease in retained earnings (revenues) of $8,000. What is the effect of this error on the accounting equation?

   A. Total assets will exceed total liabilities and stockholders' equity by $8,000.

   B. Total assets will be less than total liabilities and stockholders' equity by $8,000.

   C. Total assets will exceed total liabilities and stockholders' equity by $16,000.

   D. The error will not affect the accounting equation.

3. If total assets increased $20,000 during a period and total liabilities increased $12,000 during the same period, the amount and direction (increase or decrease) of the change in stockholders' equity for that period is:

   A. a $32,000 increase.

   B. a $32,000 decrease.

   C. an $8,000 increase.

   D. an $8,000 decrease.

4. If revenue was $90,000, expenses were $75,000, and dividends were $20,000, the amount of net income or net loss would be:

   A. $90,000 net income.

   B. $15,000 net income.

   C. $75,000 net loss.

   D. $5,000 net loss.

5. Which of the following transactions changes only the mix of assets and does not affect liabilities or stockholders' equity?

   A. Borrowed $40,000 from First National Bank

   B. Purchased land for cash

   C. Received $3,800 for fees earned

   D. Paid $4,000 for office salaries

Class Discussion Questions

1. What are the basic elements of a financial accounting system? Do these elements apply to all businesses, from a local restaurant to Google Inc.? Explain.

2. Provide an example of a transaction that affects (a) only one element of the accounting equation, (b) two elements of the accounting equation, (c) three elements of the accounting equation.

3. Indicate whether the following error would cause the accounting equation to be out of balance and, if so, indicate how it would be out of balance. The payment of utilities of $1,200 was recorded as a decrease in cash of $1,200 and a decrease in retained earnings (utilities expense) of $2,100.

4. For each of the following errors, indicate whether the error would cause the accounting equation to be out of balance and, if so, indicate how it would be out of balance. (a) The purchase of land for $85,000 cash was recorded as an increase in land of $85,000 and a decrease in cash of $58,000. (b) The receipt of $7,000 for fees earned was recorded as an increase in cash of $7,000 and an increase in liabilities of $7,000.

5. What is a primary control for determining the accuracy of a business's record keeping?

6. Capstone Consulting Services acquired land 5 years ago for $200,000. Millstone recently signed an agreement to sell the land for $375,000. In accordance with the sales agreement, the buyer transferred $375,000 to Capstone's bank account on February 20. How would elements of the accounting equation be affected by the sale?

7. (a) How does the payment of dividends of $15,000 affect the three elements of the accounting equation? (b) Is net income affected by the payment of dividends? Explain.

8. Assume that Esquire Consulting erroneously recorded the payment of $30,000 of dividends as salary expense. (a) How would this error affect the equality of the accounting equation? (b) How would this error affect the income statement, retained earnings statement, balance sheet, and statement of cash flows?

9. Assume that Larsh Realty Inc. borrowed $75,000 from Country Bank and Trust. In recording the transaction,

Larsh erroneously recorded the receipt as an increase in cash, $75,000, and an increase in fees earned, $75,000. (a) How would this error affect the equality of the accounting equation? (b) How would this error affect the income statement, retained earnings statement, balance sheet, and statement of cash flows?

10. Assume that as of January 1, 20Y8, Sylvester Consulting has total assets of $500,000 and total liabilities of $150,000. As of December 31, 20Y8, Sylvester has total

liabilities of $200,000 and total stockholders' equity of $400,000. (a) What was Sylvester's stockholders' equity as of January 1, 20Y8? (b) Assume that Sylvester did not pay any dividends during 20Y8. What was the amount of net income for 20Y8?

11. Using the January 1 and December 31, 20Y8, data given in Question 10, answer the following question: If Sylvester Consulting paid $18,000 of dividends during 20Y8, what was the amount of net income for 20Y8?

Exercises

E2-1 Accounting equation

Obj 1

✔ a. $1,000,000

Determine the missing amount for each of the following:

	Assets	=	Liabilities	+	Stockholders' Equity
a.	X	=	$250,000	+	$750,000
b.	$480,000	=	X	+	$130,000
c.	$115,000	=	$7,500	+	X

E2-2 Accounting equation

Obj 1

✔ a. $37,385

The Walt Disney Company had the following assets and liabilities (in millions) at the end of 20Y1.

Assets	$72,124
Liabilities	34,739

a. Determine the stockholders' equity of Walt Disney at the end of 20Y1.

b. If assets increased by $2,774 million and stockholders' equity increased by $2,374 million, what was the increase or decrease in liabilities for the year 20Y2?

c. What were the total assets, liabilities, and stockholders' equity at the end of 20Y2?

d. Based upon your answer to (c), does the accounting equation balance?

E2-3 Accounting equation

Obj 1

✔ a. $1,088

Campbell Soup Co. had the following assets and liabilities (in millions) at the end of 20Y1.

Assets	$6,862
Liabilities	5,774

a. Determine the stockholders' equity of Campbell Soup at the end of 20Y1.

b. If assets decreased by $332 million and liabilities decreased by $142 million, what was the increase or decrease in stockholders' equity for the year 20Y2?

c. What were the total assets, liabilities, and stockholders' equity at the end of 20Y2?

d. Based upon your answer to (c), does the accounting equation balance?

E2-4 Accounting equation

Obj 1

✔ (a) $11,610

One item is omitted in each of the following recent year summaries of balance sheet and income statement data (in millions) for Google and Verizon Communications as of December 31, Year 1 and Year 2.

	Google	Verizon
Year 1:		
Assets	$57,851	(e)
Liabilities	(a)	(f)
Stockholders' equity	(b)	$ 86,912
Increase (Decrease) in assets, liabilities, and stockholders' equity during Year 2:		
Assets	$14,723	(g)
Liabilities	2,819	$ 11,460
Stockholders' equity	11,904	(h)
Year 2:		
Assets	(c)	$230,461
Liabilities	$14,429	(i)
Stockholders' equity	(d)	85,908

Determine the amounts of the missing items (a) through (i).

Obj **1**

✔ b. $635,000

E2-5   Accounting equation

Mila Keyes is the sole stockholder and operator of Tune-In, Tune-On, a motivational consulting business. At the end of its accounting period, December 31, 20Y7, Tune-In, Tune-On has assets of $750,000 and liabilities of $200,000. Using the accounting equation and considering each case independently, determine the following amounts:

a. Stockholders' equity, as of December 31, 20Y7.

b. Stockholders' equity, as of December 31, 20Y8, assuming that assets increased by $125,000 and liabilities increased by $40,000 during 20Y8.

c. Stockholders' equity, as of December 31, 20Y8, assuming that assets decreased by $80,000 and liabilities increased by $36,000 during 20Y8.

d. Stockholders' equity, as of December 31, 20Y8, assuming that assets increased by $140,000 and liabilities decreased by $25,000 during 20Y8.

e. Net income (or net loss) during 20Y8, assuming that as of December 31, 20Y8, assets were $950,000, liabilities were $270,000, and there were no dividends and no additional capital stock was issued.

Obj **2, 4**

E2-6   Effects of transactions on stockholders' equity

For **Target Corporation**, indicate whether the following transactions would (1) increase, (2) decrease, or (3) have no effect on stockholders' equity.

a. Borrowed money from the bank.

b. Paid creditors.

c. Made cash sales to customers.

d. Purchased store equipment.

e. Paid dividends.

f. Paid store rent.

g. Paid interest expense.

h. Sold store equipment at a gain.

i. Received interest revenue.

j. Paid taxes.

Obj **1, 2, 4**

E2-7   Effects of transactions on accounting equation

Describe how the following business transactions affect the three elements of the accounting equation.

a. Received cash for services performed.

b. Paid for utilities used in the business.

c. Borrowed cash at local bank.

d. Issued capital stock for cash.

e. Purchased land for cash.

E2-8   Effects of transactions on accounting equation

A vacant lot acquired for $300,000, on which there is a balance owed of $120,000, is sold for $415,000 in cash. The seller pays the $120,000 owed. What is the effect of these transactions on the total amount of the seller's (1) assets, (2) liabilities, and (3) stockholders' equity?

Obj **1, 2, 4**

✔ (1) Assets decreased by $5,000

E2-9   Effects of transactions on stockholders' equity

Indicate whether each of the following types of transactions will (a) increase stockholders' equity or (b) decrease stockholders' equity.

Obj **2, 4**

a. Issued capital stock for cash.

b. Received cash for fees earned.

c. Paid cash for utilities expense.

d. Paid cash for rent expense.

e. Paid cash dividends.

E2-10   Transactions

Speedy Delivery Service had the following selected transactions during April:

Obj **1, 2, 4**

1. Received cash from issuance of capital stock, $100,000.
2. Paid rent for April, $4,200.
3. Paid advertising expense, $3,000.
4. Received cash for providing delivery services, $27,000.
5. Purchased supplies for cash, $2,500.
6. Billed customers for delivery services on account, $81,200.
7. Paid creditors on account, $8,300.
8. Received cash from customers on account, $25,600.
9. Determined that the cost of supplies on hand was $900; therefore, $1,600 of supplies had been used during the month.
10. Paid dividends, $3,000.

Indicate the effect of each transaction on the accounting equation by listing the numbers identifying the transactions, (1) through (10), in a vertical column, and inserting at the right of each number the appropriate letter from the following list:

a. Increase in an asset, decrease in another asset.

b. Increase in an asset, increase in a liability.

c. Increase in an asset, increase in stockholders' equity.

d. Decrease in an asset, decrease in a liability.

e. Decrease in an asset, decrease in stockholders' equity.

E2-11   Nature of transactions

Cheryl Alder operates her own catering service. Summary financial data for March are presented in equation form as follows. Each line designated by a number indicates the effect of a transaction on the balance sheet. Each increase and decrease in stockholders' equity, except transaction (4), affects net income.

Obj **1, 2, 4**

✔ b. $11,000 decrease

	Cash	+	Land	=	Liabilities	+	Capital Stock	+	Retained Earnings
Bal.	40,000		100,000		16,000		24,000		100,000
1.	+28,000								+28,000
2.	−20,000		+20,000						
3.	−18,000								−18,000
4.	−1,000								−1,000
Bal.	29,000		120,000		16,000		24,000		109,000

a. Describe each transaction.

b. What is the amount of net decrease in cash during the month?

c. What is the amount of net increase in retained earnings during the month?

d. What is the amount of the net income for the month?

e. How much of the net income for the month was retained in the business?

f. What is the amount of net cash flows from operating activities?

g. What is the amount of net cash flows from investing activities?

h. What is the amount of net cash flows from financing activities?

Obj **3, 5**

E2-12   Net income and dividends

The income statement of a corporation for the month of February indicates a net income of $32,000. During the same period, $40,000 in cash dividends were paid.

Would it be correct to say that the business incurred a net loss of $8,000 during the month? Discuss.

Obj **1, 3, 5**

✔ Company
Yankee: Net
income, $86,000

E2-13   Net income and stockholders' equity for four businesses

Four different companies, Sierra, Tango, Yankee, and Zulu, show the same balance sheet data at the beginning and end of a year. These data, exclusive of the amount of stockholders' equity, are summarized as follows:

	Total Assets	Total Liabilities
Beginning of the year	$490,000	$175,000
End of the year	770,000	294,000

On the basis of the preceding data and the following additional information for the year, determine the net income (or loss) of each company for the year. (*Suggestion:* First determine the amount of increase or decrease in stockholders' equity during the year.)

Sierra: No additional capital stock was issued, and no dividends were paid.

Tango: No additional capital stock was issued, but dividends of $55,000 were paid.

Yankee: Capital stock of $75,000 was issued, but no dividends were paid.

Zulu: Capital stock of $75,000 was issued, and dividends of $55,000 were paid.

Obj **1, 3, 5**

✔ (a) 76,500

E2-14   Missing amounts from balance sheet and income statement data

One item is omitted from each of the following summaries of balance sheet and income statement data for four different corporations.

	Carbon	Krypton	Fluorine	Radium
Beginning of the year:				
Assets	$333,000	$250,000	$100,000	(d)
Liabilities	118,000	130,000	76,000	$120,000
End of the year:				
Assets	495,000	350,000	90,000	248,000
Liabilities	160,000	110,000	80,000	136,000
During the year:				
Additional issuance of capital stock	(a)	50,000	10,000	40,000
Dividends	7,500	16,000	(c)	60,000
Revenue	90,000	(b)	115,000	112,000
Expenses	39,000	64,000	122,500	128,000

Determine the amounts of the missing items, identifying them by letter. (*Suggestion:* First determine the amount of increase or decrease in stockholders' equity during the year.)

E2-15   Net income, retained earnings, and dividends

Use the following data (in millions) for Dell, Inc., for a recent year to answer the questions below:

Retained earnings, beginning of year	$24,744
Retained earnings, end of year	28,236
Net cash flows from operating activities	5,527
Net decrease in cash	(61)
Net cash flows from financing activities	578

Obj **3, 5**

✔ a. $3,492

a. Determine the amount of earnings retained in Dell for the year.

b. Determine the net cash flows used for investing activities for the year.

E2-16   Balance sheet, net income, and cash flows

Financial information related to Abby's Interiors for October and November of 20Y6 is as follows:

	October 31, 20Y6	November 30, 20Y6
Notes payable	$200,000	$250,000
Land	500,000	575,000
Capital stock	75,000	90,000
Retained earnings	?	?
Cash	50,000	175,000

Obj **3, 5**

✔ b. $147,000

a. Prepare balance sheets for Abby's Interiors as of October 31 and November 30, 20Y6.

b. Determine the amount of net income for November, assuming that dividends of $12,000 were paid.

c. Determine the net cash flows from operating activities for November.

d. Determine the net cash flows from investing activities for November.

e. Determine the net cash flows from financing activities for November.

f. Determine the net increase or decrease in cash for November.

E2-17   Income statement

After its first month of operation, the following amounts were taken from the accounting records of Benjamin Realty Inc. as of April 30, 20Y9.

Capital stock	$25,000	Notes payable	$ 35,000
Cash	53,000	Rent expense	5,000
Dividends	10,000	Retained earnings	0
Interest expense	2,000	Salaries expense	75,000
Land	42,000	Sales commissions	145,000
Miscellaneous expense	3,000	Utilities expense	15,000

Obj **3, 5**

✔ Net income, $45,000

Prepare an income statement for the month ending April 30, 20Y9.

E2-18   Retained earnings statement

Using the financial data shown in Exercise 2-17 for Benjamin Realty Inc., prepare a retained earnings statement for the month ending April 30, 20Y9.

Obj **3, 5**

✔ Retained earnings, April 30, 20Y9, $35,000

E2-19   Balance sheet

Using the financial data shown in Exercise 2-17 for Benjamin Realty Inc., prepare a balance sheet as of April 30, 20Y9.

Obj **3, 5**

✔ Total assets, $95,000

Note: The spreadsheet icon indicates an Excel template is available on the student companion site.

Obj | **3, 5**

✔ Net cash flows
from operating
activities, $45,000

E2-20   Statement of cash flows

Using the financial data shown in Exercise 2-17 for Benjamin Realty Inc., prepare a statement of cash flows for the month ending April 30, 20Y9.

Obj | **1, 2, 4**

E2-21   Effects of transactions on accounting equation

Describe how the following transactions of Sun Microsystems, Inc., would affect the three elements of the accounting equation.

a. Paid research and development expenses for the current year.

b. Purchased machinery and equipment for cash.

c. Received cash from issuing stock.

d. Received cash from the issuance of long-term debt.

e. Made cash sales.

f. Paid selling expenses.

g. Paid employee pension expenses for the current year.

h. Received proceeds from selling a portion of manufacturing operations for a gain on the sale.

i. Paid officer salaries.

j. Paid taxes.

k. Paid off long-term debt.

l. Paid dividends.

Obj | **3, 5**

E2-22   Statement of cash flows

Based upon the financial transactions for Sun Microsystems, Inc., shown in Exercise 2-21, indicate whether the transaction would be reported in the cash flows from operating, investing, or financing sections of the statement on cash flows.

Problems

Obj | **1, 2, 3**

✔ 3. Net income,
$18,000

P2-1   Transactions and financial statements

Van Jordan established an insurance agency on March 1, 20Y5, and completed the following transactions during March:

a. Opened a business bank account in the name of Jordan Insurance Inc., with a deposit of $50,000 in exchange for capital stock.

b. Borrowed $25,000 by issuing a note payable.

c. Received cash from fees earned, $28,000.

d. Paid rent on office and equipment for the month, $3,000.

e. Paid automobile expense for the month, $1,800, and miscellaneous expense, $900.

f. Paid office salaries, $4,200.

g. Paid interest on the note payable, $100.

h. Purchased land as a future building site, paying cash of $55,000.

i. Paid dividends, $4,000.

Instructions

1. Indicate the effect of each transaction and the balances after each transaction, using the integrated financial statement framework.

2. Briefly explain why the stockholders' investments and revenues increased stockholders' equity, while dividends and expenses decreased stockholders' equity.

3. Prepare an income statement and retained earnings statement for March.

4. Prepare a balance sheet as of March 31, 20Y5.

5. Prepare a statement of cash flows for March.

P2-2   Transactions and financial statements

Obj **1, 2, 3**

James Nesbitt established Up-Date Computer Services on August 1, 20Y4. The effect of each transaction and the balances after each transaction for August are shown below in the integrated financial statement framework.

Instructions

✔ 1. Net income, $18,000

1. Prepare an income statement for the month ended August 31, 20Y4.
2. Prepare a retained earnings statement for the month ended August 31, 20Y4.
3. Prepare a balance sheet as of August 31, 20Y4.
4. Prepare a statement of cash flows for the month ended August 31, 20Y4.

Statement of Cash Flows	Assets		=	Liabilities +	Stockholders' Equity		Income Statement
	Cash +	Land	=	Notes Payable +	Capital Stock +	Retained Earnings	
a. Investment	25,000				25,000		
b. Fees earned	27,000					27,000	b.
Balances	52,000				25,000	27,000	
c. Rent expense	−2,500					−2,500	c.
Balances	49,500				25,000	24,500	
d. Issued notes payable	10,000			10,000			
Balances	59,500			10,000	25,000	24,500	
e. Purchased land	−40,000	40,000					
Balances	19,500	40,000		10,000	25,000	24,500	
f. Paid expenses	−1,900					−1,900	f.
Balances	17,600	40,000		10,000	25,000	22,600	
g. Paid salary expense	−4,600					−4,600	g.
Balances	13,000	40,000		10,000	25,000	18,000	
h. Paid dividends	−3,000					−3,000	
Balances, Aug. 31	10,000	40,000		10,000	25,000	15,000	

Balance Sheet (header spanning Assets/Liabilities/Stockholders' Equity)

Statement of Cash Flows

a. Financing	25,000
b. Operating	27,000
c. Operating	−2,500
d. Financing	10,000
e. Investing	−40,000
f. Operating	−1,900
g. Operating	−4,600
h. Financing	−3,000
Increase in cash	10,000

Income Statement

b. Fees earned	27,000
c. Rent expense	−2,500
f. Auto expense	−1,200
f. Misc. expense	−700
g. Salary expense	−4,600
Net income	18,000

Obj | 3

✔ 1. Net income,
$113,000

P2-3   Financial statements

The following amounts were taken from the accounting records of Hargrove Services, Inc., as of May 31, 20Y7. Hargrove Services began its operations on June 1, 20Y6.

Capital stock	$ 30,000
Cash	62,000
Dividends	13,000
Fees earned	300,000
Interest expense	2,000
Land	98,000
Miscellaneous expense	8,000
Notes payable	30,000
Rent expense	28,000
Salaries expense	87,000
Taxes expense	22,000
Utilities expense	40,000

Instructions

1. Prepare an income statement for the year ending May 31, 20Y2.
2. Prepare a retained earnings statement for the year ending May 31, 20Y7.
3. Prepare a balance sheet as of May 31, 20Y7.
4. Prepare a statement of cash flows for the year ending May 31, 20Y7.

Obj | 5

✔ 1. Net income,
$230,000

P2-4   Financial statements

After its second year of operations, the following amounts were taken from the accounting records of Hargrove Services, Inc., as of May 31, 20Y8. Hargrove Services began its operations on June 1, 20Y6 (see Problem 2-3).

Capital stock	$ 55,000
Cash	?
Dividends	40,000
Fees earned	515,000
Interest expense	3,000
Land	240,000
Miscellaneous expense	11,000
Notes payable	40,000
Rent expense	36,000
Salaries expense	155,000
Taxes expense	28,000
Utilities expense	52,000

Instructions

1. Prepare an income statement for the year ending May 31, 20Y8.
2. Prepare a retained earnings statement for the year ending May 31, 20Y8. (*Note:* The retained earnings at June 1, 20Y7, was $100,000.)
3. Prepare a balance sheet as of May 31, 20Y8.
4. Prepare a statement of cash flows for the year ending May 31, 20Y8. (*Hint:* You should compare the asset and liability amounts of May 31, 20Y8, with those of May 31, 20Y7, to determine cash used in investing and financing activities. See Problem 2-3 for the May 31, 20Y7, balance sheet amounts.)

Obj | 3, 5

✔ a. $125,000

P2-5   Missing amounts from financial statements

The financial statements at the end of Network Realty, Inc.'s first month of operation are shown below. By analyzing the interrelationships among the financial statements, fill in the proper amounts for (a) through (s).

NETWORK REALTY, INC.
Income Statement
For the Month Ended December 31, 20Y4

Fees earned		$ (a)
Operating expenses:		
Wages expense	$33,120	
Rent expense	18,000	
Utilities expense	(b)	
Interest expense	1,800	
Miscellaneous expense	3,960	
Total operating expenses		67,500
Net income		$ (c)

NETWORK REALTY, INC.
Retained Earnings Statement
For the Month Ended December 31, 20Y4

Retained earnings, December 1, 20Y4		$(d)
Net income for December	$ 57,500	
Less dividends	(e)	(f)
Retained earnings, December 31, 20Y4		$(g)

NETWORK REALTY, INC.
Balance Sheet
December 31, 20Y4

Assets

Cash		$ (h)
Land		175,000
Total assets		$225,500

Liabilities

Notes payable		$105,000

Stockholders' Equity

Capital stock	$(i)	
Retained earnings	(j)	
Total stockholders' equity		(k)
Total liabilities and stockholders' equity		$ (l)

NETWORK REALTY, INC.
Statement of Cash Flows
For the Month Ended December 31, 20Y4

Cash flows from operating activities:		
Cash received from customers	$125,000	
Deduct cash payments for expenses	67,500	
Net cash flows from operating activities		$ (m)
Cash flows used in investing activities:		
Cash payment for purchase of land		(175,000)
Cash flows from financing activities:		
Cash received from sale of capital stock	$75,000	
Cash received from issuing notes payable	(n)	$ (o)
Deduct cash dividends	12,000	
Net cash flows from financing activities		(p)
Net increase in cash		$ (q)
December 1, 20Y4, cash balance		(r)
December 31, 20Y4, cash balance		$ (s)

P2-6   Financial statements

Alpine Realty, Inc., organized July 1, 20Y8, is operated by Angela Griffin. How many errors can you find in the following financial statements for Alpine Realty, Inc., prepared after its first month of operation?

ALPINE REALTY, INC.
Income Statement
July 31, 20Y8

Sales commissions...		$60,000
Operating expenses:		
Office salaries expense..................................	$20,000	
Rent expense..	6,000	
Automobile expense.....................................	3,500	
Dividends...	2,000	
Miscellaneous expense..................................	1,500	
Total operating expenses............................		33,000
Net income		$27,000

ANGELA GRIFFIN
Retained Earnings Statement
July 31, 20Y7

Net income for the month	$27,000
Retained earnings, July 31, 20Y7	$27,000

Balance Sheet
For the Month Ended July 31, 20Y7

Assets

Cash		$32,000
Notes payable		20,000
Total assets		$52,000

Liabilities

Land..		$30,000

Stockholders' Equity

Capital stock..	$15,000	
Retained earnings	27,000	
Total stockholders' equity		42,000
Total liabilities and stockholders' equity....................		$72,000

ALPINE REALTY, INC.
Statement of Cash Flows
July 31, 20Y8

Cash flows from operating activities:	
Cash receipts from sales commissions.............................	$ 60,000
Cash flows used for investing activities:	
Cash payments for land...	(30,000)
Cash flows from financing activities:	
Cash receipts from retained earnings.............................	27,000
Net increase in cash during July	$ 57,000
Cash as of July 1, 20Y8	0
Cash as of July 31, 20Y8	$ 57,000

Financial Analysis

FA2-1   Common-sized income statements

Obj 6

Safeway Inc. operates over 1,700 supermarkets throughout the United States. Income statements (in millions) for Safeway Inc. shown below were adapted from its recent financial statements.

	Year 2	Year 1
Sales	$ 43,630	$ 41,050
Cost of sales	(31,836)	(29,443)
Gross profit	$ 11,794	$ 11,607
Operating expenses	(10,659)	(10,448)
Operating income	$ 1,135	$ 1,159
Other income (expense)		
Interest expense	$ (272)	$ (298)
Tax expense	(364)	(291)
Other income.....................	18	20
Net income..........................	$ 517	$ 590

1. Prepare common-sized income statements for Years 2 and 1. Round to one decimal place.
2. Using (1), analyze the performance of Safeway in Year 2.

FA2-2   Common-sized income statements

Obj 6

Using your answer to FA2-1, compare and analyze the Safeway common-sized income statements to those of The Kroger Co. The Kroger common-sized income statements are described and illustrated on page 61 of this chapter.

FA2-3   Common-sized income statements

Obj 6

Kellogg Company produces, markets, and distributes cereal and food products including Cheez-It, Coco Pops, Rice Krispies, and Pringles. The following partial income statements (in millions) were adapted from recent financial statements.

	Year 2	Year 1
Sales	$13,198	$ 12,397
Cost of sales	(7,750)	(7,108)
Gross profit	$ 5,448	$ 5,289
Operating expenses	(3,472)	(3,299)
Operating income	$ 1,976	$ 1,990

1. Prepare common-sized income statements for Years 2 and 1. Round to one decimal place.
2. Using (1), analyze the performance of Kellogg in Year 2.

FA2-4   Common-sized income statements

Obj 6

General Mills Inc. produces, markets, and distributes cereal and food products including Cheerios, Wheaties, Cocoa Puffs, Yoplait, and Pillsbury branded products. The following partial income statements (in millions) were adapted from recent financial statements.

	Year 2	Year 1
Sales	$ 16,658	$14,880
Cost of sales	(10,613)	(8,927)
Gross profit	$ 6,045	$ 5,953
Operating expenses	(3,482)	(3,179)
Operating income	$ 2,563	$ 2,774

1. Prepare common-sized income statements for Years 2 and 1. Round to one decimal place.
2. Using (1), analyze the performance of General Mills in Year 2.

Obj | **6**

FA2-5 Common-sized income statements

Using your answer to FA2-3 and FA2-4, compare and analyze Year 2 common-sized income statements of Kellogg to those of General Mills.

Obj | **6**

FA2-6 Common-sized balance sheets

The following end-of-the-year balance sheets (in millions) were adapted from recent financial statements of The Kroger Co.

	Year 2	Year 1
Current assets:		
Cash	$ 974	$ 1,491
Accounts receivable	949	845
Inventories	5,114	4,966
Prepaid and other assets	288	319
Total current assets	$ 7,325	$ 7,621
Fixed assets:		
Property, plant, and equipment	$14,464	$14,147
Intangibles	1,138	1,140
Other assets	549	597
Total fixed assets	$16,151	$15,884
Total assets	$23,476	$23,505
Current liabilities:		
Accounts payable	$ 4,329	$ 4,227
Salaries and wages payable	1,056	888
Debt due within one year	1,315	588
Other liabilities	2,405	2,367
Total current liabilities	$ 9,105	$ 8,070
Long-term liabilities:		
Debt and other financing obligations	$ 6,850	$ 7,304
Other liabilities	3,555	2,833
Total long-term liabilities	$10,405	$10,137
Total liabilities	$19,510	$18,207
Stockholders' Equity		
Capital stock	$ 4,386	$ 4,353
Retained earnings	7,727	7,675
Other equity items	(8,147)	(6,730)
Total stockholders' equity	$ 3,966	$ 5,298
Total liabilities and stockholders' equity	$23,476	$23,505

1. Prepare common-sized balance sheets for Kroger for Years 2 and 1. Round to one decimal place.

2. Comment on your answer in (1).

Cases

GROUP PROJECT

Case 2-1 Business emphasis

Assume that you are considering developing a nationwide chain of women's clothing stores. You have contacted a Seattle-based firm that specializes in financing new business ventures and enterprises. Such firms, called venture capital firms, finance new businesses in exchange for a percentage of the ownership.

1. In groups of four or five, discuss the different business emphases that you might use in your venture.

2. For each emphasis you listed in (1), provide an example of a real-world business using the same emphasis.

3. What percentage of the ownership would you be willing to give the venture capital firm in exchange for its financing?

Case 2-2   Cash accounting

On August 1, 20Y7, Dr. Ruth Turner established SickCo, a medical practice organized as a professional corporation. The following conversation occurred the following February between Dr. Turner and a former medical school classmate, Dr. Shonna Rees, at an American Medical Association convention in New York City.

Dr. Rees: Ruth, good to see you again. Why didn't you call when you were in Denver? We could have had dinner together.

Dr. Turner: Actually, I never made it to Denver this year. My husband and kids went up to our Vail condo twice, but I got stuck in Fort Lauderdale. I opened a new consulting practice this August and haven't had any time for myself since.

Dr. Rees: I heard about it ... Sick... something ... right?

Dr. Turner: Yes, SickCo. My husband chose the name.

Dr. Rees: I've thought about doing something like that. Are you making any money? I mean, is it worth your time?

Dr. Turner: You wouldn't believe it. I started by opening a bank account with $45,000, and my January bank statement has a balance of $100,000. Not bad for six months—all pure profit.

Dr. Rees: Maybe I'll try it in Denver! Let's have breakfast together tomorrow and you can fill me in on the details.

Comment on Dr. Turner's statement that the difference between the opening bank balance ($45,000) and the January statement balance ($100,000) is pure profit.

Case 2-3   Business emphasis

Amazon.com, an Internet retailer, was incorporated in the early 1990s and opened its virtual doors on the Web shortly thereafter. On its statement of cash flows, would you expect Amazon.com's net cash flows from operating, investing, and financing activities to be positive or negative for its first three years of operation? Use the following format for your answers, and briefly explain your logic.

	Year 1	Year 2	Year 3
Net cash flows from operating activities	negative		
Net cash flows from investing activities			
Net cash flows from financing activities			

Case 2-4   Financial information

Yahoo.com's finance Internet site provides summary financial information about public companies, such as stock quotes, recent financial filings with the Securities and Exchange Commission, and recent news stories. Go to Yahoo.com's financial Web site (**http://finance.yahoo.com/**) and enter Apple, Inc.'s stock symbol, AAPL. Answer the following questions concerning Apple, Inc. by clicking on the various items under the tab "More Reports for AAPL."

1. At what price did Apple's stock last trade?
2. What is the 52-week range of Apple's stock?
3. When was the last time Apple's stock hit a 52-week high?
4. Over the last six months, has there been any insider selling or buying of Apple's stock?
5. Who is the chief executive officer of Apple Inc., and how old is the president?
6. What was the salary of the president of Apple Inc.?
7. What is the annual dividend of Apple's stock?
8. How many current broker recommendations are strong buy, buy, hold, sell, or strong sell? What is the average of the broker recommendations?
9. What is the net cash flow from operations for this year?
10. What is the operating margin for this year?

Case 2-5   Analyzing financial information

On February 25, 2009, Gabriel Madway wrote an article entitled "Apple Investors Get No Satisfaction on Jobs," which appeared on *Reuters.com*. The article raises concerns about Steve Jobs's health and the possible reoccurrence of his pancreatic cancer. The following excerpt is taken from the article:

Jobs—who co-founded Apple and is credited with transforming it into a consumer juggernaut after returning as CEO a decade ago—announced . . . he would take a five-month leave of absence, handing over the reins of the firm and saying his health problems were "more complex" than originally thought.

Answer the following questions:

1. Is the article favorable, neutral, or unfavorable regarding future prospects for Apple Inc.?

2. Assuming you owned stock in Apple Inc., would you sell your stock based only on this article? If not, what additional information would you want?

3. Would it be a prudent investment strategy to rely only on published financial statements in deciding whether to invest in a company's stock?

4. What sources do you think financial analysts use in making investment decisions and recommendations?

Answers to Self-Examination Questions

1. **D** Even though a recording error has been made, the accounting equation will balance (answer D). However, assets (cash) will be overstated by $50,000, and liabilities (notes payable) will be overstated by $50,000. Answer A is incorrect because although cash is overstated by $50,000, the accounting equation will balance. Answer B is incorrect because although notes payable are overstated by $50,000, the accounting equation will balance. Answer C is incorrect because the accounting equation will balance and assets will not exceed liabilities.

2. **C** Total assets will exceed total liabilities and stockholders' equity by $16,000. This is because stockholders' equity (retained earnings) was decreased instead of increased by $8,000. Thus, stockholders' equity will be understated by a total of $16,000.

3. **C** The accounting equation is:

    Assets = Liabilities + Stockholders' Equity

    Therefore, if assets increased by $20,000 and liabilities increased by $12,000, stockholders' equity must have increased by $8,000 (answer C), as indicated in the following computation:

Assets	= Liabilities + Stockholders' Equity
+$20,000	= $12,000 + Stockholders' Equity
+$20,000 − $12,000	= Stockholders' Equity
+$8,000	= Stockholders' Equity

4. **B** Net income is the excess of revenue over expenses, or $15,000 (answer B). If expenses exceed revenue, the difference is a net loss. Dividends are the opposite of the stockholders investing in the business and do not affect the amount of net income or net loss.

5. **B** The purchase of land for cash changes the mix of assets and does not affect liabilities or stockholders' equity (answer B). Borrowing cash from a bank (answer A) increases assets and liabilities. Receiving cash for fees earned (answer C) increases cash and stockholders' equity (retained earnings). Paying office salaries (answer D) decreases cash and stockholders' equity (retained earnings).

CHAPTER 3

Accrual Accounting Concepts

LEARNING OBJECTIVES
After studying this chapter, you should be able to:

Obj | **1** Describe basic accrual accounting concepts, including the matching concept.

Obj | **2** Use accrual concepts of accounting to analyze, record, and summarize transactions.

Obj | **3** Describe and illustrate the end-of-period adjustment process.

Obj | **4** Prepare financial statements using accrual concepts of accounting, including a classified balance sheet.

Obj | **5** Describe how the accrual basis of accounting enhances the interpretation of financial statements.

Obj | **6** Financial Analysis: Describe and illustrate the use of working capital, the current ratio, and the quick ratio in assessing a company's liquidity.

Have you ever purchased an iTunes gift card from **Best Buy** or online, which can be redeemed online at the iTunes Store? If so, when do you think **Apple Inc.** should record the revenue from the sale of the gift card?

As we discussed and illustrated in Chapter 2, sometimes revenues are earned at the point cash is received. However, in some cases, a company renders a service or delivers a product before cash is received. In other cases, cash is received before a company renders a service or delivers a product. In these cases, companies normally record revenue when the service is rendered or the product is delivered to the customer.

One company that receives cash before the service is rendered or the product delivered is Apple Inc. In the case of iTunes gift cards, Apple receives cash before the customer uses the service of downloading music, movies, or other content from

its online iTunes Store. When cash is received for the gift card, Apple defers recording the revenue until the customer redeems the card. Likewise, revenue from AppleCare, which provides computer support and repair services, is recorded over the service period covered by the AppleCare contract. For example, Apple offers AppleCare on its iPads for up to a two-year period.

In this chapter, we continue our discussion of financial statements and financial reporting systems. In doing so, we focus on accrual concepts of accounting such as how Apple would record deferred revenue. In addition, our discussions will include how to record transactions under accrual accounting concepts, update accounting records, and prepare accrual financial statements. Because all large companies, and many small ones, use accrual concepts of accounting, a thorough understanding of this topic is important for your business studies and future career.

Basic Accrual Accounting Concepts, Including the Matching Concept

Family Health Care's transactions and financial statements for September and October were illustrated in Chapter 2. These illustrations used many of the eight accounting concepts described in Chapter 1. For example, the business entity concept was used to account for Family Health Care as a separate entity, independent of the owner-manager, Dr. Lee Landry. The cost, unit of measure, going concern, accounting period, full disclosure, and objectivity concepts were also used.

The one accounting concept not used in Chapter 2 was the matching concept. This is because all the transactions in Chapter 2 were structured so that cash was either received or paid. This was done to simplify the recording of transactions and preparing of the financial statements. For example, all revenues were received in cash at the time the services were rendered and all expenses were paid in cash at the time they were incurred.

In the real world, cash may be received or paid at a different time from when revenues are earned or expenses are incurred. In fact, companies often earn revenue before or after cash is received and incur expenses before or after cash is paid.

To illustrate, a real estate company might spend months or years developing land for a business complex or subdivision. During this period, the company earns no revenues but makes payments for materials, wages, insurance, and other construction items. Thus, if revenues were recorded only when cash is received and expenses recorded only when cash is paid, the company would report a series of losses on its income statement while the land is being developed. In such cases, the income statements would not provide a realistic picture of the company's operations. In fact, the development might become highly successful and the early losses misleading.

Accrual accounting is designed to avoid misleading information arising from the timing of cash receipts and payments. Under accrual accounting, transactions are recorded as they occur and thus affect the accounting equation (assets, liabilities, and stockholders' equity). Specifically, the **accrual basis of accounting** records revenue as it is earned and matches expenses against the revenue they generate. Since the receipt or payment of cash affects assets (cash), all cash receipts and payments are recorded in the accounts under accrual accounting. Conversely, under accrual accounting, transactions are also recorded even though cash is not received or paid until a later point.

HOW BUSINESSES MAKE MONEY

NOT CUTTING CORNERS

Have you ever ordered a hamburger from **Wendy's** and noticed that the meat patty is square? The square meat patty reflects a business emphasis instilled in Wendy's by its founder, Dave Thomas. Mr. Thomas emphasized offering high-quality products at a fair price in a friendly atmosphere, without "cutting corners"; hence, the square meat patty. In the highly competitive fast-food industry, Dave Thomas's approach has enabled Wendy's to become one of the largest fast-food restaurant chains in the world.

Source: Douglas Martin, "Dave Thomas, 69, Wendy's Founder, Dies," *New York Times*, January 9, 2002.

To illustrate, Family Health Care may provide services to patients who are covered by health insurance. Periodically, Family Health Care files claims with the insurance companies requesting payment. In this case, revenue is recorded, referred to as *recognized,* when the services are provided even though the cash is to be received later. When services are provided with the cash to be received at a later time, the services are said to be provided *on account.* In such cases, an *account receivable* for the amount of the services is recorded as an asset.

Likewise, a company may purchase supplies from a supplier (vendor), with terms that allow the company to pay for the purchase at a later time. In this case, the supplies are said to be purchased *on account* and an *account payable* for the amount to be paid is recorded as a liability.

In accounting, the term *recognized* is often used to refer to when a transaction is recorded. Under accrual accounting, *revenue is recognized when it is earned.* For Family Health Care, revenue is earned when services have been provided to the patient. At this point, the revenue-earning process is complete and the patient is legally obligated to pay for the services.

The matching concept plays an important role in accrual accounting for determining when expenses are recorded. When revenues are earned and recorded, all expenses incurred in generating the revenues are also recorded. In this way, revenues and expenses are *matched* and the net income or net loss for the period is determined.

Accrual accounting also recognizes liabilities at the time the business incurs the obligation to pay for the services or goods purchased. For example, the purchase of supplies on account is recorded when the supplies are received and the business has incurred the obligation to pay for the supplies.

Using Accrual Concepts of Accounting for Family Health Care's November Transactions

Obj 2

Use accrual concepts of accounting to analyze, record, and summarize transactions.

To illustrate accrual accounting, the following November 20Y5 Family Health Care transactions are used:

a. On November 1, received $1,800 from ILS Company as rent for the use of Family Health Care's land as a temporary parking lot from November 20Y5 through March 20Y6.

b. On November 1, paid a premium of $2,400 for a two-year general business insurance policy that covers risks from fire and theft.

c. On November 1, paid $6,000 for an insurance premium on a six-month medical malpractice policy.

d. Dr. Landry invested an additional $5,000 in the business in exchange for capital stock.

e. Purchased supplies for $240 on account.

f. Purchased $8,500 of office equipment. Paid $1,700 cash as a down payment, with the remaining $6,800 ($8,500 − $1,700) due in five monthly installments of $1,360 ($6,800 ÷ 5) beginning January 1, 20Y6.

g. Provided services of $6,100 to patients on account.

h. Received $5,500 for services provided to patients who paid cash.

i. Received $4,200 from insurance companies, which paid on patients' accounts for services that have been provided.

j. Paid $100 on account for supplies that had been purchased.

k. Expenses paid during November were as follows: wages, $2,790; rent, $800; utilities, $580; interest, $100; and miscellaneous, $420.

l. Paid dividends of $1,200 to stockholders (Dr. Landry).

A listing of a company's accounts is called its chart of accounts.

In analyzing and recording the November transactions for Family Health Care, the integrated financial statement framework is used. Transactions that increase or decrease a financial statement element are recorded. These financial statement elements are referred to as **accounts**.

Transaction (a)

On November 1, received $1,800 from ILS Company as rent for the use of Family Health Care's land as a temporary parking lot from November 20Y5 through March 20Y6.

In this transaction, Family Health Care entered into a rental agreement for the use of its land. The agreement requires a payment of a rental fee of $1,800 in advance. The rental agreement also gives ILS Company the option of renewing the agreement for an additional four months.

By entering into this rental agreement and accepting the $1,800, Family Health Care has incurred a liability to make the land available for ILS's use. If Family Health Care canceled the agreement on November 1, after accepting the $1,800, it would have to repay the $1,800.

Microsoft Corporation recently reported unearned revenue of $20,059 million.

Family Health Care records this transaction as an increase in Cash and an increase in a liability for $1,800. Because the liability relates to rent that has not yet been earned, it is recorded as Unearned Revenue.

The effects of this transaction on Family Health Care's financial statements are recorded as shown below.

Statement of Cash Flows	Balance Sheet							Income Statement
	Assets	=	Liabilities	+	Stockholders' Equity			
	Cash + Land	=	Notes Payable +	Unearned Revenue +	Capital Stock +	Retained Earnings		
Balances	7,320 12,000		10,000		6,000	3,320		
a. Received rent in advance	1,800			1,800				
Balances	9,120 12,000		10,000	1,800	6,000	3,320		

Statement of Cash Flows

a. Operating   1,800

The receipt of the $1,800 of cash increases cash flows from operating activities under the Statement of Cash Flows column. Since no rental revenue has yet been earned, there are no entries under the Income Statement column.

As time passes, Family Health Care will earn the rental revenue. For example, at the end of November, $360 ($1,800 ÷ 5 months) will be earned. Recording the $360 of earned rent revenue at the end of November is described and illustrated later in this chapter.

The November 1 balances shown in the preceding integrated financial statement spreadsheet are the ending balances from October. That is, the cash balance of $7,320 is the ending cash balance as of October 31, 20Y5. Likewise, the other balances are carried forward from the preceding month.

In this sense, the Balance Sheet column is a cumulative financial history of Family Health Care.

Transaction (b)

On November 1, paid a premium of $2,400 for a two-year general business insurance policy that covers risks from fire and theft.

By paying the premium, Family Health Care has purchased an asset, insurance coverage, in exchange for cash. The effects of this transaction on Family Health Care's financial statements are recorded as shown below.

Statement of Cash Flows		Balance Sheet							Income Statement
		Assets			=	Liabilities	+	Stockholders' Equity	
	Cash +	Prepaid Insurance	+ Land =	Notes Payable	+	Unearned Revenue	+	Capital Stock	+ Retained Earnings	
Balances	9,120		12,000	10,000		1,800		6,000	3,320	
b. Paid insurance for two years	−2,400	2,400								
Balances	6,720	2,400	12,000	10,000		1,800		6,000	3,320	

Statement of Cash Flows	
b. Operating	−2,400

Under the Balance Sheet column the mix of assets has changed, with Cash decreasing by $2,400 and Prepaid Insurance increasing by $2,400. The payment of cash also decreases cash flows from Operating activities under the Statement of Cash Flows column. Since no revenue or expenses are affected, there are no entries under the Income Statement column.

Prepaid insurance is unique in that it expires with the passage of time. For example, $100 ($2,400 ÷ 24 months) of Family Health Care's insurance will expire each month. Such assets are called **prepaid expenses** or **deferred expenses**.

Transaction (c)

On November 1, paid $6,000 for an insurance premium on a six-month medical malpractice policy.

This transaction is similar to transaction (b), except that Family Health Care has purchased medical malpractice insurance that is renewable every 6 months. The effects of this transaction on Family Health Care's financial statements are recorded as shown on the next page.

Balance Sheet

Statement of Cash Flows	Cash +	Prepaid Insurance	+ Land =	Notes Payable +	Unearned Revenue +	Capital Stock +	Retained Earnings	Income Statement
Balances	6,720	2,400	12,000	10,000	1,800	6,000	3,320	
c. Paid insurance for six months	–6,000	6,000						
Balances	720	8,400	12,000	10,000	1,800	6,000	3,320	

Statement of Cash Flows

c. Operating   –6,000

Transaction (d)

Dr. Landry invested an additional $5,000 in the business in exchange for capital stock.

This transaction is similar to the initial transaction in which Dr. Landry established Family Health Care. The effects of these transactions are recorded as shown below.

Balance Sheet

Statement of Cash Flows	Cash +	Prepaid Insurance	+ Land =	Notes Payable +	Unearned Revenue +	Capital Stock +	Retained Earnings	Income Statement
Balances	720	8,400	12,000	10,000	1,800	6,000	3,320	
d. Issued capital stock	5,000					5,000		
Balances	5,720	8,400	12,000	10,000	1,800	11,000	3,320	

Statement of Cash Flows

d. Financing   5,000

Transaction (e)

Purchased supplies for $240 on account.

Lowe's Companies reported accounts payable of $4,965 in a recent balance sheet.

This transaction is similar to transactions (b) and (c), in that purchased supplies are assets until they are used in the generation of revenue. Family Health Care has purchased and received the supplies, with a promise to pay in the near future. Such liabilities that are incurred in the normal operations are called **accounts payable**. The effects of this transaction on Family Health Care's financial statements are recorded as shown on the next page.

Statement of Cash Flows	Balance Sheet										Income Statement
	Assets				=	Liabilities			+	Stockholders' Equity	
	Cash +	Prepaid Insurance +	Supplies +	Land =	Notes Payable +	Accounts Payable +	Unearned Revenue +	Capital Stock +	Retained Earnings		
Balances	5,720	8,400		12,000	10,000		1,800	11,000	3,320		
e. Purchased supplies			240			240					
Balances	5,720	8,400	240	12,000	10,000	240	1,800	11,000	3,320		

Under the Balance Sheet column, the asset Supplies increases by $240 and the liability Accounts Payable increases by $240. Since no cash is paid or received, there are no entries under the Statement of Cash Flows column. Likewise, since no revenue or expenses are affected, there are no entries under the Income Statement column.

Transaction (f)

Purchased $8,500 of office equipment. Paid $1,700 cash as a down payment, with the remaining $6,800 ($8,500 – $1,700) due in five monthly installments of $1,360 ($6,800 ÷ 5) beginning January 1, 20Y6.

In this transaction, the asset Office Equipment increases by $8,500, Cash decreases by $1,700, and Notes Payable increases by $6,800. Since cash was paid, cash flows from Investing activities is decreased by $1,700 under the Statement of Cash Flows column. No revenues or expenses are affected, so no entries under the Income Statement column are necessary.

The effects of transaction (f) on Family Health Care's financial statements are recorded as shown below.

Statement of Cash Flows	Balance Sheet											Income Statement
	Assets					=	Liabilities			+	Stockholders' Equity	
	Cash +	Prepaid Insur. +	Supp. +	Office Equip. +	Land =	Notes Pay. +	Accts. Pay. +	Unearned Revenue +	Capital Stock +	Retained Earnings		
Balances	5,720	8,400	240		12,000	10,000	240	1,800	11,000	3,320		
f. Purchased office equip.	−1,700			8,500		6,800						
Balances	4,020	8,400	240	8,500	12,000	16,800	240	1,800	11,000	3,320		

Statement of Cash Flows

f. Investing   −1,700

Transaction (g)

Provided services of $6,100 to patients on account.

This transaction is similar to the revenue transactions recorded for Family Health Care in September and October. This transaction is different in that instead of receiving cash, the services were provided *on account*.

Pepsico, Inc. reported net receivables of $6,912 in a recent balance sheet.

Family Health Care will collect cash from the patients' insurance companies in the future. Such amounts that are to be collected in the future and that arise from the normal operations are called **accounts receivable**. Since a valid claim exists for future collection, accounts receivable are assets. Thus, the asset Accounts Receivable is increased by $6,100 under the Balance Sheet column. In addition, Retained Earnings are increased under the Balance Sheet column and Fees earned is increased under the Income Statement column.

The effects of transaction (g) on Family Health Care's financial statements are recorded as shown below.

Statement of Cash Flows	Balance Sheet											Income Statement
	Assets					=	Liabilities		+	Stockholders' Equity		
	Cash +	Accts. Rec. +	Prepaid Insur. +	Supp. +	Office Equip. +	Land =	Notes Pay. +	Accts. Pay. +	Unearned Revenue +	Capital Stock +	Retained Earnings	
Balances	4,020		8,400	240	8,500	12,000	16,800	240	1,800	11,000	3,320	
g. Fees earned on acct.		6,100									6,100	g.
Balances	4,020	6,100	8,400	240	8,500	12,000	16,800	240	1,800	11,000	9,420	

Income Statement

g. Fees earned   6,100

Transaction (h)

Received $5,500 for services provided to patients who paid cash.

This transaction is similar to the revenue transactions that Family Health Care recorded in September and October. The effects of this transaction on Family Health Care's financial statements are recorded as shown:

Statement of Cash Flows	Balance Sheet											Income Statement
	Assets					=	Liabilities		+	Stockholders' Equity		
	Cash +	Accts. Rec. +	Prepaid Insur. +	Supp. +	Office Equip. +	Land =	Notes Pay. +	Accts. Pay. +	Unearned Revenue +	Capital Stock +	Retained Earnings	
Balances	4,020	6,100	8,400	240	8,500	12,000	16,800	240	1,800	11,000	9,420	
h. Fees earned for cash	5,500										5,500	h.
Balances	9,520	6,100	8,400	240	8,500	12,000	16,800	240	1,800	11,000	14,920	

Statement of Cash Flows

h. Operating   5,500

Income Statement

h. Fees earned   5,500

Transaction (i)

Received $4,200 from insurance companies, which paid on patients' accounts for services that have been provided.

This transaction is similar to transaction (b) in that only the mix of assets changes. Cash is increased and Accounts Receivable is decreased by $4,200 under the

Balance Sheet column. The effects of this transaction on Family Health Care's financial statements are recorded as shown below.

Statement of Cash Flows	Balance Sheet											Income Statement
	Assets						= Liabilities			+ Stockholders' Equity		
	Cash +	Accts. Rec. +	Prepaid Insur. +	Supp. +	Office Equip. +	Land =	Notes Pay. +	Accts. Pay. +	Unearned Revenue +	Capital Stock +	Retained Earnings	
Balances	9,520	6,100	8,400	240	8,500	12,000	16,800	240	1,800	11,000	14,920	
i. Collected cash on account	4,200	–4,200										
Balances	13,720	1,900	8,400	240	8,500	12,000	16,800	240	1,800	11,000	14,920	

Statement of Cash Flows

i. Operating	4,200

Transaction (j)

Paid $100 on account for supplies that had been purchased.

The cash was paid for supplies purchased on account. Thus, this transaction decreases Cash and Accounts Payable by $100 under the Balance Sheet column. Since the supplies are used in the normal operations of Family Health Care, cash flows from Operating activities is also decreased under the Statement of Cash Flows column.

The effects of transaction (j) on Family Health Care's financial statements are recorded as shown below:

Statement of Cash Flows	Balance Sheet											Income Statement
	Assets						= Liabilities			+ Stockholders' Equity		
	Cash +	Accts. Rec. +	Prepaid Insur. +	Supp. +	Office Equip. +	Land =	Notes Pay. +	Accts. Pay. +	Unearned Revenue +	Capital Stock +	Retained Earnings	
Balances	13,720	1,900	8,400	240	8,500	12,000	16,800	240	1,800	11,000	14,920	
j. Paid on account	–100							–100				
Balances	13,620	1,900	8,400	240	8,500	12,000	16,800	140	1,800	11,000	14,920	

Statement of Cash Flows

j. Operating	–100

Transaction (k)

Expenses paid during November were as follows: wages, $2,790; rent, $800; utilities, $580; interest, $100; and miscellaneous, $420.

This transaction is similar to the September and October expense transactions for Family Health Care. The effects of this transaction on Family Health Care's financial statements are recorded as shown on the next page.

Statement of Cash Flows	Balance Sheet											Income Statement
	Assets						= Liabilities			+ Stockholders' Equity		
	Cash +	Accts. Rec. +	Prepaid Insur. +	Supp. +	Office Equip. +	Land =	Notes Pay. +	Accts. Pay. +	Unearned Revenue +	Capital Stock +	Retained Earnings	
Balances	13,620	1,900	8,400	240	8,500	12,000	16,800	140	1,800	11,000	14,920	
k. Paid expenses	−4,690										−4,690	k.
Balances	8,930	1,900	8,400	240	8,500	12,000	16,800	140	1,800	11,000	10,230	

Statement of Cash Flows			Income Statement	
k. Operating	−4,690		k. Wages expense	−2,790
			Rent expense	−800
			Utilities expense	−580
			Interest expense	−100
			Misc. expense	−420

Transaction (l)

Paid dividends of $1,200 to stockholders (Dr. Landry).

This transaction is similar to Family Health Care's dividend transactions of September and October. The effects of this transaction on Family Health Care's financial statements are recorded as shown below.

Statement of Cash Flows	Balance Sheet											Income Statement
	Assets						= Liabilities			+ Stockholders' Equity		
	Cash +	Accts. Rec. +	Prepaid Insur. +	Supp. +	Office Equip. +	Land =	Notes Pay. +	Accts. Pay. +	Unearned Revenue +	Capital Stock +	Retained Earnings	
Balances	8,930	1,900	8,400	240	8,500	12,000	16,800	140	1,800	11,000	10,230	
l. Paid dividends	−1,200										−1,200	
Balances	7,730	1,900	8,400	240	8,500	12,000	16,800	140	1,800	11,000	9,030	

Statement of Cash Flows	
l. Financing	−1,200

Obj 3

Describe and illustrate the end-of-period adjustment process.

The Adjustment Process

Accrual accounting requires the updating of the accounting records prior to preparing financial statements. This updating is called the **adjustment process**. The adjustment process is needed to match revenues and expenses, which is an application of the matching concept.

Adjustments are necessary because, at any point in time, some accounts (elements) of the accounting equation are not up to date. For example, as time passes, prepaid insurance expires and supplies are used. However, it is not efficient to record the daily expiration of prepaid insurance or the daily use of supplies. Instead, the accounting records are normally updated just prior to preparing financial statements.

Family Health Care's September and October financial statements were prepared in Chapter 2 without recording any adjustments. This is because Family Health Care only entered into cash transactions in September and October. When all of a company's transactions are cash transactions, no adjustments are necessary.

During November, however, Family Health Care entered into several accrual transactions. As a result, Family Health must adjust its accounts before preparing financial statements.

Deferrals and Accruals

Two types of accounts require adjustments as follows:

1. **Deferrals**, which are created by recording a transaction in a way that delays or defers the recognition of an expense or revenue.

2. **Accruals**, which are created when a revenue or expense has been earned or incurred but has not been recorded.

Common deferrals include prepaid expenses and unearned revenues.

Prepaid expenses or **deferred expenses** are initially recorded as assets but become expenses over time or through normal operations of the business. For Family Health Care, prepaid insurance is an example of a deferral that requires adjustment. Other examples include supplies, prepaid advertising, and prepaid interest.

Unearned revenues or **deferred revenues** are initially recorded as liabilities but become revenues over time or through normal operations of the business. For Family Health Care, unearned rent is an example of a deferral that requires adjustment. Other examples include tuition received in advance; an attorney's annual retainer fee; insurance premiums received in advance; and magazine subscriptions received in advance.

Common accruals include accrued expenses and accrued revenues.

Accrued expenses or **accrued liabilities** are expenses that have been incurred but are not recorded in the accounts. For Family Health Care, unpaid wages at

McDonald's Corporation reported prepaid and other current assets of $616 million in a recent balance sheet.

Integrity, Objectivity, and Ethics in Business

DAVE'S LEGACY

When Dave Thomas, founder of **Wendy's**, died in 2002, he left behind a corporate culture of integrity and high ethical conduct. When asked to comment on Dave's death, Jack Schuessler, chairman and chief executive officer of Wendy's, stated:

"People (could) relate to Dave, that he was honest and has integrity and he really cares about people. . . . There is no replacing Dave Thomas. . . . So you are left with . . . the values that he gave us . . . and you take care of the customer every day like Dave would want us to and good things will happen."

"He's [Dave Thomas] taught us so much that when we get stuck, we can always look back and ask ourselves, how would Dave handle it?"

In a recent discussion of corporate earnings with analysts, Kerrii Anderson, then chief financial officer of Wendy's, stated: "We're confident about the future because of our unwavering commitment to our core values, such as quality food, superior restaurant operations, continuous improvement, and *integrity to doing the right thing* [emphasis added]."

Sources: Neil Cavuto, "Wendy's CEO—Interview," *Fox News: Your World*, February 11, 2002; "Q1 2003 Wendy's International Earnings Conference Call—Final," *Financial Disclosure Wire*, April 24, 2003.

The Home Depot, Inc. reported accrued salaries and related expenses of $1,372 in a recent balance sheet.

the end of November are an example of an accrued expense. Other examples include accrued interest, utility expenses, and taxes.

Accrued revenues or **accrued assets** are revenues that have been earned but are not recorded in the accounts. For Family Health Care, revenue for patient services that have been earned but not billed at the end of November is an example of accrued revenue. Other examples include accrued interest on notes receivable and accrued rent on property rented to others.

Deferrals are normally the result of cash being received or paid *before* the revenue is earned or the expense is incurred. In contrast, accruals are normally the result of cash being received or paid *after* revenue has been earned or an expense has been incurred. Exhibit 1 summarizes the nature of deferrals and accruals.

EXHIBIT 1
Deferrals and Accruals

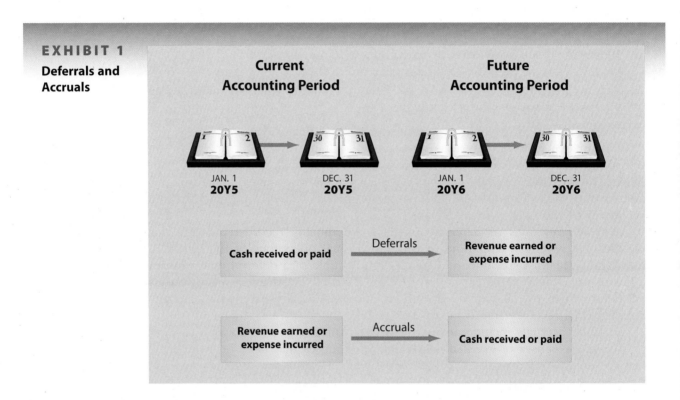

Adjustments for Family Health Care

On November 30, the following adjustment data have been gathered for Family Health Care.

Deferred expenses:
1. Prepaid insurance expired, $1,100.
2. Supplies used, $150.
3. Depreciation on office equipment, $160.

Deferred revenue:
4. Unearned revenue earned, $360.

Accrued expense:
5. Wages owed but not paid to employees, $220.

Accrued revenue:
6. Services provided but not billed to insurance companies, $750.

Adjustment 1

Prepaid insurance expired, $1,100.

During November, a portion of the prepaid insurance purchased on November 1 has expired. On November 1, Family Health Care paid for the following two policies:

1. General business policy for $2,400 (transaction b)
2. Malpractice policy for $6,000 (transaction c)

The general business policy is a two-year policy expiring at a rate of $100 ($2,400 ÷ 24) per month. The malpractice policy is a six-month policy that expires at a rate of $1,000 ($6,000 ÷ 6) per month. Thus, a total of $1,100 ($100 + $1,000) of prepaid insurance has expired by the end of November.

Adjustment 1 is recorded by decreasing the asset Prepaid Insurance and decreasing Retained Earnings under the Balance Sheet column. In addition, Insurance expense under the Income Statement column is recorded as −$1,100. Since no cash was received or paid, no entries are necessary in the Statement of Cash Flows column.

The effects of Adjustment 1 on Family Health Care's financial statements are recorded as shown below.

Statement of Cash Flows	Balance Sheet											Income Statement
	Assets						= Liabilities			+ Stockholders' Equity		
	Cash +	Accts. Rec. +	Prepaid Insur. +	Supp. +	Office Equip. +	Land =	Notes Pay. +	Accts. Pay. +	Unearned Revenue +	Capital Stock +	Retained Earnings	
Balances	7,730	1,900	8,400	240	8,500	12,000	16,800	140	1,800	11,000	9,030	
a1. Insurance expense			−1,100								−1,100	a1.
Balances	7,730	1,900	7,300	240	8,500	12,000	16,800	140	1,800	11,000	7,930	

Income Statement

a1. Insurance exp.   −1,100

All adjustments affect the balance sheet and income statement, and thus, adjusting entries are recorded in the Balance Sheet and Income Statement columns. In contrast, *no adjustment* affects cash or the statement of cash flows, and thus, no adjusting entries are recorded in the Statement of Cash Flows column.

Adjustment 2

Supplies used, $150.

For November, supplies of $150 were used. This leaves $90 ($240 − $150) of supplies on hand as of November 30.

Adjustment 2 is recorded by decreasing the asset Supplies and decreasing Retained Earnings under the Balance Sheet column. In addition, Supplies expense under the Income Statement column is recorded as −$150.

The effects of Adjustment 2 on Family Health Care's financial statements are recorded as shown below.

Statement of Cash Flows	**Balance Sheet**											Income Statement
	Assets					=	Liabilities			+	Stockholders' Equity	
	Cash +	Accts. Rec. +	Prepaid Insur. +	Supp. +	Office Equip. +	Land =	Notes Pay. +	Accts. Pay. +	Unearned Revenue +	Capital Stock +	Retained Earnings	
Balances	7,730	1,900	7,300	240	8,500	12,000	16,800	140	1,800	11,000	7,930	
a2. Supplies expense				−150							−150	a2.
Balances	7,730	1,900	7,300	90	8,500	12,000	16,800	140	1,800	11,000	7,780	

Income Statement
a2. Supplies exp.   −150

Adjustment 3

Depreciation on office equipment, $160.

Fixed assets such as office equipment lose their ability to provide service over time. This reduction in the ability of a fixed asset to provide service is called **depreciation**. However, it is difficult to objectively determine the physical decline in a fixed asset's ability to provide service. For this reason, depreciation is estimated based on the asset's useful life. Methods of estimating depreciation are covered in Chapter 7. In this chapter, the November depreciation for the office equipment is assumed to be $160.

A record of the initial cost of a fixed asset must be maintained for tax and other purposes. For this reason, the fixed asset account is not reduced directly for depreciation. Instead, an offsetting or *contra asset account*, called **accumulated depreciation**, is added to the Balance Sheet column. On the balance sheet, the accumulated depreciation is subtracted from the cost of the fixed asset.

Adjustment 3 is recorded by decreasing the asset Office Equipment in the Accumulated Depreciation (Acc. Dep.) column under Assets in the Balance Sheet column. Thus, accumulated depreciation is recorded as −$160. Retained Earnings is also decreased under the Balance Sheet column by −$160. In addition, Depreciation expense under the Income Statement column is recorded as −$160.

The effects of Adjustment 3 on Family Health Care's financial statements are recorded as shown below.

Statement of Cash Flows	**Balance Sheet**												Income Statement
	Assets						=	Liabilities			+	Stockholders' Equity	
	Cash +	Accts. Rec. +	Prepaid Insur. +	Supp. +	Office Equip. −	Acc. Depr. +	Land =	Notes Pay. +	Accts. Pay. +	Unearned Revenue +	Capital Stock +	Retained Earnings	
Balances	7,730	1,900	7,300	90	8,500		12,000	16,800	140	1,800	11,000	7,780	
a3. Depreciation exp.						−160						−160	a3.
Balances	7,730	1,900	7,300	90	8,500	−160	12,000	16,800	140	1,800	11,000	7,620	

Income Statement
a3. Depreciation exp.   −160

Three other points related to depreciation are:

1. Land is not depreciated, because it usually does not lose its ability to provide service.
2. The cost of the equipment is a type of deferred expense that is recognized as an expense over the fixed asset's useful life.
3. The cost of the fixed asset less the balance of its accumulated depreciation is called the asset's **book value**, or *carrying value*. For example, the book value of Family Health Care's office equipment, after the preceding adjustment, is $8,340 ($8,500 − $160).

Adjustment 4

Unearned revenue earned, $360.

This adjustment recognizes that a portion of the unearned revenue is earned by the end of November. That is, of the $1,800 received for rental of the land for five months (November through March), one-fifth, or $360, would have been earned as of November 30.

Adjustment 4 is recorded by decreasing the liability Unearned Revenue by $360 under the Balance Sheet column. In addition, Rent revenue is increased by $360 under the Income Statement column.

The effects of Adjustment 4 on Family Health Care's financial statements are recorded as shown below.

Statement of Cash Flows	Balance Sheet												Income Statement
	Assets						=	Liabilities		+	Stockholders' Equity		
	Cash +	Accts. Rec. +	Prepaid Insur. +	Supp. +	Office Equip. −	Acc. Depr. +	Land =	Notes Pay. +	Accts. Pay. +	Unearned Revenue +	Capital Stock +	Retained Earnings	
Balances	7,730	1,900	7,300	90	8,500	−160	12,000	16,800	140	1,800	11,000	7,620	
a4. Rent revenue										−360		360	a4.
Balances	7,730	1,900	7,300	90	8,500	−160	12,000	16,800	140	1,440	11,000	7,980	

Income Statement	
a4. Rent revenue	360

Adjustment 5

Wages owed but not paid to employees, $220.

It is rare that employees are paid the same day that the accounting period ends. Thus, at the end of an accounting period, it is normal for businesses to owe wages to their employees.

Adjustment 5 recognizes that as of November 30, employees of Family Health Care have not been paid $220 for work they have performed. This adjustment is recorded by increasing the liability Wages Payable by $220 and decreasing Retained Earnings by $220 under the Balance Sheet column. In addition, Wages expense under the Income Statement column is recorded as −$220.

Statement of Cash Flows	Balance Sheet														Income Statement
	Assets						=	Liabilities			+	Stockholders' Equity			
	Cash +	Accts. Rec. +	Prepaid Insur. +	Supp. +	Office Equip. −	Acc. Depr. +	Land =	Notes Pay. +	Accts. Pay. +	Wages Pay. +	Unearned Revenue +	Capital Stock +	Retained Earnings	
Balances	7,730	1,900	7,300	90	8,500	−160	12,000	16,800	140		1,440	11,000	7,980	
a5. Wages exp.										220			−220	a5.
Balances	7,730	1,900	7,300	90	8,500	−160	12,000	16,800	140	220	1,440	11,000	7,760	

Income Statement

a5. Wages expense   −220

Adjustment 6

Services provided but not billed to insurance companies, $750.

This adjustment recognizes that Family Health Care has provided services of $750 to patients who have not yet been billed. Such services are usually provided near the end of the month.

This adjustment is recorded by increasing the asset Accounts Receivable (Accts. Rec.) and increasing Retained Earnings by $750 under the Balance Sheet column. In addition, Fees earned under the Income Statement column is recorded as $750.

The effects of Adjustment 6 on Family Health Care's financial statements are as shown below.

Statement of Cash Flows	Balance Sheet														Income Statement
	Assets						=	Liabilities			+	Stockholders' Equity			
	Cash +	Accts. Rec. +	Prepaid Insur. +	Supp. +	Office Equip. −	Acc. Depr. +	Land =	Notes Pay. +	Accts. Pay. +	Wages Pay. +	Unearned Revenue +	Capital Stock +	Retained Earnings	
Balances	7,730	1,900	7,300	90	8,500	−160	12,000	16,800	140	220	1,440	11,000	7,760	
a6. Fees earned		750											750	a6.
Balances	7,730	2,650	7,300	90	8,500	−160	12,000	16,800	140	220	1,440	11,000	8,510	

Income Statement

a6. Fees earned   750

The November transactions and adjustments for Family Health Care are summarized in Exhibit 2.

Obj 4

Prepare financial statements using accrual concepts of accounting, including a classified balance sheet.

Financial Statements

Based on the summary of transactions and adjustments shown in Exhibit 2, Family Health Care's financial statements for November are described and illustrated in this section. These financial statements are shown in Exhibits 3, 4, 5, and 6.

Family Health Care Summary of Transactions and Adjustments for November   EXHIBIT 2

Statement of Cash Flows	Balance Sheet													Income Statement
	Assets							= Liabilities				+ Stockholders' Equity		
	Cash +	Accts. Rec. +	Prepaid Insur. +	Supp. +	Office Equip. −	Acc. Depr. +	Land =	Notes Pay. +	Accts. Pay. +	Wages Pay. +	Unearned Revenue +	Capital Stock +	Retained Earnings	
Balances, Nov. 1	7,320						12,000	10,000				6,000	3,320	
a. Rent revenue	1,800										1,800			
b. Paid insurance	−2,400		2,400											
c. Paid insurance	−6,000		6,000											
d. Investment	5,000											5,000		
e. Pur. supplies				240					240					
f. Pur. off. equip.	−1,700				8,500				6,800					
g. Fees earned		6,100											6,100	g.
h. Fees earned	5,500												5,500	h.
i. Collected cash	4,200	−4,200												
j. Paid on acct.	−100								−100					
k. Paid expenses	−4,690												−4,690	k.
l. Dividends	−1,200												−1,200	
a1. Insurance exp.			−1,100										−1,100	a1.
a2. Supplies exp.				−150									−150	a2.
a3. Depr. exp.						−160							−160	a3.
a4. Rent revenue											−360		360	a4.
a5. Wages exp.										220			−220	a5.
a6. Fees earned		750											750	a6.
Balances, Nov. 30	7,730	2,650	7,300	90	8,500	−160	12,000	10,000	6,940	220	1,440	11,000	8,510	

Statement of Cash Flows

a. Operating	1,800
b. Operating	−2,400
c. Operating	−6,000
d. Financing	5,000
f. Investing	−1,700
h. Operating	5,500
i. Operating	4,200
j. Operating	−100
k. Operating	−4,690
l. Financing	−1,200
Increase in cash	410
Nov. 1 cash bal.	7,320
Nov. 30 cash bal.	7,730

Income Statement

g.	Fees earned	6,100
h.	Fees earned	5,500
k.	Wages exp.	−2,790
	Rent exp.	−800
	Utilities exp.	−580
	Interest exp.	−100
	Misc exp.	−420
a1.	Insur. exp.	−1,100
a2.	Supplies exp.	−150
a3.	Depr. exp.	−160
a4.	Rent revenue	360
a5.	Wages exp.	−220
a6.	Fees earned	750
	Net income	6,390

Income Statement

The income statement is shown in Exhibit 3, on page 98. It is prepared by summarizing the revenue and expense transactions listed under the Income Statement column of Exhibit 2.

Revenues are a result of providing services or selling products to customers. Examples of revenues include fees earned, fares earned, commissions revenue, interest revenue, and rent revenue.

EXHIBIT 3

Family Health Care Income Statement for November

Family Health Care, P.C. Income Statement For the Month Ended November 30, 20Y5		
Fees earned...		$12,350
Operating expenses:		
Wages expense..	$3,010	
Insurance expense..	1,100	
Rent expense..	800	
Utilities expense..	580	
Depreciation expense....................................	160	
Supplies expense...	150	
Interest expense..	100	
Miscellaneous expense..................................	420	
Total operating expenses....................................		6,320
Operating income..		$ 6,030
Other income:		
Rent revenue..		360
Net income..		$ 6,390

Revenues from the primary operations of the business are reported separately from other revenue. For example, Family Health Care has two types of revenues for November fees earned and rent revenue. Since the primary operation of the business is providing services to patients, rent revenue is reported under the heading of "Other income."

Expenses are assets used up or services consumed in the process of generating revenues. Expenses are matched against their related revenues to determine the net income or net loss for a period. Examples of typical expenses include wages expense, rent expense, utilities expense, supplies expense, and miscellaneous expense. Expenses are normally listed on the income statement from largest to smallest except for miscellaneous expense, which is always listed last. Expenses not related to the primary operations of the business are reported as "Other expenses."

Operating income is determined by deducting the operating expenses from the fees earned. Family Health Care has operating income of $6,030 in November. Other income consisting of $360 in rental revenue is then added to determine the net income for November of $6,390.

Retained Earnings Statement

The retained earnings statement shown in Exhibit 4 is prepared by adding the November net income of $6,390 (from the income statement), less dividends of $1,200, to the beginning amount of retained earnings of $3,320. The result is the ending amount of retained earnings of $8,510, which is included on Family Health Care's November 30, 20Y5, balance sheet.

Balance Sheet

The balance sheet shown in Exhibit 5 is prepared from the ending balances shown in the Balance Sheet columns of Exhibit 2. The balance sheet shown in

Family Health Care, P.C.
Retained Earnings Statement
For the Month Ended November 30, 20Y5

Retained earnings, November 1, 20Y5..		$3,320
Net income for November..	$6,390	
Less dividends	1,200	5,190
Retained earnings, November 30, 20Y5		$8,510

EXHIBIT 4

Family Health Care Retained Earnings Statement for November

Exhibit 5 is a **classified balance sheet**. As the term implies, a classified balance sheet is prepared with various sections, subsections, and captions.

Family Health Care, P.C.
Balance Sheet
November 30, 20Y5

Assets

Current assets:			
Cash		$ 7,730	
Accounts receivable.....................................		2,650	
Prepaid insurance.......................................		7,300	
Supplies..		90	
Total current assets			$17,770
Fixed assets:			
Office equipment	$8,500		
Less accumulated depreciation.........................	160	$ 8,340	
Land...		12,000	
Total fixed assets			20,340
Total assets			$38,110

Liabilities

Current liabilities:			
Accounts payable.......................................		$ 140	
Wages payable..		220	
Notes payable		6,800	
Unearned revenue		1,440	
Total current liabilities..............................			$ 8,600
Long-term liabilities:			
Notes payable			10,000
Total liabilities			$18,600

Stockholders' Equity

Capital stock...		$11,000	
Retained earnings.......................................		8,510	
Total stockholders' equity...............................			19,510
Total liabilities and stockholders' equity			$38,110

EXHIBIT 5

Family Health Care Balance Sheet for November

A classified balance sheet normally reports assets as:

1. Current assets
2. Fixed assets
3. Intangible assets

Current assets are cash and other assets that are expected to be converted to cash or sold or used up within one year or less, through normal operations. In addition to cash, the current assets normally include accounts receivable, notes receivable, supplies, and prepaid expenses.

Accounts receivable and notes receivable are current assets because they are normally converted to cash within one year or less. **Notes receivable** are written claims against debtors who promise to pay the amount of the note plus interest. From the creditor's point of view, a note receivable is a note payable.

Exhibit 5 indicates that Family Health Care has current assets of cash, accounts receivable, prepaid insurance, and supplies as of November 30, 20Y5. These current assets total $17,770.

Fixed assets are physical assets of a long-term nature. The fixed assets may also be reported on the balance sheet as *property, plant, and equipment*, or *plant assets*. Fixed assets include equipment, machinery, buildings, and land. Except for land, fixed assets depreciate over a period of time. The cost less accumulated depreciation for each major type of fixed asset is normally reported on the classified balance sheet.

Exhibit 5 indicates that Family Health Care has fixed assets of office equipment and land. The book value, cost less accumulated depreciation, of the office equipment is $8,340. The land is reported at its cost of $12,000, which when added to the book value of the office equipment yields total fixed assets of $20,340.

FedEx Corporation reported goodwill of $2,387 on a recent balance sheet.

Intangible assets represent rights of a long-term nature, such as patent rights, copyrights, and goodwill. Goodwill arises from such factors as name recognition, location, product quality, reputation, and managerial skill. Goodwill is recorded and reported on the balance sheet when a company purchases another company at a price above the normal market value of the purchased company's assets. As shown in Exhibit 5, Family Health Care has no intangible assets.

A classified balance sheet normally reports liabilities as:

1. Current liabilities
2. Long-term liabilities

Current liabilities are due within a short time (usually one year or less) and are to be paid out of current assets. Common current liabilities include accounts payable and notes payable. Other current liabilities include wages payable, interest payable, taxes payable, and unearned revenue.

Exhibit 5 indicates that Family Health Care has total current liabilities of $8,600 that include accounts payable, wages payable, and notes payable. Unearned revenue (rent) is also reported as a current liability, since the revenue has not yet been earned.

Long-term liabilities are not due for a long time (usually more than one year). Long-term liabilities are reported following the current liabilities.

As long-term liabilities come due and are to be paid within one year, they are reported as current liabilities. If they are to be renewed rather than paid, they would continue to be classified as long term. When an asset is pledged as security for a long-term liability, the obligation may be called a *mortgage note payable* or a *mortgage payable*.

Exhibit 5 indicates that Family Health Care has total long-term liabilities of $10,000, which consists of notes payable. These notes payable are not due until 20Y9. However, $6,800 of notes payable are due within the next year and thus are reported as a current liability.

A classified balance sheet normally reports stockholders' equity as:

1. Capital stock, which has been invested in the company by the stockholders
2. Retained earnings, which is net income that has been retained in the corporation

Exhibit 5 indicates Family Health Care has capital stock of $11,000, which results from $6,000 of capital stock on November 1 plus an additional investment of $5,000 by Dr. Landry during November. The retained earnings of $8,510 is the ending balance of retained earnings as reported on the November retained earnings statement shown in Exhibit 4.

Statement of Cash Flows

The statement of cash flows shown in Exhibit 6 is prepared by summarizing the November cash transactions. These cash transactions are shown in the Statement of Cash Flows column of Exhibit 2.

The *Cash flows from operating activities* section is prepared from the Statement of Cash Flows column of Exhibit 2 by summarizing the *Operating* activity transactions. The cash receipts from revenue transactions are added, and the cash payments for operating transactions are subtracted.

Exhibit 6 indicates that the cash received from revenue transactions consists of $9,700 ($5,500 + $4,200) received from patients and $1,800 received from rental of the land. The cash payments for operating transactions of $13,190 ($2,400 + $6,000 + $100 + $4,690) is determined by adding the negative cash payments for operating activities shown in Exhibit 2.

The *Cash flows from investing activities* is prepared from the Statement of Cash Flows column of Exhibit 2 by summarizing the *Investing* activity transactions. During November, Family Health Care has only one investing transaction of $1,700 for the purchase of office equipment.

The *Cash flows from financing activities* section is prepared from the Statement of Cash Flows column of Exhibit 2 by summarizing the *Financing* activity transactions. During November, Family Health Care received an additional investment from Dr. Landry of $5,000 and paid dividends of $1,200.

EXHIBIT 6

Family Health Care Statement of Cash Flows for November

Family Health Care P.C. Statement of Cash Flows For the Month Ended November 30, 20Y5		
Cash flows used for operating activities:		
Cash received from patients	$ 9,700	
Cash received from rental of land	1,800	
		$ 11,500
Deduct cash payments for expenses		(13,190)
Net cash flow used in operating activities		$ (1,690)
Cash flows used for investing activities:		
Purchase of office equipment		(1,700)
Cash flows from financing activities:		
Additional issuance of capital stock	$ 5,000	
Deduct cash dividends	(1,200)	
Net cash flow from financing activities		3,800
Net increase in cash		$ 410
November 1, 20Y5, cash balance		7,320
November 30, 20Y5, cash balance		$ 7,730

Integration of Financial Statements

Exhibit 7 shows the integration of Family Health Care's financial statements for November. The reconciliation of net income and net cash flows from operations is shown in the appendix at the end of this chapter.

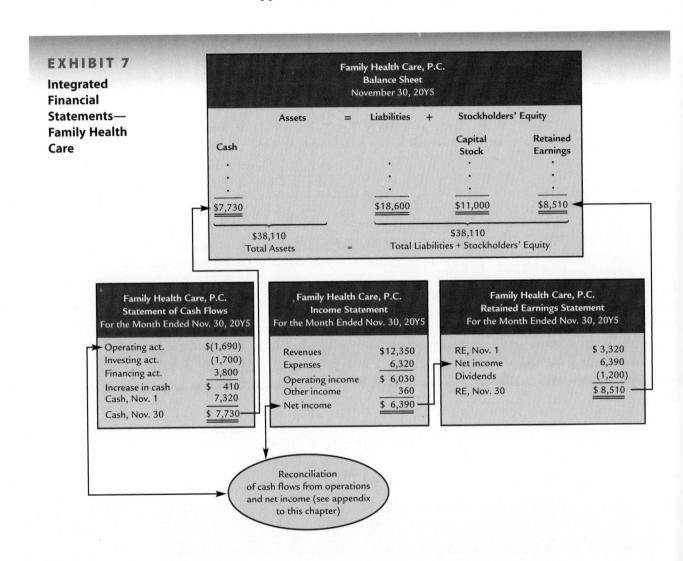

EXHIBIT 7

Integrated Financial Statements— Family Health Care

Family Health Care, P.C.
Balance Sheet
November 30, 20Y5

Assets	=	Liabilities	+	Stockholders' Equity	
				Capital Stock	Retained Earnings
Cash					
·		·		·	·
·		·		·	·
·		·		·	·
$7,730		$18,600		$11,000	$8,510

| $38,110 | | $38,110 | | | |
| Total Assets | = | Total Liabilities + Stockholders' Equity | | | |

Family Health Care, P.C.
Statement of Cash Flows
For the Month Ended Nov. 30, 20Y5

Operating act.	$(1,690)
Investing act.	(1,700)
Financing act.	3,800
Increase in cash	$ 410
Cash, Nov. 1	7,320
Cash, Nov. 30	$ 7,730

Family Health Care, P.C.
Income Statement
For the Month Ended Nov. 30, 20Y5

Revenues	$12,350
Expenses	6,320
Operating income	$ 6,030
Other income	360
Net income	$ 6,390

Family Health Care, P.C.
Retained Earnings Statement
For the Month Ended Nov. 30, 20Y5

RE, Nov. 1	$ 3,320
Net income	6,390
Dividends	(1,200)
RE, Nov. 30	$ 8,510

Reconciliation of cash flows from operations and net income (see appendix to this chapter)

Obj | **5**

Describe how the accrual basis of accounting enhances the interpretation of financial statements.

Accrual and Cash Bases of Accounting

The financial statements of Family Health Care for November were prepared under accrual accounting concepts. Companies that use accrual accounting concepts for recording transactions and preparing financial statements are said to use the **accrual basis of accounting**. The accrual basis of accounting is used by large companies and is required of corporations whose stock is publicly traded.

Companies that record transactions only when cash is received or paid are said to use the **cash basis of accounting**.[1] Individuals and small businesses often use the cash basis of accounting.

1. Some companies use a modified-cash basis of accounting, which includes some accrual accounting concepts. These bases of accounting are covered in advanced accounting texts.

Using the Cash Basis of Accounting

Under the cash basis of accounting, a company records only transactions involving increases or decreases of cash. Thus, revenue is recorded only when cash is received, and expenses are recorded only when cash is paid.

To illustrate, assume that a real estate agency sells a $300,000 piece of property on December 28, 20Y4, earning a commission of 8% of the selling price. However, the agency did not receive the $24,000 ($300,000 × 8%) commission until January 3, 20Y5. Under the cash basis, the real estate agency will not record the commission revenue until January 3, 20Y5. Likewise, a December cellular phone bill paid in January is recorded as a January expense, not a December expense.

Under the cash basis, the matching concept is not used. That is, expenses are recorded when paid in cash, not necessarily in the period when the revenue is earned. As a result, adjusting entries to properly match revenues and expenses are not required under the cash basis.

Using the Accrual Basis of Accounting

Under the accrual basis of accounting, a company records transactions using accrual accounting concepts. Thus, revenue is recorded as it is earned, regardless of when cash is received.

To illustrate, the real estate agency in the preceding example would record the $24,000 commission revenue on December 28, 20Y4. This is because the commission has been earned on December 28, 20Y4, even though the cash is not received until January 3, 20Y5.

Once revenue has been earned and recorded, any expenses incurred in generating the revenue are recorded. In this way, the expenses are matched against the revenue they generated. For example, in the preceding example, the December cellular phone bill would be recorded in December even though it was not paid until January.

The accrual basis of accounting was used to record Family Health Care's November transactions. As a result, adjusting entries were used to update the accounting records at the end of November.

Exhibit 8 summarizes the basic differences of how revenue and expenses are recorded under the cash and accrual bases of accounting.

	Cash Basis	Accrual Basis
Revenue is recorded	When cash is received	When revenue is earned
Expense is recorded	When cash is paid	When expense is incurred in generating revenue
Adjusting entries	Not required	Required in order to prepare financial statements

EXHIBIT 8
Cash versus Accrual Accounting

Cash and Accrual Bases of Accounting

All the September and October transactions for Family Health Care in Chapter 2 involved the receipt or payment of cash. As a result, the financial statements shown in Exhibit 4 and Exhibit 7 in Chapter 2 are the same as those that would be reported under the cash basis of accounting.

In November, Family Health Care entered into transactions that used accrual accounting concepts. As a result, the November financial statements shown in Exhibits 3 through 6 of this chapter use the accrual basis of accounting.

One of the major differences between accrual and cash basis financial statements is the reporting of net income and net cash flows from operations. Specifically, the following differences exist:

1. Under the cash basis of accounting, net income and net cash flows from operating activities are equal.
2. Under the accrual basis of accounting, net income and net cash flows from operating activities may be significantly different.

The net income and net cash flows from operating activities for Family Health Care are shown below.

	Net Cash Flows from Operating Activities	Net Income
September (Cash basis)	$ 2,600	$2,600
October (Cash basis)	3,220	3,220
November (Accrual basis)	(1,690)	6,390

The difference between the November net cash flows from operating activities and net income is due to the effects of accruals and deferrals.[2]

Importance of Accrual Basis of Accounting

Understanding the accrual basis of accounting is essential to assessing and interpreting the financial performance of a company. To illustrate, Family Health Care's November financial statements are used.

If the *cash basis* of accounting is used, Family Health Care's November financial statements report negative net cash flows from operating activities and net income (loss) of $(1,690). This is because under the cash basis, net cash flows from operating activities are equal to net income. When compared to September's net income of $2,600 and October's net income of $3,220, November's operations indicate an unfavorable trend.

If the *accrual basis* of accounting is used, Family Health Care's November financial statements report negative net cash flows from operating activities of $(1,690), but a positive net income of $6,390. When compared to September's net income of $2,600 and October's net income of $3,220, November's operations indicate a favorable trend. For example, since September, revenues have more than doubled, increasing from $5,500 to $12,350. As a result, net income has also more than doubled. Thus, Family Health Care is a profitable, rapidly expanding business.

The preceding Family Health Care illustration shows why generally accepted accounting principles (GAAP) require accrual accounting for all but the very smallest businesses. That is, accrual accounting is generally a better predictor of the profitability of a company than is net cash flows from operating activities and the cash basis of accounting.

Net cash flow from operating activities, however, is useful. For example, in the long run, a business cannot survive if it continually reports negative cash flows from operating activities. This is true even though the company may report net income. In other words, a business *must* generate positive cash flows from

2. A reconciliation of net cash flows from operations and the net income is shown in the appendix at the end of this chapter. This reconciliation considers the effects of accruals and deferrals on net income.

operating activities in the long term in order to survive. For this reason, generally accepted accounting principles (GAAP) require reporting net cash flows from operating activities as well as net income.

Family Health Care's negative cash flows from operations of $(1,690) for November was largely due to prepaying insurance premiums of $8,400. This suggests that Family Health Care's negative cash flows from operations is temporary and not of major concern.

Family Health Care also illustrates why the financial statements must be analyzed and interpreted together rather than individually. This is the primary reason the integrated financial statements approach is used throughout this text. For example, long-run profitability is best analyzed using accrual accounting and net income. The ability of the company to pay debts as they become due is best analyzed using net cash flows from operating activities.

The Accounting Cycle for the Accrual Basis of Accounting

The **accounting cycle** is the process that begins with analyzing transactions and ends with preparing financial statements. The basic steps in the accounting cycle are as follows:

1. Identifying, analyzing, and recording the effects of transactions on the accounting equation (financial statement elements and accounts)
2. Identifying, analyzing, and recording adjustment data
3. Preparing financial statements

Steps 1–3 have been described and illustrated in this chapter. Using the integrated financial statement framework, the ending balances for the Balance Sheet elements (columns) become the beginning balances for the next accounting period. Steps 1–3 are then repeated for the next accounting period.[3]

Financial Analysis: Working Capital, Current Ratio, and Quick Ratio

Obj | 6

Describe and illustrate the use of working capital, the current ratio, and the quick ratio in assessing a company's liquidity.

A company's **liquidity** is its ability to convert assets to cash. A company's liquidity is important for a variety of reasons including the ability to pay liabilities as they become due. Three measures useful in assessing liquidity and the ability of a company to pay its current liabilities are working capital, the current ratio, and the quick ratio.

Working capital is current assets less current liabilities. Current assets include cash and other assets that are expected to be converted to cash, sold, or used up within one year or less through normal operations. Since a company uses cash to pay its current liabilities, the larger the amount of working capital, the more likely a company will be able to pay its current liabilities.

The **current ratio** is computed as current assets divided by current liabilities. Like working capital, the current ratio measures a company's ability to pay its current liabilities. The advantage of the current ratio is that it facilitates comparisons across companies. While working capital measures a dollar amount, the current ratio measures a relationship among amounts, and like all ratios, facilitates comparisons among companies of different sizes.

3. In double-entry accounting systems such as described in Appendix A, at the end of the text, another step is necessary to complete the accounting cycle. This fourth step, called the closing process, involves transferring balances of revenues, expenses, and dividends to retained earnings. This step is unnecessary when using the integrated financial statements framework.

The **quick ratio** is computed as quick assets divided by current liabilities. **Quick assets** include cash and other current assets such as receivables and short-term investments that can be easily (and quickly) converted to cash. Inventories and prepaid assets such as prepaid rent and insurance are not included as part of quick assets. Inventories are excluded because the inventory must first be sold. If the inventory is sold on account, a receivable must then be collected. Prepaid assets such as prepaid rent and insurance are excluded because often times they are nonrefundable or only partially refundable after cancellation notices are processed.

To illustrate the value of the quick ratio, the following data for Fly Creek Company and Huron Inc. are used.

	Fly Creek Company	Huron Inc.
Cash	$ 60,000	$ 80,000
Accounts receivable	120,000	200,000
Inventories	202,000	100,000
Prepaid assets	18,000	20,000
Total current assets	$400,000	$400,000
Less current liabilities	200,000	200,000
Working capital	$200,000	$200,000

Fly Creek Company and Huron Inc. have the same working capital of $200,000. They also have the same current ratio of 2.0, computed as follows:

$$\text{Current Ratio} = \frac{\text{Current Assets}}{\text{Current Liabilities}} = \frac{\$400,000}{\$200,000} = 2$$

However, the quick ratios for each company differ significantly, as shown below.

Fly Creek Company

$$\text{Quick Ratio} = \frac{\text{Quick Assets}}{\text{Current Liabilities}} = \frac{(\$60,000 + \$120,000)}{\$200,000} = \frac{\$180,000}{\$200,000} = 0.9$$

Huron Inc.

$$\text{Quick Ratio} = \frac{\text{Quick Assets}}{\text{Current Liabilities}} = \frac{(\$80,000 + \$200,000)}{\$200,000} = \frac{\$280,000}{\$200,000} = 1.4$$

The quick ratios indicate that Huron Inc. is in a stronger liquidity position than Fly Creek. This is because Fly Creek has significantly more inventory than does Huron Inc. Fly Creek's quick ratio of less than 1.0 raises concerns as to whether Fly Creek will be able to pay its current liabilities on time.

Although working capital, current ratios, and quick ratios vary by industry, a current ratio of at least 2:1 is typical. In addition, a quick ratio of less than 1.0, as illustrated for Fly Creek Company, raises liquidity concerns for creditors.

Appendix

Reconciliation: Net Cash Flows from Operations and Net Income[4]

Chapter 2 illustrates the financial statements for Family Health Care for September and October 20Y5. Because all the September and October transactions were cash

---

4. This reconciliation is referred to as the indirect method of reporting cash flows from operations.

transactions, the net cash flows from operating activities shown on the statement of cash flows equals the net income shown in the income statements as follows:

	Net Cash Flows from Operating Activities	Net Income
September (Cash basis)	$2,600	$2,600
October (Cash basis)	3,220	3,220

When all of a company's transactions are cash transactions or when a company uses the cash basis of accounting, net cash flows from operating activities always equals net income. This is not true, however, under the accrual basis of accounting.

During November and December, Family Health Care used the accrual basis of accounting. The November financial statements are illustrated in Exhibit 3 through Exhibit 6 of this chapter. The December financial statements for Family Health Care are illustrated in the Illustrative Problem at the end of this chapter. The net cash flows from operating activities and net income for November and December are shown below.

	Net Cash Flows from Operating Activities	Net Income
November (Cash basis)	$(1,690)	$ 6,390
December (Cash basis)	8,760	10,825

As shown above, net cash flows from operating activities will normally not be the same as net income under accrual accounting. Any difference can be reconciled by considering the effects of accruals and deferrals on the income statement.

Exhibit 9 illustrates the November reconciliation of Family Health Care's net income with operating cash flows from operations.

Net income..		$ 6,390
Add:		
Depreciation expense.........................	$ 160	
Increase in accounts payable.............	140	
Increase in wages payable..................	220	
Increase in unearned revenue............	1,440	1,960
Deduct:		
Increase in accounts receivable	$(2,650)	
Increase in prepaid insurance...........	(7,300)	
Increase in supplies...........................	(90)	(10,040)
Net cash flows from operating activities		$ (1,690)

EXHIBIT 9

November's Reconciliation of Net Income and Cash Flows from Operations

Exhibit 9 begins with net income and then adds or deducts the effects of accruals or deferrals that affect net income but do not result in the receipt or payment of cash. By doing so, Exhibit 9 ends with net cash flows from operating activities.

The effect of an accrual or deferral on net income is a net increase or decrease during the period. For example, during November, depreciation expense of $160 was recorded (a deferred expense) and thus deducted in arriving at net income. Yet no cash was paid. Thus, to arrive at cash flows from operations, depreciation expense is added back to net income.

Accounts payable also increased during November by $140, and a related expense was recorded. But again, no cash was paid. Similarly, wages payable increased during November by $220, and the related wages expense was deducted in arriving at net income. However, the $220 was not paid until the next month. Thus, for November, the increases of $140 in accounts payable and $220 in wages payable are added back to net income.

Unearned revenue increased by $1,440 during November, which represents land rented to ILS Company. ILS Company initially paid Family Health Care $1,800 in advance. Of the $1,800, one-fifth ($360) was recorded as revenue for November. However, under the cash basis, the entire $1,800 would have been recorded as revenue. Thus, $1,440 (the increase in the unearned revenue) is added back to net income to arrive at net cash flows from operating activities.

Accounts receivable increased by $2,650 during November and thus was recorded as part of revenue in arriving at net income. However, no cash was received. Thus, this increase in accounts receivable is deducted in arriving at net cash flows from operations.

Prepaid insurance increased by $7,300 during November. This represents an $8,400 payment of cash for insurance premiums less $1,100 of premiums deducted in arriving at net income. Thus, the remaining $7,300 (the increase in prepaid insurance) is deducted in arriving at net cash flows from operations. Similarly, the increase in supplies of $90 is deducted.

The reconciliation of net income to net cash flows from operations is normally prepared as shown in Exhibit 10.

EXHIBIT 10

Reconciling Items

Net income		$XXX
Add:		
Depreciation expense	$XXX	
Increases in current liabilities from operations	XXX	
Decreases in current assets from operations	XXX	XXX
Deduct:		
Increases in current assets from operations	$XXX	
Decreases in current liabilities from operations	XXX	XXX
Net cash flows from operations		$XXX

During November, all the current assets are related to Family Health Care's operations. In addition, current liabilities for accounts payable and wages payable are also related to Family Health Care's operations. However, the increase in the current liability for notes payable, which increased by $6,800, is not included in the reconciliation shown in Exhibit 9. This is because the notes payable is related to the purchase of office equipment, which is an investing activity rather than an operating activity.

During November, Family Health Care did not have any decreases in current assets or current liabilities. Thus, the effects of these items are not shown in Exhibit 9. Normally, however, both increases and decreases in current assets and liabilities are included in reconciling net income and net cash flows from operating activities. For example, Family Health Care's December reconciliation, shown in the Illustrative Problem on page 113, includes increases and decreases in current assets and current liabilities.

Key Points

1. Describe basic accrual accounting concepts, including the matching concept.

Under accrual concepts of accounting, revenue is recognized when it is earned. When revenues are earned and recorded, all expenses incurred in generating the revenues are recorded so that revenues and expenses are properly matched in determining the net income or loss for the period. Liabilities are recorded at the time a business incurs the obligation to pay for the services or goods purchased.

2. Use accrual concepts of accounting to analyze, record, and summarize transactions.

Using the integrated financial statement framework, November transactions for Family Health Care were recorded. Family Health Care's November transactions involved accrual accounting transactions.

3. Describe and illustrate the end-of-period adjustment process.

The accrual concepts of accounting require the accounting records to be updated prior to preparing financial statements. This updating process, called the adjustment process, is necessary to match revenues and expenses. The adjustment process involves two types of adjustments—deferrals and accruals. Adjustments for deferrals may involve deferred expenses or deferred revenues. Adjustments for accruals may involve accrued expenses or accrued revenues.

4. Prepare financial statements using accrual concepts of accounting, including a classified balance sheet.

A classified balance sheet includes sections for current assets; property, plant, and equipment (fixed assets); and intangible assets. Liabilities are classified as current liabilities or long-term liabilities. The income statement normally reports sections for revenues, operating expenses, other income and expense, and net income.

5. Describe how the accrual basis of accounting enhances the interpretation of financial statements.

The net cash flows from operating activities and net income will differ under the accrual basis of accounting. Under the accrual basis, net income is a better indicator of the long-term profitability of a business. For this reason, the accrual basis of accounting is required by generally accepted accounting principles (GAAP), except for very small businesses. The accrual basis reports the effects of operations on cash flows through the reporting of net cash flows from operating activities on the statement of cash flows.

The accounting cycle is the process that begins with analyzing transactions and ends with preparing the accounting records for the next accounting period. The basic steps in the accounting cycle are (1) identifying, analyzing, and recording the effects of transactions on the accounting equation; (2) identifying, analyzing, and recording adjustment data; and (3) preparing financial statements.

6. Describe and illustrate the use of working capital, the current ratio, and the quick ratio in assessing a company's liquidity.

A company's liquidity is its ability to convert assets to cash. Working capital, the current ratio, and quick ratio are useful in assessing a company's liquidity. Working capital is current assets less current liabilities. The current ratio is current assets divided by current liabilities. The quick ratio is quick assets divided by current liabilities. Quick assets are normally cash, receivables, and short-term investments. The higher working capital, current ratio, and quick ratio are, the more liquid the company and the better its ability to pay current liabilities as they become due.

Key Terms

Account (84)	Accrued liabilities (91)	Current assets (100)	Liquidity (105)
Accounting cycle (105)	Accrued revenues (92)	Current liabilities (100)	Long-term liabilities (100)
Accounts payable (86)	Accumulated depreciation	Current ratio (105)	Notes receivable (100)
Accounts receivable (88)	(94)	Deferrals (91)	Prepaid expenses (85)
Accrual basis of accounting	Adjustment process (90)	Deferred expenses (85)	Quick assets (106)
(82)	Book value (95)	Deferred revenues (91)	Quick ratio (106)
Accruals (91)	Cash basis of accounting	Depreciation (94)	Unearned revenues (91)
Accrued assets (92)	(102)	Fixed assets (100)	Working capital (105)
Accrued expenses (91)	Classified balance sheet (99)	Intangible assets (100)	

Illustrative Problem

Assume that the December transactions for Family Health Care are as follows:

a. Received cash of $1,900 from patients for services provided on account during November.

b. Provided services of $10,800 on account.

c. Received $6,500 for services provided for patients who paid cash.

d. Purchased supplies on account, $400.

e. Received $6,900 from insurance companies that paid on patients' accounts for services that had been previously billed.

f. Paid $310 on account for supplies that had been purchased.

g. Expenses paid during December were as follows: wages, $4,200, including $220 accrued at the end of November; rent, $800; utilities, $610; interest, $100; and miscellaneous, $520.

h. Paid dividends of $1,200 to stockholders (Dr. Landry).

Instructions

1. Record the December transactions, using the integrated financial statement framework as shown on the following page. The beginning balances of December 1 have already been entered. After each transaction, you should enter a balance for each item. The transactions are recorded similarly to those for November. You should note that in transaction (g), the $4,200 of wages paid includes wages of $220 that were accrued at the end of November. Thus, only $3,980 ($4,200 − $220) should be recorded as wages expense for December. The remaining $220 reduces the wages payable. You should also note that the balance of retained earnings on December 1, $8,510, is the balance on November 30.

Statement of Cash Flows	Balance Sheet													Income Statement
	Assets						=	Liabilities			+	Stockholders' Equity		
	Cash +	Accts. Rec. +	Prepaid Insur. +	Supp. +	Office Equip. −	Acc. Depr. +	Land =	Notes Pay. +	Accts. Pay. +	Wages Pay. +	Unearned Revenue +	Capital Stock +	Retained Earnings	
Balances, Dec. 1	7,730	2,650	7,300	90	8,500	−160	12,000	16,800	140	220	1,440	11,000	8,510	

2. The adjustment data for December are as follows:

Deferred expenses:

1. Prepaid insurance expired, $1,100.
2. Supplies used, $275.
3. Depreciation on office equipment, $160.

Deferred revenues:

4. Unearned revenue earned, $360.

Accrued expense:

5. Wages owed employees but not paid, $340.

Accrued revenue:

6. Services provided but not billed to insurance companies, $1,050.

Enter the adjustments in the integrated financial statement framework. Identify each adjustment by "a" and the number of the related adjustment item. For example, the adjustment for prepaid insurance should be identified as (a1).

3. Prepare the December financial statements, including the income statement, retained earnings statement, balance sheet, and statement of cash flows.

4. (Appendix) Reconcile the December net income with the net cash flows from operations. (*Note:* In computing increases and decreases in amounts, use adjusted balances.)

Solution

1. and 2. Family Health Care summary of transactions and adjustments for December:

Statement of Cash Flows	Cash +	Accts. Rec. +	Prepaid Insur. +	Supp. +	Office Equip. −	Acc. Depr. +	Land =	Notes Pay. +	Accts. Pay. +	Wages Pay. +	Unearned Revenue +	Capital Stock +	Retained Earnings	Income Statement
Balances, Dec. 1	7,730	2,650	7,300	90	8,500	−160	12,000	16,800	140	220	1,440	11,000	8.510	
a. Collected cash	1,900	−1,900												
Balances	9,630	750	7,300	90	8,500	−160	12,000	16,800	140	220	1,440	11,000	8.510	
b. Fees earned		10,800											10,800	b.
Balances	9,630	11,550	7,300	90	8,500	−160	12,000	16,800	140	220	1,440	11,000	19,310	
c. Fees earned	6,500												6,500	c.
Balances	16,130	11,550	7,300	90	8,500	−160	12,000	16,800	140	220	1,440	11,000	25,810	
d. Pur. supplies				400					400					
Balances	16,130	11,550	7,300	490	8,500	−160	12,000	16,800	540	220	1,440	11,000	25,810	
e. Collected cash	6,900	−6,900												
Balances	23,030	4,650	7,300	490	8,500	−160	12,000	16,800	540	220	1,440	11,000	25,810	
f. Paid accts. pay.	−310								−310					
Balances	22,720	4,650	7,300	490	8,500	−160	12,000	16,800	230	220	1,440	11,000	25,810	
g. Paid expenses	−6,230									−220			−6,010	g.
Balances	16,490	4,650	7,300	490	8,500	−160	12,000	16,800	230	0	1,440	11,000	19,800	
h. Paid dividends	−1,200												−1,200	
Balances	15,290	4,650	7,300	490	8,500	−160	12,000	16,800	230	0	1,440	11,000	18,600	
a1. Insurance exp.			−1,100										−1,100	a1.
Balances	15,290	4,650	6,200	490	8,500	−160	12,000	16,800	230	0	1,440	11,000	17,500	
a2. Supplies exp.				−275									−275	a2.
Balances	15,290	4,650	6,200	215	8,500	−160	12,000	16,800	230	0	1,440	11,000	17,225	
a3. Depr. exp.						−160							−160	a3.
Balances	15,290	4,650	6,200	215	8,500	−320	12,000	16,800	230	0	1,440	11,000	17,065	
a4. Rent revenue											−360		360	a4.
Balances	15,290	4,650	6,200	215	8,500	−320	12,000	16,800	230	0	1,080	11,000	17,425	
a5. Wages exp.										340			−340	a5.
Balances	15,290	4,650	6,200	215	8,500	−320	12,000	16,800	230	340	1,080	11,000	17,085	
a6. Fees earned		1,050											1,050	a6.
Balances, Dec. 31	15,290	5,700	6,200	215	8,500	−320	12,000	16,800	230	340	1,080	11,000	18,135	

Balance Sheet (Assets = Liabilities + Stockholders' Equity)

Statement of Cash Flows

a. Operating	1,900
c. Operating	6,500
e. Operating	6,900
f. Operating	−310
g. Operating	−6,230
h. Financing	−1,200
Net increase in cash	7,560
Beginning cash bal.	7,730
Ending cash bal.	15,290

Income Statement

b.	Fees earned	10,800
c.	Fees earned	6,500
g.	Wages exp.	−3,980
	Rent exp.	−800
	Utilities exp.	−610
	Interest exp.	−100
	Misc exp.	−520
a1.	Insur. exp.	−1,100
a2.	Supplies exp.	−275
a3.	Depr. exp.	−160
a4.	Rent revenue	360
a5.	Wages exp.	−340
a6.	Fees earned	1,050
	Net income	10,825

3.

FAMILY HEALTH CARE, P.C.
Income Statement
For the Month Ended December 31, 20Y5

Fees earned		$18,350
Operating expenses:		
Wages expense	$4,320	
Insurance expense	1,100	
Rent expense	800	
Utilities expense	610	
Supplies expense	275	
Depreciation expense.............................	160	
Interest expense	100	
Miscellaneous expense............................	520	
Total operating expenses.........................		7,885
Operating income		$10,465
Other income:		
Rent revenue		360
Net income..		$10,825

FAMILY HEALTH CARE, P.C.
Retained Earnings Statement
For the Month Ended December 31, 20Y5

Retained earnings, December 1, 20Y5		$ 8,510
Net income for December	$10,825	
Less dividends..	1,200	9,625
Retained earnings, December 31, 20Y5...................		$18,135

FAMILY HEALTH CARE, P.C.
Balance Sheet
December 31, 20Y5

Assets

Current assets:			
Cash		$15,290	
Accounts receivable		5,700	
Prepaid insurance		6,200	
Supplies.....................................		215	
Total current assets			$27,405
Fixed assets:			
Office equipment............................	$8,500		
Less accumulated depreciation	320	$ 8,180	
Land		12,000	
Total fixed assets			20,180
Total assets			$47,585

Liabilities

Current liabilities:			
Accounts payable		$ 230	
Wages payable		340	
Notes payable...............................		6,800	
Unearned revenue...........................		1,080	
Total current liabilities			$ 8,450
Long-term liabilities:			
Notes payable..............................			10,000
Total liabilities			$18,450

Stockholders' Equity

Capital stock......................................		$11,000	
Retained earnings................................		18,135	
Total stockholders' equity			29,135
Total liabilities and stockholders' equity...........			$47,585

FAMILY HEALTH CARE, P.C.
Statement of Cash Flows
For the Month Ended December 31, 20Y5

Cash flows from operating activities:	
Cash received from patients	$15,300
Deduct cash payments for expenses	(6,540)
Net cash flows from operating activities	$ 8,760
Cash flows from financing activities:	
Deduct cash dividends	(1,200)
Net increase in cash	$ 7,560
December 1, 20Y5, cash balance	7,730
December 31, 20Y5, cash balance	$15,290

Appendix
4. December's reconciliation of net income with net cash flows from operations:

Net income		$10,825
Add:		
Depreciation expense	$ 160	
Increase in accounts payable	90	
Increase in wages payable	120	
Decrease in prepaid insurance	1,100	1,470
Deduct:		
Increase in accounts receivable	$(3,050)	
Increase in supplies	(125)	
Decrease in unearned revenue	(360)	(3,535)
Net cash flows from operating activities		$ 8,760

Self-Examination Questions *(Answers appear at the end of chapter)*

1. Assume that a lawyer bills her clients $15,000 on June 30, for services rendered during June. The lawyer collects $8,500 of the billings during July and the remainder in August. Under the accrual basis of accounting, when would the lawyer record the revenue for the fees?

   A. June, $15,000; July, $0; and August, $0

   B. June, $0; July, $6,500; and August, $8,500

   C. June, $8,500; July, $6,500; and August, $0

   D. June, $0; July, $8,500; and August, $6,500

2. On January 24, 20Y8, Niche Consulting collected $5,700 it had billed its clients for services rendered on December 31, 20Y7. How would you record the January 24 transaction, using the accrual basis?

   A. Increase Cash, $5,700; decrease Fees Earned, $5,700

   B. Increase Accounts Receivable, $5,700; increase Fees Earned, $5,700

   C. Increase Cash, .$5,700; decrease Accounts Receivable, $5,700

   D. Increase Cash, $5,700; increase Fees Earned, $5,700

3. Which of the following items represents a deferral?

   A. Prepaid insurance

   B. Wages payable

   C. Fees earned

   D. Accumulated depreciation

4. If the supplies account indicated a balance of $2,250 before adjustment on May 31 and supplies on hand at May 31 totaled $950, the adjustment would be:

   A. Increase Supplies, $950; decrease Supplies Expense, $950.

   B. Increase Supplies, $1,300; decrease Supplies Expense, $1,300.

   C. Increase Supplies Expense, $950; decrease Supplies, $950.

   D. Increase Supplies Expense, $1,300; decrease Supplies, $1,300.

5. The balance in the unearned rent account for Jones Co. as of December 31 is $1,200. If Jones Co. failed to record the adjusting entry for $600 of rent earned during December, the effect on the balance sheet and income statement for December would be:

A. Assets understated by $600; net income overstated by $600

B. Liabilities understated by $600; net income understated by $600

C. Liabilities overstated by $600; net income understated by $600

D. Liabilities overstated by $600; net income overstated by $600

Class Discussion Questions

1. Would AT&T and Microsoft use the cash basis or the accrual basis of accounting? Explain.

2. How are revenues and expenses reported on the income statement under (a) the cash basis of accounting and (b) the accrual basis of accounting?

3. Fees for services provided are billed to a customer during 20Y6. The customer remits the amount owed in 20Y7. During which year would the revenues be reported on the income statement under (a) the cash basis? (b) the accrual basis?

4. Employees performed services in 20Y8, but the wages were not paid until 20Y9. During which year would the wages expense be reported on the income statement under (a) the cash basis? (b) the accrual basis?

5. Which of the following accounts would appear only in an accrual basis accounting system, and which could appear in either a cash basis or an accrual basis accounting system? (a) Capital Stock, (b) Fees Earned, (c) Accounts Receivable, (d) Land, (e) Utilities Expense, and (f) Wages Payable.

6. Is the Land balance before the accounts have been adjusted the amount that should normally be reported on the balance sheet? Explain.

7. Is the Supplies balance before the accounts have been adjusted the amount that should normally be reported on the balance sheet? Explain.

8. Why are adjustments needed at the end of an accounting period?

9. Identify the four different categories of adjustments frequently required at the end of an accounting period.

10. If the effect of an adjustment is to increase the balance of a liability account, which of the following statements describes the effect of the adjustment on the other account?
   a. Increases the balance of a revenue account
   b. Increases the balance of an expense account
   c. Increases the balance of an asset account

11. If the effect of an adjustment is to increase the balance of an asset account, which of the following statements describes the effect of the adjustment on the other account?
   a. Increases the balance of a revenue account
   b. Increases the balance of a liability account
   c. Increases the balance of an expense account

12. Does every adjustment have an effect on determining the amount of net income for a period? Explain.

13. (a) Explain the purpose of the accounts Depreciation Expense and Accumulated Depreciation. (b) Is it customary for the balances of the two accounts to be equal? (c) In what financial statements, if any, will each account appear?

14. Describe the nature of the assets that compose the following sections of a balance sheet: (a) current assets, (b) property, plant, and equipment.

Exercises

E3-1 Transactions using accrual accounting

Obj **2**

Chris Vining organized The Herbal Shoppe at the beginning of February 20Y4. During February, The Herbal Shoppe entered into the following transactions:

a. Chris Vining invested $25,000 in The Herbal Shoppe in exchange for capital stock.

b. Paid $4,200 on February 1 for an insurance premium on a 1-year policy.

c. Purchased supplies on account, $1,200.

d. Received fees of $36,500 during February.

e. Paid expenses as follows: wages, $12,000; rent, $2,000; utilities, $1,000; and miscellaneous, $1,100.

f. Paid dividends of $7,500.

Record the preceding transactions using the integrated financial statement framework. After each transaction, you should enter a balance for each item.

E3-2 Adjustment process

Obj **3**

Using the data from Exercise 3-1, record the adjusting entries at the end of February to record the insurance expense and supplies expense. There was $900 of supplies on hand as of February 28. Identify the adjusting entry for insurance as (a1) and supplies as (a2).

E3-3 Financial statements

Obj **4**

✔ Net income, $19,750

Using the data from Exercises 3-1 and 3-2, prepare financial statements for February, including income statement, retained earnings statement, balance sheet, and statement of cash flows.

E3-4 Reconcile net income and net cash flows from operations.

Using the income statement and statement of cash flows you prepared in Exercise 3-3, reconcile net income with the net cash flows from operations.

E3-5 Accrual basis of accounting

Obj **2**

Troy Reece established Reece Services, P.C., a professional corporation, in July of the current year. Reece Services offers financial planning advice to its clients. The effect of each transaction on the balance sheet and the balances after each transaction for July are as follows. Each increase or decrease in stockholders' equity, except transaction (h), affects net income.

Statement of Cash Flows	Balance Sheet											Income Statement
	Assets					=	Liabilities	+	Stockholders' Equity			
	Cash	+	Accounts Receivable	+	Supplies	=	Accounts Payable	+	Capital Stock	+	Retained Earnings	
a.	50,000								50,000			
b.					1,500		1,500					
Bal.	50,000				1,500		1,500		50,000			
c.	−1,000						−1,000					
Bal.	49,000				1,500		500		50,000			
d.	35,000										35,000	d.
Bal.	84,000				1,500		500		50,000		35,000	
e.	−21,000										−21,000	e.
Bal.	63,000				1,500		500		50,000		14,000	
f.					−1,100						−1,100	f.
Bal.	63,000				400		500		50,000		12,900	
g.			10,000								10,000	g.
Bal.	63,000		10,000		400		500		50,000		22,900	
h.	−8,000										−8,000	
Bal.	55,000		10,000		400		500		50,000		14,900	

Statement of Cash Flows

a. Financing	50,000
c. Operating	−1,000
d. Operating	35,000
e. Operating	−21,000
h. Financing	−8,000
	55,000

Income Statement

d. Fees earned	35,000
e. Expenses	−21,000
f. Expenses	−1,100
g. Fees earned	10,000
	22,900

a. Describe each transaction.

b. What is the amount of the net income for July?

Obj 3

E3-6 Classify accruals and deferrals

Classify the following items as (a) deferred expense (prepaid expense), (b) deferred revenue (unearned revenue), (c) accrued expense (accrued liability), or (d) accrued revenue (accrued asset).

1. Subscriptions received in advance by a magazine publisher.
2. A three-year premium paid on a fire insurance policy.
3. Fees received but not yet earned.

4. Fees earned but not yet received.

5. Utilities owed but not yet paid.

6. Supplies on hand.

7. Salary owed but not yet paid.

8. Taxes owed but payable in the following period.

E3-7   Classify adjustments

Obj | **3**

The following accounts were taken from the unadjusted trial balance of Inter Circle Co., a congressional lobbying firm. Indicate whether or not each account would normally require an adjusting entry. If the account normally requires an adjusting entry, use the following notations to indicate the type of adjustment:

> AE—Accrued Expense
> AR—Accrued Revenue
> DR—Deferred Revenue
> DE—Deferred Expense

To illustrate, the answer for the first account is as follows.

Account	Answer
Accounts Receivable	Normally requires adjustment (AR)
Accumulated Depreciation	
Capital Stock	
Dividends	
Interest Payable	
Interest Receivable	
Land	
Office Equipment	
Prepaid Rent	
Supplies	
Unearned Fees	
Wages Expense	

E3-8   Adjustment for supplies

Obj | **3**
✔ a. $2,250

Answer each of the following independent questions concerning supplies and the adjustment for supplies.

a. The balance in the supplies account, before adjustment at the end of the year, is $4,000. What is the amount of the adjustment if the amount of supplies on hand at the end of the year is $1,750?

b. The supplies account has a balance of $1,100, and the supplies expense account has a balance of $3,100 at the end of the first year of operations. What was the amount of supplies purchased during the year?

E3-9   Adjustment for prepaid insurance

Obj | **3**

The prepaid insurance account had a balance of $14,400 at the beginning of the year. The account was increased for $9,600 for premiums on policies purchased during the year. What is the adjustment required at the end of the year for each of the following independent situations? Indicate each account affected, whether the account is increased or decreased, and the amount of the increase or decrease.

a. The amount of unexpired insurance applicable to future periods is $13,500.

b. The amount of insurance expired during the year is $18,300.

Obj **3**

E3-10 Adjustment for unearned fees

The balance in the unearned fees account, before adjustment at the end of the year, is $275,000. What is the adjustment if the amount of unearned fees at the end of the year is $165,000? Indicate each account affected, whether the account is increased or decreased, and the amount of the increase or decrease.

Obj **3**

E3-11 Adjustment for unearned revenue

For a recent year, **Microsoft Corporation** reported short-term unearned revenue of $18,653 million. For the same year, Microsoft also reported total revenues of $73,723 million.

a. Assuming that Microsoft recognized $6,000 million of unearned revenue as revenue during the year, what entry for unearned revenue did Microsoft make during the year? Indicate each account affected, whether the account is increased or decreased, and the amount of the increase or decrease.

b. What percentage of total revenues is the short-term unearned revenue? Round to one decimal place.

Obj **3**

E3-12 Effect of omitting adjustment

At the end of August, the first month of the business year, the usual adjustment transferring rent earned of $36,750 to a revenue account from the unearned rent account was omitted. Indicate which items will be incorrectly stated, because of the error, on (a) the income statement for August and (b) the balance sheet as of August 31. Also indicate whether the items in error will be overstated or understated.

Obj **3**

E3-13 Adjustment for accrued salaries

North Slope Realty Co. pays weekly salaries of $7,900 on Friday for a five-day week ending on that day. What is the adjustment at the end of the accounting period, assuming that the period ends (a) on Wednesday, (b) on Thursday? Indicate each account affected, whether the account is increased or decreased, and the amount of the increase or decrease.

Obj **3**

E3-14 Determine wages paid

The balances of the two wages accounts at October 31, after adjustments at the end of the first year of operations, are Wages Payable, $11,900, and Wages Expense, $825,000. Determine the amount of wages paid during the year.

Obj **3**

E3-15 Effect of omitting adjustment

Accrued salaries of $6,750 owed to employees for December 30 and 31 are not considered in preparing the financial statements for the year ended December 31, 20Y4. Indicate which items will be erroneously stated, because of the error, on (a) the income statement for December 20Y4 and (b) the balance sheet as of December 31, 20Y4. Also indicate whether the items in error will be overstated or understated.

Obj **3**

E3-16 Effect of omitting adjustment

Assume that the error in Exercise 3-15 was not corrected and that the $6,750 of accrued salaries was included in the first salary payment in January 20Y7. Indicate which items will be erroneously stated, because of failure to correct the initial error, on (a) the income statement for January 20Y7 and (b) the balance sheet as of January 31, 20Y7.

Obj **3**

E3-17 Effects of errors on financial statements

For a recent year, the balance sheet for **The Campbell Soup Company** includes accrued expenses of $598,000,000. The income before taxes for the year was $1,106,000,000.

a. Assume the accruals apply to the current year and were not recorded at the end of the year. By how much would income before taxes have been misstated?

b. What is the percentage of the misstatement in (a) to the reported income of $1,106,000,000? Round to one decimal place.

E3-18   Effects of errors on financial statements

Obj 3

The accountant for Healthy Medical Co., a medical services consulting firm, mistakenly omitted adjusting entries for (a) unearned revenue earned during the year ($175,000) and (b) accrued wages ($12,300). Indicate the effect of each error, considered individually, on the income statement for the current year ended August 31. Also indicate the effect of each error on the August 31 balance sheet. Set up a table similar to the following, and record your answers by inserting the dollar amount in the appropriate spaces. Insert a zero if the error does not affect the item.

✔ 1. (a) Revenue understated, $175,000

	Error (a)		Error (b)	
	Over-stated	Under-stated	Over-stated	Under-stated
1. Revenue for the year would be	$ _____	$ _____	$ _____	$ _____
2. Expenses for the year would be	$ _____	$ _____	$ _____	$ _____
3. Net income for the year would be	$ _____	$ _____	$ _____	$ _____
4. Assets at August 31 would be	$ _____	$ _____	$ _____	$ _____
5. Liabilities at August 31 would be	$ _____	$ _____	$ _____	$ _____
6. Stockholders' equity at August 31 would be	$ _____	$ _____	$ _____	$ _____

E3-19   Effects of errors on financial statements

Obj 3

If the net income for the current year had been $2,224,600 in Exercise 3-18, what would have been the correct net income if the proper adjustments had been made?

E3-20   Adjustment for accrued fees

Obj 3

At the end of the current year, $47,700 of fees have been earned but not billed to clients.

a. What is the adjustment to record the accrued fees? Indicate each account affected, whether the account is increased or decreased, and the amount of the increase or decrease.

b. If the cash basis rather than the accrual basis had been used, would an adjustment have been necessary? Explain.

E3-21   Adjustments for unearned and accrued fees

Obj 3

The balance in the unearned fees account, before adjustment at the end of the year, is $440,000. Of these fees, $50,000 have been earned. In addition, $80,000 of fees have been earned but not billed to clients. What are the adjustments (a) to adjust the unearned fees account and (b) to record the accrued fees? Indicate each account affected, whether the account is increased or decreased, and the amount of the increase or decrease.

E3-22   Effect on financial statements of omitting adjustment

Obj 3

The adjustment for accrued fees of $13,400 was omitted at July 31, the end of the current year. Indicate which items will be in error, because of the omission, on (a) the income statement for the current year and (b) the balance sheet as of July 31. Also indicate whether the items in error will be overstated or understated.

E3-23   Adjustment for depreciation

Obj 3

The estimated amount of depreciation on equipment for the current year is $133,000.

a. How is the adjustment recorded? Indicate each account affected, whether the account is increased or decreased, and the amount of the increase or decrease.

b. If the adjustment in (a) was omitted, which items would be erroneously stated on (1) the income statement for the year and (2) the balance sheet as of December 31?

Obj | 3

E3-24   Adjustments

Clean Air Company is a consulting firm specializing in pollution control. The following adjustments were made for Clean Air Company:

	Adjustments
Account	Increase (Decrease)
Accounts Receivable	$11,250
Supplies	(1,350)
Prepaid Insurance	(1,800)
Accumulated Depreciation—Equipment	7,500
Wages Payable	4,500
Unearned Rent	(9,000)
Fees Earned	11,250
Wages Expense	4,500
Supplies Expense	1,350
Rent Revenue	9,000
Insurance Expense	1,800
Depreciation Expense	7,500

Identify each of the six pairs of adjustments. For each adjustment, indicate the account, whether the account is increased or decreased, and the amount of the adjustment. No account is affected by more than one adjustment. Use the following format. The first adjustment is shown as an example.

Adjustment	Account	Increase or Decrease	Amount
1.	Accounts Receivable	Increase	$11,250
	Fees Earned	Increase	11,250

Obj | 4

E3-25   Book value of fixed assets

For a recent year, **Barnes & Noble Inc.** reported (in thousands) *Property and Equipment* of $2,983,797 and *Accumulated Depreciation* of $2,361,142.

a. What was the book value of the fixed assets?

b. Would the book values of Barnes & Noble's fixed assets normally approximate their fair market values?

Obj | 4

E3-26   Classify assets

Identify each of the following as (a) a current asset or (b) property, plant, and equipment:

1. Accounts Receivable
2. Building
3. Cash
4. Office Equipment
5. Prepaid Insurance
6. Supplies

Obj | 4

E3-27   Balance sheet classification

At the balance sheet date, a business owes a five-year mortgage note payable of $480,000, the terms of which provide for monthly payments of $8,000. Explain how the liability should be classified on the balance sheet.

Obj | 4

✔ Total assets,
$1,185,000

E3-28   Classified balance sheet

Pounds-Away Services Co. offers personal weight reduction consulting services to individuals. On November 30, 20Y9, the balances of selected accounts of Pounds-Away Services Co. are as follows:

Accounts Payable	$135,600	Prepaid Insurance	$ 28,800
Accounts Receivable	129,000	Prepaid Rent	21,600
Accum. Depreciation—Equipment	120,000	Retained Earnings	855,000
Capital Stock	150,000	Salaries Payable	26,400
Cash	?	Supplies	48,000
Equipment	990,000	Unearned Fees	18,000

Prepare a classified balance sheet that includes the correct balance for Cash.

E3-29 Classified balance sheet

Obj **4**

✔ Total assets,
$593,455

La-Z-Boy Inc. is one of the world's largest manufacturers of furniture and is best known for its reclining chairs. The following data (in thousands) were adapted from recent financial statements:

Accounts payable	$ 49,537
Accounts receivable	161,299
Accrued expenses	77,447
Accumulated depreciation	301,199
Capital stock	256,322
Cash	115,262
Intangible assets (trade names)	3,100
Inventories	138,444
Debt due within one year	5,120
Long-term debt	29,937
Other current assets	17,218
Other long-term assets	37,529
Other long-term liabilities	67,274
Property, plant, and equipment	421,802
Retained earnings	107,818

Prepare a classified balance sheet as of April 30, 20Y8.

E3-30 Balance sheet

Obj **4**

List any errors you can find in the following balance sheet. Prepare a corrected balance sheet.

ATLAS SERVICES CO.
Balance Sheet
For the Year Ended May 31, 20Y5

Assets

Current assets:		
Cash ...	$ 12,000	
Accounts payable	47,900	
Supplies	4,800	
Prepaid insurance	17,400	
Land	400,000	
Total current assets		$482,100
Property, plant, and equipment:		
Building	$225,000	
Equipment	90,000	
Total property, plant, and equipment		315,000
Total assets		$797,100

Liabilities

Current liabilities:		
Accounts receivable	$ 40,800	
Accumulated depreciation—building	54,600	
Accumulated depreciation—equipment	32,400	
Net loss	44,200	
Total liabilities		$172,000

Stockholders' Equity

Wages Payable	$ 8,100	
Capital Stock	200,000	
Retained Earnings	447,000	
Total Stockholders' Equity		655,100
Total liabilities and stockholders' equity		$797,100

Problems

P3-1   Accrual basis accounting

Oasis Health Care Inc. is owned and operated by Dr. George Hancock, the sole stockholder. During January 20Y6, Oasis Health Care entered into the following transactions:

Jan. 1   Received $15,000 from Rivers Company as rent for the use of a vacant office in Oasis Health Care's building. Rivers paid the rent six months in advance.

1   Paid $4,200 for an insurance premium on a general business policy.

6   Purchased supplies of $1,800 on account.

9   Collected $27,500 for services provided to customers on account.

11   Paid creditors $3,000 on account.

18   Invested an additional $25,000 in the business in exchange for capital stock.

20   Billed patients $62,000 for services provided on account.

25   Received $12,900 for services provided to customers who paid cash.

30   Paid expenses as follows: wages, $24,000; utilities, $6,000; rent on medical equipment, $5,000; interest, $200; and miscellaneous, $2,500.

30   Paid dividends of $15,000 to stockholders (Dr. Hancock).

Instructions

Analyze and record the January transactions for Oasis Health Care Inc., using the integrated financial statement framework. Record each transaction by date, and show the balance for each item after each transaction. The January 1, 20Y6, balances for the balance sheet are shown below.

		Assets					=	Liabilities			+	Stockholders' Equity	
Cash	+ Accts. Rec.	+ Pre. Ins.	+ Supp.	+ Building	− Acc. Depr.	+ Land	= Accts. Pay.	+ Un. Rev.	+ Wages Pay.	+ Notes Pay.	+ Capital Stock	+ Retained Earnings	
Bal., Jan. 1 20,000	34,500	700	1,000	150,000	− 11,200	120,000	7,500	0	0	30,000	50,000	227,500	

P3-2   Adjustment process

Adjustment data for Oasis Health Care Inc. for January are as follows:

1. Insurance expired, $800.
2. Supplies on hand on January 31, $1,100.
3. Depreciation on building, $2,000.
4. Unearned rent revenue earned, $2,500.
5. Wages owed employees but not paid, $1,700.
6. Services provided but not billed to patients, $10,000.

Instructions

Based on the transactions recorded in January for Problem 3-1, record the adjustments for January using the integrated financial statement framework.

P3-3   Financial statements

Data for Oasis Health Care for January are provided in Problems 3-1 and 3-2.

Instructions

✔ 1. Net income, $43,500

Prepare an income statement, retained earnings statement, and a classified balance sheet for January. The note payable is due in ten years.

P3-4 Statement of cash flows

Obj **4**

Data for Oasis Health Care for January are provided in Problems 3-1, 3-2, and 3-3.

Instructions

1. Prepare a statement of cash flows for January.
2. Reconcile the net cash flows from operating activities with the net income for January. (*Hint:* See the appendix to this chapter and use adjusted balances in computing increases and decreases in accounts.)

✔ Net cash flows from operating activities, $10,500

P3-5 Adjustments and errors

Obj **3**

At the end of May, the first month of operations, the following selected data were taken from the financial statements of Julie Mortenson, Attorney at Law, P.C.:

Net income for May	$127,500
Total assets at May 31	480,000
Total liabilities at May 31	150,000
Total stockholders' equity at May 31	330,000

✔ Corrected net income, $127,075

In preparing the financial statements, adjustments for the following data were overlooked:

a. Unbilled fees earned at May 31, $9,700
b. Depreciation of equipment for May, $8,000
c. Accrued wages at May 31, $1,150
d. Supplies used during May, $975

Instructions

Determine the correct amount of net income for May and the total assets, liabilities, and stockholders' equity at May 31. In addition to indicating the corrected amounts, indicate the effect of each omitted adjustment by setting up and completing a columnar table similar to the one shown below. Adjustment (a) is presented as an example.

	Net Income	Total Assets	=	Total Liabilities	+	Total Stockholders' Equity
Reported amounts	$127,500	$480,000		$150,000		$330,000
Corrections:						
Adjustment (a)	+9,700	+9,700		0		+9,700
Adjustment (b)	_____	_____		_____		_____
Adjustment (c)	_____	_____		_____		_____
Adjustment (d)	_____	_____		_____		_____
Corrected amounts	======	======		======		======

P3-6 Adjustment process and financial statements

Obj **3, 4**

Adjustment data for Ms. Ellen's Laundry Inc. for the year ended December 31, 20Y8, are as follows:

a. Wages accrued but not paid at December 31, $2,150
b. Depreciation of equipment during the year, $12,500
c. Laundry supplies on hand at December 31, $1,500
d. Insurance premiums expired, $4,600

✔ 2. Net income, $82,750

Instructions

1. Using the following integrated financial statement framework, record each adjustment to the appropriate accounts, identifying each adjustment by its letter. After all adjustments are recorded, determine the balances.

Statement of Cash Flows	Balance Sheet									Income Statement
	Assets					= Liabilities	+	Stockholders' Equity		
	Cash +	Laundry Supplies +	Prepaid Insurance +	Laundry Equip. +	Acc. Depr. –	Accts. Payable +	Wages Payable +	Capital Stock +	Retained Earnings	
Balances, Dec. 31, 2013	53,000	9,000	6,000	250,000	–65,000	7,000	0	50,000	196,000	

Statement of Cash Flows

Operating (Revenues)	275,000
Financing (Capital Stock)	25,000
Operating (Expenses)	–200,000
Investing (Equipment)	–50,000
Financing (Dividends)	–15,000
Net increase in cash	35,000
Beginning cash bal., Jan. 1, 2013	18,000
Ending cash bal., Dec. 31, 2013	$53,000

Income Statement

Laundry revenue	275,000
Wages expense	–110,000
Rent expense	–30,000
Utilities expense	–18,000
Misc. expense	–7,500

2. Prepare an income statement and retained earnings statement for the year ended December 31, 20Y8. The retained earnings balance as of January 1, 20Y8, was $101,500.

3. Prepare a classified balance sheet as of December 31, 20Y8.

4. Prepare a statement of cash flows for the year ended December 31, 20Y8.

Financial Analysis: Working Capital, Current Ratio, and Quick Ratio

Obj 8

FA3-1   Working capital, current ratio, quick ratio

GameStop Corporation has over 6,000 retail stores worldwide and sells new and used video games. The following asset and liability data (in millions) were adapted from recent financial statements.

	Year 2	Year 1
Current assets		
Cash	$ 655	$ 711
Accounts receivable	109	94
Inventory	1,137	1,258
Prepaid and other current assets	96	92
Total current assets	$1,997	$2,155
Total current liabilities	$1,634	$1,748

1. Compute working capital for Years 2 and 1.

2. Compute the current ratio for Years 2 and 1. Round to one decimal place.

3. Compute the quick ratio for Years 2 and 1. Round to one decimal place.

4. Analyze and assess any changes in liquidity for Years 2 and 1.

5. Comment on any competitive pressures that you think GameStop may be experiencing.

Obj 6

FA3-2   Working capital, current ratio, quick ratio

The Gap Inc. operates over 3,000 specialty retail stores under such brand names as GAP, Old Navy, and Banana Republic. The following asset and liability data (in millions) were adapted from recent financial statements.

	Year 2	Year 1
Current assets		
Cash	$1,885	$1,661
Accounts receivable	297	205
Inventory	1,615	1,620
Prepaid and other current assets	512	440
Total current assets	$4,309	$3,926
Total current liabilities	$2,128	$2,095

1. Compute working capital for Years 2 and 1.

2. Compute the current ratio for Years 2 and 1. Round to one decimal place.

3. Compute the quick ratio for Years 2 and 1. Round to one decimal place.

4. Analyze and assess any changes in liquidity for Years 2 and 1.

FA3-3   Working capital, current ratio, quick ratio

Obj | **6**

American Eagle Outfitters Inc. operates over 1,000 specialty retail stores, selling clothing such as denim, sweaters, t-shirts, and fleece outerwear. The following asset and liability data (in millions) were adapted from recent financial statements.

	Year 2	Year 1
Current assets		
Cash	$ 745	$ 734
Accounts receivable	89	85
Inventory	378	301
Prepaid and other current assets	75	54
Total current assets	$1,287	$1,174
Total current liabilities	$ 405	$ 388

1. Compute working capital for Years 2 and 1.

2. Compute the current ratio for Years 2 and 1. Round to one decimal place.

3. Compute the quick ratio for Years 2 and 1. Round to one decimal place.

4. Analyze and assess any changes in liquidity for Years 2 and 1.

FA3-4   Working capital, current ratio, quick ratio

Obj | **6**

Compare The Gap Inc. (FA3-2) and American Eagle Outfitters Inc. (FA3-3) liquidity positions for Year 2. Comment on the differences.

FA3-5   Working capital, current ratio, quick ratio

Obj | **6**

Walmart Stores Inc. operates over 10,000 retail stores throughout the world. In contrast, Google Inc. is a technology company that provides a variety of online services.

1. Do you think Walmart or Google has a higher current ratio?

2. Do you think Walmart or Google has a higher quick ratio?

3. Using the following data (in millions) adapted from financial statements of a recent year, compute the current and quick ratios for Walmart and Google. Round to one decimal place.

	Walmart	Google Inc.
Current assets	$54,975	$52,758
Quick assets	12,487	44,626
Total current liabilities	62,300	14,429

4. Explain the results in (3).

Cases

Case 3-1   Accrued revenue

The following is an excerpt from a conversation between Monte Trask and Jamie Palk just before they boarded a flight to Berlin on American Airlines. They are going to Berlin to attend their company's annual sales conference.

Monte: Jamie, aren't you taking an introductory accounting course at college?

Jamie: Yes, I decided it's about time I learned something about accounting. You know, our annual bonuses are based on the sales figures that come from the accounting department.

Monte: I guess I never really thought about it.

Jamie: You should think about it! Last year, I placed a $900,000 order on December 27. But when I got my bonus, the $900,000 sale wasn't included. They said it hadn't been shipped until January 5, so it would have to count in next year's bonus.

Monte: A real bummer!

Jamie: Right! I was counting on that bonus including the $900,000 sale.

Monte: Did you complain?

Jamie: Yes, but it didn't do any good. Sophia, the head accountant, said something about matching revenues and expenses. Also, something about not recording revenues until the sale is final. I figured I'd take the accounting course and find out whether she's just jerking me around.

Monte: I never really thought about it. When do you think American Airlines will record its revenues from this flight?

Jamie: Hmmm, I guess it could record the revenue when it sells the ticket ... or when the boarding passes are taken at the door ... or when we get off the plane ... or when our company pays for the tickets ... or I don't know. I'll ask my accounting instructor.

Discuss when American Airlines should recognize the revenue from ticket sales to properly match revenues and expenses.

Case 3-2   Adjustments for financial statements

Several years ago, your brother opened Ready Appliance Repairs. He made a small initial investment and added money from his personal bank account as needed. He withdrew money for living expenses at irregular intervals. As the business grew, he hired an assistant. He is now considering adding more employees, purchasing additional service trucks, and purchasing the building he now rents. To secure funds for the expansion, your brother submitted a loan application to the bank and included the most recent financial statements (shown below) prepared from accounts maintained by a part-time bookkeeper.

READY APPLIANCE REPAIRS
Income Statement
For the Year Ended March 31, 20Y6

Service revenue...		$182,500
Less: Rent paid	$41,200	
Wages paid	34,750	
Supplies paid	7,000	
Utilities paid	6,500	
Insurance paid	3,600	
Miscellaneous payments	9,100	102,150
Net income...		$ 80,350

READY APPLIANCE REPAIRS
Balance Sheet
March 31, 20Y6

Assets

Cash...	$ 25,900
Amounts due from customers..	18,750
Truck	55,350
Total assets	$100,000

Equities

Owner's equity...	$100,000

After reviewing the financial statements, the loan officer at the bank asked your brother if he used the accrual basis of accounting for revenues and expenses. Your brother responded that he did and that is why he included an account for "Amounts Due from Customers." The loan officer then asked whether or not the accounts were adjusted prior to the preparation of the statements. Your brother answered that they had not been adjusted.

a. Why do you think the loan officer suspected that the accounts had not been adjusted prior to the preparation of the statements?

b. Indicate possible accounts that might need to be adjusted before an accurate set of financial statements could be prepared.

Case 3-3   Business emphasis

Assume that you and two friends are debating whether to open an automotive and service retail chain that will be called Auto-Mart. Initially, Auto-Mart will open three stores locally, but the business plan anticipates going nationwide within five years.

Currently, you and your future business partners are debating whether to focus Auto-Mart on a "do-it-yourself" or "do-it-for-me" business. A do-it-yourself business emphasizes the sale of retail auto parts that customers will use themselves to repair and service their cars. A do-it-for-me business emphasizes the offering of maintenance and service for customers.

1. In groups of three or four, discuss whether to implement a do-it-yourself or do-it-for-me business emphasis. List the advantages of each emphasis, and arrive at a conclusion as to which emphasis to implement.

2. Provide examples of real-world businesses that use do-it-yourself or do-it-for-me business emphases.

Case 3-4   Cash basis income statement

The following operating data (in millions) were adapted from recent financial statements of CVS Caremark Corporation and Walgreen Co.

	CVS		Walgreens	
	Year 2	**Year 1**	**Year 2**	**Year 1**
Accounts receivable	$6,550	$5,436	$2,167	$2,497
Accounts payable	7,663	7,096	7,403	8,070

1. Using the preceding data, adjust the operating income for CVS and Walgreens to an adjusted cash basis. For Year 2, the operating income for CVS was $3,461 and for Walgreens it was $2,127 (in millions). (*Hint:* To convert to a cash basis, you need to compute the change in each accrual accounting item shown and then either add or subtract the change to determine the operating income.)

2. Compute the net difference between the operating income under the accrual and cash bases.

3. Express the net difference in (2) as a percentage of operating income under the accrual basis.

4. Which company's operating income, CVS's or Walgreens's, is closer to the cash basis? Round to one decimal place.

5. Do you think most analysts focus on operating income or net income in assessing the long-term profitability of a company? Explain.

Case 3-5 Analysis of income and cash flows

The following data (in millions) were taken from http://finance.yahoo.com.

	Year 3	Year 2	Year 1
Company A			
Revenues	$48,077	$34,204	$24,509
Operating income	862	1,406	1,129
Net income	631	1,152	902
Net cash flows from operating activities	3,903	3,495	3,293
Net cash flows from investing activities	(1,930)	(3,360)	(2,337)
Net cash flows from financing activities	(482)	181	(280)
Total assets	25,278	18,797	13,813
Company B			
Revenues	$35,115	$31,755	$28,063
Operating income (loss)	1,975	2,217	(324)
Net income (loss)	854	593	(1,237)
Net cash flows from operating activities	2,834	2,832	1,379
Net cash flows from investing activities	(1,498)	(2,026)	(1,008)
Net cash flows from financing activities	(1,571)	(2,521)	(19)
Total assets	43,499	43,188	43,789
Company C			
Revenues	$46,542	$35,119	$30,990
Operating income	10,154	8,449	8,231
Net income	9,262	11,809	6,824
Net cash flows from operating activities	9,474	9,532	8,186
Net cash flows from investing activities	(2,524)	(4,405)	(4,149)
Net cash flows from financing activities	(2,234)	(3,465)	(2,293)
Total assets	79,974	72,921	48,671
Company D			
Revenues	$90,374	$82,189	$76,733
Operating income (loss)	1,278	2,182	1,091
Net income (loss)	602	1,116	70
Net cash flows from operating activities	2,658	3,366	2,922
Net cash flows from investing activities	(1,908)	(1,961)	(2,327)
Net cash flows from financing activities	(1,387)	(1,004)	(434)
Total assets	23,476	23,505	23,126

1. Match each of the following companies with the data for Company A, B, C, or D:

   Amazon.com

   Coca-Cola Inc.

   Delta Air Lines

   Kroger

2. Explain the logic underlying your matches.

Answers to Self-Examination Questions

1. **A** Under the accrual basis of accounting, revenues are recorded when the services are rendered. Since the services were rendered during June, all the fees should be recorded on June 30 (answer A). This is an example of accrued revenue. Under the cash basis of accounting, revenues are recorded when the cash is collected, not necessarily when the fees are earned. Thus, no revenue would be recorded in June, $8,500 of revenue would be recorded in July, and $6,500 of revenue would be recorded in August (answer D). Answers B and C are incorrect and are not used under either the accrual or cash basis.

2. **C** The collection of a $5,700 accounts receivable is recorded as an increase in Cash, $5,700, and a decrease in Accounts Receivable, $5,700 (answer C). The initial recording of the fees earned on account is recorded as an increase in Accounts Receivable and an increase in Fees Earned (answer B). Services rendered for cash are recorded as an increase in Cash and an increase in Fees Earned (answer D). Answer A is incorrect and would result in the accounting equation being out of balance because total assets would exceed total liabilities and stockholders' equity by $11,400.

3. **A** A deferral is the delay in recording an expense already paid, such as prepaid insurance (answer A). Wages payable (answer B) is considered an accrued expense or accrued liability. Fees earned (answer C) is a revenue item. Accumulated depreciation (answer D) is a contra account to a fixed asset.

4. **D** The balance in the supplies account, before adjustment, represents the amount of supplies available during the period. From this amount, $2,250, is subtracted the amount of supplies on hand, $950, to determine the supplies used, $1,300. The used supplies is recorded as an increase in Supplies Expense, $1,300, and a decrease in Supplies, $1,300 (answer D).

5. **C** The failure to record the adjusting entry increasing Rent Revenue, $600, and decreasing Unearned Rent, $600, would have the effect of overstating liabilities by $600 and understating net income by $600 (answer C).

CHAPTER 4

Accounting for Merchandising Businesses

LEARNING OBJECTIVES
After studying this chapter, you should be able to:

Obj | **1** Distinguish the activities and financial statements of a service business from those of a merchandising business.

Obj | **2** Describe and illustrate the financial statements of a merchandising business.

Obj | **3** Describe the accounting for the sale of merchandise.

Obj | **4** Describe the accounting for the purchase of merchandise.

Obj | **5** Describe the accounting for freight and sales taxes.

Obj | **6** Illustrate the dual nature of merchandising transactions.

Obj | **7** Describe the accounting for merchandise shrinkage.

Obj | **8** Financial Analysis: Describe and illustrate the gross profit percent, average markup percent, and ratio of sales to assets in assessing a company's financial performance.

Twenty years ago, music was purchased at the "record store." No longer. Today, CDs can be purchased at retail stores such as **Best Buy**, **Walmart**, and **Disc Exchange**; through online retailers, such as **CD Universe** and **CDNow**; and as individual MP3 downloads from services such as **Apple**'s iTunes© and **Real**'s Rhapsody©. The way goods (and services) are purchased has undergone significant changes and will continue to change with consumer tastes and technology. For example, an established retailer like **JCPenney** is faced with a rapidly changing competitive landscape with the emergence of (1) discount merchandising, (2) category killers, and (3) Internet retailing.

Walmart, which led the development of discount merchandising, has become the world's largest retailer. Walmart's growth is centered on providing the consumer with everyday discount pricing over a broad array of household products. Category killers include **Toys"R"Us** (toys), Best Buy (electronics), **Home Depot** (home improvement), and **Office Depot** (office supplies), which provide a wide selection of attractively priced goods within a particular product segment. Internet retailers, such as **Amazon.com** and **Lands' End** (now part of **Sears**), allow time-conscious consumers to shop quickly and effortlessly. JCPenney has had to adapt its retailing model in order to respond to all these changes. Merchandising will undoubtedly continue to evolve as consumer lifestyles and technologies change in the future. In this chapter, the accounting issues unique to merchandisers are introduced. Merchandisers are emphasized because merchandising is significant in its own right, and because even nonmerchandisers have accounting issues similar to those discussed in this chapter.

Merchandise Operations

Prior chapters described and illustrated how businesses report their financial condition and changes in financial condition using the cash and accrual bases of accounting. Those chapters focused on service businesses. This chapter describes and illustrates the accounting for merchandise operations.[1]

The activities of a service business differ from those of a merchandising business. These differences are illustrated in the following condensed income statements:

Service Business		Merchandising Business	
Fees earned	$XXX	Sales	$XXX
Operating expenses	–XXX	Cost of merchandise sold	–XXX
Net income	$XXX	Gross profit	$XXX
		Operating expenses	–XXX
		Net income	$XXX

The revenue activities of a service business involve providing services to customers. On the income statement for a service business, the revenues from services are reported as *fees earned*. The operating expenses incurred in providing the services are subtracted from the fees earned to arrive at *net income*.

In contrast, the revenue activities of a merchandising business involve the buying and selling of merchandise. A merchandising business first purchases merchandise to sell to its customers. When this merchandise is sold, the revenue is reported as sales, and its cost is recognized as an expense. This expense is

The Operating Cycle

The operations of a merchandising business involve the purchase of merchandise for sale (purchasing), the sale of the products to customers (sales), and the receipt of cash from customers (collection). This overall process is referred to as the operating cycle. Thus, the operating cycle begins with spending cash, and it ends with receiving cash from customers. The operating cycle for a merchandising business is shown to the right. Operating cycles for retailers are usually shorter than they are for manufacturers because retailers purchase goods in a form ready for sale to the customer. Of course, some retailers will have shorter operating cycles than others because of the nature of their products. For example, a jewelry store or an automobile dealer normally has a longer operating cycle than a consumer electronics store or a grocery store. Businesses with longer operating cycles normally have higher profit margins on their products than businesses with shorter operating cycles. For example, it is not unusual for jewelry stores to price their jewelry at 30%–50% above cost. In contrast, grocery stores operate on very small profit margins, often below 5%. Grocery stores make up the difference by selling their products more quickly.

1. The closing process, which is not illustrated, is similar to that for a service business, which is referenced in Chapter 3, footnote 3, on page 105.

called the **cost of merchandise sold**. The cost of merchandise sold is subtracted from sales to arrive at gross profit. This amount is called **gross profit** because it is the profit *before* deducting operating expenses.

Merchandise on hand (not sold) at the end of an accounting period is called **merchandise inventory**. Merchandise inventory is reported as a current asset on the balance sheet.

Financial Statements for a Merchandising Business

Obj **2**

Describe and illustrate the financial statements of a merchandising business.

In this section, the financial statements for TechUSA, a retailer of computer hardware and software, are illustrated. Chris Clark organized TechUSA with a business strategy of offering personalized service to individuals and small businesses who are upgrading or purchasing new computer systems. TechUSA's personal service includes a no-obligation, on-site assessment of the customer's computer needs. By providing personalized service and follow-up, Chris feels that TechUSA can compete effectively against such retailers as Best Buy and Office Depot, Inc.

Multiple-Step Income Statement

The 20Y7 income statement for TechUSA is shown in Exhibit 1. This form of income statement, called a **multiple-step income statement**, contains several sections, subsections, and subtotals.

HOW BUSINESSES MAKE MONEY

UNDER ONE ROOF AT JCPENNEY

Most businesses cannot be all things to all people. Businesses must seek a position in the marketplace to serve a unique customer need. Companies that are unable to do this can be squeezed out of the marketplace. The mall-based department store has been under pressure from both ends of the retail spectrum. At the discount store end of the market, Walmart has been a formidable competitor. At the high end, specialty retailers have established strong presence in identifiable niches, such as electronics and apparel. Over a decade ago, JCPenney abandoned its "hard goods," such as electronics and sporting goods, in favor of providing "soft goods" because of the emerging strength of specialty retailers in the hard goods segments. JCPenney is positioning itself against these forces by *"exceeding the fashion, quality, selection, and service components of the discounter, equaling the merchandise intensity of the specialty store, and providing the selection and 'under one roof' shopping convenience of the department store."* JCPenney's merchandise emphasis is focused toward customers it terms the "modern spender" and "starting outs." It views these segments as most likely to value its higher-end merchandise offered under the convenience of "one roof."

EXHIBIT 1

Multiple-Step Income Statement

TechUSA
Income Statement
For the Year Ended December 31, 20Y7

Revenue from sales:			
Sales		$720,185	
Less: Sales returns and allowances	$ 6,140		
Sales discounts	5,790	11,930	
Net sales			$708,255
Cost of merchandise sold			525,305
Gross profit			$182,950
Operating expenses:			
Selling expenses:			
Sales salaries expense	$53,430		
Advertising expense	10,860		
Depreciation expense—store equipment	3,100		
Delivery expense	2,800		
Miscellaneous selling expense	630		
Total selling expenses		$ 70,820	
Administrative expenses:			
Office salaries expense	$21,020		
Rent expense	8,100		
Depreciation expense—office equipment	2,490		
Insurance expense	1,910		
Office supplies expense	610		
Miscellaneous administrative expense	760		
Total administrative expenses		34,890	
Total operating expenses			105,710
Income from operations			$ 77,240
Other income and expense:			
Rent revenue		$ 600	
Interest expense		(2,440)	(1,840)
Net income			$ 75,400

Revenue from Sales

This section of the multiple-step income statement consists of sales, sales returns and allowances, sales discounts, and net sales. This section, as shown in Exhibit 1, is as follows:

Revenue from sales:			
Sales		$720,185	
Less: Sales returns and allowances	$6,140		
Sales discounts	5,790	11,930	
Net sales			$708,255

Sales is the total amount charged customers for merchandise sold, including cash sales and sales on account. During 20Y7, TechUSA sold merchandise of $720,185 for cash or on account.

Sales returns and allowances are granted by the seller to customers for damaged or defective merchandise. In such cases, the customer may either return the merchandise or accept an allowance from the seller. TechUSA reported $6,140 of sales returns and allowances during 20Y7.

Sales discounts are granted by the seller to customers for early payment of amounts owed. For example, a seller may offer a customer a 2% discount on a sale of $10,000 if the customer pays within 10 days. If the customer pays within the 10-day period, the seller receives cash of $9,800, and the buyer receives a discount of $200 ($10,000 × 2%). TechUSA reported $5,790 of sales discounts during 20Y7.

Net sales is determined by subtracting sales returns and allowances and sales discounts from sales. As shown in Exhibit 1, TechUSA reported $708,255 of net sales during 20Y7. Some companies report only net sales and report sales, sales returns and allowances, and sales discounts in notes to the financial statements.

Cost of Merchandise Sold

The cost of merchandise sold is the cost of the merchandise sold to customers. TechUSA reported cost of merchandise sold of $525,305 during 20Y7. To illustrate how cost of merchandise sold is determined, data from when TechUSA began its merchandising operations are used.

For many merchandising businesses, the cost of merchandise sold is usually the largest expense. For example, the approximate percentage of cost of merchandise sold to sales is 60% for **JCPenney** and 66% for **The Home Depot**.

Purchases July 1–December 31, 20Y6	$340,000
Merchandise inventory on December 31, 20Y6	59,700

Since TechUSA had only $59,700 of merchandise left on December 31, 20Y6, it must have sold merchandise that cost $280,300 during 20Y6, as shown below.

Purchases	$340,000
Less merchandise inventory, December 31, 20Y6	59,700
Cost of merchandise sold	$280,300

To continue, assume the following 20Y7 data for TechUSA:

Purchases of merchandise	$521,980
Purchases returns and allowances	9,100
Purchases discounts	2,525
Freight in on merchandise purchased	17,400

Sellers may grant a buyer sales returns and allowances for returned or damaged merchandise. From a buyer's perspective, such allowances are called **purchases returns and allowances**. Likewise, sellers may grant a buyer a sales discount for early payment of the amount owed. From a buyer's perspective, such discounts are called **purchases discounts**. Purchases returns and allowances and purchases discounts are subtracted from purchases to arrive at **net purchases**, as shown below for TechUSA.

Purchases		$521,980
Less: Purchases returns and allowances	$9,100	
Purchases discounts	2,525	11,625
Net purchases		$510,355

Freight costs incurred in obtaining the merchandise increase the cost of the merchandise purchased. These costs are called **freight in**. Adding freight in to net purchases yields the **cost of merchandise purchased**, as shown below for TechUSA.

Net purchases	$510,355
Add freight in	17,400
Cost of merchandise purchased	$527,755

The beginning inventory is added to the cost of merchandise purchased to determine the **merchandise available for sale** for the period. The ending inventory of TechUSA on December 31, 20Y6, $59,700, becomes the beginning (January 1, 20Y7) inventory for 20Y7. Thus, the merchandise available for sale for TechUSA during 20Y7 is $587,455, as shown below.

Merchandise inventory, January 1, 20Y7	$ 59,700
Cost of merchandise purchased	527,755
Cost of merchandise available for sale	$587,455

The ending inventory is then subtracted from the merchandise available for sale to yield the cost of merchandise sold. Assuming the ending inventory on December 31, 20Y7, is $62,150, the cost of merchandise sold for TechUSA is $525,305, as shown in Exhibit 1 and below.

Cost of merchandise available for sale	$587,455
Less merchandise inventory, December 31, 20Y7	62,150
Cost of merchandise sold	$525,305

In the preceding computation, merchandise inventory at the end of the period is subtracted from the merchandise available for sale to determine the cost of merchandise sold. The merchandise inventory at the end of the period is determined by taking a physical count of inventory on hand. This method of determining the cost of merchandise sold and the amount of merchandise on hand is called the **periodic inventory system**. Under the periodic inventory system, the inventory records do not show the amount available for sale or the amount sold during the period. Instead, the cost of merchandise sold is computed and reported as shown in Exhibit 2.

EXHIBIT 2

Cost of Merchandise Sold

Merchandise inventory, January 1, 20Y7			$ 59,700
Purchases		$521,980	
Less: Purchases returns and allowances	$9,100		
Purchases discounts	2,525	11,625	
Net purchases		$510,355	
Add freight in		17,400	
Cost of merchandise purchased			527,755
Merchandise available for sale			$587,455
Less merchandise inventory, December 31, 20Y7			62,150
Cost of merchandise sold			$525,305

Under the **perpetual inventory system** of accounting, each purchase and sale of merchandise is recorded in the inventory and the cost of merchandise sold accounts. As a result, the amounts of merchandise available for sale and sold are continuously (perpetually) updated in the inventory records. Because many retailers use computerized systems, the perpetual inventory system is widely used. For example, such systems may use bar codes, such as the one on the back of this textbook. An optical scanner reads the bar code to record merchandise purchased and sold.

Businesses using a perpetual inventory system report the cost of merchandise sold as a single line on the income statement. An example of such reporting is illustrated in Exhibit 1 for TechUSA. Because of its wide use, the perpetual inventory system is used in the remainder of this chapter.

Retailers, such as **Best Buy, Sears Holding Corporation,** and **Walmart,** and grocery store chains, such as **Winn-Dixie Stores, Inc.** and **Kroger,** use bar codes and optical scanners as part of their computerized inventory systems.

Gross Profit

Gross profit is computed by subtracting the cost of merchandise sold from net sales, as shown below.

Net sales	$708,255
Cost of merchandise sold	525,305
Gross profit	$182,950

As shown above and in Exhibit 1, TechUSA has gross profit of $182,950 in 20Y7.

Income from Operations

Income from operations, sometimes called **operating income**, is determined by subtracting operating expenses from gross profit. Operating expenses are normally classified as either selling expenses or administrative expenses.

Selling expenses are incurred directly in the selling of merchandise. Examples of selling expenses include sales salaries, store supplies used, depreciation of store equipment, delivery expense, and advertising.

Administrative expenses, sometimes called **general expenses**, are incurred in the administration or general operations of the business. Examples of administrative expenses include office salaries, depreciation of office equipment, and office supplies used.

Each selling and administrative expense may be reported separately, as shown in Exhibit 1. However, many companies report selling, administrative, and operating expenses as single line items, as shown below for TechUSA.

Gross profit		$182,950
Operating expenses:		
Selling expenses	$70,820	
Administrative expenses	34,890	
Total operating expenses		105,710
Income from operations		$ 77,240

Other Income and Expense

Other income and expense items are not related to the primary operations of the business. **Other income** is revenue from sources other than the primary operating activity of a business. Examples of other income include income from interest, rent, and gains resulting from the sale of fixed assets. **Other expense** is an expense that cannot be traced directly to the normal operations of the business.

Examples of other expenses include interest expense and losses from disposing of fixed assets.

Other income and other expense are offset against each other on the income statement. If the total of other income exceeds the total of other expense, the difference is added to income from operations to determine net income. If the reverse is true, the difference is subtracted from income from operations. The other income and expense items of TechUSA are reported as shown below and in Exhibit 1.

Income from operations		$77,240
Other income and expense:		
Rent revenue	$ 600	
Interest expense	(2,440)	(1,840)
Net income		$75,400

Single-Step Income Statement

An alternate form of income statement is the **single-step income statement**. As shown in Exhibit 3, the income statement for TechUSA deducts the total of all expenses *in one step* from the total of all revenues.

EXHIBIT 3

Single-Step Income Statement

TechUSA
Income Statement
For the Year Ended December 31, 20Y7

Revenues:		
Net sales		$708,255
Rent revenue		600
Total revenues		$708,855
Expenses:		
Cost of merchandise sold	$525,305	
Selling expenses	70,820	
Administrative expenses	34,890	
Interest expense	2,440	
Total expenses		633,455
Net income		$ 75,400

The single-step form emphasizes total revenues and total expenses in determining net income. A criticism of the single-step form is that gross profit and income from operations are not reported.

Retained Earnings Statement

The retained earnings statement for TechUSA is shown in Exhibit 4. This statement is prepared in the same manner as for a service business.

Balance Sheet

As discussed and illustrated in Chapters 1–3, the balance sheet may be presented in a downward sequence in three sections. This form of balance sheet is called the **report form**.[2] The report form of balance sheet for TechUSA is shown in

2 The balance sheet may be presented with assets on the left-hand side and liabilities and stockholders' equity on the right-hand side. This form of the balance sheet is called the **account form.**

EXHIBIT 4

Retained Earnings Statement for Merchandising Business

TechUSA		
Retained Earnings Statement		
For the Year Ended December 31, 20Y7		
Retained earnings, January 1, 20Y7...		$128,800
Net income for the year..	$75,400	
Less dividends...	18,000	
Increase in retained earnings		57,400
Retained earnings, December 31, 20Y7...		$186,200

Exhibit 5. In Exhibit 5, merchandise inventory is reported as a current asset and the current portion of the note payable of $5,000 is reported as a current liability.

EXHIBIT 5

Report Form of Balance Sheet

TechUSA		
Balance Sheet		
December 31, 20Y7		
Assets		
Current assets:		
Cash	$ 52,950	
Accounts receivable............................	91,080	
Merchandise inventory	62,150	
Office supplies..................................	480	
Prepaid insurance...............................	2,650	
Total current assets.........................		$209,310
Property, plant, and equipment:		
Land..	$ 20,000	
Store equipment................$27,100		
Less accumulated depreciation.......5,700	21,400	
Office equipment $15,570		
Less accumulated depreciation 4,720	10,850	
Total property, plant, and equipment..........		52,250
Total assets..		$261,560
Liabilities		
Current liabilities:		
Accounts payable................................	$ 22,420	
Note payable (current portion).....................	5,000	
Salaries payable	1,140	
Unearned rent..................................	1,800	
Total current liabilities.........................		$ 30,360
Long-term liabilities:		
Note payable (final payment due in ten years)......		20,000
Total liabilities.......................................		$ 50,360
Stockholders' Equity		
Capital stock	$ 25,000	
Retained earnings	186,200	
Total stockholders' equity...........................		211,200
Total liabilities and stockholders' equity		$261,560

Statement of Cash Flows

The statement of cash flows for TechUSA is shown in Exhibit 6. It indicates that cash increased during 20Y7 by $11,450. This increase is generated from a positive cash flow from operating activities of $47,120, which is partially offset by negative cash flows from investing and financing activities of $12,670 and $23,000, respectively.

The net cash flows from operating activities is shown in Exhibit 6 using a method known as the **indirect method**. This method, which reconciles net income with net cash flows from operating activities, is widely used among publicly held corporations.[3] Note that the December 31, 20Y7, cash balance reported on the statement of cash flows agrees with the amount reported for cash on the December 31, 20Y7, balance sheet shown in Exhibit 5.

The integration of TechUSA's financial statements is shown in Exhibit 7.

EXHIBIT 6

Statement of Cash Flows for Merchandising Business

TechUSA
Statement of Cash Flows
For the Year Ended December 31, 20Y7

Cash flows from operating activities:		
Net income		$ 75,400
Add:		
Depreciation expense—store equipment	$ 3,100	
Depreciation expense—office equipment	2,490	
Decrease in office supplies	120	
Decrease in prepaid insurance	350	
Increase in accounts payable	8,150	14,210
Deduct:		
Increase in accounts receivable	$(39,080)	
Increase in merchandise inventory	(2,450)	
Decrease in salaries payable	(360)	
Decrease in unearned rent	(600)	(42,490)
Net cash flows from operating activities		$ 47,120
Cash flows used for investing activities:		
Purchase of store equipment	$ (7,100)	
Purchase of office equipment	(5,570)	
Net cash flows from investing activities		(12,670)
Cash flows used for financing activities:		
Payment of note payable	$ (5,000)	
Payment of dividends	(18,000)	
Net cash flows from financing activities		(23,000)
Net increase in cash		$ 11,450
January 1, 20Y7, cash balance		41,500
December 31, 20Y7, cash balance		$ 52,950

3 The preparation of the statement of cash flows using the indirect method is further discussed and illustrated in the appendix to this chapter.

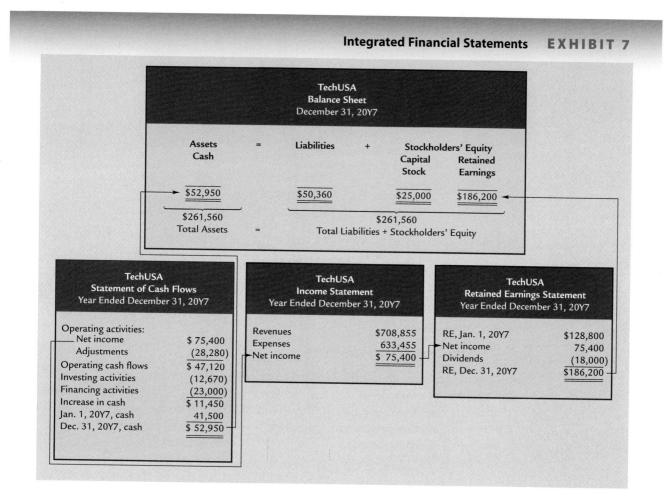

Integrated Financial Statements   **EXHIBIT 7**

Sales Transactions

Obj **3**
Describe the accounting for the sale of merchandise.

In the remainder of this chapter, transactions that affect the financial statements of a merchandising business are illustrated. These transactions affect the reporting of net sales, cost of merchandise sold, gross profit, and merchandise inventory.

Sales

A business may sell merchandise for cash. Cash sales are normally rung up (entered) on a cash register and recorded in the accounts by increasing cash and sales. Under the perpetual inventory system, the cost of merchandise sold and the reduction in merchandise inventory should also be recorded at the time of sale. In this way, the merchandise inventory account will indicate the amount of merchandise on hand (not sold). To illustrate, assume that on January 3, TechUSA sells merchandise for $1,800 that cost $1,200. The effect on the accounts and financial statements of these cash sales is shown at the top of the next page.

Sales made to customers using credit cards issued by banks, such as Master-Card or VISA, are treated as *cash sales*. The record of the sale is electronically sent to a clearinghouse for credit card transactions. The clearinghouse processes the sale by contacting the bank that issued the credit card. Within one or two days, the seller's bank account is increased by the amount of the sale.

Statement of Cash Flows	Balance Sheet				Income Statement
	Assets	= Liabilities	+ Stockholders' Equity		
	Cash +	Merchandise Inventory =		Retained Earnings	
Jan. 3.	1,800	−1,200		600	Jan. 3.

Statement of Cash Flows

Jan. 3. Operating   1,800

Income Statement

Jan. 3. Sales	1,800
Cost of merch. sold	−1,200
Net income	600

Retailers are charged service fees for credit card sales. The seller records these service fees as increases to an expense account and decreases to Cash.

A business can sell merchandise on account. The effect of sales on account is similar to that for cash sales except that Accounts Receivable is increased instead of Cash. When the customer pays the amount, Accounts Receivable is decreased and Cash is increased.

Sales Discounts

The terms of a sale are normally indicated on the **invoice** or bill that the seller sends to the buyer. An example of a sales invoice for TechUSA is shown in Exhibit 8.

The terms for when payments for merchandise are to be made, agreed on by the buyer and the seller, are called the **credit terms**. If payment is required on delivery, the terms are *cash* or *net cash*. Otherwise, the buyer is allowed an amount of time in which to pay, known as the **credit period**.

The credit period usually begins with the date of the sale as shown on the invoice. If payment is due within a stated number of days after the date of the invoice, such as 30 days, the terms are *net 30 days*. These terms may be written as *n/30*.[4] If payment is due by the end of the month in which the sale was made, the terms are written as *n/eom*.

EXHIBIT 8   Invoice

Invoice
106-8

TechUSA
5101 Washington Ave.
Cincinnati, OH 45227–5101

SOLD TO	CUSTOMER'S ORDER NO.	DATE
Alpha Technologies 1000 Matrix Blvd. San Jose, CA 95116–1000	412	May 29, 20Y7

DATE SHIPPED	HOW SHIPPED AND ROUTE	TERMS	INVOICE DATE
June 3, 20Y7	US Express Trucking Co.	2/10, n/30	June 3, 20Y7

FROM	F.O.B.		
Cincinnati	Cincinnati		

QUANTITY	DESCRIPTION	UNIT PRICE	AMOUNT
10	3COM Megahertz Wireless PC Card	150.00	1,500.00

4 The word *net* as used here does not have the usual meaning of a number after deductions have been subtracted, as in *net income*.

As a means of encouraging the buyer to pay before the end of the credit period, the seller may offer a discount. For example, a seller may offer a 2% discount if the buyer pays within 10 days of the invoice date. If the buyer does not take the discount, the total amount is due within 30 days. These terms are expressed as *2/10, n/30* and are read as *2% discount if paid within 10 days, net amount due within 30 days.* Using the information from the invoice in Exhibit 8, the credit terms of 2/10, n/30 are summarized below.

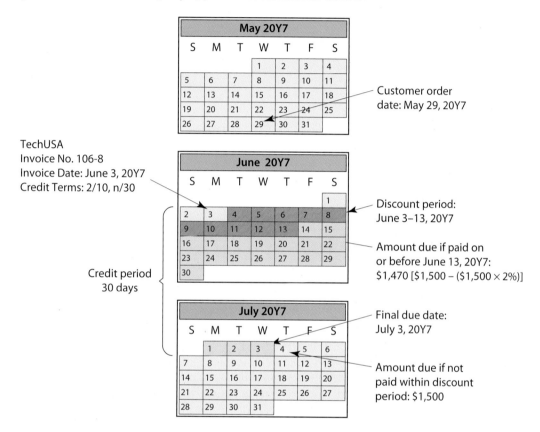

Discounts taken by the buyer for early payment are recorded as sales discounts by the seller. Since managers may want to know the amount of the sales discounts for a period, the seller normally records the sales discounts in a separate account. The sales discounts account is a *contra* (or *offsetting*) account to Sales. To illustrate, assume that cash is received within the discount period on June 13 from the credit sale of $1,500, shown on the invoice in Exhibit 8. The effect on the accounts and financial statements of the receipt of the cash is as follows:

Statement of Cash Flows	Balance Sheet				Income Statement
	Assets		= Liabilities +	Stockholders' Equity	
	Cash +	Accounts Receivable	=	Retained Earnings	
June 13.	1,470	−1,500		−30	*June 13.*

Statement of Cash Flows		Income Statement	
June 13. Operating	1,470	*June 13.* Sales discounts	−30

Sales Returns and Allowances

Merchandise sold may be returned to the seller (sales return). In addition, because of defects or for other reasons, the seller may reduce the initial price at which the goods were sold (sales allowance). If the return or allowance is for a sale on account, the seller usually issues the buyer a **credit memorandum**. This memorandum shows the amount of and the reason for the seller's credit to an account receivable. A credit memorandum issued by TechUSA is illustrated below.

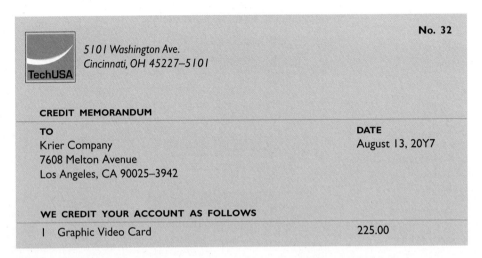

> **No. 32**
>
> **TechUSA** 5101 Washington Ave.
> Cincinnati, OH 45227–5101
>
> **CREDIT MEMORANDUM**
>
> **TO**   **DATE**
> Krier Company   August 13, 20Y7
> 7608 Melton Avenue
> Los Angeles, CA 90025–3942
>
> **WE CREDIT YOUR ACCOUNT AS FOLLOWS**
>
> 1   Graphic Video Card   225.00

Like sales discounts, sales returns and allowances reduce sales revenue. They also result in additional shipping and other expenses. Since managers often want to know the amount of returns and allowances for a period, the seller records sales returns and allowances in a separate account. Sales Returns and Allowances is a *contra* (or *offsetting*) account to Sales.

The seller increases Sales Returns and Allowances for the amount of the return or allowance. If the original sale was on account, the seller decreases Accounts Receivable. Since the merchandise inventory is kept up to date in a perpetual system, the seller adds the cost of the returned merchandise to the merchandise inventory account. The seller must also decrease the cost of returned merchandise to the cost of merchandise sold account, since this account was increased when the original sale was recorded. To illustrate, assume that the cost of the merchandise returned in the preceding credit memorandum was $140. The effect on the accounts and financial statements of the issuance of the credit memorandum and the receipt of the returned merchandise is as follows:

Statement of Cash Flows	Balance Sheet				Income Statement
	Assets		= Liabilities + Stockholders' Equity		
	Accounts Receivable +	Merchandise Inventory =		Retained Earnings	
Aug. 13.	−225	140		−85	Aug. 13.

Income Statement	
Aug. 13. Sales returns & allowances	−225
Cost of merch. sold	140
Net income	−85

What if the buyer pays for the merchsandise and the merchandise is later returned? In this case, the seller may issue a credit and apply it against other accounts receivable owed by the buyer, or the cash may be refunded. If the credit is applied against the buyer's other receivables, the seller records entries similar to those preceding. If cash is refunded for merchandise returned or for an allowance, the seller increases Sales Returns and Allowances and decreases Cash.

Purchase Transactions

Obj 4

Describe the accounting for the purchase of merchandise.

As indicated earlier in this chapter, most large retailers and many small merchandising businesses use computerized perpetual inventory systems. Under the perpetual inventory system, cash purchases of merchandise are recorded as follows:

Statement of Cash Flows	Balance Sheet			Income Statement
	Assets	**= Liabilities + Stockholders' Equity**		
	Cash +	Merchandise Inventory		
Sept. 3.	−2,510	2,510		

Statement of Cash Flows	
Sept. 3. Operating	−2,510

Purchases of merchandise on account are recorded as increases of Merchandise Inventory and Accounts Payable.

Purchases Discounts

Purchases discounts taken by the buyer for early payment of an invoice reduce the cost of the merchandise purchased. Under the perpetual inventory system, the buyer initially increases the merchandise inventory account for the amount of the invoice. When paying the invoice, the buyer decreases the merchandise inventory account for the amount of the discount. In this way, the merchandise inventory shows the *net* cost to the buyer. For example, the effects on the accounts and financial statements of paying the invoice shown in Exhibit 8 on June 13 within the discount period are as follows:

Statement of Cash Flows	Balance Sheet			Income Statement
	Assets	**= Liabilities + Stockholders' Equity**		
	Cash +	Merchandise Inventory	= Accounts Payable	
June 13.	−1,470	−30	−1,500	

Statement of Cash Flows	
June 13. Operating	−1,470

If the invoice shown in Exhibit 8 is not paid during the discount period, the payment is recorded as a decrease in Cash and Accounts Payable for $1,500.

Purchases Returns and Allowances

When merchandise is returned (purchase return) or a price adjustment is requested (purchase allowance), the buyer (debtor) usually sends the seller a letter or a debit memorandum. A **debit memorandum**, shown below, informs the seller of the amount the buyer proposes to decrease to the account payable due the seller. It also states the reasons for the return or the request for a price reduction.

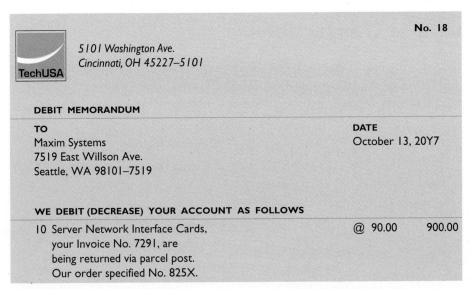

No. 18

TechUSA
5101 Washington Ave.
Cincinnati, OH 45227–5101

DEBIT MEMORANDUM

TO	**DATE**
Maxim Systems	October 13, 20Y7
7519 East Willson Ave.	
Seattle, WA 98101–7519	

WE DEBIT (DECREASE) YOUR ACCOUNT AS FOLLOWS

| 10 Server Network Interface Cards, your Invoice No. 7291, are being returned via parcel post. Our order specified No. 825X. | @ 90.00 | 900.00 |

The buyer may use a copy of the debit memorandum as the basis for recording the return or allowance or wait for approval from the seller (creditor). In either case, the buyer must decrease Accounts Payable and increase Merchandise Inventory. To illustrate, the effect on the accounts and financial statements of the return of the merchandise indicated in the preceding debit memorandum is shown below.

Statement of Cash Flows	Balance Sheet			Income Statement
	Assets	= Liabilities	+ Stockholders' Equity	
	Merchandise Inventory	=	Accounts Payable	
Oct. 7.	–900		–900	

Integrity, Objectivity, and Ethics in Business

THE CASE OF THE FRAUDULENT PRICE TAGS

One of the challenges for a retailer is policing its sales return policy. There are many ways in which customers can unethically or illegally abuse such policies. In one case, a couple was accused of attaching Marshall's store price tags to cheaper merchandise bought or obtained elsewhere. The couple then returned the cheaper goods and received the substantially higher refund amount. Company security officials discovered the fraud and had the couple arrested after they had allegedly bilked the company for over $1 million.

When a buyer returns merchandise or has been granted an allowance prior to paying the invoice, the amount of the debit memorandum is deducted from the invoice amount. The amount is deducted before the purchase discount is computed. For example, assume that on November 2, TechUSA purchases $5,000 of merchandise from Delta Data Link, subject to terms 2/10, n/30. On November 4, TechUSA returns $3,000 of the merchandise, and on November 12, TechUSA pays the original invoice less the return. TechUSA would pay Delta Data Link $1,960 as shown below.

Invoice...	$5,000
Less return	3,000
Amount due before discount	$2,000
Less discount ($2,000 × 2%)	40
Amount due within discount period	$1,960

The effect on the accounts and financial statements of paying the invoice on November 12 is as follows:

Statement of Cash Flows	Balance Sheet			Income Statement
	Assets	= Liabilities + Stockholders' Equity		
	Cash +	Merchandise Inventory =	Accounts Payable	
Nov. 12.	−1,960	−40	−2,000	

Statement of Cash Flows	
Nov. 12. Operating	−1,960

Freight and Sales Taxes

Obj 5
Describe the accounting for freight and sales taxes.

Merchandise businesses incur freight in selling and purchasing merchandise. In addition, a retailer must collect sales taxes in most states. In this section, the unique aspects of accounting for freight costs and sales taxes are discussed.

Freight

The terms of a sale should indicate when the ownership (title) of the merchandise passes to the buyer. This point determines which party, the buyer or the seller, must pay the transportation costs.[5]

The ownership of the merchandise may pass to the buyer when the seller delivers the merchandise to the freight carrier or transportation company. In this case, the terms are said to be **FOB (free on board) shipping point**. This term means that the buyer pays the freight costs from the shipping point (factory) to the final destination. Such costs are part of the buyer's total cost of purchasing inventory and should be added to the cost of the inventory by increasing Merchandise Inventory.

To illustrate, assume that on December 10, TechUSA buys merchandise from Magna Data on account, $900, terms FOB shipping point, and pays the freight

5 The passage of title also determines whether the buyer or seller must pay other costs, such as the cost of insurance, while the merchandise is in transit.

cost of $50. The effect on the accounts and financial statements of these transactions is as follows:

Statement of Cash Flows	Balance Sheet			Income Statement
	Assets	= Liabilities +	Stockholders' Equity	
	Cash +	Merchandise Inventory	= Accounts Payable	
Dec. 10.	−50	950	900	

Statement of Cash Flows	
Dec. 10. Operating	−50

The ownership of the merchandise may pass to the buyer when the buyer receives the merchandise. In this case, the terms are said to be **FOB (free on board) destination**. This term means that the seller delivers the merchandise to the buyer's final destination, free of freight charges to the buyer. The seller thus pays the freight costs to the final destination. The seller increases Delivery Expense, or Freight Out, which is reported on the seller's income statement as an expense.

Shipping terms, the passage of title, and whether the buyer or seller is to pay the transportation costs are summarized in Exhibit 9.

EXHIBIT 9
Freight Terms

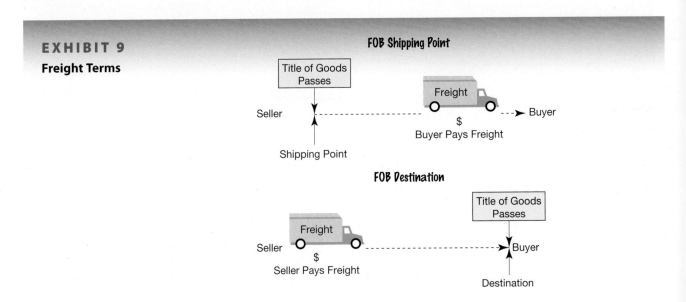

Sales Taxes

Almost all states and many other taxing units levy a tax on sales of merchandise.[6] The liability for the sales tax is incurred when the sale is made. At the time of a cash sale, the seller collects the sales tax. When a sale is made on account, the seller charges the buyer by increasing Accounts Receivable. The seller increases the sales account for the amount of the sale and increases Sales Tax Payable for the amount of the tax. Normally on a regular basis, the seller pays to the taxing

6 Businesses that purchase merchandise for resale to others are normally exempt from paying sales taxes on their purchases. Only final buyers of merchandise normally pay sales taxes.

unit the amount of the sales tax collected. The seller records such a payment by decreasing Sales Tax Payable and Cash.

Dual Nature of Merchandise Transactions

Obj 6

Illustrate the dual nature of merchandising transactions.

Each merchandising transaction affects a buyer and a seller. The following illustration shows how the same transactions would be recorded by both the seller and the buyer. In this example, the seller is Scully Company and the buyer is Burton Co.

On July 1, Scully Company sold merchandise on account to Burton Co., $7,500, terms FOB destination; 2/10, n/30. The cost of the merchandise sold was $4,500.

Scully Company (Seller)

Statement of Cash Flows	Balance Sheet			Income Statement
	Assets	= Liabilities + Stockholders' Equity		
	Accounts Receivable +	Merchandise Inventory =	Retained Earnings	
July 1.	7,500	−4,500	3,000	July 1.

Income Statement

July 1. Sales	7,500
Cost of merch. sold	−4,500
Net income	3,000

Burton Co. (Buyer)

Statement of Cash Flows	Balance Sheet		Income Statement
	Assets	= Liabilities + Stockholders' Equity	
	Merchandise Inventory	= Accounts Payable	
July 1.	7,500	7,500	

On July 5, Scully Company pays transportation charges of $300 for delivery of the merchandise sold on July 1 to Burton Co.

Scully Company (Seller)

Statement of Cash Flows	Balance Sheet		Income Statement
	Assets	= Liabilities + Stockholders' Equity	
	Cash	= Retained Earnings	
July 5.	−300	−300	July 5.

Statement of Cash Flows		Income Statement	
July 5. Operating	−300	July 5. Delivery exp.	−300

Burton Co. (Buyer) No effect on the accounts and financial statements.

On July 6, Scully Company issues a credit memorandum for $1,000 for merchandise returned by Burton Co. The cost of the merchandise returned was $600.

Scully Company (Seller)

Statement of Cash Flows	Balance Sheet					Income Statement
	Assets		= Liabilities + Stockholders' Equity			
	Accounts Receivable	+ Merchandise Inventory	=		Retained Earnings	
July 6.	−1,000	600			−400	July 6.

Income Statement	
July 6. Sales retns. & allow.	−1,000
Cost of merch. sold	600
Net income	−400

Burton Co. (Buyer)

Statement of Cash Flows	Balance Sheet			Income Statement
	Assets	= Liabilities + Stockholders' Equity		
	Merchandise Inventory	= Accounts Payable		
July 6.	−1,000	−1,000		

On July 11, Scully Company received payment from Burton Co. less discount.

Scully Company (Seller)

Statement of Cash Flows	Balance Sheet				Income Statement
	Assets		= Liabilities + Stockholders' Equity		
	Cash +	Accounts Receivable	=	Retained Earnings	
July 11.	6,370	−6,500		−130	July 11.

Statement of Cash Flows		Income Statement	
July 11. Operating	6,370	July 11. Sales discounts	−130

Burton Co. (Buyer)

Statement of Cash Flows	Balance Sheet			Income Statement
	Assets	= Liabilities + Stockholders' Equity		
	Cash + Merchandise Inventory	= Accounts Payable		
July 11.	−6,370 −130	−6,500		

Statement of Cash Flows

July 11. Operating   −6,370

Merchandise Shrinkage

Under the perpetual inventory system, the merchandise inventory account is continually updated for purchase and sales transactions. As a result, the balance of the merchandise inventory account is the amount of merchandise available for sale at that point in time. However, retailers normally experience some loss of inventory due to shoplifting, employee theft, or errors. Thus, the physical inventory on hand at the end of the accounting period is usually less than the balance of Merchandise Inventory. This difference is called **inventory shrinkage** or **inventory shortage**.

To illustrate, TechUSA's inventory records indicate the following on December 31, 20Y7:

Obj 7

Describe the accounting for merchandise shrinkage.

	Dec. 31, 20Y7
Account balance of Merchandise Inventory	$63,950
Physical merchandise inventory on hand	62,150
Inventory shrinkage	$ 1,800

The effect of the shrinkage on the accounts and financial statements is as follows.

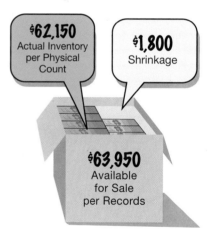

Statement of Cash Flows	Balance Sheet			Income Statement
	Assets	= Liabilities + Stockholders' Equity		
	Merchandise Inventory	=	Retained Earnings	
Dec. 31.	−1,800		−1,800	Dec. 31.

Income Statement

Dec. 31. Cost of merch. sold   −1,800

After the shrinkage is recorded, the balance of Merchandise Inventory agrees with the physical inventory on hand at the end of the period. Since inventory shrinkage cannot be totally eliminated, it is considered a normal cost of operations and is included in the cost of merchandise sold. If, however, the amount of the shrinkage is unusually large, it may be disclosed separately on the income statement. In such cases, the shrinkage may be recorded in a separate account, such as Loss from Merchandise Inventory Shrinkage.

Obj | 8

Describe and illustrate the gross profit percent, average markup percent, and ratio of sales to assets in assessing a company's financial performance.

Financial Analysis: Gross Profit Percent, Average Markup Percent, and Ratio of Sales to Assets

The gross profit percent, average markup percent, and ratio of sales to assets are useful in analyzing and assessing a company's financial performance. These measures are especially useful in assessing the operations and performance of merchandising businesses.

Gross Profit Percent and Average Markup Percent

Gross profit is defined as sales less cost of merchandise sold. The **gross profit percent** is computed as shown below.

$$\text{Gross Profit Percent} = \frac{\text{Gross Profit}}{\text{Net Sales}}$$

The gross profit percent is a measure of profitability before other operating expenses are deducted. The gross profit can also be used to compute the average markup percent on the cost of merchandise sold. The **average markup percent** is computed as shown below.[7]

$$\text{Average Markup Percent} = \frac{\text{Gross Profit}}{\text{Cost of Merchandise Sold}}$$

To illustrate, data (in millions) for Walgreen Co. are used. The following data were taken from two recent years financial statements of Walgreen.

	Year 2	Year 1
Net sales	$71,633	$72,184
Cost of merchandise sold	51,291	51,692
Gross profit	$20,342	$20,492
Average total assets	$30,458	$26,865

The gross profit percent and average markup percent, rounded to one decimal place, for Years 1 and 2 are shown below.

	Year 2	Year 1
Gross profit percent:		
($20,342 ÷ $71,633)	28.4%	
($20,492 ÷ $72,184)		28.4%
Average markup percent:		
($20,342 ÷ $51,291)	39.7%	
($20,492 ÷ $51,692)		39.6%

As shown above, the gross profit percent and average markup percent did not change significantly from Year 1 to Year 2. At the end of this chapter,

---

7 The markup percent can also be computed as follows: Markup percent = Gross profit percent × (Net sales ÷ Cost of merchandise sold).

FA 4-1 compares Walgreen's gross profit percent and markup percent to those of its competitor, CVS Caremark Corporation.

Ratio of Sales to Assets

The **ratio of sales to assets** is useful in assessing how efficiently a company generates sales from its assets. The ratio of sales to assets is computed as shown below.

$$\text{Ratio of Sales to Assets} = \frac{\text{Net Sales}}{\text{Average Total Assets}}$$

Any significant non operating assets such as investments are normally excluded from total assets in computing the ratio of sales to assets. This is because net sales are generated by operating assets. In most cases, however, non operating assets are insignificant. Thus, total assets are used in the computation.

To illustrate, the preceding data for Walgreen Co. are used. The ratio of sales to assets (rounded to two decimal places) for Years 1 and 2 is shown below.

	Year 2	Year 1
Net sales	$71,633	$72,184
Average total assets	30,458	26,865
Ratio of sales to assets:		
($71,633 ÷ $30,458)	2.35	
($72,184 ÷ $26,865)		2.69

The ratio of sales to assets indicates that Walgreen was slightly less efficient in using its assets to generate sales in Year 2. In Year 1, Walgreen generated $2.69 of sales per asset dollar, while in Year 2 it generated only $2.35 of sales per asset dollar. The causes of this decline, which could be due to a depressed economy, should be investigated or corrected if possible.

Appendix

Statement of Cash Flows: The Indirect Method

TechUSA's statement of cash flows for the year ended December 31, 20Y7, is shown in Exhibit 6, on page 140. The operating activities section of this statement was prepared using a method known as the indirect method. This method is used by over 90% of publicly held companies.

The use of the indirect method only affects net cash flows from operating activities. The other method of preparing the net cash flows from operating activities section is called the *direct method*. The direct method analyzes each transaction and its effect on cash flows. The direct method was used in preparing the statement of cash flows in Chapters 2 and 3. In contrast, the indirect method analyzes only the changes in accounts.

A major reason that the indirect method is so popular is that it is normally less costly to use. However, regardless of whether the indirect or direct method is used, the reporting of net cash flows from investing and financing activities is not affected. In this appendix, the use of the indirect method of preparing the statement of cash flows is illustrated.

The indirect method reconciles net income with net cash flows from operating activities. Net income is adjusted for the effects of accruals and deferrals that affected the net income but did not result in the receipt or payment of cash. The resulting amount is the net cash flows from operating activities.

The indirect method converts net income determined under the accrual basis of accounting to what it would have been under the cash basis of accounting. In other words, net cash flows from operating activities is equivalent to net income using the cash basis of accounting.

The typical adjustments to convert net income to net cash flows from operating activities, using the indirect method, are shown in Exhibit 10.

EXHIBIT 10
Indirect Method

	Increase (Decrease)
Net income (loss)	$ XXX
Depreciation of fixed assets	XXX
Changes in current operating assets and liabilities:	
Increases in noncash current operating assets	(XXX)
Decreases in noncash current operating assets	XXX
Increases in current operating liabilities	XXX
Decreases in current operating liabilities	(XXX)
Net cash flow from operating activities	$ XXX

Subtract
Increases in accounts receivable
Increases in inventory
Increases in prepaid expenses
Decreases in accounts payable
Decreases in accrued expenses payable

Add
Decreases in accounts receivable
Decreases in inventory
Decreases in prepaid expenses
Increases in accounts payable
Increases in accrued expenses payable

You should note that, except for depreciation, the adjustments in Exhibit 10 are for changes in the current assets and the current liabilities. This is because changes in the current assets and the current liabilities are related to operations and thus net income. For example, changes in inventories are related to sales, while changes in accounts payable are related to expenses.

Depreciation expense is deducted in arriving at net income but does not involve any cash payments. Thus, depreciation expense is added to net income under the indirect method. Likewise, assume that accounts receivable increases during the period by $10,000. This increase is included in the period's revenue and thus increases net income. However, cash was not collected. Thus, an increase in accounts receivable must be deducted from net income under the indirect method.

Cash Flows from Operating Activities

To prepare the operating activities section for TechUSA's statement of cash flows, depreciation and the changes in the current assets and the liabilities during the year must be determined. This information is determined using comparative balance sheets.

Comparative balance sheets for TechUSA as of December 31, 20Y7 and 20Y6 and related changes are shown in Exhibit 11. Based on Exhibit 11, the net cash flows from operating activities is shown below.

Net income..		$ 75,400
Depreciation expense—store equipment	$ 3,100	
Depreciation expense—office equipment................................	2,490	5,590
Changes in current operating assets and liabilities:		
Increase in accounts receivable.......................................	$(39,080)	
Increase in merchandise inventory....................................	(2,450)	
Decrease in office supplies	120	
Decrease in prepaid insurance.......................................	350	
Increase in accounts payable	8,150	
Decrease in salaries payable	(360)	
Decrease in unearned rent	(600)	(33,870)
Net cash flows from operating activities................................		$ 47,120

EXHIBIT 11

TechUSA Comparative Balance Sheets

TechUSA
Balance Sheet

	December 31, 20Y7	December 31, 20Y6	Changes Increase (Decrease)
Assets			
Current assets:			
Cash	$ 52,950	$ 41,500	$11,450
Accounts receivable........................	91,080	52,000	39,080
Merchandise inventory.....................	62,150	59,700	2,450
Office supplies.............................	480	600	(120)
Prepaid insurance..........................	2,650	3,000	(350)
Total current assets	$209,310	$156,800	$52,510
Property, plant, and equipment:			
Land	$ 20,000	$ 20,000	$ 0
Store equipment...........................	27,100	20,000	7,100
Accumulated depreciation—store equipment	(5,700)	(2,600)	(3,100)
Office equipment	15,570	10,000	5,570
Accumulated depreciation—office equipment	(4,720)	(2,230)	(2,490)
Total property, plant, and equipment........	$ 52,250	$ 45,170	$ 7,080
Total assets	$261,560	$201,970	$59,590
Liabilities			
Current liabilities:			
Accounts payable..........................	$ 22,420	$ 14,270	$ 8,150
Notes payable (current portion).............	5,000	5,000	0
Salaries payable	1,140	1,500	(360)
Unearned rent............................	1,800	2,400	(600)
Total current liabilities......................	$ 30,360	$ 23,170	$ 7,190
Long-term liabilities:			
Notes payable (final payment due in ten years)	20,000	25,000	(5,000)
Total liabilities	$ 50,360	$ 48,170	$ 2,190
Stockholders' Equity			
Capital stock....................................	$ 25,000	$ 25,000	$ 0
Retained earnings...............................	186,200	128,800	57,400
Total stockholders' equity.......................	$211,200	$153,800	$57,400
Total liabilities and stockholders' equity..........	$261,560	$201,970	$59,590

The depreciation expense of $3,100 for store equipment is determined from the increase in the accumulated depreciation for store equipment. Likewise, the depreciation expense of $2,490 for office equipment is determined from the increase in the accumulated depreciation for office equipment. The changes in the current assets and the current liabilities are also taken from Exhibit 11.

Cash Flows Used for Investing Activities

The cash flows for investing activities section can also be prepared by analyzing the changes in the accounts shown in Exhibit 11. For TechUSA, the cash flows used for investing activities is composed of two items. First, additional store equipment of $7,100 was purchased, as shown by the increase in the store equipment. Likewise, additional office equipment of $5,570 was purchased. Thus, cash of $12,670 was used for investing activities, as shown in Exhibit 6, on page 140.

Cash Flows Used for Financing Activities

The cash flows for financing activities can also be determined from Exhibit 11. For TechUSA, the cash flows used for financing activities is composed of two items. First, dividends of $18,000 are reported on the retained earnings statement shown in Exhibit 4, on page 139. Since no dividends payable appears on the balance sheets, cash dividends of $18,000 must have been paid during the year. In addition, notes payable decreased by $5,000 during the year, so cash must have been used in paying off $5,000 of the notes. Thus, cash of $23,000 was used for financing activities, as shown in Exhibit 6.

Key Points

1. Distinguish the activities and financial statements of a service business from those of a merchandising business.

The revenue activities of a service enterprise involve providing services to customers. In contrast, the revenue activities of a merchandising business involve the buying and selling of merchandise.

2. Describe and illustrate the financial statements of a merchandising business.

The multiple-step income statement of a merchandiser reports sales, sales returns and allowances, sales discounts, and net sales. The cost of the merchandise sold is subtracted from net sales to determine the gross profit. The cost of merchandise sold is determined by using either the periodic or perpetual inventory methods. Operating income is determined by subtracting operating expenses from gross profit. Operating expenses are normally classified as selling or administrative expenses. Net income is determined by subtracting income taxes and other expense and adding other income. The income statement may also be reported in a single-step form. The retained earnings statement and the statement of cash flows are similar to those for a service business. The balance sheet reports merchandise inventory at the end of the period as a current asset.

3. Describe the accounting for the sale of merchandise.

Sales of merchandise for cash or on account are recorded by increasing Sales. The cost of merchandise sold and the reduction in merchandise inventory are also recorded for the sale. For sales of merchandise on account, the credit terms can allow sales discounts for early payment. Such discounts are recorded by the seller as an increase in Sales Discounts. Sales discounts are reported as a deduction from the amount initially recorded in Sales. Likewise, when merchandise is returned or a price adjustment is granted, the seller increases Sales Returns and Allowances.

Under the perpetual inventory system, the cost of merchandise sold and the reduction of merchandise inventory on hand are recorded at the time of sale. In this way, the merchandise inventory account indicates the amount of merchandise on hand at all times. Likewise, any returned merchandise is recorded in the merchandise inventory account with a related reduction in the cost of merchandise sold.

4. Describe the accounting for the purchase of merchandise.

Purchases of merchandise for cash or on account are recorded by increasing Merchandise Inventory. For purchases of merchandise on account, the credit terms can allow cash discounts for early payment. Such purchases discounts are viewed as a reduction in the cost of the merchandise purchased. When merchandise is returned or a price adjustment is granted, the buyer decreases Merchandise Inventory.

5. Describe the accounting for freight and sales taxes.

When merchandise is shipped FOB shipping point, the buyer pays the freight and increases Merchandise Inventory. When merchandise is shipped FOB destination, the seller pays the freight and increases Delivery Expense or Freight Out.

The liability for sales tax is incurred when the sale is made and is recorded by the seller as an increase in the sales tax payable account. When the amount of the sales tax is paid to the taxing unit, Sales Tax Payable and Cash are decreased.

6. Illustrate the dual nature of merchandising transactions.

Each merchandising transaction affects a buyer and a seller. The illustration in this chapter shows how the same transactions would be recorded by both.

7. Describe the accounting for merchandise shrinkage.

The physical inventory taken at the end of the accounting period could differ from the amount of inventory shown in the inventory records. The difference, called *inventory shrinkage*, requires an adjusting entry increasing Cost of Merchandise Sold and decreasing Merchandise Inventory. After this entry has been recorded, the adjusted Merchandise Inventory (book inventory) in the accounting records agrees with the actual physical inventory at the end of the period.

8. Describe and illustrate the gross profit percent, average markup percent, and ratio of sales to assets in assessing a company's financial performance.

The gross profit percent, average markup percent, and ratio of sales to assets are useful in analyzing a company's financial performance. The gross profit percent is computed as gross profit divided by net sales. Gross profit can also be used to compute the average markup percent, which is gross profit divided by cost of merchandise sold. The ratio of sales to assets is computed as net sales divided by average total assets.

Key Terms

Account form (138)
Administrative expenses (137)
Average markup percent (152)
Cost of merchandise purchased (136)
Cost of merchandise sold (133)
Credit memorandum (144)
Credit period (142)
Credit terms (142)
Debit memorandum (146)
FOB (free on board) destination (148)

FOB (free on board) shipping point (147)
Freight in (136)
General expenses (137)
Gross profit (133)
Gross profit percent (152)
Income from operations (137)
Indirect method (140)
Inventory shortage (151)
Inventory shrinkage (151)
Invoice (142)
Merchandise available for sale (136)

Merchandise inventory (133)
Multiple-step income statement (133)
Net purchases (135)
Net sales (135)
Operating income (137)
Other expense (137)
Other income (137)
Periodic inventory system (136)
Perpetual inventory system (137)
Purchases discounts (135)

Purchases returns and allowances (135)
Ratio of sales to assets (153)
Report form (138)
Sales (134)
Sales discounts (135)
Sales returns and allowances (135)
Selling expenses (137)
Single-step income statement (138)

Illustrative Problem

The following selected accounts and their current balances appear in the ledger of Sciatic Co. for the fiscal year ended July 31, 20Y5:

Cash	$123,000	Sales	$1,028,000
Accounts receivable	96,800	Sales returns and allowances	18,480
Merchandise inventory	140,000	Sales discounts	17,520
Office supplies	4,480	Cost of merchandise sold	620,000
Prepaid insurance	2,720	Sales salaries expense	138,560
Office equipment	68,000	Advertising expense	35,040
Accumulated depreciation—		Depreciation expense—	
office equipment	10,240	store equipment	5,120
Store equipment	122,400	Miscellaneous selling expense	1,280
Accumulated depreciation—		Office salaries expense	67,320
store equipment	27,360	Rent expense	25,080
Accounts payable	44,480	Depreciation expense—	
Salaries payable	1,920	office equipment	10,160
Note payable (final		Insurance expense	3,120
payment due in seven years)	44,800	Office supplies expense	1,040
Capital stock	75,000	Miscellaneous administrative	
Retained earnings	301,600	expense	1,280
Dividends	28,000	Interest expense	4,000

Instructions

1. Prepare a single-step income statement.
2. Prepare a multiple-step income statement.
3. Prepare a retained earnings statement.
4. Prepare a report form of balance sheet, assuming that the current portion of the note payable is $6,000.

Solution

1.

SCIATIC CO.
Income Statement
For the Year Ended July 31, 20Y5

Revenues:		
Net sales..		$992,000
Expenses:		
Cost of merchandise sold	$620,000	
Selling expenses	180,000	
Administrative expenses................................	108,000	
Interest expense	4,000	
Total expenses		912,000
Net income		$ 80,000

2.

SCIATIC CO.
Income Statement
For the Year Ended July 31, 20Y5

Revenue from sales:			
Sales		$1,028,000	
Less: Sales returns and allowances	$ 18,480		
Sales discounts	17,520	36,000	
Net sales			$992,000
Cost of merchandise sold			620,000
Gross profit			$372,000
Operating expenses:			
Selling expenses:			
Sales salaries expense	$138,560		
Advertising expense	35,040		
Depreciation expense—store equipment	5,120		
Miscellaneous selling expense	1,280		
Total selling expenses		$ 180,000	
Administrative expenses:			
Office salaries expense	$ 67,320		
Rent expense	25,080		
Depreciation expense—office equipment	10,160		
Insurance expense	3,120		
Office supplies expense	1,040		
Miscellaneous administrative expense	1,280		
Total administrative expenses		108,000	
Total operating expenses			288,000
Income from operations			$ 84,000
Other expense:			
Interest expense			4,000
Net income			$ 80,000

3.

SCIATIC CO.
Retained Earnings Statement
For the Year Ended July 31, 20Y5

Retained earnings, August 1, 20Y4		$301,600
Net income for the year	$80,000	
Less dividends	28,000	
Increase in retained earnings		52,000
Retained earnings, July 31, 20Y5		$353,600

4.

SCIATIC CO.
Balance Sheet
July 31, 20Y5

Assets

Current assets:

Cash		$123,000
Accounts receivable		96,800
Merchandise inventory		140,000
Office supplies		4,480
Prepaid insurance		2,720
Total current assets		$367,000

Property, plant, and equipment:

Office equipment	$ 68,000		
Less accumulated depreciation	10,240	$ 57,760	
Store equipment	$122,400		
Less accumulated depreciation	27,360	95,040	
Total property, plant, and equipment			152,800
Total assets			$519,800

Liabilities

Current liabilities:

Accounts payable	$ 44,480	
Note payable (current portion)	6,000	
Salaries payable	1,920	
Total current liabilities		$ 52,400

Long-term liabilities:

Note payable (final payment due in seven years)	38,800
Total liabilities	$ 91,200

Stockholders' Equity

Capital stock	$ 75,000	
Retained earnings	353,600	
Total stockholders' equity		428,600
Total liabilities and stockholders' equity		$519,800

Self-Examination Questions *(Answers appear at the end of chapter)*

1. If merchandise purchased on account is returned, the buyer can inform the seller of the details by issuing:
   A. a debit memorandum
   B. a credit memorandum
   C. an invoice
   D. a bill

2. If merchandise is sold on account to a customer for $1,000, terms FOB shipping point, 1/10, n/30, and the seller prepays $50 in freight, the amount of the discount for early payment would be:
   A. $0
   B. $5.00
   C. $10.00
   D. $10.50

3. The income statement in which the total of all expenses is deducted from the total of all revenues is termed:
   A. multiple-step form
   B. single-step form
   C. account form
   D. report form

4. On a multiple-step income statement, the excess of net sales over the cost of merchandise sold is called:
   A. operating income
   B. income from operations
   C. gross profit
   D. net income

texam!

5. As of December 31, 20Y4, Ames Corporation's physical inventory was $275,000 and its book inventory was $290,000. The effect of the inventory shrinkage on the accounts is:

A. to increase Cost of Merchandise Sold and Inventory by $15,000.

B. to increase Cost of Merchandise Sold and decrease Inventory by $15,000.

C. to decrease Cost of Merchandise Sold and increase Inventory by $15,000.

D. to decrease Cost of Merchandise Sold and Inventory by $15,000.

Class Discussion Questions

1. What distinguishes a merchandising business from a service business?

2. Can a business earn a gross profit but incur a net loss? Explain.

3. In computing the cost of merchandise sold, does each of the following items increase or decrease that cost? (a) freight, (b) beginning merchandise inventory, (c) purchases discounts, (d) ending merchandise inventory.

4. Describe how the periodic method differs from the perpetual method of accounting for merchandise inventory.

5. Differentiate between the multiple and single-step forms of the income statement.

6. What are the major advantages and disadvantages of the single-step form of income statement compared to the multiple-step statement?

7. What type of revenue is reported in the "Other income" section of the multiple-step income statement?

8. How are sales to customers using MasterCard and VISA recorded?

9. What is the meaning of (a) 2/10, n/30; (b) n/90; (c) n/eom?

10. What is the nature of (a) a credit memorandum issued by the seller of merchandise and (b) a debit memorandum issued by the buyer of merchandise?

11. Who bears the freight when the terms of sale are (a) FOB shipping point or (b) FOB destination?

12. When you purchase a new car, the "sticker price" includes a "destination" charge. Are you purchasing the car FOB shipping point or FOB destination? Explain.

13. Office Outfitters Inc., which uses a perpetual inventory system, experienced a normal inventory shrinkage of $3,750. What accounts would be increased and decreased to record the adjustment for the inventory shrinkage at the end of the accounting period?

14. Assume that Office Outfitters Inc. in Question 13 experienced an abnormal inventory shrinkage of $56,900. Office Outfitters Inc. has decided to record the abnormal inventory shrinkage so that it would be separately disclosed on the income statement. What account would be increased for the abnormal inventory shrinkage?

Exercises

E4-1 Determining gross profit

Obj 1

During the current year, merchandise is sold for $3,750,000. The cost of the merchandise sold is $2,550,000.

a. What is the amount of the gross profit?

b. Compute the gross profit percentage (gross profit divided by sales).

c. Will the income statement necessarily report a net income? Explain.

E4-2 Determining cost of merchandise sold

Obj 1

For a recent year, Target Corporation reported revenue of $69,865 million. Its gross profit was $22,005 million. What was the amount of Target's cost of merchandise sold?

Obj 2

E4-3   Identify items missing in determining cost of merchandise sold

For (a) through (d), identify the items designated by "X" and "Y."

a. Purchases − (X + Y) = Net purchases.

b. Net purchases + X = Cost of merchandise purchased.

c. Merchandise inventory (beginning) + Cost of merchandise purchased = X.

d. Merchandise available for sale − X = Cost of merchandise sold.

Obj 2

✔ a. Cost of merchandise sold, $1,310,000

E4-4   Cost of merchandise sold and related items

The following data were extracted from the accounting records of Catz Company for the year ended April 30, 20Y2:

Merchandise inventory, May 1, 20Y1	$ 175,000
Merchandise inventory, April 30, 20Y2	240,000
Purchases	1,400,000
Purchases returns and allowances	20,000
Purchases discounts	18,000
Sales	2,250,000
Freight in	13,000

a. Prepare the cost of merchandise sold section of the income statement for the year ended April 30, 20Y2, using the periodic inventory system.

b. Determine the gross profit to be reported on the income statement for the year ended April 30, 20Y2.

Obj 2

✔ Correct cost of merchandise sold, $840,000

E4-5   Cost of merchandise sold

Identify the errors in the following schedule of cost of merchandise sold for the current year ended May 31, 20Y9:

Cost of merchandise sold:			
Merchandise inventory, May 31, 20Y9			$ 155,000
Purchases		$875,000	
Plus: Purchases returns and allowances	$12,000		
Purchases discounts	8,000	20,000	
Gross purchases		$895,000	
Less freight in		15,000	
Cost of merchandise purchased			880,000
Merchandise available for sale			$1,035,000
Less merchandise inventory, June 1, 20Y8			125,000
Cost of merchandise sold			$ 910,000

Obj 2

E4-6   Income statement for merchandiser

For the fiscal year, sales were $12,140,000, sales discounts were $250,000, sales returns and allowances were $80,000, and the cost of merchandise sold was $7,000,000.

a. What was the amount of net sales?

b. What was the amount of gross profit?

E4-7 Income statement for merchandiser

Obj **2**

The following expenses were incurred by a merchandising business during the year. In which expense section of the income statement should each be reported: (a) selling, (b) administrative, or (c) other?

1. Advertising expense
2. Depreciation expense on store equipment
3. Insurance expense on office equipment
4. Interest expense on notes payable
5. Rent expense on office building
6. Salaries of office personnel
7. Salary of sales manager
8. Sales supplies used

E4-8 Single-step income statement

Obj **2**

✔ Net income:
$3,100,000

Summary operating data for Eco-Windows Company during the current year ended June 30, 20Y6, are as follows: cost of merchandise sold, $3,800,000; administrative expenses, $1,200,000; interest expense, $100,000; rent revenue, $200,000; net sales, $9,300,000; and selling expenses, $1,300,000. Prepare a single-step income statement.

E4-9 Multiple-step income statement

Obj **2**

✔ a. Net income:
$500,000

On October 31, 20Y5, the balances of the accounts appearing in the ledger of Quality Interiors Company, a furniture wholesaler, are as follows:

Administrative Expenses	$ 600,000	Office Supplies	$ 5,000
Building	2,000,000	Retained Earnings	903,000
Capital Stock	300,000	Salaries Payable	12,000
Cash	175,000	Sales	5,000,000
Cost of Merchandise Sold	2,500,000	Sales Discounts	400,000
Dividends	20,000	Sales Returns and Allowances	100,000
Interest Expense	50,000	Selling Expenses	850,000
Merchandise Inventory	400,000	Store Supplies	15,000
Notes Payable	900,000		

a. Prepare a multiple-step income statement for the year ended October 31, 20Y5.

b. Compare the major advantages and disadvantages of the multiple-step and single-step forms of income statements.

E4-10 Determining amounts for items omitted from income statement

Obj **2**

✔ a $40,000
✔ h. $900,000

Two items are omitted in each of the following four lists of income statement data. Determine the amounts of the missing items, identifying them by letter.

Sales	$360,000	$1,200,000	$980,000	$ (g)
Sales returns and allowances	(a)	250,000	(e)	400,000
Sales discounts	30,000	200,000	35,000	300,000
Net sales	290,000	(c)	870,000	(h)
Cost of merchandise sold	(b)	350,000	(f)	400,000
Gross profit	115,000	(d)	370,000	500,000

E4-11   Multiple-step income statement

Identify the errors in the following income statement and prepare a corrected income statement:

CARLSBAD COMPANY
Income Statement
For the Year Ended February 28, 20Y9

Revenue from sales:			
Sales..		$4,400,000	
Add: Sales returns and allowances	$120,000		
Sales discounts................................	60,000	180,000	
Gross sales.......................................			$4,580,000
Cost of merchandise sold			2,650,000
Income from operations............................			$1,930,000
Expenses:			
Selling expenses		$ 800,000	
Administrative expenses...........................		600,000	
Delivery expense......................................		50,000	
Total expenses			1,450,000
Other expense:			$ 480,000
Interest revenue....................................			40,000
Gross profit			$ 440,000

E4-12   Sales-related transactions, including the use of credit cards

Illustrate the effects on the accounts and financial statements of recording the following transactions:

a. Sold merchandise for cash, $62,500. The cost of the merchandise sold was $30,000.

b. Sold merchandise on account, $27,800. The cost of the merchandise sold was $16,000.

c. Sold merchandise to customers who used MasterCard and VISA, $287,500. The cost of the merchandise sold was $170,000.

E4-13   Sales returns and allowances

During the year, sales returns and allowances totaled $90,000. The cost of the merchandise returned was $54,000. The accountant recorded all the returns and allowances by decreasing the sales account and decreasing Cost of Merchandise Sold for $90,000.

Was the accountant's method of recording returns acceptable? Explain. In your explanation, include the advantages of using a sales returns and allowances account.

E4-14   Sales-related transactions

After the amount due on a sale of $40,000, terms 2/10, n/eom, is received from a customer within the discount period, the seller consents to the return of the entire shipment. The cost of the merchandise returned was $24,000. (a) What is the amount of the refund owed to the customer? (b) Illustrate the effects on the accounts and financial statements of the return and the refund.

E4-15   Sales-related transactions

Merchandise is sold on account to a customer for $12,500, terms FOB shipping point, 1/10, n/30. The seller paid the freight of $250. Determine the following: (a) amount of the sale, (b) amount debited to Accounts Receivable, (c) amount of the discount for early payment, and (d) amount due within the discount period.

E4-16 Purchase-related transaction

Obj 4

Top Notch Company purchased merchandise on account from a supplier for $13,500, terms 2/10, n/30. Top Notch Company returned $4,000 of the merchandise before payment was made and received full credit.

a. If Top Notch Company pays the invoice within the discount period, what is the amount of cash required for the payment?

b. Under a perpetual inventory system, what account is decreased by Top Notch Company to record the return?

E4-17 Purchase-related transactions

Obj 4

A retailer is considering the purchase of 100 units of a specific item from either of two suppliers. Their offers are as follows:

A: $390 a unit, total of $39,000, 1/10, n/30, plus freight of $750.

B: $400 a unit, total of $40,000, 2/10, n/30, no charge for freight.

Which of the two offers, A or B, yields the lower price?

E4-18 Purchase-related transactions

Obj 4

✔ c. Cash, decreased $101,920

Milan Co., a women's clothing store, purchased $120,000 of merchandise from a supplier on account, terms FOB destination, 2/10, n/30. Milan Co. returned $16,000 of the merchandise, receiving a credit memorandum, and then paid the amount due within the discount period. Illustrate the effects on the accounts and financial statements of Milan Co. to record (a) the purchase, (b) the merchandise return, and (c) the payment.

E4-19 Purchase-related transactions

Obj 4

✔ e. Cash, increased $14,200

Illustrate the effects on the accounts and financial statements of the following related transactions of CT Diagnostic Company:

a. Purchased $560,000 of merchandise from Schultz Co. on account, terms 2/10, n/30.

b. Paid the amount owed on the invoice within the discount period.

c. Discovered that $40,000 of the merchandise was defective and returned items, receiving credit.

d. Purchased $25,000 of merchandise from Schultz Co. on account, terms n/30.

e. Received a check for the balance owed from the return in (c), after deducting for the purchase in (d).

E4-20 Determining amounts to be paid on invoices

Obj 5

✔ a. $7,227

Determine the amount to be paid in full settlement of each of the following invoices, assuming that credit for returns and allowances was received prior to payment and that all invoices were paid within the discount period.

	Merchandise	Freight Paid by Seller		Returns and Allowances
a.	$ 8,250	—	FOB shipping point, 1/10, n/30	$ 950
b.	2,900	$125	FOB shipping point, 2/10, n/30	400
c.	15,000	600	FOB destination, n/30	800
d.	10,000	400	FOB shipping point, 2/10, n/30	1,200
e.	3,850	175	FOB destination, 2/10, n/30	—

E4-21   Sales tax

A sale of merchandise on account for $6,400 is subject to a 7% sales tax. (a) Should the sales tax be recorded at the time of sale or when payment is received? (b) What is the amount of the sale? (c) What is the amount of the increase to Accounts Receivable? (d) What is the title of the account in which the $448 ($6,400 × 7%) is recorded?

E4-22   Sales tax transactions

Illustrate the effects on the accounts and financial statements of recording the following selected transactions:

a. Sold $11,250 of merchandise on account, subject to a sales tax of 6%. The cost of the merchandise sold was $6,750.

b. Paid $63,120 to the state sales tax department for taxes collected.

E4-23   Sales-related transactions

Steritech Co., a furniture wholesaler, sells merchandise to Butler Co. on account, $86,000, terms 2/10, n/30. The cost of the merchandise sold is $51,600. Steritech Co. issues a credit memorandum for $9,000 for merchandise returned and subsequently receives the amount due within the discount period. The cost of the merchandise returned is $5,000. Illustrate the effects on the accounts and financial statements of Steritech Co. for (a) the sale, including the cost of the merchandise sold, (b) the credit memorandum, including the cost of the returned merchandise, and (c) the receipt of the check for the amount due from Butler Co.

E4-24   Purchase-related transactions

Based on the data presented in Exercise 4-23, illustrate the effects on the accounts and financial statements of Butler Co. for (a) the purchase, (b) the return of the merchandise for credit, and (c) the payment of the invoice within the discount period.

E4-25   Adjusting entry for merchandise inventory shrinkage

Intrax Inc.'s perpetual inventory records indicate that $815,400 of merchandise should be on hand on December 31, 20Y4. The physical inventory indicates that $798,300 of merchandise is actually on hand. Illustrate the effects on the accounts and financial statements of the inventory shrinkage for Intrax Inc. for the year ended December 31, 20Y4.

Problems

P4-1   Multiple-step income statement and report form of balance sheet

The following selected accounts and their current balances appear in the ledger of Aqua Co. for the fiscal year ended June 30, 20Y8:

Obj 2

✔ 1. Net income,
$775,000

Cash	$ 83,500	Sales	$3,625,000
Accounts Receivable	150,000	Sales Returns and Allowances	37,800
Merchandise Inventory	380,000	Sales Discounts	20,200
Office Supplies	15,000	Cost of Merchandise Sold	2,175,000
Prepaid Insurance	12,000	Sales Salaries Expense	388,800
Office Equipment	115,200	Advertising Expense	45,900
Accumulated Depreciation—		Depreciation Expense—	
Office Equipment	49,500	Store Equipment	8,300
Store Equipment	511,500	Miscellaneous Selling Expense	2,000
Accumulated Depreciation—		Office Salaries Expense	77,400
Store Equipment	186,700	Rent Expense	39,900
Accounts Payable	48,600	Insurance Expense	22,950
Salaries Payable	9,600	Depreciation Expense—	
Note Payable		Office Equipment	16,200
(final payment due in five years)	54,000	Office Supplies Expense	1,650
Capital Stock	15,000	Miscellaneous Administrative	
Retained Earnings	253,800	Expense	1,900
Dividends	125,000	Interest Expense	12,000

Instructions

1. Prepare a multiple-step income statement.
2. Prepare a retained earnings statement.
3. Prepare a report form of balance sheet, assuming that the current portion of the note payable is $8,000.
4. Briefly explain (a) how multiple-step and single-step income statements differ and (b) how report-form and account-form balance sheets differ.

P4-2   Single-step income statement

Obj 2

Selected accounts and related amounts for Aqua Co. for the fiscal year ended June 30, 20Y8, are presented in Problem 4-1.

Instructions

1. Prepare a single-step income statement in the format shown in Exhibit 3.
2. Prepare a retained earnings statement.

P4-3   Sales-related transactions

Obj 3, 5

The following selected transactions were completed by Affordable Supplies Co., which sells supplies primarily to wholesalers and occasionally to retail customers.

Jan. 6. Sold merchandise on account, $14,000, terms FOB shipping point, n/eom. The cost of merchandise sold was $8,400.

    8. Sold merchandise on account, $20,000, terms FOB destination, 1/10, n/30. The cost of merchandise sold was $14,000.

Note: The spreadsheet icon [icon] indicates an Excel template is available on the student companion site.

Jan. 16. Sold merchandise on account, $19,500, terms FOB shipping point, 1/10, n/30. The cost of merchandise sold was $11,700.

18. Received check for amount due for sale on January 8.

19. Issued credit memorandum for $4,500 for merchandise returned from sale on January 16. The cost of the merchandise returned was $2,700.

26. Received check for amount due for sale on January 16 less credit memorandum of January 19 and discount.

31. Paid Cashell Delivery Service $3,000 for merchandise delivered during January to customers under shipping terms of FOB destination.

31. Received check for amount due for sale of January 6.

Instructions

Illustrate the effects of each of the preceding transactions on the accounts and financial statements of Affordable Supplies Co. Identify each transaction by date.

Obj | **4, 5**

P4-4 Purchase-related transactions

The following selected transactions were completed by Epic Co. during August of the current year:

Aug. 3. Purchased merchandise for $33,400, terms FOB destination, 2/10, n/30.

9. Issued debit memorandum for $7,000 of merchandise returned from purchase on August 3.

10. Purchased merchandise, $25,000, terms FOB shipping point, n/eom. Paid freight of $600 on purchase.

13. Paid for invoice of August 3, less debit memorandum of August 9 and discount.

31. Paid for invoice of August 10.

Instructions

Illustrate the effects of each of the preceding transactions on the accounts and financial statements of Epic Co. Identify each transaction by date.

Obj | **6**

P4-5 Sales and purchase-related transactions for seller and buyer

The following selected transactions were completed during June between Snipes Company and Beejoy Company:

June 8. Snipes Company sold merchandise on account to Beejoy Company, $18,250, terms FOB destination, 2/15, n/eom. The cost of the merchandise sold was $10,000.

8. Snipes Company paid transportation costs of $400 for delivery of merchandise sold to Beejoy Company on June 8.

12. Beejoy Company returned $5,000 of merchandise purchased on account on June 8 from Snipes Company. The cost of the merchandise returned was $3,000.

23. Beejoy Company paid Snipes Company for purchase of June 8, less discount and less return of June 12.

24. Snipes Company sold merchandise on account to Beejoy Company, $15,000, terms FOB shipping point, n/eom. The cost of the merchandise sold was $9,000.

26. Beejoy Company paid transportation charges of $375 on June 24 purchase from Snipes Company.

30. Beejoy Company paid Snipes Company on account for purchase of June 24.

Instructions

Illustrate the effects of each of the preceding transactions on the accounts and financial statements of (1) Snipes Company and (2) Beejoy Company. Identify each transaction by date.

P4-6   Statement of cash flows using indirect method

For the year ending March 31, 20Y5, Omega Systems Inc. reported net income of $105,450 and paid dividends of $7,500. Comparative balance sheets as of March 31, 20Y5 and 20Y4, are as follows:

✔ 1. Net cash flows from operating activities: $98,605

app

OMEGA SYSTEMS INC.
Balance Sheets

	March 31, 20Y5	March 31, 20Y4	Changes Increase (Decrease)
Assets			
Current assets:			
Cash	$ 39,500	$ 29,250	$ 10,250
Accounts receivable	114,120	78,000	36,120
Merchandise inventory	133,150	122,550	10,600
Office supplies	4,255	4,435	(180)
Prepaid insurance	3,975	4,500	(525)
Total current assets	$ 295,000	$238,735	$ 56,265
Property, plant, and equipment:			
Land	$ 30,000	$ 30,000	$ 0
Store equipment	350,000	285,000	65,000
Accumulated depreciation— store equipment	(118,550)	(93,900)	(24,650)
Office equipment	23,355	15,000	8,355
Accumulated depreciation—office equipment	(7,080)	(3,345)	(3,735)
Total property, plant, and equipment	$ 277,725	$232,755	$ 44,970
Total assets	$ 572,725	$471,490	$101,235
Liabilities			
Current liabilities:			
Accounts payable	$ 33,630	$ 21,405	$ 12,225
Notes payable (current portion)	7,500	7,500	0
Salaries payable	1,710	2,250	(540)
Unearned rent	2,700	3,600	(900)
Total current liabilities	$ 45,540	$ 34,755	$ 10,785
Long-term liabilities:			
Notes payable (final payment due in eight years)	30,000	37,500	(7,500)
Total liabilities	$ 75,540	$ 72,255	$ 3,285
Stockholders' Equity			
Capital stock	$ 37,500	$ 37,500	$ 0
Retained earnings	459,685	361,735	97,950
Total stockholders' equity	$ 497,185	$399,235	$ 97,950
Total liabilities and stockholders' equity	$ 572,725	$471,490	$101,235

Instructions

1. Prepare a statement of cash flows, using the indirect method.
2. Why is depreciation added to net income in determining net cash flows from operating activities? Explain.

Financial Analysis

FA 4-1   Gross profit percent, average markup percent, and ratio of sales to assets

CVS Caremark Corporation operates over 7,000 pharmacies and is a major competitor of Walgreen Co. The following data (in millions) were adapted from recent financial statements of CVS.

	Year 2	Year 1
Net sales	$107,100	$95,778
Cost of merchandise sold	86,539	75,559
Gross profit	$ 20,561	$20,219
Average total assets	$ 63,356	$61,905

1. Compute the gross profit percent for Years 1 and 2. Round to one decimal place.
2. Compute the average markup percent for Years 1 and 2. Round to one decimal place.
3. Compute the ratio of sales to assets for Years 1 and 2. Round to two decimal places.
4. Compare the results in parts (1), (2), and (3) for Years 1 and 2. Comment on your comparison.

FA 4-2   Gross profit percent, average markup percent, and ratio of sales to assets

Compare the CVS results in FA 4-1 with those of Walgreen shown in the chapter illustration. Comment on the differences.

FA 4-3   Gross profit percent, average markup percent, and ratio of sales to assets

Deere & Company produces and sells tractors, loaders, combines, lawnmowers, and a variety of other equipment. The following data (in millions) were adapted from recent financial statements of Deere.

	Year 2	Year 1
Net sales	$36,157	$32,012
Cost of merchandise sold	25,008	21,919
Gross profit	$11,149	$10,093
Average total assets*	$52,028	$45,514

* Excluding long-term investments

1. Compute the gross profit percent for Years 1 and 2. Round to one decimal place.
2. Compute the average markup percent for Years 1 and 2. Round to one decimal place.
3. Compute the ratio of sales to assets for Years 1 and 2. Round to two decimal places.
4. Compare the results in parts (1), (2), and (3) for Years 1 and 2. Comment on your comparison.

FA 4-4   Gross profit percent, average markup percent, and ratio of sales to assets

Caterpillar Inc. produces and sells various types of equipment, including tractors, loaders, and mining equipment. The following data (in millions) were adapted from recent financial statements of Caterpillar.

	Year 2	Year 1
Net sales	$60,138	$42,588
Cost of merchandise sold	44,404	31,281
Gross profit	$15,734	$11,307
Average total assets*	$60,017	$49,241

* Excluding long-term investments

1. Compute the gross profit percent for Years 1 and 2. Round to one decimal place.
2. Compute the average markup percent for Years 1 and 2. Round to one decimal place.
3. Compute the ratio of sales to assets for Years 1 and 2. Round to two decimal places.
4. Compare the results in parts (1), (2), and (3) for Years 1 and 2. Comment on your comparison.

FA 4-5 Gross profit percent, average markup percent, and ratio of sales to assets

Obj 8

Compare the gross profit percent, average markup percent, and ratio of sales to assets for **Deere & Company** and **Caterpillar Inc.** using the results of FA 4-3 and FA 4-4. Comment on any differences.

FA 4-6 Gross profit percent, average markup percent, and ratio of sales to assets

Obj 8

Companies with low gross profit and markup percents often have high ratios of sales to assets. Conversely, companies with high gross profit and markup percents often have low ratios of sales to assets.

1. Comment on the preceding statements.
2. The following data (in millions) were adapted from recent financial statements of **The Kroger Co.** and **Tiffany & Co.** Kroger operates supermarkets, while Tiffany designs and sells jewelry, china, watches, and other expensive merchandise.

	Kroger	Tiffany
Net sales	$90,374	$3,643
Cost of merchandise sold	71,494	1,492
Gross profit	$18,880	$2,151
Average total assets	$23,491	$3,948

Compute the gross profit percent, average markup percent, and ratio of sales to assets for Kroger and Tiffany. Round the gross profit percent and average markup percent to one decimal place. Round the ratio of sales to asset to two decimal places.

3. Comment on the results in part (2).

Cases

Case 4-1 Ethics and professional conduct in business

On July 29, 20Y1, Ever Green Company, a garden retailer, purchased $12,000 of seed, terms 2/10, n/30, from Fleck Seed Co. Even though the discount period had expired, Mary Jasper subtracted the discount of $240 when she processed the documents for payment on August 13, 20Y1.

Discuss whether Mary Jasper behaved in a professional manner by subtracting the discount, even though the discount period had expired.

Case 4-2 Purchases discounts and accounts payable

The Laurel Co. is owned and operated by Paul Laurel. The following is an excerpt from a conversation between Paul Laurel and Maria Fuller, the chief accountant for Laurel Co.

Paul: Maria, I've got a question about this recent balance sheet.

Maria: Sure, what's your question?

Paul: Well, as you know, I'm applying for a bank loan to finance our new store in Clinton, and I noticed that the accounts payable are listed as $180,000.

Maria: That's right. Approximately $150,000 of that represents amounts due our suppliers, and the remainder is miscellaneous payables to creditors for utilities, office equipment, supplies, etc.

Paul: That's what I thought. But we normally receive a 2% discount from our suppliers for earlier payment, and we always try to take the discount.

Maria: That's right. I can't remember the last time we missed a discount.

Paul: Well, in that case, it seems to me the accounts payable should be listed minus the 2% discount. Let's list the accounts payable due suppliers as $147,000, rather than $150,000. Every little bit helps. You never know. It might make the difference between getting the loan and not.

How would you respond to Paul Laurel's request?

Case 4-3 Determining cost of purchase

The following is an excerpt from a conversation between Eric Jackson and Carlie Miller. Eric is debating whether to buy a stereo system from First Audio, a locally owned electronics store, or Dynamic Sound Systems, an online electronics company.

Eric: Carlie, I don't know what to do about buying my new stereo.

Carlie: What's the problem?

Eric: Well, I can buy it locally at First Audio for $890.00. But Dynamic Sound Systems has the same system listed for $899.99.

Carlie: So what's the big deal? Buy it from First Audio.

Eric: It's not quite that simple. Dynamic Sound Systems said something about not having to pay sales tax, since I was out of state.

Carlie: Yes, that's a good point. If you buy it at First Audio, they'll charge you 6% sales tax.

Eric: But Dynamic Sound Systems charges $13.99 for shipping and handling. If I have them send it next-day air, it'll cost $44.99 for shipping and handling.

Carlie: I guess it is a little confusing.

Eric: That's not all. First Audio will give an additional 1% discount if I pay cash. Otherwise, they will let me use my VISA, or I can pay it off in three monthly installments.

Carlie: Anything else???

Eric: Well ... Dynamic Sound Systems says I have to charge it on my VISA. They don't accept checks.

Carlie: I am not surprised. Many online stores don't accept checks.

Eric: I give up. What would you do?

1. Assuming that Dynamic Sound Systems doesn't charge sales tax on the sale to Eric, which company is offering the best buy?

2. What might be some considerations other than price that might influence Eric's decision on where to buy the stereo system?

Case 4-4 Sales discounts

Your sister operates Harbor Ready Parts Company, an online boat parts distributorship that is in its third year of operation. The income statement is shown below and was recently prepared for the year ended October 31, 20Y6.

HARBOR READY PARTS COMPANY
Income Statement
For the Year Ended October 31, 20Y6

Revenues:		
Net sales		$1,200,000
Interest revenue		15,000
Total revenues		$1,215,000
Expenses:		
Cost of merchandise sold	$800,000	
Selling expenses	135,000	
Administrative expenses	75,000	
Interest expense	21,650	
Total expenses		1,031,650
Net income		$ 183,350

Your sister is considering a proposal to increase net income by offering sales discounts of 2/15, n/30, and by shipping all merchandise FOB shipping point. Currently, no sales discounts are allowed and merchandise is shipped FOB destination. It is estimated that these credit terms will increase net sales by 15%. The ratio of the cost of merchandise sold to net sales is expected to be 65%. All selling and administrative expenses are expected to remain unchanged, except for store supplies, miscellaneous selling, office supplies, and miscellaneous administrative expenses, which are expected to increase proportionately with increased net sales. The amounts of these preceding items for the year ended October 31, 20Y6, were as follows:

Store supplies expense	$18,000	Office supplies expense	$4,000
Miscellaneous selling expense	5,000	Miscellaneous administrative expense	2,000

The other income and other expense items will remain unchanged. The shipment of all merchandise FOB shipping point will eliminate all delivery expenses, which for the year ended October 31, 20Y6, were $28,000.

1. Prepare a projected single-step income statement for the year ending October 31, 20Y7, based on the proposal. Assume all sales are collected within the discount period.

2. Based on the projected income statement in part (1), would you recommend implementation of the proposed changes?

3. Describe any possible concerns you may have related to the proposed changes described in part (1).

GROUP PROJECT

Case 4-5 Shopping for a television

Assume that you are planning to purchase a Samsung LED-LCD, 55-inch television. In groups of three or four, determine the lowest cost for the television, considering the available alternatives and the advantages and disadvantages of each alternative. For example, you could purchase locally, through mail order, or through an Internet shopping service. Consider such factors as delivery charges, interest-free financing, discounts, coupons, and availability of warranty services. Prepare a report for presentation to the class.

Answers to Self-Examination Questions

1. **A** A debit memorandum (answer A), issued by the buyer, indicates the amount the buyer proposes to decrease the accounts payable account. A credit memorandum (answer B), issued by the seller, indicates the amount the seller proposes to decrease the accounts receivable account. An invoice (answer C) or a bill (answer D), issued by the seller, indicates the amount and terms of the sale.

2. **C** The amount of discount for early payment is $10 (answer C), or 1% of $1,000. Although the $50 of transportation costs paid by the seller increases the customer's account, the customer is not entitled to a discount on that amount.

3. **B** The single-step form of income statement (answer B) is so named because the total of all expenses is deducted in one step from the total of all revenues. The multiple-step form (answer A) includes numerous

sections and subsections with several subtotals. The account form (answer C) and the report form (answer D) are two common forms of the balance sheet.

4. **C** Gross profit (answer C) is the excess of net sales over the cost of merchandise sold. Operating income (answer A) or income from operations (answer B) is the excess of gross profit over operating expenses. Net income (answer D) is the final figure on the income statement after all revenues and expenses have been reported.

5. **B** The inventory shrinkage, $15,000, is the difference between the book inventory, $290,000, and the physical inventory, $275,000. The effect of the inventory shrinkage on the accounts is to increase Cost of Merchandise Sold and decrease Inventory by $15,000.

CHAPTER 5

Sarbanes-Oxley, Internal Control, and Cash

LEARNING OBJECTIVES
After studying this chapter, you should be able to:

Obj **1** Describe the Sarbanes-Oxley Act and its impact on internal controls and financial reporting.

Obj **2** Describe and illustrate the objectives and elements of internal control.

Obj **3** Describe and illustrate the application of internal controls to cash.

Obj **4** Describe the nature of a bank account and its use in controlling cash.

Obj **5** Describe and illustrate the use of a bank reconciliation in controlling cash.

Obj **6** Describe the accounting for special-purpose cash funds.

Obj **7** Describe and illustrate the reporting of cash and cash equivalents in the financial statements.

Obj **8** Financial Analysis: Describe and illustrate the ratio of cash to monthly cash expenses in assessing the ability of a company to continue operating.

Controls are a part of your everyday life. At one extreme, laws are used to limit your behavior. For example, the speed limit is a control on your driving, designed for traffic safety. In addition, you are also affected by many nonlegal controls. For example, recording checks in your checkbook is a control that you can use at the end of the month to verify the accuracy of your bank statement. In addition, banks give you a personal identification number (PIN) as a control against unauthorized access to your cash if you lose your automated teller machine (ATM) card. As you can see, you use and encounter controls every day.

Just as there are many examples of controls throughout society, businesses must also implement controls to help guide the behavior of their managers, employees, and customers. For example, **eBay Inc.** maintains an Internet-based marketplace for the sale of goods and services. Using eBay's online platform, buyers and sellers can browse, buy, and sell a wide variety of items including antiques and used cars. However, in order to maintain the integrity and trust of its buyers and sellers, eBay must have controls to ensure that buyers pay for their items and sellers don't misrepresent their items or fail to deliver sales. One such control eBay uses is a feedback forum that establishes buyer and seller reputations. A prospective buyer or seller can view the member's reputation and feedback comments before completing a transaction. Dishonest or unfair trading can lead to a negative reputation and even suspension or cancellation.

This chapter discusses controls that can be included in accounting systems to provide reasonable assurance that the financial statements are reliable. Controls over cash that you can use to determine whether your bank has made any errors in your account are also discussed. This chapter begins by discussing the Sarbanes-Oxley Act and its impact on controls and financial reporting.

Obj | **1**

Describe the Sarbanes-Oxley Act and its impact on internal controls and financial reporting.

The ex-CEO of WorldCom, Bernard Ebbers, was sentenced to 25 years in prison.

Sarbanes-Oxley Act

During recent financial scandals, stockholders, creditors, and other investors lost billions of dollars.[1] As a result, the U.S. Congress passed the **Sarbanes-Oxley Act**. This act, often referred to as *Sarbanes-Oxley,* is one of the most important laws affecting U.S. companies in recent history. The purpose of Sarbanes-Oxley is to restore public confidence and trust in the financial reporting of companies.

Sarbanes-Oxley applies only to companies whose stock is traded on public exchanges, referred to as *publicly held companies.* However, Sarbanes-Oxley highlighted the importance of assessing the financial controls and reporting of all companies. As a result, companies of all sizes have been influenced by Sarbanes-Oxley.

Sarbanes-Oxley emphasizes the importance of effective internal control.[2] **Internal control** is defined as the procedures and processes used by a company to:

1. Safeguard its assets.
2. Process information accurately.
3. Ensure compliance with laws and regulations.

Sarbanes-Oxley requires companies to maintain effective internal controls over the recording of transactions and the preparing of financial statements. Such controls are important because they deter fraud and prevent misleading financial statements as shown below.

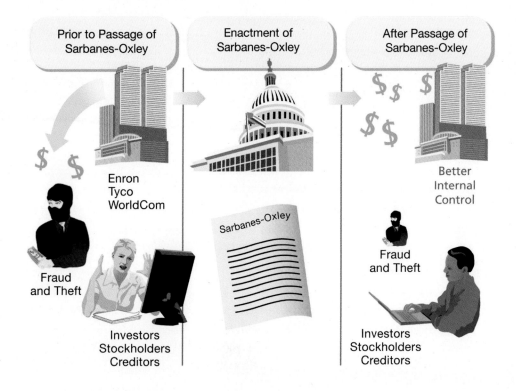

Sarbanes-Oxley also requires companies and their independent accountants to report on the effectiveness of the company's internal controls.[3] These reports are

---

1. Exhibit 13 in Chapter 1 briefly summarizes these scandals.

2. Sarbanes-Oxley also has important implications for corporate governance and the regulation of the public accounting profession. This chapter, however, focuses on the internal control implications of Sarbanes-Oxley.

3. These reporting requirements are required under Section 404 of the act. As a result, these requirements and reports are often referred to as 404 requirements and 404 reports.

required to be filed with the company's annual 10-K report with the Securities and Exchange Commission. Companies are also encouraged to include these reports in their annual reports to stockholders. An example of such a report by the management of Dell Inc. is shown in Exhibit 1.

Management's Report on Internal Control over Financial Reporting

Management, under the supervision of the Chief Executive Officer and the Chief Financial Officer, is responsible for establishing and maintaining adequate internal control over financial reporting. Internal control over financial reporting . . . is a process designed to provide reasonable assurance regarding the reliability of financial reporting and the preparation of financial statements for external purposes in accordance with GAAP. Internal control over financial reporting includes those policies and procedures which (a) pertain to the maintenance of records that, in reasonable detail, accurately and fairly reflect the transactions and dispositions of assets, (b) provide reasonable assurance that transactions are recorded as necessary to permit preparation of financial statements in accordance with GAAP, (c) provide reasonable assurance that receipts and expenditures are being made only in accordance with appro-

priate authorization of management and the board of directors, and (d) provide reasonable assurance regarding prevention or timely detection of unauthorized acquisition, use, or disposition of assets that could have a material effect on the financial statements.

In connection with the preparation of this Report, our management, under the supervision and with the participation of our Chief Executive Officer and Chief Financial Officer, conducted an evaluation of the effectiveness of our internal control over financial reporting . . . based on the criteria established in Internal Control—Integrated Framework issued by the Committee of Sponsoring Organizations of the Treadway Commission. As a result of that evaluation, management has concluded that our internal control over financial reporting was effective. . . .

Source: Dell Inc., Form 10-K.

EXHIBIT 1

Sarbanes-Oxley Report of Dell

Exhibit 1 indicates that Dell based its evaluation of internal controls on *Internal Control—Integrated Framework,* which was issued by the Committee of Sponsoring Organizations (COSO) of the Treadway Commission. This framework is the standard by which companies design, analyze, and evaluate internal controls.

It is estimated that companies spend millions each year to comply with the requirements of Sarbanes-Oxley.

Internal Control

Obj | 2

Describe and illustrate the objectives and elements of internal control.

Internal Control—Integrated Framework is used as the basis for discussing internal controls.[4] In this section, the objectives of internal control are described, followed by a discussion of how these objectives can be achieved through the *Integrated Framework*'s five elements of internal control.

Objectives of Internal Control

The objectives of internal control are to provide reasonable assurance that:

1. Assets are safeguarded and used for business purposes.
2. Business information is accurate.
3. Employees and managers comply with laws and regulations.

Information on *Internal Control—Integrated Framework* can be found on COSO's Web site at http://www.coso.org/.

---

4. *Internal Control—Integrated Framework* by the Committee of Sponsoring Organizations of the Treadway Commission, 1992.

These objectives are illustrated below.

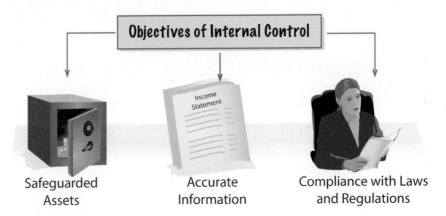

The Association of Certified Fraud Examiners has estimated that globally businesses will lose more than $3.5 trillion, or around 5% of revenue, to employee fraud.

Source: *2012 Report to the Nation: Occupational Fraud and Abuse*, Association of Certified Fraud Examiners.

Internal control can safeguard assets by preventing theft, fraud, misuse, or misplacement. A serious concern of internal control is preventing employee fraud. **Employee fraud** is the intentional act of deceiving an employer for personal gain. Such fraud may range from minor overstating of a travel expense report to stealing millions of dollars. Employees stealing from a business often adjust the accounting records in order to hide their fraud. Thus, employee fraud usually affects the accuracy of business information.

Accurate information is necessary to successfully operate a business. Businesses must also comply with laws, regulations, and financial reporting standards. Examples of such standards include environmental regulations, safety regulations, and generally accepted accounting principles (GAAP).

Elements of Internal Control

The three internal control objectives can be achieved by applying the five **elements of internal control** set forth by the *Integrated Framework*.[5] These elements are as follows:

1. Control environment
2. Risk assessment
3. Control procedures
4. Monitoring
5. Information and communication

The elements of internal control are illustrated in Exhibit 2. In this exhibit, the elements of internal control form an umbrella over the business to protect it from control threats. The control environment is the size of the umbrella. Risk assessment, control procedures, and monitoring are the fabric of the umbrella, which keep it from leaking. Information and communication connect the umbrella to management.

Control Environment

The control environment is the overall attitude of management and employees about the importance of controls. Three factors influencing a company's control environment are listed on the next page.

5. Ibid., pp. 12–14.

EXHIBIT 2

Elements of Internal Control

1. Management's philosophy and operating style
2. The company's organizational structure
3. The company's personnel policies

Management's philosophy and operating style relates to whether management emphasizes the importance of internal controls. An emphasis on controls and adherence to control policies creates an effective control environment. In contrast, overemphasizing operating goals and tolerating deviations from control policies creates an ineffective control environment.

The business's *organizational structure* is the framework for planning and controlling operations. For example, a retail store chain might organize each of its stores as separate business units. Each store manager has full authority over pricing and other operating activities. In such a structure, each store manager has the responsibility for establishing an effective control environment.

The business's *personnel policies* involve the hiring, training, evaluation, compensation, and promotion of employees. In addition, job descriptions, employee codes of ethics, and conflict-of-interest policies are part of the personnel policies. Such policies can enhance the internal control environment if they provide reasonable assurance that only competent, honest employees are hired and retained.

Risk Assessment

All businesses face risks such as changes in customer requirements, competitive threats, regulatory changes, and changes in economic factors. Management should identify such risks, analyze their significance, assess their likelihood of occurring, and take any necessary actions to minimize them.

Control Procedures

Control procedures provide reasonable assurance that business goals will be achieved, including the prevention of fraud. Control procedures, which constitute one of the most important elements of internal control, include the following:

1. Competent personnel, rotating duties, and mandatory vacations
2. Separating responsibilities for related operations
3. Separating operations, custody of assets, and accounting
4. Proofs and security measures

A bank officer who was not required to take vacations stole almost $5 million by printing fake certificates of deposit. The theft was discovered when the bank began requiring all employees to take vacations.

Competent Personnel, Rotating Duties, and Mandatory Vacations A successful company needs competent employees who are able to perform the duties that they are assigned. Procedures should be established for properly training and supervising employees. It is also advisable to rotate duties of accounting personnel and mandate vacations for all employees. In this way, employees are encouraged to adhere to procedures. Cases of employee fraud are often discovered when a long-term employee, who never took vacations, missed work because of an illness or another unavoidable reason.

Separating Responsibilities for Related Operations The responsibility for related operations should be divided among two or more persons. This decreases the possibility of errors and fraud. For example, if the same person orders supplies, verifies the receipt of the supplies, and pays the supplier, the following abuses may occur:

An accounting clerk for the Grant County (Washington) Alcoholism Program was in charge of collecting money, making deposits, and keeping the records. While the clerk was away on maternity leave, the replacement clerk discovered a fraud: $17,800 in fees had been collected but had been hidden for personal gain.

1. Orders may be placed on the basis of friendship with a supplier, rather than on price, quality, and other objective factors.
2. The quantity and quality of supplies received may not be verified; thus, the company may pay for supplies not received or that are of poor quality.
3. Supplies may be stolen by the employee.
4. The validity and accuracy of invoices may not be verified; hence, the company may pay false or inaccurate invoices.

For the preceding reasons, the responsibilities for purchasing, receiving, and paying for supplies should be divided among three persons or departments.

Separating Operations, Custody of Assets, and Accounting The responsibilities for operations, custody of assets, and accounting should be separated. In this way, the accounting records serve as an independent check on the operating managers and the employees who have custody of assets.

To illustrate, employees who handle cash receipts should not record cash receipts in the accounting records. To do so would allow employees to borrow or steal cash and hide the theft in the accounting records. Likewise, operating managers should not also record the results of operations. To do so would allow the managers to distort the accounting reports to show favorable results, which might allow them to receive larger bonuses.

An accounts payable clerk created false invoices and submitted them for payment. The clerk obtained the checks, cashed them, and stole thousands of dollars.

Proofs and Security Measures Proofs and security measures are used to safeguard assets and ensure reliable accounting data. Proofs involve procedures such as authorization, approval, and reconciliation. For example, an employee planning to travel on company business may be required to complete a "travel request" form for a manager's authorization and approval.

Documents used for authorization and approval should be prenumbered, accounted for, and safeguarded. Prenumbering of documents helps prevent transactions from being recorded more than once or not at all. In addition, accounting for and safeguarding prenumbered documents helps prevent fraudulent transactions from being recorded. For example, blank checks are prenumbered and safeguarded. Once a payment has been properly authorized and approved, the checks are filled out and issued.

Reconciliations are also an important control. Later in this chapter, the use of bank reconciliations as an aid in controlling cash is described and illustrated.

Security measures involve measures to safeguard assets. For example, cash on hand should be kept in a cash register or safe. Inventory not on display should be stored in a locked storeroom or warehouse. Accounting records such as the accounts receivable subsidiary ledger should also be safeguarded to prevent their loss. For example, electronically maintained accounting records should be safeguarded with access codes and backed up so that any lost or damaged files could be recovered if necessary.

A 24-hour convenience store could use a security guard, video cameras, and an alarm system to deter robberies.

Monitoring

Monitoring the internal control system is used to locate weaknesses and improve controls. Monitoring often includes observing employees' behavior and the accounting system for indicators of control problems. Some such indicators are shown in Exhibit 3.[6]

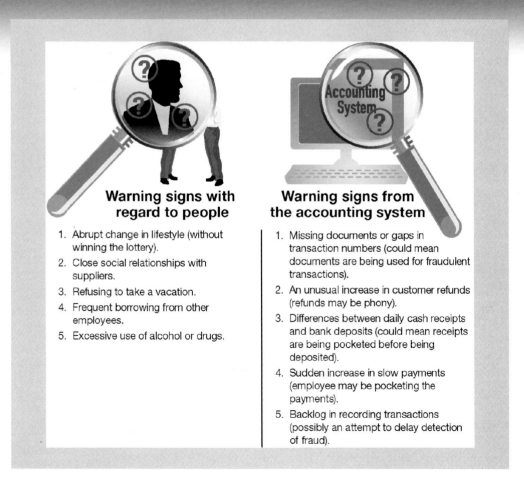

EXHIBIT 3

Warning Signs of Internal Control Problems

Warning signs with regard to people

1. Abrupt change in lifestyle (without winning the lottery).
2. Close social relationships with suppliers.
3. Refusing to take a vacation.
4. Frequent borrowing from other employees.
5. Excessive use of alcohol or drugs.

Warning signs from the accounting system

1. Missing documents or gaps in transaction numbers (could mean documents are being used for fraudulent transactions).
2. An unusual increase in customer refunds (refunds may be phony).
3. Differences between daily cash receipts and bank deposits (could mean receipts are being pocketed before being deposited).
4. Sudden increase in slow payments (employee may be pocketing the payments).
5. Backlog in recording transactions (possibly an attempt to delay detection of fraud).

6. Edwin C. Bliss, "Employee Theft," *Boardroom Reports,* July 15, 1994, pp. 5–6.

Evaluations of controls are often performed when there are major changes in strategy, senior management, business structure, or operations. Internal auditors, who are independent of operations, usually perform such evaluations. Internal auditors are also responsible for day-to-day monitoring of controls. External auditors also evaluate and report on internal control as part of their annual financial statement audit.

Information and Communication

Information and communication is an essential element of internal control. Information about the control environment, risk assessment, control procedures, and monitoring is used by management for guiding operations and ensuring compliance with reporting, legal, and regulatory requirements. Management also uses external information to assess events and conditions that impact decision making and external reporting. For example, management uses pronouncements of the Financial Accounting Standards Board (FASB) to assess the impact of changes in reporting standards on the financial statements.

Limitations of Internal Control

Internal control systems can provide only reasonable assurance for safeguarding assets, processing accurate information, and compliance with laws and regulations. In other words, internal controls are not a guarantee. This is due to the following factors:

1. The human element of controls
2. Cost-benefit considerations

The *human element* recognizes that controls are applied and used by humans. As a result, human errors can occur because of fatigue, carelessness, confusion, or misjudgment. For example, an employee may unintentionally shortchange a customer or miscount the amount of inventory received from a supplier. In addition, two or more employees may collude together to defeat or circumvent

Integrity, Objectivity, and Ethics in Business

TIPS ON PREVENTING EMPLOYEE FRAUD IN SMALL COMPANIES

- Do not have the same employee write company checks and keep the books. Look for payments to vendors you don't know or payments to vendors whose names appear to be misspelled.
- If your business has a computer system, restrict access to accounting files as much as possible. Also, keep a backup copy of your accounting files and store it at an off-site location.
- Be wary of anybody working in finance that declines to take vacations. They may be afraid that a replacement will uncover fraud.

- Require and monitor supporting documentation (such as vendor invoices) before signing checks.
- Track the number of credit card bills you sign monthly.
- Limit and monitor access to important documents and supplies, such as blank checks and signature stamps.
- Check W-2 forms against your payroll annually to make sure you're not carrying any fictitious employees.
- Rely on yourself, not on your accountant, to spot fraud.

Source: Steve Kaufman, "Embezzlement Common at Small Companies," Knight-Ridder Newspapers, reported in *Athens Daily News/Athens Banner-Herald,* March 10, 1996, p. 4D.

internal controls. This latter case often involves fraud and the theft of assets. For example, the cashier and the accounts receivable clerk might collude to steal customer payments on account.

Cost-benefit considerations recognize that costs of internal controls should not exceed their benefits. For example, retail stores could eliminate shoplifting by searching all customers before they leave the store. However, such a control procedure would upset customers and result in lost sales. Instead, retailers use cameras or signs saying they prosecute all shoplifters.

Cash Controls Over Receipts and Payments

Obj | 3

Describe and illustrate the application of internal controls to cash.

Cash includes coins, currency (paper money), checks, and money orders. Money on deposit with a bank or other financial institution that is available for withdrawal is also considered cash. Normally, you can think of cash as anything that a bank would accept for deposit in your account. For example, a check made payable to you could normally be deposited in a bank and thus is considered cash.

Businesses usually have several bank accounts. For example, a business might have one bank account for general cash payments and another for payroll. For example, a general bank account at City Bank could be identified as *Cash in Bank—City Bank*. To simplify, we will assume in this chapter that a company has only one bank account, which is identified as *Cash*.

Cash is the asset most likely to be stolen or used improperly in a business. For this reason, businesses must carefully control cash and cash transactions.

The Internet has given rise to a form of cash called "cybercash," which is used for Internet transactions, such as with **PayPal**.

Control of Cash Receipts

To protect cash from theft and misuse, a business must control cash from the time it is received until it is deposited in a bank. Businesses normally receive cash from two main sources.

1. Customers purchasing products or services
2. Customers making payments on account

Cash Received from Cash Sales An important control to protect cash received in over-the-counter sales is a cash register. The use of a cash register to control cash is shown at the top of the following page.

A cash register controls cash as follows:

1. At the beginning of every work shift, each cash register clerk is given a cash drawer containing a predetermined amount of cash. This amount is used for making change for customers and is sometimes called a *change fund*.
2. When a salesperson enters the amount of a sale, the cash register displays the amount to the customer. This allows the customer to verify that the clerk has charged the correct amount. The customer also receives a cash receipt.
3. At the end of the shift, the clerk and the supervisor count the cash in the clerk's cash drawer. The amount of cash in each drawer should equal the beginning amount of cash plus the cash sales for the day.

Fast-food restaurants, such as **McDonald's**, receive cash primarily from over-the-counter sales. Internet retailers, such as **Amazon.com**, receive cash primarily through electronic funds transfers from credit card companies.

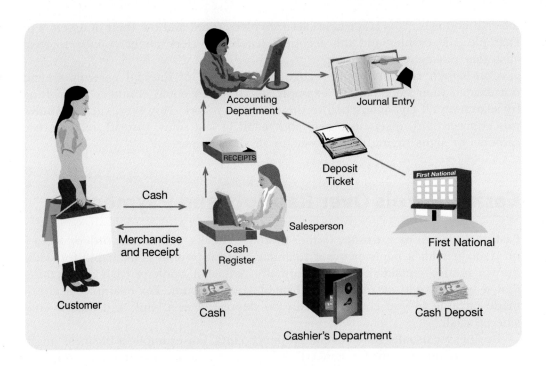

4. The supervisor takes the cash to the Cashier's Department where it is placed in a safe.

5. The supervisor forwards the clerk's cash register receipts to the Accounting Department.

6. The cashier prepares a bank deposit ticket.

7. The cashier deposits the cash in the bank, or the cash is picked up by an armored car service, such as Wells Fargo.

8. The Accounting Department summarizes the cash receipts and records the day's cash sales.

9. When cash is deposited in the bank, the bank normally stamps a duplicate copy of the deposit ticket with the amount received. This bank receipt is returned to the Accounting Department, where it is compared to the total amount that should have been deposited. This control helps ensure that all the cash is deposited and that no cash is lost or stolen on the way to the bank. Any shortages are thus promptly detected.

Salespersons may make errors in making change for customers or in ringing up cash sales. As a result, the amount of cash on hand may differ from the amount of cash sales. Such differences are recorded in a **cash short and over**.

To illustrate, assume the following cash register data for May 3:

Cash register total for cash sales	$35,690
Cash receipts from cash sales	35,668

The cash sales are recorded in the normal manner. The cash shortage of $22 ($35,690 − $35,668) is recorded as a normal operating expense. This is done by recording a negative $22 under the account titled Cash Short and Over.

A cash overage is recorded as a positive amount in Cash Short and Over. At the end of the period, a negative balance in Cash Short and Over is reported as a Miscellaneous operating expense. A positive balance in Cash Short and Over is reported as Other income.

Cash Received in the Mail Cash is received in the mail when customers pay their bills. This cash is usually in the form of checks and money orders. Most companies design their invoices so that customers return a portion of the invoice, called a *remittance advice,* with their payment. Remittance advices may be used to control cash received in the mail as follows:

1. An employee opens the incoming mail and compares the amount of cash received with the amount shown on the remittance advice. If a customer does not return a remittance advice, the employee prepares one. The remittance advice serves as a record of the cash initially received. It also helps ensure that the posting to the customer's account is for the amount of cash received.
2. The employee opening the mail stamps checks and money orders "For Deposit Only" in the bank account of the business.
3. The remittance advices and their summary totals are delivered to the Accounting Department.
4. All cash and money orders are delivered to the Cashier's Department.
5. The cashier prepares a bank deposit ticket.
6. The cashier deposits the cash in the bank, or the cash is picked up by an armored car service, such as Wells Fargo.
7. An accounting clerk records the cash received and posts the amounts to the customer accounts.
8. When cash is deposited in the bank, the bank normally stamps a duplicate copy of the deposit ticket with the amount received. This bank receipt is returned to the Accounting Department, where it is compared to the total amount that should have been deposited. This control helps ensure that all cash is deposited and that no cash is lost or stolen on the way to the bank. Any shortages are thus promptly detected.

Separating the duties of the Cashier's Department, which handles cash, and the Accounting Department, which records cash, is a control. If Accounting Department employees both handle and record cash, an employee could steal cash and change the accounting records to hide the theft.

Cash Received by EFT Cash also may be received from customers through **electronic funds transfer (EFT)**. For example, customers may authorize automatic electronic transfers from their checking accounts to pay monthly bills for such items as cell phone, Internet, and electric services. In such cases, the company sends the customer's bank a signed form from the customer authorizing the monthly electronic transfers. Each month, the company notifies the customer's bank of the amount of the transfer and the date the transfer should take place. On the due date, the company records the electronic transfer as a receipt of cash to its bank account and posts the amount paid to the customer's account.

Companies encourage customers to use EFT for the following reasons:

1. EFTs cost less than receiving cash payments through the mail.
2. EFTs enhance internal controls over cash since the cash is received directly by the bank without any employees handling cash.
3. EFTs reduce late payments from customers and speed up the processing of cash receipts.

Howard Schultz & Associates (HS&A) specializes in reviewing cash payments for its clients. HS&A searches for errors, such as duplicate payments, failures to take discounts, and inaccurate computations. Amounts recovered for clients range from thousands to millions of dollars.

Control of Cash Payments

The control of cash payments should provide reasonable assurance that:

1. Payments are made for only authorized transactions.
2. Cash is used effectively and efficiently. For example, controls should ensure that all available purchase discounts are taken.

In a small business, an owner/manager may authorize payments based on personal knowledge. In a large business, however, purchasing goods, inspecting the goods received, and verifying the invoices are usually performed by different employees. These duties must be coordinated to ensure that proper payments are made to creditors. One system used for this purpose is the voucher system.

Voucher System A **voucher system** is a set of procedures for authorizing and recording liabilities and cash payments. A **voucher** is any document that serves as proof of authority to pay cash or issue an electronic funds transfer. An invoice that has been approved for payment could be considered a voucher. In many businesses, however, a voucher is a special form used to record data about a liability and the details of its payment.

In a manual system, a voucher is normally prepared after all necessary supporting documents have been received. For the purchase of goods, a voucher is supported by the supplier's invoice, a purchase order, and a receiving report. After a voucher is prepared, it is submitted for approval. Once approved, the voucher is recorded in the accounts and filed by due date. Upon payment, the voucher is recorded in the same manner as the payment of an account payable.

In a computerized system, data from the supporting documents (such as purchase orders, receiving reports, and suppliers' invoices) are entered directly into computer files. At the due date, the checks are automatically generated and mailed to creditors. At that time, the voucher is electronically transferred to a paid voucher file.

Cash Paid by EFT Cash also can be paid by electronic funds transfer systems. For example, many companies pay their employees by EFT. Under such a system, employees authorize the deposit of their payroll checks directly into their checking accounts. Each pay period, the company transfers the employees' net pay to their checking accounts through the use of EFT. Many companies also use EFT systems to pay their suppliers and other vendors.

Many businesses and individuals are now using Internet banking services, which provide for the payment of funds electronically.

Obj 4

Describe the nature of a bank account and its use in controlling cash.

Bank Accounts

A major reason that companies use bank accounts is for internal control. Some of the control advantages of using bank accounts are as follows:

1. Bank accounts reduce the amount of cash on hand.
2. Bank accounts provide an independent recording of cash transactions. Reconciling the balance of the cash account in the company's records with the cash balance according to the bank is an important control.
3. Use of bank accounts facilitates the transfer of funds using EFT systems.

Bank Statement

Banks usually maintain a record of all checking account transactions. A summary of all transactions, called a **bank statement**, is mailed, usually each month, to the company (depositor) or made available online. The bank statement shows the beginning balance, additions, deductions, and the ending balance. A typical bank statement is shown in Exhibit 4.

EXHIBIT 4
Bank Statement

MEMBER FDIC — PAGE 1

Mariner National Bank
5000 NE 75th Street
Bellevue, WA 98005

ACCOUNT NUMBER 1627042

FROM 6/30/20Y7 TO 7/31/20Y7

BALANCE 4,218.60

Colter Inc.
200 West Main Street
Bozeman, MT 59715

22 DEPOSITS 13,749.75

52 WITHDRAWALS 14,698.57

3 OTHER DEBITS AND CREDITS 90.00CR

NEW BALANCE 3,359.78

* – – CHECKS AND OTHER DEBITS – – – – – – – – *					– – – – – – – DEPOSITS *–DATE * BALANCE *		
No. 850	819.40	No. 852	122.54		585.75	07/01	3,862.41
No. 854	369.50	No. 853	20.15		421.53	07/02	3,894.29
No. 851	600.00	No. 856	190.70	No. 857 52.50	781.30	07/03	3,832.39
No. 855	25.93	No. 858	160.00		662.50	07/05	4,308.96
No. 860	921.20	NSF	300.00		503.18	07/07	3,590.94

No. 880	32.26	No. 877	535.09		ACH 932.00	07/29	4,136.66
No. 881	21.10	No. 879	732.26	No. 882 126.20	705.21	07/30	3,962.31
		SC	18.00		MS 408.00	07/30	4,352.31
No. 874	26.12	ACH	1,615.13		648.72	07/31	3,359.78

EC — ERROR CORRECTION   ACH — AUTOMATED CLEARING HOUSE
MS — MISCELLANEOUS   SC — SERVICE CHARGE
NSF — NOT SUFFICIENT FUNDS

* * *   * * *   * * *

THE RECONCILEMENT OF THIS STATEMENT WITH YOUR RECORDS IS ESSENTIAL.
ANY ERROR OR EXCEPTION SHOULD BE REPORTED IMMEDIATELY.

Checks or copies of the checks listed in the order that they were paid by the bank may accompany the bank statement. If paid checks are returned, they are stamped "Paid," together with the date of payment. Many banks no longer return checks or check copies. Instead, the check payment information is available online.

The depositor's checking account balance in the bank records is a liability. A credit memo entry on the bank statement indicates an increase in the depositor's account. Likewise, a debit memo entry on the bank statement indicates a decrease in the depositor's account. This relationship is shown at the top of the following page.

A bank issues credit memos for the following:

1. Deposits made by electronic funds transfer (EFT)
2. Collections of note receivable for the company
3. Proceeds for a loan made to the company by the bank
4. Interest earned on the company's account
5. Correction (if any) of bank errors

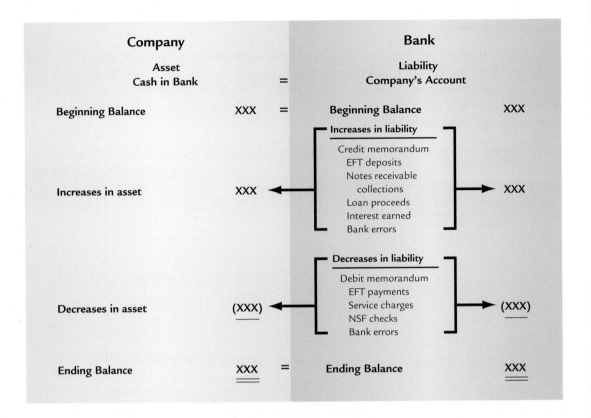

A bank issues debit memos for the following:

1. Payments made by electronic funds transfer (EFT)
2. Service charges
3. Customer checks returned for not sufficient funds
4. Correction (if any) of bank errors

Customers' checks returned for not sufficient funds, called *NSF checks,* are customer checks that were initially deposited but not paid by the customer's bank. Since the company's bank increased the company's account when the customer's check was deposited, the bank decreases the company's account (issues a debit memo) when the check is returned without payment.

The reason for a credit or debit memo entry is indicated on the bank statement. Exhibit 4 identifies the following types of credit and debit memo entries:

EC: Error correction to correct bank error
NSF: Not sufficient funds check
SC: Service charge
ACH: Automated clearing house entry for electronic funds transfer
MS: Miscellaneous item such as collection of a note receivable on behalf of the company or receipt of a loan by the company from the bank

The above list includes the notation "ACH" for electronic funds transfers. ACH is a network for clearing electronic funds transfers among individuals, companies, and banks.[7] Because electronic funds transfers may be either deposits or payments, ACH entries may indicate either a positive or negative entry to the company's account. Likewise, entries to correct bank errors and miscellaneous items may indicate a positive or negative entry to the company's account.

---

7. For further information on ACH, go to http://www.nacha.org/. Click on "ACH Network" and then click on "Intro to the ACH Network."

Integrity, Objectivity, and Ethics in Business

CHECK FRAUD

Check fraud involves counterfeiting, altering, or otherwise manipulating the information on checks in order to fraudulently cash a check. According to the National Check Fraud Center, check fraud and counterfeiting are among the growing problems affecting the financial system, generating over $10 billion in losses annually.

Criminals perpetrate the fraud by taking blank checks from your checkbook, finding a canceled check in the garbage, or removing a check you have mailed to pay bills. Consumers can prevent check fraud by carefully storing blank checks, placing outgoing mail in postal mailboxes, and shredding canceled checks.

Using the Bank Statement as a Control Over Cash

The bank statement is a primary control that a company uses over cash. A company uses the bank's statement as a control by comparing the company's recording of cash transactions to those recorded by the bank.

The cash balance shown by a bank statement is usually different from the company's cash balance, as shown in Exhibit 5.

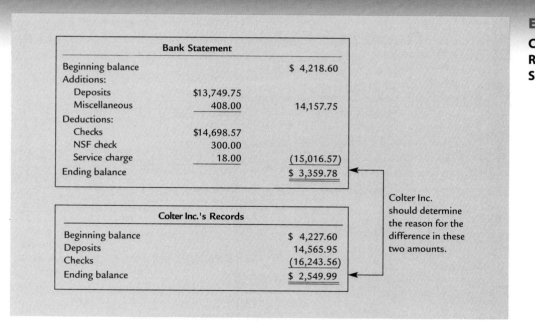

EXHIBIT 5

Colter Inc.'s Records and Bank Statement

Differences between the company and bank balances may arise because of a delay by either the company or bank in recording transactions. For example, there is normally a time lag of one or more days between the date a check is written and the date that it is paid by the bank. Likewise, there is normally a time lag between when the company mails a deposit to the bank (or uses the night depository) and when the bank receives and records the deposit.

Differences may also arise because the bank has increased or decreased the company's account for transactions that the company will not know about until the bank statement is received. Finally, differences may arise from errors made by either the company or the bank. For example, the company may incorrectly post to Cash a check written for $4,500 as $450. Further, a bank may incorrectly record the amount of a check.

Obj | **5**

Describe and illustrate
the use of a bank
reconciliation in
controlling cash.

Bank Reconciliation

A **bank reconciliation** is an analysis of the items and amounts that result in the cash balance reported in the bank statement differing from the balance of the cash account in the ledger. The adjusted cash balance determined in the bank reconciliation is reported on the balance sheet.

A bank reconciliation is usually divided into two sections as follows:

1. The *bank section* begins with the cash balance according to the bank statement and ends with the *adjusted balance*.
2. The *company section* begins with the cash balance according to the company's records and ends with the *adjusted balance*.

The *adjusted balance* from bank and company sections must be equal. The format of the bank reconciliation is shown below.

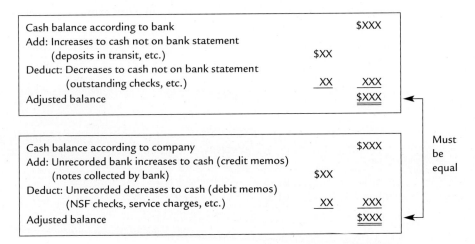

A bank reconciliation is prepared using the following steps:

Bank Section of Reconciliation

Step 1. Enter the *Cash balance according to bank* from the ending cash balance according to the bank statement.

Step 2. *Add deposits not recorded by the bank.* Identify deposits not recorded by the bank by comparing each deposit listed on the bank statement with unrecorded deposits appearing in the preceding period's reconciliation and with the current period's deposits. Examples: Deposits in transit at the end of the period.

Step 3. *Deduct outstanding checks that have not been paid by the bank.* Identify outstanding checks by comparing paid checks with outstanding checks appearing on the preceding period's reconciliation and with recorded checks. Examples: Outstanding checks at the end of the period.

Step 4. Determine the *Adjusted balance* by adding Step 2 and deducting Step 3.

Company Section of Reconciliation

Step 5. Enter the *Cash balance according to company* from the ending cash balance in the ledger.

Step 6. *Add increases to cash (credit memos) that have not been recorded.* Identify the bank credit memos that have not been recorded by comparing the bank statement credit memos to entries in the journal. Examples: A note receivable and interest that the bank has collected for the company.

Step 7. *Deduct decreases to cash (debit memos) that have not been recorded.* Identify the bank debit memos that have not been recorded by comparing the bank statement debit memos to entries in the journal. Examples: Customers' not sufficient funds (NSF) checks; bank service charges.

Step 8. Determine the *Adjusted balance* by adding Step 6 and deducting Step 7.

Verify that Adjusted Balances Are Equal

Step 9. Verify that the Adjusted balances determined in Steps 4 and 8 are equal.

The adjusted balances in the bank and company sections of the reconciliation must be equal. If the balances are not equal, an item has been overlooked and must be found.

Sometimes the adjusted balances are not equal because either the company or the bank has made an error. In such cases, the error is often discovered by comparing the amount of each item (deposit and check) on the bank statement with that in the company's records.

Any bank or company errors discovered should be added to or deducted from the bank or company section of the reconciliation depending on the nature of the error. For example, assume that the bank incorrectly recorded a company check for $50 as $500. This bank error of $450 ($500 − $50) would be added to the bank balance in the bank section of the reconciliation. In addition, the bank would be notified of the error so that it could be corrected. On the other hand, assume that the company recorded a deposit of $1,200 as $2,100. This company error of $900 ($2,100 − $1,200) would be deducted from the cash balance in the company section of the bank reconciliation. The company would later correct the error in its records.

To illustrate, we will use the bank statement for Colter Inc. in Exhibit 5. This bank statement shows a balance of $3,359.78 as of July 31. The cash balance in Colter Inc.'s ledger on the same date is $2,549.99. Using the preceding steps, the following reconciling items were identified:

Step 2. Deposit of July 31, not recorded on bank statement: $816.20
Step 3. Outstanding checks:

Check No. 812	$1,061.00
Check No. 878	435.39
Check No. 883	48.60
Total	$1,544.99

Step 6. Note receivable of $400 plus interest of $8 collected by bank, but not recorded by the company as indicated by a credit memo of $408.

Step 7. Check from customer (Thomas Ivey) for $300 returned by bank because of insufficient funds (NSF) as indicated by a debit memo of $300.00. Bank service charges of $18, but not recorded by the company as indicated by a debit memo of $18.00.

In addition, an error of $9 was discovered. This error occurred when Check No. 879 for $732.26 to Taylor Co., on account, was recorded by the company as $723.26.

The bank reconciliation, based on the Exhibit 4 bank statement and the preceding reconciling items, is shown in Exhibit 6.

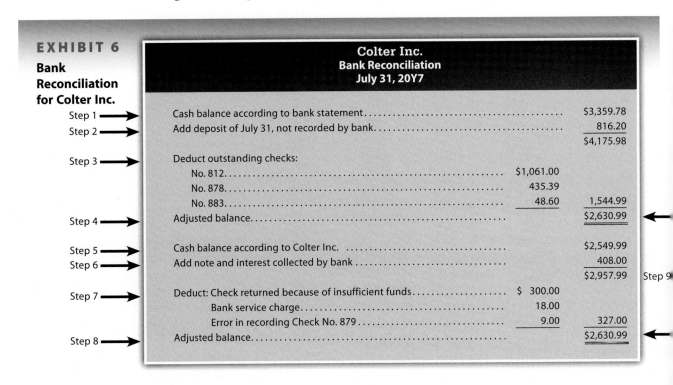

EXHIBIT 6

Bank Reconciliation for Colter Inc.

Colter Inc.
Bank Reconciliation
July 31, 20Y7

Step 1 →	Cash balance according to bank statement..		$3,359.78
Step 2 →	Add deposit of July 31, not recorded by bank....................................		816.20
			$4,175.98
Step 3 →	Deduct outstanding checks:		
	No. 812..	$1,061.00	
	No. 878..	435.39	
	No. 883..	48.60	1,544.99
Step 4 →	Adjusted balance..		$2,630.99
Step 5 →	Cash balance according to Colter Inc.		$2,549.99
Step 6 →	Add note and interest collected by bank		408.00
			$2,957.99
Step 7 →	Deduct: Check returned because of insufficient funds....................	$ 300.00	
	Bank service charge...	18.00	
	Error in recording Check No. 879.............................	9.00	327.00
Step 8 →	Adjusted balance..		$2,630.99

Step 9

The company's records do not need to be updated for any items in the *bank section* of the reconciliation. This section begins with the cash balance according to the bank statement. However, the bank should be notified of any errors that need to be corrected.

The company's records do need to be updated for any items in the *company section* of the bank reconciliation. For example, entries should be made for any unrecorded bank memos and any company errors.

The effects of the adjustments on the accounts and financial statements of Colter Inc. based on the bank reconciliation in Exhibit 6, are as follows:

Statement of Cash Flows	Balance Sheet			Income Statement
	Assets	= **Liabilities** +	**Stockholders' Equity**	
	Cash +	Notes Receivable =	Retained Earnings	
July 31.	408	−400	8	July 31.

Statement of Cash Flows		Income Statement	
July 31. Operating	408	July 31. Interest income	8

Statement of Cash Flows	Balance Sheet				Income Statement
	Assets	= Liabilities +	Stockholders' Equity		
	Cash +	Accounts Receivable	= Accounts Payable +	Retained Earnings	
July 31.	−327	300	−9	−18	July 31.

Statement of Cash Flows		Income Statement	
July 31. Operating	−327	July 31. Misc. expense	−18

After the preceding entries are recorded, the cash account will have a balance of $2,630.99. This cash balance agrees with the adjusted balance shown on the bank reconciliation. This is the amount of cash on July 31 and is the amount that is reported on Colter Inc.'s July 31 balance sheet.

Businesses may reconcile their bank accounts in a slightly different format from that shown in Exhibit 6. Regardless, the objective is to control cash by reconciling the company's records with the bank statement. In doing so, any errors or misuse of cash may be detected.

To enhance internal control, the bank reconciliation should be prepared by an employee who does not take part in or record cash transactions. Otherwise, mistakes may occur, and it is more likely that cash will be stolen or misapplied. For example, an employee who handles cash and also reconciles the bank statement could steal a cash deposit, omit the deposit from the accounts, and omit it from the reconciliation.

Bank reconciliations are also important in computerized systems where deposits and checks are stored in electronic files and records. Some systems use computer software to determine the difference between the bank statement and company cash balances. The software then adjusts for deposits in transit and outstanding checks. Any remaining differences are reported for further analysis.

Special-Purpose Cash Funds

Obj **6**

Describe the accounting for special-purpose cash funds.

A company often has to pay small amounts for such items as postage, office supplies, or minor repairs. Although small, such payments may occur often enough to total a significant amount. Thus, it is desirable to control such payments. However, writing a check for each small payment is not practical. Instead, a special cash fund, called a **petty cash fund**, is used.

Integrity, Objectivity, and Ethics in Business

BANK ERROR IN YOUR FAVOR

At some point, you might experience a bank error in your favor, such as a misposted deposit. Such errors are not a case of "found money," as in the Monopoly® game. Bank control systems

©stephenkirsh/Shutterstock.com

quickly discover most errors and make automatic adjustments. Even so, you have a legal responsibility to report the error and return the money to the bank.

A petty cash fund is established by estimating the amount of payments needed from the fund during a period, such as a week or a month. A check is then written and cashed for this amount. The money obtained from cashing the check is then given to an employee, called the *petty cash custodian*. The petty cash custodian disburses monies from the fund as needed. For control purposes, the company may place restrictions on the maximum amount and the types of payments that can be made from the fund. Each time money is paid from petty cash, the custodian records the details on a petty cash receipts form.

The petty cash fund is normally replenished at periodic intervals, when it is depleted, or reaches a minimum amount. When a petty cash fund is replenished, the accounts are updated by summarizing the petty cash receipts. A check is then written for this amount, payable to Petty Cash.

To illustrate normal petty cash fund entries, assume that a petty cash fund of $500 is established on August 1. The effect on the accounts and financial statements of recording this transaction is as follows:

Statement of Cash Flows	Balance Sheet			Income Statement
	Assets	= Liabilities + Stockholders' Equity		
	Cash +	Petty Cash =		
Aug. 1.	−500	500		

At the end of August, the petty cash receipts indicate expenditures for the following items:

Office supplies	$380
Postage (debit Office Supplies)	22
Store supplies	35
Miscellaneous administrative expense	30
Total	$467

The effect on the accounts and financial statements of replenishing the petty cash fund on August 31 is as follows:

Statement of Cash Flows	Balance Sheet				Income Statement
	Assets			= Liabilities + Stockholders' Equity	
	Cash +	Office Supplies +	Store Supplies =	Retained Earnings	
Aug. 31.	−467	402	35	−30	Aug. 31.

Statement of Cash Flows		Income Statement	
Aug. 31. Operating	−467	Aug. 31. Misc. admin. expense	−30

Replenishing the petty cash fund restores the fund to its original amount of $500. There is no adjustment to Petty Cash when the fund is replenished. Petty Cash is adjusted only if the amount of the fund is later increased or decreased.

Companies often use other cash funds for special needs, such as payroll or travel expenses. Such funds are called **special-purpose funds**. For example, each salesperson might be given $1,000 for travel-related expenses. Periodically, each salesperson submits an expense report, and the fund is replenished. Special-purpose funds are established and controlled in a manner similar to that of the petty cash fund.

Financial Statement Reporting of Cash

Obj | 7

Describe and illustrate the reporting of cash and cash equivalents in the financial statements.

Cash is normally listed as the first asset in the Current Assets section of the balance sheet. Most companies present only a single cash amount on the balance sheet by combining all their bank and cash fund accounts.

A company may temporarily have excess cash. In such cases, the company normally invests in highly liquid investments in order to earn interest. These investments are called **cash equivalents**.[8] Examples of cash equivalents include U.S. Treasury bills, notes issued by major corporations (referred to as commercial paper), and money market funds. In such cases, companies usually report *Cash and cash equivalents* as one amount on the balance sheet.

To illustrate, Microsoft Corp. disclosed the details of its cash and cash equivalents in the notes to a recent financial statement as follows:

Current assets:

Cash and cash equivalents	$ 6,938
Short-term investments	56,102
Total cash and short-term investments	$63,040

The cash and cash equivalents of $6,938 million are further described in the notes to the financial statements, as shown below.

Cash and equivalents:

Cash	$ 2,019
Mutual funds	820
Commercial paper	96
Certificates of deposit	342
U.S. government and agency securities	561
Foreign government bonds	575
Corporate notes and bonds	2,525
Total cash and equivalents	$ 6,938

Banks may require that companies maintain minimum cash balances in their bank accounts. Such a balance is called a **compensating balance**. This is often required by the bank as part of a loan agreement or line of credit. A *line of credit* is a preapproved amount the bank is willing to lend to a customer upon request. Compensating balance requirements are normally disclosed in notes to the financial statements.

8. To be classified as a cash equivalent, according to *FASB Accounting Standards Codification*, Section 305.10, the investment is expected to be converted to cash within three months.

Obj 8

Describe and illustrate the ratio of cash to monthly cash expenses in assessing the ability of a company to continue operating.

Financial Analysis: Ratio of Cash to Monthly Cash Expenses

The statement of cash flows reports "Net cash flows from operating activities." It is generally expected that a company will generate positive cash flows from operations. While a company may occasionally experience economic downturns that generate negative cash flows from operations, a company must generate positive cash flows from operations in the long term to continue in business.

When a company reports negative net cash flows from operations, one measure that is useful in assessing the ability of the company to continue to operate is the ratio of cash to monthly cash expenses. The **ratio of cash to monthly cash expenses** is computed as follows:

$$\text{Ratio of Cash to Monthly Cash Expenses} = \frac{\text{Cash and Cash Equivalents}}{\text{Monthly Cash Expenses}}$$

In the preceding computation, the numerator includes short-term investments that are reported under current assets as cash equivalents. Cash and cash equivalents is the amount reported on the end-of-period balance sheet for which the net cash flows from operations is reported.

The **monthly cash expenses** are computed as follows:

$$\text{Monthly Cash Expenses} = \frac{\text{Net Cash Flows from Operations}}{12}$$

The ratio of cash to monthly cash expenses is especially useful when assessing the ability of new companies to continue operating. A primary cause of failure of new companies is that they are undercapitalized. That is, the companies don't have sufficient funding (cash) from debt or equity financing to operate long enough to generate positive cash flows from operations.

To illustrate, XOMA Corporation is a biotechnology company that develops antibodies for a variety of diseases and illnesses. The following data (in thousands) were adapted from recent financial statements of XOMA.

	Year 2	Year 1
Net cash flows from operating activities	$(29,062)	$(52,537)
End of the year cash and cash equivalents	48,344	37,304

The monthly cash expenses (rounded to nearest thousand) and ratio of cash to monthly cash expenses (rounded to one decimal place) are computed for Years 1 and 2 as follows:

	Year 2	Year 1
Monthly cash expenses:		
$(29,062) ÷ 12	$(2,422)	
$(52,537) ÷ 12		$(4,378)
Ratio of cash to monthly cash expenses:		
$48,344 ÷ $(2,422)	20.0 months	
$37,304 ÷ $(4,378)		8.5 months

At the end of Year 1, XOMA had only enough cash to continue its operations for 8.5 months. In order to continue beyond 8.5 months, XOMA needed to do one or more of the following:

1. Generate positive net cash flows from operations
2. Obtain additional financing from issuing stock or debt

During Year 2, XOMA raised additional cash by issuing stock of $15,143 and debt of $28,836. By doing so, XOMA increased its cash and cash equivalents to $48,344 by the end of Year 2. As a result, it had enough cash to continue its operations 20.0 months at the end of Year 2. In the long term, however, XOMA must generate positive cash flows from operations to continue its operations.

Key Points

1. Describe the Sarbanes-Oxley Act and its impact on internal controls and financial reporting.

The purpose of the Sarbanes-Oxley Act is to restore public confidence and trust in the financial statements of companies. Sarbanes-Oxley requires companies to maintain strong and effective internal controls over the recording of transactions and the preparing of financial statements. Sarbanes-Oxley also requires companies and their independent accountants to report on the effectiveness of a company's internal controls.

2. Describe and illustrate the objectives and elements of internal control.

The objectives of internal control are to provide reasonable assurance that (1) assets are safeguarded and used for business purposes, (2) business information is accurate, and (3) compliance with laws and regulations is met. The elements of internal control are the control environment, risk assessment, control procedures, monitoring, and information and communication.

3. Describe and illustrate the application of internal controls to cash.

One of the most important controls to protect cash received in over-the-counter sales is a cash register. A remittance advice is a control for cash received through the mail. Separating the duties of handling cash and recording cash is also a control. A voucher system is a control system for cash payments that uses a set of procedures for authorizing and recording liabilities and cash payments. Many companies use electronic funds transfers to enhance their control over cash receipts and cash payments.

4. Describe the nature of a bank account and its use in controlling cash.

Businesses use bank accounts as a means of controlling cash. Bank accounts reduce the amount of cash on hand and facilitate the transfer of cash between businesses and locations. In addition, banks send monthly statements to their customers, summarizing all of the transactions for the month. The bank statement allows a business to reconcile the cash transactions recorded in the accounting records to those recorded by the bank.

5. Describe and illustrate the use of a bank reconciliation in controlling cash.

The first section of the bank reconciliation begins with the cash balance according to the bank statement. This balance is adjusted for the company's changes in cash that do not appear on the bank statement and for any bank errors. The second section begins with the cash balance according to the company's records. This balance is adjusted for the bank's changes in cash that do not appear on the company's records and for any company errors. The adjusted balances for the two sections must be equal. No adjustments are necessary on the company's records as a result of the information included in the bank section of the bank reconciliation. However, the items in the company section require adjustments on the company's records.

6. Describe the accounting for special-purpose cash funds.

Businesses often use special-purpose cash funds, such as a petty cash fund or travel funds, to meet specific needs. Each fund is initially established by cashing a check for the amount of cash needed. The cash is then given to a custodian who is authorized to disburse monies from the fund. At periodic intervals or when it is depleted or reaches a minimum amount, the fund is replenished and the disbursements recorded.

7. Describe and illustrate the reporting of cash and cash equivalents in the financial statements.

Cash is listed as the first asset in the Current Assets section of the balance sheet. Companies that have invested excess cash in highly liquid investments usually report *Cash and cash equivalents* on the balance sheet.

8. Describe and illustrate the ratio of cash to monthly cash expenses in assessing the ability of a company to continue operating.

The ratio of cash to monthly cash expenses can be used to assess how long a company with negative cash flows from operations can continue to operate. It is computed as cash and cash equivalents divided by monthly cash expenses. Monthly cash expenses is computed as net cash flows from operations divided by 12.

Key Terms

Bank reconciliation (190)
Bank statement (187)
Cash (183)
Cash equivalents (195)
Cash short and over (184)

Compensating balance (195)
Electronic funds transfer (EFT) (185)
Elements of internal control (178)
Employee fraud (178)

Internal control (176)
Monthly cash expenses (196)
Petty cash fund (193)
Ratio of cash to monthly cash expenses (196)

Sarbanes-Oxley Act (176)
Special-purpose funds (195)
Voucher (186)
Voucher system (186)

Illustrative Problem

The bank statement for Urethane Company for June 30, 20Y5, indicates a balance of $9,143.11. All cash receipts are deposited each evening in a night depository, after banking hours.

The accounting records indicate the following summary data for cash receipts and payments for June:

Cash balance as of June 1	$ 3,943.50
Total cash receipts for June	28,971.60
Total amount of checks issued in June	28,388.85

Comparing the bank statement and the accompanying canceled checks and memorandums with the records reveals the following reconciling items:

a. The bank had collected for Urethane Company $1,030 on a customer's note left for collection. The face of the note was $1,000.

b. A deposit of $1,852.21, representing receipts of June 30, had been made too late to appear on the bank statement.

c. Checks outstanding totaled $5,265.27.

d. A check drawn for $157 had been incorrectly charged by the bank as $175.

e. A check for $30 returned with the statement had been recorded in the company's records as $300. The check was for the payment of an obligation to Avery Equipment Company for the purchase of office supplies on account.

f. Bank service charges for June amounted to $78.20.

Instructions

1. Prepare a bank reconciliation for June.

2. Record the effects on the accounts and financial statements that should be made by Urethane Company based upon the bank reconciliation.

Solution

1.

URETHANE COMPANY

Bank Reconciliation June 30, 20Y5

Cash balance according to bank statement		$ 9,143.11
Add: Deposit of June 30 not recorded by bank	$1,852.21	
Bank error in charging check as $175 instead of $157	18.00	1,870.21
		$11,013.32
Deduct: Outstanding checks		5,265.27
Adjusted balance		$ 5,748.05
Cash balance according to company's records		$ 4,526.25*
Add: Proceeds of note collected by bank, including $30 interest	$1,030.00	
Error in recording check	270.00	1,300.00
		$ 5,826.25
Deduct: Bank service charges		78.20
Adjusted balance		$ 5,748.05

*$3,943.50 + $28,971.60 − $28,388.85

2.

Statement of Cash Flows	Balance Sheet					Income Statement
	Assets		= **Liabilities** +	**Stockholders' Equity**		
	Cash +	Notes Receivable	= Accounts Payable +	Retained Earnings		
June 30.	1,300.00	−1,000.00	270.00	30.00		June 30.

Statement of Cash Flows		Income Statement
June 30. Operating	1,240.00	June 30. Interest revenue 30.00

Statement of Cash Flows	Balance Sheet			Income Statement
	Assets	= **Liabilities** +	**Stockholders' Equity**	
	Cash	=	Retained Earnings	
June 30.	−78.20		−78.20	June 30.

Statement of Cash Flows		Income Statement
June 30. Operating	−78.20	June 30. Misc. admin. exp. −78.20

Self-Examination Questions (Answers appear at the end of chapter)

1. Which of the following is not an element of internal control?
   A. Control environment
   B. Monitoring
   C. Compliance with laws and regulations
   D. Control procedures

2. The bank erroneously charged Tropical Services' account for $450.50 for a check that was correctly written and recorded by Tropical Services as $540.50. To reconcile the bank account of Tropical Services at the end of the month, you would:
   A. add $90 to the cash balance according to the bank statement.
   B. add $90 to the cash balance according to Tropical Services' records.
   C. deduct $90 from the cash balance according to the bank statement.
   D. deduct $90 from the cash balance according to Tropical Services' records.

3. In preparing a bank reconciliation, the amount of checks outstanding would be:
   A. added to the cash balance according to the bank statement.
   B. deducted from the cash balance according to the bank statement.
   C. added to the cash balance according to the company's records.
   D. deducted from the cash balance according to the company's records.

4. Adjustments to the company's records based on the bank reconciliation are required for:
   A. additions to the cash balance according to the company's records.
   B. deductions from the cash balance according to the company's records.
   C. both A and B.
   D. neither A nor B.

5. A petty cash fund is:
   A. used to pay relatively small amounts.
   B. established by estimating the amount of cash needed for disbursements of relatively small amounts during a specified period.
   C. reimbursed when the amount of money in the fund is reduced to a predetermined minimum amount.
   D. all of the above.

Class Discussion Questions

1. (a) Why did Congress pass the Sarbanes-Oxley Act? (b) What was the purpose of the Sarbanes-Oxley Act?

2. Define internal control.

3. (a) Name and describe the five elements of internal control. (b) Is any one element of internal control more important than another?

4. How does a policy of rotating clerical employees from job to job aid in strengthening the control procedures within the control environment? Explain.

5. Why should the responsibility for a sequence of related operations be divided among different persons? Explain.

6. Why should the employee who handles cash receipts not have the responsibility for maintaining the accounts receivable records? Explain.

7. In an attempt to improve operating efficiency, one employee was made responsible for all purchasing, receiving, and storing of supplies. Is this organizational change wise from an internal control standpoint? Explain.

8. The ticket seller at a movie theater doubles as a ticket taker for a few minutes each day while the ticket taker is on a break. Which control procedure of a business's system of internal control is violated in this situation?

9. Why should the responsibility for maintaining the accounting records be separated from the responsibility for operations? Explain.

10. Assume that Leslie Hunter, accounts payable clerk for Campland Inc., stole $185,000 by paying fictitious invoices for goods that were never received. The clerk set up accounts in the names of the fictitious companies and cashed the checks at a local bank. Describe a control procedure that would have prevented or detected the fraud.

11. Before a voucher for the purchase of merchandise is approved for payment, supporting documents should be compared to verify the accuracy of the

liability. Give an example of a supporting document for the purchase of merchandise.

12. The accounting clerk pays all obligations by pre-numbered checks. What are the strengths and weaknesses in the internal control over cash payments in this situation?

13. The balance of Cash is likely to differ from the bank statement balance. What two factors are likely to be responsible for the difference?

14. What is the purpose of preparing a bank reconciliation?

15. Do items reported as a credit memorandum on the bank statement represent (a) additions made by the bank to the company's balance or (b) deductions made by the bank from the company's balance? Explain.

16. Seatow Inc. has a petty cash fund of $2,500. (a) Since the petty cash fund is only $2,500, should Seatow Inc. implement controls over petty cash? (b) What controls, if any, could be used for the petty cash fund?

17. (a) How are cash equivalents reported in the financial statements? (b) What are some examples of cash equivalents?

Exercises

E5-1   Sarbanes-Oxley internal control report

Obj 1

Using Wikipedia (www.wikipedia.org.), look up the entry for the Sarbanes-Oxley Act. Look over the table of contents and find the section that describes Section 404. What does Section 404 require of management's internal control report?

E5-2   Internal controls

Obj 2, 3

Abby Bergen has recently been hired as the manager of Stella's Coffee, a national chain of franchised coffee shops. During her first month as store manager, Abby encountered the following internal control situations:

a. Since only one employee uses the cash register, that employee is responsible for counting the cash at the end of the shift and verifying that the cash in the drawer matches the amount of cash sales recorded by the cash register. Abby expects each cashier to balance the drawer to the penny *every* time—no exceptions.

b. Abby caught an employee putting a case of single-serving tea bags in her car. Not wanting to create a scene, Abby smiled and said, "I don't think you're putting those tea bags on the right shelf. Don't they belong inside the coffee shop?" The employee returned the tea bags to the stockroom.

c. Stella's Coffee has one cash register. Prior to Abby's joining the coffee shop, each employee working on a shift would take a customer order, accept payment, and then prepare the order. Abby made one employee on each shift responsible for taking orders and accepting the customer's payment. Other employees prepare the orders.

State whether you agree or disagree with Abby's method of handling each situation and explain your answer.

E5-3   Internal controls

Obj 2, 3

Lili's Creations is a retail store specializing in women's clothing. The store has established a liberal return policy for the holiday season in order to encourage gift purchases. Any item purchased during November and December may be returned through January 31, with a receipt, for cash or exchange. If the customer does not have a receipt, cash will still be refunded for any item under $100. If the item is more than $100, a check is mailed to the customer.

Whenever an item is returned, a store clerk completes a return slip, which the customer signs. The return slip is placed in a special box. The store manager visits the return counter approximately once every two hours to authorize the return slips. Clerks are instructed to place the returned merchandise on the proper rack on the selling floor as soon as possible.

This year, returns at Lili's Creations reached an all-time high. There are a large number of returns under $100 without receipts.

a. How can sales clerks employed at Lili's Creations use the store's return policy to steal money from the cash register?

b. What internal control weaknesses do you see in the return policy that make cash thefts easier?

c. Would issuing a store credit in place of a cash refund for all merchandise returned without a receipt reduce the possibility of theft? List some advantages and disadvantages of issuing a store credit in place of a cash refund.

d. Assume that Lili's Creations is committed to the current policy of issuing cash refunds without a receipt. What changes could be made in the store's procedures regarding customer refunds in order to improve internal control?

Obj 2, 3

E5-4   Internal controls

Republic City Bank provides loans to businesses in the community through its Commercial Lending Department. Small loans (less than $250,000) may be approved by an individual loan officer, while larger loans (greater than $250,000) must be approved by a board of loan officers. Once a loan is approved, the funds are made available to the loan applicant under agreed-upon terms. The president of Republic City Bank has instituted a policy whereby he has the individual authority to approve loans up to $4,000,000. The president believes that this policy will allow flexibility to approve loans to valued clients much quicker than under the previous policy.

As an internal auditor of Republic City Bank, how would you respond to this change in policy?

Obj 2, 3

E5-5   Internal controls

One of the largest losses in history from unauthorized securities trading involved a securities trader for the French bank **Société Générale**. The trader was able to circumvent internal controls and create over $7 billion in trading losses in six months. The trader apparently escaped detection by using knowledge of the bank's internal control systems learned from a previous back-office monitoring job. Much of this monitoring involved the use of software to monitor trades. In addition, traders are usually kept to tight spending limits. Apparently, these controls failed in this case.

What general weaknesses in Société Générale's internal controls contributed to the occurrence and size of the losses?

Obj 2, 3

E5-6   Internal controls

An employee of **JHT Holdings, Inc.**, a trucking company, was responsible for resolving roadway accident claims under $25,000. The employee created fake accident claims and wrote settlement checks of between $5,000 and $25,000 to friends or acquaintances acting as phony "victims." One friend recruited subordinates at his place of work to cash some of the checks. Beyond this, the JHT employee also recruited lawyers, who he paid to represent both the trucking company and the fake victims in the bogus accident settlements. When the lawyers cashed the checks, they allegedly split the money with the corrupt JHT employee. This fraud went undetected for two years.

Why would it take so long to discover such a fraud?

Obj 2, 3

E5-7   Internal controls

Timeless Sound Co. discovered a fraud wherein one of its front office administrative employees used company funds to purchase goods, such as computers, digital cameras, DVD players, and other electronic items, for her own use. The fraud was discovered when employees noticed an increase in delivery frequency from vendors and the use of unusual vendors. After some investigation, it was discovered that the employee would alter the description or change the quantity on an invoice in order to explain the cost on the bill.

What general internal control weaknesses contributed to this fraud?

E5-8 Financial statement fraud

Obj 2, 3

A former chairman, CFO, and controller of Donnkenny, Inc., an apparel company that makes sportswear for Pierre Cardin and Victoria Jones, pleaded guilty to financial statement fraud. These managers used false journal entries to record fictitious sales, hid inventory in public warehouses so that it could be recorded as "sold," and required sales orders to be backdated so that the sale could be moved back to an earlier period. The combined effect of these actions caused $25 million out of $40 million in quarterly sales to be phony.

a. Why might control procedures listed in this chapter be insufficient in stopping this type of fraud?

b. How could this type of fraud be stopped?

E5-9 Internal control of cash receipts

Obj 2, 3

The procedures used for over-the-counter receipts are as follows. At the close of each day's business, the sales clerks count the cash in their respective cash drawers, after which they determine the amount recorded by the cash register and prepare the memo cash form, noting any discrepancies. An employee from the cashier's office counts the cash, compares the total with the memo, and takes the cash to the cashier's office.

a. Indicate the weak link in internal control.

b. How can the weakness be corrected?

E5-10 Internal control of cash receipts

Obj 2, 3

Kevin Clavin works at the drive-through window of Big Bad Burgers. Occasionally, when a drive-through customer orders, Kevin fills the order and pockets the customer's money. He does not ring up the order on the cash register.

Identify the internal control weaknesses that exist at Big Bad Burgers, and discuss what can be done to prevent this theft.

E5-11 Internal control of cash receipts

Obj 2, 3

The mailroom employees send all remittances and remittance advices to the cashier. The cashier deposits the cash in the bank and forwards the remittance advices and duplicate deposit slips to the Accounting Department.

a. Indicate the weak link in internal control in the handling of cash receipts.

b. How can the weakness be corrected?

E5-12 Entry for cash sales; cash short

Obj 2, 3

The actual cash received from cash sales was $41,568, and the amount indicated by the cash register total was $41,610.

a. What is the amount deposited in the bank for the day's sales?

b. What is the amount recorded for the day's sales?

c. How should the difference be recorded?

d. If a cashier is consistently over or short, what action should be taken?

Obj **2, 3**

E5-13   Recording cash sales; cash over

The actual cash received from cash sales was $19,040, and the amount indicated by the cash register total was $18,975.

a. What is the amount deposited in the bank for the day's sales?

b. What is amount recorded for the day's sales?

c. How should the difference be recorded?

d. If a cashier is consistently over or short, what action should be taken?

Obj **2, 3**

E5-14   Internal control of cash payments

Greenleaf Co. is a small merchandising company with a manual accounting system. An investigation revealed that in spite of a sufficient bank balance, a significant amount of available cash discounts had been lost because of failure to make timely payments. In addition, it was discovered that the invoices for several purchases had been paid twice.

Outline procedures for the payment of vendors' invoices, so that the possibilities of losing available cash discounts and of paying an invoice a second time will be minimized.

Obj **2, 3**

E5-15   Internal control of cash payments

Torpedo Digital Company, a communications equipment manufacturer, recently fell victim to a fraud scheme developed by one of its employees. To understand the scheme, it is necessary to review Torpedo's procedures for the purchase of services.

The purchasing agent is responsible for ordering services (such as repairs to a photocopy machine or office cleaning) after receiving a service requisition from an authorized manager. However, since no tangible goods are delivered, a receiving report is not prepared. When the Accounting Department receives an invoice billing Torpedo for a service call, the accounts payable clerk calls the manager who requested the service in order to verify that it was performed.

The fraud scheme involves Ross Dunbar, the manager of plant and facilities. Ross arranged for his uncle's company, Capo Industrial Supplies and Service, to be placed on Torpedo's approved vendor list. Ross did not disclose the family relationship.

On several occasions, Ross would submit a requisition for services to be provided by Capo Industrial Supplies and Service. However, the service requested was really not needed, and it was never performed. Capo Industrial Supplies and Service would bill Torpedo for the service and then split the cash payment with Ross.

Explain what changes should be made to Torpedo's procedures for ordering and paying for services in order to prevent such occurrences in the future.

Obj **5**

E5-16   Bank reconciliation

Identify each of the following reconciling items as: (a) an addition to the cash balance according to the bank statement, (b) a deduction from the cash balance according to the bank statement, (c) an addition to the cash balance according to the company's records, or (d) a deduction from the cash balance according to the company's records. (None of the transactions reported by bank debit and credit memos have been recorded by the company.)

1. Bank service charges, $36.

2. Check drawn by company for $375 but incorrectly recorded by company as $735.

3. Check for $50 incorrectly charged by bank as $500.

4. Check of a customer returned by bank to company because of insufficient funds, $1,200.

5. Deposit in transit, $12,375.

6. Outstanding checks, $14,770.

7. Note collected by bank, $10,600.

E5-17   Entries based on bank reconciliation

Obj 5

Which of the reconciling items listed in Exercise 5-16 are required to be recorded in the company's accounts?

E5-18   Bank reconciliation

Obj 5
✔ Adjusted
balance: $30,000

The following data were accumulated for use in reconciling the bank account of Ross Co. for March 20Y9:

a. Cash balance according to the company's records at March 31, $29,945.

b. Cash balance according to the bank statement at March 31, $29,200.

c. Checks outstanding, $11,600.

d. Deposit in transit, not recorded by bank, $12,400.

e. A check for $240 in payment of an account was erroneously recorded by Ross Co. as $420.

f. Bank debit memo for service charges, $125.

Prepare a bank reconciliation, using the format shown in Exhibit 6.

E5-19   Entries for bank reconciliation

Obj 5

Using the data presented in Exercise 5-18, record the effects on the accounts and financial statements of the company based upon the bank reconciliation.

E5-20   Entries for note collected by bank

Obj 5

Accompanying a bank statement for Nite Lighting Company is a credit memo for $26,500, representing the principal ($25,000) and interest ($1,500) on a note that had been collected by the bank. The company had been notified by the bank at the time of the collection, but had made no recording. Record the adjustment that should be made by the company to bring the accounting records up to date.

E5-21   Bank reconciliation

Obj 5
✔ Adjusted
balance: $15,310

An accounting clerk for Westwind Co. prepared the following bank reconciliation:

WESTWIND CO.
Bank Reconciliation
August 31, 20Y6

Cash balance according to company's records		$ 6,800
Add: Outstanding checks	$4,190	
Error by Westwind Co. in recording Check No. 01-115 as $830 instead of $380	450	
Note for $7,500 collected by bank, including interest	8,100	12,740
	$2,175	$19,540
Deduct: Deposit in transit on August 31		
Bank service charges	40	2,215
Cash balance according to bank statement		$17,325

a. From the bank reconciliation data, prepare a new bank reconciliation for Westwind Co., using the format shown in the illustrative problem.

b. If a balance sheet were prepared for Westwind Co. on August 31, 20Y6, what amount should be reported for cash?

Obj 5

✔ Corrected
adjusted balance:
$24,110

E5-22 Bank reconciliation

Identify the errors in the following bank reconciliation:

DAKOTA CO.
Bank Reconciliation
For the Month Ended June 30, 20Y3

Cash balance according to bank statement			$22,900
Add outstanding checks:			
No. 7715		$1,450	
7760		915	
7764		1,850	
7765		775	4,990
			$27,890
Deduct deposit of June 30, not recorded by bank			6,200
Adjusted balance			$21,690
Cash balance according to company's records			$15,625
Add: Proceeds of note collected by bank:			
Principal	$6,000		
Interest	360	$6,360	
Service charges		30	6,390
			$22,015
Deduct: Check returned because of insufficient funds		$ 545	
Error in recording June 20 deposit of $5,200 as $2,500		2,700	3,245
Adjusted balance			$18,770

Obj 2, 3, 5

E5-23 Using bank reconciliation to determine cash receipts stolen

Pala Co. records all cash receipts on the basis of its cash register tapes. Pala Co. discovered during April 20Y1 that one of its sales clerks had stolen an undetermined amount of cash receipts when she took the daily deposits to the bank. The following data have been gathered for April:

Cash in bank according to the company records	$19,565
Cash according to the April 30, 20Y1, bank statement	28,175
Outstanding checks as of April 30, 20Y1	12,100
Bank service charges for April	75
Note receivable, including interest collected by bank in April	3,710

No deposits were in transit on April 30.

a. Determine the amount of cash receipts stolen by the sales clerk.

b. What accounting controls would have prevented or detected this theft?

Obj 6

E5-24 Recording petty cash fund transactions

Illustrate the effect on the accounts and financial statements of the following transactions:

a. Established a petty cash fund of $750.

b. The amount of cash in the petty cash fund is now $140. Replenished the fund, based on the following summary of petty cash receipts: office supplies, $325; miscellaneous selling expense, $200; miscellaneous administrative expense, $85.

E5-25 Recording petty cash fund transactions

Illustrate the effect on the accounts and financial statements of the following transactions:

a. Established a petty cash fund of $500.

b. The amount of cash in the petty cash fund is now $45. Replenished the fund, based on the following summary of petty cash receipts: office supplies, $175; miscellaneous selling expense, $190; miscellaneous administrative expense, $90.

E5-26 Variation in cash flows

Mattel, Inc., designs, manufactures, and markets toy products worldwide. Mattel's toys include Barbie™ fashion dolls and accessories, Hot Wheels™, and Fisher-Price brands. For a recent year, Mattel reported the following net cash flows from operating activities (in thousands):

First quarter ending March 31	$ 171,506
Second quarter ending June 30	(232,557)
Third quarter ending September 30	(40,109)
Fourth quarter December 31	986,778

Explain why Mattel reports negative net cash flows from operating activities during the first three quarters, yet reports positive cash flows for the fourth quarter and net positive cash flows for the year.

Problems

P5-1 Evaluate internal control of cash

The following procedures were recently installed by The China Shop:

a. All sales are rung up on the cash register, and a receipt is given to the customer. All sales are recorded on a record locked inside the cash register.

b. At the end of a shift, each cashier counts the cash in his or her cash register, unlocks the cash register record, and compares the amount of cash with the amount on the record to determine cash shortages and overages.

c. Checks received through the mail are given daily to the accounts receivable clerk for recording collections on account and for depositing in the bank.

d. Disbursements are made from the petty cash fund only after a petty cash receipt has been completed and signed by the payee.

e. Each cashier is assigned a separate cash register drawer to which no other cashier has access.

f. The bank reconciliation is prepared by the accountant.

g. Vouchers and all supporting documents are perforated with a PAID designation after being paid by the treasurer.

Instructions

Indicate whether each of the procedures of internal control over cash represents (1) a strength or (2) a weakness. For each weakness, indicate why it exists.

Obj | 5

✔ 1. Adjusted
balance: $21,470

P5-2   Bank reconciliation and entries

The cash account for Recreational Systems at March 31, 20Y6, indicated a balance of $12,435. The bank statement indicated a balance of $27,150 on March 31, 20Y6. Comparing the bank statement and the accompanying canceled checks and memos with the records reveals the following reconciling items:

a. Checks outstanding totaled $9,675.

b. A deposit of $4,175, representing receipts of March 31, had been made too late to appear on the bank statement.

c. The bank had collected $8,480 on a note left for collection. The face of the note was $8,000.

d. A check for $180 returned with the statement had been incorrectly recorded by Recreational Systems as $810. The check was for the payment of an obligation to Jones Co. for the purchase of office supplies on account.

e. A check drawn for $750 had been incorrectly charged by the bank as $570.

f. Bank service charges for March amounted to $75.

Instructions

1. Prepare a bank reconciliation.

2. Illustrate the effects on the accounts and financial statements of the bank reconciliation.

Obj | 5

✔ 1. Adjusted
balance: $34,885

P5-3   Bank reconciliation and entries

The cash account for All American Sports Co. on April 1, 20Y5, indicated a balance of $23,600. During April, the total cash deposited was $80,150, and checks written totaled $72,800. The bank statement indicated a balance of $40,360 on April 30, 20Y5. Comparing the bank statement, the canceled checks, and the accompanying memos with the records revealed the following reconciling items:

a. Checks outstanding totaled $14,300.

b. A deposit of $9,275, representing receipts of April 30, had been made too late to appear on the bank statement.

c. A check for $720 had been incorrectly charged by the bank as $270.

d. A check for $110 returned with the statement had been recorded by All American Sports Co. as $1,100. The check was for the payment of an obligation to Garber Co. on account.

e. The bank had collected for All American Sports Co. $4,320 on a note left for collection. The face of the note was $4,000.

f. Bank service charges for April amounted to $75.

g. A check for $1,300 from Bishop Co. was returned by the bank because of insufficient funds.

Instructions

1. Prepare a bank reconciliation as of April 30.

2. Illustrate the effects on the accounts and financial statements of the bank reconciliation.

Obj | 5

✔ 1. Adjusted
balance: $10,798.88

P5-4   Bank reconciliation and entries

Rancho Foods deposits all cash receipts each Wednesday and Friday in a night depository, after banking hours. The data required to reconcile the bank statement as of May 31 have been taken from various documents and records and are reproduced as follows. The sources of the data are printed in capital letters. All checks were written for payments on account.

Note: The spreadsheet icon indicates an Excel template is available on the student companion site.

CASH ACCOUNT:

Balance as of May 1	$9,578.00

CASH RECEIPTS FOR MONTH OF MAY	$5,255.89

DUPLICATE DEPOSIT TICKETS:

Date and amount of each deposit in May:

Date	Amount	Date	Amount	Date	Amount
May 2	$569.50	May 12	$580.70	May 23	$ 731.45
5	701.80	16	600.10	26	601.50
9	189.24	19	701.26	31	580.34

CHECKS WRITTEN:

Number and amount of each check issued in May:

Check No.	Amount	Check No.	Amount	Check No.	Amount
614	$243.50	621	$309.50	628	$ 837.70
615	350.10	622	Void	629	329.90
616	279.90	623	Void	630	882.80
617	395.50	624	707.01	631	1,081.56
618	435.40	625	185.63	632	62.40
619	320.10	626	550.03	633	310.08
620	238.87	627	318.73	634	503.30

Total amount of checks issued in May	$8,342.01

```
                          MEMBER FDIC                          PAGE   1

  A        AMERICAN NATIONAL BANK        ACCOUNT NUMBER
  N B          OF DETROIT                FROM  5/01/20Y8  TO  5/31/20Y8

  DETROIT, MI 48201-2500   (313)933-8547   BALANCE         9,422.80

                                        9 DEPOSITS         6,086.35

                                       20 WITHDRAWALS      7,462.11

         Rancho Foods                   4 OTHER DEBITS
                                          AND CREDITS      3,650.00CR

                                          NEW BALANCE     11,697.04

  * – – – – – CHECKS AND OTHER DEBITS – – – – – * –  DEPOSITS – * – DATE – * – BALANCE– *

  No.580  310.10   No.612    92.50            780.80    05/01     9,801.00
  No.602   85.50   No.614   243.50            569.50    05/03    10,041.50
  No.615  350.10   No.616   279.90            701.80    05/06    10,113.30
  No.617  395.50   No.618   435.40            819.24    05/11    10,101.64
  No.619  320.10   No.620   238.87            580.70    05/13    10,123.37
  No.621  309.50   No.624   707.01     MS 4,000.00      05/14    13,106.86
  No.625  158.63   No.626   550.03     MS   160.00      05/14    12,558.20
  No.627  318.73   No.629   329.90            600.10    05/17    12,509.67
  No.630  882.80   No.631 1,081.56  NSF 450.00          05/20    10,095.31
  No.632   62.40   No.633   310.08            701.26    05/21    10,424.09
                                              731.45    05/24    11,155.54
                                              601.50    05/28    11,757.04
                      SC    60.00                       05/31    11,697.04

          EC — ERROR CORRECTION            OD — OVERDRAFT
          MS — MISCELLANEOUS               PS — PAYMENT STOPPED
          NSF — NOT SUFFICIENT FUNDS       SC — SERVICE CHARGE

    * * *                      * * *                      * * *
       THE RECONCILEMENT OF THIS STATEMENT WITH YOUR RECORDS IS ESSENTIAL.
         ANY ERROR OR EXCEPTION SHOULD BE REPORTED IMMEDIATELY.
```

BANK RECONCILIATION FOR PRECEDING MONTH (DATED APRIL 30):

Cash balance according to bank statement		$ 9,422.80
Add deposit of April 30, not recorded by bank		780.80
		$10,203.60
Deduct outstanding checks:		
No. 580	$310.10	
No. 602	85.50	
No. 612	92.50	
No. 613	137.50	625.60
Adjusted balance		$ 9,578.00
Cash balance according to company's records		$ 9,605.70
Deduct service charges		27.70
Adjusted balance		$ 9,578.00

Instructions

1. Prepare a bank reconciliation as of May 31. If errors in recording deposits or checks are discovered, assume that the errors were made by the company. Assume that all deposits are from cash sales except for the note receivable of $4,000 and interest of $160 collected on May 14. All checks are written to satisfy accounts payable.

2. Illustrate the effects on the accounts and financial statements of the bank reconciliation.

3. What is the amount of Cash that should appear on the balance sheet as of May 31?

4. Assume that a canceled check for $50 has been incorrectly recorded by the bank as $500. Briefly explain how the error would be included in a bank reconciliation and how it should be corrected.

Financial Analysis

Obj 8

FA 5-1   Ratio of cash to monthly cash expenses

AcelRx Pharmaceuticals, Inc., develops therapies for pain relief for a variety of patients, including cancer and trauma patients. The following data (in thousands) were adapted from recent financial statements.

	Year 2	Year 1
Net cash flows from operating activities	$(15,287)	$(12,225)
End of the year cash and cash equivalents	7,794	3,055
Short-term investments*	27,991	627

*Includes U.S. short-term government securities that are readily convertible to cash.

1. Compute the monthly cash expenses for Years 1 and 2. Round to nearest thousand.

2. Compute the ratio of cash to monthly cash expenses for Years 1 and 2, excluding short-term investments.

3. Including short-term investments as part of cash and cash equivalents, compute the ratio of cash to monthly cash expenses for Years 1 and 2. Round to one decimal place.

4. Comment on the results from parts (2) and (3).

5. AcelRx had negative cash flows from operations for Years 1 and 2, yet cash, cash equivalents, and short-term investments increased from $3,682 ($3,055 + $627) in Year 1 to $35,785 ($7,794 + $27,991) in Year 2. How could this have happened?

FA 5-2 Ratio of cash to monthly cash expenses

Pacira Pharmaceuticals Inc. develops, produces, and sells products used in hospitals and surgery centers.

The following data (in thousands) were adapted from recent financial statements.

	Year 2	Year 1
Net cash flows from operating activities	$(31,000)	$(24,880)
End of the year cash and cash equivalents	47,467	27,447
Short-term investments*	29,985	—

*Includes various short-term securities that are readily convertible to cash.

1. Compute the monthly cash expenses for Years 1 and 2. Round to nearest thousand.
2. Compute the ratio of cash to monthly cash expenses for Years 1 and 2.
3. Including short-term investments as part of cash and cash equivalents, compute the ratio of cash to monthly cash expenses for Years 1 and 2. Round to one decimal place.
4. Comment on the results from parts (2) and (3).
5. Pacira had negative cash flows from operations for Years 1 and 2, yet cash, cash equivalents, and short-term investments increased from $27,447 in Year 1 to $77,452 ($47,467 + $29,985) in Year 2. How could this have happened?

FA 5-3 Ratio of cash to monthly cash expenses

Kips Bay Medical Inc. is a medical device company that develops, produces, and sells products used in coronary surgery. The following data (in thousands) were adapted from recent financial statements.

	Year 2	Year 1
Net cash flows from operating activities	$(8,105)	$(4,378)
End of the year cash and cash equivalents	6,211	3,548
Short-term investments*	2,957	236

*Includes various short-term securities that are readily convertible to cash.

1. Compute the monthly cash expenses for Years 1 and 2. Round to nearest thousand.
2. Compute the ratio of cash to monthly cash expenses for Years 1 and 2.
3. Including short-term investments as part of cash and cash equivalents, compute the ratio of cash to monthly cash expenses for Years 1 and 2. Round to one decimal place.
4. Comment on the results from parts (2) and (3).
5. Kips Bay Medical had negative cash flows from operations for Years 1 and 2, yet cash, cash equivalents, and short-term investments increased. How could this have happened?

FA 5-4 Ratio of cash to monthly cash expenses

Boston Scientific Corporation is a competitor of Kips Bay Medical (FA 5-3). It was organized in 1979 and also develops, produces, and sells medical devices. The following data (in thousands) were adapted from Boston Scientific's recent financial statements.

	Year 2	Year 1
Net cash flows from operating activities	$1,008	$325
End of the year cash and cash equivalents	267	213

1. Compare the preceding data for Boston Scientific with Kips Bay Medical's data shown in FA 5-3.
2. Would the computation of the ratio of cash to monthly cash expenses be meaningful for Boston Scientific?

Cases

Case 5-1 Ethics and professional conduct in business

During the preparation of the bank reconciliation for Apache Grading Co., Sarah Ferrari, the assistant controller, discovered that Rocky Spring Bank incorrectly recorded a $610 check written by Apache Grading Co. as $160. Sarah has decided not to notify the bank but wait for the bank to detect the error. Sarah plans to record the $450 error as Other Income if the bank fails to detect the error within the next three months.

Discuss whether Sarah is behaving in a professional manner.

Case 5-2 Internal controls

The following is an excerpt from a conversation between two sales clerks, Tracy Rawlin and Jeff Weimer. Both Tracy and Jeff are employed by Magnum Electronics, a locally owned and operated electronics retail store.

Tracy: Did you hear the news?

Jeff: What news?

Tracy: Bridget and Ken were both arrested this morning.

Jeff: What? Arrested? You're putting me on!

Tracy: No, really! The police arrested them first thing this morning. Put them in handcuffs, read them their rights—the whole works. It was unreal!

Jeff: What did they do?

Tracy: Well, apparently they were filling out merchandise refund forms for fictitious customers and then taking the cash.

Jeff: I guess I never thought of that. How did they catch them?

Tracy: The store manager noticed that returns were twice that of last year and seemed to be increasing. When he confronted Bridget, she became flustered and admitted to taking the cash, apparently over $15,000 in just three months. They're going over the last six months' transactions to try to determine how much Ken stole. He apparently started stealing first.

Suggest appropriate control procedures that would have prevented or detected the theft of cash.

Case 5-3 Internal controls

The following is an excerpt from a conversation between the store manager of La Food Grocery Stores, Amy Locke, and Steve Meyer, president of La Food Grocery Stores.

Steve: Amy, I'm concerned about this new scanning system.

Amy: What's the problem?

Steve: Well, how do we know the clerks are ringing up all the merchandise?

Amy: That's one of the strong points about the system. The scanner automatically rings up each item, based on its bar code. We update the prices daily, so we're sure that the sale is rung up for the right price.

Steve: That's not my concern. What keeps a clerk from pretending to scan items and then simply not charging his friends? If his friends were buying 10–15 items, it would be easy for the clerk to pass through several items with his finger over the bar code or just pass the merchandise through the scanner with the wrong side showing. It would look normal for anyone observing. In the old days, we at least could hear the cash register ringing up each sale.

Amy: I see your point.

Suggest ways that La Food Grocery Stores could prevent or detect the theft of merchandise as described.

Case 5-4   Ethics and professional conduct in business

Javier Meza and Sue Quan are both cash register clerks for Healthy Markets. Ingrid Perez is the store manager for Healthy Markets. The following is an excerpt of a conversation between Javier and Sue:

Javier: Sue, how long have you been working for Healthy Markets?

Sue: Almost five years this June. You just started two weeks ago, right?

Javier: Yes. Do you mind if I ask you a question?

Sue: No, go ahead.

Javier: What I want to know is, have they always had this rule that if your cash register is short at the end of the day, you have to make up the shortage out of your own pocket?

Sue: Yes, as long as I've been working here.

Javier: Well, it's the pits. Last week I had to pay in almost $30.

Sue: It's not that big a deal. I just make sure that I'm not short at the end of the day.

Javier: How do you do that?

Sue: I just shortchange a few customers early in the day. There are a few jerks that deserve it anyway. Most of the time, their attention is elsewhere and they don't think to check their change.

Javier: What happens if you're over at the end of the day?

Sue: Ingrid lets me keep it as long as it doesn't get to be too large. I've not been short in over a year. I usually clear about $10 to $40 extra per day.

Discuss this case from the viewpoint of proper controls and professional behavior.

Case 5-5   Bank reconciliation and internal control

The records of Clairemont Company indicate an August 31, 20Y1, cash balance of $6,675, which includes undeposited receipts for August 30 and 31. The cash balance on the bank statement as of August 31 is $5,350. This balance includes a note of $3,000 plus $210 interest collected by the bank but not recorded in the journal. Checks outstanding on August 31 were as follows: No. 370, $580; No. 379, $615; No. 390, $900; No. 1148, $225; No. 1149, $300; and No. 1151, $750.

On August 9, the cashier resigned, effective at the end of the month. Before leaving on August 31, the cashier prepared the following bank reconciliation:

Cash balance per books, August 31, 20Y1		$6,675
Add outstanding checks:		
No. 1148	$225	
1149	300	
1151	750	1,175
		$7,850
Less undeposited receipts		2,500
Cash balance per bank, August 31, 20Y1		$5,350
Deduct unrecorded note with interest		3,210
True cash, August 31, 20Y1		$2,140

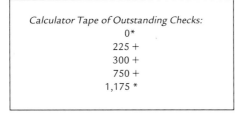

Calculator Tape of Outstanding Checks:
0*
225 +
300 +
750 +
1,175 *

Subsequently, the owner of Clairemont Company discovered that the cashier had stolen an unknown amount of undeposited receipts, leaving only $2,500 to be deposited on August 31. The owner, a close family friend, has asked your help in determining the amount that the former cashier has stolen.

1. Determine the amount the cashier stole from Clairemont Company. Show your computations in good form.
2. How did the cashier attempt to conceal the theft?
3. a. Identify two major weaknesses in internal controls that allowed the cashier to steal the undeposited cash receipts.
   b. Recommend improvements in internal controls, so that similar types of thefts of undeposited cash receipts can be prevented.

GROUP PROJECT   **Case 5-6   Observe internal controls over cash**

Select a business in your community and observe its internal controls over cash receipts and cash payments. The business could be a bank or a bookstore, restaurant, department store, or other retailer. In groups of three or four, identify and discuss the similarities and differences in each business's cash internal controls.

Answers to Self-Examination Questions

1. **C** Compliance with laws and regulations (answer C) is an objective, not an element, of internal control. The control environment (answer A), monitoring (answer B), control procedures (answer D), risk assessment, and information and communication are the five elements of internal control.

2. **C** The error was made by the bank, so the cash balance according to the bank statement needs to be adjusted. Since the bank deducted $90 ($540.50 − $450.50) too little, the error of $90 should be deducted from the cash balance according to the bank statement (answer C).

3. **B** On any specific date, the cash account in a company's records may not agree with the account in the bank's records because of delays and/or errors by either party in recording transactions. The purpose of a bank reconciliation, therefore, is to determine the reasons for any differences between the two account balances. All errors should then be corrected by the company or the bank, as appropriate. In arriving at the adjusted cash balance according to the bank state-

ment, outstanding checks must be deducted (answer B) to adjust for checks that have been written by the company but that have not yet been presented to the bank for payment.

4. **C** All reconciling items that are added to and deducted from the cash balance according to the company's records on the bank reconciliation (answer C) require that adjustments be recorded by the company to correct errors made in recording transactions or to bring the cash account up to date for delays in recording transactions.

5. **D** To avoid the delay, annoyance, and expense that is associated with paying all obligations by check, relatively small amounts (answer A) are paid from a petty cash fund. The fund is established by estimating the amount of cash needed to pay these small amounts during a specified period (answer B), and it is then reimbursed when the amount of money in the fund is reduced to a predetermined minimum amount (answer C).

CHAPTER 6

Receivables and Inventories

LEARNING OBJECTIVES
After studying this chapter, you should be able to:

Obj | **1** Describe the common classifications of receivables.

Obj | **2** Describe the nature of and the accounting for uncollectible receivables.

Obj | **3** Describe the direct write-off method of accounting for uncollectible receivables.

Obj | **4** Describe the allowance method of accounting for uncollectible receivables.

Obj | **5** Describe the common classifications of inventories.

Obj | **6** Describe three inventory cost flow assumptions and how they impact the financial statements.

Obj | **7** Compare and contrast the use of the three inventory costing methods.

Obj | **8** Describe how receivables and inventory are reported on the financial statements.

Obj | **9** Financial Analysis: Describe and illustrate accounts receivable and inventory turnover and their use in assessing the management of receivables and inventory.

What is the role of receivables in business? Unlike the individual consumer purchasing a DVD at **Walmart** for cash or by **MasterCard** or **Visa**, a business normally purchases merchandise on account. That is, the seller records a receivable and invoices the buyer for payment at a later time. For example, **The Hershey Company** will record a receivable and invoice **Kroger** supermarkets for delivery of chocolate candy to various stores. Kroger will pay for the candy after delivery according to the terms of the invoice.

What is the role of inventory in business? From a consumer's perspective, inventory allows us to compare items, touch items, purchase on impulse, and take immediate delivery of a product on purchase. For example, at **Best Buy** you can inspect television sets before deciding which set best suits your needs and tastes. To support Walmart's need for immediate product shipments, **Procter & Gamble** holds an inventory of Tide®. Inventory also provides protection against disruptions in production and transportation. For example, an unexpected strike by a supplier's employees can halt production for a manufacturer or cause lost sales for a merchandiser. Inventory also allows a business to meet unexpected increases in the demand for its product.

In this chapter, accounting and reporting issues related to receivables and inventories are described and illustrated. In doing so, the effects on the financial statements of estimating uncollectible receivables and inventory cost flow assumptions are emphasized.

Obj | **1**

Describe the common classifications of receivables.

Classification of Receivables

The receivables that result from sales on account are normally accounts receivable or notes receivable. The term **receivables** includes all money claims against other entities, including people, companies, and other organizations. Receivables are usually a significant portion of the total current assets.

Accounts Receivable

A recent balance sheet of **La-Z-Boy Incorporated** reported that receivables made up over 33% of La-Z-Boy's current assets.

The most common transaction creating a receivable is selling merchandise or services on account (on credit). The receivable is recorded as an increase to Accounts Receivable. Such **accounts receivable** are normally collected within a short period, such as 30 or 60 days. They are classified on the balance sheet as a current asset.

Notes Receivable

Notes receivable are amounts that customers owe for which a formal, written instrument of credit has been issued. If notes receivable are expected to be collected within a year, they are classified on the balance sheet as a current asset.

Notes are often used for credit periods of more than 60 days. For example, an automobile dealer may require a down payment at the time of sale and accept a note or a series of notes for the remainder. Such notes usually provide for monthly payments.

A note has some advantages over an account receivable. By signing a note, the debtor recognizes the debt and agrees to pay it according to its terms. Thus, a note is a stronger legal claim.

A promissory note receivable is a written promise to pay the face amount, usually with interest, on demand or at a date in the future.[1] Characteristics of a promissory note are as follows:

1. The *maker* is the party making the promise to pay.
2. The *payee* is the party to whom the note is payable.
3. The *face amount* is the amount the note is written for on its face.

Integrity, Objectivity, and Ethics in Business

RECEIVABLES FRAUD

Financial reporting frauds are often tied to accounts receivable, because receivables allow companies to record revenue before cash is received. Take, for example, the case of entrepreneur Michael Weinstein, who acquired **Coated Sales, Inc.**, with the dream of growing the small specialty company into a major corporation. To acquire funding that would facilitate this growth, Weinstein had to artificially boost the company's sales. He accomplished this by adding millions in false accounts receivable to existing customer accounts.

The company's auditors began to sense a problem when they called one of the company's customers to confirm a large order. When the customer denied placing the order, the auditors began to investigate the company's receivables more closely. Their analysis revealed a fraud which overstated profits by $55 million and forced the company into bankruptcy, costing investors and creditors over $160 million.

Source: Joseph T. Wells, "Follow Fraud to the Likely Perpetrator," *The Journal of Accountancy*, March 2001.

---

1. You may see references to non-interest-bearing notes. Such notes are not widely used and carry an assumed or implicit interest rate.

4. The *issuance date* is the date a note is issued.
5. The *due date* or *maturity date* is the date the note is to be paid.
6. The *term* of a note is the amount of time between the issuance and due dates.
7. The *interest rate* is that rate of interest that must be paid on the face amount for the term of the note.

Exhibit 1 illustrates a promissory note.

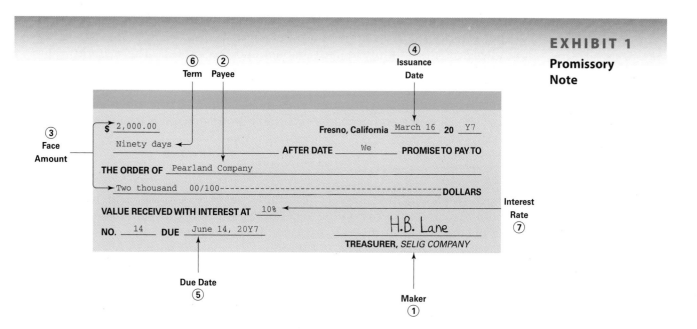

EXHIBIT 1

Promissory Note

The maker of the note is Selig Company, and the payee is Pearland Company. The face value of the note is $2,000, and the issuance date is March 16, 20Y7. The term of the note is 90 days, which results in a due date of June 14, 20Y7, as shown below.

Days in March	31 days
Minus issuance date of note	16
Days remaining in March	15 days
Add days in April	30
Add days in May	31
Add days in June (due date of June 14)	14
Term of note	90 days

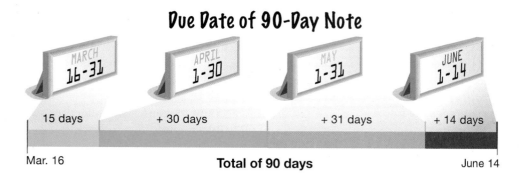

Due Date of 90-Day Note

MARCH 16–31	APRIL 1–30	MAY 1–31	JUNE 1–14
15 days	+ 30 days	+ 31 days	+ 14 days

Mar. 16   **Total of 90 days**   June 14

Your credit card balances that are not paid at the end of the month incur an interest charge expressed as a percent per month. Interest charges of 1½% per month are common. Such charges approximate an annual interest rate of 18% per year (1½% × 12). Thus, if you can borrow money at less than 18%, you are better off borrowing the money to pay off the credit card balance.

If you have purchased an automobile on credit, you probably signed a note. From your viewpoint, the note is a note payable. From the creditor's viewpoint, the note is a note receivable.

Obj | **2**

Describe the nature of and the accounting for uncollectible receivables.

In Exhibit 1, the term of the note is 90 days and it has an interest rate of 10%. The interest on a note is computed as follows:

$$\text{Interest} = \text{Face Amount} \times \text{Interest Rate} \times (\text{Term}/360 \text{ days})$$

The interest rate is stated on an annual (yearly) basis, while the term is expressed as days. Thus, the interest on the note in Exhibit 1 is computed as follows:

$$\text{Interest} = \$2,000 \times 10\% \times (90/360) = \$50$$

To simplify, 360 days per year are used in this chapter. In practice, companies such as banks and mortgage lenders use the exact number of days in a year, 365.

The **maturity value** is the amount that must be paid at the due date of the note, which is the sum of the face amount and the interest. The maturity value of the note in Exhibit 1 is $2,050 ($2,000 + $50).

Notes may be used to settle a customer's account receivable. Notes and accounts receivable that result from sales transactions are sometimes called *trade receivables*. All notes and accounts receivable in this chapter are assumed to be from sales transactions.

Other Receivables

Other receivables include interest receivable, taxes receivable, and receivables from officers or employees. Other receivables are normally reported separately on the balance sheet. If they are expected to be collected within one year, they are classified as current assets. If collection is expected beyond one year, they are classified as noncurrent assets and reported under the caption *Investments*.

Uncollectible Receivables

In prior chapters, the accounting for sales of merchandise or services on account (on credit) was described and illustrated. A major issue that has not yet been discussed is that some customers will not pay their accounts. That is, some accounts receivable will be uncollectible.

Companies may shift the risk of uncollectible receivables to other companies. For example, some retailers do not accept sales on account, but will only accept cash or credit cards. Such policies shift the risk to the credit card companies.

Companies may also sell their receivables. This is often the case when a company issues its own credit card. For example, Macy's and JCPenney issue their own credit cards. Selling receivables is called *factoring* the receivables. The buyer of the receivables is called a *factor*. An advantage of factoring is that the company selling its receivables immediately receives cash for operating and other needs. Also, depending on the factoring agreement, some of the risk of uncollectible accounts is shifted to the factor.

Regardless of how careful a company is in granting credit, some credit sales will be uncollectible. The operating expense recorded from uncollectible receivables is called **bad debt expense**, *uncollectible accounts expense,* or *doubtful accounts expense.*

There is no general rule for when an account becomes uncollectible. Some indications that an account may be uncollectible include the following:

1. The receivable is past due.
2. The customer does not respond to the company's attempts to collect.

3. The customer files for bankruptcy.
4. The customer closes its business.
5. The company cannot locate the customer.

If a customer doesn't pay, a company may turn the account over to a collection agency. After the collection agency attempts to collect payment, any remaining balance in the account is considered worthless.

The two methods of accounting for uncollectible receivables are as follows:

1. The **direct write-off method** records bad debt expense only when an account is determined to be worthless.
2. The **allowance method** records bad debt expense by estimating uncollectible accounts at the end of the accounting period.

The direct write-off method is often used by small companies and companies with few receivables.[2] Generally accepted accounting principles (GAAP), however, require companies with a large amount of receivables to use the allowance method. As a result, most well-known companies such as General Electric, Pepsi, Intel, and FedEx use the allowance method.

Adams, Stevens & Bradley, Ltd. is a collection agency that operates on a contingency basis. That is, its fees are based on what it collects.

Direct Write-Off Method for Uncollectible Accounts

Obj **3**

Describe the direct write-off method of accounting for uncollectible receivables.

Under the direct write-off method, bad debt expense is not recorded until the customer's account is determined to be worthless. At that time, the customer's account receivable is written off.

To illustrate, assume that on May 10 a $4,200 account receivable from Markieff Carson has been determined to be uncollectible. The effect on the accounts and financial statements of writing off the account is as follows:

Statement of Cash Flows	Balance Sheet				Income Statement
	Assets	=	Liabilities +	Stockholders' Equity	
	Accounts Receivable	=		Retained Earnings	
May 10.	−4,200			−4,200	May 10.

Income Statement

May 10. Bad debt expense −4,200

An account receivable that has been written off may be later collected. In such cases, the account is reinstated by reversing the write-off. The cash received in payment is then recorded as a receipt on account.

To illustrate, assume that the Markieff Carson account of $4,200 written off on May 10 is later collected on November 21. The effect on the accounts

---

2. The direct write-off method is also required for federal income tax purposes.

and financial statements of the reinstatement and the receipt of cash is as follows:

Statement of Cash Flows	Balance Sheet				Income Statement
	Assets	=	Liabilities + Stockholders' Equity		
	Accounts Receivable	=		Retained Earnings	
Nov. 21.	4,200			4,200	Nov. 21.

Income Statement

Nov. 21. Bad debt expense   4,200

Statement of Cash Flows	Balance Sheet				Income Statement
	Assets	=	Liabilities + Stockholders' Equity		
	Cash +	Accounts Receivable			
Nov. 21.	4,200	−4,200			

Statement of Cash Flows

Nov. 21. Operating   4,200

The direct write-off method is used by businesses that sell most of their goods or services for cash and accept only MasterCard or Visa, which are recorded as cash sales. In such cases, receivables are a small part of the current assets and any bad debt expense would be small. Examples of such businesses are a restaurant, a convenience store, and a small retail store.

Obj 4

Describe the allowance method of accounting for uncollectible receivables.

Allowance Method for Uncollectible Accounts

The allowance method estimates the uncollectible accounts receivable at the end of the accounting period. Based on this estimate, Bad Debt Expense is recorded by an adjustment.

To illustrate, assume that DPS Company began operations August 1. As of the end of its accounting period on December 31, 20Y6, DPS has an accounts receivable balance of $200,000. This balance includes some past due accounts. Based on industry averages, DPS estimates that $30,000 of the December 31 accounts receivable will be uncollectible. However, on December 31, DPS doesn't know which customer accounts will be uncollectible. Thus, specific customer accounts cannot be decreased or credited. Instead, a contra asset account, **Allowance for Doubtful Accounts**, is used.

Using the $30,000 estimate, the effect on the accounts and financial statements of recording the adjustment on December 31 is shown below.

Statement of Cash Flows	Balance Sheet				Income Statement
	Assets	**=**	**Liabilities + Stockholders' Equity**		
	Allowance for – Doubtful Accts.	=		Retained Earnings	
Dec. 31.	–30,000			–30,000	Dec. 31.

Income Statement
Dec. 31. Bad debt expense –30,000

The preceding adjustment affects the income statement and balance sheet. On the income statement, the $30,000 of Bad Debt Expense will be matched against the related revenues of the period. On the balance sheet, the value of the receivables is reduced to the amount that is expected to be collected or realized. This amount, $170,000 ($200,000 − $30,000), is called the **net realizable value** of the receivables.

After the preceding adjustment is recorded, Accounts Receivable still has a balance of $200,000. This balance is the total amount owed by customers on account on December 31 and is supported by the individual customer accounts.[3] The accounts receivable contra account, Allowance for Doubtful Accounts, has a negative balance of $30,000.

Write-Offs to the Allowance Account

When a customer's account is identified as uncollectible, it is written off against the allowance account. This requires the company to remove the specific accounts receivable and an equal amount from the allowance account. For example, the effect on the accounts and financial statements on January 21, 20Y7, of writing off Chandler Somers's account of $6,000 with DPS Company is as follows:

Statement of Cash Flows	Balance Sheet				Income Statement
	Assets	=	**Liabilities + Stockholders' Equity**		
	Accounts Receivable	– Allowance for Doubtful Accts.			
Jan. 21.	–6,000	6,000			

At the end of a period, the Allowance for Doubtful Accounts will normally have a balance. This is because the Allowance for Doubtful Accounts is based upon an estimate. As a result, the total write-offs to the allowance account during the period will rarely equal the balance of the account at the beginning of the period. The allowance account will have a negative balance at the end of the

3. The individual customer accounts are often maintained in a separate file or record called a subsidiary ledger. The sum of the individual customer accounts equals the balance of the accounts receivable reported in the balance sheet.

period if the write-offs during the period are less than the beginning balance. It will have a positive balance if the write-offs exceed the beginning balance. However, after the end-of-period adjustment is recorded, Allowance for Doubtful Accounts should always have a negative balance.

An account receivable that has been written off against the allowance account may be collected later. Like the direct write-off method, the account is reinstated by reversing the write-off. The cash received in payment is then recorded as a receipt on account.

To illustrate, assume that Nancy Smith's account of $5,000, which was written off on April 2, is later collected on June 10. DPS Company records the reinstatement and the collection as follows:

Statement of Cash Flows	Balance Sheet				Income Statement
	Assets	=	Liabilities	+ Stockholders' Equity	
	Accounts Receivable	Allowance for – Doubtful Accts.			
June 10.	5,000	–5,000			

Statement of Cash Flows	Balance Sheet				Income Statement
	Assets	=	Liabilities	+ Stockholders' Equity	
	Cash +	Accounts Receivable			
June 10.	5,000	–5,000			

Statement of Cash Flows		
June 10. Operating	5,000	

Estimating Uncollectibles

The allowance method requires an estimate of uncollectible accounts at the end of the period. This estimate is normally based on past experience, industry averages, and forecasts of the future.

Integrity, Objectivity, and Ethics in Business

SELLER BEWARE

A company in financial distress will still try to purchase goods and services on account. In these cases, rather than "buyer beware," it is more like "seller beware." Sellers must be careful in advancing credit to such companies, because trade creditors have low priority for cash payments in the event of bankruptcy. To help suppliers, third-party services specialize in evaluating financially distressed customers.

These services analyze credit risk for these firms by evaluating recent management payment decisions (who is getting paid and when), court actions (if in bankruptcy), and other supplier credit tightening or suspension actions. Such information helps monitor and adjust trade credit amounts and terms with the financially distressed customer.

The two methods used to estimate uncollectible accounts are as follows:

1.   percent of sales method
2.   analysis of receivables method

Percent of Sales Method   Since accounts receivable are created by credit sales, uncollectible accounts can be estimated as a percent of credit sales. If the portion of credit sales to sales is relatively constant, the percent may be applied to total sales or net sales.

To illustrate, assume the following data for DPS Company on December 31, 20Y7, before any adjustments:

Balance of Accounts Receivable	$240,000
Balance of Allowance for Doubtful Accounts	–$3,250
Total credit sales	$3,000,000
Bad debt as a percent of credit sales	¾%

Bad Debt Expense of $22,500 is estimated as follows:

Bad Debt Expense = Credit Sales × Bad Debt as a Percent of Credit Sales

Bad Debt Expense = $3,000,000 × ¾% = $22,500

The effect of the adjustment on the accounts and financial statements on December 31 is as follows:

Statement of Cash Flows	Balance Sheet			Income Statement
	Assets =	**Liabilities** +	**Stockholders' Equity**	
	Allowance for – Doubtful Accts. =		Retained Earnings	
Dec. 31.	–22,500		–22,500	Dec. 31.

Income Statement

Dec. 31. Bad debt expense –22,500

After the adjustment, Bad Debt Expense will have an adjusted balance of $22,500. Allowance for Doubtful Accounts will have a negative adjusted balance of –$25,750 ($3,250 + $22,500).

Under the percent of sales method, the amount of the adjustment is always the amount estimated for Bad Debt Expense. In the preceding example, this amount was $22,500.

Analysis of Receivables Method   The analysis of receivables method is based on the assumption that the longer an account receivable is outstanding, the less likely that it will be collected. The analysis of receivables method is applied as follows:

Step 1. The due date of each account receivable is determined.
Step 2. The number of days each account is past due is determined. This is the number of days between the due date of the account and the date of the analysis.

The percentage of uncollectible accounts will vary across companies and industries. For example, in their recent financial statements, **Target Corporation** reported 7% of its receivables as uncollectible, **Deere & Company** (manufacturer of John Deere tractors, etc.) reported only 2.0% of its dealer receivables as uncollectible, and **HCA Holdings Inc.,** a hospital management company, reported 47.5% of its receivables as uncollectible.

Step 3. Each account is placed in an aged class according to its days past due. Typical aged classes include the following:

Not past due
1–30 days past due
31–60 days past due
61–90 days past due
91–180 days past due
181–365 days past due
Over 365 days past due

Step 4. The totals for each aged class are determined.

Step 5. The total for each aged class is multiplied by an estimated percentage of uncollectible accounts for that class.

Step 6. The estimated total of uncollectible accounts is determined as the sum of the uncollectible accounts for each aged class.

The preceding steps are summarized in an aging schedule, and this overall process is called **aging the receivables**.

To illustrate, assume that DPS Company uses the analysis of receivables method instead of the percent of sales method. DPS prepared an aging schedule for its accounts receivable of $240,000 as of December 31, 20Y7, as shown in Exhibit 2.

EXHIBIT 2   Aging of Receivables Schedule, December 31, 20Y7

	A	B	C	D	E	F	G	H	I
1			**Not**				**Days Past Due**		
2			**Past**						**Over**
3	**Customer**	**Balance**	**Due**	**1–30**	**31–60**	**61–90**	**91–180**	**181–365**	**365**
4	Ashby & Co.	1,500			1,500				
5	B. T. Barr	6,100					3,500	2,600	
6	Brock Co.	4,700	4,700						
21									
22	Saxon Woods Co.	600					600		
23	Total	240,000	125,000	64,000	13,100	8,900	5,000	10,000	14,000
24	Percent uncollectible			2%	5%	10%	20%	30%	50%	80%
25	Estimate of uncollectible accounts	26,490	2,500	3,200	1,310	1,780	1,500	5,000	11,200

Steps 1–3
Step 4 → 23
Step 5 → 24
Step 6 → 25

Assume that DPS Company sold merchandise to Saxon Woods Co. on August 29, 20Y7, with terms 2/10, n/30. Thus, the due date (Step 1) of Saxon Woods' account is September 28, as shown below.

Credit terms, net	30 days
Less (31 – 29)	2 days
Days in September	28 days

As of December 31, Saxon Woods' account is 94 days past due (Step 2), as shown below.

Number of days past due in September	2 days (30 – 28)
Number of days past due in October	31 days
Number of days past due in November	30 days
Number of days past due in December	31 days
Total number of days past due	94 days

Exhibit 2 shows that the $600 account receivable for Saxon Woods Co. was placed in the 91–180 days past due class (Step 3).

The total for each of the aged classes is determined (Step 4). Exhibit 2 shows that $125,000 of the accounts receivable are not past due, while $64,000 are 1–30 days past due. DPS Company applies a different estimated percentage of uncollectible accounts to the totals of each of the aged classes (Step 5). As shown in Exhibit 2, the percent is 2% for accounts not past due, while the percent is 80% for accounts over 365 days past due.

The sum of the estimated uncollectible accounts for each aged class (Step 6) is the estimated uncollectible accounts on December 31, 20Y7. This is the desired adjusted balance for Allowance for Doubtful Accounts. For DPS Company, this amount is $26,490, as shown in Exhibit 2.

Comparing the estimate of $26,490 with the unadjusted balance of the allowance account determines the amount of the adjustment for Bad Debt Expense. For DPS, the unadjusted balance of the allowance account is a negative balance of −$3,250. The amount to be added to this balance is therefore −$23,240 ($26,490 − $3,250).

The effect of the adjustment of $23,240 on the accounts and financial statements of DPS Company is shown below.

Statement of Cash Flows	Balance Sheet			Income Statement
	Assets	=	Liabilities + Stockholders' Equity	
	Allowance for − Doubtful Accts.	=	Retained Earnings	
Dec. 31.	−23,240		−23,240	Dec. 31.

Income Statement

Dec. 31. Bad debt expense −23,240

After the preceding adjustment, Bad Debt Expense will have an adjusted balance of $23,240. Allowance for Doubtful Accounts will have an adjusted balance of $26,490, and the net realizable value of the receivables is $213,510 ($240,000 − $26,490).

Under the analysis of receivables method, the amount of the adjustment is the amount that will yield an adjusted balance for Allowance for Doubtful Accounts equal to that estimated by the aging schedule.

Comparing Estimation Methods Both the percent of sales and analysis of receivables methods estimate uncollectible accounts. However, each method has a slightly different focus and financial statement emphasis.

Under the percent of sales method, Bad Debt Expense is the focus of the estimation process. The percent of sales method places more emphasis on matching revenues and expenses and thus emphasizes the income statement. That is, the amount of the adjusting entry is based on the estimate of Bad Debt Expense for the period. Allowance for Doubtful Accounts is then adjusted by this amount.

Under the analysis of receivables method, Allowance for Doubtful Accounts is the focus of the estimation process. The analysis of receivables method places more emphasis on the net realizable value of the receivables and thus emphasizes the balance sheet. That is, the amount of the adjusting entry is the amount that will yield an adjusted balance for Allowance for Doubtful Accounts equal to that estimated by the aging schedule. Bad Debt Expense is then adjusted by this amount.

Exhibit 3 summarizes these differences between the percent of sales and the analysis of receivables methods. Exhibit 3 also shows the results of the DPS Company illustration for the percent of sales and analysis of receivables methods. The amounts shown in Exhibit 3 assume an unadjusted negative balance of –$3,250 for Allowance for Doubtful Accounts. While the methods normally yield different amounts for any one period, over several periods the amounts should be similar.

EXHIBIT 3   **Differences Between Estimation Methods**

| | | | DPS Company Example | |
Estimation Method	Focus of Method	Financial Statement Emphasis	Bad Debt Expense (Adjusting Entry Amount)	Allowance for Doubtful Accounts (After Adjusting Entry)
Percent of Sales Method	Bad Debt Expense Estimate	Income Statement	$22,500	$25,750* ($22,500 + $3,250)
Analysis of Receivables Method	Allowance for Doubtful Accounts Estimate	Balance Sheet	$23,240* ($26,490 – $3,250)	$26,490

*Indicates that the estimate was derived (sometimes called "plugged") from the estimate on which this method focuses.

Obj | **5**

Describe the common classifications of inventories.

Inventory Classification for Merchandisers and Manufacturers

In Chapter 4, a merchandiser was defined as a company that purchases products for resale, such as apparel, consumer electronics, hardware, or food items. Merchandise on hand (not sold) at the end of the period is a current asset called **merchandise inventory**. Inventory sold becomes the *cost of merchandise sold.* Merchandise inventory is a large asset for most merchandising companies, as illustrated for some well-known merchandising companies in Exhibit 4.

EXHIBIT 4

Size of Merchandise Inventory for Merchandising Businesses

	Merchandise Inventory as a Percentage of Current Assets	Merchandise Inventory as a Percentage of Total Assets
Walmart	70%	20%
Best Buy	56	33
Home Depot	79	26
Kroger	65	21

As illustrated in earlier chapters, the cost of merchandise is its purchase price less any purchase discounts. Merchandise inventory also includes other costs, such as freight, import duties, property taxes, and insurance costs.

Manufacturing companies convert raw materials into final products, which are often sold to merchandising businesses. A manufacturing company has three types of inventory:

1. **Materials inventory** consists of the cost of raw materials used in manufacturing a product.
2. **Work-in-process inventory** consists of the costs for partially completed product.
3. **Finished goods inventory** consists of all the costs for completed product.

The manufacturing costs for Hershey candy bars, illustrated in Exhibit 5, are as follows:

1. Materials inventory consists of cocoa and sugar.
2. Work-in-process inventory consists of material costs that have been put into production as well as labor costs and overhead costs. Overhead costs consist of costs such as electricity and depreciation on factory equipment.
3. Finished goods inventory consists of candy bars, which are made up of material, labor, and overhead costs.

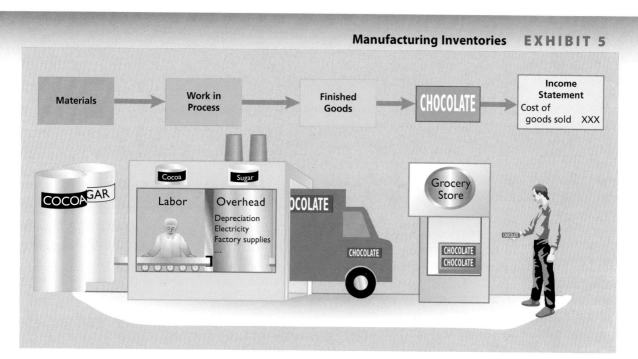

Manufacturing Inventories   **EXHIBIT 5**

When the finished goods are sold, the costs are transferred to cost of goods sold on the income statement. Manufacturers normally use the term **cost of goods sold** rather than cost of merchandise sold to describe the cost of products sold.

Manufacturing inventories are normally disclosed in the notes to the financial statements. For example, The Hershey Company recently reported inventories of $815,863 (in thousands) as follows:

Materials	$241,812
Work in process	91,956
Finished goods	482,095
Total inventories	$815,863

In this chapter, inventory accounting and analysis issues for a merchandising company are described and illustrated. However, much of this discussion also applies to manufacturing companies.

HOW BUSINESSES MAKE MONEY

THE CONSUMER ELECTRONIC WARS: BEST BUY VERSUS AMAZON.COM

Adam Hunger/Reuters/Landov

How does **Best Buy** compete against online retailers such as **Amazon.com** in the intensely competitive consumer electronic market? Best Buy believes that by offering high-quality customer service in its retail stores that it can compete effectively with online retailers like Amazon.com. An important part of this strategy is hiring, training, and retaining high-quality store employees and managers. In addition, Best Buy recently announced a "Perfect Match Promise" that provides customers (1) 30 days of free telephone support for any products purchased, (2) 30-day return policy with no restocking fees, and (3) 30 days of competitor price matching. Finally, Best Buy plans to enhance its customer loyalty program with free shipping, access to new products and technologies, free access to the Geek Squad, and an extended return and price-matching options.

Is Best Buy's strategy working? In a recent income statement, Best Buy reported a net loss of $1,231 million. However, Best Buy's founder Richard Schulze is considering buying back the company from its public stockholders and taking the company private. Mr. Schulze obviously believes that Best Buy has a bright future.

Source: Adapted from Best Buy Co., Inc.'s 10-K report.

Obj | 6

Describe three inventory cost flow assumptions and how they impact the financial statements.

Inventory Cost Flow Assumptions

An accounting issue arises when identical units of merchandise are acquired at different unit costs during a period. In such cases, when an item is sold, it is necessary to determine its cost using a cost flow assumption and related inventory cost flow method. Three common cost flow assumptions and related inventory cost flow methods are shown below.

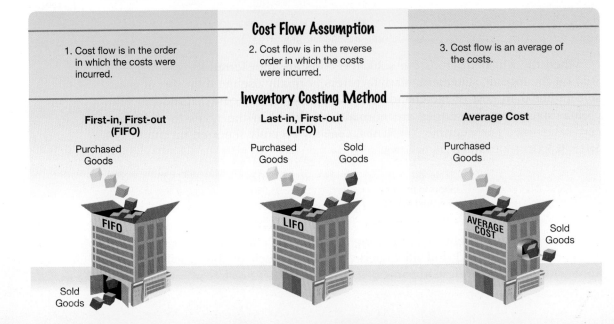

To illustrate, assume that three identical units of merchandise are purchased during May, as follows:

			Units	Cost
May	10	Purchase	1	$ 9
	18	Purchase	1	13
	24	Purchase	1	14
Total			3	$36

Average cost per unit: $12 ($36 ÷ 3 units)

Assume that one unit is sold on May 30 for $20. Depending upon which unit was sold, the gross profit varies from $11 to $6, as shown below.

	May 10 Unit Sold	May 18 Unit Sold	May 24 Unit Sold
Sales	$20	$20	$20
Cost of merchandise sold	9	13	14
Gross profit	$11	$ 7	$ 6
Ending inventory	$27	$23	$22
	($13 + $14)	($9 + $14)	($9 + $13)

Under the **specific identification inventory cost flow method**, the unit sold is identified with a specific purchase. The ending inventory is made up of the remaining units on hand. Thus, the gross profit, cost of merchandise sold, and ending inventory can vary as shown above. For example, if the May 18 unit was sold, the cost of merchandise sold is $13, the gross profit is $7, and the ending inventory is $23.

The specific identification method is not practical unless each inventory unit can be separately identified. For example, an automobile dealer may use the specific identification method since each automobile has a unique serial number. However, most businesses cannot identify each inventory unit separately. In such cases, one of the following three inventory cost flow methods is used.

Under the **first-in, first-out (FIFO) inventory cost flow method**, the first units purchased are assumed to be sold and the ending inventory is made up of the most recent purchases. In the preceding example, the May 10 unit would be assumed to have been sold. Thus, the gross profit would be $11, and the ending inventory would be $27 ($13 + $14).

Under the **last-in, first-out (LIFO) inventory cost flow method**, the last units purchased are assumed to be sold and the ending inventory is made up of the first purchases. In the preceding example, the May 24 unit would be assumed to have been sold. Thus, the gross profit would be $6, and the ending inventory would be $22 ($9 + $13).

Under the **average cost inventory cost flow method**, the cost of the units sold and in ending inventory is an average of the purchase costs. In the preceding example, the cost of the unit sold would be $12 ($36 ÷ 3 units), the gross profit would be $8 ($20 − $12), and the ending inventory would be $24 ($12 × 2 units).

The three inventory cost flow methods—FIFO, LIFO, and average cost—are shown in Exhibit 6.

The specific identification method is normally used by automobile dealerships, jewelry stores, and art galleries.

EXHIBIT 6 **Inventory Costing Methods**

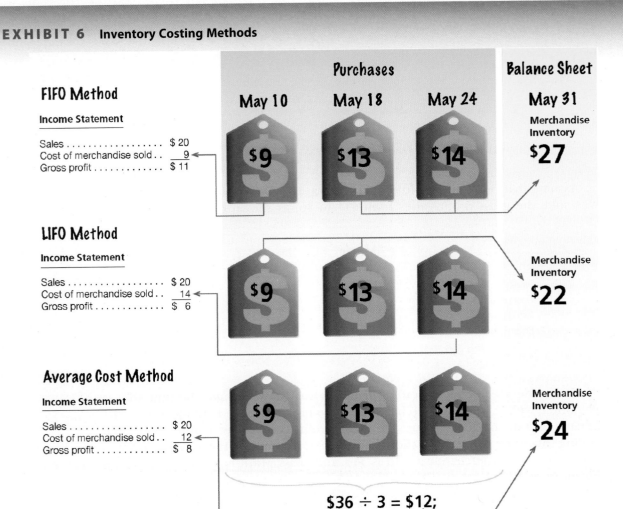

FIFO Method

Income Statement

Sales	$ 20
Cost of merchandise sold ..	9
Gross profit	$ 11

LIFO Method

Income Statement

Sales	$ 20
Cost of merchandise sold ..	14
Gross profit	$ 6

Average Cost Method

Income Statement

Sales	$ 20
Cost of merchandise sold ..	12
Gross profit	$ 8

Purchases

May 10	May 18	May 24
$9	$13	$14
$9	$13	$14
$9	$13	$14

Balance Sheet

May 31

Merchandise Inventory **$27**

Merchandise Inventory **$22**

Merchandise Inventory **$24**

$36 ÷ 3 = $12;
$12 × 2 = $24

Exhibit 7 shows the frequency with which the FIFO, LIFO, and average cost methods are used.

International Connection

IFRS PROHIBITS LIFO

While the FIFO, LIFO, and average cost methods are permitted within the United States, International Financial Reporting Standards (IFRS) prohibit the LIFO method. If IFRS were adopted within the United States, this could have a significant impact on a company's income. For example, **Deere & Company** reports its inventories using LIFO. If Deere & Company were to switch to FIFO, its income before taxes would decrease by approximately $1,398 million, which is over a 40% decrease.

EXHIBIT 7

Use of Inventory Costing Methods*

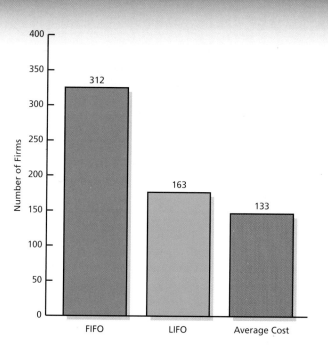

Source: *Accounting Trends and Techniques*, 66th edition, 2012 (New York: American Institute of Certified Public Accountants, Inc.).

*Firms may be counted more than once for using multiple methods.

Comparing Inventory Costing Methods

Obj | 7

Compare and contrast the use of the three inventory costing methods.

As illustrated in Exhibit 6, when prices change, the different inventory costing methods affect the income statement and balance sheet differently. That is, the methods yield different amounts for (1) the cost of the merchandise sold for the period, (2) the gross profit (and net income) for the period, and (3) the ending inventory.

Use of the First-In, First-Out (FIFO) Method

When the FIFO method is used during a period of inflation or rising prices, the earlier unit costs are lower than the more recent unit costs. Much of the benefit of the larger amount of gross profit is lost, however, because the inventory must be replaced at ever higher prices. In fact, the balance sheet will report the ending merchandise inventory at an amount that is about the same as its current replacement cost. When prices are increasing, the larger gross profits that result from the FIFO method are often called *inventory profits* or *illusory profits*. In a period of deflation or declining prices, the effect is just the opposite.

Use of the Last-In, First-Out (LIFO) Method

When the LIFO method is used during a period of inflation or rising prices, the results are opposite those of the other two methods. The LIFO method will yield a higher amount of cost of merchandise sold, a lower amount of gross profit, and a lower amount of inventory at the end of the period than will the other two methods. The reason for these effects is that the cost of the most recently acquired units is about the same as the cost of their replacement. In a period of inflation, the more recent unit costs are higher than the earlier unit costs. Thus, it can be argued that the LIFO method more nearly matches current costs with current revenues.

Integrity, Objectivity, and Ethics in Business

WHERE'S THE BONUS?

Managers are often given bonuses based on reported earnings numbers. This can create a conflict. LIFO can improve the value of the company through lower taxes. However, in periods of rising costs (prices), LIFO also produces a lower earnings number and therefore lower management bonuses. Ethically, managers should select accounting procedures that will maximize the value of the firm, rather than their own compensation. Compensation specialists can help avoid this ethical dilemma by adjusting the bonus plan for the accounting procedure differences.

The rules used for external financial reporting need not be the same as those used for income tax reporting. One exception to this general rule is the use of LIFO. If a company elects to use LIFO inventory valuation for tax purposes, then the company must also use LIFO for external financial reporting. This is called the **LIFO conformity rule**. Thus, in periods of rising prices, LIFO offers an income tax savings because it reports the lowest amount of net income of the three methods. Many managers elect to use LIFO because of the tax savings, even though the reported earnings will be lower.

Under LIFO, the ending inventory on the balance sheet may be quite different from its current replacement cost (or FIFO estimate).[4] In such cases, the financial statements will include a note that states the estimated difference between the LIFO inventory and the inventory if FIFO had been used. This difference is called the **LIFO reserve**. An example of such a note for Deere & Company is shown below.

Most inventories owned by Deere & Company and its United States equipment subsidiaries are valued at cost, on the LIFO basis. . . . If all inventories had been valued on a FIFO basis, estimated inventories by major classification . . . in millions of dollars would have been as follows:

INVENTORIES

	Year 2	Year 1
Raw materials and supplies	$1,874	$1,626
Work-in-process	652	647
Finished machines and parts	4,065	3,584
Total FIFO value	6,591	5,857
Less (LIFO reserve) adjustment to LIFO value	1,421	1,486
Inventories	$5,170	$4,371

As shown above, the LIFO reserve may be quite large. For Deere & Company, the LIFO reserve is 21.6% ($1,421 ÷ $6,591) of the total FIFO inventory for Year 2 and 25.4% ($1,486 ÷ $5,857) in Year 1.

The wide differences in the percent of LIFO reserve to FIFO are a result of two major factors: (1) price inflation of the inventory and (2) the age of the inventory. Generally, old LIFO inventory combined with rapid price inflation will result in large LIFO reserves.

If a business sells some of its old LIFO inventory, the LIFO reserve is said to be liquidated. Since old LIFO inventory is normally at low prices, selling old LIFO inventory will result in a lower cost of merchandise sold and a higher gross profit and net income.

Whenever LIFO inventory is liquidated, investors and analysts should be careful in interpreting the income statement. In such cases, most investors and analysts will adjust earnings to what they would have been under FIFO.

4. The FIFO estimate is replacement cost, which is often similar to FIFO.

Use of the Average Cost Method

As you might have already reasoned, the average cost method is, in a sense, a compromise between FIFO and LIFO. The effect of price trends is averaged in determining the cost of merchandise sold and the ending inventory. For a series of purchases, the average cost will be the same, regardless of the direction of price trends. For example, reversing the sequence of unit costs presented in Exhibit 6 would not affect the reported cost of merchandise sold, gross profit, or ending inventory.

Reporting Receivables and Inventory

Obj 8

Describe how receivables and inventory are reported on the financial statements.

Receivables and inventory are reported as current assets on the balance sheet, as shown in Exhibit 8. In addition, generally accepted accounting principles require that supplementary information for these accounts be reported in the notes accompanying the financial statements. This section focuses on the financial statement and note reporting requirements for receivables and inventory.

EXHIBIT 8

Receivables and Inventory in Balance Sheet

CRABTREE CO.
Balance Sheet
December 31, 20Y3

Assets

Current assets:		
Cash and cash equivalents		$119,500
Notes receivable		250,000
Accounts receivable	$445,000	
Less allowance for doubtful accounts	15,000	430,000
Interest receivable		14,500
Merchandise inventory—at lower of cost (first-in, first-out method) or market		216,300

Receivables

All receivables expected to be realized in cash within a year are presented in the Current Assets section of the balance sheet. These assets are normally listed in the order of their liquidity, that is, the order in which they are expected to be converted to cash during normal operations. The receivables reported on a recent Johnson & Johnson balance sheet are shown below.[5]

Assets (in millions)	Year 2	Year 1
Current assets:		
Cash and cash equivalents	$24,542	$19,355
Marketable securities	7,719	8,303
Accounts receivable, net of allowances of $361 in Year 2 and $340 in Year 1	10,581	9,774
Inventories	6,285	5,378
Prepaid expenses and other current assets	5,189	4,497
Total current assets	$54,316	$47,307

5. Adapted from Johnson & Johnson Form 10-K.

Johnson & Johnson reports net accounts receivable of $10,581 and $9,774. The allowances for doubtful accounts of $361 and $340 are subtracted from the total accounts receivable to arrive at the net receivables. Alternatively, the allowances for each year could be shown in a note to the financial statements.

Other disclosures related to receivables are presented either on the face of the financial statements or in the accompanying notes.[6] Such disclosures include the market (fair) value of the receivables if significantly different from the reported value. In addition, if unusual credit risks exist within the receivables, the nature of the risks should be disclosed. For example, if the majority of the receivables are due from one customer or are due from customers located in one area of the country or one industry, these facts should be disclosed.

To illustrate, Deere & Company reported the following credit risks in its recent financial statements:

Trade accounts and notes receivable have significant concentrations of credit risk in the agricultural and turf sector, and construction and forestry sector. . . . On a geographic basis, there is not a disproportionate concentration of credit risk in any area.

Inventory

Merchandise inventory is usually presented in the Current Assets section of the balance sheet, following receivables. The method of determining the cost of the inventory (FIFO, LIFO, or average cost) should be shown. It is not unusual for large businesses with varied activities to use different costing methods for different segments of their inventories. The details may be disclosed in parentheses on the balance sheet or in a note to the financial statements.

Valuation at Net Realizable Value Merchandise that is out of date, spoiled, or damaged can often be sold only at a price below its original cost. Such merchandise should be valued at its **net realizable value**. Net realizable value is determined as follows:

Net Realizable Value = Estimated Selling Price − Direct Costs of Disposal

Digital Theater Systems Inc. reported the following inventory write-downs: ". . . an inventory write-down of $3,871,000 (was recorded) due to . . . technological obsolescence."

Direct costs of disposal include selling expenses such as special advertising or sales commissions on the sale. To illustrate, assume the following data about an item of damaged merchandise:

Original cost	$1,000
Estimated selling price	800
Selling expenses	150

The merchandise should be valued at its net realizable value of $650 as shown below.

Net Realizable Value = $800 − $150 = $650

Inventory is valued at other than cost when (1) the cost of replacing items in inventory is below the recorded cost, and (2) the inventory is not salable at normal sales prices. This latter case may be due to imperfections, shop wear, style changes, or other causes. In either situation, the method of valuing the inventories (cost or lower of cost or market) also should be disclosed on the balance sheet.

6. FASB *Accounting Standards Codification,* Section 210-10-50.

Valuation at Lower of Cost or Market

If the cost of replacing inventory is lower than its recorded purchase cost, the **lower-of-cost-or-market (LCM) method** is used to value the inventory. *Market,* as used in *lower of cost or market,* is the cost to replace the inventory. The market value is based on normal quantities that would be purchased from suppliers.

The lower-of-cost-or-market method can be applied in one of three ways. The cost, market price, and any declines could be determined for the following:

Dell Inc. recorded over $39.3 million of charges (expenses) in writing down its inventory of notebook computers. The remaining inventories of computers were then sold at significantly reduced prices.

1. each item in the inventory
2. each major class or category of inventory
3. total inventory as a whole

The amount of any price decline is included in the cost of merchandise sold. This in turn reduces gross profit and net income in the period in which the price declines occur. This matching of price declines to the period in which they occur is the primary advantage of using the lower-of-cost-or-market method.

To illustrate, assume the following data for 400 identical units of Item A in inventory on December 31, 20Y4:

Unit purchased cost	$10.25
Replacement cost on December 31, 20Y4	9.50

Since Item A could be replaced at $9.50 a unit, $9.50 is used under the lower-of-cost-or-market method.

Exhibit 9 illustrates applying the lower-of-cost-or-market method to each inventory item (A, B, C, and D). As applied on an item-by-item basis, the total lower of cost or market is $15,070, which is a market decline of $450 ($15,520 – $15,070). This market decline of $450 is included in the cost of merchandise sold.

EXHIBIT 9
Determining Inventory at Lower of Cost or Market

	A	B	C	D	E	F	G
1			Unit	Unit		Total	
2		Inventory	Cost	Market			
3	Item	Quantity	Price	Price	Cost	Market	LCM
4	A	400	$10.25	$ 9.50	$ 4,100	$ 3,800	$ 3,800
5	B	120	22.50	24.10	2,700	2,892	2,700
6	C	600	8.00	7.75	4,800	4,650	4,650
7	D	280	14.00	14.75	3,920	4,130	3,920
8	Total				$15,520	$15,472	$15,070
9							

In Exhibit 9, Items A, B, C, and D could be viewed as a class of inventory items. If the lower-of-cost-or-market method is applied to the class, the inventory would be valued at $15,472, which is a market decline of $48 ($15,520 – $15,472). Likewise, if Items A, B, C, and D make up the total inventory, the lower-of-cost-or-market method as applied to the total inventory would be the same amount, $15,472.

Financial Analysis: Accounts Receivable and Inventory Turnover

Obj 9
Describe and illustrate accounts receivable and inventory turnover and their use in assessing the management of receivables and inventory.

For most companies, accounts receivable and inventory are the largest current assets. One of the primary objectives in managing receivables and inventory is to convert them to cash by collecting receivables and selling inventory. Accounts receivable and inventory turnover are two useful measures of how quickly a company is meeting this objective.

Accounts Receivable Turnover

The **accounts receivable turnover** is computed as follows:

$$\text{Accounts Receivable Turnover} = \frac{\text{Net Sales}}{\text{Average Accounts Receivable}}$$

Although accounts receivable are related to "credit" sales, net sales is normally used to compute accounts receivable turnover. This is because credit sales are normally not reported to external users. The average accounts receivable is computed as the beginning accounts receivable plus the ending accounts receivable for the period divided by two.

To illustrate, assume the following data for Wolf Custom Furniture Company for a recent year:

Net sales	$18,750,000
Beginning receivables	1,200,000
Ending receivables	1,800,000

The accounts receivable turnover for Wolf Custom Furniture is computed as follows:

$$\text{Accounts Receivable Turnover} = \frac{\$18,750,000}{[(\$1,200,000 + \$1,800,000) \div 2]} = \frac{\$18,750,000}{\$1,500,000} = 12.5$$

An accounts receivable turnover ratio of 12.5 means that Wolf Custom Furniture is converting its accounts receivable to cash 12.5 times per year. Assuming that Wolf Custom Furniture's credit terms net 30 days, a turnover of 12.5 is favorable. In other words, customers are paying within the credit period. Another way of expressing this is to divide 365 days by the accounts receivable turnover. This results in what is known as the **number of days' sales in receivables**. For Wolf Custom Furniture this results in 29.2 days (365 days ÷ 12.5). This means customers are paying, on average, in 29.2 days. Compared to the credit terms of net 30 days, this is a favorable result.

Inventory Turnover

The **inventory turnover** is computed as follows:

$$\text{Inventory Turnover} = \frac{\text{Cost of Merchandise Sold}}{\text{Average Inventory}}$$

The average inventory is computed as the beginning inventory plus the ending inventory for the period divided by two.

To illustrate, assume the following data for Wolf Custom Furniture Company for a recent year.

Cost of merchandise sold	$12,000,000
Beginning inventory	600,000
Ending inventory	900,000

The inventory turnover for Wolf Custom Furniture is computed as follows:

$$\text{Inventory Turnover} = \frac{\$12,000,000}{[(\$600,000 + \$900,000) \div 2]} = \frac{\$12,000,000}{\$750,000} = 16.0$$

An inventory turnover ratio of 16.0 means that Wolf Custom Furniture is converting (or turning over) its inventory 16.0 times a year. A comparison of the current period's inventory turnover with the prior period or industry averages provides feedback on how well the company is managing its inventory. For example, if Wolf Custom Furniture's inventory turnover was 14.0 in the prior period, then the company has improved its managing of inventory. In other words, it is selling its inventory faster.

Another way of expressing inventory turnover is to divide 365 days by the inventory turnover. This results in what is known as the **number of days' sales in inventory**. For Wolf Custom Furniture, this results in 22.8 days (365 days ÷ 16.0). This means that the company is selling its inventory, on average, every 22.8 days. If competitors' averages or the industry average is 33.0 days, then this is a favorable result. In other words, the company is selling its inventory faster than its competitors.

Key Points

1. Describe the common classifications of receivables.

The term *receivables* includes all money claims against other entities, including people, business firms, and other organizations. Receivables are normally classified as accounts receivable, notes receivable, or other receivables.

2. Describe the nature of and the accounting for uncollectible receivables.

The two methods of accounting for uncollectible receivables are the direct write-off method and the allowance method. The direct write-off method recognizes the expense only when the account is judged to be uncollectible. The allowance method provides in advance for uncollectible receivables.

3. Describe the direct write-off method of accounting for uncollectible receivables.

Under the direct write-off method, writing off an account increases Bad Debt Expense and decreases Accounts Receivable. Neither an allowance account nor an adjustment is needed at the end of the period.

4. Describe the allowance method of accounting for uncollectible receivables.

A year-end adjustment provides for (1) the reduction of the value of the receivables to the amount of cash expected to be realized from them in the future and (2) the allocation to the current period of the expected expense resulting from such reduction. The adjustment increases Bad Debt Expense and Allowance for Doubtful Accounts. When an account is believed to be uncollectible, it is written off against the allowance account.

When the estimate of uncollectibles is based on the amount of sales for the period, the adjustment is made without regard to the balance of the allowance account. When the estimate of uncollectibles is based on the amount and the age of the receivable accounts at the end of the period, the adjustment is recorded so that the balance of the allowance account will equal the estimated uncollectibles at the end of the period.

The allowance account, which will have a negative balance after the adjustment has been posted, is a contra asset account. The bad debt expense is generally reported on the income statement as an operating expense.

5. Describe the common classifications of inventories.

The inventory of a merchandiser is called merchandise inventory. The cost of merchandise inventory that is sold is reported on the income statement. Manufacturers typically have three types of inventory: materials, work in process, and finished goods. When finished goods are sold, the cost is reported on the income statement as cost of goods sold.

6. Describe three inventory cost flow assumptions and how they impact the financial statements.

The three common cost flow assumptions used in business are the (1) first-in, first-out method, (2) last-in, first-out method, and (3) average cost method. Each method normally yields different amounts for the cost of merchandise sold and the ending merchandise inventory. Thus, the choice of a cost flow assumption directly affects the financial statements.

7. Compare and contrast the use of the three inventory costing methods.

The three inventory costing methods will normally yield different amounts for (1) the ending inventory, (2) the cost of the merchandise sold for the period, and (3) the gross profit (and net income) for the period. During periods of inflation, the FIFO method yields the lowest amount for the cost of merchandise sold, the highest amount for gross profit (and net income), and the highest amount for the ending inventory. The LIFO method yields the opposite results. During periods of deflation, the preceding effects are reversed. The average cost method yields results that are between those of FIFO and LIFO.

8. Describe how receivables and inventory are reported on the financial statements.

All receivables that are expected to be realized in cash within a year are presented in the Current Assets section of the balance sheet. It is normal to list the assets in the order of their liquidity, which is the order in which they can be converted to cash in normal operations. In addition to the allowance for doubtful accounts, additional receivable disclosures include the market (fair) value and unusual credit risks.

Inventory is normally presented in the Current Assets section of the balance sheet following receivables. If the market price of an item of inventory is lower than its cost, the lower market price is used to compute the value of the item. Market price is the cost to replace the merchandise on the inventory date. It is possible to apply the lower of cost or market to each item in the inventory, to major classes or categories, or to the inventory as a whole.

Merchandise that can be sold only at prices below cost should be valued at net realizable value, which is the estimated selling price less any direct costs of disposal.

9. Describe and illustrate accounts receivable and inventory turnover and their use in assessing the management of receivables and inventory.

The accounts receivable and inventory turnovers are useful in assessing a company's management of its receivables and inventory. The accounts receivable turnover is computed as net sales divided by average accounts receivable. The inventory turnover is computed as cost of merchandise sold divided by average inventory.

Key Terms

Accounts receivable (216)
Accounts receivable turnover (236)
Aging the receivables (224)
Allowance for doubtful accounts (220)
Allowance method (219)
Average cost inventory cost flow method (229)
Bad debt expense (218)
Cost of goods sold (227)

Direct write-off method (219)
Finished goods inventory (227)
First-in, first-out (FIFO) inventory cost flow method (229)
Inventory turnover (236)
Last-in, first-out (LIFO) inventory cost flow method (229)

LIFO conformity rule (232)
LIFO reserve (232)
Lower-of-cost-or-market (LCM) method (235)
Materials inventory (227)
Maturity value (218)
Merchandise inventory (226)
Net realizable value (234)

Notes receivable (216)
Number of days' sales in inventory (237)
Number of days' sales in receivables (236)
Receivables (216)
Specific identification inventory cost flow method (229)
Work-in-process (WIP) inventory (227)

Illustrative Problem

Stewart Co. is a construction supply company that uses the allowance method of accounting for uncollectible accounts receivable. It is estimated that 3% of the credit sales of $1,375,000 for the year ended December 31 will be uncollectible. In addition, Stewart Co.'s beginning inventory and purchases during the year ended December 31, 20Y5, were as follows:

		Units	Unit Cost	Total Cost
January 1	Inventory	1,000	$50.00	$ 50,000
March 10	Purchase	1,200	52.50	63,000
August 30	Purchase	800	55.00	44,000
November 26	Purchase	2,000	56.00	112,000
Total		5,000		$269,000

Instructions

1. Determine the amount of the adjustment for uncollectible accounts as of December 31, 20Y5.

2. Illustrate the effects of the adjustment for uncollectible accounts on the accounts and financial statements of Stewart Co.

3. If the balance of Allowance for Doubtful Accounts was a negative $7,500, would the amount of adjustment determined in (1) change?

4. Assuming that 3,300 units were sold during the year, determine the cost of inventory on December 31, 20Y5, using each of the following inventory costing methods:

   a. First-in, first-out

   b. Last-in, first-out

   c. Average cost

Solution

1. $41,250 ($1,375,000 × 3%)

2.

Statement of Cash Flows	Balance Sheet				Income Statement
	Assets	=	Liabilities +	Stockholders' Equity	
	Allowance for – Doubtful Accts.	=		Retained Earnings	
Dec. 31.	–41,250			–41,250	*Dec. 31.*

Income Statement

Dec. 31. Bad debt expense –41,250

3. No. Under the percent of sales method, the amount of the adjustment is determined without considering the balance of Allowance for Doubtful Accounts. Under the analysis of receivables method, however, the balance of Allowance for Doubtful Accounts does affect the amount of the adjustment.

4. a. First-in, first-out method: 1,700 units at $56 = $95,200

   b. Last-in, first-out method:

1,000	units at $50.00	$50,000
700	units at $52.50	36,750
1,700		$86,750

   c. Average cost method:

   Average cost per unit: $269,000 ÷ 5,000 units = $53.80

   Inventory, December 31, 20Y5: 1,700 units at $53.80 = $91,460

Self-Examination Questions *(Answers appear at the end of chapter)*

1. At the end of the fiscal year, before the accounts are adjusted, Accounts Receivable has a balance of $200,000 and Allowance for Doubtful Accounts has a negative balance of $2,500. If the estimate of uncollectible accounts determined by aging the receivables is $8,500, the amount of bad debt expense is:

   A. $2,500

   B. $6,000

   C. $8,500

   D. $11,000

2. At the end of the fiscal year, Accounts Receivable has a balance of $100,000 and Allowance for Doubtful Accounts has a negative balance of $7,000. The expected net realizable value of the accounts receivable is:

   A. $7,000

   B. $93,000

   C. $100,000

   D. $107,000

3. The direct labor cost should be recognized first in which inventory account?

    A. Materials Inventory

    B. Merchandise Inventory

    C. Finished Goods Inventory

    D. Work-in-Process Inventory

4. The following units of a particular item were available for sale during the period:

Beginning inventory	40 units at $20
First purchase	50 units at $21
Second purchase	50 units at $22
Third purchase	50 units at $23

    What is the unit cost of the 35 units on hand at the end of the period as determined under the FIFO costing method?

    A. $20

    B. $21

    C. $22

    D. $23

5. If merchandise inventory is being valued at cost and the price level is steadily rising, the method of costing that will yield the highest net income is:

    A. LIFO

    B. FIFO

    C. average

    D. periodic

Class Discussion Questions

1. What are the three classifications of receivables?

2. What types of transactions give rise to accounts receivable?

3. In what section of the balance sheet should a note receivable be listed if its term is (a) 90 days, (b) 12 years?

4. Give two examples of other receivables.

5. Carter's Hardware is a small hardware store in the rural township of Oglethorpe that rarely extends credit to its customers in the form of an account receivable. The few customers that are allowed to carry accounts receivable are long-time residents of Oglethorpe and have a history of doing business at Carter's. What method of accounting for uncollectible receivables should Carter's Hardware use? Why?

6. Which of the two methods of accounting for uncollectible accounts provides for the recognition of the expense at the earlier date?

7. What kind of an account (asset, liability, etc.) is Allowance for Doubtful Accounts?

8. After the accounts are adjusted at the end of the fiscal year, Accounts Receivable has a balance of $475,000 and Allowance for Doubtful Accounts has a negative balance of $46,800. Describe how Accounts Receivable and Allowance for Doubtful Accounts are reported on the balance sheet.

9. A firm has consistently adjusted its allowance account at the end of the fiscal year by adding a fixed percent of the period's net sales on account. After 10 years, the balance in Allowance for Doubtful Accounts has become very large in relationship to the balance in Accounts Receivable. Give two possible explanations.

10. How are manufacturing inventories different from those of a merchandiser?

11. Do the terms *FIFO* and *LIFO* refer to techniques used in determining quantities of the various classes of merchandise on hand? Explain.

12. Does the term *last-in* in the LIFO method mean that the items in the inventory are assumed to be the most recent (last) acquisitions? Explain.

13. If merchandise inventory is being valued at cost and the price level is steadily rising, which of the three methods of costing—FIFO, LIFO, or average cost—will yield (a) the highest inventory cost, (b) the lowest inventory cost, (c) the highest gross profit, (d) the lowest gross profit?

14. Which of the three methods of inventory costing—FIFO, LIFO, or average cost—will in general yield an inventory cost most nearly approximating current replacement cost?

15. If inventory is being valued at cost and the price level is steadily rising, which of the three methods of costing—FIFO, LIFO, or average cost—will yield the lowest annual income tax expense? Explain.

16. What is the LIFO reserve, and why would an analyst be careful in interpreting the earnings of a company that has liquidated some of its LIFO reserve?

17. Under what section should accounts receivable be reported on the balance sheet?

18. Because of imperfections, an item of merchandise cannot be sold at its normal selling price. How should this item be valued for financial statement purposes?

19. How is the method of determining the cost of inventory and the method of valuing it disclosed in the financial statements?

Exercises

E6-1 Classifications of receivables

Obj 1

Boeing is one of the world's major aerospace firms, with operations involving commercial aircraft, military aircraft, missiles, satellite systems, and information and battle management systems. Recently, Boeing reported $2,950 million of receivables involving U.S. government contracts and $1,390 million of receivables involving commercial aircraft customers, such as Delta Air Lines and United Airlines.

Should Boeing report these receivables separately in the financial statements, or combine them into one overall accounts receivable amount? Explain.

E6-2 Determine due date and interest on notes

Obj 1

Determine the due date and the amount of interest due at maturity on the following notes:

✔ a. Feb. 20, $450

	Date of Note	Face Amount	Interest Rate	Term of Note
a.	January 6	$40,000	9%	45 days
b.	March 23	9,000	10	60 days
c.	May 30	12,000	12	90 days
d.	August 30	18,000	10	120 days
e.	October 1	10,500	8	60 days

E6-3 Nature of uncollectible accounts

Obj 2

MGM Resorts International owns and operates casinos including the MGM Grand and the Bellagio in Las Vegas, Nevada. For a recent year, the MGM Resorts International reported accounts and notes receivable of $592,937,000 and allowance for doubtful accounts of $101,207,000.

✔ a. 17.1%

International Business Machines (IBM) provides information technology services, including software, worldwide. For a recent year, IBM reported accounts receivable of $11,435,000,000 and allowance for doubtful accounts of $256,000,000.

a. Compute the percentage of the allowance for doubtful accounts to the accounts and notes receivable for the MGM Mirage.

b. Compute the percentage of the allowance for doubtful accounts to the accounts receivable for IBM.

c. Discuss possible reasons for the difference in the two ratios computed in (a) and (b).

E6-4 Uncollectible accounts, using direct write-off method

Obj 3

Illustrate the effects on the accounts and financial statements of the following transactions in the accounts of MedTech Co., a local hospital supply company that uses the direct write-off method of accounting for uncollectible receivables:

Feb. 14.   Received $9,000 on an account and wrote off the remainder owed of $45,000 as uncollectible.

Dec. 23.   Reinstated the account that had been written off on February 14 and received $45,000 cash in full payment.

Note: The spreadsheet icon [icon] indicates an Excel template is available on the student companion site.

Obj 4

E6-5   Uncollectible receivables, using allowance method

Illustrate the effects on the accounts and financial statements of the following transactions in the accounts of A1 Kitchen Company, a restaurant supply company that uses the allowance method of accounting for uncollectible receivables:

Jan. 31.   Received $8,000 on an account and wrote off the remainder owed of $32,000 as uncollectible.

Nov. 2.   Reinstated the account that had been written off on January 31 and received $32,000 cash in full payment.

Obj 3, 4

E6-6   Writing off accounts receivable

Intermountain Technologies, a computer consulting firm, has decided to write off the $11,575 balance of an account owed by a customer. Illustrate the effects on the accounts and financial statements to record the write-off (a) assuming that the direct write-off method is used, and (b) assuming that the allowance method is used.

E6-7   Estimating doubtful accounts

Cycle Parts International is a wholesaler of motorcycle supplies. An aging of the company's accounts receivable on December 31, 20Y3, and a historical analysis of the percentage of uncollectible accounts in each age category are as follows:

Age Interval	Balance	Percent Uncollectible
Not past due	$1,350,000	2%
1–30 days past due	600,000	3
31–60 days past due	90,000	5
61–90 days past due	40,000	15
91–180 days past due	20,000	50
Over 180 days past due	10,000	80
	$2,110,000	

Estimate what the balance of Allowance for Doubtful Accounts should be as of December 31, 20Y3.

Obj 4

E6-8   Entry for uncollectible accounts

Using the data in Exercise 6-7, assume that the allowance for doubtful accounts for Cycle Parts International had a negative balance of −$11,300 as of December 31, 20Y3.

Illustrate the effects of the adjustment for uncollectible accounts as of December 31, 20Y3, on the accounts and financial statements.

Obj 4

✔ a. $108,000

✔ b. $125,000

E6-9   Providing for doubtful accounts

At the end of the current year, the accounts receivable account has a balance of $1,800,000 and net sales for the year total $21,600,000. Determine the amount of the adjusting entry to provide for doubtful accounts under each of the following assumptions:

a.   The allowance account before adjustment has a negative balance of −$20,000. Bad debt expense is estimated at ½ of 1% of net sales.

b.   The allowance account before adjustment has a negative balance of −$20,000. An aging of the accounts in the customer ledger indicates estimated doubtful accounts of $145,000.

c.   The allowance account before adjustment has a positive balance of $18,000. Bad debt expense is estimated at ¾ of 1% of net sales.

d.   The allowance account before adjustment has a positive balance of $18,000. An aging of the accounts in the customer ledger indicates estimated doubtful accounts of $130,000.

E6-10   Effect of doubtful accounts on net income

Obj 3, 4

During its first year of operations, Williams Plumbing Supply Co. had net sales of $6,500,000, wrote off $40,000 of accounts as uncollectible using the direct write-off method, and reported net income of $590,000. Determine what the net income would have been if the allowance method had been used, and the company estimated that 1¾% of net sales would be uncollectible.

E6-11   Effect of doubtful accounts on net income

Obj 3, 4
✔ b. $119,750

Using the data in Exercise 6-10, assume that during the second year of operations Williams Plumbing Supply Co. had net sales of $7,200,000, wrote off $80,000 of accounts as uncollectible using the direct write-off method, and reported net income of $625,000.

a. Determine what net income would have been in the second year if the allowance method (using 1¾% of net sales) had been used in both the first and second years.

b. Determine what the balance of Allowance for Doubtful Accounts would have been at the end of the second year if the allowance method had been used in both the first and second years.

E6-12   Manufacturing inventories

Obj 5

Qualcomm Incorporated is a leading developer and manufacturer of digital wireless telecommunications products and services. Qualcomm reported the following inventories in the notes to recent financial statements:

	(In millions)
Raw materials	$ 19
Work in process	531
Finished goods	480
	$1,030

a. Why does Qualcomm report three different inventories?

b. What costs are included in each of the three classes of inventory?

E6-13   Film costs of DreamWorks

Obj 5

DreamWorks Animation SKG Inc. shows "film costs" as an asset on its balance sheet. In the notes to its financial statements, the following disclosure was made:

	December 31,	
Film Costs (in thousands)	Year 2	Year 1
In release:		
Animated feature films	$356,715	$328,174
Television specials	41,955	56,689
In production:		
Animated feature films	435,985	341,319
Television specials	22,034	14,359
In development	25,957	32,127
Total film costs	$882,646	$772,668

a. Interpret the film cost asset categories.

b. How are these classifications similar or dissimilar to the inventory classifications used in a manufacturing firm?

Obj **6**

✔ b. $114,480

E6-14   Inventory by three methods

The units of an item available for sale during the year were as follows:

Jan. 1	Inventory	54 units at $1,200
Mar. 6	Purchase	108 units at $1,380
July 14	Purchase	126 units at $1,560
Nov. 2	Purchase	112 units at $1,650

There are 90 units of the item in the physical inventory at December 31. The periodic inventory system is used. Determine the inventory cost by (a) the first-in, first-out method, (b) the last-in, first-out method, and (c) the average cost method.

Obj **6**

✔ a. Merchandise inventory, $7,728

E6-15   Inventory by three methods; cost of merchandise sold

The units of an item available for sale during the year were as follows:

Jan. 1	Inventory	42 units at $180
Apr. 10	Purchase	58 units at $195
Sept. 30	Purchase	20 units at $204
Dec. 12	Purchase	30 units at $210

There are 37 units of the item in the physical inventory at December 31. The periodic inventory system is used. Determine the inventory cost and the cost of merchandise sold by three methods, presenting your answers in the following form:

| | Cost | |
Inventory Method	Merchandise Inventory	Merchandise Sold
a. First-in, first-out	$	$
b. Last-in, first-out		
c. Average cost		

Obj **7**

E6-16   Comparing inventory methods

Assume that a firm separately determined inventory under FIFO and LIFO and then compared the results.

1. In each space below, place the correct sign [less than (<), greater than (>), or equal (=)] for each comparison, assuming periods of rising prices.
   a. FIFO inventory _____ LIFO inventory
   b. FIFO cost of goods sold _____ LIFO cost of goods sold
   c. FIFO net income _____ LIFO net income
   d. FIFO income tax _____ LIFO income tax

2. Why would management prefer to use LIFO over FIFO in periods of rising prices?

Obj **8**

E6-17   Receivables in the balance sheet

List any errors you can find in the following partial balance sheet:

ZABEL COMPANY
Balance Sheet
December 31, 20Y4

Assets

Current assets:		
Cash		$ 75,000
Notes receivable	$115,000	
Less interest receivable	9,000	106,000
Account receivable	$475,000	
Plus allowance for doubtful accounts	11,150	486,150

E6-18 Lower-of-cost-or-market inventory

On the basis of the following data, determine the value of the inventory at the lower of cost or market. Assemble the data in the form illustrated in Exhibit 9.

Obj 8

Commodity	Inventory Quantity	Unit Cost Price	Unit Market Price
Buffalo	35	$115	$120
Dakota	67	90	75
Frontier	8	300	280
Midwest	83	40	30
Rainbow	100	90	94

✔ LCM: $22,780

E6-19 Merchandise inventory on the balance sheet

Obj 8

Based on the data in Exercise 6-18 and assuming that cost was determined by the FIFO method, show how the merchandise inventory would appear on the balance sheet.

Problems

P6-1 Allowance method for doubtful accounts

Obj 4

Natural Hair Company supplies wigs and hair care products to beauty salons throughout Texas and the Southwest. The accounts receivable clerk for Natural Hair prepared the following aging-of-receivables schedule as of the end of business on December 31, 20Y7:

	A	B	C	D	E	F	G	H
1			Not		Days Past Due			
2			Past					
3	Customer	Balance	Due	1–30	31–60	61–90	91–120	Over 120
4	AAA Beauty	19,500	19,500					
5	Amelia's Wigs	8,000			8,000			
30	Zim's Beauty	6,100			6,100			
31	Totals	880,000	575,000	140,500	82,700	36,000	25,000	20,800

✔ 1. Estimate of uncollectible accounts, $45,966

Natural Hair Company has a past history of uncollectible accounts by age category, as follows:

Age Class	Percent Uncollectible
Not past due	1%
1–30 days past due	2
31–60 days past due	8
61–90 days past due	15
91–120 days past due	35
Over 120 days past due	80

Instructions

1. Estimate the allowance for doubtful accounts, based on the aging-of-receivables schedule.

2. Assume that the allowance for doubtful accounts for Natural Hair Company has a negative balance of –$3,500 before adjustment on December 31, 20Y7. Illustrate the effect on the accounts and financial statements of the adjustment for uncollectible accounts.

3. Natural Hair Company reported credit sales of $5,000,000 during 20Y7. Assume that instead of using the analysis of receivables method of estimating uncollectible accounts, Natural Hair Company uses the percent of sales method and estimates that 1.25% of sales will be uncollectible. Illustrate the effect on the accounts and financial statements of the adjustment for uncollectible accounts using the percent of sales method.

4. Assume that on March 4, 20Y8, Natural Hair wrote off the $4,350 account of Top Dog Images as uncollectible. Illustrate the effect on the accounts and financial statements of the write-off of the Top Dog Images account.

5. Assume that on August 17, 20Y8, Top Dog Images paid $4,350 on its account. Illustrate the effect on the accounts and financial statements of reinstating and collecting the Top Dog Images account.

6. Assume that instead of using the allowance method, Natural Hair uses the direct write-off method. Illustrate the effect on the accounts and financial statements of the following:

   a. The write-off of the Top Dog Images account on March 4, 20Y8.

   b. The reinstatement and collection of the Top Dog Images account on August 17, 20Y8.

7. Does Amazon.com use the direct write-off or allowance method of accounting for uncollectible accounts receivable? Explain.

Obj 4

✔ 1. a. 20Y2, $31,250

P6-2   Estimate uncollectible accounts

For several years, EquiPrime Co.'s sales have been on a "cash only" basis. On January 1, 20Y2, however, EquiPrime Co. began offering credit on terms of n/30. The amount of the adjusting entry to record the estimated uncollectible receivables at the end of each year has been ¼ of 1% of credit sales, which is the rate reported as the average for the industry. Credit sales and the year-end credit balances in Allowance for Doubtful Accounts for the past four years are as follows:

Year	Credit Sales	Allowance for Doubtful Accounts
20Y2	$12,500,000	$12,800
20Y3	12,600,000	23,000
20Y4	12,800,000	34,000
20Y5	13,000,000	49,000

Mandy Pulaski, president of EquiPrime Co., is concerned that the method used to account for and write off uncollectible receivables is unsatisfactory. She has asked for your advice in the analysis of past operations in this area and for recommendations for change.

1. Determine the amount of (a) the addition to Allowance for Doubtful Accounts and (b) the accounts written off for each of the four years.

2. a. Advise Mandy Pulaski as to whether the estimate of ¼ of 1% of credit sales appears reasonable.

   b. Assume that after discussing (a) with Mandy Pulaski, she asked you what action might be taken to determine what the balance of Allowance for Doubtful Accounts should be at December 31, 20Y5, and what possible changes, if any, you might recommend in accounting for uncollectible receivables. How would you respond?

Obj 3, 4

✔ 1. Year 4:
Balance of
allowance account,
end of year,
$53,750

P6-3   Compare two methods of accounting for uncollectible receivables

Cyber Space Company, which operates a chain of 65 electronics supply stores, has just completed its fourth year of operations. The direct write-off method of recording bad debt expense has been used during the entire period. Because of substantial increases in sales volume and the amount of uncollectible accounts, the firm is considering changing to the allowance method. Information is requested as to the effect that an annual provision of ½% of sales would have had on the amount of bad debt expense reported for each of the past four years. It is also considered desirable to know what the balance of Allowance for Doubtful Accounts would have been at the end of each year. The following data have been obtained from the accounts:

| | | | Year of Origin of Accounts Receivable Written Off as Uncollectible | | | |
Year	Sales	Uncollectible Accounts Written Off	1	2	3	4
1	$2,300,000	$ 5,000	$5,000			
2	4,750,000	9,000	4,000	$ 5,000		
3	9,000,000	23,000	2,000	12,000	$ 9,000	
4	9,600,000	37,500		5,500	14,500	$17,500

Instructions

1. Assemble the desired data, using the following column headings:

| | Bad Debt Expense | | | |
Year	Expense Actually Reported	Expense Based on Estimate	Increase (Decrease) in Amount of Expense	Balance of Allowance Account, End of Year

2. Experience during the first four years of operations indicated that the receivables were either collected within two years or had to be written off as uncollectible. Does the estimate of ½% of sales appear to be reasonably close to the actual experience with uncollectible accounts originating during the first two years? Explain.

P6-4   Inventory by three cost flow methods

Obj **6, 7**

✔ 1. $11,227

Details regarding the inventory of appliances at January 1, 20Y7, purchases invoices during the year, and the inventory count at December 31, 20Y7, of Icelander Appliances are summarized as follows:

Model	Inventory, January 1	Purchases Invoices 1st	2nd	3rd	Inventory Count, December 31
101Sx	9 at $213	7 at $215	6 at $222	6 at $225	9
256Br	20 at $120	12 at $130	4 at $130	4 at $140	8
378Wh	6 at $305	3 at $310	3 at $316	4 at $317	4
590Pm	2 at $520	2 at $527	2 at $530	2 at $535	4
661Qu	6 at $520	8 at $531	4 at $549	6 at $542	7
828Ts	—	4 at $222	4 at $232	—	2
913Vn	8 at $35	12 at $36	16 at $37	14 at $39	12

Instructions

1. Determine the cost of the inventory on December 31, 20Y7, by the first-in, first-out method. Present data in columnar form, using the following headings:

Model	Quantity	Unit Cost	Total Cost

   If the inventory of a particular model comprises one entire purchase plus a portion of another purchase acquired at a different unit cost, use a separate line for each purchase.

2. Determine the cost of the inventory on December 31, 20Y7, by the last-in, first-out method, following the procedures indicated in (1).

3. Determine the cost of the inventory on December 31, 20Y7, by the average cost method, using the columnar headings indicated in (1).

4. Discuss which method (FIFO or LIFO) would be preferred for income tax purposes in periods of (a) rising prices and (b) declining prices.

Obj | 8

✔ Total LCM, $41,855

P6-5 Lower-of-cost-or-market inventory

Data on the physical inventory of Moyer Company as of December 31, 20Y9, are presented below.

Description	Inventory Quantity	Unit Market Price
112Aa	38	$ 83
B300t	33	115
C39f	41	64
Echo9	125	26
F900w	18	550
H687	60	15
J023	5	390
L33y	375	6
R66b	90	18
S77x	6	235
T882m	130	18
Z55p	12	746

Quantity and cost data from the last purchases invoice of the year and the next-to-the-last purchases invoice are summarized as follows:

Description	Last Purchases Invoice Quantity Purchased	Unit Cost	Next-to-the-Last Purchases Invoice Quantity Purchased	Unit Cost
112Aa	25	$ 80	30	$ 78
B300t	35	118	20	117
C39f	20	66	25	70
Echo9	150	25	100	24
F900w	10	565	10	560
H687	100	15	100	14
J023	10	385	5	384
L33y	500	6	500	6
R66b	80	22	50	21
S77x	5	250	4	260
T882m	100	20	75	19
Z55p	9	750	9	749

Instructions

Determine the inventory at cost and also at the lower of cost or market, using the first-in, first-out method. Record the appropriate unit costs on an inventory sheet and complete the pricing of the inventory. When there are two different unit costs applicable to an item, proceed as follows:

1. Draw a line through the quantity, and insert the quantity and unit cost of the last purchase.
2. On the following line, insert the quantity and unit cost of the next-to-the-last purchase.
3. Total the cost and market columns and insert the lower of the two totals in the LCM column. The first item on the inventory sheet has been completed below as an example.

Inventory Sheet
December 31, 20Y9

Description	Inventory Quantity	Unit Cost Price	Unit Market Price	Total Cost	Market	LCM
112Aa	3̶8̶ 25	$80	$83	$2,000	$2,075	
	13	78		1,014	1,079	
				$3,014	$3,154	$3,014

Financial Analysis

FA 6-1   Accounts receivable and inventory turnover

Obj 9

The following data (in millions) were adapted from recent financial statements of Dell Inc.

	Year 2	Year 1
Net sales	$62,071	$61,494
Cost of merchandise sold	48,260	50,098
Average accounts receivable	9,970	9,340
Average inventory	1,353	1,176

1. Compute the accounts receivable turnover for Years 1 and 2. Round to one decimal place.
2. Compute the number of days' sales in receivables for Years 1 and 2. Round to one decimal place.
3. Compute the inventory turnover for Years 1 and 2. Round to one decimal place.
4. Compute the number of days' sales in inventory for Years 1 and 2. Round to one decimal place.
5. Comment on Dell's management of receivables and inventory based upon the results in parts (1), (2), (3), and (4).

FA 6-2   Accounts receivable and inventory turnover

Obj 9

The following data (in millions) were adapted from recent financial statements of Hewlett-Packard Company.

	Year 2	Year 1
Net sales	$120,357	$127,245
Cost of merchandise sold	92,385	97,418
Average accounts receivable	20,523	21,427
Average inventory	6,904	6,978

1. Compute the accounts receivable turnover for Years 1 and 2. Round to one decimal place.
2. Compute the number of days' sales in receivables for Years 1 and 2. Round to one decimal place.
3. Compute the inventory turnover for Years 1 and 2. Round to one decimal place.
4. Compute the number of days' sales in inventory for Years 1 and 2. Round to one decimal place.
5. Comment on Hewlett-Packard's management of receivables and inventory based upon the results in parts (1), (2), (3), and (4).

FA 6-3   Accounts receivable and inventory turnover

Obj 9

Compare and comment on Dell Inc. and Hewlett-Packard Company's management of receivables and inventory using the results of FA 6-1 and FA 6-2.

FA 6-4   Accounts receivable and inventory turnover

Obj 9

The following data (in millions) were adapted from recent financial statements of Johnson & Johnson.

	Year 2	Year 1
Net sales	$65,030	$61,587
Cost of merchandise sold	20,350	18,792
Average accounts receivable	12,568	12,219
Average inventory	5,832	5,279

1. Compute the accounts receivable turnover for Years 1 and 2. Round to one decimal place.
2. Compute the number of days' sales in receivables for Years 1 and 2. Round to one decimal place.

3. Compute the inventory turnover for Years 1 and 2. Round to one decimal place.

4. Compute the number of days' sales in inventory for Years 1 and 2. Round to one decimal place.

5. Comment on Johnson & Johnson's management of receivables and inventory based upon the results in parts (1), (2), (3), and (4).

Obj | **9**

FA 6-5 Accounts receivable and inventory turnover

The following data (in millions) were adapted from recent financial statements of International Paper Company and Walmart Stores Inc.

	International Paper	Walmart
Net sales	$26,034	$446,950
Cost of merchandise sold	18,960	335,127
Accounts receivable:		
Beginning of year	3,378	5,089
End of year	3,782	5,937
Inventory:		
Beginning of year	2,347	36,437
End of year	2,320	40,714

1. Compute the accounts receivable turnover for International Paper and Walmart. Round to one decimal place.

2. Compute the number of days' sales in receivables for International Paper and Walmart. Round to one decimal place.

3. Compute the inventory turnover for International Paper and Walmart. Round to one decimal place.

4. Compute the number of days' sales in inventory for International Paper and Walmart. Round to one decimal place.

5. Comment on and explain any differences in International Paper's and Walmart's management of inventories and receivables based upon the results in parts (1), (2), (3), and (4).

Cases

Case 6-1 Ethics and professional conduct in business

Sybil Crumpton, vice president of operations for Bob Marshall Wilderness Bank, has instructed the bank's computer programmer to use a 365-day year to compute interest on depository accounts (payables). Sybil also instructed the programmer to use a 360-day year to compute interest on loans (receivables).

Discuss whether Sybil is behaving in a professional manner.

Case 6-2 Collecting accounts receivable

The following is an excerpt from a conversation between the office manager, Terry Holland, and the president of Northern Construction Supplies Co., Janet Austel. Northern Construction Supplies sells building supplies to local contractors.

Terry: Janet, we're going to have to do something about these overdue accounts receivable. One-third of our accounts are over 60 days past due, and I've had accounts that have stayed open for almost a year!

Janet: I didn't realize it was that bad. Any ideas?

Terry: Well, we could stop giving credit. Make everyone pay with cash or a credit card. We accept MasterCard and Visa already, but only the walk-in customers use them. Almost all of the contractors put purchases on their bills.

Janet: Yes, but we've been allowing credit for years. As far as I know, all of our competitors allow contractors credit. If we stopped giving credit, we'd lose many of our contractors. They'd just go elsewhere. You know, some of these guys run up bills as high as $50,000 or $75,000. There's no way they could put that kind of money on a credit card.

Terry: That's a good point. But we've got to do something.

Janet: How many of the contractor accounts do you actually end up writing off as uncollectible?

Terry: Not many. Almost all eventually pay. It's just that they take so long!

    Suggest one or more solutions to Northern Construction Supplies Co.'s problem concerning the collection of accounts receivable.

Case 6-3   Ethics and professional conduct in business

Mitchell Co. is experiencing a decrease in sales and operating income for the fiscal year ending December 31, 20Y1. Gene Lumpkin, controller of Mitchell Co., has suggested that all orders received before the end of the fiscal year be shipped by midnight, December 31, 20Y1, even if the shipping department must work overtime. Since Mitchell Co. ships all merchandise FOB shipping point, it would record all such shipments as sales for the year ending December 31, 20Y1, thereby offsetting some of the decreases in sales and operating income.

    Discuss whether Gene Lumpkin is behaving in a professional manner.

Case 6-4   LIFO and inventory flow

The following is an excerpt from a conversation between Evan Eberhard, the warehouse manager for Greenbriar Wholesale Co., and its accountant, Marty Hayes. Greenbriar operates a large regional warehouse that supplies produce and other grocery products to grocery stores in smaller communities.

Evan: Marty, can you explain what's going on here with these monthly statements?

Marty: Sure, Evan. How can I help you?

Evan: I don't understand this last-in, first-out inventory procedure. It just doesn't make sense.

Marty: Well, what it means is that we assume that the last goods we receive are the first ones sold. So the inventory is made up of the items we purchased first.

Evan: Yes, but that's my problem. It doesn't work that way! We always distribute the oldest produce first. Some of that produce is perishable! We can't keep any of it very long or it'll spoil.

Marty: Evan, you don't understand. We only assume that the products we distribute are the last ones received. We don't actually have to distribute the goods in this way.

Evan: I always thought that accounting was supposed to show what really happened. It all sounds like "make believe" to me! Why not report what really happens?

    Respond to Evan's concerns.

Answers to Self-Examination Questions

1. **B** The estimate of uncollectible accounts, $8,500 (answer C), is the amount of the desired balance of Allowance for Doubtful Accounts after adjustment. The amount of the current provision to be made for bad debt expense is thus $6,000 (answer B), which is the amount that must be added to the Allowance for Doubtful Accounts negative balance of $2,500 (answer A), so that the account will have the desired balance of $8,500.

2. **B** The amount expected to be realized from accounts receivable is the balance of Accounts Receivable, $100,000, less the balance of Allowance for Doubtful Accounts, $7,000, or $93,000 (answer B).

3. **D** The direct labor costs are introduced into production initially as work in process. Once the units are completed, these costs are transferred to finished goods inventory (answer C). Materials inventory

(answer A) includes only material costs, not direct labor cost. Merchandise inventory (answer B) is not used in a manufacturing setting and thus does not include direct labor cost.

4. **D** The FIFO method of costing is based on the assumption that costs should be charged against revenue in the order in which they were incurred (first-in, first-out). Thus, the most recent costs are assigned to inventory. The 35 units would be assigned a unit cost of $23 (answer D).

5. **B** When the price level is steadily rising, the earlier unit costs are lower than recent unit costs. Under the FIFO method (answer B), these earlier costs are matched against revenue to yield the highest possible net income. The periodic inventory system (answer D) is a system and not a method of costing.

CHAPTER 7

Fixed Assets and Intangible Assets

LEARNING OBJECTIVES

After studying this chapter, you should be able to:

Obj 1 Define, classify, and account for the cost of fixed assets.

Obj 2 Compute depreciation using the straight-line and double-declining-balance methods.

Obj 3 Describe the accounting for the disposal of fixed assets.

Obj 4 Describe the accounting for depletion of natural resources.

Obj 5 Describe the accounting for intangible assets.

Obj 6 Describe how depreciation expense is reported on an income statement and prepare a balance sheet that includes fixed assets and intangible assets.

Obj 7 Financial Analysis : Describe and illustrate the fixed asset turnover in assessing a company's use of fixed assets.

D o you remember purchasing your first car? You probably didn't buy your first car like you would download songs from iTunes. Purchasing a new or used car is expensive. In addition, you would drive (use) the car for the next 3–5 years or longer. As a result, you might spend hours or weeks considering different makes and models, safety ratings, warranties, and operating costs before deciding on the final purchase.

Like buying her first car, Lovie Yancey spent a lot of time before deciding to open her first restaurant. In 1952, she created the biggest, juiciest hamburger that anyone had ever seen. She called it a Fatburger. The **Fatburger** restaurant initially started as a 24-hour operation to cater to the schedules of professional musicians. As a fan of popular music and its performers, Yancey played rhythm and blues, jazz, and blues recordings for her customers. Fatburger's popularity with entertainers was illustrated when its name was used in a 1992 rap by Ice Cube. "Two in the mornin' got the Fatburger," Cube said, in "It Was a Good Day," a track on his *Predator* album.

The demand for this incredible burger was such that, in 1980, Ms. Yancey decided to offer Fatburger franchise opportunities. In 1990, with the goal of expanding Fatburger throughout the world, Fatburger Inc. purchased the business from Ms. Yancey. Today, Fatburger has grown to a multi-restaurant chain with owners and investors such as talk show host Montel Williams, former Cincinnati Bengals' tackle Willie Anderson, comedian David Spade, and musicians Cher, Janet Jackson, and Pharrell.

So, how much would it cost you to open a Fatburger restaurant? The total investment begins at over $750,000 per restaurant. Thus, in starting a Fatburger restaurant, you would be making a significant investment that would affect your life for years to come. For more information, see **http://www.fatburger.com.**

This chapter discusses the accounting for investments in fixed assets such as those used to open a Fatburger restaurant. How to determine the portion of the fixed asset that becomes an expense over time is also discussed. Finally, the accounting for the disposal of fixed assets and accounting for intangible assets such as patents and copyrights are discussed.

Obj | 1

Define, classify, and account for the cost of fixed assets.

Nature of Fixed Assets

Fixed assets are long-term or relatively permanent assets such as equipment, machinery, buildings, and land. Other descriptive titles for fixed assets are *plant assets* or *property, plant, and equipment.* Fixed assets have the following characteristics:

1. They exist physically and thus are *tangible* assets.
2. They are owned and used by the company in its normal operations.
3. They are not offered for sale as part of normal operations.

Exhibit 1 shows the percent of fixed assets to total assets for some select companies. As shown in Exhibit 1, fixed assets are often a significant portion of the total assets of a company.

EXHIBIT 1

Fixed Assets as a Percent of Total Assets— Selected Companies

	Fixed Assets as a Percent of Total Assets
Alcoa Inc.	48%
Exxon Mobil Corporation	65
Hyatt Hotels Corporation	54
Kroger	62
Starbucks Corporation	32
United Parcel Service, Inc.	51
Verizon Communications	38
Walgreen Co.	36
Walmart	58

Classifying Costs

A cost that has been incurred may be classified as a fixed asset, an investment, or an expense. Exhibit 2 shows how to determine the proper classification of a cost and thus how it should be recorded.

As shown in Exhibit 2, classifying a cost involves the following steps:

Step 1. Is the purchased item (cost) long-lived?
If *yes,* the item is capitalized as an asset on the balance sheet as either a fixed asset or an investment. Proceed to Step 2.
If *no,* the item is classified and recorded as an *expense.*

Step 2. Is the asset used in normal operations?
If *yes,* the asset is classified and recorded as a *fixed asset.*
If *no,* the asset is classified and recorded as an *investment.*

Costs that are classified and recorded as fixed assets include the purchase of land, buildings, or equipment. Such assets normally last more than a year and are used in the normal operations. However, standby equipment for use during peak periods or when other equipment breaks down is still classified as a fixed asset even though it is not used very often. In contrast, fixed assets that have been abandoned or are no longer used in operations are not fixed assets.

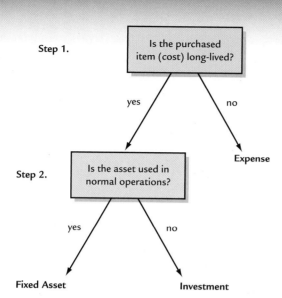

EXHIBIT 2

Classifying Costs

Although fixed assets may be sold, they should not be offered for sale as part of normal operations. For example, cars and trucks offered for sale by an automotive dealership are not fixed assets of the dealership. On the other hand, a tow truck used in the normal operations of the dealership is a fixed asset of the dealership.

Investments are long-lived assets that are not used in the normal operations and are held for future resale. Such assets are reported on the balance sheet in a section entitled *Investments*. For example, undeveloped land acquired for future resale would be classified and reported as an investment, not land.

The Cost of Fixed Assets

The costs of acquiring fixed assets include all amounts spent to get the asset in place and ready for use. For example, freight costs and the costs of installing equipment are part of the asset's total cost.

Exhibit 3 summarizes some of the common costs of acquiring fixed assets. These costs are recorded by increasing the related fixed asset account, such as Building, Machinery and Equipment, Land,[1] and Land Improvements.

Only costs necessary for preparing the fixed asset for use are included as a cost of the asset. Unnecessary costs that do not increase the asset's usefulness are recorded as an expense. For example, the following costs are recorded as an expense:

1. Vandalism
2. Mistakes in installation
3. Uninsured theft
4. Damage during unpacking and installing
5. Fines for not obtaining proper permits from governmental agencies

A company may incur costs associated with constructing a fixed asset such as a new building. The direct costs incurred in the construction, such as labor

---

1. As discussed here, land is assumed to be used only as a location or site and not for its mineral deposits or other natural resources.

EXHIBIT 3   Costs of Acquiring Fixed Assets

Building

- Architects' fees
- Engineers' fees
- Insurance costs incurred during construction
- Interest on money borrowed to finance construction
- Walkways to and around the building
- Sales taxes
- Repairs (purchase of existing building)
- Reconditioning (purchase of existing building)
- Modifying for use
- Permits from government agencies

Machinery & Equipment

- Sales taxes
- Freight
- Installation
- Repairs (purchase of used equipment)
- Reconditioning (purchase of used equipment)
- Insurance while in transit
- Assembly
- Modifying for use
- Testing for use
- Permits from government agencies

Land & Land Improvements

- Purchase price
- Sales taxes
- Permits from government agencies
- Broker's commissions
- Title fees
- Surveying fees
- Delinquent real estate taxes
- Removing unwanted buildings, less any salvage
- Grading and leveling
- Paving a public street bordering the land

- Trees and shrubs
- Paved parking areas
- Outdoor lighting
- Fences

Intel Corporation recently reported almost $6 billion of construction in progress, which was 25% of its total fixed assets.

and materials, should be capitalized by increasing an account entitled Construction in Progress. When the construction is complete, the costs are reclassified by decreasing Construction in Progress and increasing the proper fixed asset account such as Building. For some companies, construction in progress can be significant.

Capital and Revenue Expenditures

Once a fixed asset has been acquired and placed in service, costs may be incurred for ordinary maintenance and repairs. In addition, costs may be incurred for improving an asset or for extraordinary repairs that extend the asset's useful life. Costs that benefit only the current period are called **revenue expenditures**. Costs that improve the asset or extend its useful life are **capital expenditures**.

Ordinary Maintenance and Repairs Costs related to the ordinary maintenance and repairs of a fixed asset are recorded as an expense of the current period. Such expenditures are *revenue expenditures* and are recorded as increases to Repairs and Maintenance Expense. For example, $300 paid for a tune-up of a delivery truck is recorded as an increase in Repairs and Maintenance Expense and a decrease in Cash of $300.

Asset Improvements   After a fixed asset has been placed in service, costs may be incurred to improve the asset. For example, the service value of a delivery truck might be improved by adding a $5,500 hydraulic lift to allow for easier and quicker loading of cargo. Such costs are *capital expenditures* and are recorded as increases to the fixed asset account. In the case of the hydraulic lift, the expenditure is recorded as an increase in Delivery Truck and a decrease in Cash of $5,500. Because the cost of the delivery truck has increased, depreciation for the truck would also change over its remaining useful life.

Extraordinary Repairs   After a fixed asset has been placed in service, costs may be incurred to extend the asset's useful life. For example, the engine of a forklift that is near the end of its useful life may be overhauled at a cost of $4,500, extending its useful life by eight years. Such costs are *capital expenditures* and are recorded as a decrease in an accumulated depreciation account. In the case of the forklift, the expenditure is recorded as a decrease in Accumulated Depreciation—Forklift and a decrease in Cash of $4,500. Because the forklift's remaining useful life has changed, depreciation for the forklift would also change based on the new book value of the forklift.

The accounting for revenue and capital expenditures is summarized below.

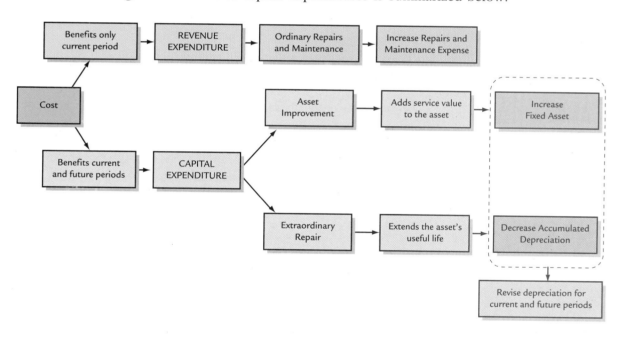

Integrity, Objectivity, and Ethics in Business

CAPITAL CRIME

One of the largest alleged accounting frauds in history involved the improper accounting for capital expenditures. WorldCom, the second largest telecommunications company in the United States at the time, improperly treated maintenance expenditures on its telecommunications network as capital expenditures. As a result, the company had to restate its prior years' earnings downward by nearly $4 billion to correct this error. The company declared bankruptcy within months of disclosing the error, and the CEO was sentenced to 25 years in prison.

Obj | **2**

Compute depreciation using the straight-line and double-declining-balance methods.

The adjusting entry to record depreciation increases Depreciation Expense and increases Accumulated Depreciation.

Would you have more cash if you depreciated your car? The answer is no. Depreciation does not affect your cash flows. Likewise, depreciation does not affect the cash flows of a business. However, depreciation is subtracted in determining net income.

Walmart depreciates buildings and improvements using 3–40 years while using 3–25 years for fixtures and equipment.

Accounting for Depreciation

Fixed assets, with the exception of land, lose their ability, over time, to provide services. Thus, the cost of fixed assets such as equipment and buildings should be recorded as an expense over their useful lives. This periodic recording of the cost of fixed assets as an expense is called **depreciation**. Because land has an unlimited life, it is not depreciated.

The adjustment to record depreciation increases *Depreciation Expense* and a *contra asset* account entitled *Accumulated Depreciation* or *Allowance for Depreciation*. The use of a contra asset account allows the original cost to remain unchanged in the fixed asset account.

Depreciation can be caused by physical or functional factors.

1. *Physical depreciation* factors include wear and tear during use or from exposure to weather.

2. *Functional depreciation* factors include obsolescence and changes in customer needs that cause the asset to no longer provide services for which it was intended. For example, equipment may become obsolete due to changing technology.

Two common misunderstandings that exist about *depreciation* as used in accounting include:

1. Depreciation does not measure a decline in the market value of a fixed asset. Instead, depreciation is an allocation of a fixed asset's cost to expense over the asset's useful life. Thus, the book value of a fixed asset (cost less accumulated depreciation) usually does not agree with the asset's market value. This is justified in accounting because a fixed asset is for use in a company's operations rather than for resale.

2. Depreciation does not provide cash to replace fixed assets as they wear out. This misunderstanding may occur because depreciation, unlike most expenses, does not require an outlay of cash when it is recorded.

Factors in Computing Depreciation Expense

Three factors determine the depreciation expense for a fixed asset. These three factors are as follows:

1. The asset's initial cost
2. The asset's expected useful life
3. The asset's estimated residual value

The initial *cost* of a fixed asset is determined using the concepts discussed and illustrated earlier in this chapter.

The *expected useful life* of a fixed asset is estimated at the time the asset is placed into service. Estimates of expected useful lives are available from industry trade associations. The Internal Revenue Service also publishes guidelines for useful lives, which may be helpful for financial reporting purposes. However, it is not uncommon for different companies to use a different useful life for similar assets.

The **residual value** of a fixed asset at the end of its useful life is estimated at the time the asset is placed into service. Residual value is sometimes referred to as *scrap value*, *salvage value*, or *trade-in value*. The difference between a fixed asset's initial cost and its residual value is called the asset's depreciable cost. The depreciable cost is the amount of the asset's cost that is allocated over its useful life as depreciation expense. If a fixed asset has no residual value, then its entire cost should be allocated to depreciation.

Exhibit 4 shows the relationship between depreciation expense and a fixed asset's initial cost, expected useful life, and estimated residual value.

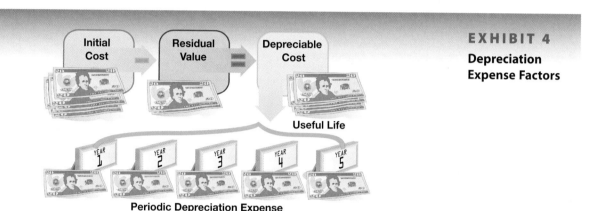

EXHIBIT 4

Depreciation Expense Factors

For an asset placed into or taken out of service during the first half of a month, many companies compute depreciation on the asset for the entire month. That is, the asset is treated as having been purchased or sold on the first day of *that* month. Likewise, purchases and sales during the second half of a month are treated as having occurred on the first day of the *next* month. To simplify, this practice is used in this chapter.

The two depreciation methods often used are:

1. Straight-line depreciation
2. Double-declining-balance depreciation

It is not necessary that a company use one method of computing depreciation for all of its fixed assets. For example, a company may use one method for depreciating equipment and another method for depreciating buildings. A company may also use different methods for determining income and property taxes.

Straight-Line Method

The **straight-line method** provides for the same amount of depreciation expense for each year of the asset's useful life. The straight-line method is the most widely used depreciation method.

To illustrate, assume that equipment was purchased on January 1 as follows:

Initial cost	$24,000
Expected useful life	5 years
Estimated residual value	$2,000

The annual straight-line depreciation of $4,400 is computed below.

$$\text{Annual Depreciation} = \frac{\text{Cost} - \text{Residual Value}}{\text{Useful Life}} = \frac{\$24,000 - \$2,000}{5 \text{ Years}} = \$4,400$$

If an asset is used for only part of a year, the annual depreciation is prorated. For example, assume that the preceding equipment was purchased and placed into service on October 1. The depreciation for the year ending December 31 would be $1,100, computed as follows:

First-Year Partial Depreciation = $4,400 × 3/12 − $1,100

The computation of straight-line depreciation may be simplified by converting the annual depreciation to a percentage of depreciable cost.[2] The straight-line percentage is determined by dividing 100% by the number of years of expected useful life, as shown below.

Expected Years of Useful Life	Straight-Line Percentage
5 years	20% (100%/5)
8 years	12.5% (100%/8)
10 years	10% (100%/10)
20 years	5% (100%/20)
25 years	4% (100%/25)

For the preceding equipment, the annual depreciation of $4,400 can be computed by multiplying the depreciable cost of $22,000 by 20% (100%/5).

As shown above, the straight-line method is simple to use. When an asset's revenues are about the same from period to period, straight-line depreciation provides a good matching of depreciation expense with the asset's revenues.

Double-Declining-Balance Method

The **double-declining-balance method** provides for a declining periodic expense over the expected useful life of the asset. The double-declining-balance method is applied in three steps.

Step 1. Determine the straight-line percentage using the expected useful life.

Step 2. Determine the double-declining-balance rate by multiplying the straight-line rate from Step 1 by two.

Step 3. Compute the depreciation expense by multiplying the double-declining-balance rate from Step 2 by the book value of the asset.

To illustrate, the equipment purchased in the preceding example is used to compute double-declining-balance depreciation. For the first year, the depreciation is $9,600, as shown below.

Step 1. Straight-line percentage = 20% (100%/5)
Step 2. Double-declining-balance rate = 40% (20% × 2)
Step 3. Depreciation expense = $9,600 ($24,000 × 40%)

For the first year, the book value of the equipment is its initial cost of $24,000. After the first year, the **book value** (cost minus accumulated depreciation) declines

2. The depreciation rate may also be expressed as a fraction. For example, the annual straight-line rate for an asset with a three-year useful life is 1/3.

and thus the depreciation also declines. The double-declining-balance depreciation for the full five-year life of the equipment is shown below.

Year	Cost	Acc. Depr. at Beginning of Year	Book Value at Beginning of Year		Double-Declining-Balance Rate	Depreciation for Year	Book Value at End of Year
1	$24,000		$24,000.00	×	40%	$9,600.00	$14,400.00
2	24,000	$ 9,600.00	14,400.00	×	40%	5,760.00	8,640.00
3	24,000	15,360.00	8,640.00	×	40%	3,456.00	5,184.00
4	24,000	18,816.00	5,184.00	×	40%	2,073.60	3,110.40
5	24,000	20,889.60	3,110.40	×	—	1,110.40	2,000.00

When the double-declining-balance method is used, the estimated residual value is *not* considered. However, the asset should not be depreciated below its estimated residual value. In the above example, the estimated residual value was $2,000. Therefore, the depreciation for the fifth year is $1,110.40 ($3,110.40 − $2,000.00) instead of $1,244.16 (40% × $3,110.40).

Like straight-line depreciation, if an asset is used for only part of a year, the annual depreciation is prorated. For example, assume that the preceding equipment was purchased and placed into service on October 1. The depreciation for the year ending December 31 would be $2,400, computed as follows:

$$\text{First-Year Partial Depreciation} = \$9,600 \times 3/12 = \$2,400$$

The depreciation for the second year would then be $8,640, computed as follows:

$$\text{Second-Year Depreciation} = \$8,640 = [40\% \times (\$24,000 - \$2,400)]$$

The double-declining-balance method provides a higher depreciation in the first year of the asset's use, followed by declining depreciation amounts. For this reason, the double-declining-balance method is called an **accelerated depreciation method**.

An asset's revenues are often greater in the early years of its use than in later years. In such cases, the double-declining-balance method provides a good matching of depreciation expense with the asset's revenues.

Comparing Depreciation Methods

The depreciation methods are summarized in Exhibit 5. Both methods allocate a portion of the total cost of an asset to an accounting period, while never depreciating an asset below its residual value. The straight-line method provides

EXHIBIT 5

Summary of Depreciation Methods

Method	Useful Life	Depreciable Cost	Depreciation Rate	Depreciation Expense
Straight-line	Years	Cost less residual value	Straight-line rate*	Constant
Double-declining-balance	Years	Declining book value, but not below residual value	Straight-line rate* × 2	Declining

*Straight-line rate = (1/Useful life)

for the same periodic amounts of depreciation expense over the life of the asset. The double-declining-balance method provides for a higher depreciation amount in the first year of the asset's use, followed by declining amounts.

The depreciation for the straight-line and double-declining-balance methods is shown in Exhibit 6. The depreciation in Exhibit 6 is based on the equipment purchased in our prior illustrations.

EXHIBIT 6

Comparing Depreciation Methods

	Depreciation Expense	
Year	Straight-Line Method	Double-Declining-Balance Method
1	$ 4,400*	$ 9,600.00 ($24,000 × 40%)
2	4,400	5,760.00 ($14,400 × 40%)
3	4,400	3,456.00 ($8,640 × 40%)
4	4,400	2,073.60 ($5,184 × 40%)
5	4,400	1,110.40**
Total	$22,000	$22,000.00

*$4,400 = ($24,000 − $2,000)/5 years
**$3,110.40 − $2,000.00 because the equipment cannot be depreciated below its residual value.

Depreciation for Federal Income Tax

Tax Code Section 179 allows a business to deduct a portion of the cost of qualified property in the year it is placed into service.

The Internal Revenue Code uses the *Modified Accelerated Cost Recovery System (MACRS)* to compute depreciation for tax purposes. MACRS has eight classes of useful life and depreciation rates for each class. Two of the most common classes are the five-year class and the seven-year class.[3] The five-year class includes automobiles and light-duty trucks. The seven-year class includes most machinery and equipment. Depreciation for these two classes is similar to that computed using the double-declining-balance method.

In using the MACRS rates, residual value is ignored. Also, all fixed assets are assumed to be put in and taken out of service in the middle of the year. For the five-year-class assets, depreciation is spread over six years, as shown below.

Year	MACRS 5-Year-Class Depreciation Rates
1	20.0%
2	32.0
3	19.2
4	11.5
5	11.5
6	5.8
	100.0%

To simplify, a company will sometimes use MACRS for both financial statement and tax purposes. This is acceptable if MACRS does not result in significantly different amounts than would have been reported using one of the depreciation methods discussed in this chapter.

3. Real estate is in either a 27½-year or a 31½-year class and is depreciated by the straight-line method.

Disposal of Fixed Assets

Obj | **3**

Describe the accounting for the disposal of fixed assets.

Fixed assets that are no longer useful may be discarded or sold.[4] In such cases, the fixed asset is removed from the accounts. Just because a fixed asset is fully depreciated, however, does not mean that it should be removed from the accounts.

If a fixed asset is still being used, its cost and accumulated depreciation should remain in the records even if the asset is fully depreciated. This maintains accountability. If the asset was removed from the records, the accounts would contain no evidence of the continued existence of the asset. In addition, cost and accumulated depreciation data on such assets are often needed for property tax and income tax reports.

The entry to record the disposal of a fixed asset removes the cost of the asset and its accumulated depreciation from the accounts.

Discarding Fixed Assets

If a fixed asset is no longer used and has no residual value, it is discarded. To illustrate, assume that fully depreciated equipment acquired at a cost of $25,000 is discarded on February 14, 20Y7. The effect on the accounts and financial statements is as follows:

Statement of Cash Flows	Balance Sheet			Income Statement
	Assets	= Liabilities + Stockholders' Equity		
	Equipment –	Acc. Depr.— Equip.		
Feb. 14.	−25,000	25,000		

If an asset has not been fully depreciated, depreciation should be recorded before removing the asset from the accounting records. To illustrate, assume that equipment costing $6,000 with no estimated residual value is depreciated at a straight-line rate of 10%. On December 31, 20Y6, the accumulated depreciation balance, after adjusting entries, is $4,750. On March 24, 20Y7, the asset is removed from service and discarded. The effect of recording the depreciation for the three months of 20Y7 before the asset is discarded is as follows:

Statement of Cash Flows	Balance Sheet			Income Statement
	Assets	= Liabilities + Stockholders' Equity		
	– Acc. Depr.— Equip.	=	Retained Earnings	
Mar. 24.	−150		−150	Mar. 24.

Income Statement

Mar. 24. Depr. expense   −150

---

4. The accounting for the exchange of fixed assets is described and illustrated in advanced accounting courses.

The effect on the accounts and financial statements of discarding the equipment is as follows:

Statement of Cash Flows	Balance Sheet				Income Statement
	Assets		= Liabilities +	Stockholders' Equity	
	Equipment −	Acc. Depr.— Equip.	=	Retained Earnings	
Mar. 24.	−6,000	4,900		−1,100	Mar. 24.

Income Statement
Mar. 24. Loss on disposal of equip.   −1,100

The loss of $1,100 is recorded because the balance of the accumulated depreciation account ($4,900) is less than the balance in the equipment account ($6,000). Losses on the discarding of fixed assets are nonoperating items and are normally reported in the Other expense section of the income statement.

Selling Fixed Assets

The entry to record the sale of a fixed asset is similar to the entries for discarding an asset. The only difference is that the receipt of cash is also recorded. If the selling price is more than the book value of the asset, a gain is recorded. If the selling price is less than the book value, a loss is recorded.

To illustrate, assume that equipment is purchased at a cost of $10,000 with no estimated residual value and is depreciated at a straight-line rate of 10%. The equipment is sold for cash on October 12 of the eighth year of its use. The balance of the accumulated depreciation account as of the preceding December 31 is $7,000. The effect on the accounts and financial statements of updating depreciation for the nine months of the current year is as follows:

Statement of Cash Flows	Balance Sheet				Income Statement
	Assets		= Liabilities +	Stockholders' Equity	
	−	Acc. Depr.— Equip.	=	Retained Earnings	
Oct. 12.		−750		−750	Oct. 12.

Income Statement
Oct. 12. Depr. exp.—equip.   −750

After the current depreciation is recorded, the book value of the asset is $2,250 ($10,000 − $7,750). The effect of the sale, assuming three different selling prices, is as follows:

Sold at book value, for $2,250. No gain or loss.

Statement of Cash Flows	Balance Sheet				Income Statement
	Assets		= Liabilities + Stockholders' Equity		
	Cash + Equipment –	Acc. Depr.—Equip.			
Oct. 12.	2,250 −10,000	−7,750			

Statement of Cash Flows	
Oct. 12. Investing	2,250

Sold below book value, for $1,000. Loss of $1,250.

Statement of Cash Flows	Balance Sheet				Income Statement
	Assets		= Liabilities + Stockholders' Equity		
	Cash + Equipment –	Acc. Depr.—Equip. =		Retained Earnings	
Oct. 12.	1,000 −10,000	−7,750		−1,250	Oct. 12.

Statement of Cash Flows		Income Statement	
Oct. 12. Investing	1,000	Oct. 12. Loss on disposal of equip.	−1,250

Sold above book value, for $2,800. Gain of $550.

Statement of Cash Flows	Balance Sheet				Income Statement
	Assets		= Liabilities + Stockholders' Equity		
	Cash + Equipment –	Acc. Depr.—Equip. =		Retained Earnings	
Oct. 12.	2,800 −10,000	7,750		550	Oct. 12.

Statement of Cash Flows		Income Statement	
Oct. 12. Investing	2,800	Oct. 12. Gain on disposal of equip.	550

Natural Resources

Obj **4**

Describe the accounting for depletion of natural resources.

The fixed assets of some companies include timber, metal ores, minerals, or other natural resources. As these resources are harvested or mined and then sold, a portion of their cost is debited to an expense account. This process of transferring the cost of natural resources to an expense account is called **depletion**.

Depletion is determined as follows:[5]

Step 1. Determine the depletion rate as:

$$\text{Depletion Rate} = \frac{\text{Cost of Resource}}{\text{Estimated Total Units of Resource}}$$

Step 2. Multiply the depletion rate by the quantity extracted from the resource during the period.

$$\text{Depletion Expense} = \text{Depletion Rate} \times \text{Quantity Extracted}$$

To illustrate, assume that Karst Company purchased mining rights as follows:

Cost of mineral deposit	$400,000
Estimated total units of resource	1,000,000 tons
Tons mined during year	90,000 tons

The depletion expense of $36,000 for the year is computed as shown below.

Step 1.

$$\text{Depletion Rate} = \frac{\text{Cost of Resource}}{\text{Estimated Total Units of Resource}}$$

$$= \frac{\$400,000}{1,000,000 \text{ Tons}} = \$0.40 \text{ per Ton}$$

Step 2.

$$\text{Depletion Expense} = \$0.40 \text{ per Ton} \times 90,000 \text{ Tons} = \$36,000$$

The effect of the depletion on the accounts and financial statements is shown below.

Statement of Cash Flows	Balance Sheet			Income Statement
	Assets =	Liabilities +	Stockholders' Equity	
	−Acc. Depletion =		Retained Earnings	
Dec. 31.	−36,000		−36,000	Dec. 31.

Income Statement
Dec. 31. Depletion exp. −36,000

Like the accumulated depreciation account, Accumulated Depletion is a *contra asset* account. It is reported on the balance sheet as a deduction from the cost of the mineral deposit.

Describe the accounting for intangible assets.

Intangible Assets

Patents, copyrights, trademarks, and goodwill are long-lived assets that are used in the operations of a business and are not held for sale. These assets are called **intangible assets** because they do not exist physically.

5. It is assumed that there is no significant residual value left after all the natural resource is extracted.

The accounting for intangible assets is similar to that for fixed assets. The major issues are:

1. Determining the initial cost
2. Determining the **amortization**, which is the amount of cost to transfer to expense

Amortization results from the passage of time or a decline in the usefulness of the intangible asset.

Apple, Inc., amortizes intangible assets over 3–10 years.

Patents

Manufacturers may acquire exclusive rights to produce and sell goods with one or more unique features. Such rights are granted by **patents**, which the federal government issues to inventors. These rights continue in effect for 20 years. A business may purchase patent rights from others, or it may obtain patents developed by its own research and development.

The initial cost of a purchased patent, including any legal fees, is recorded by increasing an asset account. This cost is written off, or amortized, over the years of the patent's expected useful life. The expected useful life of a patent may be less than its legal life. For example, a patent may become worthless due to changing technology or consumer tastes.

Patent amortization is normally computed using the straight-line method. The amortization is recorded by increasing an amortization expense account and decreasing the patents account. A separate contra asset account is usually *not* used for intangible assets.

To illustrate, assume that at the beginning of its fiscal year, a company acquires patent rights for $100,000. Although the patent will not expire for 14 years, its remaining useful life is estimated as five years. The effect of the amortization of the patent at the end of the fiscal year is as follows:

Statement of Cash Flows	Balance Sheet			Income Statement
	Assets	= Liabilities +	Stockholders' Equity	
	Patents	=	Retained Earnings	
Dec. 31.	−20,000		−20,000	Dec. 31.

Income Statement
Dec. 31. Amortization exp.—
patents −20,000

Some companies develop their own patents through research and development. In such cases, any *research and development costs* are usually recorded as current operating expenses in the period in which they are incurred. This accounting for research and development costs is justified on the basis that any future benefits from research and development are highly uncertain.

Copyrights and Trademarks

The exclusive right to publish and sell a literary, artistic, or musical composition is granted by a **copyright**. Copyrights are issued by the federal government and extend for 70 years beyond the author's death. The costs of a copyright include all costs of creating the work plus any other costs of obtaining the copyright.

Sony Corporation of America amortizes its artist contracts and music catalogs over 16 years and 21 years, respectively.

Coke® is one of the world's most recognizable trademarks. As stated in a recent issue of *Life* Magazine, "Two-thirds of the earth is covered by water; the rest is covered by Coke. If the French are known for wine and the Germans for beer, America achieved global beverage dominance with fizzy water and caramel color."

eBay recorded an impairment of $1.39 billion in the goodwill created from its purchase of **Skype™**.

A copyright that is purchased is recorded at the price paid for it. Copyrights are amortized over their estimated useful lives.

A **trademark** is a name, term, or symbol used to identify a business and its products. Most businesses identify their trademarks with the symbol ® in their advertisements and on their products.

Under federal law, businesses can protect their trademarks by registering them for 10 years and renewing the registration for 10-year periods. Like a copyright, the legal costs of registering a trademark are recorded as an asset.

If a trademark is purchased from another business, its cost is recorded as an asset. In such cases, the cost of the trademark is considered to have an indefinite useful life. Thus, trademarks are not amortized. Instead, trademarks are reviewed periodically for impaired value. When a trademark is impaired, the trademark should be written down and a loss recognized.

Goodwill

Goodwill refers to an intangible asset of a business that is created from such favorable factors as location, product quality, reputation, and managerial skill. Goodwill allows a business to earn a greater rate of return than normal.

Generally accepted accounting principles (GAAP) allow goodwill to be recorded only if it is objectively determined by a transaction. An example of such a transaction is the purchase of a business at a price in excess of the fair value of its net assets (assets – liabilities). The excess is recorded as goodwill and reported as an intangible asset.

Unlike patents and copyrights, goodwill is not amortized. However, a loss should be recorded if the future prospects of the purchased firm become impaired. This loss would normally be disclosed in the Other expense section of the income statement.

To illustrate, assume that on December 31 FaceCard Company has determined that $250,000 of the goodwill created from the purchase of Electronic Systems is impaired. The effect on the accounts and financial statements is as follows:

Statement of Cash Flows	Balance Sheet			Income Statement
	Assets	= Liabilities +	Stockholders' Equity	
	Goodwill	=	Retained Earnings	
Dec. 31.	−250,000		−250,000	Dec. 31.

Income Statement
Dec. 31. Loss from impaired
goodwill   −250,000

Exhibit 7 shows intangible asset disclosures for 600 large firms. Goodwill is the most often reported intangible asset. This is because goodwill arises from merger transactions, which are common.

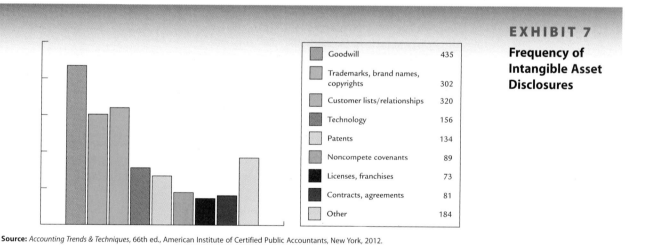

Source: *Accounting Trends & Techniques*, 66th ed., American Institute of Certified Public Accountants, New York, 2012.
Note: Some firms have multiple disclosures.

EXHIBIT 7

Frequency of Intangible Asset Disclosures

Goodwill	435
Trademarks, brand names, copyrights	302
Customer lists/relationships	320
Technology	156
Patents	134
Noncompete covenants	89
Licenses, franchises	73
Contracts, agreements	81
Other	184

Integrity, Objectivity, and Ethics in Business

WHEN DOES GOODWILL BECOME WORTHLESS?

The timing and amount of goodwill write-offs can be very subjective. Managers and their accountants should fairly estimate the value of goodwill and record goodwill impairment when it occurs. It would be unethical to delay a write-down of goodwill when it is determined that the asset is impaired.

Exhibit 8 summarizes the characteristics of intangible assets.

EXHIBIT 8

Comparison of Intangible Assets

Intangible Asset	Description	Amortization Period	Periodic Expense
Patent	Exclusive right to benefit from an innovation	Estimated useful life not to exceed legal life	Amortization expense
Copyright	Exclusive right to benefit from a literary, artistic, or musical composition	Estimated useful life not to exceed legal life	Amortization expense
Trademark	Exclusive use of a name, term, or symbol	None	Impairment loss if fair value less than carrying value (impaired)
Goodwill	Excess of purchase price of a business over the fair value of its net assets (assets – liabilities)	None	Impairment loss if fair value less than carrying value (impaired)

Obj 6

Describe how depreciation expense is reported on an income statement and prepare a balance sheet that includes fixed assets and intangible assets.

Financial Reporting for Fixed Assets and Intangible Assets

In the income statement, depreciation and amortization expense should be reported separately or disclosed in a note. A description of the methods used in computing depreciation should also be reported.

In the balance sheet, each class of fixed assets should be disclosed on the face of the statement or in the notes. The related accumulated depreciation should also be disclosed, either by class or in total. The fixed assets may be shown at their *book value* (cost less accumulated depreciation), which can also be described as their *net* amount.

If there are many classes of fixed assets, a single amount may be presented in the balance sheet, supported by a note with a separate listing. Fixed assets may be reported under the more descriptive caption of property, plant, and equipment.

The cost of mineral rights or ore deposits is normally shown as part of the Fixed assets section of the balance sheet. The related accumulated depletion should also be disclosed. In some cases, the mineral rights are shown net of depletion on the face of the balance sheet, accompanied by a note that discloses the amount of the accumulated depletion.

Intangible assets are usually reported in the balance sheet in a separate section immediately following fixed assets. The balance of each major class of intangible assets should be disclosed at an amount net of amortization taken to date. Exhibit 9 is a partial balance sheet that shows the reporting of fixed assets and intangible assets.

EXHIBIT 9

Fixed Assets and Intangible Assets in the Balance Sheet

DISCOVERY MINING CO.
Balance Sheet
December 31, 20Y9

Assets

Total current assets... $ 462,500

Property, plant, and equipment:	Cost	Acc. Depr.	Book Value	
Land......................	$ 30,000	—	$ 30,000	
Buildings..................	110,000	$ 26,000	84,000	
Factory equipment.........	650,000	192,000	458,000	
Office equipment..........	120,000	13,000	107,000	
	$ 910,000	$ 231,000		$ 679,000

Mineral deposits:	Cost	Acc. Depl.	Book Value	
Alaska deposit..........	$1,200,000	$ 800,000	$ 400,000	
Wyoming deposit.......	750,000	200,000	550,000	
	$1,950,000	$ 1,000,000		950,000

Total property, plant, and
    equipment.. 1,629,000

Intangible assets:

Patents.. $ 75,000

Goodwill 50,000

    Total intangible assets 125,000

HOW BUSINESSES MAKE MONEY

HUB-AND-SPOKE OR POINT-TO-POINT?

Southwest Airlines Co. uses a simple fare structure, featuring low, unrestricted, unlimited, everyday coach fares. These fares are made possible by Southwest's use of a point-to-point, rather than a hub-and-spoke, business approach. United Airlines, Inc., Delta Air Lines, and American Airlines employ a hub-and-spoke approach in which an airline establishes major hubs that serve as connecting links to other cities. For example, Delta has established major connecting hubs in Atlanta and Salt Lake City. In contrast, Southwest focuses on point-to-point service between select cities with over 450 one-way, nonstop city pairs with an average length of just over 640 miles and average flying time of 1.8 hours. As a result, Southwest minimizes connections, delays, and total trip time. Southwest also focuses on serving conveniently located satellite or downtown airports, such as Dallas Love Field, Houston Hobby, and Chicago Midway. Because these airports are normally less congested than hub airports, Southwest is better able to maintain high employee productivity and reliable on-time performance. This operating approach permits the company to achieve high utilization of its fixed assets, such as its 737 aircraft. For example, aircraft are scheduled to minimize time spent at the gate, thereby reducing the number of aircraft and gate facilities that would otherwise be required.

Obj|7
Describe and illustrate
the fixed asset turnover
in assessing a company's
use of fixed assets.

Financial Analysis: Fixed Asset Turnover

For many companies, fixed assets, often called property, plant, and equipment, are a large percent of total assets. For Delta Air Lines, fixed assets are over 46% of its total assets. An important objective for such companies, that require large investments in property, plant, and equipment to generate sales is to maximize the use of fixed assets to generate sales. One measure of how efficiently a company is using its fixed assets to generate sales is the fixed asset turnover.

The **fixed asset turnover** measures how efficiently a company is generating sales from its property, plant, and equipment. It is computed as follows:

$$\text{Fixed Asset Turnover} = \frac{\text{Net Sales}}{\text{Average Net Property, Plant, and Equipment}}$$

To illustrate, assume the following data (in millions) adapted from recent financial statements for Delta Air Lines are used.

	Year 2	Year 1
Net sales	$35,115	$31,755
Beginning of year property, plant, and equipment	20,307	20,433
End of year property, plant, and equipment	20,223	20,307

The fixed asset turnover (rounded to two decimal places) for Delta Air Lines is computed as follows:

	Year 2	Year 1
Net sales	$35,115	$31,755
Average net property, plant, and equipment:		
($20,307 + $20,223) ÷ 2	20,265	
($20,433 + $20,307) ÷ 2		20,370
Fixed asset turnover:		
($35,115 ÷ $20,265)	1.73	
($31,755 ÷ $20,370)		1.56

Delta Air Lines increased its fixed asset turnover from 1.56 in Year 1 to 1.73 in Year 2. Thus, Delta improved its management of fixed assets in generating sales. Another way of expressing the fixed asset turnover is that Delta generated $1.72 and $1.56 of sales per average dollar of fixed asset in Year 2 and Year 1, respectively. Normally, a high or increasing fixed asset turnover is considered favorable.

Key Points

1. Define, classify, and account for the cost of fixed assets.

Fixed assets are long-term tangible assets that are owned by the business and are used in the normal operations of the business. Examples of fixed assets are equipment, buildings, and land. The initial cost of a fixed asset includes all amounts spent to get the asset in place and ready for use. For example, sales tax, freight, insurance in transit, and installation costs are all included in the cost of a fixed asset. Once a fixed asset has been acquired and placed in service, revenue and capital expenditures may be incurred. Expenditures related to the ordinary maintenance and repairs of a fixed asset are revenue expenditures and are recorded as an expense of the current period. Expenditures to improve an asset are capital expenditures and are recorded as increases to the fixed asset account. Expenditures to extend the asset's useful life are capital expenditures and are recorded as a decrease in accumulated depreciation.

2. Compute depreciation using the straight-line and double-declining-balance methods.

In computing depreciation, three factors need to be considered: (1) the fixed asset's initial cost, (2) the useful life of the asset, and (3) the residual value of the asset.

The straight-line method spreads the initial cost less the residual value equally over the useful life. The double-declining-balance method is applied by multiplying the declining book value of the asset by twice the straight-line rate.

3. Describe the accounting for the disposal of fixed assets.

The recording of disposals of fixed assets will vary. In all cases, however, any depreciation for the current period should be recorded, and the book value of the asset is then removed from the accounts. Removing the book value from the accounts decreases the asset's accumulated depreciation account and the asset account for the cost of the asset. For assets retired from service, a loss may be recorded for any remaining book value of the asset. When a fixed asset is sold, the book value is removed and the cash or other asset received is also recorded. If the selling price is more than the book value of the asset, the transaction results in a gain. If the selling price is less than the book value, there is a loss.

4. Describe the accounting for depletion of natural resources.

The amount of periodic depletion is computed by multiplying the quantity of minerals extracted during the period by a depletion rate. The depletion rate is computed by dividing the cost of the mineral deposit by its estimated size. Recording depletion increases a depletion expense account and an accumulated depletion account.

5. Describe the accounting for intangible assets.

Long-term assets that are without physical attributes but are used in the business are classified as intangible assets. Examples of intangible assets are patents, copyrights, trademarks, and goodwill. The initial cost of an intangible asset should be recorded by increasing an asset account. For patents and copyrights, this cost should be written off, or amortized, over the years of the asset's expected usefulness by increasing an expense account and decreasing the intangible asset account. Trademarks and goodwill are not amortized but are written down only on impairment.

6. Describe how depreciation expense is reported on an income statement and prepare a balance sheet that includes fixed assets and intangible assets.

The amount of depreciation expense and the method or methods used in computing depreciation should be disclosed in the financial statements. In addition, each major class of fixed assets should be disclosed, along with the related accumulated depreciation. Intangible assets are usually presented in the balance sheet in a separate section immediately following fixed assets. Each major class of intangible assets should be disclosed at an amount net of the amortization recorded to date.

7. Describe and illustrate the fixed asset turnover in assessing a company's use of fixed assets.

The fixed asset turnover is a measure of a company's use of its fixed assets to generate sales. It is computed by dividing net sales by the average fixed assets for the period.

Key Terms

Accelerated depreciation method (261)
Amortization (267)
Book value (260)
Capital expenditures (256)
Copyright (267)
Depletion (265)
Depreciation (258)
Double-declining-balance method (260)
Fixed asset turnover (272)
Fixed assets (254)
Goodwill (268)
Intangible assets (266)
Patents (267)
Residual value (258)
Revenue expenditures (256)
Straight-line method (259)
Trademark (268)

Illustrative Problem

McCollum Company, a furniture wholesaler, acquired new equipment at a cost of $150,000 at the beginning of the fiscal year. The equipment has an estimated life of five years and an estimated residual value of $12,000. Ellen McCollum, the president, has requested information regarding alternative depreciation methods.

Instructions

Determine the annual depreciation for each of the five years of estimated useful life of the equipment, the accumulated depreciation at the end of each year, and the book value of the equipment at the end of each year by (a) the straight-line method and (b) the double-declining-balance method.

Solution

	Year	Depreciation Expense	Accumulated Depreciation, End of Year	Book Value, End of Year
a.	1	$27,600*	$ 27,600	$122,400
	2	27,600	55,200	94,800
	3	27,600	82,800	67,200
	4	27,600	110,400	39,600
	5	27,600	138,000	12,000

*$27,600 = ($150,000 − $12,000) ÷ 5

	Year	Depreciation Expense	Accumulated Depreciation, End of Year	Book Value, End of Year
b.	1	$60,000**	$ 60,000	$ 90,000
	2	36,000	96,000	54,000
	3	21,600	117,600	32,400
	4	12,960	130,560	19,440
	5	7,440***	138,000	12,000

**$60,000 = $150,000 × 40%
***The asset is not depreciated below the estimated residual value of $12,000.

Self-Examination Questions *(Answers appear at the end of chapter)*

1. Which of the following expenditures incurred in connection with acquiring machinery is a proper addition to the asset account?

    A. Freight

    B. Installation costs

    C. Both A and B

    D. Neither A nor B

2. What is the amount of depreciation, using the double-declining-balance method (twice the straight-line rate), for the second year of use for equipment costing $9,000, with an estimated residual value of $600 and an estimated life of three years?

    A. $6,000

    B. $3,000

    C. $2,000

    D. $400

3. An example of an accelerated depreciation method is:

    A. Straight-line

    B. Double-declining-balance

    C. Units-of-production

    D. Depletion balance

4. Hyde Inc. purchased mineral rights estimated at 2,500,000 tons near Great Falls, Montana, for $3,600,000 on August 7, 20Y4. During the remainder of the year, Hyde mined 175,000 tons of ore. What is the depletion expense for 20Y4?

    A. $121,528

    B. $252,000

    C. $1,500,000

    D. $3,600,000

5. Which of the following is an example of an intangible asset?

    A. Patents

    B. Goodwill

    C. Copyrights

    D. All of the above

Class Discussion Questions

1. Which of the following qualities are characteristic of fixed assets? (a) tangible, (b) capable of repeated use in the normal operations of the business, (c) not held for sale in the normal course of business, (d) not used in the operations of the business, (e) useful life must be greater than 10 years.

2. Enterprise Supplies Co. has a fleet of automobiles and trucks for use by salespersons and for delivery of office supplies and equipment. Bizarro Auto Sales Co. has automobiles and trucks for sale. Under what caption would the automobiles and trucks be reported on the balance sheet of (a) Enterprise Supplies Co. and (b) Bizarro Auto Sales Co.?

3. The Stone Store Co. acquired an adjacent vacant lot with the hope of selling it in the future at a gain. The lot is not intended to be used in The Stone Store's business operations. Where should such real estate be listed in the balance sheet?

4. Lanier Company solicited bids from several contractors to construct an addition to its office building. The lowest bid received was for $600,000. Lanier Company decided to construct the addition itself at a cost of $475,000. What amount should be recorded in the building account?

5. Distinguish between the accounting for capital expenditures and revenue expenditures.

6. Immediately after a used truck is acquired, a new motor is installed and the tires are replaced at a total cost of $4,300. Is this a capital expenditure or a revenue expenditure?

7. Classify each of the following expenditures as either a revenue or capital expenditure: (a) installation of a video messaging system on a semitrailer, (b) changing oil in a delivery truck, (c) purchase of a color copier.

8. Are the amounts at which fixed assets are reported in the balance sheet their approximate market values as of the balance sheet date? Discuss.

9. a. Does the recognition of depreciation in the accounts provide a special cash fund for the replacement of fixed assets? Explain.

   b. Describe the nature of depreciation as the term is used in accounting.

10. Backyard Company purchased a machine that has a manufacturer's suggested life of 30 years. The company plans to use the machine on a special project that will last 18 years. At the completion of the project, the machine will be sold. Over how many years should the machine be depreciated?

11. Is it necessary for a business to use the same method of computing depreciation (a) for all classes of its depreciable assets and (b) in the financial statements and in determining income taxes?

12. a. Under what conditions is the use of an accelerated depreciation method most appropriate?

    b. Why is an accelerated depreciation method often used for income tax purposes?

    c. What is the Modified Accelerated Cost Recovery System (MACRS), and under what conditions is it used?

13. For some of the fixed assets of a business, the balance in Accumulated Depreciation is exactly equal to the cost of the asset. (a) Is it permissible to record additional depreciation on the assets if they are still useful to the company? Explain. (b) When should the cost and the accumulated depreciation be removed from the accounts?

14. How is depletion determined?

15. a. Over what period of time should the cost of a patent acquired by purchase be amortized?

    b. In general, what is the required accounting treatment for research and development costs?

    c. How should goodwill be amortized?

Exercises

E7-1   Costs of acquiring fixed assets

Obj 1

Chris Baird owns and operates Baird Services. During April, Baird Services Co. incurred the following costs in acquiring two printing presses. One printing press was new, and the other was used by a business that recently filed for bankruptcy.

Costs related to new printing press:

1. Fee paid to factory representative for installation
2. Freight
3. Insurance while in transit
4. New parts to replace those damaged in unloading
5. Sales tax on purchase price
6. Special foundation

Costs related to used printing press:

7. Amount paid to attorney to review purchase agreement
8. Freight
9. Installation
10. Repair of vandalism during installation
11. Replacement of worn-out parts
12. Repair of damage incurred in reconditioning the press

a. Indicate which costs incurred in acquiring the new printing press should be recorded as an increase to the asset account.

b. Indicate which costs incurred in acquiring the used printing press should be recorded as an increase to the asset account.

Obj 1

E7-2 Determine cost of land

Absarokee Ski Co. has developed a tract of land into a ski resort. The company has cut the trees, cleared and graded the land and hills, and constructed ski lifts. (a) Should the tree cutting, land clearing, and grading costs of constructing the ski slopes be recorded as an increase in the land account? (b) If such costs are recorded as an increase in Land, should they be depreciated?

Obj 1

✔ $522,700

E7-3 Determine cost of land

Rapid Delivery Company acquired an adjacent lot to construct a new warehouse, paying $100,000 and giving a short-term note for $400,000. Legal fees paid were $4,500, delinquent taxes assumed were $12,000, and fees paid to remove an old building from the land were $7,500. Materials salvaged from the demolition of the building were sold for $1,300. A contractor was paid $1,250,000 to construct a new warehouse. Determine the cost of the land to be reported on the balance sheet.

Obj 1

E7-4 Capital and revenue expenditures

Reliable Delivery Co. incurred the following costs related to trucks and vans used in operating its delivery service:

1. Changed the oil and greased the joints of all the trucks and vans.
2. Changed the radiator fluid on a truck that had been in service for the past four years.
3. Installed a hydraulic lift to a van.
4. Installed security systems on four of the newer trucks.
5. Overhauled the engine on one of the trucks purchased three years ago.
6. Rebuilt the transmission on one of the vans that had been driven 40,000 miles. The van was no longer under warranty.
7. Removed a two-way radio from one of the trucks and installed a new radio with a greater range of communication.
8. Repaired a flat tire on one of the vans.
9. Replaced a truck's suspension system with a new suspension system that allows for the delivery of heavier loads.
10. Tinted the back and side windows of one of the vans to discourage theft of contents.

Classify each of the costs as a capital expenditure or a revenue expenditure.

E7-5   Capital and revenue expenditures

Obj 1

Gwen Jones owns and operates GJ Transport Co. During the past year, Gwen incurred the following costs related to an 18-wheel truck:

1. Changed engine oil.

2. Installed a television in the sleeping compartment of the truck.

3. Installed a wind deflector on top of the cab to increase fuel mileage.

4. Modified the factory-installed turbo charger with a special-order kit designed to add 50 more horsepower to the engine performance.

5. Removed the old GPS navigation system and replaced it with a newer model.

6. Replaced fog and cab light bulbs.

7. Replaced a headlight that had burned out.

8. Replaced a shock absorber that had worn out.

9. Replaced the hydraulic brake system that had begun to fail during her latest trip through the Rocky Mountains.

10. Replaced the old radar detector with a newer model that detects additional frequencies now used by many of the state patrol radar guns. The detector is wired directly into the cab, so that it is partially hidden. In addition, Gwen fastened the detector to the truck with a locking device that prevents its removal.

Classify each of the costs as a capital expenditure or a revenue expenditure.

E7-6   Nature of depreciation

Obj 2

Custer Construction Co. reported $8,300,000 for equipment and $4,950,000 for accumulated depreciation—equipment on its balance sheet.

Does this mean (a) that the replacement cost of the equipment is $8,300,000 and (b) that $4,950,000 is set aside in a special fund for the replacement of the equipment? Explain.

E7-7   Straight-line depreciation rates

Obj 2

✔ c. 10%

Convert each of the following estimates of useful life to a straight-line depreciation rate, stated as a percentage, assuming that the residual value of the fixed asset is to be ignored: (a) 2 years, (b) 4 years, (c) 10 years, (d) 20 years, (e) 25 years, (f) 40 years, (g) 50 years.

E7-8   Straight-line depreciation

Obj 2

✔ $3,170

A refrigerator used by a meat processor has a cost of $86,750, an estimated residual value of $7,500, and an estimated useful life of 25 years. What is the amount of the annual depreciation computed by the straight-line method?

E7-9   Depreciation by two methods

Obj 2

✔ a. First
Year, $6,000

A John Deere tractor acquired on January 7 at a cost of $240,000 has an estimated useful life of 40 years. Assuming that it will have no residual value, determine the depreciation for each of the first two years by (a) the straight-line method and (b) the double-declining-balance method.

E7-10   Depreciation by two methods

Obj 2

✔ a. $9,000

A storage tank acquired at the beginning of the fiscal year at a cost of $210,000 has an estimated residual value of $30,000 and an estimated useful life of 20 years. Determine the following: (a) the amount of annual depreciation by the straight-line method and (b) the amount of depreciation for the first and second years computed by the double-declining-balance method.

E7-11 Partial-year depreciation

Sandblasting equipment acquired at a cost of $42,000 has an estimated residual value of $6,000 and an estimated useful life of 10 years. It was placed in service on October 1 of the current fiscal year, which ends on December 31, 20Y5. Determine the depreciation for 20Y5 and for 20Y6 by (a) the straight-line method and (b) the double-declining-balance method.

E7-12 Book value of fixed assets

The following data (in millions) were adapted from recent annual reports of **United Parcel Service, Inc. (UPS)**. UPS provides delivery and freight services throughout the world.

	Year 2	Year 1
Vehicles	$ 5,981	$ 5,519
Aircraft	14,616	14,063
Land	1,114	1,081
Buildings	6,038	5,962
Equipment	8,489	8,330
Construction in progress	303	265
Less accumulated depreciation	(18,920)	(17,833)

a. Compute the net property, plant, and equipment (book value) for Years 1 and 2

b. Compare Years 1 and 2; comment on changes between years.

E7-13 Sale of asset

Equipment acquired on January 3, 20Y3, at a cost of $415,000, has an estimated useful life of 15 years, has an estimated residual value of $32,500, and is depreciated by the straight-line method.

a. What was the book value of the equipment at December 31, 20Y6, the end of the year?

b. Assuming that the equipment was sold on July 1, 20Y7, for $285,000, illustrate the effects on the accounts and financial statements of (1) depreciation for the six months until the sale date and (2) the sale of the equipment.

E7-14 Disposal of fixed asset

Equipment acquired on January 8, 20Y1, at a cost of $375,000, has an estimated useful life of 12 years and an estimated residual value of $45,000.

a. What was the annual amount of depreciation for the years 20Y1, 20Y2, and 20Y3, using the straight-line method of depreciation?

b. What was the book value of the equipment on January 1, 20Y4?

c. Assuming that the equipment was sold on January 7, 20Y4, for $280,000, illustrate the effects on the accounts and financial statements of the sale.

d. Assuming that the equipment was sold on January 7, 20Y4, for $300,000 instead of $280,000, illustrate the effects on the accounts and financial statements of the sale.

E7-15 Recording depletion

Cooper Gate Mining Co. acquired mineral rights for $16,500,000. The mineral deposit is estimated at 75,000,000 tons. During the current year, 29,800,000 tons were mined and sold.

a. Determine the amount of depletion expense for the current year.

b. Illustrate the effects on the accounts and financial statements of the depletion expense.

E7-16 Recording amortization

Quantum Technologies Company acquired patent rights on January 6, 20Y5, for $1,350,000. The patent has a useful life of 10 years. On January 7, 20Y8, Quantum Technologies successfully defended the patent in a lawsuit at a cost of $199,500.

a. Determine the patent amortization expense for the current year ended December 31, 20Y8.

b. Illustrate the effects on the accounts and financial statements to recognize the amortization.

E7-17 Goodwill impairment

Obj 5

On January 1, 20Y3, The Simmons Group, Inc., purchased the assets of NWS Insurance Co. for $36,000,000, a price reflecting an $8,000,000 goodwill premium. On December 31, 20Y9, The Simmons Group determined that the goodwill from the NWS acquisition was impaired and had a value of only $2,300,000.

a. Determine the book value of the goodwill on December 31, 20Y9, prior to making the impairment adjustment.

b. Illustrate the effects on the accounts and financial statements of the December 31, 20Y9, adjustment for the goodwill impairment.

E7-18 Book value of fixed assets

Obj 6

Apple, Inc., designs, manufactures, and markets personal computers (iPad™) and related software. Apple also manufactures and distributes music players (iPod™) along with related accessories and services, including the online distribution of third-party music. The following information was adapted from a recent annual report of Apple:

Property, Plant, and Equipment (in millions):

	Year 2	Year 1
Land and buildings	$ 2,439	$ 2,059
Machinery, equipment, and internal-use software	15,743	6,926
Office furniture and equipment	241	184
Other fixed assets related to leases	3,464	2,599
Accumulated depreciation and amortization	(6,435)	(3,991)

a. Compute the book value of the fixed assets for Years 1 and 2 and explain the differences, if any.

b. Would you normally expect the book value of fixed assets to increase or decrease during the year?

E7-19 Balance sheet presentation

Obj 6

List the errors you find in the following partial balance sheet:

CHICO COMPANY
Balance Sheet
December 31, 20Y7

Assets

Total current assets				$350,000

	Replacement Cost	Accumulated Depreciation	Book Value	
Property, plant, and equipment:				
Land	$ 250,000	$ 20,000	$230,000	
Buildings	400,000	150,000	250,000	
Factory equipment	330,000	175,200	154,800	
Office equipment	72,000	48,000	24,000	
Patents	48,000	—	48,000	
Goodwill	90,000	3,000	87,000	
Total property, plant, and equipment	$1,190,000	$ 396,200		793,800

Problems

Obj **1**

✔ Land, $470,250

P7-1 Allocate payments and receipts to fixed asset accounts

The following payments and receipts are related to land, land improvements, and buildings acquired for use in a wholesale apparel business. The receipts are identified by an asterisk.

a. Architect's and engineer's fees for plans and supervision	$ 75,000
b. Cost of filling and grading land	18,000
c. Cost of removing building purchased with land in (e)	12,500
d. Cost of paving parking lot to be used by customers	14,500
e. Cost of real estate acquired as a plant site: Land ($375,000) and Building ($25,000)	400,000
f. Cost of repairing windstorm damage during construction	7,000
g. Cost of repairing vandalism damage during construction	1,800
h. Cost of trees and shrubbery planted	12,000
i. Delinquent real estate taxes on property, assumed by purchaser	31,750
j. Fee paid to attorney for title search	1,500
k. Finder's fee paid to real estate agency	4,000
l. Interest incurred on building loan during construction	40,000
m. Money borrowed to pay building contractor	775,000*
n. Payment to building contractor for new building	800,000
o. Proceeds from insurance company for windstorm and vandalism damage	4,500*
p. Premium on one-year insurance policy during construction	6,000
q. Proceeds from sale of salvage materials from old building	6,500*
r. Refund of premium on insurance policy (p) canceled after 10 months	1,000*
s. Special assessment paid to city for extension of water main to the property	9,000

Instructions

1. Assign each payment and receipt to Land (unlimited life), Land Improvements (limited life), Building, or Other Accounts. Indicate receipts by an asterisk. Identify each item by letter and list the amounts in columnar form, as follows:

Item	Land	Land Improvements	Building	Other Accounts

2. Determine the increases to Land, Land Improvements, and Building.
3. The costs assigned to the land, which is used as a plant site, will not be depreciated, while the costs assigned to land improvements will be depreciated. Explain this seemingly contradictory application of the concept of depreciation.

Obj **2**

✔ a. 20Y4: straight-line depreciation, $45,250

P7-2 Compare three depreciation methods

Bayside Coatings Company purchased waterproofing equipment on January 2, 20Y4, for $190,000. The equipment was expected to have a useful life of four years and a residual value of $9,000.

Instructions

Determine the amount of depreciation expense for the years ended December 31, 20Y4, 20Y5, 20Y6, and 20Y7, by (a) the straight-line method and (b) the double-declining-balance method. Also determine the total depreciation expense for the four years by each method. The following columnar headings are suggested for recording the depreciation expense amounts:

	Depreciation Expense	
Year	Straight-Line Method	Double-Declining-Balance Method

P7-3   Depreciation by two methods; partial years

Knife Edge Company purchased tool sharpening equipment on July 1, 20Y5, for $16,200. The equipment was expected to have a useful life of three years and a residual value of $900.

Instructions

Determine the amount of depreciation expense for the years ended December 31, 20Y5, 20Y6, 20Y7, and 20Y8, by (a) the straight-line method and (b) the double-declining-balance method.

Obj 2

✔ a. 20Y5, $2,550

P7-4   Depreciation by two methods; sale of fixed asset

New tire retreading equipment, acquired at a cost of $140,000 at the beginning of a fiscal year, has an estimated useful life of four years and an estimated residual value of $10,000. The manager requested information regarding the effect of alternative methods on the amount of depreciation expense each year. On the basis of the data presented to the manager, the double-declining-balance method was selected.

In the first week of the fourth year, the equipment was sold for $23,300.

Obj 2,3

✔ 1. b. Year 1, $70,000 depreciation expense

Instructions

1. Determine the annual depreciation expense for each of the estimated four years of use, the accumulated depreciation at the end of each year, and the book value of the equipment at the end of each year by (a) the straight-line method and (b) the double-declining-balance method. The following columnar headings are suggested for each schedule:

Year	Depreciation Expense	Accumulated Depreciation, End of Year	Book Value, End of Year

2. Illustrate the effects on the accounts and financial statements of the sale.

3. Illustrate the effects on the accounts and financial statements of the sale, assuming a sale price of $15,250 instead of $23,300.

P7-5   Amortization and depletion entries

Data related to the acquisition of timber rights and intangible assets of Gemini Company during the current year ended December 31 are as follows:

a. On December 31, Gemini Company determined that $3,000,000 of goodwill was impaired.

b. Governmental and legal costs of $920,000 were incurred by Gemini Company on June 30 in obtaining a patent with an estimated economic life of eight years. Amortization is to be for one-half year.

c. Timber rights on a tract of land were purchased for $1,350,000 on March 6. The stand of timber is estimated at 15,000,000 board feet. During the current year, 3,300,000 board feet of timber were cut and sold.

Obj 4,5

✔ 1. b. $57,500

Instructions

1. Determine the amount of the amortization, depletion, or impairment for the current year for each of the foregoing items.

2. Illustrate the effects on the accounts and financial statements of the adjustments for each item.

Financial Analysis

Obj 7

FA 7-1 Fixed asset turnover

United Continental Holdings, Inc., which was formerly known as United Airlines, operates passenger service throughout the world. The following data (in millions) were adapted from a recent financial statement of United.

Net sales	$37,110
Beginning of year property, plant, and equipment	16,945
End of year property, plant, and equipment	16,419

1. Compute the fixed asset turnover. Round to two decimal places.
2. Compare the results from part (1) with Delta's fixed asset turnover for Year 2 of 1.73 computed on page 272.

Obj 7

FA 7-2 Fixed asset turnover

Southwest Airlines operates passenger services throughout the United States. The following data (in millions) were adapted from a recent financial statement of Southwest.

Net sales	$15,658
Beginning of year property, plant, and equipment	10,578
End of year property, plant, and equipment	12,127

1. Compute the fixed asset turnover. Round to two decimal places.
2. Compare the results from part (1) with the fixed asset turnover calculated for United in FA 7-1 and for Year 2 for of Delta calculated on page 272.

Obj 7

FA 7-3 Fixed asset turnover

JetBlue Airways Corporation operates passenger services throughout the United States. The following data (in millions) were adapted from recent financial statements of JetBlue.

	Year 2	Year 1
Net sales	$4,504	$3,779
Beginning of year property, plant, and equipment	4,641	4,638
End of year property, plant, and equipment	4,860	4,641

1. Compute the fixed asset turnover. Round to two decimal places.
2. Comment on the fixed asset turnover results from part (1).

Obj 7

FA 7-4 Fixed asset turnover

1. Compare the fixed asset turnover ratios for Delta Air Lines (see the chapter illustration on page 272), United (FA 7-1), Southwest (FA 7-2), and JetBlue (FA 7-3). Use Year 2 of Delta and JetBlue for your comparison.
2. Comment on the results from part (1).

Obj 7

FA 7-5 Fixed asset turnover

Marriott International Inc. and Intercontinental Hotels Group operate hotels worldwide. The following data (in millions) were adapted from recent financial statements of Marriott and Intercontinental.

	Marriott	Intercontinental
Net sales	$12,317	$1,768
Beginning of year property, plant, and equipment	1,307	1,690
End of year property, plant, and equipment	1,168	1,579

1. Compute the fixed asset turnover. Round to two decimal places.
2. Comment on the fixed asset turnover results from part (1).

Cases

Case 7-1   Ethics and professional conduct in business

Rowel Baylon, CPA, is an assistant to the controller of Arches Consulting Co. In his spare time, Rowel also prepares tax returns and performs general accounting services for clients. Frequently, Rowel performs these services after his normal working hours, using Arches Consulting Co.'s computers and laser printers. Occasionally, Rowel's clients will call him at the office during regular working hours.

Discuss whether Rowel is performing in a professional manner.

Case 7-2   Financial vs. tax depreciation

The following is an excerpt from a conversation between two employees of Linquest Technologies, Don Corbet and Rita Shevlin. Don is the accounts payable clerk, and Rita is the cashier.

Don: Rita, could I get your opinion on something?
Rita: Sure, Don.

Don: Do you know Margaret, the fixed assets clerk?

Rita: I know who she is, but I don't know her real well. Why?

Don: Well, I was talking to her at lunch last Tuesday about how she liked her job, etc. You know, the usual … and she mentioned something about having to keep two sets of books … one for taxes and one for the financial statements. That can't be good accounting, can it? What do you think?

Rita: Two sets of books? It doesn't sound right.

Don: It doesn't seem right to me either. I was always taught that you had to use generally accepted accounting principles. How can there be two sets of books? What could be the difference between the two?

How would you respond to Rita and Don if you were Margaret?

Case 7-3   Effect of depreciation on net income

Einstein Construction Co. specializes in building replicas of historic houses. Bree Andrus, president of Einstein Construction, is considering the purchase of various items of equipment on July 1, 20Y2, for $300,000. The equipment would have a useful life of five years and no residual value. In the past, all equipment has been leased. For tax purposes, Bree is considering depreciating the equipment by the straight-line method. She discussed the matter with her CPA and learned that although the straight-line method could be elected, it was to her advantage to use the Modified Accelerated Cost Recovery System (MACRS) for tax purposes. She asked for your advice as to which method to use for tax purposes.

1. Compute depreciation for each of the years (20Y2, 20Y3, 20Y4, 20Y5, 20Y6, and 20Y7) of useful life by (a) the straight-line method and (b) MACRS. In using the straight-line method, one-half year's depreciation should be computed for 20Y2 and 20Y7. Use the MACRS rates presented in the chapter.

2. Assuming that income before depreciation and income tax is estimated to be $800,000 uniformly per year and that the income tax rate is 40%, compute the net income for each of the years 20Y2, 20Y3, 20Y4, 20Y5, 20Y6, and 20Y7, if (a) the straight-line method is used and (b) MACRS is used.

3. What factors would you present for Bree's consideration in the selection of a depreciation method?

Case 7-4   Lease or buy

GROUP PROJECT

INTERNET PROJECT

You are planning to acquire an asset for use in your business. In groups of three or four, use the Internet to research some factors that should be considered in deciding whether to purchase or lease an asset. Summarize the considerations you have identified on purchasing or leasing an asset.

Case 7-5   Applying for patents, copyrights, and trademarks

Go to the Internet and review the procedures for applying for a patent, a copyright, and a trademark. One Internet site that is useful for this purpose is **www .idresearch.com**. Prepare a written summary of these procedures.

Case 7-6   Ethics and professional conduct in business

The following is an excerpt from a conversation between the chief executive officer, Kim Jenkins, and the chief financial officer, Steve Mueller, of Quatro Group Inc.:

Kim: Steve, as you know, the auditors are coming in to audit our year-end financial statements pretty soon. Do you see any problems on the horizon?

Steve: Well, you know about our "famous" Scher Company acquisition of a couple of years ago. We booked $9,000,000 of goodwill from that acquisition, and the accounting rules require us to recognize any impairment of goodwill.

Kim: Uh-oh.

Steve: Yeah, right. We had to shut the old Scher Company operations down this year because those products were no longer selling. Thus, our auditor is going to insist that we write off the $9,000,000 of goodwill to reflect the impaired value.

Kim: We can't have that—at least not this year! Do everything you can to push back on this one. We just can't take that kind of a hit this year. The most we could stand is $5,000,000. Steve, keep the write-off to $5,000,000 and promise anything in the future. Then we'll deal with that down the road.

How should Steve respond to Kim?

Answers to Self-Examination Questions

1. **C** All amounts spent to get a fixed asset (such as machinery) in place and ready for use are proper additions to the asset account. In the case of machinery acquired, the freight (answer A) and the installation costs (answer B) are both (answer C) proper charges to the machinery account.

2. **C** The periodic charge for depreciation under the double-declining-balance method for the second year is determined by first computing the depreciation charge for the first year. The depreciation for the first year of $6,000 (answer A) is computed by multiplying the cost of the equipment, $9,000, by 2/3 (the straight-line rate of 1/3 multiplied by 2). The depreciation for the second year of $2,000 (answer C) is then determined by multiplying the book value at the end of the first year, $3,000 (the cost of $9,000 minus the first-year depreciation of $6,000), by 2/3. The third year's depreciation is $400 (answer D). It is determined by multiplying the book value at the end of the second year, $1,000, by 2/3, thus yielding $667. However, the equipment cannot be depreciated below its residual value of $600; thus, the third-year depreciation is $400 ($1,000 − $600).

3. **B** A depreciation method that provides for a higher depreciation amount in the first year of the use of an asset and a gradually declining periodic amount thereafter is called an accelerated depreciation method. The double-declining-balance method (answer B) is an example of such a method.

4. **B** $252,000. The depletion expense is determined by first computing a depletion rate. For Hyde Inc. the depletion rate is $1.44 per ton ($3,600,000/2,500,000 tons). The depletion rate of $1.44 per ton is then multiplied by the number of tons mined during the year, or 175,000 tons, to determine the depletion expense of $252,000 (175,000 tons × $1.44).

5. **D** Long-lived assets that are useful in operations, not held for sale, and without physical qualities are called intangible assets. Patents, goodwill, and copyrights are examples of intangible assets (answer D).

CHAPTER 8

Liabilities and Stockholders' Equity

LEARNING OBJECTIVES

After studying this chapter, you should be able to:

Obj | 1 Describe how businesses finance their operations.

Obj | 2 Describe and illustrate current liabilities, notes payable, taxes, contingencies, and payroll.

Obj | 3 Describe and illustrate the financing of operations through issuance of bonds.

Obj | 4 Describe and illustrate the financing of operations through issuance of stock.

Obj | 5 Describe and illustrate the accounting for cash and stock dividends.

Obj | 6 Describe the effects of stock splits on the financial statements.

Obj | 7 Describe financial statement reporting of liabilities and stockholders' equity.

Obj | 8 Analyze the impact of debt or equity financing on earnings per share.

Obj | 9 Financial Analysis: Describe and illustrate the use of the ratio of liabilities to total assets and the price-earnings ratio in assessing a company's financial condition and prospects for future performance.

Banks and other financial institutions provide loans or credit to buyers for purchases of various items. Using credit to purchase items is probably as old as commerce itself. In fact, the Babylonians were lending money to support trade as early as 1300 B.C. The use of credit provides *individuals* convenience and buying power. Credit cards provide individuals convenience over using cash and make purchasing over the Internet easier. Credit cards also provide individuals control over cash by providing documentation of their purchases through receipt of monthly credit card statements and by allowing them to avoid carrying large amounts of cash and to purchase items before they are paid.

Short-term credit is also used by *businesses* to provide convenience in purchasing items for manufacture or resale.

More importantly, short-term credit gives a business control over the payment for goods and services. For example, **Panera Bread**, a chain of bakery-cafés located throughout the United States, uses short-term trade credit, or accounts payable, to purchase ingredients for making bread products in its bakeries. In addition to accounts payable, a business like Panera Bread can also have current liabilities related to payroll, payroll taxes, short-term notes, and contingencies. Each of these types of current liabilities is described and illustrated in this chapter.

Panera Bread also uses long-term debt and stock to finance its operations and to raise funds for future expansion of its business. In this chapter, the use of bond and stock financing is described and illustrated.

Obj | **1**

Describe how businesses finance their operations.

Financing Operations

A company may finance its operations through debt, equity, or both. Debt financing includes all liabilities of the company. For example, most companies have accounts payable due to vendors and other suppliers. In effect, these vendors and suppliers are helping finance the company. A company may also issue notes or bonds to finance its operations. In contrast to accounts payable, notes and bonds normally require the periodic payment of interest.

Some equity financing is used by all companies. A proprietorship or partnership obtains equity financing from investments by its owner(s). A corporation obtains equity financing by issuing stock.

The preceding chapters focused primarily on the asset side of the balance sheet. This chapter focuses on the right side of the accounting equation: the liabilities and stockholders' equity. The next section focuses on current liabilities, notes payable, taxes, contingencies, and payroll. This is followed by a discussion of bond and stock financing.

Obj | **2**

Describe and illustrate current liabilities, notes payable, taxes, contingencies, and payroll.

Liabilities

Liabilities are debts owed to others. Liabilities that are to be paid out of current assets and are due within a short time are reported as **current liabilities** on the balance sheet. Liabilities due beyond one year are classified as **long-term liabilities**. In addition, in some cases a company incurs a liability, called a **contingent liability**, if certain events occur in the future.

Current Liabilities

Most current liabilities arise from two basic transactions:

1. Receiving goods or services prior to making payment
2. Receiving payment prior to delivering goods or services

An example of the first type of transaction is an account payable arising from a purchase of merchandise for resale. An example of the second type of transaction is unearned rent arising from the receipt of rent in advance.

Earlier chapters described and illustrated the accounting for accounts payable and unearned liabilities transactions. The remainder of this section focuses on notes payable, tax liabilities, contingencies, and payroll liabilities.

Notes Payable

Notes payable are often issued to:

1. Satisfy an account payable
2. Purchase merchandise or other assets

The issuer of the note is called the borrower, while the party receiving the note is called the lender. The lender accounts for the note as a note receivable, which was described and illustrated in Chapter 6.[1]

---

1. The effect on the accounts and financial statements by a lender who accepts a note is exactly opposite that for the issuer of the note.

To illustrate the effects on the accounts and financial statements of issuing a note, assume the following:

Face value of note:	$1,000
Interest rate:	6%
Date of note:	August 1, 20Y5
Term of note:	90 days
Due date of note:	October 30

The effect on the accounts and financial statements of issuing and paying the note is as follows:

Issuing a 90-day, 6% note on account on August 1.

Statement of Cash Flows	Balance Sheet				Income Statement
	Assets	=	Liabilities	+ Stockholders' Equity	
			Accounts Payable + Notes Payable		
Aug. 1.			−1,000 1,000		

Paying of note on October 30.

Statement of Cash Flows	Balance Sheet				Income Statement
	Assets	= Liabilities	+	Stockholders' Equity	
	Cash	= Notes Payable	+	Retained Earnings	
Oct. 30.	−1,015	−1,000		−15	Oct. 30.

Statement of Cash Flows		Income Statement	
Oct. 30. Operating	−1,015	Oct. 30. Interest expense	−15

The interest expense is reported in the Other expense section of the income statement for the year ended December 31, 20Y5. If the accounting period ends before the maturity date of the note, interest expense to the end of the period is recorded by an adjustment.

Income Taxes

Under the U.S. tax code, corporations must pay federal income taxes.[2] Most corporations normally pay estimated federal income taxes in four installments throughout the year.

To illustrate, assume that a corporation, with a calendar-year accounting period, estimates its income tax expense for the year as $84,000. The effect on the accounts and the financial statements of the first of the four estimated tax payments of $21,000 (¼ of $84,000) is as follows:

Statement of Cash Flows	Balance Sheet			Income Statement
	Assets	**= Liabilities +**	**Stockholders' Equity**	
	Cash	=	Retained Earnings	
Mar. 15	–21,000		–21,000	*Mar. 15*

Statement of Cash Flows		Income Statement	
Mar. 15 Operating	–21,000	*Mar. 15* Income tax exp.	–21,000

At year-end, the actual taxable income and related tax are determined. If additional taxes are owed, the additional liability is recorded. If the total estimated tax payments are more than the tax liability, the overpayment is recorded as an increase in Income Tax Receivable and a decrease in Income Tax Expense.

The **taxable income** of a corporation is determined according to the tax laws. Since tax laws differ from generally accepted accounting principles, the income before taxes reported on the income statement is usually different from taxable income, as shown in Exhibit 1.

EXHIBIT 1

Taxable Income and Income Before Taxes

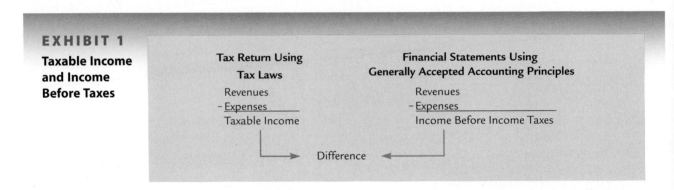

The implication of Exhibit 1 is that the tax expense shown on the tax return may differ from that shown in the financial statements. As a result, this difference may need to be allocated between financial statement periods. The difference may be created because items are recognized in one period for tax purposes and in another period for income statement purposes. Such differences, called **temporary differences**, reverse or turn around in later years. For example, such differences may be caused by a company using MACRS (Modified Accelerated Cost Recovery System) depreciation for tax purposes and the straight-line method for financial reporting purposes.

Since temporary differences reverse in later years, they do not change or reduce the total amount of taxable income over the life of a business. For example, MACRS recognizes more depreciation in the early years but less depreciation in the later years. However, the total depreciation expense is the same for MACRS and the straight-line method over the life of the asset.

Temporary differences do not change the total amount of taxes paid. Only the timing of when taxes are to be paid is affected. Companies normally use tax planning to delay or defer the payment of taxes to later years. As a result, at the end of each year, most corporations will have two tax liabilities:

1. Current income tax liability, which is due on the current year's taxable income.
2. Postponed or deferred tax liability, which is due in the future when the temporary differences reverse.

To illustrate, assume the following data for the first year of a corporation's operations:

Income before income taxes (income statement)	$300,000
Less temporary differences	200,000
Taxable income (tax return)	$100,000
Income tax rate	40%

Based on the preceding data, the income tax expense reported on the income statement is $120,000 ($300,000 × 40%). However, the current income tax liability (income tax due for the year) reported on the corporate tax return is only $40,000 ($100,000 × 40%). The $80,000 ($120,000 − $40,000) difference is the deferred tax liability that will be paid in future years as shown below.

Income tax expense based on $300,000 reported income at 40%	$120,000
Income tax payable based on $100,000 taxable income at 40%	40,000
Income tax deferred to future years	$ 80,000

On the income statement, income tax expense of $120,000 ($300,000 × 40%) is reported. This is done so that the current year's expenses (including income tax) are properly matched against the current year's revenue. Of this amount, $40,000 is currently due and $80,000 will be due in (deferred to) future years.

The effect on the accounts and financial statements of recording the preceding tax expense is as follows:

Statement of Cash Flows	Balance Sheet			
	Assets =	Liabilities		+ Stockholders' Equity
		Income Tax Payable +	Deferred Income Tax Payable +	Retained Earnings
		40,000	80,000	−120,000

Income Statement

Income tax exp.   −120,000

The balance of deferred income tax payable is reported as a liability. The amount due within one year is reported as a current liability and the remainder is reported as a long-term liability.[3]

---

3. In some cases, a deferred tax asset can arise for tax benefits to be received in the future. Such items, as well as additional disclosures for deferred taxes, are discussed in advanced accounting texts.

Differences between taxable income and income (before taxes) reported on the income statement may also arise because some revenues are exempt from tax or some expenses are not deductible. Such differences, called **permanent differences**, create no special financial reporting issues. This is because the amount of income tax determined according to the tax laws is the same amount reported on the income statement.

Contingent Liabilities

Some liabilities may arise from past transactions if certain events occur in the future. These *potential* liabilities are called *contingent liabilities.*

As shown in Exhibit 2, the accounting for contingent liabilities depends on the following two factors:

1. Likelihood of occurring: Probable, reasonably possible, or remote
2. Measurement: Estimable or not estimable

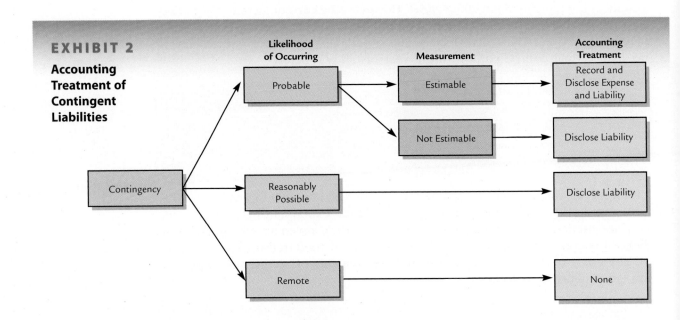

EXHIBIT 2

Accounting Treatment of Contingent Liabilities

Probable and Estimable If a contingent liability is *probable* and the amount of the liability can be *reasonably estimated,* it is recorded and disclosed. The liability is recorded by increasing an expense and a liability.

The estimated costs of warranty work on new car sales are a contingent liability for **Ford Motor Company**.

To illustrate, assume that during June a company sold a product for $60,000 that includes a 36-month warranty for repairs. The average cost of repairs over the warranty period is 5% of the sales price.

Warranty expense of $3,000 ($60,000 × 5%) is recorded by increasing Warranty Expense and increasing Product Warranty Payable. In doing so, the warranty expense is recorded in the same period in which the related product sale is recorded. In other words, the warranty expense is matched with the related revenue (sales). When a defective product is repaired, the repair costs are recorded by decreasing Product Warranty Payable and decreasing Cash, Supplies, or other appropriate accounts.

Probable and Not Estimable A contingent liability may be probable, but cannot be estimated. In this case, the contingent liability is disclosed in the notes to the financial statements. For example, a company may have accidentally polluted a local river by dumping waste products. At the end of the period, the cost of the cleanup and any fines may not be able to be estimated.

Reasonably Possible A contingent liability may be only possible. For example, a company may have lost a lawsuit for infringing on another company's patent rights. However, the verdict is under appeal and the company's lawyers feel that the verdict will be reversed or significantly reduced. In this case, the contingent liability is disclosed in the notes to the financial statements.

Remote A contingent liability may be remote. For example, a ski resort may be sued for injuries incurred by skiers. In most cases, the courts have found that a skier accepts the risk of injury when participating in the activity of skiing. Thus, unless the ski resort is grossly negligent, the resort will not incur a liability for ski injuries. In such cases, no disclosure needs to be made in the notes to the financial statements.

Disclosure of Contingent Liabilities Common examples of contingent liabilities disclosed in notes to the financial statements are litigation, environmental matters, guarantees, and contingencies from the sale of receivables.

An example of a contingent liability disclosure from a recent annual report of Google Inc. is shown below.

—*We have had patent, copyright, and trademark infringement lawsuits filed against us claiming that certain of our products, services, and technologies, including **Android, Google WebSearch, Google AdWords, Google AdSense, Google News, Google Image Search, Google Chrome, Google Talk, Google Voice,** and **YouTube,** infringe the intellectual property rights of others. Adverse results in these lawsuits may include awards of substantial monetary damages, costly royalty or licensing agreements, or orders preventing us from offering certain features, functionalities, products, or services, and may also result in a change in our business practices, and require development of non-infringing products or technologies, which could result in a loss of revenues for us and otherwise harm our business.*

—*Although the results of such claims, suits, government investigations, and proceedings cannot be predicted with certainty, we believe that the final outcome of the matters discussed above will not have a material adverse effect on our business, consolidated financial position, results of operations, or cash flows.*

Professional judgment is necessary in distinguishing among classes of contingent liabilities. This is especially the case when distinguishing between probable and reasonably possible contingent liabilities.

Payroll

The term **payroll** refers to the amount paid to employees for the services they provide during a period. Payroll can include either salaries or wages or both. *Salary* refers to payment for managerial, administrative, or similar services.

Integrity, Objectivity, and Ethics in Business

TODAY'S MISTAKES CAN BE TOMORROW'S LIABILITY

Environmental and public health claims are quickly growing into some of the largest contingent liabilities facing companies. As a result, managers must be careful that today's decisions do not become tomorrow's nightmares. For example, tobacco, asbestos, and environmental cleanup claims have reached billions of dollars and have led to a number of corporate bankruptcies.

Durabla Manufacturing Co., which produced sealing products, had over 100,000 asbestos lawsuits filed against it. As a result, Durabla filed for bankruptcy.

The rate of salary is normally expressed in terms of a month or a year. *Wages* refers to payment for manual labor, both skilled and unskilled. The rate of wages is normally stated on an hourly or a weekly basis.

The total earnings of an employee for a payroll period, including bonuses and overtime pay, is called **gross pay**. From this amount is subtracted one or more deductions to arrive at the net pay. **Net pay** is the amount the employer must pay the employee. The deductions for federal taxes are usually the largest deduction. Deductions may also be required for state or local income taxes. Still other deductions may be made for FICA tax, medical insurance, contributions to pensions, and items authorized by individual employees.

The FICA tax withheld from employees contributes to two federal programs. The first program, called *social security,* is for old age, survivors, and disability insurance (OASDI). The second program, called *Medicare,* is health insurance for senior citizens. The FICA tax rate and the amounts subject to the tax are established annually by law.[4]

To illustrate recording payroll, assume that McDermott Co. had a gross payroll of $13,800 for the week ending April 11. Assume that the FICA tax was 7.5% of the gross payroll and that federal and state withholding were $1,655 and $280, respectively. The effect on the accounts and financial statements of McDermott Co. of recording the payroll follows:

Statement of Cash Flows	Balance Sheet					Income Statement
	Assets =	Liabilities			+ Stockholders' Equity	
	Cash =	FICA Tax Payable +	Employee Federal Income Tax Payable +	Employee State Income Tax Payable +	Retained Earnings	
Apr. 11.	−10,830	1,035	1,655	280	−13,800	*Apr. 11.*

Statement of Cash Flows	
Apr. 11. Operating	−10,830

Income Statement	
Apr. 11. Wages and salary exp.	−13,800

The FICA, federal, and state taxes withheld from the employees' earnings are not expenses to the employer. Rather, these amounts are withheld on the

---

4. The social security tax portion of the FICA tax is limited to a specific amount of the annual compensation for each individual. The 2013 limitation is $113,700. The Medicare portion is not subject to a limitation. To simplify, it is assumed that all compensation is within the social security limitation. By doing so, we express social security and Medicare as a single assumed rate of 7.5%. The actual combined social security and Medicare rate for 2013 is 7.65%.

behalf of employees. These amounts must be remitted periodically to the state and federal agencies.

Most employers are subject to federal and state payroll taxes. Such taxes are an operating expense of the business. For example, employers are required to match employees' contributions to social security and Medicare. In addition, most businesses must pay federal and state unemployment taxes.

The Federal Unemployment Tax Act (FUTA) provides for temporary payments to those who become unemployed as a result of layoffs or other causes beyond their control. The FUTA tax rate and maximum earnings of each employee subject to the tax are established annually by law.

State Unemployment Tax Acts (SUTA) provide for payments to unemployed workers. The amounts paid as benefits are obtained, for the most part, from a tax on employers only. The employment experience and the status of each employer's tax account are reviewed annually, and the tax rates are adjusted accordingly by each state.

The employer's payroll taxes become liabilities when the related payroll is *paid* to employees. The prior payroll information of McDermott Co. indicates that the amount of FICA tax withheld is $1,035 on April 11. Since the employer must match the employees' FICA contributions, the employer's social security payroll tax will also be $1,035. Furthermore, assume that the FUTA and SUTA taxes are $145 and $25, respectively. The effect on the accounts and financial statements of McDermott Co. of recording the payroll tax liabilities for the week follows:

Statement of Cash Flows	Balance Sheet					Income Statement
	Assets =	Liabilities			+ Stockholders' Equity	
		FICA Tax Payable +	FUTA Tax Payable +	SUTA Tax Payable +	Retained Earnings	
Apr. 11.		1,035	145	25	−1,205	Apr. 11.

Income Statement

Apr. 11. Payroll tax exp. −1,205

Payroll tax liabilities are paid to appropriate taxing authorities on a quarterly basis by decreasing Cash and the related taxes payable.

Many companies provide their employees a variety of benefits in addition to salary and wages earned. Such **fringe benefits** can take many forms, including vacations; pension plans; and health, life, and disability insurance coverage. When the employer pays part or all of the cost of the fringe benefits, these costs must be recognized as expenses. To properly match revenues and expenses, the estimated cost of these benefits should be recorded as an expense during the period in which the employee earns the benefit. In recording the expense, the related liability is also recorded.

Bonds

Many large corporations finance their long-term operations through the issuance of bonds. A **bond** is simply a form of an interest-bearing note. Like a note, a bond requires periodic interest payments, with the face amount payable at the maturity date.

Obj **3**

Describe and illustrate the financing of operations through issuance of bonds.

A corporation that issues bonds enters into a contract, called a **bond indenture** or trust indenture, with the bondholders. A bond issue is normally divided into a number of individual bonds. Usually, the face value of each bond, called the *principal,* is $1,000 or a multiple of $1,000. The interest on bonds may be payable annually, semiannually, or quarterly. Most bonds pay interest semiannually.

The prices of bonds are quoted on bond exchanges as a percentage of the bonds' face value. Thus, investors could purchase or sell bonds quoted at 109⅞ for $1,098.75. Likewise, bonds quoted at 110 could be purchased or sold for $1,100.

When a corporation issues bonds, the price that buyers are willing to pay for the bonds depends on these three factors:

1. The face amount of the bonds due at the maturity date
2. The periodic interest to be paid on the bonds
3. The market rate of interest

The periodic interest to be paid on the bonds is identified in the bond indenture and is expressed as a percentage of the face amount of the bond. This percentage or rate of interest is called the **contract rate** or *coupon rate.* The **market rate of interest**, sometimes called the *effective rate of interest,* is determined by transactions between buyers and sellers of similar bonds. If the contract rate of interest is the same as the market rate of interest, the bonds sell for their face amount.

To illustrate, assume that on January 1 a corporation issues for cash $100,000 of 6%, 5-year bonds, with interest of $3,000 payable semiannually. The market rate of interest at the time the bonds are issued is 6%.

Since the contract rate and the market rate of interest are the same, the bonds will sell at their face amount. The effect on the accounts and financial statements of issuing the bonds, paying the semiannual interest, and paying off the bonds at the maturity date is shown here.

Issuance of bonds payable at face amount on January 1.

Statement of Cash Flows	Balance Sheet			Income Statement
	Assets	=	Liabilities + Stockholders' Equity	
	Cash	=	Bonds Payable	
Jan. 1.	100,000		100,000	

Statement of Cash Flows		
Jan. 1. Financing	100,000	

Payment of semiannual interest on June 30. (Interest: $100,000 \times 0.06 \times \frac{1}{2} = \$3,000$)

Statement of Cash Flows	Balance Sheet				Income Statement
	Assets	**= Liabilities**	**+**	**Stockholders' Equity**	
	Cash	=		Retained Earnings	
June 30.	–3,000			–3,000	June 30.

Statement of Cash Flows		Income Statement	
June 30. Operating	–3,000	June 30. Interest expense	–3,000

Payment of face value of bond at maturity.

Statement of Cash Flows	Balance Sheet				Income Statement
	Assets	**= Liabilities**	**+**	**Stockholders' Equity**	
	Cash	=	Bonds Payable		
Dec. 31.	–100,000	–100,000			

Statement of Cash Flows	
Dec. 31. Financing	–100,000

The market and contract rates of interest determine whether the selling price of a bond will be equal to, less than, or more than the bond's face amount.

1. Market Rate = Contract Rate

   Selling Price = Face Amount of Bonds

2. Market Rate > Contract Rate

   Selling Price < Face Amount of Bonds

   The face amount of bonds less the selling price is called a **discount on bonds payable**.

3. Market Rate < Contract Rate

   Selling Price > Face Amount of Bonds

   The selling price less the face amount of the bonds is called a **premium on bonds payable**.

A bond sells at a discount because buyers are only willing to pay less than the face amount for bonds whose contract rate is less than the market rate. A bond sells at a premium because buyers are willing to pay more than the face amount for bonds whose contract rate is higher than the market rate.

Generally accepted accounting principles require that bond discounts and premiums be amortized to Interest Expense over the life of the bond. The amortization of a discount increases Interest Expense, and the amortization of a premium reduces Interest Expense.

Obj | **4**

Describe and illustrate the financing of operations through issuance of stock.

Stock

A major means of equity financing for a corporation is issuing stock. The equity in the assets that results from issuing stock is called *paid-in capital* or *contributed capital*. Another major means of equity financing for a corporation's operations is through retaining net income in the business, called *retained earnings*. The accounting for retained earnings has been described and illustrated in earlier chapters.

The number of shares of stock that a corporation is authorized to issue is stated in its charter filed in its state of incorporation. The term *issued* refers to the shares issued to the stockholders. A corporation may reacquire some of the stock that it has issued. The stock remaining in the hands of stockholders is then called **outstanding stock**. The relationship between authorized, issued, and outstanding stock is shown in the margin.

Shares of stock are often assigned a monetary amount, called **par**. Upon request, a corporation may issue stock certificates to stockholders to document their ownership. Printed on a stock certificate is the par value of the stock, the name of the stockholder, and the number of shares owned. Stock can also be issued without par, in which case it is called *no-par stock*. Some states require the board of directors to assign a **stated value** to no-par stock.

Number of shares authorized, issued, and outstanding

Because corporations have limited liability, creditors have no claim against the personal assets of stockholders. However, some state laws require that corporations maintain a minimum stockholder contribution to protect creditors. This minimum amount is called *legal capital*. The amount of required legal capital varies among the states, but it usually includes the amount of par or stated value of the shares of stock issued.

The major rights that accompany ownership of a share of stock are as follows:

1. The right to vote in matters concerning the corporation
2. The right to share in distributions of earnings
3. The right to share in assets upon liquidation

Common and Preferred Stock

When only one class of stock is issued, it is called **common stock**. Each share of common stock has equal rights.

A corporation may also issue one or more classes of stock with various preference rights such as a preference to dividends. Such stock is called **preferred stock**. The dividend rights of preferred stock are stated either as dollars per share or as a percent of par. For example, a $50 par value preferred stock with a $4-per-share dividend may be described as either:

$4 preferred stock, $50 par

or

8% preferred stock, $50 par

The payment of dividends is authorized by the corporation's board of directors. When authorized, the directors are said to have *declared* a dividend. Because they have first rights (preference) to any dividends, preferred stockholders have a greater chance of receiving dividends than common stockholders. However, since dividends are normally based on earnings, a corporation cannot guarantee dividends even to preferred stockholders.

Issuance of Stock

Because different classes of stock have different rights, a separate account is used for recording the amount of each class of stock issued to investors. Stock is often issued by a corporation at a price other than its par.

The price at which stock is sold depends on a variety of factors such as:

1. The financial condition, earnings record, and dividend record of the corporation
2. Investor expectations of the corporation's potential earning power
3. General business and economic conditions and prospects

Normally, stock is issued for a price that is more than its par. In this case, it is sold at a **premium**.[5] Thus, if stock with a par of $50 is issued for a price of $60, the stock is sold at a premium of $10.

When stock is issued at a premium, Cash (or other asset) is increased for the amount received. Common Stock or Preferred Stock is then increased for the par amount. The excess of the amount received over par is a part of the capital contributed by the stockholders of the corporation. This amount is recorded in an account entitled Paid-In Capital in Excess of Par.

To illustrate, assume that Caldwell Company issues 2,000 shares of $1 par common stock for cash at $55 on November 1. The effects on the accounts and financial statements follow:

Statement of Cash Flows	Balance Sheet				Income Statement
	Assets	= Liabilities +	Stockholders' Equity		
	Cash	=	Common Stock	+ Paid-In Capital in Excess of Par	
Nov. 1.	110,000		2,000	108,000	

Statement of Cash Flows	
Nov. 1. Financing	110,000

When stock is issued in exchange for assets other than cash, such as land, buildings, and equipment, the assets acquired are recorded at their fair market value. If this value cannot be objectively determined, the fair market price of the stock issued may be used.

In most states, both preferred and common stock may be issued without a par value. When no-par stock is issued, the entire proceeds are recorded in the stock account. In some states, no-par stock may be assigned a stated value per share. The stated value is recorded like a par value, and the excess of the amount received over the stated value is recorded in Paid-In Capital in Excess of Stated Value.

---

5. When stock is issued for a price that is less than its par, the stock is sold at a discount. Many states do not permit stock to be issued at a discount. In others, it may be done only under unusual conditions. For these reasons, we assume that stock is sold at par or at a premium in this text.

Reacquired Stock

Treasury stock is stock that a corporation has issued and then reacquired. A corporation may reacquire (purchase) its own stock for a variety of reasons including:

1. To provide shares for resale to employees
2. To reissue as bonuses to employees
3. To support the market price of the stock

The purchase of treasury stock increases Treasury Stock and decreases Cash by the cost of the repurchased shares. At the end of the year, the balance of the treasury stock account is reported as a reduction of stockholders' equity. When treasury stock is sold or reissued, Cash is increased by the proceeds from the sale and Treasury Stock is decreased by the cost of its repurchase. Any difference increases or decreases an account called Paid-In Capital from Treasury Stock.

Obj | **5**

Describe and illustrate the accounting for cash and stock dividends.

Dividends

When a board of directors declares a cash dividend, it authorizes the distribution of cash to stockholders. When a board of directors declares a stock dividend, it authorizes the distribution of its stock. In both cases, declaring a dividend decreases the retained earnings of the corporation.[6]

Cash Dividends

A cash distribution of earnings by a corporation to its shareholders is a **cash dividend**. Although dividends may be paid in other assets, cash dividends are the most common.

Three conditions for a cash dividend are as follows:

1. Sufficient retained earnings
2. Sufficient cash
3. Formal action by the board of directors

There must be a sufficient (large enough) balance in Retained Earnings to declare a cash dividend. However, a large Retained Earnings balance does not mean that there is cash available to pay dividends. This is because the balances of Cash and Retained Earnings are often unrelated.

Even if there are sufficient retained earnings and cash, a corporation's board of directors is not required to pay dividends. Nevertheless, many corporations pay quarterly cash dividends to make their stock more attractive to investors. *Special* or *extra* dividends may also be paid when a corporation experiences higher than normal profits.

Three dates included in a dividend announcement are as follows:

1. Date of declaration
2. Date of record
3. Date of payment

---

6. In rare cases, when a corporation is reducing its operations or going out of business, a dividend may be a distribution of paid-in capital. Such a dividend is called a liquidating dividend.

The *date of declaration* is the date the board of directors formally authorizes the payment of the dividend. On this date, the corporation incurs the liability to pay the amount of the dividend.

The *date of record* is the date the corporation uses to determine which stockholders will receive the dividend. During the period of time between the date of declaration and the date of record, the stock price is quoted as selling *with-dividends*. This means that any investors purchasing the stock before the date of record will receive the dividend.

The *date of payment* is the date the corporation will pay the dividend to the stockholders who owned the stock on the date of record. During the period of time between the record date and the payment date, the stock price is quoted as selling *ex-dividends*. This means that since the date of record has passed, any new investors will not receive the dividend.

To illustrate, assume that on *December 1*, Hiber Corporation's board of directors declares the following quarterly cash dividend. The date of record is *January 10*, and the date of payment is *February 2*.

Microsoft Corporation recently declared on June 12 a quarterly cash dividend of $0.23 to common stockholders of record as of the close of business on August 15, payable on September 12.

	Dividend per Share	Total Dividends
Preferred stock, $100 par, 5,000 shares outstanding	$2.50	$12,500
Common stock, $10 par, 100,000 shares outstanding	$0.30	30,000
Total		$42,500

The effect of the declaration of the dividend on the accounts and financial statements is as follows:

Date of Declaration	Date of Record	Date of Payment

| December 1 | January 10 | February 2 |

Board of directors takes action to declare dividends.   Owners of the shares on this date receive dividends.   Dividend is paid.

No entry

Dec. 1 Increase Cash Dividends $42,500
         Increase Dividends Payable   −42,500

Jan. 10 No entry

Feb. 2 Decrease Cash   −$42,500
         Decrease Dividends Payable   42,500

Statement of Cash Flows	Balance Sheet				Income Statement
	Assets	=	Liabilities	+ Stockholders' Equity	
			Dividends Payable	+ Retained Earnings	
Dec. 1.			42,500	−42,500	

Note that the date of record, January 10, does not affect the accounts or the financial statements, since this date merely determines which stockholders will receive the dividend. The payment of the dividend on February 2 decreases Cash and Dividends Payable.

If a corporation holding treasury stock declares a cash dividend, the dividends are not paid on the treasury shares. To do so would place the corporation in the position of earning income through dealing with itself. For example, if Hiber Corporation in the preceding illustration had held 5,000 shares of its own common stock, the cash dividends on the common stock would have been $28,500 [(100,000 − 5,000) × $0.30] instead of $30,000.

Integrity, Objectivity, and Ethics in Business

THE PROFESSOR WHO KNEW TOO MUCH

A major Midwestern university released a quarterly "American Customer Satisfaction Index" based on its research of customers of popular U.S. products and services. Before the release of the index to the public, the professor in charge of the research bought and sold stocks of some of the companies in the report. The professor was quoted as saying that he thought it was important to test his theories of customer satisfaction with "real" [his own] money.

Is this proper or ethical? Apparently, the dean of the Business School didn't think so. In a statement to the press, the dean stated: "I have instructed anyone affiliated with the (index) not to make personal use of information gathered in the course of producing the quarterly index, prior to the index's release to the general public, and they [the researchers] have agreed."

Sources: Jon E. Hilsenrath and Dan Morse, "Researcher Uses Index to Buy, Short Stocks," *The Wall Street Journal*, February 18, 2003; and Jon E. Hilsenrath, "Satisfaction Theory: Mixed Results," *The Wall Street Journal*, February 19, 2003.

Stock Dividends

A **stock dividend** is a distribution of shares of stock to stockholders. Stock dividends are normally declared only on common stock and issued to common stockholders.

The effect of a stock dividend on the stockholders' equity of the issuing corporation is to transfer retained earnings to paid-in capital. For public corporations, the amount transferred from the retained earnings account to the paid-in capital account is normally the fair value (market price) of the shares issued in the stock dividend.[7]

A stock dividend does not change the assets, liabilities, or total stockholders' equity of a corporation. Likewise, a stock dividend does not change an individual stockholder's proportionate interest (equity) in the corporation.

To illustrate, assume a stockholder owns 1,000 of a corporation's 10,000 shares outstanding. If the corporation declares a 6% stock dividend, the stockholder's proportionate interest will not change, as shown below.

	Before Stock Dividend	After Stock Dividend
Total shares issued	10,000	10,600 [10,000 + (10,000 × 6%)]
Number of shares owned	1,000	1,060 [1,000 + (1,000 × 6%)]
Proportionate ownership	10% (1,000/10,000)	10% (1,060/10,600)

Stock Splits

Obj **6**

Describe the effects of stock splits on the financial statements.

A **stock split** is a process by which a corporation reduces the par or stated value of its common stock and issues a proportionate number of additional shares. A stock split applies to all common shares including the unissued, issued, and treasury shares.

A major objective of a stock split is to reduce the market price per share of the stock. This, in turn, attracts more investors to the stock and broadens the types and numbers of stockholders.

---

7. The use of fair market value is justified as long as the number of shares issued for the stock dividend is small (less than 25% of the shares outstanding).

To illustrate, assume that Rojek Corporation has 10,000 shares of $100 par common stock outstanding with a current market price of $150 per share. The board of directors declares the following stock split:

1. Each common shareholder will receive 5 shares for each share held. This is called a 5-for-1 stock split. As a result, 50,000 shares (10,000 shares × 5) will be outstanding.

2. The par of each share of common stock will be reduced to $20 ($100/5).

The par value of the common stock outstanding is $1,000,000 both before and after the stock split as shown below.

	Before Split	After Split
Number of shares	10,000	50,000
Par value per share	× $100	× $20
Total	$1,000,000	$1,000,000

In addition, each Rojek Corporation shareholder owns the same total par amount of stock before and after the stock split. For example, a stockholder who owned 4 shares of $100 par stock before the split (total par of $400) would own 20 shares of $20 par stock after the split (total par of $400). Only the number of shares and the par value per share have changed.

Since there are more shares outstanding after the stock split, the market price of the stock should decrease. For example, in the preceding example, there would be 5 times as many shares outstanding after the split. Thus, the market price of the stock would be expected to fall from $150 to about $30 ($150/5).

Stock splits do not affect any financial statement accounts, since only the par (or stated) value and number of shares outstanding have changed. However, the details of stock splits are normally disclosed in the notes to the financial statements.

Before Stock Split

4 shares, $100 par

$400 total par value

After 5:1 Stock Split

20 shares, $20 par

$400 total par value

When **Nature's Sunshine Products, Inc.**, declared a 2-for-1 stock split, the company president said: *We believe the split will place our stock price in a range attractive to both individual and institutional investors, broadening the market for the stock.*

Reporting Liabilities and Stockholders' Equity

Obj | 7

Describe financial statement reporting of liabilities and stockholders' equity.

Liabilities that are expected to be paid within one year are presented in the Current Liabilities section of the balance sheet. Thus, any notes or bonds payable maturing within one year are reported as current liabilities. However, if the notes or bonds are to be paid from noncurrent assets or if the notes or bonds are going to be refinanced, they are reported as noncurrent liabilities. The detailed descriptions, including terms, due dates, and interest rates for notes or bonds, are reported either on the balance sheet or in a note. Also, the fair market value of notes or bonds is disclosed. Exhibit 3 illustrates the reporting of liabilities on the balance sheet.

Contingent liabilities that are probable but cannot be reasonably estimated or are only possible are disclosed in the notes to the financial statements.

Although stockholders' equity is reported on the balance sheet, significant changes in stockholders' equity during the year should also be disclosed. Changes in retained earnings may be presented in a separate retained earnings statement. Changes in paid-in capital during the year may be reported on the face of the balance sheet or in the notes. Some companies prepare a separate statement of stockholders' equity that includes changes in both paid-in capital and retained earnings. An example of a statement of stockholders' equity is shown in Exhibit 4.

EXHIBIT 3

Partial Balance Sheet with Liabilities and Stockholders' Equity

Bergstom Corporation
Balance Sheet
December 31, 20Y8

Liabilities

Current liabilities:		
Accounts payable	$ 488,200	
Notes payable (9% due on March 1, 20Y9)	250,000	
Accrued interest payable	15,000	
Accrued salaries and wages payable	13,500	
Other accrued liabilities	9,850	
Total current liabilities		$ 776,550
Long-term liabilities:		
Debenture 8% bonds payable, due in 15 years		
(Market value, $950,000)		1,000,000
Total liabilities		$1,776,550

Stockholders' Equity

Paid-in capital:		
Preferred 10% stock, $50 par (20,000 shares authorized and issued)	$1,000,000	
Common stock, $20 par (250,000 shares authorized, 100,000 shares issued)	2,000,000	
Additional paid-in capital in excess of par	520,000	
Total paid-in capital	$3,520,000	
Retained earnings	4,580,500	
Total	$8,100,500	
Deduct treasury stock (1,000 shares at cost)	75,000	
Total stockholders' equity		8,025,500
Total liabilities and stockholders' equity		$9,802,050

EXHIBIT 4   **Statement of Stockholders' Equity**

Heise Inc.
Statement of Stockholders' Equity
For the Year Ended December 31, 20Y8

	Preferred Stock	Common Stock	Paid-In Capital in Excess of Par—Common Stock	Retained Earnings	Treasury (Common) Stock	Total
Balance, January 1	$5,000,000	$10,000,000	$3,000,000	$2,000,000	$(500,000)	$19,500,000
Net income				850,000		850,000
Dividends on preferred stock				(250,000)		(250,000)
Dividends on common stock				(400,000)		(400,000)
Issuance of additional common stock		500,000	50,000			550,000
Purchase of treasury stock					(30,000)	(30,000)
Balance, December 31	$5,000,000	$10,500,000	$3,050,000	$2,200,000	$(530,000)	$20,220,000

International Connection

REPORTING LIABILITIES AND STOCKHOLDERS' EQUITY UNDER IFRS

In the United States, liabilities are reported in the order that they will become due, with current liabilities reported first followed by long-term liabilities. On the balance sheet, stockholders' equity is reported after liabilities. Typically, companies reporting under IFRS report stockholders' equity before liabilities on the balance sheet. In addition, long-term liabilities are reported before current liabilities. That is, liabilities are reported in the reverse order in which they become due, with liabilities due within one year reported last.

Earnings per Share

One of the many factors that influence the decision of whether to finance operations using debt or equity is the effect on earnings per share. Earnings per share is a major profitability measure that is reported in the financial statements and is followed closely by the financial press. As a result, corporate managers closely monitor the impact of decisions on earnings per share.

Earnings per share (EPS) measures the income earned by each share of common stock.[8] It is computed as follows:

$$\text{Earning per Share} = \frac{\text{Net Income} - \text{Preferred Dividends}}{\text{Number of Common Shares Outstanding}}$$

To illustrate, assume the following data for Lincoln Corporation:

	Year 2	Year 1
Shares of common stock outstanding	50,000	50,000
Shares of 9%, $100 par preferred stock outstanding	100,000	100,000
Net income	$91,000	$76,500

The earnings per share for Year 2 and Year 1 is computed below.

Year 2:

$$\text{Earnings per Share} = \frac{\text{Net Income} - \text{Preferred Dividends}}{\text{Number of Common Shares Outstanding}}$$

$$= \frac{\$91,000 - \$9,000}{50,000 \text{ Shares}} = \$1.64 \text{ per Share}$$

Year 1:

$$\text{Earnings per Share} = \frac{\text{Net Income} - \text{Preferred Dividends}}{\text{Number of Common Shares Outstanding}}$$

$$= \frac{\$76,500 - \$9,000}{50,000 \text{ Shares}} = \$1.35 \text{ per Share}$$

Obj **8**

Analyze the impact of debt or equity financing on earnings per share.

---

8. Earnings per share is further discussed in Chapter 9, "Financial Statement Analysis."

To illustrate the impact of financing of long-term operations on earnings per share, assume Huckadee Corporation is considering the following plans to issue debt and equity:

	Plan 1		Plan 2		Plan 3	
	Amount	Percent	Amount	Percent	Amount	Percent
Issue 6% bonds	—	0%	—	0%	$2,000,000	50%
Issue 4% preferred stock, $50 par value	—	0	$2,000,000	50	1,000,000	25
Issue common stock, $10 par value	$4,000,000	100	2,000,000	50	1,000,000	25
Total amount of financing	$4,000,000	100%	$4,000,000	100%	$4,000,000	100%

Each of the preceding plans finances some of the corporation's operations by issuing common stock. However, the percentage financed by common stock varies from 100% (Plan 1) to 25% (Plan 3).

In addition, assume the following data for Huckadee Corporation:

1. Earnings before interest and income taxes are $400,000.
2. The tax rate is 40%.
3. All bonds or stocks are issued at their par or face amount.

The effect of the preceding financing plans on Huckadee's net income and earnings per share is shown in Exhibit 5. Exhibit 5 indicates that Plan 3 yields the highest earnings per share on common stock and thus is the most attractive for common stockholders. If the estimated earnings are more than $400,000, the difference between the earnings per share to common stockholders under Plans 1 and 3 is even greater.[9]

EXHIBIT 5

Effect of Alternative Financing Plans— $400,000 Earnings

	Plan 1	Plan 2	Plan 3
6% bonds	—	—	$2,000,000
Preferred 4% stock, $50 par	—	$2,000,000	1,000,000
Common stock, $10 par	$ 4,000,000	2,000,000	1,000,000
Total	$ 4,000,000	$4,000,000	$4,000,000
Earnings before interest and income tax	$ 400,000	$ 400,000	$ 400,000
Deduct interest on bonds	—	—	120,000
Income before income tax	$ 400,000	$ 400,000	$ 280,000
Deduct income tax	160,000	160,000	112,000
Net income	$ 240,000	$ 240,000	$ 168,000
Dividends on preferred stock	—	80,000	40,000
Available for dividends on common stock	$ 240,000	$ 160,000	$ 128,000
Shares of common stock outstanding	÷ 400,000	÷ 200,000	÷ 100,000
Earnings per share on common stock	$ 0.60	$ 0.80	$ 1.28

If smaller earnings occur, however, Plans 1 and 2 become more attractive to common stockholders. To illustrate, the effect of earnings of $200,000 rather than $400,000 is shown in Exhibit 6.

9. The higher earnings per share under Plan 3 is due to a finance concept known as leverage. This concept is discussed further in Chapter 9.

EXHIBIT 6

How to Search Publish Sources of Secondary Data

	Plan 1	Plan 2	Plan 3
6% bonds	—	—	$ 2,000,000
Preferred 4% stock, $50 par	—	$ 2,000,000	1,000,000
Common stock, $10 par	$ 4,000,000	2,000,000	1,000,000
Total	$ 4,000,000	$ 4,000,000	$ 4,000,000
Earnings before interest and income tax	$ 200,000	$ 200,000	$ 200,000
Deduct interest on bonds	—	—	120,000
Income before income tax	$ 200,000	$ 200,000	$ 80,000
Deduct income tax	80,000	80,000	32,000
Net income	$ 120,000	$ 120,000	$ 48,000
Dividends on preferred stock	—	80,000	40,000
Available for dividends on common stock	$ 120,000	$ 40,000	$ 8,000
Shares of common stock outstanding	÷ 400,000	÷ 200,000	÷ 100,000
Earnings per share on common stock	$ 0.30	$ 0.20	$ 0.08

In addition to earnings per share, the corporation should consider other factors in deciding among the financing plans. For example, once bonds are issued, the interest and the face value of the bonds at maturity must be paid. If these payments are not made, the bondholders could seek court action and force the company into bankruptcy. In contrast, a corporation is not legally obligated to pay dividends on preferred or common stock.

Financial Analysis: Ratio of Liabilities to Total Assets and Price-Earnings Ratio

Obj | **9**

Describe and illustrate the use of the ratio of liabilities to total assets and the price-earnings ratio in assessing a company's financial condition and prospects for future performance.

The ratio of liabilities to total assets is useful in assessing a company's financial condition and risk to its creditors. The price-earnings ratio is useful in revealing the market's assessment of the financial prospects for a company.

Ratio of Liabilities to Total Assets

The **ratio of liabilities to total assets**, sometimes called the debt ratio, indicates the percent of a company's total assets that are financed with debt. A high ratio of liabilities to total assets indicates the company is financing its operations with a high percent of debt. This, in turn, increases the risk that if operating performance declines the company may not be able to pay its liabilities. In addition, a high ratio indicates that the company may not be able to easily borrow additional funds, which could prevent such opportunities as expanding into new product lines.

The ratio of liabilities to total assets is computed as follows:

$$\text{Ratio of Liabilities to Total Assets} = \frac{\text{Total Liabilities}}{\text{Total Assets}}$$

To illustrate, Lowe's is used. Lowe's is a home improvement retailer with over 1,700 stores in United States, Canada, and Mexico. The following data (in millions) were taken from two of its recent financial statements.

	Year 2	Year 1
Total assets	$33,559	$33,699
Total liabilities	17,026	15,587
Total stockholders' equity	16,533	18,112

The ratio of liabilities to total assets, rounded to one decimal place, for Years 1 and 2 is shown below.

	Ratio of Liabilities to Total Assets
Year 1 ($15,587 ÷ $33,699)	46.3
Year 2 ($17,026 ÷ $33,559)	50.7%

As shown above, the ratio of liabilities to total assets increased from 46.3% to 50.7% during Year 2. As a result, Lowe's finances slightly more than half of its operations through debt.

Since total liabilities plus total stockholders' equity equals total assets, 100.0% minus the ratio of liabilities to total assets equals the **ratio of stockholders' equity to total assets**. In other words, in Year 1, Lowe's financed 53.7% (100.0 − 46.3) of its operations with equity financing. In Year 2, Lowe's financed 49.3% (100.0 − 50.7) of its operations with equity financing.

The relationship between liabilities and equity financing for a company can also be expressed as the **ratio of liabilities to stockholders' equity**. It is computed as follows:[10]

$$\text{Ratio of Liabilities to Stockholders' Equity} = \frac{\text{Total Liabilities}}{\text{Total Stockholders' Equity}}$$

To illustrate, Lowe's ratio of liabilities to stockholders' equity (rounded to two decimal places) is 1.03 ($17,026 ÷ $16,533) in Year 2 and 0.86 ($15,587 ÷ $18,112) in Year 1. In other words, Lowe's financed its operations almost equally with debt and equity financing in Year 2 and with more equity than debt financing in Year 1.

Price-Earnings Ratio

The market's assessment of the future earnings potential of a company is indicated by the **price-earnings ratio**. The price-earnings ratio, sometimes called the earnings multiple, is computed as follows:

$$\text{Price-Earnings Ratio} = \frac{\text{Market Price per Share of Common Stock}}{\text{Earnings per Share of Common Stock}}$$

To illustrate, Lowe's earnings per share of common stock for Year 2 was $1.43. With a market price of $38.44, the price-earnings ratio is 26.9 ($38.44 ÷ $1.43), which means that investors are willing to pay 26.9 times current earnings per share. The price-earnings ratio cannot be computed for companies with losses or no income.

The higher a company's price-earnings ratio, the more favorable the market's assessment of the future earnings potential and growth of the company. A price-

10. The ratio of liabilities to stockholders' equity can also be computed as (Ratio of total liabilities to total assets) ÷ (1 − Ratio of total liabilities to total assets).

earnings ratio less than 10 is often interpreted as indicating a company that has declining earnings or is undervalued. A price-earnings ratio over 25 usually indicates an expanding company with high earnings potential or a company that is overvalued.

Price-earnings ratios are often compared over time or with other companies within the same industry. To illustrate, Lowe's earnings per share for Year 1 was $1.42. With a market price of $26.35, Lowe's price-earnings ratio was 18.6 ($26.35 ÷ $1.42). Thus, the market's assessment of Lowe's future earnings potential has increased since Year 1. This is consistent with an improving U.S. housing industry which has shown increases in new housing and renovations of existing houses.

Key Points

1. Describe how businesses finance their operations.

A business must finance its operations through either debt or equity. Debt financing includes all liabilities owed by a business, including both current and long-term liabilities. A corporation may also finance its operations by issuing stock. Corporations may issue different classes of stock that contain different rights and privileges, such as rights to dividend payments.

2. Describe and illustrate current liabilities, notes payable, taxes, contingencies, and payroll.

Liabilities that are to be paid out of current assets and are due within a short time, usually within one year, are called *current liabilities*. Most current liabilities arise from either receiving goods or services prior to making payment or receiving payment prior to delivering goods or services. Current liabilities can also arise from notes payable, taxes, contingencies, and payroll. Warranties are examples of liabilities arising from contingencies. Wages and salaries payable and employee and employer payroll taxes are examples of liabilities arising from payroll. Deferred income taxes arise from temporary differences between taxable income and income before taxes as reported on the income statement.

3. Describe and illustrate the financing of operations through issuance of bonds.

Many large corporations finance their operations through the issuance of bonds. A bond is simply a form of an interest-bearing note that requires periodic interest payments and the repayment of the face amount at the maturity date. When the contract rate of interest differs from the market rate of interest, bonds are issued at discounts or premiums. The amortization of discounts and premiums affects interest expense.

4. Describe and illustrate the financing of operations through issuance of stock.

A corporation may finance its operations by issuing either preferred or common stock. Preferred stock has preferential rights, including the right to receive dividends ahead of the common stockholders. When stock is issued at a premium, Cash or another asset account is increased for the amount received. Common Stock or Preferred Stock is increased for the par amount. The excess of the amount paid over par is a part of the paid-in capital and is normally recorded in an account entitled Paid-In Capital in Excess of Par.

Stock that a corporation has once issued and then reacquires is called *treasury stock*. It decreases stockholders' equity.

5. Describe and illustrate the accounting for cash and stock dividends.

When a board of directors declares a cash dividend, it authorizes the distribution of a portion of the corporation's cash to stockholders. When a board of directors declares a stock dividend, it authorizes the distribution of a portion of the stock. In both cases, the declaration of a dividend reduces the retained earnings of the corporation.

6. Describe the effects of stock splits on the financial statements.

Corporations sometimes reduce the par or stated value of their common stock and issue a proportionate number of additional shares in what is called a *stock split*. Since a stock split changes only the par or stated value and the number of shares outstanding, it is not recorded. However, the details of stock splits are normally disclosed in the notes to the financial statements.

7. Describe financial statement reporting of liabilities and stockholders' equity.

Liabilities that are expected to be paid within one year are presented in the Current Liabilities section of the balance sheet. Notes or bonds payable not maturing within one year should be shown as noncurrent liabilities. The detailed descriptions including terms, due dates, and interest rates for notes or bonds should be reported either on the balance sheet or in an accompanying note. Also, the fair market value of notes or bonds should be disclosed.

The notes should disclose any contingent liabilities that cannot be reasonably estimated or are only possible. Significant changes in stockholders' equity during the year should also be reported.

8. Analyze the impact of debt or equity financing on earnings per share.

One of the many factors that influence the decision of whether to finance operations using debt or equity is the effect of each alternative on earnings per share. If a corporation has issued only common stock, earnings per share is computed by dividing net income by the number of shares of common stock outstanding. If preferred and common stock have been issued, the net income must first be reduced by the amount of preferred dividends.

9. Describe and illustrate the use of the ratio of liabilities to total assets and the price-earnings ratio in assessing a company's financial condition and prospects for future performance.

The ratio of liabilities to total assets indicates the percent of a company's operations that are financed by debt. The higher the ratio, the higher the financial leverage and more risk to creditors. The price-earnings ratio measures the market's assessment of the future earnings potential of the company. It is computed as the market price per share of common stock divided by the earnings per share of common stock. The higher the price-earnings ratio, the greater the market's expectations of future earnings.

Key Terms

Bond (293)
Bond indenture (294)
Cash dividend (298)
Common stock (296)
Contingent liabilities (286)
Contract rate (294)
Current liabilities (286)
Discount on bonds payable (295)
Earnings per share (EPS) (303)

Fringe benefits (293)
Gross pay (292)
Long-term liabilities (286)
Market rate of interest (294)
Net pay (292)
Outstanding stock (296)
Par (296)
Payroll (291)
Permanent differences (290)

Preferred stock (296)
Premium on bonds payable (295)
Premium on stock (297)
Price-earnings ratio (306)
Ratio of liabilities to stockholders' equity (306)
Ratio of liabilities to total assets (305)

Ratio of stockholders' equity to total assets (306)
Stated value (296)
Stock dividend (300)
Stock split (300)
Taxable income (288)
Temporary differences (288)
Treasury stock (298)

Illustrative Problem

Differences between the accounting methods applied to accounts and financial reports and those used in determining taxable income yielded the following amounts for the first four years of a corporation's operations:

	First Year	Second Year	Third Year	Fourth Year
Income before income taxes	$400,000	$480,000	$600,000	$520,000
Taxable income	300,000	420,000	630,000	600,000

The income tax rate for each of the four years was 40% of taxable income, and each year's taxes were promptly paid.

Instructions

1. Determine for each year the amounts described by the following captions, presenting the information in the form indicated:

Year	Income Tax Deducted on Income Statement	Income Tax Payments for the Year	Deferred Income Tax Payable	
			Year's Addition (Deduction)	Year-End Balance

2. Total the first three amount columns.

Solution

1. and 2.

Year	Income Tax Deducted on Income Statement	Income Tax Payments for the Year	Deferred Income Tax Payable	
			Year's Addition (Deduction)	Year-End Balance
First	$160,000	$120,000	$ 40,000	$40,000
Second	192,000	168,000	24,000	64,000
Third	240,000	252,000	(12,000)	52,000
Fourth	208,000	240,000	(32,000)	20,000
Total	$800,000	$780,000	$ 20,000	

Self-Examination Questions *(Answers appear at the end of chapter)*

1. A business issued a $5,000, 60-day, 12% note to the bank. The amount due at maturity is:
   A. $4,900
   B. $5,000
   C. $5,100
   D. $5,600

2. Which of the following taxes are employers usually not required to withhold from employees?
   A. Federal income tax
   B. Federal unemployment compensation tax
   C. FICA tax
   D. State and local income taxes

3. Employers do not incur an expense for which of the following payroll taxes?
   A. FICA tax
   B. Federal unemployment compensation tax
   C. State unemployment compensation tax
   D. Employees' federal income tax

4. If a corporation plans to issue $1,000,000 of 7% bonds when the market rate for similar bonds is 6%, the bonds can be expected to sell at:
   A. Their face amount
   B. A premium
   C. A discount
   D. A price below their face amount

5. A corporation has issued 25,000 shares of $100 par common stock and holds 3,000 of these shares as treasury stock. If the corporation declares a $2-per-share cash dividend, what amount will be recorded as cash dividends?
   A. $22,000
   B. $25,000
   C. $44,000
   D. $50,000

Class Discussion Questions

1. What two types of transactions cause most current liabilities?

2. When are short-term notes payable issued?

3. When should the liability associated with a product warranty be recorded? Discuss.

4. **Deere & Company**, a company well known for manufacturing farm equipment, reported more than $800 million of product warranties in recent financial statements. How would costs of repairing a defective product be recorded?

5. **Delta Air Lines'** SkyMiles program allows frequent flyers to earn credit toward free tickets and other amenities.
   a. Does Delta Air Lines have a contingent liability for award redemption by its SkyMiles members?
   b. When should a contingent liability be recorded?

6. For each of the following payroll-related taxes, indicate whether it generally applies to (1) employees only, (2) employers only, or (3) both employees and employers:
   a. Federal income tax
   b. Federal unemployment compensation tax
   c. Medicare tax
   d. Social security tax
   e. State unemployment compensation tax

7. To match revenues and expenses properly, should the expense for employee vacation pay be recorded in the period during which the vacation privilege is earned or during the period in which the vacation is taken? Discuss.

8. Identify the two distinct obligations incurred by a corporation when issuing bonds.

9. A corporation issues $40,000,000 of 6% bonds to yield an effective interest rate of 8%.
   a. Was the amount of cash received from the sale of the bonds more or less than $40,000,000?
   b. Identify the following amounts related to the bond issue: (1) face amount, (2) market rate of interest, (3) contract rate of interest, and (4) maturity amount.

10. The following data relate to an $8,000,000, 7% bond issue for a selected semiannual interest period:

Bond carrying amount at beginning of period	$8,190,000
Interest paid at end of period	560,000
Interest expense allocable to the period	540,500

   a. Were the bonds issued at a discount or at a premium?
   b. What expense account was decreased to amortize the discount or premium?

11. Of two corporations organized at approximately the same time and engaged in competing businesses, one issued $75 par common stock, and the other issued $1 par common stock. Do the par designations provide any indication as to which stock is preferable as an investment? Explain.

12. When a corporation issues stock at a premium, is the premium income? Explain.

13. a. In what respect does treasury stock differ from unissued stock?
    b. How should treasury stock be presented on the balance sheet?

14. A corporation reacquires 18,000 shares of its own $50 par common stock for $2,250,000, recording it at cost.
    a. What effect does this transaction have on revenue or expense of the period?
    b. What effect does it have on stockholders' equity?

15. The treasury stock in Question 14 is resold for $2,400,000.
    a. What is the effect on the corporation's revenue of the period?
    b. What is the effect on stockholders' equity?

16. A corporation with preferred stock and common stock outstanding has a substantial balance in its retained earnings account at the beginning of the current fiscal year. Although net income for the current year is sufficient to pay the preferred dividend of $150,000 each quarter and a common dividend of $40,000 each quarter, the board of directors declares dividends only on the preferred stock. Suggest possible reasons that the board passes the dividends on the common stock.

17. An owner of 300 shares of Colorado Spring Company common stock receives a stock dividend of 6 shares.
    a. What is the effect of the stock dividend on the stockholder's proportionate interest (equity) in the corporation?
    b. How does the total equity of 306 shares compare with the total equity of 300 shares before the stock dividend?

18. What is the primary purpose of a stock split?

Exercises

Obj **2, 7**

✔ Total current liabilities, $892,000

E8-1   Current liabilities

Carabiner Co. sold 28,000 annual magazine subscriptions for $40 during December 20Y4. These new subscribers will receive monthly issues, beginning in January 20Y5. In addition, the business had taxable income of $130,000 during the first calendar quarter of 20Y5. The federal tax rate is 40%. A quarterly tax payment will be made on April 15, 20Y5.

Prepare the Current Liabilities section of the balance sheet for Carabiner Co. on March 31, 20Y5.

E8-2 Notes payable

Obj 2

A business issued a 90-day, 6% note for $25,000 to a creditor on account. Illustrate the effects on the accounts and financial statements of recording (a) the issuance of the note and (b) the payment of the note at maturity, including interest.

E8-3 Recording income taxes

Obj 2

Illustrate the effects on the accounts and financial statements of recording the following selected transactions of Sid's Leather Co.:

Apr. 15. Paid the first installment of the estimated income tax for the current fiscal year ending December 31, $29,000. No entry had been made to record the liability.

Dec. 31. Recorded the estimated income tax liability for the year just ended and the deferred income tax liability, based on the April 15 transaction and the following data:

Income tax rate	40%
Income before income tax	$300,000
Taxable income according to tax return	$280,000

Assume that the June 15 and September 15 installments of $29,000 were also paid.

E8-4 Deferred income taxes

Obj 2

Warehouse System Inc. recognized service revenue of $960,000 on its financial statements in 20Y7. Assume, however, that the tax code requires this amount to be recognized for tax purposes in 20Y8. The taxable income for 20Y7 and 20Y8 is $7,100,000 and $8,900,000, respectively. Assume a tax rate of 40%.

Illustrate the effects on the accounts and financial statements of the tax expense, deferred taxes, and taxes payable for 20Y7 and 20Y8, respectively.

E8-5 Accrued product warranty

Obj 2

Stealth Devices Inc. warrants its products for one year. The estimated product warranty is 4% of sales. Assume that sales were $450,000 for July. In August, a customer received warranty repairs requiring $13,600 of parts.

a. Determine the warranty liability at July 31, the end of the first month of the current year.

b. What accounts are decreased for the warranty work provided in August?

E8-6 Accrued product warranty

Obj 2

Ford Motor Company disclosed the following estimated product warranty payable for two recent years.

	December 31,	
	Year 2	Year 1
	(in millions)	
Product warranty payable	$3,915	$3,855

Ford's sales in its automotive sector were $128,168 million in Year 2 and $119,280 million in Year 1. Assume that the total paid on warranty claims during Year 2 was $2,799 million.

a. Illustrate the effects on the accounts and financial statements for the Year 2 product warranty expense.

b. Explain the $60 ($3,915 − $3,855) million increase in the total warranty liability from Year 1 to Year 2.

E8-7 Contingent liabilities

Obj 2

Several months ago, Maltese Chemical Company experienced a hazardous materials spill at one of its plants. As a result, the Environmental Protection Agency (EPA) fined the company $750,000. The company is contesting the fine. In addition, an employee is seeking $300,000 damages related to the spill. Lastly, a homeowner has sued the company for $180,000. The homeowner lives 15 miles from the plant, but believes that the incident has reduced the home's resale value by $180,000.

Maltese's legal counsel believes that it is probable that the EPA fine will stand. In addition, counsel indicates that an out-of-court settlement of $90,000 has recently been reached with the employee. The final papers will be signed next week. Counsel believes that the homeowner's case is much weaker and will be decided in favor of Maltese. Other litigation related to the spill is possible, but the damage amounts are uncertain.

a. Illustrate the effects of the contingent liabilities associated with the hazardous materials spill on the accounts and financial statements.

b. Prepare a note disclosure relating to this incident.

Obj 2

E8-8   Contingent liabilities

The following note accompanied financial statements for **Goodyear Tire and Rubber Company**:

> *We are a defendant in numerous lawsuits alleging various asbestos-related personal injuries purported to result from alleged exposure to certain asbestos products manufactured by us or present in certain of our facilities. Typically, these lawsuits have been brought against multiple defendants in state and federal courts. To date, we have disposed of approximately 90,700 claims by defending and obtaining the dismissal thereof or by entering into a settlement. The sum of our accrued asbestos-related liability, . . . including legal costs totaled approximately $365 million . . .*

a. Illustrate the effects on the accounts and financial statements of recording the contingent liability of $365,000,000.

b. Why was the contingent liability recorded?

Obj 2

✔ b. Net pay, $1,749.75

E8-9   Calculate payroll

An employee earns $35 per hour and 1.5 times that rate for all hours in excess of 40 hours per week. Assume that the employee worked 52 hours during the week, and that the gross pay prior to the current week totaled $62,000. Assume further that the social security tax rate was 6.0% (on earnings up to $100,000), the Medicare tax rate was 1.5%, and federal income tax to be withheld was $128.

a. Determine the gross pay for the week.

b. Determine the net pay for the week.

Obj 2

✔ (3) Total earnings, $786,000

E8-10   Summary payroll data

In the following summary of data for a payroll period, some amounts have been intentionally omitted:

Earnings:	
1. At regular rate	?
2. At overtime rate	$113,000
3. Total earnings	?
Deductions:	
4. FICA tax	54,375
5. Income tax withheld	144,750
6. Medical insurance	72,875
7. Union dues	?
8. Total deductions	294,750
9. Net amount paid	491,250
Accounts increased:	
10. Factory Wages	551,500
11. Sales Salaries	?
12. Office Salaries	100,000

Calculate the amounts omitted in lines (1), (3), (7), and (11).

E8-11 Recording payroll taxes

Obj 2

According to a summary of the payroll of Zumwalt Co., $345,000 was subject to the 7.5% FICA tax. Also, $30,000 was subject to state and federal unemployment taxes.

a. Calculate the employer's payroll taxes, using the following rates: state unemployment, 4.3%; federal unemployment, 0.8%.

b. Illustrate the effects on the accounts and financial statements of recording the accrual of payroll taxes.

E8-12 Accrued vacation pay

Obj 2

A business provides its employees with varying amounts of vacation per year, depending on the length of employment. The estimated amount of the current year's vacation pay is $518,400. Illustrate the effects on the accounts and financial statements of the adjustment required on January 31, the end of the first month of the current year, to record the accrued vacation pay.

E8-13 Bond price

Obj 3

Walt Disney 7% bonds due in 2032 were recently selling for 149.01. Were the bonds selling at a premium or at a discount? Explain.

E8-14 Issuing bonds

Obj 3

Cyber Tech Inc. produces and distributes fiber optic cable for use by telecommunications companies. Cyber Tech Inc. issued $50,000,000 of 20-year, 6% bonds on March 1 at their face amount, with interest payable on March 1 and September 1. The fiscal year of the company is the calendar year. Illustrate the effects on the accounts and financial statements of recording the following selected transactions for the current year:

Mar. 1. Issued the bonds for cash at their face amount.
Sept. 1. Paid the interest on the bonds.
Dec. 31. Recorded accrued interest for four months.

E8-15 Dividends per share

Obj 4, 5

✔ Preferred stock, Ist year: $0.80

Scan Tech Inc., a developer of radiology equipment, has stock outstanding as follows: 24,000 shares of 2% preferred stock of $75 par, and 100,000 shares of $8 par common. During its first four years of operations, the following amounts were distributed as dividends: first year, $19,200; second year, $30,000; third year, $75,000; fourth year, $120,000. Calculate the dividends per share on each class of stock for each of the four years.

E8-16 Dividends per share

Obj 4, 5

✔ Preferred stock, 3rd year: $0.15

Sea Horse Inc., a software development firm, has stock outstanding as follows: 80,000 shares of 1% preferred stock of $15 par, and 200,000 shares of $65 par common. During its first four years of operations, the following amounts were distributed as dividends: first year, $4,000; second year, $10,400; third year, $40,000; fourth year, $90,000. Calculate the dividends per share on each class of stock for each of the four years.

E8-17 Issuing par stock

Obj 4

On January 29, Quality Marble Inc., a marble contractor, issued for cash 75,000 shares of $10 par common stock at $23, and on May 31, it issued for cash 100,000 shares of $4 par preferred stock at $6.

a. Illustrate the effects on the accounts and financial statements of the January 29 and May 31 transactions.

b. What is the total amount invested (total paid-in capital) by all stockholders as of May 31?

Obj 4

E8-18 Issuing stock for assets other than cash

On August 7, Easy Up Corporation, a wholesaler of hydraulic lifts, acquired land in exchange for 20,000 shares of $10 par common stock with a current market price of $14.

Illustrate the effect on the accounts and financial statements of the purchase of the land.

Obj 4

E8-19 Treasury stock transactions

Calgary Water Supply Inc. bottles and distributes spring water. On September 9 of the current year, Calgary Water Supply reacquired 20,000 shares of its common stock at $44 per share.

a. What is the balance of Treasury Stock on December 31 of the current year?

b. Where will the balance of Treasury Stock be reported on the balance sheet?

c. For what reasons might Calgary Water Supply have purchased the treasury stock?

Obj 4

E8-20 Treasury stock transactions

Sun Dance Gardens Inc. develops and produces spraying equipment for lawn maintenance and industrial uses. On June 3 of the current year, Sun Dance Gardens Inc. reacquired 28,000 shares of its common stock at $37 per share.

a. What is the balance of Treasury Stock on December 31 of the current year?

b. How will the balance in Treasury Stock be reported on the balance sheet?

c. Assume that Sun Dance Gardens sold 10,000 shares of its treasury stock at $40 on November 2. What accounts would be affected by the sale of the treasury stock?

Obj 4

E8-21 Treasury stock transactions

Banff Water Inc. bottles and distributes spring water. On April 2 of the current year, Banff Water Inc. reacquired 30,000 shares of its common stock at $33 per share.

a. What is the balance of Treasury Stock on December 31 of the current year?

b. Where will the balance of Treasury Stock be reported on the balance sheet?

c. For what reasons might Banff Water Inc. have purchased the treasury stock?

d. Assume that on January 25 of the following year, Banff Water Inc. sold 20,000 shares of its treasury stock for $40 per share. Illustrate the effects on the accounts and financial statements of the sale of the treasury stock.

Obj 5

E8-22 Cash dividends

The dates of importance in connection with a cash dividend declared and paid of $375,000 on a corporation's common stock are June 6, July 15, and August 14. Illustrate the effects on the accounts and financial statements for each date.

Obj 5, 6

E8-23 Effect of cash dividend and stock split

Indicate whether the following actions would (+) increase, (−) decrease, or (0) not affect Ballistic Scientific Inc.'s total assets, liabilities, and stockholders' equity:

	Assets	Liabilities	Stockholders' Equity
(1) Declaring a cash dividend	_____	_____	_____
(2) Paying the cash dividend declared in (1)	_____	_____	_____
(3) Authorizing and issuing stock certificates in a stock split	_____	_____	_____
(4) Declaring a stock dividend	_____	_____	_____
(5) Issuing stock certificates for the stock dividend declared in (4)	_____	_____	_____

E8-24 Effect of stock split

Obj **6**

Papa's Restaurant Corporation wholesales ovens and ranges to restaurants throughout the Northeast. Papa's Restaurant Corporation, which had 18,000 shares of common stock outstanding, declared a 4-for-1 stock split (3 additional shares for each share issued).

a. What will be the number of shares outstanding after the split?

b. If the common stock had a market price of $280 per share before the stock split, what would be an approximate market price per share after the split?

E8-25 Stockholders' Equity section of balance sheet

Obj **7**

✔ Total stockholders' equity, $8,616,000

The following accounts and their balances appear in the ledger of Amazon Properties Inc. on April 30 of the current year:

Common Stock, $25 par	$ 900,000
Paid-In Capital in Excess of Par	216,000
Paid-In Capital from Sale of Treasury Stock	24,000
Retained Earnings	7,680,000
Treasury Stock	204,000

Prepare the Stockholders' Equity section of the balance sheet as of April 30. Fifty thousand shares of common stock are authorized, and 4,000 shares have been reacquired.

E8-26 Stockholders' Equity section of balance sheet

Obj **7**

✔ Total stockholders' equity, $22,818,000

Premium Imports Inc. retails racing products for BMWs, Porsches, and Ferraris. The following accounts and their balances appear in the ledger of Premium Imports Inc. on November 30, the end of the current year:

Common Stock, $8 par	$ 3,200,000
Paid-In Capital in Excess of Par—Common Stock	700,000
Paid-In Capital in Excess of Par—Preferred Stock	182,000
Paid-In Capital from Sale of Treasury Stock—Common	150,000
Preferred 2% Stock, $80 par	2,080,000
Retained Earnings	17,250,000
Treasury Stock—Common	744,000

Forty thousand shares of preferred and 500,000 shares of common stock are authorized. There are 62,000 shares of common stock held as treasury stock.

Prepare the Stockholders' Equity section of the balance sheet as of November 30, the end of the current year.

E8-27 Effect of financing on earnings per share

Obj **8**

✔ a. $0.60

BSF Co., which produces and sells skiing equipment, is financed as follows:

Bonds payable, 8% (issued at face amount)	$7,500,000
Preferred 2% stock, $10 par	7,500,000
Common stock, $50 par	7,500,000

Income tax is estimated at 40% of income.

Determine the earnings per share of common stock, assuming that the income before bond interest and income tax is (a) $1,000,000, (b) $3,000,000, and (c) $4,500,000.

E8-28 Evaluate alternative financing plans

Obj **8**

Based on the data in Exercise 8-27, discuss factors other than earnings per share that should be considered in evaluating such financing plans.

Problems

Obj 2

✔ 1. Year-end
balance, 3rd year,
$150,000

P8-1   Income tax allocation

Differences between the accounting methods applied to accounts and financial reports and those used in determining taxable income yielded the following amounts for the first four years of a corporation's operations:

	First Year	Second Year	Third Year	Fourth Year
Income before income taxes	$425,000	$750,000	$900,000	$1,350,000
Taxable income	350,000	650,000	700,000	1,725,000

The income tax rate for each of the four years was 40% of taxable income, and each year's taxes were promptly paid.

Instructions

1. Determine for each year the amounts described by the following captions, presenting the information in the form indicated:

Year	Income Tax Deducted on Income Statement	Income Tax Payments for the Year	Deferred Income Tax Payable	
			Year's Addition (Deduction)	Year-End Balance

2. Total the first three amount columns.

3. Illustrate the effects of recording the current and deferred tax liabilities on the accounts and financial statements for the first year.

Obj 2
✔ 1. $46,875

P8-2   Recording payroll and payroll taxes

The following information about the payroll for the week ended July 17 was obtained from the records of Anaconda Mining Co.:

Salaries:		Deductions:	
Sales salaries	$315,000	Income tax withheld	$98,000
Warehouse salaries	185,000	U.S. savings bonds	15,000
Office salaries	125,000	Group insurance	12,500
	$625,000		

Tax rates assumed:
FICA tax, 7.5% of employee annual earnings
State unemployment (employer only), 4.2%
Federal unemployment (employer only), 0.8%

Instructions

1. For the July 17 payroll, determine the employee FICA tax payable.

2. Illustrate the effect on the accounts and financial statements of paying and recording the July 17 payroll.

3. Determine the following amounts for the employer payroll taxes related to the July 17 payroll: (a) FICA tax payable, (b) state unemployment tax payable, and (c) federal unemployment tax payable.

4. Illustrate the effect on the accounts and financial statements of recording the liability for the July 17 payroll taxes.

P8-3   Bond premium; bonds payable transactions

Obj **3**

Beaufort Vaults Corporation produces and sells burial vaults. On July 1, 20Y3, Beaufort Vaults Corporation issued $25,000,000 of 10-year, 8% bonds at par. Interest on the bonds is payable semiannually on December 31 and June 30. The fiscal year of the company is the calendar year.

Instructions

1. Illustrate the effects of the issuance of the bonds on July 1, 20Y3, on the accounts and financial statements.

2. Illustrate the effects of the first semiannual interest payment on December 31, 20Y3, on the accounts and financial statements.

3. Illustrate the effects of the payment of the face value of bonds at maturity on the accounts and financial statements.

4. If the market rate of interest were 7% on July 1, 20Y3, would the bonds have sold at a discount or premium?

P8-4   Stock transactions for corporate expansion

Obj **4**

Vaga Optics produces medical lasers for use in hospitals. The accounts and their balances appear in the ledger of Vaga Optics on December 31 of the current year as follows:

Preferred 2% Stock, $120 par (50,000 shares authorized, 25,000 shares issued)	$ 3,000,000
Paid-In Capital in Excess of Par—Preferred Stock	400,000
Common Stock, $75 par (500,000 shares authorized, 300,000 shares issued)	22,500,000
Paid-In Capital in Excess of Par—Common Stock	540,000
Retained Earnings	55,000,000

At the annual stockholders' meeting on January 31, the board of directors presented a plan for modernizing and expanding plant operations at a cost of approximately $9,500,000. The plan provided (a) that the corporation borrow $4,500,000, (b) that 20,000 shares of the unissued preferred stock be issued through an underwriter, and (c) that a building, valued at $1,200,000, and the land on which it is located, valued at $900,000, be acquired in accordance with preliminary negotiations by the issuance of 27,400 shares of common stock. The plan was approved by the stockholders and accomplished by the following transactions:

Mar. 8.   Borrowed $4,500,000 from Conrad National Bank, giving a 6% mortgage note.
     13.   Issued 20,000 shares of preferred stock, receiving $130 per share in cash.
     26.   Issued 27,400 shares of common stock in exchange for land and a building, according to the plan.

No other transactions occurred during March.

Instructions

Illustrate the effects on the accounts and financial statements of each of the preceding transactions.

P8-5   Dividends on preferred and common stock

Obj **4, 5**

Yukon Bike Corp. manufactures mountain bikes and distributes them through retail outlets in Canada, Montana, Idaho, Oregon, and Washington. Yukon Bike Corp. has declared the following annual dividends over a six-year period ending December 31 of each year: Year 1, $28,000; Year 2, $44,000; Year 3, $48,000; Year 4, $60,000; Year 5, $76,000; and Year 6, $140,000. During the entire period, the outstanding stock of the company was composed of 40,000 shares of 2% preferred stock, $65 par, and 50,000 shares of common stock, $1 par.

✔ 1. Preferred
dividends in
Year 2: $44,000

Instructions

1. Determine the total dividends and the per-share dividends declared on each class of stock for each of the six years. Summarize the data in tabular form, using the following column headings:

Year	Total Dividends	Preferred Dividends		Common Dividends	
		Total	Per Share	Total	Per Share
Year 1	$ 28,000				
Year 2	44,000				
Year 3	48,000				
Year 4	60,000				
Year 5	76,000				
Year 6	140,000				

2. Calculate the average annual dividend per share for each class of stock for the six-year period.

3. Assuming that the preferred stock was sold at $57.50 and common stock was sold at $5.00 at the beginning of the six-year period, calculate the average annual percentage return on initial shareholders' investment, based on the average annual dividend per share (a) for preferred stock and (b) for common stock.

....

Obj | 8

✔ 1. Plan 3: $1.72

P8-6   Effect of financing on earnings per share

Three different plans for financing a $5,000,000 corporation are under consideration by its organizers. Under each of the following plans, the securities will be issued at their par or face amount, and the income tax rate is estimated at 40% of income.

	Plan 1	Plan 2	Plan 3
8% bonds	—	—	$2,500,000
Preferred 4% stock, $100 par	—	$2,500,000	1,250,000
Common stock, $5 par	$5,000,000	2,500,000	1,250,000
Total	$5,000,000	$5,000,000	$5,000,000

Instructions

1. Determine for each plan the earnings per share of common stock, assuming that the income before bond interest and income tax is $1,000,000.

2. Determine for each plan the earnings per share of common stock, assuming that the income before bond interest and income tax is $300,000.

3. Discuss the advantages and disadvantages of each plan.

Financial Analysis

....

Obj | 9

FA 8-1   Ratio of stockholders' equity to total assets; price-earnings ratio

The Home Depot, Inc. operates over 2,200 home improvement retail stores and is a competitor of **Lowe's.** The following data (in millions) were adapted from a recent financial statement of The Home Depot.

	Year 2	Year 1
Total assets	$40,518	$40,125
Total liabilities	22,620	21,236
Total stockholders' equity	17,898	18,889
Earnings per share	2.49	2.03

1. Compute the ratio of liabilities to total assets for Years 1 and 2. Round to one decimal place.

2. Given your answer to part (1), what is the ratio of stockholders' equity to total assets? Round to one decimal place.

3. Compute the ratio of liabilities to stockholders' equity. Round to one decimal place.

4. Are Home Depot's operations financed primarily with liabilities or equity?

5. Comparing Years 1 and 2, should creditors feel more or less safe in Year 2?

6. With a market price of $66.60, compute the price-earnings ratio for Year 2.

7. With a market price of $44.20, compute the price-earnings ratio for Year 1.

8. Compare the results from parts (6) and (7). Comment on any differences.

FA 8-2   Ratio of stockholders' equity to total assets; price-earnings ratio

Obj 9

1. Compare the ratio of liabilities to total assets for Lowe's (see the chapter illustration on page 306) and The Home Depot (FA 8-1). Comment on any differences.

2. Compare the price-earnings ratios of Lowe's (see the chapter illustration on pages 306–307) and The Home Depot (FA 8-1). Comment on any differences.

FA 8-3   Ratio of stockholders' equity to total assets; price-earnings ratio

Obj 9

Google Inc. is a technology company that offers users Internet search and e-mail services. Google also developed the Android operating system for use with cell phones and other mobile devices. The following data (in millions) were adapted from a recent financial statement of Google.

	Year 2	Year 1
Total assets	$93,798	$72,574
Total liabilities	22,083	14,429
Total stockholders' equity	71,715	58,145
Earnings per share	32.81	29.76

1. Compute the ratio of liabilities to total assets for Years 1 and 2. Round to one decimal place.

2. Given your answer to part (1), what is the ratio of stockholders' equity to total assets? Round to one decimal place.

3. Compute the ratio of liabilities to stockholders' equity. Round to one decimal place.

4. Are Google's operations financed primarily with liabilities or equity?

5. Comparing Years 1 and 2, should creditors feel more or less safe in Year 2?

6. With a market price of $762.10, compute the price-earnings ratio for Year 2.

7. With a market price of $596.33, compute the price-earnings ratio for Year 1.

8. Compare the results from parts (6) and (7). Comment on any differences.

FA 8-4   Ratio of stockholders' equity to total assets; price-earnings ratio

Obj 9

Apple Inc. is a technology company that designs, produces, and sells a variety of digital devices, including the iPod, iPhone, and iPad. The following data (in millions) were adapted from a recent financial statement of Apple.

	Year 2	Year 1
Total assets	$176,064	$116,371
Total liabilities	57,854	39,756
Total stockholders' equity	118,210	76,615
Earnings per share	44.64	28.05

1. Compute the ratio of liabilities to total assets for Years 1 and 2. Round to one decimal place.

2. Given your answer to part (1), what is the ratio of stockholders' equity to total assets? Round to one decimal place.

3. Compute the ratio of liabilities to stockholders' equity. Round to one decimal place.

4. Are Apple's operations financed primarily with liabilities or equity?

5. Comparing Years 1 and 2, should creditors feel more or less safe in Year 2?

6. With a market price of $444.38, compute the price-earnings ratio for Year 2.

7. With a market price of $459.68, compute the price-earnings ratio for Year 1.

8. Compare the results from parts (6) and (7). Comment on any differences.

Obj 9

FA 8-5 Ratio of stockholders' equity to total assets; price-earnings ratio

For each of the following companies, indicate whether you think the ratio of liabilities to total assets is more than 50%. Also, indicate whether you think the price-earnings ratio is above 10.

	Ratio of Liabilities to Total Assets More than 50% (Yes, No)	Price-Earnings Ratio Above 10 (Yes, No)
Alcoa		
Boeing		
Dell		
McDonald's		
Nike		
Walmart		

Cases

Case 8-1 Ethics and professional conduct in business

Jas Carillo was discussing summer employment with Maria Perez, president of Valparaiso Construction Service:

Maria: I'm glad that you're thinking about joining us for the summer. We could certainly use the help.

Jas: Sounds good. I enjoy outdoor work, and I could use the money to help with next year's school expenses.

Maria: I've got a plan that can help you out on that. As you know, I'll pay you $8 per hour; but in addition, I'd like to pay you with cash. Since you're only working for the summer, it really doesn't make sense for me to go to the trouble of formally putting you on our payroll system. In fact, I do some jobs for my clients on a strictly cash basis, so it would be easy to just pay you that way.

Jas: Well, that's a bit unusual, but I guess money is money.

Maria: Yeah, not only that, it's tax-free!

Jas: What do you mean?

Maria: Didn't you know? Any money that you receive in cash is not reported to the IRS on a W-2 form; therefore, the IRS doesn't know about the income—hence, it's the same as tax-free earnings.

1. Why does Maria Perez want to conduct business transactions using cash (not check or credit card)?

2. How should Jas respond to Maria's suggestion?

INTERNET PROJECT

Case 8-2 Contingent liabilities

Altria Group, Inc., has a note dedicated to describing contingent liabilities in its recent financial statements. This note includes extensive descriptions of multiple contingent liabilities. Go to the Web site **http://www.sec.gov/edgar/searchedgar/companysearch.html**, enter MO as the ticker symbol, click on 10-K Documents, and click on Form 10-K. Using the Table of Contents and excerpts from the annual report, answer the following questions.

1. What are the major business units of Altria Group?

2. Based on your understanding of this company, why would Altria Group require a note on contingent liabilities?

Case 8-3   Issuing stock

Sahara Unlimited Inc. began operations on January 2, 20Y4, with the issuance of 250,000 shares of $8 par common stock. The sole stockholders of Sahara Unlimited Inc. are Karina Takemoto and Dr. Noah Grove, who organized Sahara Unlimited Inc. with the objective of developing a new flu vaccine. Dr. Grove claims that the flu vaccine, which is nearing the final development stage, will protect individuals against 80% of the flu types that have been medically identified. To complete the project, Sahara Unlimited Inc. needs $25,000,000 of additional funds. The banks have been unwilling to loan the funds because of the lack of sufficient collateral and the riskiness of the business. The following is a conversation between Karina Takemoto, the chief executive officer of Sahara Unlimited Inc., and Dr. Noah Grove, the leading researcher:

Karina: What are we going to do? The banks won't loan us any more money, and we've got to have $25 million to complete the project. We are so close! It would be a disaster to quit now. The only thing I can think of is to issue additional stock. Do you have any suggestions?

Noah: I guess you're right. But if the banks won't loan us any more money, how do you think we can find any investors to buy stock?

Karina: I've been thinking about that. What if we promise the investors that we will pay them 2% of net sales until they have received an amount equal to what they paid for the stock?

Noah: What happens when we pay back the $25 million? Do the investors get to keep the stock? If they do, it'll dilute our ownership.

Karina: How about, if after we pay back the $25 million, we make them turn in their stock for what they paid for it? Plus, we could pay them an additional $50 per share. That's a $50 profit per share for the investors.

Noah: It could work. We get our money, but don't have to pay any interest or dividends until we start generating net sales. At the same time, the investors could get their money back plus $50 per share.

Karina: We'll need current financial statements for the new investors. I'll get our accountant working on them and contact our attorney to draw up a legally binding contract for the new investors. Yes, this could work.

In late 20Y4, the attorney and the various regulatory authorities approved the new stock offering, and shares of common stock were privately sold to new investors for $25,000,000.

In preparing financial statements for 20Y4, Karina Takemoto and Glenn Bergum, the controller for Sahara Unlimited Inc., have the following conversation:

Glenn: Karina, I've got a problem.

Karina: What's that, Glenn?

Glenn: Issuing common stock to raise that additional $25 million was a great idea. But …

Karina: But what?

Glenn: I've got to prepare the 20Y4 annual financial statements, and I am not sure how to classify the common stock.

Karina: What do you mean? It's common stock.

Glenn: I'm not so sure. I called the auditor and explained how we are contractually obligated to pay the new stockholders 2% of net sales until they receive what they paid for the stock. Then, we may be obligated to pay them $50 per share.

Karina: So …

Glenn: So the auditor thinks that we should classify the additional issuance of $25 million as debt, not stock! And, if we put the $25 million on the balance sheet as debt, we will violate our other loan agreements with the banks. And, if these agreements are violated, the banks may call in all our debt immediately. If they do that, we are in deep trouble. We'll probably have to file for bankruptcy. We just don't have the cash to pay off the banks.

1. Discuss the arguments for and against classifying the issuance of the $25 million of stock as debt.
2. What do you think might be a practical solution to this classification problem?

Case 8-4   Preferred stock vs. bonds

Living Smart Inc. has decided to expand its operations to owning and operating long-term health care facilities. The following is an excerpt from a conversation between the chief executive officer, Mark Vierra, and the vice president of finance, Jolin Kilcup.

Mark: Jolin, have you given any thought to how we're going to finance the acquisition of St. George Health Care?

Jolin: Well, the two basic options, as I see it, are to issue either preferred stock or bonds. The equity market is a little depressed right now. The rumor is that the Federal Reserve Bank may increase the interest rates either this month or next.

Mark: Yes, I've heard the rumor. The problem is that we can't wait around to see what's going to happen. We'll have to move on this next week if we want any chance to complete the acquisition of St. George.

Jolin: Well, the bond market is strong right now. Maybe we should issue debt this time around.

Mark: That's what I would have guessed as well. St. George's financial statements look pretty good, except for the volatility of its income and cash flows. But that's characteristic of the industry.

Discuss the advantages and disadvantages of issuing preferred stock versus bonds.

Case 8-5   Financing business expansion

You hold a 30% common stock interest in the family-owned business, a vending machine company. Your sister, who is the manager, has proposed an expansion of plant facilities at an expected cost of $6,000,000. Two alternative plans have been suggested as methods of financing the expansion. Each plan is briefly described as follows:

Plan 1. Issue $6,000,000 of 15-year, 8% notes at face amount.
Plan 2. Issue an additional 100,000 shares of $20 par common stock at $25 per share, and $3,500,000 of 15-year, 8% notes at face amount.

The balance sheet as of the end of the previous fiscal year is as follows:

MOJAVE OASIS, INC.
Balance Sheet
December 31, 20Y6

Assets	
Current assets	$10,000,000
Property, plant, and equipment	15,000,000
Total assets	$25,000,000
Liabilities and Stockholders' Equity	
Liabilities	$ 7,000,000
Common stock, $20	8,000,000
Paid-in capital in excess of par	300,000
Retained earnings	9,700,000
Total liabilities and stockholders' equity	$25,000,000

Net income has remained relatively constant over the past several years. The expansion program is expected to increase yearly income before bond interest and income tax from $900,000 in the previous year to $1,200,000 for this year. Your sister has asked you, as the company treasurer, to prepare an analysis of each financing plan.

1. Prepare a table indicating the expected earnings per share on the common stock under each plan. Assume an income tax rate of 25%.

2. a. Discuss the factors that should be considered in evaluating the two plans.

   b. Which plan offers the greater benefit to the present stockholders? Give reasons for your opinion.

Case 8-6   Profiling a corporation

GROUP PROJECT

INTERNET PROJECT

Select a public corporation you are familiar with or which interests you. Using the Internet, your school library, and other sources, develop a short (one to two pages) profile of the corporation. Include in your profile the following information:

1. Name of the corporation
2. State of incorporation
3. Nature of its operations
4. Total assets for the most recent balance sheet
5. Total revenues for the most recent income statement
6. Net income for the most recent income statement
7. Classes of stock outstanding
8. Market price of the stock outstanding
9. High and low price of the stock for the past year
10. Dividends paid for each share of stock during the past year

In groups of three or four, discuss each corporate profile. Select one of the corporations, assuming that your group has $100,000 to invest in its stock. Summarize why your group selected the corporation it did and how financial accounting information may have affected your decision. Keep track of the performance of your corporation's stock for the remainder of the term.

Note: Most major corporations maintain "home pages" on the Internet. This home page provides a variety of information on the corporation and often includes the corporation's financial statements. In addition, the New York Stock Exchange Web site (**http://www.nyse.com**) includes links to the home pages of many listed companies. Financial statements also can be accessed using EDGAR, the electronic archives of financial statements filed with the Securities and Exchange Commission (SEC).

SEC documents can also be retrieved using the EdgarScan™ service at **http://www.sec.gov/edgar/searchedgar/webusers.htm**. To obtain annual report information, key in a company name in the appropriate space. EDGAR will list the reports available to you for the company you've selected. Select the most recent annual report filing, identified as a 10-K or 10-K405.

Answers to Self-Examination Questions

1. **C**   The maturity value is $5,100, determined as follows:

Face amount of note	$5,000
Plus interest ($5,000 × 0.12 × 60/360)	100
Maturity value	$5,100

2. **B**   Employers are usually required to withhold a portion of their employees' earnings for payment of federal income taxes (answer A), FICA tax (answer C), and state and local income taxes (answer D). Generally, federal unemployment compensation taxes (answer B) are levied against the employer only and thus are not deducted from employee earnings.

3. **D**   The employer incurs an expense for FICA tax (answer A), federal unemployment compensation tax (answer B), and state unemployment compensation tax (answer C). The employees' federal income tax (answer D) is not an expense of the employer. It is withheld from the employees' earnings.

4. **B** Since the contract rate on the bonds is higher than the prevailing market rate, a rational investor would be willing to pay more than the face amount, or a premium (answer B), for the bonds. If the contract rate and the market rate were equal, the bonds could be expected to sell at their face amount (answer A). Likewise, if the market rate is higher than the contract rate, the bonds would sell at a price below their face amount (answer D) or at a discount (answer C).

5. **C** If a corporation that holds treasury stock declares a cash dividend, the dividends are not paid on the treasury shares. To do so would place the corporation in the position of earning income through dealing with itself. Thus, the corporation will record $44,000 (answer C) as cash dividends [(25,000 shares issued less 3,000 shares held as treasury stock) $\times$ $2 per share dividend].

CHAPTER 9

Financial Statement Analysis

LEARNING OBJECTIVES
After studying this chapter, you should be able to:

Obj | **1** Describe basic financial statement analytical methods.

Obj | **2** Use financial statement analysis to assess the liquidity and solvency of a business.

Obj | **3** Use financial statement analysis to assess the profitability of a business.

Obj | **4** Describe the contents of corporate annual reports.

" Just do it." These three words identify one of the most recognizable brands in the world, Nike. While this phrase inspires athletes to "compete and achieve their potential," it also defines the company.

Nike began in 1964 as a partnership between University of Oregon track coach Bill Bowerman and one of his former student-athletes, Phil Knight. The two began by selling shoes imported from Japan out of the back of Knight's car to athletes at track and field events. As sales grew, the company opened retail outlets and began to develop its own shoes. In 1971, the company, originally named Blue Ribbon Sports, commissioned a graphic design student at Portland State University to develop the Nike Swoosh logo for a fee of $35. In 1978, the company changed its name to Nike, and in 1980, it sold its first shares of stock to the public.

Nike would have been a great company in which to have invested. If you had invested in Nike's common stock back in 1990, you would have paid $5 per share. Recently, Nike's stock sold for $96 per share. Unfortunately, you can't invest using hindsight.

How then should you select companies in which to invest? Like any significant purchase, you should do some research to guide your investment decision. If you were buying a car, for example, you might go to **Edmunds.com** to obtain reviews, ratings, prices, specifications, options, and fuel economy across a number of vehicles. In deciding whether to invest in a company, you can use financial analysis to gain insight into a company's past performance and future prospects. This chapter describes and illustrates common financial data that can be analyzed to assist you in making investment decisions such as whether or not to invest in Nike's stock.

Source: http://www.nikebiz.com/.

Obj | 1

Describe basic financial
statement analytical
methods.

Basic Analytical Methods

Users analyze a company's financial statements using a variety of analytical methods. Three such methods are as follows:

1. Horizontal analysis
2. Vertical analysis
3. Common-sized statements

Horizontal Analysis

The percentage analysis of increases and decreases in related items in comparative financial statements is called **horizontal analysis**. Each item on the most recent statement is compared with the related item on one or more earlier statements in terms of the following:

1. *Amount* of increase or decrease
2. *Percent* of increase or decrease

When comparing statements, the earlier statement is normally used as the base for computing increases and decreases.

Exhibit 1 illustrates horizontal analysis for the December 31, 20Y6 and 20Y5 balance sheets of Mooney Company. In Exhibit 1, the December 31, 20Y5, balance sheet (the earliest year presented) is used as the base.

Exhibit 1 indicates that total assets decreased by $91,000 (7.4%), liabilities decreased by $133,000 (30.0%), and stockholders' equity increased by $42,000 (5.3%). It appears that most of the decrease in long-term liabilities of $100,000 was achieved through the sale of long-term investments.

EXHIBIT 1

**Comparative
Balance Sheet—
Horizontal
Analysis**

Mooney Company
Comparative Balance Sheet
December 31, 20Y6 and 20Y5

	Dec. 31, 20Y6	Dec. 31, 20Y5	Increase (Decrease) Amount	Percent
Assets				
Current assets	$ 550,000	$ 533,000	$ 17,000	3.2%
Long-term investments	95,000	177,500	(82,500)	(46.5%)
Property, plant, and equipment (net)	444,500	470,000	(25,500)	(5.4%)
Intangible assets	50,000	50,000	—	—
Total assets	$1,139,500	$1,230,500	$ (91,000)	(7.4%)
Liabilities				
Current liabilities	$ 210,000	$ 243,000	$ (33,000)	(13.6%)
Long-term liabilities	100,000	200,000	(100,000)	(50.0%)
Total liabilities	$ 310,000	$ 443,000	$(133,000)	(30.0%)
Stockholders' Equity				
Preferred 6% stock, $100 par	$ 150,000	$ 150,000	—	—
Common stock, $10 par	500,000	500,000	—	—
Retained earnings	179,500	137,500	$ 42,000	30.5%
Total stockholders' equity	$ 829,500	$ 787,500	$ 42,000	5.3%
Total liabilities and stockholders' equity	$1,139,500	$1,230,500	$ (91,000)	(7.4%)

The balance sheets in Exhibit 1 may be expanded or supported by a separate schedule that includes the individual asset and liability accounts. For example, Exhibit 2 is a supporting schedule of Mooney's current asset accounts.

Exhibit 2 indicates that while cash and temporary investments increased, accounts receivable and inventories decreased. The decrease in accounts receivable could be caused by improved collection policies, which would increase cash. The decrease in inventories could be caused by increased sales.

	Dec. 31, 20Y6	Dec. 31, 20Y5	Increase (Decrease) Amount	Percent
Cash	$ 90,500	$ 64,700	$ 25,800	39.9%
Temporary investments	75,000	60,000	15,000	25.0%
Accounts receivable (net)	115,000	120,000	(5,000)	(4.2%)
Inventories	264,000	283,000	(19,000)	(6.7%)
Prepaid expenses	5,500	5,300	200	3.8%
Total current assets	$550,000	$533,000	$ 17,000	3.2%

Mooney Company
Comparative Schedule of Current Assets
December 31, 20Y6 and 20Y5

EXHIBIT 2

Comparative Schedule of Current Assets— Horizontal Analysis

Exhibit 3 illustrates horizontal analysis for the 20Y6 and 20Y5 income statements of Mooney Company. Exhibit 3 indicates an increase in sales of $296,500, or 24.0%. However, the percentage increase in sales of 24.0% was accompanied by an even greater percentage increase in the cost of goods (merchandise) sold

Mooney Company
Comparative Income Statement
For the Years Ended December 31, 20Y6 and 20Y5

	20Y6	20Y5	Increase (Decrease) Amount	Percent
Sales	$1,530,500	$1,234,000	$296,500	24.0%
Sales returns and allowances	32,500	34,000	(1,500)	(4.4%)
Net sales	$1,498,000	$1,200,000	$298,000	24.8%
Cost of goods sold	1,043,000	820,000	223,000	27.2%
Gross profit	$ 455,000	$ 380,000	$ 75,000	19.7%
Selling expenses	$ 191,000	$ 147,000	$ 44,000	29.9%
Administrative expenses	104,000	97,400	6,600	6.8%
Total operating expenses	$ 295,000	$ 244,400	$ 50,600	20.7%
Income from operations	$ 160,000	$ 135,600	$ 24,400	18.0%
Other income	8,500	11,000	(2,500)	(22.7%)
	$ 168,500	$ 146,600	$ 21,900	14.9%
Other expense (interest)	6,000	12,000	(6,000)	(50.0%)
Income before income tax	$ 162,500	$ 134,600	$ 27,900	20.7%
Income tax expense	71,500	58,100	13,400	23.1%
Net income	$ 91,000	$ 76,500	$ 14,500	19.0%

EXHIBIT 3

Comparative Income Statement— Horizontal Analysis

of 27.2%.[1] Thus, gross profit increased by only 19.7% rather than by the 24.0% increase in sales.

Exhibit 3 also indicates that selling expenses increased by 29.9%. Thus, the 24.0% increase in sales could have been caused by an advertising campaign, which increased selling expenses. Administrative expenses increased by only 6.8%, total operating expenses increased by 20.7%, and income from operations increased by 18.0%. Interest expense decreased by 50.0%. This decrease was probably caused by the 50.0% decrease in long-term liabilities (Exhibit 1). Overall, net income increased by 19.0%, a favorable result.

Exhibit 4 illustrates horizontal analysis for the 20Y6 and 20Y5 retained earnings statements of Mooney Company. Exhibit 4 indicates that retained earnings increased by 30.5% for the year. The increase is due to net income of $91,000 for the year, less dividends of $49,000.

EXHIBIT 4

Comparative Retained Earnings Statement— Horizontal Analysis

Mooney Company Comparative Retained Earnings Statement For the Years Ended December 31, 20Y6 and 20Y5			Increase (Decrease)	
	20Y6	20Y5	Amount	Percent
Retained earnings, January 1	$137,500	$100,000	$37,500	37.5%
Net income for the year	91,000	76,500	14,500	19.0%
Total	$228,500	$176,500	$52,000	29.5%
Dividends:				
On preferred stock	$ 9,000	$ 9,000	—	—
On common stock	40,000	30,000	$10,000	33.3%
Total	$ 49,000	$ 39,000	$10,000	25.6%
Retained earnings, December 31	$179,500	$137,500	$42,000	30.5%

Vertical Analysis

The percentage analysis of the relationship of each component in a financial statement to a total within the statement is called **vertical analysis**. Although vertical analysis is applied to a single statement, it may be applied on the same statement over time. This enhances the analysis by showing how the percentages of each item have changed over time.

In vertical analysis of the balance sheet, the percentages are computed as follows:

1. Each asset item is stated as a percent of the total assets.
2. Each liability and stockholders' equity item is stated as a percent of the total liabilities and stockholders' equity.

Exhibit 5 illustrates the vertical analysis of the December 31, 20Y6 and 20Y5 balance sheets of Mooney Company. Exhibit 5 indicates that current assets have increased from 43.3% to 48.3% of total assets. Long-term investments decreased from 14.4% to 8.3% of total assets. Stockholders' equity increased from 64.0% to 72.8% with a comparable decrease in liabilities.

1. The term *cost of goods sold* is often used in practice in place of *cost of merchandise sold*. Such usage is followed in this chapter.

EXHIBIT 5

Comparative Balance Sheet— Vertical Analysis

Mooney Company
Comparative Balance Sheet
December 31, 20Y6 and 20Y5

	Dec. 31, 20Y6		Dec. 31, 20Y5	
	Amount	Percent	Amount	Percent
Assets				
Current assets	$ 550,000	48.3%	$ 533,000	43.3%
Long-term investments	95,000	8.3	177,500	14.4
Property, plant, and equipment (net)	444,500	39.0	470,000	38.2
Intangible assets	50,000	4.4	50,000	4.1
Total assets	$1,139,500	100.0%	$1,230,500	100.0%
Liabilities				
Current liabilities	$ 210,000	18.4%	$ 243,000	19.7%
Long-term liabilities	100,000	8.8	200,000	16.3
Total liabilities	$ 310,000	27.2%	$ 443,000	36.0%
Stockholders' Equity				
Preferred 6% stock, $100 par	$ 150,000	13.2%	$ 150,000	12.2%
Common stock, $10 par	500,000	43.9	500,000	40.6
Retained earnings	179,500	15.7	137,500	11.2
Total stockholders' equity	$ 829,500	72.8%	$ 787,500	64.0%
Total liabilities and stockholders' equity	$1,139,500	100.0%	$1,230,500	100.0%

In a vertical analysis of the income statement, each item is stated as a percent of net sales. Exhibit 6 illustrates the vertical analysis of the 20Y6 and 20Y5 income statements of Mooney Company.

EXHIBIT 6

Comparative Income Statement— Vertical Analysis

Mooney Company
Comparative Income Statement
For the Years Ended December 31, 20Y6 and 20Y5

	20Y6		20Y5	
	Amount	Percent	Amount	Percent
Sales	$1,530,500	102.2%	$1,234,000	102.8%
Sales returns and allowances	32,500	2.2	34,000	2.8
Net sales	$1,498,000	100.0%	$1,200,000	100.0%
Cost of goods sold	1,043,000	69.6	820,000	68.3
Gross profit	$ 455,000	30.4%	$ 380,000	31.7%
Selling expenses	$ 191,000	12.8%	$ 147,000	12.3%
Administrative expenses	104,000	6.9	97,400	8.1
Total operating expenses	$ 295,000	19.7%	$ 244,400	20.4%
Income from operations	$ 160,000	10.7%	$ 135,600	11.3%
Other income	8,500	0.6	11,000	0.9
	$ 168,500	11.3%	$ 146,600	12.2%
Other expense (interest)	6,000	0.4	12,000	1.0
Income before income tax	$ 162,500	10.9%	$ 134,600	11.2%
Income tax expense	71,500	4.8	58,100	4.8
Net income	$ 91,000	6.1%	$ 76,500	6.4%

Exhibit 6 indicates a decrease of the gross profit rate from 31.7% in 20Y5 to 30.4% in 20Y6. Although this is only a 1.3 percentage points (31.7% − 30.4%) decrease, in dollars of potential gross profit, it represents a decrease of about $19,500 (1.3% × $1,498,000). Thus, a small percentage decrease can have a large dollar effect.

Common-Sized Statements

In a **common-sized statement**, all items are expressed as percentages with no dollar amounts shown. Common-sized statements are often useful for comparing one company with another or for comparing a company with industry averages.

Exhibit 7 illustrates common-sized income statements for Mooney Company and Lowell Corporation.

EXHIBIT 7

Common-Sized Income Statement

	Mooney Company	Lowell Corporation
Sales	102.2%	102.3%
Sates returns and allowances	2.2	2.3
Net sales	100.0%	100.0%
Cost of goods sold	69.6	70.0
Gross profit	30.4%	30.0%
Selling expenses	12.8%	11.5%
Administrative expenses	6.9	4.1
Total operating expenses	19.7%	15.6%
Income from operations	10.7%	14.4%
Other income	0.6	0.6
	11.3%	15.0%
Other expense (interest)	0.4	0.5
Income before income tax	10.9%	14.5%
Income tax expense	4.8	5.5
Net income	6.1%	9.0%

The percentages of gross profit and net income to sales for a recent year for **Target** and **Walmart** are shown below.

	Target	Walmart
Gross profit to sales	31.5%	25.0%
Net income to sales	4.2%	3.5%

Walmart has a significantly lower gross profit margin percentage than does Target, which is likely due to Walmart's aggressive pricing strategy. However, Target's gross profit margin advantage shrinks when comparing the net income to sales ratio. Target must have larger selling and administrative expenses to sales than does Walmart. Even so, Target's net income to sales is still 0.7 percentage point better than Walmart's net income to sales.

Exhibit 7 indicates that Mooney Company has a slightly higher rate of gross profit (30.4%) than Lowell Corporation (30.0%). However, Mooney has a higher percentage of selling expenses (12.8%) and administrative expenses (6.9%) than does Lowell (11.5% and 4.1%). As a result, the income from operations of Mooney (10.7%) is less than that of Lowell (14.4%).

The unfavorable difference of 3.7 (14.4% − 10.7%) percentage points in income from operations would concern the managers and other stakeholders of Mooney. The underlying causes of the difference should be investigated and possibly corrected. For example, Mooney Company may decide to outsource some of its administrative duties so that its administrative expenses are more comparative to those of Lowell Corporation.

Other Analytical Measures

Other relationships may be expressed in ratios and percentages. Often, these relationships are compared within the same statement and thus are a type of vertical analysis. Comparing these items with items from earlier periods is a type of horizontal analysis.

Analytical measures are not ends in themselves. They are only guides in evaluating financial and operating data. Many other factors, such as trends in the industry and general economic conditions, should also be considered when analyzing a company.

Liquidity and Solvency Analysis

All users of financial statements are interested in the ability of a company to do the following:

1. Maintain liquidity and solvency
2. Earn income, called **profitability**

The ability to convert assets into cash is called **liquidity**, while the ability of a business to pay its debts is called **solvency**. Liquidity, solvency, and profitability are interrelated. For example, a company that cannot convert assets into cash may have difficulty taking advantage of profitable courses of action requiring immediate cash outlays. Likewise, a company that cannot pay its debts will have difficulty obtaining credit. The lack of credit will, in turn, limit the company's ability to purchase merchandise or expand operations, which decreases its profitability.

Liquidity and solvency are normally assessed using the following:

1. Current position analysis
        Working capital
        Current ratio
        Quick ratio
2. Accounts receivable analysis
        Accounts receivable turnover
        Number of days' sales in receivables
3. Inventory analysis
        Inventory turnover
        Number of days' sales in inventory
4. The ratio of fixed assets to long-term liabilities
5. The ratio of liabilities to stockholders' equity
6. The number of times interest charges are earned

The Mooney Company financial statements presented earlier are used to illustrate the preceding analyses.

Current Position Analysis

A company's ability to pay its current liabilities is called **current position analysis**. It is of special interest to short-term creditors and includes the computation and analysis of the following:

1. Working capital
2. Current ratio
3. Quick ratio

Working Capital A company's **working capital** is computed as follows:

$$\text{Working Capital} = \text{Current Assets} - \text{Current Liabilities}$$

To illustrate, the working capital for Mooney Company for 20Y6 and 20Y5 is computed below.

	20Y6	20Y5
Current assets	$550,000	$533,000
Less current liabilities	210,000	243,000
Working capital	$340,000	$290,000

The working capital is used to evaluate a company's ability to pay current liabilities. A company's working capital is often monitored monthly, quarterly, or yearly by creditors and other debtors. However, it is difficult to use working capital to compare companies of different sizes. For example, working capital of $250,000 may be adequate for a local hardware store, but it would be inadequate for The Home Depot.

Current Ratio The **current ratio**, sometimes called the *working capital ratio* or *bankers' ratio,* is computed as follows:

$$\text{Current Ratio} = \frac{\text{Current Assets}}{\text{Current Liabilities}}$$

To illustrate, the current ratio for Mooney Company is computed below.

	20Y6	20Y5
Current assets	$550,000	$533,000
Current liabilities	$210,000	$243,000
Current ratio	2.6 ($550,000 ÷ $210,000)	2.2 ($533,000 ÷ $243,000)

The current ratio is a more reliable indicator of the ability to pay current liabilities than is working capital. To illustrate, assume that as of December 31, 20Y6, the working capital of a competitor is much greater than $340,000, but its current ratio is only 1.3. Considering these facts alone, Mooney Company, with its current ratio of 2.6, is in a more favorable position to obtain short-term credit than the competitor, which has the greater amount of working capital.

Quick Ratio One limitation of working capital and the current ratio is that they do not consider the makeup of the current assets. Because of this, two companies may have the same working capital and current ratios, but differ significantly in their ability to pay their current liabilities.

To illustrate, the current assets and liabilities for Mooney Company and Wendt Corporation as of December 31, 20Y6, are as follows:

	Mooney Company	Wendt Corporation
Current assets:		
Cash	$ 90,500	$ 45,500
Temporary investments	75,000	25,000
Accounts receivable (net)	115,000	90,000
Inventories	264,000	380,000
Prepaid expenses	5,500	9,500
Total current assets	$550,000	$550,000
Total current assets	$550,000	$550,000
Less current liabilities	210,000	210,000
Working capital	$340,000	$340,000
Current ratio ($550,000/$210,000)	2.6	2.6

Mooney and Wendt both have a working capital of $340,000 and current ratios of 2.6. Wendt, however, has more of its current assets in inventories. These inventories must be sold and the receivables collected before all the current liabilities can be paid. This takes time. In addition, if the market for its product declines, Wendt may have difficulty selling its inventory. This, in turn, could impair its ability to pay its current liabilities.

In contrast, Mooney's current assets contain more cash, temporary investments, and accounts receivable, which can easily be converted to cash. Thus, Mooney is in a stronger current position than Wendt to pay its current liabilities.

A ratio that measures the "instant" debt-paying ability of a company is the **quick ratio**, sometimes called the *acid-test ratio*. The quick ratio is computed as follows:

$$\text{Quick Ratio} = \frac{\text{Quick Assets}}{\text{Current Liabilities}}$$

Microsoft Corporation maintains a high quick ratio—2.5 for a recent year. Microsoft's stable and profitable software business has allowed it to develop a strong cash position coupled with no short-term notes payable.

Quick assets are cash and other current assets that can be easily converted to cash. Quick assets normally include cash, temporary investments, and receivables. To illustrate, the quick ratio for Mooney Company is computed below.

	20Y6	20Y5
Quick assets:		
Cash	$ 90,500	$ 64,700
Temporary investments	75,000	60,000
Accounts receivable (net)	115,000	120,000
Total quick assets	$280,500	$244,700
Current liabilities	$210,000	$243,000
Quick ratio	1.3*	1.0**

*1.3 = $280,500 ÷ $210,000
**1.0 = $244,700 ÷ $243,000

Accounts Receivable Analysis

A company's ability to collect its accounts receivable is called **accounts receivable analysis**. It includes the computation and analysis of the following:

1. Accounts receivable turnover
2. Number of days' sales in receivables

Collecting accounts receivable as quickly as possible improves a company's liquidity. In addition, the cash collected from receivables may be used to improve or expand operations. Quick collection of receivables also reduces the risk of uncollectible accounts.

Accounts Receivable Turnover The **accounts receivable turnover** is computed as follows:

$$\text{Accounts Receivable Turnover} = \frac{\text{Net Sales}[2]}{\text{Average Accounts Receivable}}$$

To illustrate, the accounts receivable turnover for Mooney Company for 20Y6 and 20Y5 is computed below.

	20Y6	20Y5
Net sales	$1,498,000	$1,200,000
Accounts receivable (net):		
Beginning of year	$ 120,000	$ 140,000
End of year	115,000	120,000
Total	$ 235,000	$ 260,000
Average accounts receivable	$117,500 ($235,000 ÷ 2)	$130,000 ($260,000 ÷ 2)
Accounts receivable turnover	12.7 ($1,498,000 ÷ $117,500)	9.2 ($1,200,000 ÷ $130,000)

The increase in Mooney's accounts receivable turnover from 9.2 to 12.7 indicates that the collection of receivables has improved during 20Y6. This may be due to a change in how credit is granted, collection practices, or both.

For Mooney Company, the average accounts receivable was computed using the accounts receivable balance at the beginning and the end of the year. When sales are seasonal and thus vary throughout the year, monthly balances of receivables are often used. Also, if sales on account include notes receivable as well as accounts receivable, notes and accounts receivable are normally combined for analysis.

Number of Days' Sales in Receivables The **number of days' sales in receivables** is computed as follows:[3]

$$\text{Number of Days' Sales in Receivables} = \frac{\text{Average Accounts Receivable}}{\text{Average Daily Sales}}$$

where

$$\text{Average Daily Sales} = \frac{\text{Net Sales}}{365 \text{ days}}$$

---

2. If known, credit sales should be used in the numerator. Because credit sales are not normally known by external users, net sales is used in the numerator.

3. The number of days' sales in receivables can also be computed as: $\dfrac{365 \text{ Days}}{\text{Accounts Receivable Turnover}}$

To illustrate, the number of days' sales in receivables for Mooney Company is computed below.

	20Y6	20Y5
Average accounts receivable	$117,500 ($235,000 ÷ 2)	$130,000 ($260,000 ÷ 2)
Average daily sales	$4,104 ($1,498,000 ÷ 365)	$3,288 ($1,200,000 ÷ 365)
Number of days' sales in receivables	28.6 ($117,500 ÷ $4,104)	39.5 ($130,000 ÷ $3,288)

The number of days' sales in receivables is an estimate of the time (in days) that the accounts receivable have been outstanding. The number of days' sales in receivables is often compared with a company's credit terms to evaluate the efficiency of the collection of receivables.

To illustrate, if Mooney's credit terms are 2/10, n/30, then Mooney was very *inefficient* in collecting receivables in 20Y5. In other words, receivables should have been collected in 30 days or less, but were being collected in 39.5 days. Although collections improved during 20Y6 to 28.6 days, there is probably still room for improvement. On the other hand, if Mooney's credit terms are n/45, then there is probably little room for improving collections.

Inventory Analysis

A company's ability to manage its inventory effectively is evaluated using **inventory analysis**. It includes the computation and analysis of the following:

1. Inventory turnover
2. Number of days' sales in inventory

Excess inventory decreases liquidity by tying up funds (cash) in inventory. In addition, excess inventory increases insurance expense, property taxes, storage costs, and other related expenses. These expenses further reduce funds that could be used elsewhere to improve or expand operations.

Excess inventory also increases the risk of losses because of price declines or obsolescence of the inventory. On the other hand, a company should keep enough inventory in stock so that it doesn't lose sales because of lack of inventory.

Inventory Turnover The **inventory turnover** is computed as follows:

$$\text{Inventory Turnover} = \frac{\text{Cost of Goods Sold}}{\text{Average Inventory}}$$

To illustrate, the inventory turnover for Mooney Company for 20Y6 and 20Y5 is computed below.

	20Y6	20Y5
Cost of goods sold	$1,043,000	$820,000
Inventories:		
Beginning of year	$ 283,000	$311,000
End of year	264,000	283,000
Total	$ 547,000	$594,000
Average inventory	$273,500 ($547,000 ÷ 2)	$297,000 ($594,000 ÷ 2)
Inventory turnover	3.8 ($1,043,000 ÷ $273,500)	2.8 ($820,000 ÷ $297,000)

The increase in Mooney's inventory turnover from 2.8 to 3.8 indicates that the management of inventory has improved in 20Y6. The inventory turnover improved because of an increase in the cost of goods sold, which indicates more sales, and a decrease in the average inventories.

What is considered a good inventory turnover varies by type of inventory, companies, and industries. For example, grocery stores have a higher inventory turnover than jewelers or furniture stores. Likewise, within a grocery store, perishable foods have a higher turnover than the soaps and cleansers.

Number of Days' Sales in Inventory The **number of days' sales in inventory** is computed as follows:[4]

$$\text{Number of Days' Sales in Inventory} = \frac{\text{Average Inventory}}{\text{Average Daily Cost of Goods Sold}}$$

where

$$\text{Average Daily Cost of Goods Sold} = \frac{\text{Cost of Goods Sold}}{365 \text{ days}}$$

To illustrate, the number of days' sales in inventory for Mooney Company is computed below.

	20Y6	20Y5
Average inventory	$273,500 ($547,000 ÷ 2)	$297,000 ($594,000 ÷ 2)
Average daily cost of goods sold	$2,858 ($1,043,000 ÷ 365)	$2,247 ($820,000 ÷ 365)
Number of days' sales in inventory	95.7 ($273,500 ÷ $2,858)	132.2 ($297,000 ÷ $2,247)

The number of days' sales in inventory is a rough measure of the length of time it takes to purchase, sell, and replace the inventory. Mooney's number of days' sales in inventory improved from 132.2 days to 95.7 days during 20Y6. This is a major improvement in managing inventory.

Ratio of Fixed Assets to Long-Term Liabilities

The **ratio of fixed assets to long-term liabilities** provides a measure of whether noteholders or bondholders will be paid. Since fixed assets are often pledged as security for long-term notes and bonds, it is computed as follows:

$$\text{Ratio of Fixed Assets to Long-Term Liabilities} = \frac{\text{Fixed Assets (net)}}{\text{Long-Term Liabilities}}$$

To illustrate, the ratio of fixed assets to long-term liabilities for Mooney Company is computed below.

	20Y6	20Y5
Fixed assets (net)	$444,500	$470,000
Long-term liabilities	$100,000	$200,000
Ratio of fixed assets to long-term liabilities	4.4 ($444,500 ÷ $100,000)	2.4 ($470,000 ÷ $200,000)

4. The number of days' sales in inventory can also be computed as: $\dfrac{365 \text{ Days}}{\text{Inventory Turnover}}$

During 20Y6, Mooney's ratio of fixed assets to long-term liabilities increased from 2.4 to 4.4. This increase was due primarily to Mooney paying off one-half of its long-term liabilities in 20Y6.

Ratio of Liabilities to Stockholders' Equity

The **ratio of liabilities to stockholders' equity** measures how much of the company is financed by debt and equity. It is computed as follows:

$$\text{Ratio of Liabilities to Stockholders' Equity} = \frac{\text{Total Liabilities}}{\text{Total Stockholders' Equity}}$$

To illustrate, the ratio of liabilities to stockholders' equity for Mooney Company is computed below.

	20Y6	20Y5
Total liabilities	$310,000	$443,000
Total stockholders' equity	$829,500	$787,500
Ratio of liabilities to stockholders' equity	0.4 ($310,000 ÷ $829,500)	0.6 ($443,000 ÷ $787,500)

Mooney's ratio of liabilities to stockholders' equity decreased from 0.6 to 0.4 during 20Y6. This is an improvement and indicates that Mooney's creditors have an adequate margin of safety.

The ratio of liabilities to stockholders' equity varies across industries as in the following examples:

Delta Air Lines   47.1
Procter & Gamble 1.1

Number of Times Interest Charges Earned

The **number of times interest charges are earned**, sometimes called the *fixed charge coverage ratio,* measures the risk that interest payments will not be made if earnings decrease. It is computed as follows:

$$\frac{\text{Number of Times Interest}}{\text{Charges Are Earned}} = \frac{\text{Income Before Income Tax} + \text{Interest Expense}}{\text{Interest Expense}}$$

Interest expense is paid before income taxes. In other words, interest expense is deducted in determining taxable income and, thus, income tax. For this reason, income *before taxes* is used in computing the number of times interest charges are earned.

The *higher* the ratio, the more likely interest payments will be paid if earnings decrease. To illustrate, the number of times interest charges are earned for Mooney Company is computed below.

	20Y6	20Y5
Income before income tax	$162,500	$134,600
Add interest expense	6,000	12,000
Amount available to pay interest	$168,500	$146,600
Number of times interest charges earned	28.1 ($168,500 ÷ $6,000)	12.2 ($146,600 ÷ $12,000)

The number of times interest charges are earned improved from 12.2 to 28.1 during 20Y6. This indicates that Mooney Company has sufficient earnings to pay interest expense.

The number of times interest charges are earned can be adapted for use with dividends on preferred stock. In this case, the *number of times preferred dividends are earned* is computed as follows:

$$\text{Number of Times Preferred Dividends Are Earned} = \frac{\text{Net Income}}{\text{Preferred Dividends}}$$

Since dividends are paid after taxes, net income is used in computing the number of times preferred dividends are earned. The *higher* the ratio, the more likely preferred dividend payments will be paid if earnings decrease.

Obj 3

Use financial statement analysis to assess the profitability of a business.

Profitability Analysis

Profitability analysis focuses on the ability of a company to earn profits. This ability is reflected in the company's operating results, as reported in its income statement. The ability to earn profits also depends on the assets the company has available for use in its operations, as reported in its balance sheet. Thus, income statement and balance sheet relationships are often used in evaluating profitability.

Common profitability analyses include the following:

1. Ratio of net sales to assets
2. Rate earned on total assets
3. Rate earned on stockholders' equity
4. Rate earned on common stockholders' equity
5. Earnings per share on common stock
6. Price-earnings ratio
7. Dividends per share
8. Dividend yield

Ratio of Net Sales to Assets

The **ratio of net sales to assets** measures how effectively a company uses its assets. It is computed as follows:

$$\text{Ratio of Net Sales to Assets} = \frac{\text{Net Sales}}{\substack{\text{Average Total Assets} \\ \text{(excluding long-term investments)}}}$$

As shown above, any long-term investments are excluded in computing the ratio of net sales to assets. This is because long-term investments are unrelated to normal operations and net sales.

To illustrate, the ratio of net sales to assets for Mooney Company is computed below.

	20Y6	20Y5
Net sales	$1,498,000	$1,200,000
Total assets		
(excluding long-term investments):		
Beginning of year	$1,053,000	$1,010,000
End of year	1,044,500	1,053,000
Total	$2,097,500	$2,063,000
Average total assets	$1,048,750 ($2,097,500 ÷ 2)	$1,031,500 ($2,063,000 ÷ 2)
Ratio of net sales to assets	1.4 ($1,498,000 ÷ $1,048,750)	1.2 ($1,200,000 ÷ $1,031,500)

For Mooney Company, the average total assets was computed using total assets (excluding long-term investments) at the beginning and the end of the year. The average total assets could also be based on monthly or quarterly averages.

The ratio of net sales to assets indicates that Mooney's use of its operating assets has improved in 20Y6. This was primarily due to the increase in net sales in 20Y6.

Rate Earned on Total Assets

The **rate earned on total assets** measures the profitability of total assets, without considering how the assets are financed. In other words, this rate is not affected by the portion of assets financed by creditors or stockholders. It is computed as follows:

$$\text{Rate Earned on Total Assets} = \frac{\text{Net Income} + \text{Interest Expense}}{\text{Average Total Assets}}$$

The rate earned on total assets is computed by adding interest expense to net income. By adding interest expense to net income, the effect of whether the assets are financed by creditors (debt) or stockholders (equity) is eliminated. Because net income includes any income earned from long-term investments, the average total assets includes long-term investments as well as the net operating assets.

To illustrate, the rate earned on total assets by Mooney Company is computed below.

	20Y6	20Y5
Net income	$ 91,000	$ 76,500
Plus interest expense	6,000	12,000
Total	$ 97,000	$ 88,500
Total assets:		
Beginning of year	$1,230,500	$1,187,500
End of year	1,139,500	1,230,500
Total	$2,370,000	$2,418,000
Average total assets	$1,185,000 ($2,370,000 ÷ 2)	$1,209,000 ($2,418,000 ÷ 2)
Rate earned on total assets	8.2% ($97,000 ÷ $1,185,000)	7.3% ($88,500 ÷ $1,209,000)

The rate earned on total assets improved from 7.3% to 8.2% during 20Y6.

The *rate earned on operating assets* is sometimes computed when there are large amounts of nonoperating income and expense. It is computed as follows:

$$\text{Rate Earned on Operating Assets} = \frac{\text{Income from Operations}}{\text{Average Operating Assets}}$$

Since Mooney Company does not have a significant amount of nonoperating income and expense, the rate earned on operating assets is not illustrated.

Rate Earned on Stockholders' Equity

The **rate earned on stockholders' equity** measures the rate of income earned on the amount invested by the stockholders. It is computed as follows:

$$\text{Rate Earned on Stockholders' Equity} = \frac{\text{Net Income}}{\text{Average Total Stockholders' Equity}}$$

To illustrate, the rate earned on stockholders' equity for Mooney Company is computed below.

	20Y6	20Y5
Net income	$ 91,000	$ 76,500
Stockholders' equity:		
Beginning of year	$ 787,500	$ 750,000
End of year	829,500	787,500
Total	$1,617,000	$1,537,500
Average stockholders' equity	$808,500 ($1,617,000 ÷ 2)	$768,750 ($1,537,500 ÷ 2)
Rate earned on stockholders' equity	11.3% ($91,000 ÷ $808,500)	10.0% ($76,500 ÷ $768,750)

The approximate rates earned on assets and stockholders' equity for **Molson Coors Brewing Company** and **Anheuser-Busch InBev SA/NV** for a recent fiscal year are shown below.

	Molson Coors	Anheuser-Busch
Rate earned on assets	6.3%	10.2%
Rate earned on stockholders' equity	8.8%	21.9%

Anheuser-Busch has been more profitable and has benefited from a greater use of leverage than has Molson Coors.

The rate earned on stockholders' equity improved from 10.0% to 11.3% during 20Y6.

Leverage involves using debt to increase the return on an investment. The rate earned on stockholders' equity is normally higher than the rate earned on total assets. This is because of the effect of leverage.

For Mooney Company, the effect of leverage for 20Y6 is 3.1%, computed as follows:

Rate earned on stockholders' equity	11.3%
Less rate earned on total assets	8.2
Effect of leverage	3.1%

Exhibit 8 shows the 20Y6 and 20Y5 effects of leverage for Mooney Company.

EXHIBIT 8
Effect of Leverage

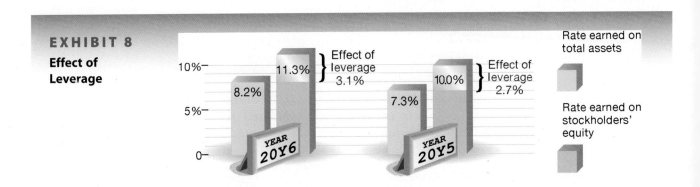

Rate Earned on Common Stockholders' Equity

The **rate earned on common stockholders' equity** measures the rate of profits earned on the amount invested by the common stockholders. It is computed as follows:

$$\text{Rate Earned on Common Stockholders' Equity} = \frac{\text{Net Income} - \text{Preferred Dividends}}{\text{Average Common Stockholders' Equity}}$$

Because preferred stockholders rank ahead of the common stockholders in their claim on earnings, any preferred dividends are subtracted from net income in computing the rate earned on common stockholders' equity.

To illustrate, the rate earned on common stockholders' equity for Mooney Company is computed below.

	20Y6	**20Y5**
Net income	$ 91,000	$ 76,500
Less preferred dividends	9,000	9,000
Total	$ 82,000	$ 67,500
Common stockholders' equity:		
Beginning of year	$ 637,500	$ 600,000
End of year	679,500	637,500
Total	$1,317,000	$1,237,500
Average common stockholders' equity	$658,500 ($1,317,000 ÷ 2)	$618,750 ($1,237,500 ÷ 2)
Rate earned on common stockholders' equity	12.5% ($82,000 ÷ $658,500)	10.9% ($67,500 ÷ $618,750)

Mooney Company had $150,000 of 6% preferred stock outstanding on December 31, 20Y6 and 20Y5. Thus, preferred dividends of $9,000 ($150,000 × 6%) were deducted from net income. Mooney's common stockholders' equity was determined as follows:

	December 31		
	20Y6	**20Y5**	**20Y4**
Common stock, $10 par	$500,000	$500,000	$500,000
Retained earnings	179,500	137,500	100,000
Common stockholders' equity	$679,500	$637,500	$600,000

The retained earnings on December 31, 20Y4, of $100,000 is the same as the retained earnings on January 1, 20Y5, as shown in Mooney's retained earnings statement in Exhibit 4.

Mooney Company's rate earned on common stockholders' equity improved from 10.9% to 12.5% in 20Y6. This rate differs from the rates earned by Mooney Company on total assets and stockholders' equity as shown below.

	20Y6	**20Y5**
Rate earned on total assets	8.2%	7.3%
Rate earned on stockholders' equity	11.3%	10.0%
Rate earned on common stockholders' equity	12.5%	10.9%

These rates differ because of leverage, as discussed in the preceding section.

Earnings per Share on Common Stock

Earnings per share (EPS) on common stock measures the share of profits that are earned by a share of common stock. Generally accepted accounting principles (GAAP) require the reporting of earnings per share on the income statement.[5] As a result, earnings per share (EPS) is often reported in the financial press. It is computed as follows:

$$\text{Earnings per Share (EPS) on Common Stock} = \frac{\text{Net Income} - \text{Preferred Dividends}}{\text{Shares of Common Stock Outstanding}}$$

5. FASB, *Accounting Standards Codification*, Section 260.10.

When preferred and common stock are outstanding, preferred dividends are subtracted from net income to determine the income related to the common shares. Mooney Company had $150,000 of 6% preferred stock outstanding on December 31, 20Y6 and 20Y5. Thus, preferred dividends of $9,000 ($150,000 × 6%) are deducted from net income in computing earnings per share on common stock.

To illustrate, the earnings per share (EPS) of common stock for Mooney Company is computed below.

	20Y6	20Y5
Net income	$91,000	$76,500
Preferred dividends	9,000	9,000
Total	$82,000	$67,500
Shares of common stock outstanding	50,000	50,000
Earnings per share on common stock	$1.64 ($82,000 ÷ 50,000)	$1.35 ($67,500 ÷ 50,000)

As shown above, Mooney's earnings per share (EPS) on common stock improved from $1.35 to $1.64 during 20Y6. Mooney did not issue any additional shares of common stock in 20Y6. If Mooney had issued additional shares in 20Y6, a weighted average of common shares outstanding during the year would have been used.

Mooney Company has a simple capital structure with only common stock and preferred stock outstanding. Many corporations, however, have complex capital structures with various types of equity securities outstanding, such as convertible preferred stock, stock options, and stock warrants. In such cases, the possible effects of such securities on the shares of common stock outstanding are considered in reporting earnings per share. These possible effects are reported separately as *earnings per common share assuming dilution* or *diluted earnings per share*.[6] This topic is described and illustrated in advanced accounting courses and textbooks.

Price-Earnings Ratio

The **price-earnings (P/E) ratio** on common stock measures a company's future earnings prospects. It is often quoted in the financial press and is computed as follows:

$$\text{Price-Earnings (P/E) Ratio} = \frac{\text{Market Price per Share of Common Stock}}{\text{Earnings per Share on Common Stock}}$$

To illustrate, the price-earnings (P/E) ratio for Mooney Company is computed below.

	20Y6	20Y5
Market price per share of common stock	$41.00	$27.00
Earnings per share on common stock	$1.64	$1.35
Price-earnings ratio on common stock	25 ($41 ÷ $1.64)	20 ($27 ÷ $1.35)

The price-earnings ratio improved from 20 to 25 during 20Y6. In other words, a share of common stock of Mooney Company was selling for 20 times earnings per share at the end of 20Y5. At the end of 20Y6, the common stock was selling for 25 times earnings per share. This indicates that the market expects Mooney to experience favorable earnings in the future.

6. Ibid., Section 260.10.

Dividends per Share

Dividends per share measures the extent to which earnings are being distributed to common shareholders. It is computed as follows:

$$\text{Dividends per Share} = \frac{\text{Dividends}}{\text{Shares of Common Stock Outstanding}}$$

The dividends per share, dividend yield, and P/E ratio of a common stock are normally quoted on the daily listing of stock prices in *The Wall Street Journal* and on Yahoo!'s finance Web site.

To illustrate, the dividends per share for Mooney Company are computed below.

	20Y6	20Y5
Dividends	$40,000	$30,000
Shares of common stock outstanding	50,000	50,000
Dividends per share of common stock	$0.80 ($40,000 ÷ 50,000)	$0.60 ($30,000 ÷ 50,000)

The dividends per share of common stock increased from $0.60 to $0.80 during 20Y6.

Dividends per share are often reported with earnings per share. Comparing the two per-share amounts indicates the extent to which earnings are being retained for use in operations. To illustrate, the dividends and earnings per share for Mooney Company are shown in Exhibit 9.

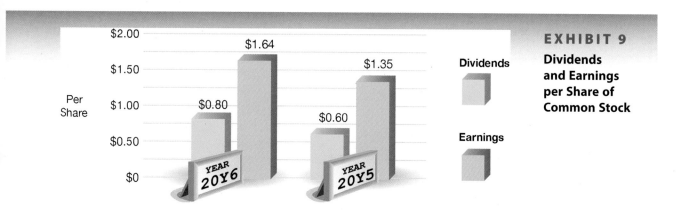

EXHIBIT 9

Dividends and Earnings per Share of Common Stock

Dividend Yield

The **dividend yield** on common stock measures the rate of return to common stockholders from cash dividends. It is of special interest to investors, whose objective is to earn revenue (dividends) from their investment. It is computed as follows:

$$\text{Dividend Yield} = \frac{\text{Dividends per Share of Common Stock}}{\text{Market Price per Share of Common Stock}}$$

To illustrate, the dividend yield for Mooney Company is computed below.

	20Y6	20Y5
Dividends per share of common stock	$0.80	$0.60
Market price per share of common stock	$41.00	$27.00
Dividend yield on common stock	2.0% ($0.80 ÷ $41)	2.2% ($0.60 ÷ $27)

The dividend yield declined slightly from 2.2% to 2.0% in 20Y6. This decline was primarily due to the increase in the market price of Mooney's common stock.

Summary of Analytical Measures

Exhibit 10 shows a summary of the liquidity, solvency, and profitability measures discussed in this chapter. The type of industry and the company's operations usually affect which measures are used. In many cases, additional measures are

EXHIBIT 10 **Summary of Analytical Measures**

	Method of Computation	
Liquidity and solvency measures:		
Working Capital	Current Assets − Current Liabilities	To indicate the ability to meet currently maturing obligations
Current Ratio	$\dfrac{\text{Current Assets}}{\text{Current Liabilities}}$	
Quick Ratio	$\dfrac{\text{Quick Assets}}{\text{Current Liabilities}}$	To indicate instant debt-paying
Accounts Receivable Turnover	$\dfrac{\text{Net Sales}}{\text{Average Accounts Receivable}}$	To assess the efficiency in collecting receivables and in the management of credit
Numbers of Days' Sales in Receivables	$\dfrac{\text{Average Accounts Receivable}}{\text{Average Daily Sales}}$	
Inventory Turnover	$\dfrac{\text{Cost of Goods Sold}}{\text{Average Inventory}}$	To assess the efficiency in the management of inventory
Number of Days' Sales in Inventory	$\dfrac{\text{Average Inventory}}{\text{Average Daily Cost of Goods Sold}}$	
Ratio of Fixed Assets to Long-Term Liabilities	$\dfrac{\text{Fixed Assets (net)}}{\text{Long-Term Liabilities}}$	To indicate the margin of safety to long-term creditors
Ratio of Liabilities to Stockholders' Equity	$\dfrac{\text{Total Liabilities}}{\text{Total Stockholders' Equity}}$	To indicate the margin of safety to creditors
Number of Times Interest Charges Are Earned	$\dfrac{\text{Income Before Income Tax + Interest Expense}}{\text{Interest Expense}}$	To assess the risk to debtholders in terms of number of times interest charges were earned
Profitability measures:		
Ratio of Net Sales to Assets	$\dfrac{\text{Net Sales}}{\text{Average Total Assets (excluding long-term investments)}}$	To assess the effectiveness in the use of assets
Rate Earned on Total Assets	$\dfrac{\text{Net Income ÷ Interest Expense}}{\text{Average Total Assets}}$	To assess the profitability of the assets
Rate Earned on Stockholders' Equity	$\dfrac{\text{Net Income}}{\text{Average Total Stockholders' Equity}}$	To assess the profitability of the investment by stockholders
Rate Earned on Common Stockholders' Equity	$\dfrac{\text{Net Income − Preferred Dividends}}{\text{Average Common Stockholders' Equity}}$	To assess the profitability of the investment by common stockholders
Earnings per Share on Common Stock	$\dfrac{\text{Net Income − Preferred Dividends}}{\text{Shares of Common Stock Outstanding}}$	
Price-Earnings Ratio	$\dfrac{\text{Market Price per Share of Common Stock}}{\text{Earnings per Share on Common Stock}}$	To indicate future earnings prospects, based on the relationship between market value of common stock and earnings
Dividends per Share	$\dfrac{\text{Dividends}}{\text{Shares of Common Stock Outstanding}}$	To indicate the extent to which earnings are being distributed to common stockholders
Dividend Yield	$\dfrac{\text{Dividends per Share of Common Stock}}{\text{Market Price per Share of Common Stock}}$	To indicate the rate of return to common stockholders in terms of dividends

Integrity, Objectivity, and Ethics in Business

ONE BAD APPLE

A recent survey by *CFO* magazine reported that 47% of chief financial officers have been pressured by the chief executive officer to use questionable accounting. In addition, only 38% of those surveyed feel less pressure to use aggressive accounting today than in years past, while 20% believe there is more pressure. Perhaps more troublesome is the chief financial officers' confidence in the quality of financial information, with only 27% being "very confident" in the quality of financial information presented by public companies.

Source: D. Durfee, "It's Better (and Worse) Than You Think," *CFO*, May 3, 2004.

used for a specific industry. For example, airlines use *revenue per passenger mile* and *cost per available seat* as profitability measures. Likewise, hotels use *occupancy rates* as a profitability measure.

The analytical measures shown in Exhibit 10 are a useful starting point for analyzing a company's liquidity, solvency, and profitability. However, they are not a substitute for sound judgment. For example, the general economic and business environment should always be considered in analyzing a company's future prospects. In addition, any trends and interrelationships among the measures should be carefully studied.

Corporate Annual Reports

Obj **4**

Describe the contents of corporate annual reports.

Public corporations issue annual reports summarizing their operating activities for the past year and plans for the future. Such annual reports include the financial statements and the accompanying notes. In addition, annual reports normally include the following sections:

1. Management's discussion and analysis
2. Report on internal control
3. Report on fairness of the financial statements

Management's Discussion and Analysis

Management's Discussion and Analysis (MD&A) is required in annual reports filed with the Securities and Exchange Commission. It includes management's analysis of current operations and its plans for the future. Typical items included in the MD&A include the following:

1. Management's analysis and explanations of any significant changes between the current and prior years' financial statements.
2. Important accounting principles or policies that could affect interpretation of the financial statements, including the effect of changes in accounting principles or the adoption of new accounting principles.
3. Management's assessment of the company's liquidity and the availability of capital to the company.
4. Significant risk exposures that might affect the company.
5. Any "off-balance-sheet" arrangements such as leases not included directly in the financial statements. Such arrangements are discussed in advanced accounting courses and textbooks.

HOW BUSINESSES MAKE MONEY

INVESTING STRATEGIES

How do people make investment decisions? Investment decisions, like any major purchase, must meet the needs of the buyer. For example, if you have a family of five and are thinking about buying a new car, you probably wouldn't buy a two-seat sports car. It just wouldn't meet your objectives or fit your lifestyle. Alternatively, if you are a young single person, a minivan might not meet your immediate needs. Investors buy stocks in the same way, buying stocks that match their investment style and their financial needs. Two common approaches are value and growth investing.

Value Investing

Value investors search for undervalued stocks. That is, the investor tries to find companies whose value is not reflected in their stock price. These are typically quiet, "boring" companies with excellent financial performance that are temporarily out of favor in the stock market. This investment approach assumes that the stock's price will eventually rise to match the company's value. The most successful investor of all time, Warren Buffett, uses this approach almost exclusively. Naturally, the key to successful value investing is to accurately determine a stock's value. This will often include analyzing a company's financial ratios, as discussed in this chapter, compared to target ratios and industry norms. For example, the stock of **Deckers Outdoor Corporation**, the maker of TEVA™ sport sandals, was selling for $27.43 several years ago, a value relative to its earnings per share of $2.58. Over the next two years, the company's stock price increased more than 500%, reaching $166.50.

OLIVER BERG/DPA/Landov

Growth Investing

The growth investor tries to identify companies that have the potential to grow sales and earnings through new products, markets, or opportunities. Growth companies are often newer companies that are still unproven but that possess unique technologies or capabilities. The strategy is to purchase these companies before their potential becomes obvious, hoping to profit from relatively large increases in the company's stock price. This approach, however, carries the risk that the growth may not occur. Growth investors use many of the ratios discussed in this chapter to identify high-potential growth companies. For example, **Research in Motion Limited**, maker of the popular BlackBerry® handheld mobile device, reported earnings per share of $0.37, when the company's stock price was trading near $62 per share. In the following two years, the company's sales increased by 125%, earnings increased to $1.14 per share, and the company's stock price rose above $135 per share.

Report on Internal Control

The Sarbanes-Oxley Act requires management to prepare a report on internal control. The report states management's responsibility for establishing and maintaining internal control. In addition, management's assessment of the effectiveness of internal controls over financial reporting is included in the report.

Sarbanes-Oxley also requires a public accounting firm to verify management's conclusions on internal control. Thus, two reports on internal control, one by management and one by a public accounting firm, are included in the annual report. In some situations, these may be combined into a single report on internal control.

Report on Fairness of the Financial Statements

All publicly held corporations are required to have an independent audit (examination) of their financial statements. The Certified Public Accounting (CPA) firm that conducts the audit renders an opinion, called the *Report of Independent Registered Public Accounting Firm,* on the fairness of the statements.

An opinion stating that the financial statements present fairly the financial position, results of operations, and cash flows of the company is said to be an *unqualified opinion,* sometimes called a *clean opinion.* Any report other than an unqualified opinion raises a "red flag" for financial statement users and requires further investigation as to its cause.

Appendix

Unusual Items on the Income Statement

Generally accepted accounting principles require that unusual items be reported separately on the income statement. This is because such items do not occur frequently and often are unrelated to current operations. Without separate reporting of these items, users of the financial statements might be misled about current and future operations.

Unusual items affecting the current period's income statement include the following:

1. Discontinued operations
2. Extraordinary items

Discontinued Operations

A company may discontinue a segment of its operations by selling or abandoning the operations. For example, a retailer might decide to sell its product only online and thus discontinue selling its merchandise at its retail outlets (stores).

Any gain or loss on discontinued operations is reported on the income statement as a *Gain (or loss) from discontinued operations.* It is reported immediately following *Income from continuing operations.*[7]

To illustrate, assume that Jones Corporation produces and sells electrical products, hardware supplies, and lawn equipment. Because of lack of profits, Jones discontinues its electrical products operation and sells the remaining inventory and other assets at a loss of $100,000. Exhibit 11 illustrates the reporting of the loss on discontinued operations.[8]

In addition, a note accompanying the income statement should describe the operations sold, including such details as the date operations were discontinued, the assets sold, and the effect (if any) on current and future operations.

7. FASB, *Accounting Standards Codification*, Section 260.20.

8. The gain or loss on discontinued operations is reported net of any tax effects. To simplify, the tax effects are not specifically identified in Exhibit 11.

EXHIBIT 11

Unusual Items in the Income Statement

Jones Corporation
Income Statement
For the Year Ended December 31, 20Y6

Net sales	$12,350,000
Cost of merchandise sold	5,800,000
Gross profit	$ 6,550,000
Selling and administrative expenses	5,240,000
Income from continuing operations before income tax	$ 1,310,000
Income tax expense	620,000
Income from continuing operations	$ 690,000
Loss on discontinued operations	100,000
Income before extraordinary items	$ 590,000
Extraordinary items:	
Gain on condemnation of land	150,000
Net income	$ 740,000

Extraordinary Items

An **extraordinary item** is defined as an event or a transaction with the following characteristics:

1. Unusual in nature
2. Infrequent in occurrence

Gains and losses from natural disasters such as floods, earthquakes, and fires are normally reported as extraordinary items, provided that they occur infrequently. Gains or losses from land or buildings taken (condemned) for public use are also reported as extraordinary items.

Any gain or loss from extraordinary items is reported on the income statement as *Gain (or loss) from extraordinary item*. It is reported immediately following *Income from continuing operations* and any *Gain (or loss) on discontinued operations*.

To illustrate, assume that land owned by Jones Corporation was condemned by the local government. The condemnation of the land resulted in a gain of $150,000. Exhibit 11 illustrates the reporting of the extraordinary gain.[9]

Reporting Earnings per Share

Earnings per common share should be reported separately for discontinued operations and extraordinary items. Assuming 200,000 shares of common stock are outstanding, a partial income statement for Jones Corporation is shown in Exhibit 12.

Exhibit 12 reports earnings per common share for income from continuing operations, discontinued operations, and extraordinary items. However, only earnings per share for income from continuing operations and net income are required by generally accepted accounting principles (GAAP). The other per-share amounts may be presented in the notes to the financial statements.[10]

---

9. The gain or loss on extraordinary operations is reported net of any tax effects.

10. FASB, *Accounting Standards Codification*, Section 260.10.

Jones Corporation	
Income Statement	
For the Year Ended December 31, 20Y6	

EXHIBIT 12

Income Statement with Earnings per Share

Earnings per common share:	
Income from continuing operations	$3.45
Loss on discontinued operations	0.50
Income before extraordinary items	$2.95
Extraordinary items:	
Gain on condemnation of land	0.75
Net income	$3.70

Key Points

1. Describe basic financial statement analytical methods.

The analysis of percentage increases and decreases in related items in comparative financial statements is called horizontal analysis. The analysis of percentages of component parts to the total in a single statement is called vertical analysis. Financial statements in which all amounts are expressed in percentages for purposes of analysis are called common-sized statements.

2. Use financial statement analysis to assess the liquidity and solvency of a business.

The primary focus of financial statement analysis is the assessment of liquidity, solvency, and profitability. All users are interested in the ability of a business to convert assets to cash (liquidity), pay its debts as they come due (solvency), and earn income (profitability). Liquidity, solvency, and profitability are interrelated. Liquidity and solvency are normally assessed by examining the following: (1) current position analysis, (2) accounts receivable analysis, (3) inventory analysis, (4) the ratio of fixed as-

sets to long-term liabilities, (5) the ratio of liabilities to stockholders' equity, and (6) the number of times interest charges are earned.

3. Use financial statement analysis to assess the profitability of a business.

Profitability analysis focuses mainly on the relationship between operating results (income statement) and resources available (balance sheet). Major analyses used in assessing profitability include (1) the ratio of net sales to assets, (2) the rate earned on total assets, (3) the rate earned on stockholders' equity, (4) the rate earned on common stockholders' equity, (5) earnings per share on common stock, (6) the price-earnings ratio, (7) dividends per share, and (8) dividend yield.

4. Describe the contents of corporate annual reports.

Corporate annual reports normally include financial statements and the accompanying notes, the Management's Discussion and Analysis, the Report on Internal Control, and the Report on Fairness of the Financial Statements.

Key Terms

Accounts receivable analysis (333)
Accounts receivable turnover (334)
Common-sized statement (330)
Current position analysis (331)
Current ratio (332)
Dividend yield (343)
Dividends per share (343)
Earnings per share (EPS) on common stock (341)

Extraordinary item (348)
Horizontal analysis (326)
Inventory analysis (335)
Inventory turnover (335)
Liquidity (331)
Management's Discussion and Analysis (MD&A) (345)
Number of days' sales in inventory (336)
Number of days' sales in receivables (334)

Number of times interest charges are earned (337)
Price-earnings (P/E) ratio (342)
Profitability (331)
Quick assets (333)
Quick ratio (333)
Rate earned on common stockholders' equity (340)
Rate earned on stockholders' equity (339)

Rate earned on total assets (339)
Ratio of fixed assets to long-term liabilities (336)
Ratio of liabilities to stockholders' equity (337)
Ratio of net sales to assets (338)
Solvency (331)
Vertical analysis (328)
Working capital (332)

Illustrative Problem

Esmeralda Paint Co.'s comparative financial statements for the years ending December 31, 20Y4 and 20Y3, are as follows. The market price of Esmeralda Paint Co.'s common stock was $30 on December 31, 20Y3, and $25 on December 31, 20Y4.

ESMERALDA PAINT CO.
Comparative Income Statement
For the Years Ended December 31, 20Y4 and 20Y3

	20Y4	20Y3
Sales	$5,125,000	$3,257,600
Sales returns and allowances	125,000	57,600
Net sales	$5,000,000	$3,200,000
Cost of goods sold	3,400,000	2,080,000
Gross profit	$1,600,000	$1,120,000
Selling expenses	$ 650,000	$ 464,000
Administrative expenses	325,000	224,000
Total operating expenses	$ 975,000	$ 688,000
Income from operations	$ 625,000	$ 432,000
Other income	25,000	19,200
	$ 650,000	$ 451,200
Other expenses (interest)	105,000	64,000
Income before income tax	$ 545,000	$ 387,200
Income tax expenses	300,000	176,000
Net income	$ 245,000	$ 211,200

ESMERALDA PAINT CO.
Comparative Retained Earnings Statement
For the Years Ended December 31, 20Y4 and 20Y3

	20Y4	20Y3
Retained earnings, January 1	$723,000	$581,800
Add net income for year	245,000	211,200
Total	$968,000	$793,000
Deduct dividends:		
On preferred stock	$ 40,000	$ 40,000
On common stock	45,000	30,000
Total	$ 85,000	$ 70,000
Retained earnings, December 31	$883,000	$723,000

ESMERALDA PAINT CO.
Comparative Balance Sheet
December 31, 20Y4 and 20Y3

	Dec. 31, 20Y4	Dec. 31, 20Y3
Assets		
Current assets:		
Cash	$ 175,000	$ 125,000
Temporary investments	150,000	50,000
Accounts receivable (net)	425,000	325,000
Inventories	720,000	480,000
Prepaid expenses	30,000	20,000
Total current assets	$1,500,000	$1,000,000
Long-term investments	250,000	225,000
Property, plant, and equipment (net)	2,093,000	1,948,000
Total assets	$3,843,000	$3,173,000

	Dec. 31, 20Y4	Dec. 31, 20Y3
Liabilities		
Current liabilities	$ 750,000	$ 650,000
Long-term liabilities:		
Mortgage note payable, 10%, due in eight years	$ 410,000	—
Bonds payable, 8%, due in 15 years	800,000	$ 800,000
Total long-term liabilities	$1,210,000	$ 800,000
Total liabilities	$1,960,000	$1,450,000
Stockholders' Equity		
Preferred 8% stock, $100 par	$ 500,000	$ 500,000
Common stock, $10 par	500,000	500,000
Retained earnings	883,000	723,000
Total stockholders' equity	$1,883,000	$1,723,000
Total liabilities and stockholders' equity	$3,843,000	$3,173,000

Instructions

Determine the following measures for 20Y4:

1. Working capital
2. Current ratio
3. Quick ratio
4. Accounts receivable turnover
5. Number of days' sales in receivables
6. Inventory turnover
7. Number of days' sales in inventory
8. Ratio of fixed assets to long-term liabilities
9. Ratio of liabilities to stockholders' equity
10. Number of times interest charges are earned
11. Number of times preferred dividends earned
12. Ratio of net sales to assets
13. Rate earned on total assets
14. Rate earned on stockholders' equity
15. Rate earned on common stockholders' equity
16. Earnings per share on common stock
17. Price-earnings ratio
18. Dividends per share
19. Dividend yield

Solution

(Ratios are rounded to the nearest single digit after the decimal point.)

1. Working capital: $750,000
   $1,500,000 − $750,000

2. Current ratio: 2.0
   $1,500,000 ÷ $750,000

3. Quick ratio: 1.0
   $750,000 ÷ $750,000

4. Accounts receivable turnover: 13.3
   $5,000,000 ÷ [($425,000 + $325,000) ÷ 2]

5. Number of days' sales in receivables: 27.4 days
   $5,000,000 ÷ 365 days = $13,699
   $375,000 ÷ $13,699

6. Inventory turnover: 5.7
   $3,400,000 ÷ [($720,000 + $480,000) ÷ 2]

7. Number of days' sales in inventory: 64.4 days
   $3,400,000 ÷ 365 days = $9,315
   $600,000 ÷ $9,315

8. Ratio of fixed assets to long-term liabilities: 1.7
   $2,093,000 ÷ $1,210,000

9. Ratio of liabilities to stockholders' equity: 1.0
   $1,960,000 ÷ $1,883,000

10. Number of times interest charges are earned: 6.2
    ($545,000 + $105,000) ÷ $105,000

11. Number of times preferred dividends earned: 6.1
$245,000 ÷ $40,000

12. Ratio of net sales to assets: 1.5
$5,000,000 ÷ [($3,593,000 + $2,948,000) ÷ 2]

13. Rate earned on total assets: 10.0%
($245,000 + $105,000) ÷ [($3,843,000 + $3,173,000) ÷ 2]

14. Rate earned on stockholders' equity: 13.6%
$245,000 ÷ [($1,883,000 + $1,723,000) ÷ 2]

15. Rate earned on common stockholders' equity: 15.7%
($245,000 − $40,000) ÷ [($1,383,000 + $1,223,000) ÷ 2]

16. Earnings per share on common stock: $4.10
($245,000 − $40,000) ÷ 50,000 shares

17. Price-earnings ratio: 6.1
$25 ÷ $4.10

18. Dividends per share: $0.90
$45,000 ÷ 50,000 shares

19. Dividend yield: 3.6%
$0.90 ÷ $25

Self-Examination Questions *(Answers appear at the end of chapter)*

1. What type of analysis is indicated by the following?

	Amount	Percent
Current assets	$100,000	20%
Property, plant, and equipment	400,000	80
Total assets	$500,000	100%

A. Vertical analysis
B. Horizontal analysis
C. Profitability analysis
D. Contribution margin analysis

2. Which of the following measures indicates the ability of a firm to pay its current liabilities?
A. Working capital
B. Current ratio
C. Quick ratio
D. All of the above

3. The ratio determined by dividing total current assets by total current liabilities is:
A. the current ratio.
B. the working capital ratio.
C. the bankers' ratio.
D. all of the above.

4. The ratio of the quick assets to current liabilities, which indicates the "instant" debt-paying ability of a firm, is the:
A. current ratio.
B. working capital ratio.
C. quick ratio.
D. bankers' ratio.

5. A measure useful in evaluating efficiency in the management of inventories is the:
A. working capital ratio.
B. quick ratio.
C. number of days' sales in inventory.
D. ratio of fixed assets to long-term liabilities.

Class Discussion Questions

1. What is the difference between horizontal and vertical analysis of financial statements?

2. What is the advantage of using comparative statements for financial analysis rather than statements for a single date or period?

3. The current year's amount of net income (after income tax) is 9% larger than that of the preceding year. Does this indicate an improved operating performance? Discuss.

4. How would you respond to a horizontal analysis that showed an expense increasing by over 70%?

5. How would the current and quick ratios of a service business compare?

6. For Belzer Corporation, the working capital at the end of the current year is $24,000 more than the working capital at the end of the preceding year, reported as follows:

	Current Year	Preceding Year
Current assets:		
Cash, temporary investments, and receivables	$ 81,000	$ 72,000
Inventories	171,000	126,000
Total current assets	$252,000	$198,000
Current liabilities	90,000	60,000
Working capital	$162,000	$138,000

Has the current position improved? Explain.

7. Why would the accounts receivable turnover ratio be different between Walmart and Procter & Gamble?

8. A company that grants terms of n/30 on all sales has a yearly accounts receivable turnover, based on monthly averages, of 9. Is this a satisfactory turnover? Discuss.

9. a. Why is it advantageous to have a high inventory turnover?

   b. Is it possible for the inventory turnover to be too high? Discuss.

   c. Is it possible to have a high inventory turnover and a high number of days' sales in inventory? Discuss.

10. What do the following data taken from a comparative balance sheet indicate about the company's ability to borrow additional funds on a long-term basis in the current year as compared to the preceding year?

	Current Year	Preceding Year
Fixed assets (net)	$1,800,000	$1,260,000
Total long-term liabilities	450,000	350,000

11. a. How does the rate earned on total assets differ from the rate earned on stockholders' equity?

    b. Which ratio is normally higher? Explain.

12. a. Why is the rate earned on stockholders' equity by a thriving business ordinarily higher than the rate earned on total assets?

    b. Should the rate earned on common stockholders' equity normally be higher or lower than the rate earned on total stockholders' equity? Explain.

13. The net income (after income tax) of Fleming Inc. was $4.80 per common share in the latest year and $7.50 per common share for the preceding year. At the beginning of the latest year, the number of shares outstanding was doubled by a stock split. There were no other changes in the amount of stock outstanding. What were the earnings per share in the preceding year, adjusted for comparison with the latest year?

14. The price-earnings ratio for the common stock of In-Work Company was 15 at December 31, the end of the current fiscal year. What does the ratio indicate about the selling price of the common stock in relation to current earnings?

15. Why would the dividend yield differ significantly from the rate earned on common stockholders' equity?

16. Favorable business conditions may bring about certain seemingly unfavorable ratios, and unfavorable business operations may result in apparently favorable ratios. For example, Shaddox Company increased its sales and net income substantially for the current year, yet the current ratio at the end of the year is lower than at the beginning of the year. Discuss some possible causes of the apparent weakening of the current position, while sales and net income have increased substantially.

17. Describe two reports provided by independent auditors in the annual report to shareholders.

Exercises

Obj 1

✔ a. 20Y8 net
income: $85,500;
9.5% of sales

E9-1 Vertical analysis of income statement

Revenue and expense data for Searle Technologies Co. are as follows:

	20Y8	20Y7
Sales	$900,000	$725,000
Cost of goods sold	558,000	435,000
Selling expenses	117,000	116,000
Administrative expenses	63,000	65,250
Income tax expense	76,500	58,000

a. Prepare an income statement in comparative form, stating each item for both 20Y8 and 20Y7 as a percent of sales. Round to one decimal place.

b. Comment on the significant changes disclosed by the comparative income statement.

Obj 1

✔ a. Year 2 income
from continuing
operations before
taxes, 3.5%
of revenues

E9-2 Vertical analysis of income statement

The following comparative income statement (in thousands of dollars) for two recent years was adapted from the annual report of Speedway Motorsports, Inc., owner and operator of several major motor speedways, such as the Atlanta, Texas, and Las Vegas Motor Speedways.

	Year 2	Year 1
Revenues:		
Admissions	$130,239	$139,125
Event-related revenue	163,621	156,691
NASCAR broadcasting revenue	185,394	178,722
Other operating revenue	26,591	27,705
Total revenue	$505,845	$502,243
Expenses and other:		
Direct expense of events	$106,204	$100,843
NASCAR purse and sanction fees	120,146	120,273
General and administrative	89,384	85,717
Depreciation and amortization	54,004	52,762
Other expenses	118,187	71,563
Total expenses and other	$487,925	$431,158
Income from continuing operations before taxes	$ 17,920	$ 71,085

a. Prepare a comparative income statement for Years 1 and 2 in vertical form, stating each item as a percent of revenues. Round to one decimal place.

b. Comment on the significant changes.

Note: The spreadsheet icon indicates an Excel template is available on the student companion site.

E9-3   Common-sized income statement

Revenue and expense data for the current calendar year for Garrity Electronics Company and for the electronics industry are as follows. The Garrity Electronics Company data are expressed in dollars. The electronics industry averages are expressed in percentages.

	Garrity Electronics Company	Electronics Industry Average
Sales	$4,728,800	102.5%
Sales returns and allowances	128,800	2.5
Net sales	$4,600,000	100.0%
Cost of goods sold	2,668,000	61.0
Gross profit	$1,932,000	39.0%
Selling expenses	$1,472,000	23.0%
Administrative expenses	368,000	10.0
Total operating expenses	$1,840,000	33.0%
Operating income	$ 92,000	6.0%
Other income	138,000	3.0
	$ 230,000	9.0%
Other expense	46,000	1.0
Income before income tax	$ 184,000	8.0%
Income tax expense	115,000	2.5
Net income	$ 69,000	5.5%

a. Prepare a common-sized income statement comparing the results of operations for Garrity Electronics Company with the industry average.

b. As far as the data permit, comment on significant relationships revealed by the comparisons.

E9-4   Vertical analysis of balance sheet

Balance sheet data for Otter Creek Company on December 31, the end of the fiscal year, are shown below.

	20Y2	20Y1
Current assets	$700,000	$504,000
Property, plant, and equipment	945,000	770,000
Intangible assets	105,000	126,000
Current liabilities	280,000	294,000
Long-term liabilities	595,000	560,000
Common stock	140,000	140,000
Retained earnings	735,000	406,000

Prepare a comparative balance sheet for 20Y2 and 20Y1, stating each asset as a percent of total assets and each liability and stockholders' equity item as a percent of the total liabilities and stockholders' equity.

✔ Net income
increase, 18.7%

E9-5 Horizontal analysis of the income statement

Income statement data for Montana Images Company for the years ended December 31, 20Y5 and 20Y4, are as follows:

	20Y5	20Y4
Sales	$579,000	$500,000
Cost of goods sold	343,500	300,000
Gross profit	$235,500	$200,000
Selling expenses	$ 46,000	$ 40,000
Administrative expenses	11,000	10,000
Total operating expenses	$ 57,000	$ 50,000
Income before income tax	$178,500	$150,000
Income tax expense	45,000	37,500
Net income	$133,500	$112,500

a. Prepare a comparative income statement with horizontal analysis, indicating the increase (decrease) for 20Y5 when compared with 20Y4. Round to one decimal place.

b. What conclusions can be drawn from the horizontal analysis?

✔ 20Y9 working
capital, $700,000

E9-6 Current position analysis

The following data were taken from the balance sheet of Tiger Shapes Company:

	Dec. 31, 20Y9	Dec. 31, 20Y8
Cash	$ 100,000	$ 80,000
Temporary investments	150,000	40,000
Accounts and notes receivable (net)	400,000	360,000
Inventories	525,000	380,000
Prepaid expenses	25,000	20,000
Total current assets	$1,200,000	$ 880,000
Accounts and notes payable (short-term)	$ 425,000	$ 340,000
Accrued liabilities	75,000	60,000
Total current liabilities	$ 500,000	$ 400,000

a. Determine for each year (1) the working capital, (2) the current ratio, and (3) the quick ratio.

b. What conclusions can be drawn from these data as to the company's ability to meet its currently maturing debts?

✔ a. (1) Year 1
current ratio, 1.1

E9-7 Current position analysis

PepsiCo, Inc., the parent company of Frito-Lay™ snack foods and Pepsi beverages, had the following current assets and current liabilities at the end of two recent years:

	Year 2 (in millions)	Year 1 (in millions)
Cash and cash equivalents	$ 4,067	$ 5,943
Short-term investments, at cost	358	426
Accounts and notes receivable, net	6,912	6,323
Inventories	3,827	3,372
Prepaid expenses and other current assets	2,277	1,505
Short-term obligations (liabilities)	6,205	4,898
Accounts payable and other current liabilities	11,757	10,923
Income taxes payable	192	71

a. Determine the (1) current ratio and (2) quick ratio for both years. Round to one decimal place.

b. What conclusions can you draw from these data?

E9-8   Current position analysis

Obj 2

The bond indenture for the 10-year, 8% debenture bonds dated January 2, 20Y8, required working capital of $200,000, a current ratio of 2.0, and a quick ratio of 1.0 at the end of each calendar year until the bonds mature. At December 31, 20Y9, the three measures were computed as follows:

1. Current assets:

Cash	$120,000	
Temporary investments	150,000	
Accounts and notes receivable (net)	240,000	
Inventories	190,000	
Prepaid expenses	50,000	
Intangible assets	30,000	
Property, plant, and equipment	540,000	
Total current assets (net)		$1,320,000
Current liabilities:		
Accounts and short-term notes payable	$440,000	
Accrued liabilities	160,000	
Total current liabilities		600,000
Working capital		$ 720,000

2. Current ratio	2.2	$1,320,000 ÷ $600,000
3. Quick ratio	1.5	$660,000 ÷ $440,000

a. List the errors in the determination of the three measures of current position analysis.

b. Is the company satisfying the terms of the bond indenture?

E9-9   Accounts receivable analysis

Obj 2

The following data are taken from the financial statements of Amazing Technology Inc. Terms of all sales are 2/10, n/30.

✔ a. Accounts receivable turnover, Year 3, 13.2

	Year 3	Year 2	Year 1
Accounts receivable, end of year	$ 350,000	$ 290,000	$250,000
Net sales on account	4,224,000	3,456,000	

a. For Years 2 and 3, determine (1) the accounts receivable turnover and (2) the number of days' sales in receivables. Round to nearest dollar and one decimal place.

b. What conclusions can be drawn from these data concerning accounts receivable and credit policies?

E9-10   Accounts receivable analysis

Obj 2

Bassett Stores Company and Fox Stores Inc. are large retail department stores. Both companies offer credit to their customers through their own credit card operations. Information from the financial statements for both companies for two recent years is as follows (all numbers are in millions):

	Bassett	Fox
Merchandise sales	$726,000	$2,470,000
Credit card receivables—beginning	75,000	350,000
Credit card receviables—ending	90,000	410,000

a. Determine (1) the accounts receivable turnover and (2) the number of days' sales in receivables for both companies. Round to nearest dollar and one decimal place.

b. Compare the two companies with regard to their credit card policies.

Obj 2

✓ a. Inventory
turnover, current
year, 12.0

E9-11   Inventory analysis

The following data were extracted from the income statement of Brecca Systems Inc.:

	Current Year	Preceding Year
Sales	$9,700,000	$7,175,000
Beginning inventories	420,000	400,000
Cost of goods sold	5,820,000	4,305,000
Ending inventories	550,000	420,000

a. Determine for each year (1) the inventory turnover and (2) the number of days' sales in inventory. Round to nearest dollar and one decimal place.

b. What conclusions can be drawn from these data concerning the inventories?

Obj 2

✓ a. Dell inventory
turnover, 35.7

E9-12   Inventory analysis

Dell Inc. and Hewlett-Packard Company (HP) compete with each other in the personal computer market. Dell's primary strategy is to assemble computers to customer orders, rather than for inventory. Thus, for example, Dell will build and deliver a computer within days of a customer entering an order on a Web page. Hewlett-Packard, on the other hand, builds some computers prior to receiving an order, then sells from this inventory once an order is received. Below is selected financial information for both companies from a recent year's financial statements (in millions):

	Dell Inc.	Hewlett-Packard Company
Sales	$62,071	$120,857
Cost of goods sold	48,260	92,385
Inventory, beginning of period	1,301	7,490
Inventory, end of period	1,404	6,317

a. Determine for both companies (1) the inventory turnover and (2) the number of days' sales in inventory. Round to one decimal place.

b. Interpret the inventory ratios by considering Dell's and Hewlett-Packard's operating strategies.

Obj 2

✓ a. Ratio of
liabilities to
stockholders'
equity, Dec. 31,
20Y6, 0.6

E9-13   Ratio of liabilities to stockholders' equity and number of times interest charges earned

The following data were taken from the financial statements of Starr Construction Inc. for December 31, 20Y6 and 20Y5:

	Dec. 31, 20Y6	Dec. 31, 20Y5
Accounts payable and other liabilities	$ 1,700,000	$2,325,000
Current maturities of bonds payable	500,000	500,000
Serial bonds payable, 8%, issued 2008, due in five years	5,000,000	5,500,000
Common stock, $5 par value	250,000	250,000
Paid-in capital in excess of par	1,500,000	1,500,000
Retained earnings	10,250,000	7,500,000

The income before income tax was $2,816,000 and $2,640,000 for the years 20Y6 and 20Y5, respectively.

a. Determine the ratio of liabilities to stockholders' equity at the end of each year.

b. Determine the number of times the bond interest charges are earned during the year for both years.

c. What conclusions can be drawn from these data as to the company's ability to meet its currently maturing debts?

E9-14 Ratio of liabilities to stockholders' equity and number of times interest charges earned

Obj **2**

✔ a. Hasbro, 1.9

Hasbro and Mattel, Inc., are the two largest toy companies in North America. Condensed liabilities and stockholders' equity from a recent balance sheet are shown for each company as follows (in millions):

	Hasbro	Mattel
Current liabilities	$ 942	$ 1,039
Long-term debt	1,771	2,022
Total liabilities	$ 2,713	$ 3,061
Shareholders' equity:		
Common stock	$ 105	$ 441
Additional paid-in capital	630	1,690
Retained earnings	3,205	3,168
Accumulated other equity items	(36)	(447)
Treasury stock, at cost	(2,486)	(2,242)
Total stockholders' equity	$ 1,418	$ 2,610
Total liabilities and stockholders' equity	$ 4,131	$ 5,671

The income from operations and interest expense from the income statement for both companies were as follows (in millions):

	Hasbro	Mattel
Income from operations before tax	$486	$971
Interest expense	89	75

a. Determine the ratio of liabilities to stockholders' equity for both companies. Round to one decimal place.

b. Determine the number of times interest charges are earned for both companies. Round to one decimal place.

c. Interpret the ratio differences between the two companies.

E9-15 Ratio of liabilities to stockholders' equity and ratio of fixed assets to long-term liabilities

Obj **2**

✔ a. H.J. Heinz, 3.3

Recent balance sheet information for two companies in the food industry, H.J. Heinz Company and The Hershey Company, is as follows (in millions of dollars):

	H.J. Heinz	Hershey
Net property, plant, and equipment	$2,484	$1,560
Current liabilities	2,648	1,174
Long-term debt	4,780	1,749
Other long-term liabilities	1,683	641
Stockholders' equity	2,759	849

a. Determine the ratio of liabilities to stockholders' equity for both companies. Round to one decimal place.

b. Determine the ratio of fixed assets to long-term liabilities for both companies. Round to two decimal places.

c. Interpret the ratio differences between the two companies.

E9-16 Ratio of net sales to assets

Three major segments of the transportation industry are motor carriers (YRC Worldwide), railroads (Union Pacific), and transportation arrangement services (C.H. Robinson Worldwide Inc.). Recent financial statement information for these three companies is shown as follows (in millions of dollars):

	YRC Worldwide	Union Pacific	C.H. Robinson Worldwide Inc.
Net sales	$4,869	$19,557	$10,336
Average total assets	2,529	44,092	2,067

a. Determine the ratio of net sales to assets for all three companies. Round to one decimal place.

b. Assume that the ratio of net sales to assets for each company represents that company's respective industry segment. Interpret the differences in the ratio of net sales to assets in terms of the operating characteristics of each of the respective segments.

E9-17 Profitability ratios

The following selected data were taken from the financial statements of The O'Malley Group Inc. for December 31, 20Y5, 20Y4, and 20Y3:

	December 31		
	20Y5	20Y4	20Y3
Total assets	$2,900,000	$2,400,000	$2,000,000
Notes payable (5% interest)	800,000	800,000	800,000
Common stock	250,000	250,000	250,000
Preferred $4 stock, $50 par (no change during year)	400,000	400,000	400,000
Retained earnings	1,450,000	950,000	550,000
Net income	530,000	430,000	330,000

No dividends on common stock were declared between 20Y3 and 20Y5.

a. Determine the rate earned on total assets, the rate earned on stockholders' equity, and the rate earned on common stockholders' equity for the years 20Y4 and 20Y5. Round to one decimal place.

b. What conclusions can be drawn from these data as to the company's profitability?

E9-18 Profitability ratios

Macy's, Inc., sells merchandise through company-owned retail stores and Internet Web sites. Recent financial information for Macy's is provided below (all numbers in millions).

	Year 3	Year 2
Net income	$1,335	$1,256
Interest expense	425	447

	Year 3	Year 2	Year 1
Total assets	$20,991	$22,095	$20,631
Total stockholders' equity	6,051	5,933	5,530

Assume the apparel industry average rate earned on total assets is 8.2%, and the average rate earned on stockholders' equity is 10.0% for Year 3.

a. Determine the rate earned on total assets for Macy's for Years 2 and 3. Round to one decimal place.

b. Determine the rate earned on stockholders' equity for Macy's for Years 2 and 3. Round to one decimal place.

c. Evaluate the two-year trend for the profitability ratios determined in (a) and (b).

E9-19 Six measures of liquidity or profitability

Obj **2, 3**

✔ c. Ratio of net sales to assets, 2.6

The following data were taken from the financial statements of Whiting Enterprises Inc. for the current fiscal year. Assuming that long-term investments totaled $1,000,000 for the past two years and that total assets were $14,400,000 at the beginning of the year, determine the following: (a) ratio of fixed assets to long-term liabilities, (b) ratio of liabilities to stockholders' equity, (c) ratio of net sales to assets, (d) rate earned on total assets, (e) rate earned on stockholders' equity, and (f) rate earned on common stockholders' equity. Round to one decimal place.

Property, plant, and equipment (net)			$ 7,000,000
Liabilities:			
Current liabilities		$ 200,000	
Mortgage note payable, 8%, ten-year note issued two years ago		5,000,000	
Total liabilities			$ 5,200,000
Stockholders' equity:			
Preferred $2 stock, $20 par (no change during year)			$ 3,000,000
Common stock, $2 par (no change during year)			500,000
Retained earnings:			
Balance, beginning of year	$6,525,000		
Net income	725,000	$7,250,000	
Preferred dividends	$ 300,000		
Common dividends	50,000	350,000	
Balance, end of year			6,900,000
Total stockholders' equity			$10,400,000
Net sales			$36,400,000
Interest expense			$ 400,000

E9-20 Six financial ratios

Obj **2, 3**

✔ d. Price-earnings ratio, 12.5

The balance sheet for Shryer Industries Inc. at the end of 20Y9 indicated the following:

Bonds payable, 5% (due in 30 years)	$ 8,000,000
Preferred $4 stock, $75 par	15,000,000
Common stock, $7 par	3,500,000

Income before income tax was $3,400,000, and income taxes were $1,000,000 for the current year. Cash dividends paid on common stock during the current year totaled $100,000. The common stock was selling for $8 per share at the end of the year. Determine each of the following: (a) number of times bond interest charges are earned, (b) number of times preferred dividends are earned, (c) earnings per share on common stock, (d) price-earnings ratio, (e) dividends per share of common stock, and (f) dividend yield. Round to one decimal place except earnings per share, which should be rounded to two decimal places.

E9-21 Earnings per share, price-earnings ratio, dividend yield

Obj **2, 3**

✔ b. Price-earnings ratio, 8.0

The following information was taken from the financial statements of Monarch Resources Inc. for December 31 of the current year:

Common stock, $125 par value (no change during the year)	$12,500,000
Preferred $6 stock, $90 par (no change during the year)	2,250,000

The net income was $1,300,000, and the declared dividends on the common stock were $460,000 for the current year. The market price of the common stock is $92 per share.

For the common stock, determine (a) the earnings per share, (b) the price-earnings ratio, (c) the dividends per share, and (d) the dividend yield.

Obj 3

E9-22 Price-earnings ratio, dividend yield

The table below shows recent stock prices, earnings per share, and dividends per share for three companies.

	Price	Earnings per Share	Dividends per Share
McDonald's Corporation	$95.19	$5.33	$2.53
eBay Inc.	56.40	2.02	0.00
The Coca-Cola Company	38.59	3.75	1.88

a. Determine the price-earnings ratio and dividend yield for the three companies. Round to one decimal place.

b. Explain the differences in these ratios across the three companies.

✔ b. Earnings per
share on common
stock, $15.68

app

E9-23 Earnings per share

The net income reported on the income statement of Bellach Co. was $4,100,000. There were 250,000 shares of $40 par common stock and 60,000 shares of $3 preferred stock par value $100 outstanding throughout the current year. The income statement included two extraordinary items: a $600,000 gain from condemnation of land and a $150,000 loss arising from flood damage, both after applicable income tax. Determine the per-share figures for common stock for (a) income before extraordinary items and (b) net income.

app

E9-24 Unusual income statement items

Assume that the amount of each of the following items is material to the financial statements. Classify each item as either normally recurring (NR) or unusual items. If unusual item, then specify if it is a discontinued operations item (DI) or extraordinary (E).

a. Interest revenue on notes receivable.

b. Gain on sale of land condemned by the local government for a public works project.

c. Gain on sale of segment of the company's operations that manufactures bottling equipment.

d. Loss on sale of investments in stocks and bonds.

e. Uncollectible accounts expense.

f. Uninsured loss on building due to hurricane damage. The building was purchased by the company twenty years ago and had not previously incurred hurricane damage.

g. Uninsured flood loss. (Flood insurance is unavailable because of periodic flooding in the area.)

app

E9-25 Income statement and earnings per share for extraordinary items and discontinued operations

Leadbetter Inc. reports the following for 20Y3:

Income from continuing operations before income tax	$766,250
Extraordinary property loss from hurricane	$60,000*
Gain from discontinued operations	$180,000*
Applicable tax rate	40%

*Net of any tax effect.

a. Prepare a partial income statement for Leadbetter Inc. beginning with income from continuing operations before income tax.

b. Assuming 75,000 shares, calculate the earnings per common share for Leadbetter Inc. including per-share amounts for unusual items.

Problems

P9-1   Horizontal analysis for income statement

Obj | 1

For 20Y3, Greyhound Technology Company reported its most significant decline in net income in years. At the end of the year, Duane Vogel, the president, is presented with the following condensed comparative income statement:

✔ 1. Net sales, 9.8% increase

GREYHOUND TECHNOLOGY COMPANY
Comparative Income Statement
For the Years Ended December 31, 20Y3 and 20Y2

	20Y3	20Y2
Sales	$880,000	$800,000
Sales returns and allowances	18,000	15,000
Net sales	$862,000	$785,000
Cost of goods sold	650,000	500,000
Gross profit	$212,000	$285,000
Selling expenses	$ 44,000	$ 40,000
Administrative expenses	27,000	25,000
Total operating expenses	$ 71,000	$ 65,000
Income from operations	$141,000	$220,000
Other income	2,300	2,000
Income before income tax	$143,300	$222,000
Income tax expense	13,000	20,000
Net income	$130,300	$202,000

Instructions

1. Prepare a comparative income statement with horizontal analysis for the two-year period, using 20Y2 as the base year. Round to one decimal place.

2. To the extent the data permit, comment on the significant relationships revealed by the horizontal analysis prepared in (1).

P9-2   Vertical analysis for income statement

Obj | 1

For 20Y6, Blue Buffalo Company initiated a sales promotion campaign that included the expenditure of an additional $60,000 for advertising. At the end of the year, Tamara Wasnuk, the president, is presented with the following condensed comparative income statement:

✔ 1. Net income, 20Y6, 10.6%

BLUE BUFFALO COMPANY
Comparative Income Statement
For the Years Ended December 31, 20Y6 and 20Y5

	20Y6	20Y5
Sales	$1,545,000	$1,224,000
Sales returns and allowances	45,000	24,000
Net sales	$1,500,000	$1,200,000
Cost of goods sold	960,000	780,000
Gross profit	$ 540,000	$ 420,000
Selling expenses	$ 285,000	$ 216,000
Administrative expenses	90,000	96,000
Total operating expenses	$ 375,000	$ 312,000
Income from operations	$ 165,000	$ 108,000
Other income	36,000	36,000
Income before income tax	$ 201,000	$ 144,000
Income tax expense	42,000	28,800
Net income	$ 159,000	$ 115,200

Instructions

1. Prepare a comparative income statement for the two-year period, presenting an analysis of each item in relationship to net sales for each of the years.

2. To the extent the data permit, comment on the significant relationships revealed by the vertical analysis prepared in (1).

Obj 2

✔ 2. c. Current
ratio, 2.3

P9-3   Effect of transactions on current position analysis

Data pertaining to the current position of Newlan Company are as follows:

Cash	$ 80,000
Temporary investments	160,000
Accounts and notes receivable (net)	235,000
Inventories	190,000
Prepaid expenses	10,000
Accounts payable	158,000
Notes payable (short-term)	80,000
Accrued expenses	12,000

Instructions

1. Compute (a) the working capital, (b) the current ratio, and (c) the quick ratio.

2. List the following captions on a sheet of paper:

Transaction	Working Capital	Current Ratio	Quick Ratio

Compute the working capital, the current ratio, and the quick ratio after each of the following transactions, and record the results in the appropriate columns. Consider each transaction separately and assume that only that transaction affects the data given above. Round to one decimal place.

a. Sold temporary investments at no gain or loss, $50,000.

b. Paid accounts payable, $40,000.

c. Purchased goods on account, $75,000.

d. Paid notes payable, $30,000.

e. Declared a cash dividend, $15,000.

f. Declared a stock dividend on common stock, $24,000.

g. Borrowed cash from bank on a long-term note, $150,000.

h. Received cash on account, $72,000.

i. Issued additional shares of stock for cash, $300,000.

j. Paid cash for prepaid expenses, $10,000.

Obj 2, 3

✔ 5. Number
of days' sales in
receivables, 33.2

P9-4   Nineteen measures of liquidity, solvency, and profitability

The comparative financial statements of Tec Solutions Inc. are as follows. The market price of Tec Solutions Inc. common stock was $89.75 on December 31, 20Y8.

TEC SOLUTIONS INC.
Comparative Income Statement
For the Years Ended December 31, 20Y8 and 20Y7

	20Y8	20Y7
Sales	$1,940,000	$1,450,000
Sales returns and allowances	15,000	10,000
Net sales	$1,925,000	$1,440,000
Cost of goods sold	780,000	575,000
Gross profit	$1,145,000	$ 865,000
Selling expenses	$ 385,000	$ 365,000
Administrative expenses	215,000	200,000
Total operating expenses	$ 600,000	$ 565,000
Income from operations	$ 545,000	$ 300,000
Other income	25,000	43,000
	$ 570,000	$ 343,000
Other expense (interest)	115,000	75,000
Income before income tax	$ 455,000	$ 268,000
Income tax expense	91,000	40,000
Net income	$ 364,000	$ 228,000

TEC SOLUTIONS INC.
Comparative Retained Earnings Statement
For the Years Ended December 31, 20Y8 and 20Y7

	20Y8	20Y7
Retained earnings, January 1	$381,000	$168,000
Add net income for year	364,000	228,000
Total	$745,000	$396,000
Deduct dividends:		
On preferred stock	$ 5,000	$ 5,000
On common stock	40,000	10,000
Total	$ 45,000	$ 15,000
Retained earnings, December 31	$700,000	$381,000

TEC SOLUTIONS INC.
Comparative Balance Sheet
December 31, 20Y8 and 20Y7

	Dec. 31, 20Y8	Dec. 31, 20Y7
Assets		
Current assets:		
Cash	$ 175,000	$ 200,000
Temporary investments	250,000	292,000
Accounts receivable (net)	190,000	160,000
Inventories	300,000	260,000
Prepaid expenses	50,000	13,000
Total current assets	$ 965,000	$ 925,000
Long-term investments	400,000	100,000
Property, plant, and equipment (net)	1,135,000	875,000
Total assets	$2,500,000	$1,900,000
Liabilities		
Current liabilities	$ 200,000	$ 419,000
Long-term liabilities:		
Mortgage note payable, 8%, due in 15 years	$ 500,000	—
Bonds payable, 10%, due in 20 years	750,000	$ 750,000
Total long-term liabilities	$1,250,000	$ 750,000
Total liabilities	$1,450,000	$1,169,000
Stockholders' Equity		
Preferred $5 stock, $100 par	$ 100,000	$ 100,000
Common stock, $5 par	250,000	250,000
Retained earnings	700,000	381,000
Total stockholders' equity	$1,050,000	$ 731,000
Total liabilities and stockholders' equity	$2,500,000	$1,900,000

Instructions

Determine the following measures for 20Y8, rounding to one decimal place:
1. Working capital
2. Current ratio
3. Quick ratio
4. Accounts receivable turnover
5. Number of days' sales in receivables
6. Inventory turnover
7. Number of days' sales in inventory
8. Ratio of fixed assets to long-term liabilities
9. Ratio of liabilities to stockholders' equity
10. Number of times interest charges earned

11. Number of times preferred dividends earned
12. Ratio of net sales to assets
13. Rate earned on total assets
14. Rate earned on stockholders' equity
15. Rate earned on common stockholders' equity
16. Earnings per share on common stock
17. Price-earnings ratio
18. Dividends per share of common stock
19. Dividend yield

Obj 2, 3

P9-5 Trend analysis

Critelli Company has provided the following comparative information:

	Year 5	Year 4	Year 3	Year 2	Year 1
Net income	$1,785,000	$1,330,000	$ 990,000	$ 768,800	$ 664,000
Interest expense	400,000	350,000	300,000	240,000	200,000
Income tax expense	615,000	340,000	270,000	71,200	16,000
Average total assets	9,500,000	8,000,000	6,000,000	5,200,000	4,500,000
Average stockholders' equity	5,400,000	4,300,000	3,100,000	2,650,000	2,200,000

You have been asked to evaluate the historical performance of the company over the last five years.

Selected industry ratios have remained relatively steady at the following levels for the last five years:

	Industry Ratios
Rate earned on total assets	15%
Rate earned on stockholders' equity	18%
Number of times interest charges earned	3.5

Instructions

1. Prepare three line graphs, with the ratio on the vertical axis and the years on the horizontal axis for the following three ratios (rounded to one decimal place):

   a. Rate earned on total assets

   b. Rate earned on stockholders' equity

   c. Number of times interest charges earned

   Display both the company ratio and the industry benchmark on each graph. That is, each graph should have two lines.

2. Prepare an analysis of the graphs in (1).

Cases

Case 9-1 Analysis of financing corporate growth

Assume that the president of Elkhead Brewery made the following statement in the Annual Report to Shareholders:

"The founding family and majority shareholders of the company do not believe in using debt to finance future growth. The founding family learned from hard experience during Prohibition and the Great Depression that debt can cause loss of flexibility and eventual loss of corporate control. The company will not place itself at such risk. As such, all future growth will be financed either by stock sales to the public or by internally generated resources."

As a public shareholder of this company, how would you respond to this policy?

Case 9-2 Receivables and inventory turnover

Thornby Inc. has completed its fiscal year on December 31. The auditor, Kim Holmes, has approached the CFO, Brad Potter, regarding the year-end receivables and inventory levels of Thornby Inc. The following conversation takes place:

Kim: We are beginning our audit of Thornby Inc. and have prepared ratio analyses to determine if there have been significant changes in operations or financial position. This helps us guide the audit process. This analysis indicates that the inventory turnover has decreased from 5.1 to 3.8, while the accounts receivable turnover has decreased from 12.5 to 9. I was wondering if you could explain this change in operations.

Brad: There is little need for concern. The inventory represents computers that we were unable to sell during the holiday buying season. We are confident, however, that we will be able to sell these computers as we move into the next fiscal year.

Kim: What gives you this confidence?

Brad: We will increase our advertising and provide some very attractive price concessions to move these machines. We have no choice. Newer technology is already out there, and we have to unload this inventory.

Kim: ... and the receivables?

Brad: As you may be aware, the company is under tremendous pressure to expand sales and profits. As a result, we lowered our credit standards to our commercial customers so that we would be able to sell products to a broader customer base. As a result of this policy change, we have been able to expand sales by 28%.

Kim: Your responses have not been reassuring to me.

Brad: I'm a little confused. Assets are good, right? Why don't you look at our current ratio? It has improved, hasn't it? I would think that you would view that very favorably.

Why is Kim concerned about the inventory and accounts receivable turnover ratios and Brad's responses to them? What action may Kim need to take? How would you respond to Brad's last comment?

Case 9-3 Vertical analysis

The condensed income statements through income from operations for Apple Inc. and Dell Inc. are reproduced below for recent fiscal years (numbers in millions of dollars).

	Apple Inc.	Dell Inc.
Sales (net)	$156,508	$62,071
Cost of sales	87,846	48,260
Gross profit	$ 68,662	$13,811
Selling, general, and administrative expenses	$ 10,040	$ 8,524
Research and development expenses	3,381	856
Operating expenses	$ 13,421	$ 9,380
Income from operations	$ 55,241	$ 4,431

Prepare comparative common-sized statements, rounding percents to one decimal place. Interpret the analyses.

Case 9-4 Profitability and stockholder ratios

Harley-Davidson, Inc., is a leading motorcycle manufacturer in the United States. The company manufactures and sells a number of different types of motorcycles, a complete line of motorcycle parts, and brand-related accessories, clothing, and collectibles. In recent years, Harley-Davidson has attempted to expand its dealer network and product lines internationally.

The following information is available for three recent years (in millions except per-share amounts):

	Year 3	Year 2	Year 1
Net income (loss)	$599	$147	$(55)
Preferred dividends	$0.00	$0.00	$0.00
Interest expense	$45	$90	$22
Shares outstanding for computing earnings per share	233	233	233
Cash dividend per share	$0.475	$0.40	$0.40
Average total assets	$9,552	$9,293	$8,493
Average stockholders' equity	$2,314	$2,157	$2,112
Average stock price per share	$36.43	$29.94	$21.09

1. Calculate the following ratios for each year:

   a. Rate earned on total assets

   b. Rate earned on stockholders' equity

   c. Earnings per share

   d. Dividend yield

   e. Price-earnings ratio

2. What is the ratio of average liabilities to average stockholders' equity for Years 1, 2, and 3?

3. Explain the direction of the dividend yield and price-earnings ratio in light of Harley-Davidson's profitability trend.

4. Based on these data, evaluate Harley-Davidson's strategy to expand to international markets.

Case 9-5 Comprehensive profitability and solvency analysis

Starwood Hotels & Resorts Worldwide and Wyndham Worldwide Corporation are two major owners and managers of lodging and resort properties in the United States. Financial data (in millions) for a recent year for the two companies are as follows:

	Starwood	Wyndham
Income statement data:		
Interest expense	$ 216	$ 152
Income before income tax expense	414	650
Net income	487*	417
Balance sheet data:		
Total assets	$9,560	$9,023
Total liabilities	6,605	6,791
Total stockholders' equity	2,955	2,232

*Starwood had a tax credit (refund).

The average liabilities, stockholders' equity, and total assets were as follows:

	Starwood	Wyndham
Average total assets	$9,668	$9,220
Average total liabilities	6,956	6,645
Average total stockholders' equity	2,712	2,575

1. Determine the following ratios for both companies (round to one decimal place after the whole percent):

   a. Rate earned on total assets

   b. Rate earned on total stockholders' equity

   c. Number of times interest charges are earned

   d. Ratio of liabilities to stockholders' equity

2. Analyze and compare the two companies, using the information in (1).

Answers to Self-Examination Questions

1. **A** Percentage analysis indicating the relationship of the component parts to the total in a financial statement, such as the relationship of current assets to total assets (20% to 100%) in the question, is called vertical analysis (answer A). Percentage analysis of increases and decreases in corresponding items in comparative financial statements is called horizontal analysis (answer B). An example of horizontal analysis would be the presentation of the amount of current assets in the preceding balance sheet, along with the amount of current assets at the end of the current year, with the increase or decrease in current assets between the periods expressed as a percentage. Profitability analysis (answer C) is the analysis of a firm's ability to earn income. Contribution margin analysis (answer D) is discussed in a later managerial accounting chapter.

2. **D** Various liquidity and solvency measures, categorized as current position analysis, indicate a firm's ability to meet currently maturing obligations. Each measure contributes to the analysis of a firm's current position and is most useful when viewed with other measures and when compared with similar measures for other periods and for other firms. Working capital (answer A) is the excess of current assets over current liabilities; the current ratio (answer B) is the ratio of current assets to current liabilities; and the quick ratio (answer C) is the ratio of the sum of cash, receivables, and temporary investments to current liabilities.

3. **D** The ratio of current assets to current liabilities is usually called the current ratio (answer A). It is sometimes called the working capital ratio (answer B) or bankers' ratio (answer C).

4. **C** The ratio of the sum of cash, receivables, and temporary investments (sometimes called quick assets) to current liabilities is called the quick ratio (answer C) or acid-test ratio. The current ratio (answer A), working capital ratio (answer B), and bankers' ratio (answer D) are terms that describe the ratio of current assets to current liabilities.

5. **C** The number of days' sales in inventory (answer C), which is determined by dividing the average inventory by the average daily cost of goods sold, expresses the relationship between the cost of goods sold and inventory. It indicates the efficiency in the management of inventory. The working capital ratio (answer A) indicates the ability of the business to meet currently maturing obligations (debt). The quick ratio (answer B) indicates the "instant" debt-paying ability of the business. The ratio of fixed assets to long-term liabilities (answer D) indicates the margin of safety for long-term creditors.

CHAPTER 10

Accounting Systems for Manufacturing Businesses

LEARNING OBJECTIVES
After studying this chapter, you should be able to:

Obj | 1   Describe the differences between financial and managerial accounting.

Obj | 2   Distinguish the activities of a manufacturing business from those of a merchandising or service business.

Obj | 3   Define and illustrate materials, factory labor, and factory overhead costs.

Obj | 4   Describe cost accounting systems used by manufacturing businesses.

Obj | 5   Describe and illustrate a job order cost accounting system.

Obj | 6   Use job order cost information for decision making.

Obj | 7   Describe the flow of costs for a service business that uses a job order cost accounting system.

Obj | 8   Describe just-in-time manufacturing practices.

Obj | 9   Describe and illustrate the use of activity-based costing in a service business.

D an Donegan, guitarist for the rock band *Disturbed*, entertains millions of fans each year playing his guitar. His guitar was built by **Washburn Guitars** in Chicago. Washburn Guitars is well-known in the music industry and has been in business for over 120 years.

Staying in business for 120 years requires a thorough understanding of how to manufacture high-quality guitars. In addition, it requires knowledge of how to account for the costs of making guitars. For example, Washburn needs cost information to answer the following questions:

How much should be charged for its guitars?

How many guitars does it have to sell in a year to cover its costs and earn a profit?

How many employees should the company have working on each stage of the manufacturing process?

How would purchasing automated equipment affect the costs of its guitars?

Washburn Guitars can answer these questions with the aid of cost information. This chapter introduces cost concepts used in managerial accounting that help answer questions like those above. In addition, the development of cost information and its use in manufacturing a product will be described and illustrated.

This chapter begins by describing the nature of manufacturing businesses. We then introduce basic cost terms and describe accounting systems for manufacturing businesses. Using this as a basis, a job order cost accounting system is described and illustrated. This chapter concludes by focusing on recent trends in manufacturing and the design of manufacturing accounting systems.

Obj 1

Describe the differences between financial and managerial accounting.

Financial and Managerial Accounting

Chapters 1–9 have dealt primarily with financial accounting. **Financial accounting** is the area of accounting that focuses on recording transactions and events so that general-purpose financial statements can be prepared. These general-purpose financial statements include the income statement, retained earnings statement, balance sheet, and statement of cash flows. While the management of a company may use general-purpose financial statements in making decisions, financial statements are primarily prepared for stakeholders that are external to the company. Such stakeholders include creditors, stockholders, and government agencies. For example, Chapter 9 focused on the use of financial statements in financial analysis by creditors and stockholders.

Managerial accounting is the area of accounting that focuses on recording and reporting information for use by a company's management in decision making. For example, managers must make decisions such as the following:

- What is the cost of manufacturing a product, and how can it be reduced?
- How much does the company have to sell of a product to make a profit?
- What should be the selling price of a product?
- When two or more products use limited resources, how much of each product should be produced?
- Should the company purchase or lease an asset?
- Should the company discontinue an unprofitable segment?
- With limited investment monies, which of two projects should the company invest in for the long term?

Since managerial accounting focuses on preparing information that is useful for management, it is not constrained by rules such as generally accepted accounting principles. That is, managerial accounting information often reports information that is not recorded using generally accepted accounting principles. For example, managerial accountants might prepare reports that involve more subjective data such as the possibility of competitors' reactions to a company's new sales prices or marketing campaign. Also, managerial accounting is not constrained to report data in periodic intervals, but instead often prepares "as needed" by management.

Some of the ways financial and managerial accounting differ are summarized in Exhibit 1.

EXHIBIT 1

Financial and Managerial Accounting Differences

	Managerial Accounting	Financial Accounting
Type of information	Information that is useful to management for its decision making, which varies by type of decision and is not restricted by specific rules such as generally accepted accounting principles (GAAP).	Transactions and events recorded and reported using generally accepted accounting principles.
When reported	As needed by management for its decision making.	Required to be reported annually, but may be reported monthly or quarterly.
Focus of report	Varies by type of decision and may be an employee, manufacturing unit or process, or product as well as the company as a whole or segments within the company.	Company as a whole or segments within the company.

The remainder of this text focuses on managerial accounting topics. For example, this chapter focuses on determining the cost of manufacturing a product. Such information would be used by management in setting prices and in determining the profitability of a product.

Nature of Manufacturing Businesses

Obj **2**

Distinguish the activities of a manufacturing business from those of a merchandising or service business.

Chapters 2 and 3 described and illustrated accounting systems for service businesses. Chapter 4 described and illustrated accounting systems for merchandising businesses. This chapter focuses on manufacturing businesses. Examples of manufacturing businesses include General Motors and Intel Corporation.

The revenue activities of a service business involve providing services to customers. The revenue activities of a merchandising business involve the buying and selling of merchandise. In contrast, a manufacturing business first produces the products it sells. A manufacturing business converts materials into finished products through the use of machinery and labor.

Like merchandising businesses, a manufacturing business reports sales from selling its products. The cost of the products sold is normally reported as **cost of goods sold**, whereas a merchandising business reports these costs as cost of merchandise sold. The subtraction of the cost of goods sold from sales is reported as gross profit. Operating expenses are deducted from gross profit to arrive at net income.

Materials, products in the process of being manufactured, and finished products are reported on the manufacturer's balance sheet as inventories. Like merchandise inventory, these inventories are reported as current assets.

Manufacturing Cost Terms

Obj **3**

Define and illustrate materials, factory labor, and factory overhead costs.

Managers rely on managerial accountants to provide useful *cost* information to support decision making. What is a cost? A **cost** is a payment of cash or its equivalent or the commitment to pay cash in the future for the purpose of generating revenues. A cost provides a benefit that is used immediately or deferred to a future period of time. If the benefit is used immediately, then the cost is an expense, such as salary expense. If the benefit is deferred, then the cost is an asset, such as equipment. As the asset is used, an expense, such as depreciation expense, is recognized.

This section illustrates manufacturing costs for Quixote Guitars, a manufacturing firm. A *manufacturing business* converts materials into a finished product through the use of machinery and labor. Quixote Guitars manufactures guitars as shown in Exhibit 2.

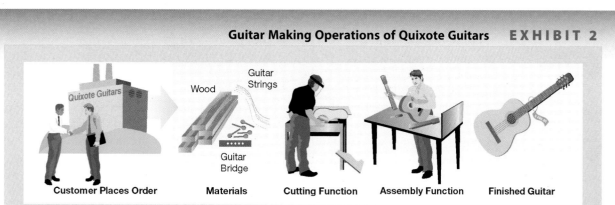

Guitar Making Operations of Quixote Guitars   **EXHIBIT 2**

Customer Places Order   Materials   Cutting Function   Assembly Function   Finished Guitar

Quixote's guitar-making process begins when a customer places an order for a guitar. Once the order is accepted, the manufacturing process begins when the necessary materials are obtained. An employee then cuts the body and neck of the guitar out of raw lumber. Once the wood is cut, the body and neck of the guitar are assembled. When the assembly is complete, the guitar is painted and finished.

The cost of a manufactured product includes the cost of materials used in making the product. In addition, the cost of a manufactured product includes the cost of converting the materials into a finished product. For example, Quixote Guitars uses employees and machines to convert wood (and other supplies) into finished guitars. Thus, the cost of a finished guitar (the cost object) includes the following:

1. Direct materials cost
2. Direct labor cost
3. Factory overhead cost

Direct Materials Cost

Manufactured products begin with raw materials that are converted into finished products. The cost of any material that is an integral part of the finished product is classified as a **direct materials cost**. For Quixote Guitars, direct materials cost includes the cost of the wood used in producing each guitar. Other examples of direct materials costs include the cost of electronic components for a television, silicon wafers for microcomputer chips, and tires for an automobile.

To be classified as a direct materials cost, the cost must be *both* of the following:

1. An integral part of the finished product
2. A significant portion of the total cost of the product

For Quixote Guitars, the cost of the guitar strings is not a direct materials cost. This is because the cost of guitar strings is an insignificant part of the total cost of each guitar. Instead, the cost of guitar strings is classified as a factory overhead cost, which is discussed later.

Materials costs such as the cost of the guitar strings are referred to as indirect materials costs. Another example of an indirect cost for Quixote Guitars is glue. As noted above, indirect materials costs are included in factory overhead.

Direct Labor Cost

Most manufacturing processes use employees to convert materials into finished products. The cost of employee wages that is an integral part of the finished product is classified as **direct labor cost**. For Quixote Guitars, direct labor cost includes the wages of the employees who cut each guitar out of raw lumber and assemble it. Other examples of direct labor costs include mechanics' wages for repairing an automobile, machine operators' wages for manufacturing tools, and assemblers' wages for assembling a laptop computer.

Like a direct materials cost, a direct labor cost must be *both* of the following:

1. An integral part of the finished product
2. A significant portion of the total cost of the product

For Quixote Guitars, the wages of the janitors who clean the factory are not a direct labor cost. This is because janitorial costs are not an integral part or a significant cost of each guitar. Instead, janitorial costs are classified as a factory overhead cost, which is discussed next.

Such labor costs as janitorial costs are referred to as indirect labor costs. Another example of an indirect labor cost for Quixote Guitars is salaries of maintenance employees and plant supervisors. As noted above, indirect labor costs are included in factory overhead.

Factory Overhead Cost

Costs other than direct materials cost and direct labor cost that are incurred in the manufacturing process are combined and classified as **factory overhead cost**. Factory overhead is sometimes called *manufacturing overhead* or *factory burden.*

All factory overhead costs are indirect costs of the product. Some factory overhead costs include the following:

1. Heating and lighting the factory
2. Repairing and maintaining factory equipment
3. Property taxes on factory buildings and land
4. Insurance on factory buildings
5. Depreciation on factory plant and equipment

Factory overhead cost also includes materials and labor costs that do not enter directly into the finished product. Examples include the cost of oil used to lubricate machinery and the wages of janitorial and supervisory employees. Also, if the costs of direct materials or direct labor are not a significant portion of the total product cost, these costs may be classified as factory overhead costs.

For Quixote Guitars, the costs of guitar strings and janitorial wages are factory overhead costs. Additional factory overhead costs of making guitars are as follows:

As manufacturing processes have become more automated, direct labor costs may become so small that they are included as part of factory overhead.

1. Sandpaper
2. Buffing compound
3. Glue
4. Power (electricity) to run the machines
5. Depreciation of the machines and building
6. Salaries of production supervisors

Prime Costs and Conversion Costs

Direct materials, direct labor, and factory overhead costs may be grouped together for analysis and reporting. Two such common groupings are as follows:

1. **Prime costs**, which consist of direct materials and direct labor costs
2. **Conversion costs**, which consist of direct labor and factory overhead costs

Conversion costs are the costs of converting the materials into a finished product. Direct labor is both a prime cost and a conversion cost, as shown in Exhibit 3.

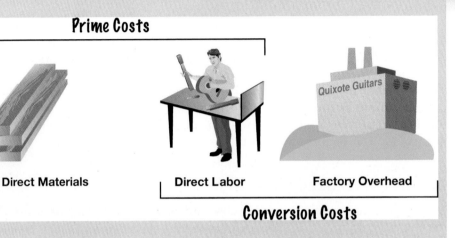

Product Costs and Period Costs

For financial reporting purposes, costs are classified as product costs or period costs.

1. **Product costs** consist of manufacturing costs: direct materials, direct labor, and factory overhead.
2. **Period costs** consist of selling and administrative expenses. *Selling expenses* are incurred in marketing the product and delivering the product to customers. *Administrative expenses* are incurred in managing the company and are not directly related to the manufacturing or selling functions.

Examples of product costs and period costs for Quixote Guitars are presented in Exhibit 4.

To facilitate control, selling and administrative expenses may be reported by level of responsibility. For example, selling expenses may be reported by products, salespersons, departments, divisions, or territories. Likewise, administrative expenses may be reported by areas such as human resources, computer services, legal, accounting, or finance.

The impact on the financial statements of product and period costs is summarized in Exhibit 5. As product costs are incurred, they are recorded and reported on the balance sheet as *inventory*. When the inventory is sold, the cost of the manufactured product sold is reported as *cost of goods sold* on the income statement. Period costs are reported as *expenses* on the income statement in the period in which they are incurred and thus never appear on the balance sheet.

Examples of Product Costs and Period Costs—Quixote Guitars   **EXHIBIT 4**

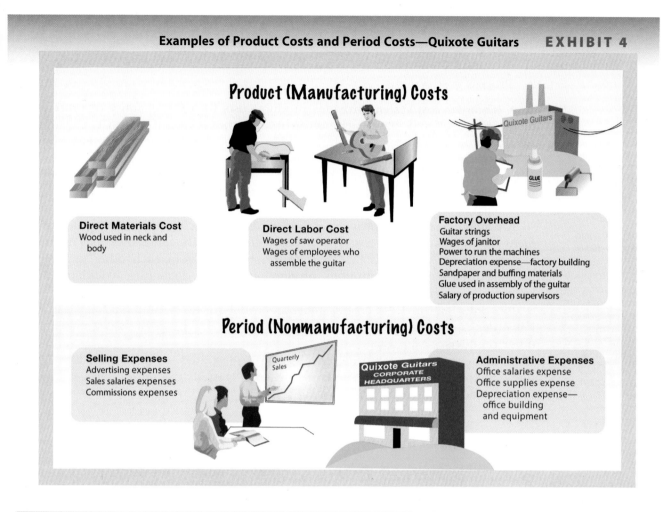

Product (Manufacturing) Costs

Direct Materials Cost
Wood used in neck and
body

Direct Labor Cost
Wages of saw operator
Wages of employees who
assemble the guitar

Factory Overhead
Guitar strings
Wages of janitor
Power to run the machines
Depreciation expense—factory building
Sandpaper and buffing materials
Glue used in assembly of the guitar
Salary of production supervisors

Period (Nonmanufacturing) Costs

Selling Expenses
Advertising expenses
Sales salaries expenses
Commissions expenses

Administrative Expenses
Office salaries expense
Office supplies expense
Depreciation expense—
office building
and equipment

EXHIBIT 5

**Product Costs,
Period Costs,
and the Financial
Statements**

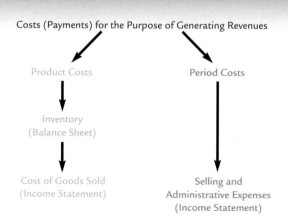

Costs (Payments) for the Purpose of Generating Revenues

Product Costs

Period Costs

Inventory
(Balance Sheet)

Cost of Goods Sold
(Income Statement)

Selling and
Administrative Expenses
(Income Statement)

Cost Accounting System Overview

Cost accounting systems measure, record, and report product costs. Managers use product costs for setting product prices, controlling operations, and developing financial statements.

Obj **4**

Describe cost
accounting systems
used by manufacturing
businesses.

The two main types of cost accounting systems for manufacturing operations are:

1. Job order cost systems
2. Process cost systems

A **job order cost system** provides product costs for each quantity of product that is manufactured. Each quantity of product that is manufactured is called a *job.* Job order cost systems are often used by companies that manufacture custom products for customers or batches of similar products. Manufacturers that use a job order cost system are sometimes called *job shops.* An example of a job shop would be an apparel manufacturer, such as Levi Strauss & Co., or a guitar manufacturer such as Washburn Guitars.

A **process cost system** provides product costs for each manufacturing department or process. Process cost systems are often used by companies that manufacture units of a product that are indistinguishable from each other and are manufactured using a continuous production process. Examples would be oil refineries, paper producers, chemical processors, and food processors.

Job order and process cost systems are widely used. A company may use a job order cost system for some of its products and a process cost system for other products.

In this chapter, the job order cost system is illustrated. As a basis for illustration, Quixote Guitars, a manufacturer of guitars, is used. The process cost system is described and illustrated in Appendix B.

Warner Bros. and other movie studios use job order cost systems to accumulate movie production and distribution costs. Costs such as actor salaries, production costs, movie print costs, and marketing costs are accumulated in a job account for a particular movie.

Obj | **5**

Describe and illustrate a job order cost accounting system.

Job Order Cost Systems for Manufacturing Businesses

A job order cost system records and summarizes manufacturing costs by jobs. The flow of manufacturing costs in a job order system is illustrated in Exhibit 6.

The **materials inventory**, sometimes called *raw materials inventory,* consists of the costs of the direct and indirect materials that have not yet entered the manufacturing process. For Quixote Guitars, the materials inventory would consist of wood, guitar strings, guitar bridges, and glue.

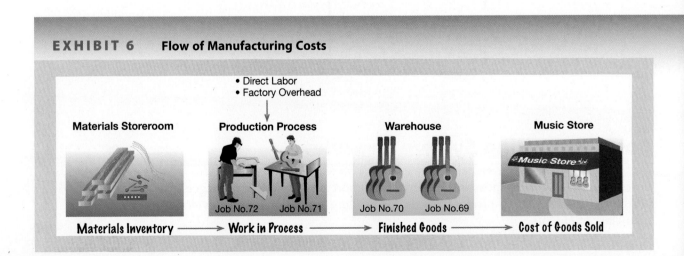

EXHIBIT 6   Flow of Manufacturing Costs

The **work-in-process inventory** consists of direct materials costs, direct labor costs, and factory overhead costs that have entered the manufacturing process but are associated with products that have not been completed. For example, although the materials for Jobs 71 and 72 have been added, they are still in the production process. Thus, Jobs 71 and 72 are in Work-in-Process Inventory as shown in Exhibit 6.

The **finished goods inventory** consists of completed jobs that have not been sold. Jobs 69 and 70 have been completed and are included in Finished Goods Inventory as shown in Exhibit 6.

Upon sale, a manufacturer records the cost of the sale as *cost of goods sold*. An example is the guitars sold to the music store in Exhibit 6. The cost of goods sold for a manufacturer is comparable to the cost of merchandise sold for a merchandising business.

In a job order cost accounting system, perpetual inventory records are maintained for materials, work-in-process, and finished goods inventories. For example, materials inventory is supported by subsidiary inventory accounts that record the increase, decrease, and amount on hand for each type of material. These subsidiary materials accounts are kept in a ledger, called a **subsidiary ledger**. The sum of the subsidiary ledger accounts equals the balance of the materials account, called the **controlling account**.[1]

The controlling accounts and subsidiary ledgers for materials, work-in-process, and finished goods inventories are illustrated below for Quixote Guitars.

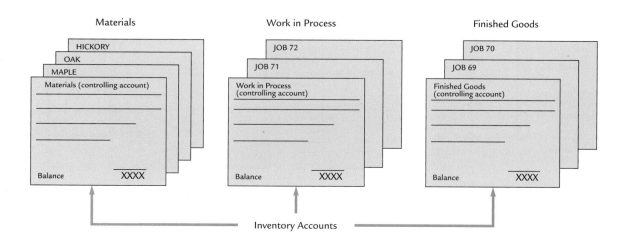

Materials

The materials account is a controlling account. A separate account for each type of material is maintained in a subsidiary **materials ledger**.

Exhibit 7 shows Quixote Guitars' materials subsidiary ledger account for maple. Increases and decreases to the account are as follows:

1. Increases are based on *receiving reports* such as Receiving Report No. 196 for $10,500, which is supported by the supplier's invoice.
2. Decreases are based on *materials requisitions* such as Requisition No. 672 for $2,000 for Job 71 and Requisition No. 704 for $11,000 for Job 72.

Many companies use bar code scanning devices in place of receiving reports to record and electronically transmit incoming materials data.

---

1. In addition to inventory, controlling accounts and subsidiary ledgers are also normally maintained for accounts receivable; accounts payable; property, plant, and equipment; and capital stock.

EXHIBIT 7

Materials Information and Cost Flows

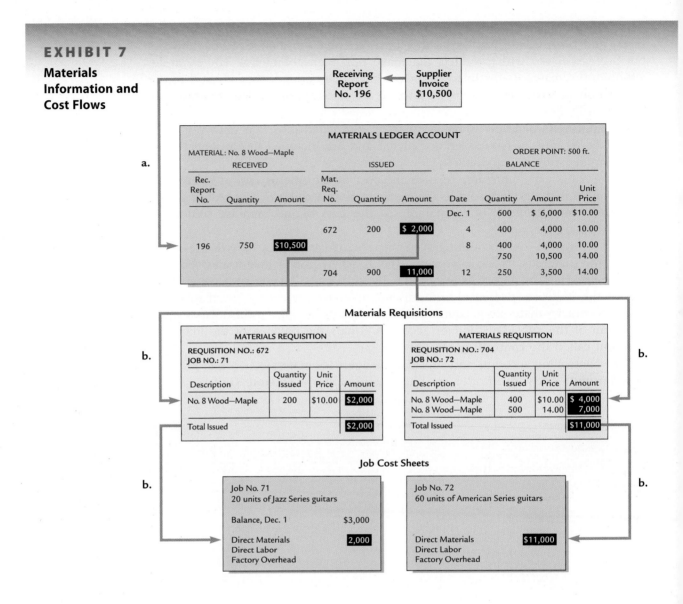

A **receiving report** is prepared when materials that have been ordered are received and inspected. The quantity received and the condition of the materials are entered on the receiving report. When the supplier's invoice is received, it is compared to the receiving report. If there are no discrepancies, the purchase is recorded.

The effect on the accounts and financial statements of recording the supplier invoice and Receiving Report No. 196 is shown below.

Statement of Cash Flows	Balance Sheet			Income Statement
	Assets	**= Liabilities**	**+ Stockholders' Equity**	
	Materials	=	**Accounts Payable**	
a.	10,500		10,500	

The storeroom releases materials for use in manufacturing when a **materials requisition** is received. An example of a materials requisition is shown in Exhibit 7.

The materials requisitions for each job serve as the basis for recording materials used. For direct materials, the quantities and amounts from the materials requisitions are recorded on job cost sheets. **Job cost sheets**, which are illustrated in Exhibit 7, make up the work-in-process subsidiary ledger.

For many manufacturing firms, the direct materials cost can be greater than 50% of the total cost to manufacture a product. This is why controlling materials costs is very important.

Exhibit 7 shows the posting of $2,000 of direct materials to Job 71 and $11,000 of direct materials to Job 72.[2] Job 71 is an order for 20 units of Jazz Series guitars, while Job 72 is an order for 60 units of American Series guitars.

A summary of the materials requisitions is used as a basis for recording the materials of $13,000 ($2,000 + $11,000) used for the month. The effect on the accounts and financial statements of the materials used in December is shown below.

Statement of Cash Flows	Balance Sheet					Income Statement
	Assets		= Liabilities + Stockholders' Equity			
	Materials +	Work in Process				
b.	−13,000	13,000				

Many companies use computerized information processes to record the use of materials. In such cases, storeroom employees electronically record the release of materials, which automatically updates the materials ledger and job cost sheets.

Factory Labor

When employees report for work, they may use *clock cards, in-and-out cards,* or *electronic badges* to clock in. When employees work on an individual job, they use **time tickets**. Exhibit 8 illustrates time tickets for Jobs 71 and 72.

Exhibit 8 shows that on December 13, 20Y7, D. McInnis spent six hours working on Job 71 at an hourly rate of $10 for a cost of $60 (6 hrs. × $10). Exhibit 8 also indicates that a total of 350 hours was spent by employees on Job 71 during December for a total cost of $3,500. This total direct labor cost of $3,500 is recorded on the job cost sheet for Job 71, as shown in Exhibit 8.

Integrity, Objectivity, and Ethics in Business

PHONY INVOICE SCAMS

A popular method for defrauding a company is to issue a phony invoice. The scam begins by initially contacting the target firm to discover details of key business contacts, business operations, and products. The swindler then uses this information to create a fictitious invoice. The invoice will include names, figures, and other details to give it the appearance of legitimacy. This type of scam can be avoided if invoices are matched with receiving documents prior to issuing a check.

2. To simplify, Exhibit 7 and this chapter use the first-in, first-out cost flow method.

EXHIBIT 8

Labor Information and Cost Flows

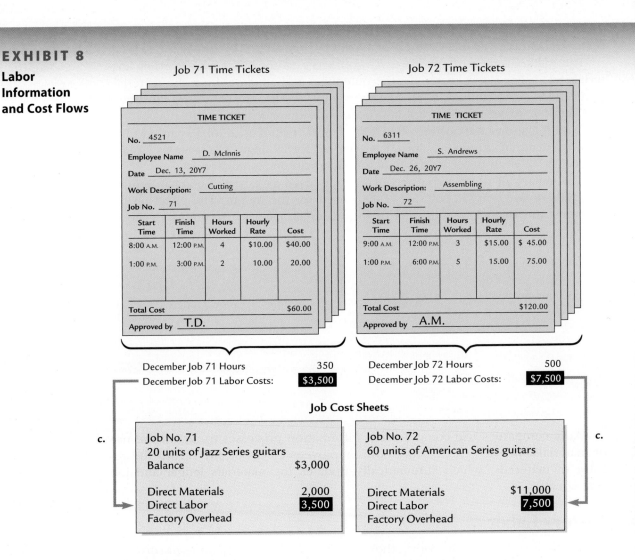

Likewise, Exhibit 8 shows that on December 26, 20Y7, S. Andrews spent eight hours on Job 72 at an hourly rate of $15 for a cost of $120 (8 hrs. × $15). A total of 500 hours was spent by employees on Job 72 during December for a total cost of $7,500. This total direct labor cost of $7,500 is posted to the job cost sheet for Job 72, as shown in Exhibit 8.

A summary of the time tickets is used as the basis for recording direct labor of $11,000 ($3,500 + $7,500) for the month. The direct labor costs that flow into production increase Work in Process and Wages Payable. The effect on the accounts and financial statements of recording the direct labor for December is shown below.

Statement of Cash Flows	Balance Sheet			Income Statement
	Assets	= Liabilities	+ Stockholders' Equity	
	Work in Process	=	Wages Payable	
c.	11,000		11,000	

Integrity, Objectivity, and Ethics in Business

GHOST EMPLOYEES

Companies must guard against the fraudulent creation and cashing of payroll checks. Numerous payroll frauds involve supervisors adding fictitious employees to or failing to remove departing employees from the payroll and then cashing the check. This type of fraud can be minimized by requiring proper authorization and approval of employee additions, removals, or changes in pay rates.

As with direct materials, many businesses use computerized information processing to record direct labor. In such cases, employees may log their time directly into computer terminals at their workstations. In other cases, employees may be issued magnetic cards, much like credit cards, to log in and out of work assignments.

Factory Overhead Cost

Factory overhead includes all manufacturing costs except direct materials and direct labor. A summary of factory overhead costs comes from a variety of sources including the following:

1. *Indirect materials* comes from a summary of materials requisitions.
2. *Indirect labor* comes from the salaries of production supervisors and the wages of other employees such as janitors.
3. *Factory power* comes from utility bills.
4. *Factory depreciation* comes from Accounting Department computations of depreciation.

Shell Group uses a magnetic card system to track the work of maintenance crews in its refinery operations.

To illustrate the recording of factory overhead, assume that Quixote Guitars incurred $4,600 of overhead in December. The effect on the accounts and financial statements is shown below.

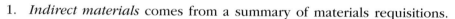

Statement of Cash Flows	Balance Sheet						Income Statement
	Assets			=	Liabilities	+ Stockholders' Equity	
	Materials +	Factory Overhead	− Accumulated Depreciation	=	Wages Payable +	Utilities Payable	
d.	−500	4,600	−1,200		2,000	900	

Allocating Factory Overhead Factory overhead is different from direct labor and direct materials in that it is *indirectly* related to the jobs. That is, factory overhead costs cannot be identified with or traced to specific jobs. For this reason, factory overhead costs are allocated to jobs. The process by which factory overhead or other costs are assigned to a cost object, such as a job, is called **cost allocation**.

The factory overhead costs are *allocated* to jobs using a common measure related to each job. This measure is called an **activity base**, *allocation base*, or *activity driver.* The activity base used to allocate overhead should reflect the consumption or use of factory overhead costs. For example, production supervisor salaries could be allocated on the basis of direct labor hours or direct labor cost of each job.

Predetermined Factory Overhead Rate Factory overhead costs are normally allocated or *applied* to jobs using a **predetermined factory overhead rate**. The predetermined factory overhead rate is computed as follows:

$$\frac{\text{Predetermined Factory}}{\text{Overhead Rate}} = \frac{\text{Estimated Total Factory Overhead Costs}}{\text{Estimated Activity Base}}$$

To illustrate, assume that Quixote Guitars estimates the total factory overhead cost as $50,000 for the year and the activity base as 10,000 direct labor hours. The predetermined factory overhead rate of $5 per direct labor hour is computed as follows:

$$\frac{\text{Predetermined Factory}}{\text{Overhead Rate}} = \frac{\text{Estimated Total Factory Overhead Costs}}{\text{Estimated Activity Base}}$$

$$\frac{\text{Predetermined Factory}}{\text{Overhead Rate}} = \frac{\$50,000}{10,000 \text{ direct labor hours}} = \$5 \text{ per direct labor hour}$$

As shown above, the predetermined overhead rate is computed using *estimated* amounts at the beginning of the period. This is because managers need timely information on the product costs of each job. If a company waited until all overhead costs were known at the end of the period, the allocated factory overhead would be accurate, but not timely. Only through timely reporting can managers adjust manufacturing methods or product pricing.

Many companies are using **activity-based costing** for accumulating and allocating factory overhead costs. This method uses a different overhead rate for each type of factory overhead activity, such as inspecting, moving, and machining. Activity-based costing is discussed and illustrated at the end of this chapter.

A survey conducted by the Cost Management Group of the Institute for Management Accountants found that 20% of survey respondents had adopted activity-based costing.

Applying Factory Overhead to Work in Process Quixote Guitars applies factory overhead using a rate of $5 per direct labor hour. The factory overhead applied to each job is recorded on the job cost sheets, as shown in Exhibit 9.

Exhibit 9 shows that 850 direct labor hours were used in Quixote Guitars' December operations. Based on the time tickets, 350 hours can be traced to Job 71, and 500 hours can be traced to Job 72.

Using a factory overhead rate of $5 per direct labor hour, $4,250 of factory overhead is applied as follows:

	Direct Labor Hours	Factory Overhead Rate	Factory Overhead Applied
Job 71	350	$5	$1,750 (350 hrs. × $5)
Job 72	500	5	2,500 (500 hrs. × $5)
Total	850		$4,250

As shown in Exhibit 9, the applied overhead is recorded on each job cost sheet. Factory overhead of $1,750 is posted to Job 71, which results in a total product

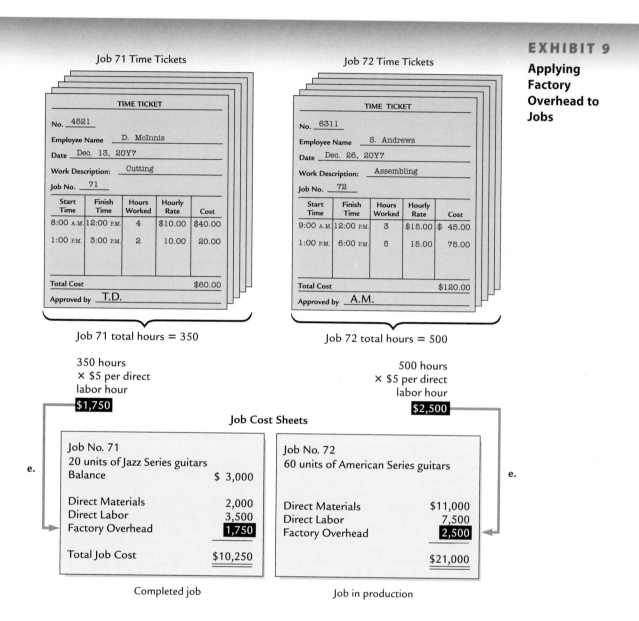

EXHIBIT 9

Applying Factory Overhead to Jobs

cost on December 31, 20Y7, of $10,250. Factory overhead of $2,500 is posted to Job 72, which results in a total product cost on December 31, 20Y7, of $21,000.

The factory overhead costs applied to production increase the work-in-process account and decrease the factory overhead account. The effect of applying the $4,250 ($1,750 + $2,500) of factory overhead to production on the accounts and financial statements for Quixote Guitars is shown below.

Statement of Cash Flows	Balance Sheet			Income Statement
	Assets	= Liabilities + Stockholders' Equity		
	Work in Process	+	Factory Overhead	
e.	4,250		−4,250	

To summarize, the factory overhead account is:

1. Increased for the *actual overhead* costs incurred, as shown earlier for transaction (d) on page 383.
2. Decreased for the *applied overhead,* as shown on the previous page for transaction (e).

The actual and applied overhead usually differ because the actual overhead costs are normally different from the estimated overhead costs. Depending on whether actual overhead is greater or less than applied overhead, the factory overhead account will either have a positive or negative ending balance as follows:

1. If the applied overhead is *less than* the actual overhead incurred, the factory overhead account will have a positive balance. This positive balance is called **underapplied factory overhead** or *underabsorbed factory overhead.*
2. If the applied overhead is *more than* the actual overhead incurred, the factory overhead account will have a negative balance. This negative balance is called **overapplied factory overhead** or *overabsorbed factory overhead.*

If the balance of factory overhead (either underapplied or overapplied) becomes large, the balance and related overhead rate should be investigated. For example, a large balance could be caused by changes in manufacturing methods. In this case, the factory overhead rate should be revised.

Disposal of Factory Overhead Balance During the year, the balance in the factory overhead account is carried forward and reported as a positive or negative amount on the monthly (interim) balance sheets. However, any balance in the factory overhead account should not be carried over to the next year. This is because any such balance applies only to operations of the current year.

If the estimates for computing the predetermined overhead rate are reasonably accurate, the ending balance of Factory Overhead should be relatively small. For this reason, the balance of Factory Overhead at the end of the year is disposed of by transferring it to the cost of goods sold account as follows:[3]

1. An ending positive balance (underapplied overhead) in the factory overhead account is disposed of by increasing Cost of Goods Sold and decreasing Factory Overhead.
2. An ending negative balance (overapplied overhead) in the factory overhead account is disposed of by increasing Factory Overhead and decreasing Cost of Goods Sold.

To illustrate, the effect on the accounts and financial statements of eliminating an underapplied (positive) overhead balance of $150 at the end of the year for Quixote Guitars is as shown below.

Statement of Cash Flows	Balance Sheet			Income Statement
	Assets	= Liabilities +	Stockholders' Equity	
	Factory Overhead	=	Retained Earnings	
f.	−150		−150	f.

Income Statement	
f. Cost of goods sold	−150

---

3. An ending balance in the factory overhead account also may be allocated among the work-in-process, finished goods, and cost of goods sold accounts. This brings these accounts into agreement with the actual costs incurred. This approach is rarely used and is only required for large ending balances in the factory overhead account. For this reason, it will not be used in this text.

Work in Process

During the period, Work in Process is increased for the following:

1. Direct materials cost
2. Direct labor cost
3. Applied factory overhead cost

To illustrate, the balance of work in process for Quixote Guitars on December 1, 20Y7 (beginning balance), was $3,000. This balance relates to Job 71, which was the only job in process on this date. During December, Work in Process was increased for the following:

1. Direct materials cost of $13,000 [transaction (b)] based on materials requisitions.
2. Direct labor cost of $11,000 [transaction (c)] based on time tickets.
3. Applied factory overhead of $4,250 [transaction (e)] based on the predetermined overhead rate of $5 per direct labor hour.

The preceding increases in Work in Process are supported by the job cost sheets for Jobs 71 and 72, as shown in Exhibit 10.

Job Cost Sheets and the Work-in-Process Controlling Accounts EXHIBIT 10

Job Cost Sheets

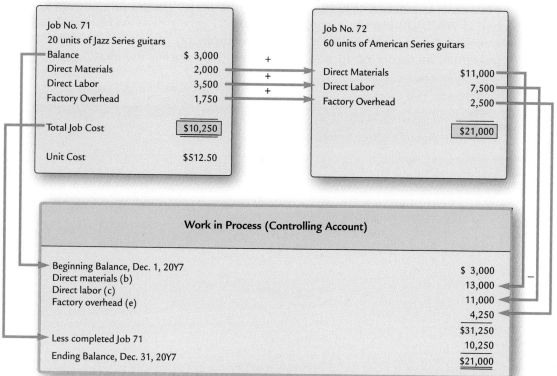

During December, Job 71 was completed. Upon completion, the product costs (direct materials, direct labor, factory overhead) are totaled. This total is divided by the number of units produced to determine the cost per unit. Thus, the 20 Jazz Series guitars produced as Job 71 cost $512.50 ($10,250/20) per guitar.

After completion, Job 71 is transferred from Work in Process to Finished Goods. For Job 71, this transfer of costs affects the accounts and financial statements as follows:

Statement of Cash Flows	Balance Sheet			Income Statement
	Assets	= Liabilities + Stockholders' Equity		
	Work in Process +	Finished Goods		
g.	−10,250	10,250		

Job 72 was started in December, but was not completed by December 31, 20Y7. Thus, Job 72 is still part of work in process on December 31, 20Y7. As shown in Exhibit 10, the balance of the job cost sheet for Job 72 ($21,000) is also the December 31, 20Y7, balance of Work in Process.

Finished Goods

The finished goods account is a controlling account for the subsidiary **finished goods ledger** or *stock ledger*. Each account in the finished goods ledger contains cost data for the units manufactured, units sold, and units on hand.

Exhibit 11 illustrates the finished goods ledger account for Jazz Series guitars. This exhibit indicates that there were 40 Jazz Series guitars on hand on December 1, 20Y7. During the month, 20 additional Jazz guitars were completed and transferred to Finished Goods from the completion of Job 71. In addition, the beginning inventory of 40 Jazz guitars were sold during the month.

EXHIBIT 11   Finished Goods Ledger Account

ITEM: *Jazz Series guitars*

Manufactured			Shipped			Balance			
Job Order No.	Quantity	Amount	Ship Order No.	Quantity	Amount	Date	Quantity	Amount	Unit Cost
						Dec. 1	40	$20,000	$500.00
			643	40	$20,000	9	—	—	—
71	20	$10,250				31	20	10,250	512.50

Sales and Cost of Goods Sold

Sales for a manufacturing business and a merchandising business have the same effect on the accounts and financial statements. To illustrate, assume that Quixote

Guitars sold the 40 Jazz Series guitars during December for $850 per unit. These guitars have a cost of $500 per unit. The cost data can be obtained from the finished goods ledger. The effect of selling the 40 Jazz guitars on the accounts and financial statements is as follows:

Statement of Cash Flows	Balance Sheet					Income Statement
	Assets		= Liabilities +	**Stockholders' Equity**		
	Accounts Receivable	+ Finished Goods =		Retained Earnings		
h.	34,000	−20,000		14,000		h.

Income Statement

h. Sales	34,000
Cost of goods sold	−20,000
Net income	14,000

Period Costs

Period costs are used in generating revenue during the current period, but are not involved in the manufacturing process. Period costs are recorded as expenses of the current period as either selling or administrative expenses.

Selling expenses are incurred in marketing the product and delivering sold products to customers. Administrative expenses are incurred in managing the company, but are not related to the manufacturing or selling functions.

Service companies, such as telecommunications, insurance, banking, broadcasting, and hospitality, typically have a large portion of their total costs as period costs with few product costs.

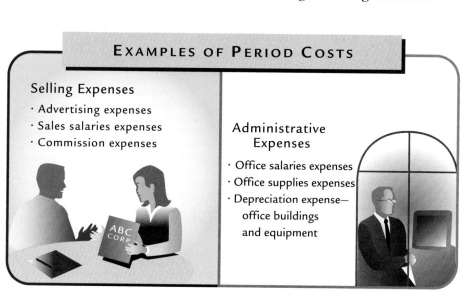

EXAMPLES OF PERIOD COSTS

Selling Expenses
· Advertising expenses
· Sales salaries expenses
· Commission expenses

Administrative Expenses
· Office salaries expenses
· Office supplies expenses
· Depreciation expense—office buildings and equipment

During December, Quixote Guitars incurred sales salaries of $2,000 and office salaries of $1,500. The effect on the accounts and financial statements of recording the December salaries is shown on the following page.

Statement of Cash Flows	Balance Sheet			Income Statement
	Assets	= Liabilities +	Stockholders' Equity	
		Salaries Payable +	Retained Earnings	
i.		3,500	−3,500	i.

Income Statement

i. Sales salaries exp.	−2,000	
Office salaries exp.	−1,500	
Net income	−3,500	

Summary of Cost Flows for Quixote Guitars

Exhibit 12 shows the cost flows through the manufacturing accounts of Quixote Guitars for December. In Exhibit 12, increases are shown on the left side and decreases are shown on the right side of the accounts. In addition, summary details of the following subsidiary ledgers are shown:

1. *Materials Ledger*—the subsidiary ledger for Materials.
2. *Job Cost Sheets*—the subsidiary ledger for Work in Process.
3. *Finished Goods Ledger*—the subsidiary ledger for Finished Goods.

Entries in the accounts shown in Exhibit 12 are identified by letters. These letters refer to the entries described and illustrated in the chapter. Entry (h) is not shown because it does not involve a cost flow.

As shown in Exhibit 12, the balances of Materials, Work in Process, and Finished Goods are supported by their subsidiary ledgers. These balances are as follows:

Controlling Account	Balance and Total of Related Subsidiary Ledger
Materials	$ 3,500
Work in Process	21,000
Finished Goods	10,250

The income statement for Quixote Guitars is shown in Exhibit 13 on page 392.

Job Order Costing for Decision Making

Obj | **6**

Use job order cost information for decision making.

A job order cost accounting system accumulates and records product costs by jobs. The resulting total and unit product costs can be compared to similar jobs, compared over time, or compared to expected costs. In this way, a job order cost system can be used by managers for cost evaluation and control.

To illustrate, Exhibit 14 on page 392 shows the direct materials used for Jobs 54 and 63 for Quixote Guitars. The wood used in manufacturing guitars is measured in board feet. Since Jobs 54 and 63 produced the same type and number of guitars, the direct materials cost per unit should be about the same. However, the materials cost per guitar for Job 54 is $100, while for Job 63 it is $125. Thus, the materials costs are significantly more for Job 63.

EXHIBIT 12   Flow of Manufacturing Costs for Quixote Guitars

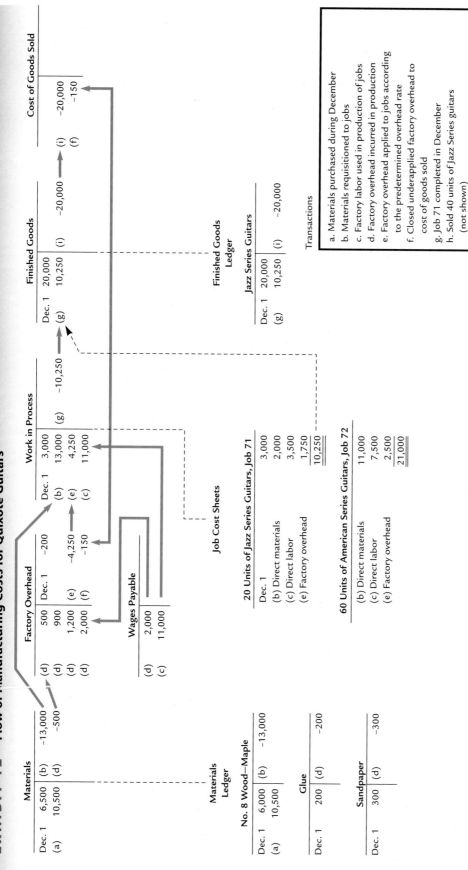

Materials

Dec. 1	6,500	(b)	−13,000
(a)	10,500	(d)	−500

Materials Ledger

No. 8 Wood—Maple

Dec. 1	6,000	(b)	−13,000
(a)	10,500		

Glue

Dec. 1	200	(d)	−200

Sandpaper

Dec. 1	300	(d)	−300

Factory Overhead

	500	Dec. 1	−200
(d)	900		
(d)	1,200	(e)	−4,250
(d)	2,000	(f)	−150

Wages Payable

(d)	2,000	
(c)	11,000	

Work in Process

Dec. 1	3,000		
(b)	13,000	(g)	−10,250
(e)	4,250		
(c)	11,000		

Job Cost Sheets

20 Units of Jazz Series Guitars, Job 71

Dec. 1	3,000
(b) Direct materials	2,000
(c) Direct labor	3,500
(e) Factory overhead	1,750
	10,250

60 Units of American Series Guitars, Job 72

(b) Direct materials	11,000
(c) Direct labor	7,500
(e) Factory overhead	2,500
	21,000

Finished Goods

Dec. 1	20,000		
(g)	10,250	(i)	−20,000

Finished Goods Ledger

Jazz Series Guitars

Dec. 1	20,000		
(g)	10,250	(i)	−20,000

Cost of Goods Sold

(i)	−20,000	
(f)	−150	

Transactions

a. Materials purchased during December
b. Materials requisitioned to jobs
c. Factory labor used in production of jobs
d. Factory overhead incurred in production
e. Factory overhead applied to jobs according to the predetermined overhead rate
f. Closed underapplied factory overhead to cost of goods sold
g. Job 71 completed in December
h. Sold 40 units of Jazz Series guitars (not shown)
i. Cost of 40 units of Jazz Series guitars sold

EXHIBIT 13

Income Statement of Quixote Guitars

Quixote Guitars
Income Statement
For the Month Ended December 31, 20Y7

Sales		$34,000
Cost of goods sold		20,150
Gross profit		$13,850
Selling and administrative expenses:		
Sales salaries expenses	$2,000	
Office salaries expense	1,500	
Total selling and administrative expenses		3,500
Income from operations		$10,350

EXHIBIT 14

Comparing Data from Job Cost Sheets

Job 54
Item: 40 Jazz Series guitars

	Materials Quantity (board feet)	Materials Price	Materials Amount	Materials per Guitar
Direct materials:				
No. 8 Wood—Maple	400	$10.00	$4,000	$100

Job 63
Item: 40 Jazz Series guitars

	Materials Quantity (board feet)	Materials Price	Materials Amount	Materials per Guitar
Direct materials:				
No. 8 Wood—Maple	500	$10.00	$5,000	$125

Major electric utilities such as **Tennessee Valley Authority, Consolidated Edison Inc.,** and **Pacific Gas and Electric Company** use job order accounting to control the costs associated with major repairs and overhauls that occur during maintenance shutdowns.

The job cost sheets shown in Exhibit 14 can be analyzed for possible reasons for the increased materials cost for Job 63. Since the materials price did not change ($10 per board foot), the increased materials cost must be related to wood consumption.

Comparing wood consumed for Jobs 54 and 63 shows that 400 board feet were used in Job 54 to produce 40 guitars. In contrast, Job 63 used 500 board feet to produce the same number of guitars. Thus, an investigation should be undertaken to determine the cause of the extra 100 board feet used for Job 63. Possible explanations could include the following:

1. A new employee, who was not properly trained, cut the wood for Job 63. As a result, there was excess waste and scrap.

2. The wood used for Job 63 was purchased from a new supplier. The wood was of poor quality, which created excessive waste and scrap.

3. The cutting tools needed repair and were not properly maintained. As a result, the wood was miscut, which created excessive waste and scrap.

4. The instructions attached to the job were incorrect. The wood was cut according to the instructions. The incorrect instructions were discovered later in assembly. As a result, the wood had to be recut and the initial cuttings scrapped.

Job Order Cost Systems for Service Businesses

Obj **7**

Describe the flow of costs for a service business that uses a job order cost accounting system.

A job order cost accounting system may be used for a professional service business. For example, an advertising agency, an attorney, and a physician provide services to individual customers, clients, or patients. In such cases, the customer, client, or patient can be viewed as a job for which costs are accumulated and reported.

The primary product costs for a service business are direct labor and overhead costs. Any materials or supplies used in rendering services are normally insignificant. As a result, materials and supply costs are included as part of the overhead cost.

Like a manufacturing business, direct labor and overhead costs of rendering services to clients are accumulated in a work-in-process account. *Work in Process* is supported by a cost ledger with a job cost sheet for each client.

When a job is completed and the client is billed, the costs are transferred to a cost of services account. *Cost of Services* is similar to the cost of merchandise sold account for a merchandising business or the cost of goods sold account for a manufacturing business. A finished goods account and related finished goods ledger are not necessary. This is because the revenues for the services are recorded only after the services are provided.

The flow of costs through a service business using a job order cost accounting system is shown in Exhibit 15.

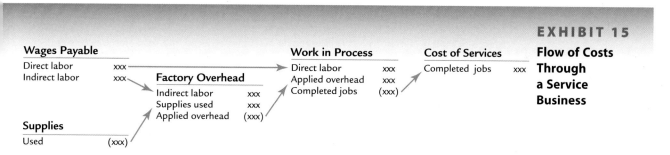

EXHIBIT 15

Flow of Costs Through a Service Business

In practice, other considerations unique to service businesses may need to be considered. For example, a service business may bill clients on a weekly or monthly basis rather than when a job is completed. In such cases, a portion of the costs related to each billing is transferred from the work-in-process account to the cost of services account. A service business may also bill clients for services in advance, which would be accounted for as deferred revenue until the services are completed.

Just-in-Time Practices

Obj **8**

Describe just-in-time manufacturing practices.

The objective of most manufacturers is to produce products with high quality, low cost, and instant availability. In attempting to achieve this objective, many manufacturers have implemented just-in-time processing. **Just-in-time (JIT) processing**, sometimes called *lean manufacturing,* is a philosophy that focuses on reducing time and cost, and eliminating poor quality.

Exhibit 16 lists just-in-time manufacturing and the traditional manufacturing practices. Each of the just-in-time practices is discussed in this section.

EXHIBIT 16

Operating Principles of Just-in-Time versus Traditional Manufacturing

Issue	Just-in-Time Manufacturing	Traditional Manufacturing
Inventory	Reduces inventory.	Increases inventory to protect against process problems.
Lead time	Reduces lead time.	Increases lead time to protect against uncertainty.
Setup time	Reduces setup time.	Disregards setup time as an improvement priority.
Production layout	Emphasizes product-oriented layout.	Emphasizes process-oriented layout.
Role of the employee	Emphasizes team-oriented employee involvement.	Emphasizes work of individuals, following manager instructions.
Production scheduling policy	Emphasizes pull manufacturing.	Emphasizes push manufacturing.
Quality	Emphasizes zero defects.	Tolerates defects.
Suppliers and customers	Emphasizes supply chain management.	Treats suppliers and customers as "arm's-length," independent entities.

HOW BUSINESSES MAKE MONEY

MAKING MONEY IN THE MOVIE BUSINESS

Movie making is a high risk venture. The movie must be produced and marketed before the first dollar is received from the box office. If the movie is a hit, then all is well; but if the movie is a bomb, money will be lost. This is termed a "Blockbuster" business strategy and is common in businesses that have large up-front costs in the face of uncertain follow-up revenues, such as pharmaceuticals, video games, and publishing.

The profitability of a movie depends on its revenue and cost. A movie's cost is determined using job order costing; however, how costs are assigned to a movie is often complex and may be subject to disagreement. For example, in Hollywood's competitive environment, studios often negotiate payments to producers and actors based on a percentage of the film's gross revenues. This is termed "contingent compensation." As movies become hits, compensation costs increase in proportion to the movie's revenues, which eats into a hit's profitability.

As the dollars involved get bigger, disagreements often develop between movie studios and actors or producers over the amount of contingent compensation. For example, the producer

of the hit movie *Chicago* sued **Miramax Film Corp.** for failing to include foreign receipts and DVD sales in the revenue that was used to determine his payments. The controversial nature of contingent compensation is illustrated by the suit's claim that the accounting for contingent compensation led to confusing and meaningless results.

iStockPhoto.com/miflippo

Integrity, Objectivity, and Ethics in Business

THE INVENTORY SHIFT

Some managers take a shortcut to reducing inventory by shifting inventory to their suppliers. With this tactic, the hard work of improving processes is avoided. Enlightened managers realize that such tactics often have short-lived savings.

Suppliers will eventually increase their prices to compensate for the additional inventory holding costs, thus resulting in no savings. Therefore, shifting a problem doesn't eliminate a problem.

Reducing Inventory

Just-in-time (JIT) manufacturing views inventory as wasteful and unnecessary. As a result, JIT emphasizes reducing or eliminating inventory.

Under traditional manufacturing, inventory often hides underlying production problems. For example, if machine breakdowns occur, work-in-process inventories can be used to keep production running in other departments while the machines are being repaired. Likewise, inventories can be used to hide problems caused by a shortage of trained employees, unreliable suppliers, or poor quality.

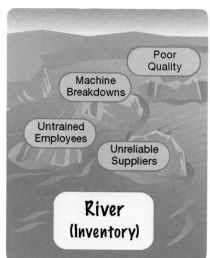

In contrast, just-in-time manufacturing attempts to solve and remove production problems. In this way, raw materials, work-in-process, and finished goods inventories are reduced or eliminated.

The role of inventory in manufacturing can be illustrated using a river. Inventory is the water in a river. The rocks at the bottom of the river are production problems. When the water (inventory) is high, the rocks (production problems) at the bottom of the river are hidden. As the water level (inventory) drops, the rocks (production problems) become visible, one by one. JIT manufacturing reduces the water level (inventory), exposes the rocks (production problems), and removes the rocks so that the river can flow smoothly.

Reducing Lead Times

Lead time, sometimes called *throughput time,* measures the time between when a product enters production (is started) and when it is completed (finished). In other words, lead time measures how long it takes to manufacture a product. For example, if a product enters production at 1:00 P.M. and is completed at 5:00 P.M., the lead time is four hours.

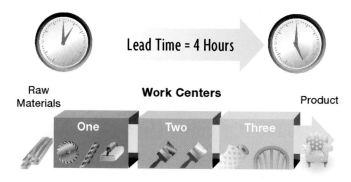

The lead time can be classified as one of the following:

1. **Value-added lead time**, which is the time spent in converting raw materials into a finished unit of product
2. **Non-value-added lead time**, which is the time spent while the unit of product is waiting to enter the next production process or is moved from one process to another

Exhibit 17 illustrates value-added and non-value-added lead time.

EXHIBIT 17   **Components of Lead Time**

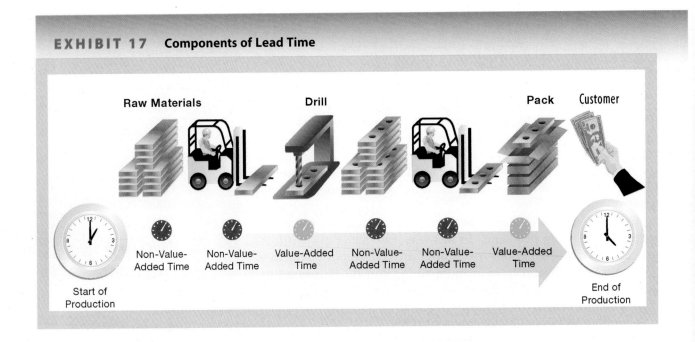

Crown Audio reduced the lead time between receiving a customer order and delivering it from 30 days to 12 hours by using just-in-time principles.

The time spent drilling and packing the unit of product is value-added time. The time spent waiting to enter the next process or the time spent moving the unit of product from one process to another is non-valued-added time.

Just-in-time manufacturing reduces or eliminates non-value-added time. In contrast, traditional manufacturing processes may have a value-added ratio as small as 5%.

Reducing Setup Time

A **setup** is the effort spent preparing an operation or process for a production run. If setups are long and costly, the batch size (number of units) for the related production run is normally large. Large batch sizes allow setup costs to be spread over more units and thus reduce the cost per unit. However, large batch sizes increase inventory and lead time.

Emphasizing Product-Oriented Layout

Manufacturing processes can be organized around a product, which is called a **product-oriented layout** (or *product cells*). Alternatively, manufacturing processes can be organized around a process, which is called a **process-oriented layout**.

HOW BUSINESSES MAKE MONEY

P&G'S "PIT STOPS"

What do **Procter & Gamble (P&G)** and **Formula One** racing have in common? The answer begins with P&G's Packing Department, which is where detergents and other products are filled on a "pack line." Containers move down the pack line and are filled with products from a packing machine. When it was time to change from a 36-oz. to a 54-oz. Tide box, for example, the changeover involved stopping the line, adjusting guide rails, retrieving items from the tool room, placing items back in the tool room, changing and cleaning the pack heads, and performing routine maintenance. Changing the pack line could be a very difficult process and typically took up to several hours.

Management realized that it was important to reduce this time significantly in order to become more flexible and cost efficient in packing products. Where could they learn how to do setups faster? They turned to Formula One racing, reasoning that a pit stop was much like a setup. As a result, P&G videotaped actual Formula One pit stops. These videos were used to form the following principles for conducting a fast setup:

- Position the tools near their point of use on the line prior to stopping the line, to reduce time going back and forth to the tool room.
- Arrange the tools in the exact order of work, so that no time is wasted looking for a tool.
- Have each employee perform a very specific task during the setup.
- Design the workflow so that employees don't interfere with each other.
- Have each employee in position at the moment the line is stopped.
- Train each employee, and practice, practice, practice.
- Put a stop watch on the setup process.
- Plot improvements over time on a visible chart.

As a result of these changes, P&G was able to reduce pack-line setup time from several hours to 20 minutes. This allowed the company to reduce lead time and to improve the cost performance of the Packing Department.

AP PHOTO/PAUL SAKUMA

Just-in-time normally organizes manufacturing around products rather than processes. Organizing work around products reduces:

1. Moving materials and products between processes
2. Work-in-process inventory
3. Lead time
4. Production costs

In addition, a product-oriented layout improves coordination among operations.

Emphasizing Employee Involvement

Employee involvement is a management approach that grants employees the responsibility and authority to make decisions about operations. Employee involvement is often applied in a just-in-time operation by organizing employees into *product cells*. Within each product cell, employees are organized as teams where the employees are *cross-trained* to perform any operation within the product cell.

Yamaha manufactures musical instruments such as trumpets, horns, saxophones, clarinets, and flutes using product-oriented layouts.

Sony has organized a small team of four employees to completely assemble a camcorder, doing everything from soldering to testing. The new line reduces assembly time from 70 minutes to 15 minutes per camera.

To illustrate, employees learn how to operate several different machines within their product cell. In addition, team members are trained to perform functions traditionally performed by centralized service departments. For example, product cell employees may perform their own equipment maintenance, quality control, and housekeeping.

Emphasizing Pull Manufacturing

Kenney Manufacturing Company, a manufacturer of window shades, estimated that 50% of its window shade process was non-value-added. By using pull manufacturing and changing the line layout, it was able to reduce inventory by 82% and lead time by 84%.

Pull manufacturing (or *make-to-order*) is an important just-in-time practice. In pull manufacturing, products are manufactured only as they are needed by the customer. Products can be thought of as being pulled through the manufacturing process. In other words, the status of the next operation determines when products are moved or produced. If the next operation is busy, production stops so that work in process does not pile up in front of the busy operation. When the next operation is ready, the product is moved to that operation.

A system used in pull manufacturing is *kanban,* which is Japanese for "cards." Electronic cards or containers signal production quantities to be filled by the preceding operation. The cards link the customer's order for a product back through each stage of production. In other words, when a consumer orders a product, a kanban card triggers the manufacture of the product.

In contrast, the traditional approach to manufacturing is based on estimated customer demand. This principle is called **push manufacturing** (or *make-to-stock*) manufacturing. In push manufacturing, products are manufactured according to a production schedule that is based upon estimated sales. The schedule "pushes" product into inventory before customer orders are received. As a result, push manufacturers normally have more inventory than pull manufacturers.

Emphasizing Zero Defects

Just-in-time manufacturing attempts to eliminate poor quality. Poor quality creates:

1. Scrap
2. Rework, which is fixing product made wrong the first time
3. Disruption in the production process
4. Dissatisfied customers
5. Warranty costs and expenses

Motorola has claimed over $17 billion in savings from Six Sigma.

One way to improve product quality and manufacturing processes is Six Sigma. **Six Sigma** was developed by Motorola Corporation and consists of five steps: define, measure, analyze, improve, and control (DMAIC).[4] Since its development, Six Sigma has been adopted by thousands of organizations worldwide.

Emphasizing Supply Chain Management

Toyota Motor often works with supply chain partners to maximize the use of just-in-time.

Supply chain management coordinates and controls the flow of materials, services, information, and finances with suppliers, manufacturers, and customers. Supply chain management partners with suppliers using long-term agreements. These agreements ensure that products are delivered with the right quality, at the right cost, at the right time.

---

4. The term "Six Sigma" refers to a statistical property where a process has less than 3.4 defects per 1 million items.

To enhance the interchange of information between suppliers and customers, supply chain management often uses:

1. **Electronic data interchange (EDI)**, which uses computers to electronically communicate orders, relay information, and make or receive payments from one organization to another.

2. **Radio frequency identification devices (RFID)**, which are electronic tags (chips) placed on or embedded within products that can be read by radio waves that allow instant monitoring of product location.

3. **Enterprise resource planning (ERP)** systems, which are used to plan and control internal and supply chain operations.

Hyundai/Kia Motors Group will use 20 million RFID tags annually to track automotive parts through the supply chain.

Activity-Based Costing

Obj **9**

Describe and illustrate the use of activity-based costing in a service business.

In today's complex manufacturing systems, product costs can be distorted if inappropriate factory overhead rates are used. One way to avoid this distortion is by using the *activity-based costing (ABC) method*. This approach allocates factory overhead more accurately than does the single, plantwide overhead rate that was illustrated earlier in this chapter.

The activity-based costing method uses cost of activities to determine product costs. Under this method, factory overhead costs are initially accounted for in **activity cost pools**. These cost pools are related to a given activity, such as machine usage, inspections, moving, production setups, and engineering activities.

In order to simplify, a service business is used to illustrate the principles of activity-based costing. Like manufacturing businesses, service companies need to determine the cost of services in order to make pricing, promotional, and other decisions. Many service companies find that a single overhead rate can lead to service cost distortions. Thus, many service companies are now using activity-based costing for determining the cost of providing services to customers.

To illustrate, assume that Hopewell Hospital uses activity-based costing to allocate hospital overhead to patients. Hopewell Hospital applies activity-based costing by:

1. Identifying activity cost pools
2. Determining activity rates for each cost pool
3. Allocating overhead costs to patients based upon activity usage

Hopewell Hospital has identified the following activity cost pools:

1. Admission
2. Radiological testing
3. Operating room
4. Pathological testing
5. Dietary and laundry

Owens & Minor, a medical distributor, uses activity-based costing information to price distribution services to customers, based on the number of orders and the number of items per order.

Each activity cost pool has an estimated patient activity-base usage. Based on the budgeted costs for each activity and related estimated activity-base usage, the activity rates shown in Exhibit 18 were developed.

To illustrate, assume the following data for radiological testing:

Budgeted costs	$960,000
Total estimated activity-base usage	3,000 images

EXHIBIT 18 **Activity-Based Costing Method—Hopewell Hospital**

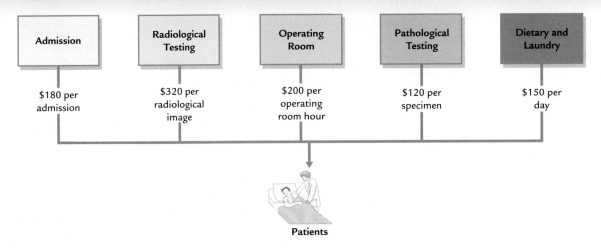

Admission	Radiological Testing	Operating Room	Pathological Testing	Dietary and Laundry
$180 per admission	$320 per radiological image	$200 per operating room hour	$120 per specimen	$150 per day

Patients

The activity rate of $320 per radiological image is computed as:

$$\text{Radiological Testing Activity Rate} = \frac{\text{Budgeted Activity Cost}}{\text{Activity-Base Usage}}$$

$$= \frac{\$960,000}{3,000 \text{ images}} = \$320 \text{ per image}$$

The activity rates for the other activities are determined in a similar manner. These activity rates along with the patient activity usage are used to allocate costs to patients as follows:

Activity Cost Allocated to Patient = Patient Activity Usage × Activity Rate

To illustrate, assume that Mia Wilson was a patient of the hospital. The hospital overhead services (activities) performed for Mia Wilson are shown below.

	Patient (Mia Wilson) Activity Usage
Admission	1 admission
Radiological testing	2 images
Operating room	4 hours
Pathological testing	1 specimen
Dietary and laundry	7 days

Based on the preceding services (activities), the Hopewell Hospital overhead costs allocated to Mia Wilson total $2,790, as computed below.

	A	B	C	D	E	F
1	Patient Name: Mia Wilson					
2		Activity-Base		Activity		Activity
3	Activity	Usage	×	Rate	=	Cost
4						
5	Admission	1 admission		$180/admission		$ 180
6	Radiological testing	2 images		$320/image		640
7	Operating room	4 hours		$200/hour		800
8	Pathological testing	1 specimen		$120/specimen		120
9	Dietary and laundry	7 days		$150/day		1,050
10	Total					$2,790
11						

The patient activity costs can be combined with the direct costs, such as drugs and supplies. These costs and the related revenues can be reported for each patient in a patient (customer) profitability report. A partial patient profitability report for Hopewell Hospital is shown in Exhibit 19.

EXHIBIT 19

Customer Profitability Report

	Adcock, Kim	Birini, Brian	Conway, Don		Wilson, Mia
Revenues	$9,500	$ 21,400	$5,050		$3,300
Less patient costs:					
Drugs and supplies	$ 400	$ 1,000	$ 300		$ 200
Admission	180	180	180		180
Radiological testing	1,280	2,560	1,280		640
Operating room	2,400	6,400	1,600		800
Pathological testing	240	600	120		120
Dietary and laundry	4,200	14,700	1,050		1,050
Total patient costs	$8,700	$ 25,440	$4,530		$2,990
Income from operations	$ 800	$ (4,040)	$ 520		$ 310

Hopewell Hospital
Patient (Customer) Profitability Report
For the Period Ending December 31, 20Y5

Exhibit 19 can be used by hospital administrators for decisions on pricing or services. For example, there was a large loss on services provided to Brian Birini. Investigation might reveal that some of the services provided to Birini were not reimbursed by insurance. As a result, Hopewell might lobby the insurance company to reimburse these services or request higher insurance reimbursement on other services.

Integrity, Objectivity, and Ethics in Business

UNIVERSITY AND COMMUNITY PARTNERSHIP— LEARNING YOUR ABC'S

Students at Harvard's Kennedy School of Government joined with the city of Somerville, Massachusetts, in building an activity-based cost system for the city. The students volunteered several hours a week in four-person teams, interviewing city officials within 18 departments. The students were able to determine activity costs, such as the cost of filling a pothole, processing a building permit, or responding to a four-alarm fire. Their study was used by the city in forming the city budget. As stated by some of the students participating in this project: "It makes sense to use the resources of the university for community building. . . . Real-world experience is a tremendous thing to have in your back pocket. We learned from the mayor and the fire chief, who are seasoned professionals in their own right."

Source: Kennedy School Bulletin, Spring 2005, "Easy as A-B-C: Students Take on the Somerville Budget Overhaul."

HOW BUSINESSES MAKE MONEY

FINDING THE RIGHT NICHE

Businesses often attempt to divide a market into its unique characteristics, called market segmentation. Once a market segment is identified, product, price, promotion, and location strategies are tailored to fit that market. This is a better approach for many products and services than following a "one size fits all" strategy. Activity-based costing can be used to help tailor organizational effort toward different segments. For example, Fidelity Investments uses activity-based costing to tailor its sales and marketing strategies to different wealth segments. Thus, a higher wealth segment could rely on personal sales activities, while less wealthy segments would rely on less costly sales activities, such as mass mail. The following table lists popular forms of segmentation and their common characteristics:

Form of Segmentation	Characteristics
Demographic	Age, education, gender, income, race
Geographic	Region, city, country
Psychographic	Lifestyle, values, attitudes
Benefit	Benefits provided
Volume	Light vs. heavy use

Examples for each of these forms of segmentation are as follows:

Demographic: Growth investments are marketed to younger consumers while less aggressive investments are marketed to older consumers.

Geographic: Pro sports teams offer merchandise in their home cities.

Psychographic: The Body Shop markets all-natural beauty products to consumers who value cosmetic products that have not been animal-tested.

Benefit: Cold Stone Creamery sells a premium ice cream product with customized toppings.

Volume: Delta Air Lines provides additional benefits, such as class upgrades, free air travel, and boarding priority, to its frequent fliers.

Key Points

1. Describe the differences between financial and managerial accounting.

Managerial accounting records and reports information for use by management in decision making. The information is reported when needed and varies in nature by the type of decision. In addition, the information may be for any item within the company such as an employee, product, or process. In contrast, financial accounting normally reports financial statements annually, monthly, or quarterly for the company as a whole using generally accepted accounting principles.

2. Distinguish the activities of a manufacturing business from those of a merchandising or service business.

A manufacturing business must first produce the products it sells. A manufacturing business converts materials into a finished product through the use of machinery and labor. Materials, products in the process of being manufactured, and finished products are reported on the balance sheet as inventories under the Current Assets caption.

3. Define and illustrate materials, factory labor, and factory overhead costs.

A manufacturer converts materials into a finished product by using machinery and labor. The cost of materials that are an integral part of the manufactured product is direct materials cost. The cost of wages of employees who are involved in converting materials into the manufactured product is direct labor cost. Costs other than direct materials and direct labor costs are factory overhead costs, including indirect materials and labor. Direct labor and factory overhead are termed conversion costs. Direct materials, direct labor, and factory overhead costs are associated with products and are called product costs.

4. Describe cost accounting systems used by manufacturing businesses.

A cost accounting system accumulates product costs. The cost accounting system is used by management to determine the proper product cost for inventory valuation on the financial statements, to support product pricing decisions, and to identify opportunities for cost reduction and improved production efficiency. The two primary cost accounting systems are job order and process cost systems.

5. Describe and illustrate a job order cost accounting system.

A job order cost system provides for a separate record of the cost of each particular quantity of product that passes through the factory. Direct materials, direct labor, and factory overhead costs are accumulated in a subsidiary cost ledger, in which each account is represented by a job cost sheet. Work in Process is the controlling account for the cost ledger. As a job is finished, its costs are transferred to the finished goods ledger, for which Finished Goods is the controlling account.

6. Use job order cost information for decision making.

Job order cost information can support pricing and cost analysis. Managers can use job cost information to identify unusual trends and areas for cost improvement.

7. Describe the flow of costs for a service business that uses a job order cost accounting system.

A cost flow diagram for a service business using a job order cost accounting system is shown in Exhibit 15, on page 393. For a service business, the cost of materials or supplies used is normally included as part of the overhead. The direct labor and overhead costs of rendering services are accumulated in a work-in-process account. When a job is completed and the client is billed, the costs are transferred to a cost of services account.

8. Describe just-in-time manufacturing practices.

The just-in-time manufacturing philosophy uses different principles than do traditional manufacturing methods. Just-in-time attempts to reduce lead time, while traditional methods lengthen lead time to provide a time buffer for uncertainty. Just-in-time emphasizes a product-oriented production layout rather than a process-oriented layout. Just-in-time emphasizes a team-oriented work environment; the traditional approach is more individual oriented. Just-in-time views setup time reduction as a high-priority item. With reduced setup times, just-in-time manufacturers can emphasize pull manufacturing rather than push manufacturing. Just-in-time manufacturers must emphasize high quality, since there is very little inventory to protect production against quality problems. Finally, just-in-time manufacturers emphasize supplier partnering to improve the quality and delivery of incoming materials.

9. Describe and illustrate the use of activity-based costing in a service business.

Activity-based costing can be applied in service settings to determine the cost of individual service offerings. Service costs are determined by multiplying activity rates by the amount of activity-base quantities consumed by the customer using the service offering. Such information can support service pricing and profitability analysis.

Key Terms

Activity base (driver) (383)
Activity-based costing (384)
Activity cost pools (399)
Controlling account (379)
Conversion costs (375)
Cost (373)
Cost accounting system (377)

Cost allocation (383)
Cost of goods sold (373)
Direct labor cost (375)
Direct materials cost (374)
Electronic data interchange (EDI) (399)

Employee involvement (397)
Enterprise resource planning (ERP) (399)
Factory overhead cost (375)
Financial accounting (372)
Finished goods inventory (379)

Finished goods ledger (388)
Job cost sheet (381)
Job order cost system (378)
Just-in-time (JIT) processing (393)
Lead time (395)

Managerial accounting (372)
Materials inventory (378)
Materials ledger (379)
Materials requisition (381)
Non-value-added lead time (396)
Overapplied factory overhead (386)

Period costs (376)
Predetermined factory overhead rate (384)
Prime costs (375)
Process cost system (378)
Process-oriented layout (396)
Product costs (376)
Product-oriented layout (396)

Pull manufacturing (398)
Push manufacturing (398)
Radio frequency identification devices (RFID) (399)
Receiving report (380)
Setup (396)
Six Sigma (398)
Subsidiary ledger (379)

Supply chain management (398)
Time tickets (381)
Underapplied factory overhead (386)
Value-added lead time (396)
Work-in-process inventory (379)

Illustrative Problem

Derby Music Company specializes in producing and packaging compact discs (CDs) for the music recording industry. Derby uses a job order cost system. The following data summarize the operations related to production for March, the first month of operations:

a. Materials purchased on account, $15,500.

b. Materials requisitioned and labor used:

	Materials	Factory Labor
Job No. 100	$2,650	$1,770
Job No. 101	1,240	650
Job No. 102	980	420
Job No. 103	3,420	1,900
Job No. 104	1,000	500
Job No. 105	2,100	1,760
For general factory use	450	650

c. Factory overhead costs incurred on account, $2,700.

d. Depreciation of machinery, $1,750.

e. Factory overhead is applied at a rate of 70% of direct labor cost.

f. Jobs completed: Nos. 100, 101, 102, 104.

g. Jobs 100, 101, and 102 were shipped, and customers were billed for $8,100, $3,800, and $3,500, respectively.

Instructions

1. Prepare a schedule summarizing manufacturing costs by job during the month. Use the following form:

Job	Direct Materials	Direct Labor	Factory Overhead	Total

2. Prepare a schedule of jobs finished.

3. Prepare a schedule of jobs sold.

4. Prepare a schedule of completed jobs on hand at the end of the month.

5. Prepare a schedule of unfinished jobs at the end of the month.

Solution

1. Schedule of manufacturing costs incurred during month:

Job	Direct Materials	Direct Labor	Factory Overhead	Total
Job No. 100	$ 2,650	$1,770	$1,239	$ 5,659
Job No. 101	1,240	650	455	2,345
Job No. 102	980	420	294	1,694
Job No. 103	3,420	1,900	1,330	6,650
Job No. 104	1,000	500	350	1,850
Job No. 105	2,100	1,760	1,232	5,092
	$11,390	$7,000	$4,900	$23,290

2. Schedule of the cost of jobs finished:

Job	Direct Materials	Direct Labor	Factory Overhead	Total
Job No. 100	$2,650	$1,770	$1,239	$ 5,659
Job No. 101	1,240	650	455	2,345
Job No. 102	980	420	294	1,694
Job No. 104	1,000	500	350	1,850
				$11,548

3. Schedule of the cost of jobs sold:

Job No. 100	$5,659
Job No. 101	2,345
Job No. 102	1,694
	$9,698

4.

Schedule of Completed Jobs

Job No. 104:	
Direct materials	$1,000
Direct labor	500
Factory overhead	350
Balance of Finished Goods, March, 31	$1,850

5.

Schedule of Unfinished Jobs

Job	Direct Materials	Direct Labor	Factory Overhead	Total
Job No. 103	$3,420	$1,900	$1,330	$ 6,650
Job No. 105	2,100	1,760	1,232	5,092
Balance of Work in Process, March 31				$11,742

Self-Examination Questions (Answers appear at the end of chapter)

1. Which of the following is *not* considered a cost of manufacturing a product?
   A. Direct materials cost
   B. Factory overhead cost
   C. Sales salaries
   D. Direct labor cost

2. Which of the following costs would be included as part of the factory overhead costs of a computer manufacturer?
   A. The cost of memory chips
   B. Depreciation of testing equipment
   C. Wages of computer assemblers
   D. The cost of disk drives

3. A company estimated $420,000 of factory overhead cost and 16,000 direct labor hours for the period. During the period, a job was completed with $4,500 of direct materials and $3,000 of direct labor. The direct labor rate was $15 per hour. What is the factory overhead applied to this job?

   A. $2,100

   B. $5,250

   C. $78,750

   D. $420,000

4. If the factory overhead account has a negative balance, factory overhead is said to be:

   A. underapplied.

   B. overapplied.

   C. underabsorbed.

   D. in error.

5. Which of the following is *not* a characteristic of the just-in-time philosophy?

   A. Product-oriented layout

   B. Push manufacturing (make-to-stock)

   C. Short lead times

   D. Reducing setup time as a critical improvement priority

Class Discussion Questions

1. List three differences in how managerial accounting differs from financial accounting.

2. For a company that produces desktop computers, would memory chips be considered a direct or an indirect materials cost of each computer produced?

3. How is product cost information used by managers?

4. a. Name two principal types of cost accounting systems.

   b. Which system provides for a separate record of each particular quantity of product that passes through the factory?

   c. Which system accumulates the costs for each department or process within the factory?

5. What kind of firm would use a job order cost system?

6. **Hewlett-Packard Company** assembles inkjet printers in which a high volume of standardized units are assembled and tested. Is the job order cost system appropriate in this situation?

7. How does the use of the materials requisition help control the issuance of materials from the storeroom?

8. a. Differentiate between the clock card and the time ticket.

   b. Why should the total time reported on an employee's time tickets for a payroll period be compared with the time reported on the employee's clock cards for the same period?

9. Describe the source of the data for increasing Work in Process for (a) direct materials, (b) direct labor, and (c) factory overhead.

10. Discuss how the predetermined factory overhead rate can be used in job order cost accounting to assist management in pricing jobs.

11. a. How is a predetermined factory overhead rate calculated?

    b. Name three common bases used in calculating the rate.

12. a. What is (1) overapplied factory overhead and (2) underapplied factory overhead?

    b. If the factory overhead account has a positive balance, was factory overhead underapplied or overapplied?

13. At the end of the fiscal year, there was a relatively minor balance in the factory overhead account. What procedure can be used for disposing of the balance in the account?

14. What is the difference between a product cost and a period cost?

15. How can job cost information be used to identify cost improvement opportunities?

16. Describe how a job order cost system can be used for professional service businesses.

17. What is the benefit of just-in-time processing?

18. What are some examples of non-value-added lead time?

19. Why do just-in-time manufacturers favor pull or make-to-order manufacturing?

20. Why would a just-in-time manufacturer strive to produce zero defects?

21. How is supplier partnering different from traditional supplier relationships?

22. How can activity-based costing be used in service companies?

Exercises

E10-1 Classifying costs as materials, labor, or factory overhead

Obj **3**

Indicate whether each of the following costs of an airplane manufacturer would be classified as direct materials cost, direct labor cost, or factory overhead cost:

a. Aircraft engines
b. Controls for flight deck
c. Depreciation of welding equipment
d. Salary of test pilot
e. Steel used in landing gear
f. Tires
g. Wages of assembly line worker
h. Welding machinery lubricants

E10-2 Classifying costs as materials, labor, or factory overhead

Obj **3**

Indicate whether the following costs of **Colgate-Palmolive Company** would be classified as direct materials cost, direct labor cost, or factory overhead cost:

a. Wages paid to Packaging Department employees
b. Maintenance supplies
c. Plant manager salary for the Morristown, Tennessee, toothpaste plant
d. Packaging materials which are a significant product cost
e. Depreciation on production machinery
f. Salary of process engineers
g. Depreciation on the Clarksville, Indiana, soap plant
h. Resins for soap and shampoo products
i. Scents and fragrances
j. Wages of production line employees

E10-3 Classifying costs as factory overhead

Obj **3**

Which of the following items are properly classified as part of factory overhead for **Caterpillar**?

a. Factory supplies used in the Morganton, North Carolina, engine parts plant
b. Amortization of patents on new assembly process
c. Steel plate
d. Vice president of finance's salary
e. Sales incentive fees to dealers
f. Depreciation on Peoria, Illinois, headquarters building
g. Interest expense on debt
h. Plant manager's salary at Aurora, Illinois, manufacturing plant
i. Consultant fees for a study of production line employee productivity
j. Property taxes on the Danville, Kentucky, tractor tread plant

Obj | **3, 5**

E10-4 Classifying costs as product or period costs

For apparel manufacturer Ann Taylor, Inc., classify each of the following costs as either a product cost or a period cost:

a. Sales commissions

b. Advertising expenses

c. Fabric used during production

d. Property taxes on factory building and equipment

e. Depreciation on sewing machines

f. Factory janitorial supplies

g. Depreciation on office equipment

h. Wages of sewing machine operators

i. Repairs and maintenance costs for sewing machines

j. Salary of production quality control supervisor

k. Salaries of distribution center personnel

l. Research and development costs

m. Oil used to lubricate sewing machines

n. Corporate controller's salary

o. Utility costs for office building

p. Travel costs of salespersons

q. Factory supervisors' salaries

Obj | **3, 5**

E10-5 Concepts and terminology

From the choices presented in the parentheses, choose the appropriate term for completing each of the following sentences:

a. Advertising expenses are usually viewed as (period, product) costs.

b. An example of factory overhead is (plant depreciation, sales office depreciation).

c. Direct labor costs combined with factory overhead costs are called (prime, conversion) costs.

d. Implementing automatic factory robotics equipment normally (increases, decreases) the factory overhead component of product costs.

e. Materials that are an integral part of the manufactured product are classified as (direct materials, materials inventory).

f. Payments of cash or its equivalent or the commitment to pay cash in the future for the purpose of generating revenues are (costs, expenses).

g. The balance sheet of a manufacturer would include an account for (cost of goods sold, work-in-process inventory).

h. The wages of an assembly worker are normally considered a (period, product) cost.

Obj | **5**

E10-6 Transactions in a job order cost system

Five selected transactions for the current month are indicated by letters in the following accounts in a job order cost accounting system:

Materials	Work in Process
(a) decrease	(a) increase
	(b) increase
	(c) increase
	(d) decrease

Wages Payable	Finished Goods
(b) increase	(d) increase
	(e) decrease

Factory Overhead	Cost of Goods Sold
(a) increase	(e) increase
(b) increase	
(c) decrease	

Describe each of the five transactions.

E10-7 Cost flow relationships

Obj 5
✔ c. $173,200

The following information is available for the first month of operations of Beek Inc., a manufacturer of art and craft items:

Sales	$478,000
Gross profit	286,800
Indirect labor	48,000
Indirect materials	11,300
Other factory overhead	14,700
Materials purchased	124,000
Total manufacturing costs for the period	325,000
Materials inventory, end of period	34,900

Using the above information, determine the following:

a. Cost of goods sold

b. Direct materials cost

c. Direct labor cost

E10-8 Cost of materials issuances

Obj 5

An incomplete subsidiary ledger of wire cable for July is as follows:

✔ b. $2,560

RECEIVED			ISSUED			BALANCE			
Receiving Report Number	Quantity	Unit Price	Materials Requisition Number	Quantity	Amount	Date	Quantity	Amount	Unit Price
						July 1	250	$1,500	$6.00
309	400	$7.50				July 5			
			7401	480		July 10			
422	800	8.00				July 20			
			7639	650		July 26			

a. Complete the materials issuances and balances for the wire cable subsidiary ledger.

b. Determine the balance of wire cable at the end of July.

c. Determine the total amount of materials transferred to Work in Process for July.

d. Explain how the materials ledger might be used as an aid in maintaining inventory quantities on hand.

Note: The spreadsheet icon  indicates an Excel template is available on the student companion site.

Obj 5

E10-9 Recording issuing of materials

Materials issued for the current month are as follows:

Requisition No.	Material	Job No.	Amount
945	Fiberglass	78	$17,600
946	Plastic	93	8,600
947	Glue	Indirect	955
948	Wood	99	3,150
949	Aluminium	108	33,450

a. Determine the amount of materials transferred to Work in Process and Factory Overhead for the current month.

b. Illustrate the effect on the accounts and financial statements of the materials transferred in (a).

Obj 5

✔ c. Fabric, $10,690

E10-10 Amounts for materials

Cherokee Furniture Company manufactures furniture. Cherokee Furniture uses a job order cost system. Balances on April 1 from the materials ledger are as follows:

Fabric	$ 6,140
Polyester filling	5,900
Lumber	17,400
Glue	1,800

The materials purchased during April are summarized from the receiving reports as follows:

Fabric	$67,750
Polyester filling	40,000
Lumber	92,350
Glue	8,000

Materials were requisitioned to individual jobs as follows:

	Fabric	Polyester Filling	Lumber	Glue	Total
Job 304	$12,460	$ 5,175	$18,300		$ 35,935
Job 305	19,170	10,225	29,950		59,345
Job 306	31,570	26,100	40,250		97,920
Factory overhead—indirect materials				$7,350	7,350
Total	$63,200	$41,500	$88,500	$7,350	$200,550

The glue is not a significant cost, so it is treated as indirect materials (factory overhead).

a. Determine the total purchase of materials in April.

b. Determine the amounts of materials transferred to Work in Process and Factory Overhead for the requisition of materials in April.

c. Determine the April 30 balances that would be shown in the materials ledger accounts.

E10-11   Recording factory labor costs

Obj 5

A summary of the time tickets for October is as follows:

Job No.	Amount	Job No.	Amount
3467	$ 4,350	3478	$ 5,800
3470	2,190	3480	6,300
3471	7,180	3497	8,050
Indirect labor	13,600	3501	11,130

a. Determine the amounts of factory labor costs transferred to Work in Process and Factory Overhead for October.

b. Illustrate the effect on the accounts and financial statements of the factory labor costs transferred in (a).

E10-12   Recording factory labor costs

Obj 5

The weekly time tickets indicate the following distribution of labor hours for three direct labor employees:

	Job 560A	Job 560B	Job 560C	Process Improvement
Eva Leavitt	15	15	6	4
Micah Stone	10	15	13	2
Travis Hendrix	12	14	10	4

The direct labor rate earned by the three employees is as follows:

Leavitt	$31
Stone	28
Hendrix	20

The process improvement category includes training, quality improvement, housekeeping, and other indirect tasks.

a. Determine the amounts of factory labor costs transferred to Work in Process and Factory Overhead for the week.

b. Assume that Jobs 560A and 560B were completed but not sold during the week and that Job 560C remained incomplete at the end of the week. How would the direct labor costs for all three jobs be reflected on the financial statements at the end of the week?

E10-13   Recording direct labor and factory overhead

Obj 5

Chamlee Industries Inc. manufactures recreational vehicles. Chamlee Industries uses a job order cost system. The time tickets from May jobs are summarized below.

Job 5-100	$6,400
Job 5-101	3,900
Job 5-102	4,800
Job 5-103	2,900
Factory supervision	1,750

Factory overhead is applied to jobs on the basis of a predetermined overhead rate of $30 per direct labor hour. The direct labor rate is $25 per hour.

a. Determine the total factory labor costs transferred to Work in Process and Factory Overhead for May.

b. Determine the amount of factory overhead applied to production for May.

c. Illustrate the effects of the factory overhead applied in (b) on the accounts and financial statements.

Obj | 5

✔ b. $9.50 per
direct labor hour

E10-14   Factory overhead rates and account balances

Prostheses Industries operates two factories. The manufacturing operation of Factory 1 is machine intensive, while the manufacturing operation of Factory 2 is labor intensive. The company applies factory overhead to jobs on the basis of machine hours in Factory 1 and on the basis of direct labor hours in Factory 2. Estimated factory overhead costs, direct labor hours, and machine hours are as follows:

	Factory 1	Factory 2
Estimated factory overhead cost for fiscal year beginning August 1	$375,200	$2,660,000
Estimated direct labor hours for year		280,000
Estimated machine hours for year	22,400	
Actual factory overhead costs for August	$28,700	$230,000
Actual direct labor hours for August		24,000
Actual machine hours for August	1,800	

a. Determine the factory overhead rate for Factory 1.

b. Determine the factory overhead rate for Factory 2.

c. Determine the factory overhead applied to production in each factory for January.

d. Determine the balances of the factory accounts for each factory as of January 31, and indicate whether the amounts represent overapplied or underapplied factory overhead.

e. Explain why Factory 1 might use machine hours to allocate factory overhead while Factory 2 uses direct labor hours.

Obj | 5

E10-15   Predetermined factory overhead rate

Ace Engine Shop uses a job order cost system to determine the cost of performing engine repair work. Estimated costs and expenses for the coming period are as follows:

Engine parts	$325,000
Shop direct labor	296,000
Shop and repair equipment depreciation	18,000
Shop supervisor salaries	110,000
Shop property taxes	20,500
Shop supplies	7,500
Advertising expense	30,000
Administrative office salaries	75,000
Administrative office depreciation expense	8,000
Total costs and expenses	$890,000

The average shop direct labor rate is $18.50 per hour. Determine the predetermined shop overhead rate per direct labor hour.

E10-16 Predetermined factory overhead rate

Obj 5

✔ a. $300 per hour

St. Lukes Medical Center has a single operating room that is used by local physicians to perform surgical procedures. The cost of using the operating room is accumulated by each patient procedure and includes the direct materials costs (drugs and medical devices), physician surgical time, and operating room overhead. On July 1 of the current year, the annual operating room overhead is estimated to be:

Disposable supplies	$ 330,000
Depreciation expense	59,400
Utilities	34,100
Nurse salaries	496,500
Technician wages	151,000
Total operating room overhead	$1,071,000

The overhead costs will be assigned to procedures based on the number of surgical room hours. St. Lukes Medical Center expects to use the operating room an average of 10 hours per day, seven days per week. In addition, the operating room will be shut down one week per year for general and maintenance repairs.

a. Determine the predetermined operating room overhead rate for the year.

b. Vivian Kau had a 3.8-hour procedure on July 23. How much operating room overhead would be charged to her procedure, using the rate determined in part (a)?

c. During July, the operating room was used 280 hours. The actual overhead costs incurred for July were $83,175. Determine the overhead under- or overapplied for the period.

E10-17 Recording jobs completed

Obj 5

✔ b. $85,000

The following account appears in the ledger after only part of the postings have been completed for October:

Work in Process

Balance, October 1	$ 42,600
Direct materials	360,000
Direct labor	400,400
Factory overhead	107,000

Jobs finished during October are summarized as follows:

Job 1004	$180,000	Job 1037	$140,000
Job 1030	225,000	Job 1041	280,000

a. Determine the cost of jobs completed.

b. Determine the cost of the unfinished jobs at October 31.

E10-18 Determining manufacturing costs

Obj 5

✔ d. $34,000

Steuben Printing Inc. began printing operations on March 1. Jobs 3-01 and 3-02 were completed during the month, and all costs applicable to them were recorded on the related cost sheets. Jobs 3-03 and 3-04 are still in process at the end of the month, and all applicable costs except factory overhead have been recorded on the related cost sheets. In addition to the materials and labor charged directly to the jobs, $3,300 of indirect materials and $4,800 of indirect labor were used during the month. The cost sheets for the four jobs entering production during the month are as follows, in summary form:

Job 3-01

Direct materials	14,000
Direct labor	5,000
Factory overhead	3,750
Total	22,750

Job 3-02

Direct materials	6,000
Direct labor	3,000
Factory overhead	2,250
Total	11,250

Job 3-03

Direct materials	19,000
Direct labor	5,800
Factory overhead	?

Job 3-04

Direct materials	4,400
Direct labor	1,000
Factory overhead	?

Determine each of the following for March:

a. Direct and indirect materials used.

b. Direct and indirect labor used.

c. Factory overhead applied (a single overhead rate is used based on direct labor cost).

d. Cost of completed Jobs 3-01 and 3-02.

e. Assume that in addition to indirect materials and indirect labor, factory overhead of $3,700 was incurred during March. Determine the overapplied or underapplied overhead for March.

Obj 5

✔ a. Income from operations, $155,500

E10-19   Financial statements of a manufacturing firm

The following events took place for Bridger Bikes Inc. during July 20Y6, the first month of operations, as a producer of road bikes:

- Purchased $340,000 of materials.
- Used $329,000 of direct materials in production.
- Incurred $160,000 of direct labor wages.
- Applied factory overhead at a rate of 80% of direct labor cost.
- Transferred $590,000 of work in process to finished goods.
- Sold goods with a cost of $550,000.
- Sold goods for $918,000.
- Incurred $132,500 of selling expenses.
- Incurred $80,000 of administrative expenses.

a. Prepare the July income statement for Bridger Bikes Inc. Assume that Bridger Bikes uses the perpetual inventory method.

b. Determine the inventory balances at the end of the first month of operations.

E10-20 Decision making with job order costs

Colfax Manufacturing Inc. is a job shop. The management of Colfax Manufacturing uses the cost information from the job sheets to assess its cost performance. Information on the total cost, product type, and quantity of items produced is as follows:

Date	Job No.	Quantity	Product	Amount
Jan. 13	1	180	Mercury	$ 4,500
Jan. 29	26	1,020	Venus	8,160
Feb. 3	38	1,330	Venus	13,300
Mar. 14	49	550	Mercury	12,100
Mar. 24	65	1,500	Pluto	6,000
May 11	74	1,750	Pluto	10,500
June 12	83	400	Mercury	7,200
Aug. 18	92	2,200	Pluto	19,800
Sept. 5	100	600	Venus	4,800
Nov. 14	109	725	Mercury	10,150
Dec. 15	116	2,000	Pluto	24,000

a. Develop a graph for *each* product (three graphs), with Job No. (in date order) on the horizontal axis and unit cost on the vertical axis. Use this information to determine Colfax Manufacturing's cost performance over time for the three products.

b. What additional information would you require to investigate Colfax Manufacturing's cost performance more precisely?

E10-21 Decision making with job order costs

Creative Trophies Inc. uses a job order cost system for determining the cost to manufacture award products (plaques and trophies). Among the company's products is an engraved plaque that is awarded to participants who complete an executive education program at a local university. The company sells the plaque to the university for $40 each.

Each plaque has a brass plate engraved with the name of the participant. Engraving requires approximately 20 minutes per name. Improperly engraved names must be redone. The plate is screwed to a walnut backboard. This assembly takes approximately 10 minutes per unit. Improper assembly must be redone using a new walnut backboard.

During the first half of the year, the university had two separate executive education classes. The job cost sheets for the two separate jobs indicated the following information:

Job 9-08	September 9		
	Cost per Unit	Units	Job Cost
Direct materials:			
Wood	$ 8.00/unit	60 units	$ 480
Brass	6.00/unit	60 units	360
Engraving labor	15.00/hr.	20 hrs.	300
Assembly labor	12.00/hr.	10 hrs.	120
Factory overhead	9.00/hr.	30 hrs.	270
			$1,530
Plaques shipped			÷ 60
Cost per plaque			$25.50

Job 10-34	October 29		
	Cost per Unit	Units	Job Cost
Direct materials:			
Wood	$ 8.00/unit	58 units	$ 464
Brass	6.00/unit	58 units	348
Engraving labor	15.00/hr.	18 hrs.	270
Assembly labor	12.00/hr.	9 hrs.	108
Factory overhead	9.00/hr.	27 hrs.	243
			$1,433
Plaques shipped			÷ 50
Cost per plaque			$28.66

a. Why did the cost per plaque increase from $25.50 to $28.66?

b. What improvements would you recommend for Creative Trophies Inc.?

Obj 7

✔ d. Cost of services completed, $1,377,000

E10-22 Job order cost accounting entries for a service business

Media Connect Inc. provides advertising services for clients across the nation. Media Connect is presently working on four projects, each for a different client. Media Connect accumulates costs for each account (client) on the basis of both direct costs and allocated indirect costs. The direct costs include the charged time of professional personnel and media purchases (air time and ad space). Overhead is allocated to each project as a percentage of media purchases. The predetermined overhead rate is 40% of media purchases. On April 1, the four advertising projects had the following accumulated costs:

	April 1 Balances
First Bank	$40,000
Reliable Airlines	18,000
Motel 26	33,000
Blue Mountain Beverages	27,000

During April, Media Connect incurred the following direct labor and media purchase costs related to preparing advertising for each of the four accounts:

	Direct Labor	Media Purchases
First Bank	$115,000	$ 480,000
Reliable Airlines	84,000	320,000
Motel 26	110,000	200,000
Blue Mountain Beverages	125,000	300,000
Total	$434,000	$1,300,000

At the end of April, both the First Bank and Reliable Airlines campaigns were completed. The costs of completed campaigns are added to the cost of services account.

Determine each of the following for the month:

a. Direct labor costs.

b. Media purchases.

c. Overhead applied.

d. Cost of completed First Bank and Reliable Airlines campaigns.

E10-23   Just-in-time principles

Obj | **8**

The chief executive officer (CEO) of Kankakee Industries has just returned from a management seminar describing the benefits of the just-in-time philosophy. The CEO issued the following statement after returning from the conference:

> *This company will become a just-in-time manufacturing company. Presently, we have too much inventory. To become just-in-time we need to eliminate the excess inventory. Therefore, I want all employees to begin reducing inventories until we are just-in-time. Thank you for your cooperation.*

How would you respond to the CEO's statement?

E10-24   Just-in-time as a strategy

Obj | **8**

The American textile industry has moved much of its operations offshore in the pursuit of lower labor costs. Over the past 50 years, textile imports have risen from 2% of all textile production to over 70%. Offshore manufacturers make long runs of standard mass-market apparel items. These are then brought to the United States in container ships, requiring significant time between original order and delivery. As a result, retail customers must accurately forecast market demands for imported apparel items.

Assuming that you work for a U.S.-based textile company, how would you recommend responding to the low-cost imports?

E10-25   Lead time reduction—service company

Obj | **8**

Onsite Insurance Company takes 10 days to make payments on insurance claims. Claims are processed through three departments: Data Input, Claims Audit, and Claims Adjustment. The three departments are on different floors, approximately one hour apart from each other. Claims are processed in batches of 100. Each batch of 100 claims moves through the three departments on a wheeled cart. Management is concerned about customer dissatisfaction caused by the long lead time for claim payments.

How might this process be changed so that the lead time could be reduced significantly?

E10-26   Just-in-time principles

Obj | **8**

Jupiter Shirt Company manufactures various styles of men's casual wear. Shirts are cut and assembled by a workforce that is paid by piece rate. This means that workers are paid according to the amount of work completed during a period of time. To illustrate, if the piece rate is $0.18 per sleeve assembled, and the worker assembles 1,000 sleeves during the day, then the worker would be paid $180 (1,000 $\times$ $0.18) for the day's work.

The company is considering adopting a just-in-time manufacturing philosophy by organizing work cells around various types of products and employing pull manufacturing. However, no change is expected in the compensation policy. On this point, the manufacturing manager stated the following:

> *Piecework compensation provides an incentive to work fast. Without it, the workers will just goof off and expect a full day's pay. We can't pay straight hourly wages—at least not in this industry.*

How would you respond to the manufacturing manager's comments?

Obj | 8

E10-27 Supply chain management

The following is an excerpt from a recent article discussing supplier relationships with the Big Three North American automakers.

> *"The Big Three select suppliers on the basis of lowest price and annual price reductions," said Neil De Koker, president of the* Original Equipment Suppliers Association. *"They look glob-ally for the lowest parts prices from the lowest cost countries," De Koker said. "There is little trust and respect. Collaboration is missing." Japanese auto makers want long-term supplier relationships. They select suppliers as a person would a mate. The Big Three are quick to beat down prices with methods such as electronic auctions or rebidding work to a competitor. The Japanese are equally tough on price but are committed to maintaining supplier continuity. "They work with you to arrive at a competitive price, and they are willing to pay because they want long-term partnering," said Carl Code, a vice president at* Ernie Green Industries. *"They [Honda and Toyota] want suppliers to make enough money to stay in business, grow and bring them innovation." The Big Three's supply chain model is not much different from the one set by Henry Ford. In 1913, he set up the system of independent supplier firms operating at arm's length on short-term contracts. One consequence of the Big Three's low-price-at-all-costs men-tality is that suppliers are reluctant to offer them their cutting-edge technology out of fear the contract will be resourced before the research and development costs are recouped.*

a. Contrast the Japanese supply chain model with that of the Big Three.

b. Why might a supplier prefer the Japanese model?

c. What benefits might accrue to the Big Three by adopting the Japanese supply chain practices?

Source: Robert Sherefkin and Amy Wilson, "Suppliers Prefer Japanese Business Model," *Rubber & Plastics News*, March 17, 2003, Vol. 24, No. 11.

Obj | 8

E10-28 Employee involvement

Quickie Designs Inc. uses teams in the manufacture of lightweight wheelchairs. Two features of its team approach are team hiring and peer reviews. Under team hiring, the team recruits, interviews, and hires new team members from within the organization. Using peer reviews, the team evaluates each member of the team with regard to quality, knowledge, teamwork, goal performance, attendance, and safety. These reviews provide feedback to the team member for improvement.

How do these two team approaches differ from using managers to hire and evaluate employees?

Obj | 9

✔ a. Patient
Mims, $2,320

E10-29 Activity-based costing for a hospital

Hall Regional Hospital plans to use activity-based costing to assign hospital indirect costs to the care of patients. The hospital has identified the following activities and activity rates for the hospital indirect costs:

Activity	Activity Rate
Room and meals	$125 per day
Radiology	$180 per image
Pharmacy	$15 per physician order
Chemistry lab	$90 per test
Operating room	$1,200 per operating room hour

The records of two representative patients were analyzed, using the activity rates. The activity information associated with the two patients is as follows:

	Patient Mims	Patient Slater
Number of days	2 days	4 days
Number of images	4 images	7 images
Number of physician orders	6 orders	10 orders
Number of tests	2 tests	5 tests
Number of operating room hours	0.9 hour	3.1 hours

a. Determine the activity cost associated with each patient.

b. Why is the total activity cost different for the two patients?

E10-30 Activity-based costing in an insurance company

Umbrella Insurance Company carries three major lines of insurance: auto, workers' compensation, and homeowners. The company has prepared the following report for 20Y2:

Obj **9**

✔ a. Auto, $1,440,500

UMBRELLA INSURANCE COMPANY
Product Profitability Report
For the Year Ended December 31, 20Y2

	Auto	Workers' Compensation	Homeowners
Premium revenue	$ 7,200,000	$6,500,000	$9,200,000
Less estimated claims	5,040,000	4,550,000	6,440,000
Underwriting income	$2,160,000	$1,950,000	$2,760,000
Underwriting income as a percent of premium revenue	30%	30%	30%

Management is concerned that the administrative expenses may make some of the insurance lines unprofitable. However, the administrative expenses have not been allocated to the insurance lines. The controller has suggested that the administrative expenses could be assigned to the insurance lines using activity-based costing. The administrative expenses are comprised of five activities. The activities and their rates are as follows:

	Activity Rates
New policy processing	$160 per new policy
Cancellation processing	$240 per cancellation
Claim audits	$500 per claim audit
Claim disbursements processing	$120 per disbursement
Premium collection processing	$ 25 per premium collected

Activity-base usage data for each line of insurance were retrieved from the corporate records and are shown below.

	Auto	Workers' Comp.	Homeowners
Number of new policies	1,500	1,450	4,100
Number of canceled policies	350	250	2,000
Number of audited claims	320	100	700
Number of claim disbursements	400	180	750
Number of premiums collected	7,500	1,500	12,000

a. Complete the product profitability report through the administrative activities.

b. Determine the underwriting income as a percent of premium revenue.

c. Determine the income from operations as a percent of premium revenue, rounded to one decimal.

d. Interpret the report.

Problems

P10-1 Classifying costs

The following is a list of costs that were incurred in the production and sale of all-terrain vehicles (ATVs).

a. Attorney fees for drafting a new lease for headquarters offices.

b. Cash paid to outside firm for janitorial services for factory.

c. Commissions paid to sales representatives, based on the number of ATVs sold.

d. Cost of advertising in a national magazine.

e. Cost of boxes used in packaging ATVs.

f. Electricity used to run the robotic machinery.

g. Engine oil used in engines prior to shipment.

h. Factory cafeteria cashier's wages.

i. Filter for spray gun used to paint the ATVs.

j. Gasoline engines used for ATVs.

k. Hourly wages of operators of robotic machinery used in production.

l. License fees for use of patent for transmission assembly, based on the number of ATVs produced.

m. Maintenance costs for new robotic factory equipment, based on hours of usage.

n. Paint used to coat the ATVs.

o. Payroll taxes on hourly assembly line employees.

p. Plastic for outside housing of ATVs.

q. Premiums on insurance policy for factory buildings.

r. Property taxes on the factory building and equipment.

s. Salary of factory supervisor.

t. Salary of quality control supervisor who inspects each ATV before it is shipped.

u. Salary of vice president of marketing.

v. Steering wheels for ATVs.

w. Straight-line depreciation on the robotic machinery used to manufacture the ATVs.

x. Steel used in producing the ATVs.

y. Telephone charges for company controller's office.

z. Tires for ATVs.

Instructions

Classify each cost as either a product cost or a period cost. Indicate whether each product cost is a direct materials cost, a direct labor cost, or a factory overhead cost. Indicate whether each period cost is a selling expense or an administrative expense. Use the following tabular headings for your answer, placing an "X" in the appropriate column.

	Product Costs			Period Costs	
Cost	Direct Materials Cost	Direct Labor Cost	Factory Overhead Cost	Selling Expense	Administrative Expense

P10-2   Entries and schedules for unfinished jobs and completed jobs

Shenandoah Equipment Company uses a job order cost system. The following data summarize the operations related to production for June 20Y4, the first month of operations:

a. Materials purchased on account, $93,600.

b. Materials requisitioned and factory labor used:

✔ 5. Work in Process, balance, $89,160

Job	Materials	Factory Labor
No. 6001	$ 9,400	$ 8,800
No. 6002	11,500	11,880
No. 6003	7,600	5,960
No. 6004	25,800	21,840
No. 6005	16,400	16,600
No. 6006	11,920	10,600
For general factory use	3,440	13,000

c. Factory overhead costs incurred on account, $18,000.

d. Depreciation of machinery and equipment, $6,240.

e. The factory overhead rate is $50 per machine hour. Machine hours used:

Job	Machine Hours
No. 6001	72
No. 6002	120
No. 6003	96
No. 6004	300
No. 6005	132
No. 6006	80
Total	800

f. Jobs completed: 6001, 6002, 6003, and 6005.

g. Jobs were shipped and customers were billed as follows: Job 6001, $26,000; Job 6002, $36,000; Job 6003, $48,000.

Instructions

1. Prepare a schedule summarizing manufacturing costs by job for June. Use the following form:

Job	Direct Materials	Direct Labor	Factory Overhead	Total

2. Prepare a schedule of jobs finished in June.

3. Prepare a schedule of jobs sold in June. What account does this schedule support for the month of June?

4. Prepare a schedule of completed jobs on hand as of June 30, 20Y4. What account does this schedule support?

5. Prepare a schedule of unfinished jobs as of June 30, 20Y4. What account does this schedule support?

6. Determine the gross profit for June based upon the jobs sold.

P10-3 Job order cost sheet

Hallmark Furniture Company refinishes and reupholsters furniture. Hallmark Furniture uses a job order cost system. When a prospective customer asks for a price quote on a job, the estimated cost data are inserted on an unnumbered job cost sheet. If the offer is accepted, a number is assigned to the job, and the costs incurred are recorded in the usual manner on the job cost sheet. After the job is completed, reasons for the variances between the estimated and actual costs are noted on the sheet. The data are then available to management in evaluating the efficiency of operations and in preparing quotes on future jobs.

On February 14, 20Y1, an estimate of $897.60 for reupholstering a chair and couch was given to Millard Schmidt. The estimate was based on the following data:

Estimated direct materials:	
12 meters at $9 per meter	$108.00
Estimated direct labor:	
32 hours at $16 per hour	512.00
Estimated factory overhead (25% of direct labor cost)	128.00
Total estimated costs	$748.00
Markup (20% of production costs)	149.60
Total estimate	$897.60

On February 17, the chair and couch were picked up from the residence of Millard Schmidt, 315 White Oak Drive, Columbus, Georgia, with a commitment to return them on March 15. The job was completed on March 9.

The related materials requisitions and time tickets are summarized as follows:

Materials Requisition No.	Description	Amount
122	9 meters at $9	$81
129	7 meters at $9	63

Time Ticket No.	Description	Amount
T344	20 hours at $14	$280
T348	18 hours at $14	252

Instructions

1. Prepare a job order cost sheet showing the estimate given to the customer. Use the format shown on the next page.

2. Assign number 02-019 to the job, record the costs incurred, and complete the job order cost sheet. Comment on the reasons for the variances between actual costs and estimated costs. For this purpose, assume that four meters of materials were spoiled, the factory overhead rate has been proved to be satisfactory, and an inexperienced employee performed the work.

JOB ORDER COST SHEET

Customer _____   Date _____

Address _____   Date wanted _____

_____   Date completed _____

Item _____   Job No. _____

ESTIMATE

Direct Materials		Direct Labor		Summary	
	Amount		Amount		Amount
____ meters at $_____	_____	____ hours at $_____	_____	Direct materials	_____
____ meters at $_____	_____	____ hours at $_____	_____	Direct labor	_____
____ meters at $_____	_____	____ hours at $_____	_____	Factory overhead	_____
____ meters at $_____	_____	____ hours at $_____	_____		
Total	_____	Total	_____	Total cost	_____

ACTUAL

Mat. Req. No.	Description	Amount	Time Tick. No.	Description	Amount	Item	Amount
____	____ meters at $__	_____	____	____ hours at $__	_____	Direct materials	_____
____	____ meters at $__	_____	____	____ hours at $__	_____	Direct labor	_____
____	____ meters at $__	_____	____	____ hours at $__	_____	Factory overhead	_____
____	____ meters at $__	_____	____	____ hours at $__	_____		
Total		_____	Total		_____	Total cost	_____

COMMENTS

P10-4   Analyzing manufacturing cost accounts

Summer Boards Company manufactures surf boards in a wide variety of sizes and styles. The following incomplete ledger accounts refer to transactions that are summarized for May:

Obj | 5

✔ 1. (G) $176,610

Materials

May	1	Balance	9,000
	31	Purchases	40,000
	31	Requisitions	(A)

Work in Process

May	1	Balance	(B)
	31	Materials	(C)
	31	Direct labor	(D)
	31	Factory overhead applied	(E)
	31	Completed jobs	(F)

Finished Goods

May	1	Balance	0
	31	Completed jobs	(F)
	31	Cost of goods sold	(G)

Wages Payable

| May | 31 | Wages incurred | 110,000 |

Factory Overhead

May	1	Balance	−3,000
	31	Indirect labor	(H)
	31	Indirect materials	2,500
	31	Other overhead	102,900
	31	Factory overhead applied	(E)

In addition, the following information is available:

a. Materials and direct labor were applied to six jobs in May:

Job No.	Style	Quantity	Direct Materials	Direct Labor
No. 0521	SX	100	$ 5,000	$15,000
No. 0522	SJ	200	8,500	26,000
No. 0523	SK	100	3,500	8,000
No. 0524	T3	125	7,500	25,000
No. 0525	T6	90	5,600	17,500
No. 0526	SX	70	2,000	4,500
	Total	685	$32,100	$96,000

b. Factory overhead is applied to each job at a rate of 120% of direct labor cost.

c. The May 1 Work in Process balance consisted of two jobs, as follows:

Job No.	Style	Work in Process, May 1
Job 0521	SX	$1,500
Job 0522	SJ	4,000
Total		$5,500

d. Customer jobs completed and units sold in May were as follows:

Job No.	Style	Completed in May	Units Sold in May
No. 0521	SX	X	80
No. 0522	SJ	X	160
No. 0523	SK		0
No. 0524	T3	X	105
No. 0525	T6	X	75
No. 0526	SX		0

Instructions

1. Determine the missing amounts associated with each letter. Provide supporting calculations by completing a table with the following headings:

Job No.	Quantity	May 1 Work in Process	Direct Materials	Direct Labor	Factory Overhead	Total Cost	Unit Cost	Units Sold	Cost of Goods Sold

2. Determine the May 31 balances for each of the inventory accounts and factory overhead.

P10-5 Flow of costs and income statement

Obj **5**

R-Tunes Inc. is in the business of developing, promoting, and selling musical talent online and with compact discs (CDs). The company signed a new group, called *Cyclone Panic,* on January 1, 20Y8. For the first six months of 20Y8, the company spent $1,000,000 on a media campaign for *Cyclone Panic* and $175,000 in legal costs. The CD production began on April 1, 20Y8.

R-Tunes uses a job order cost system to accumulate costs associated with a CD title. The unit direct materials cost for the CD is:

✔ 1. Income from operations, $184,500

Blank CD	$0.40
Case	0.25
Song lyric insert	0.18

The production process is straightforward. First, the blank CDs are brought to a production area where the digital soundtrack is copied onto the CD. The copying machine requires one hour per 3,600 CDs.

After the CDs are copied, they are brought to an assembly area where an employee packs the CD with a case and song lyric insert. The direct labor cost is $0.37 per unit.

The CDs are sold to record stores. Each record store is given promotional materials, such as posters and aisle displays. Promotional materials cost $30 per record store. In addition, shipping costs average $0.28 per CD.

Total completed production was 500,000 units during the year. Other information is as follows:

Number of customers (record stores)	50,000
Number of CDs sold	475,000
Wholesale price (to record store) per CD	$8

Factory overhead cost is applied to jobs at the rate of $1,800 per copy machine hour. There were an additional 18,000 copied CDs, packages, and inserts waiting to be assembled on December 31, 20Y8.

Instructions

1. Prepare an annual income statement for the *Cyclone Panic* CD, including supporting calculations, from the information above.
2. Determine the balances in the work-in-process and finished goods inventories for the *Cyclone Panic* CD on December 31, 20Y8.

Cases

Case 10-1 Ethics and professional conduct in business

Ebenezer Manufacturing Company allows employees to purchase, at cost, manufacturing materials, such as metal and lumber, for personal use. To purchase materials for personal use, an employee must complete a materials requisition form, which must then be approved by the employee's immediate supervisor. Beth Turner, an assistant cost accountant, charges the employee an amount based on Ebenezer's net purchase cost.

Beth Turner is in the process of replacing a deck on her home and has requisitioned lumber for personal use, which has been approved in accordance with company policy. In computing the cost of the lumber, Beth reviewed all the purchase invoices for the past year. She then used the lowest price to compute the amount due the company for the lumber.

Discuss whether Beth behaved in an ethical manner.

Case 10-2   Financial vs. managerial accounting

The following statement was made by the vice president of finance of Electro Inc.: "The managers of a company should use the same information as the shareholders of the firm. When managers use the same information in guiding their internal operations as shareholders use in evaluating their investments, the managers will be aligned with the stockholders' profit objectives."

Respond to the vice president's statement.

Case 10-3   Classifying costs

Reboot Inc. provides computer repair services for the community. Ashley DaCosta's computer was not working, and she called Reboot for a home repair visit. The Reboot Inc. technician arrived at 2:00 P.M. to begin work. By 4:00 P.M., the problem was diagnosed as a failed circuit board. Unfortunately, the technician did not have a new circuit board in the truck, since the technician's previous customer had the same problem, and a board was used on that visit. Replacement boards were available back at Reboot's shop. Therefore, the technician drove back to the shop to retrieve a replacement board. From 4:00 to 5:00 P.M., Reboot's technician drove the round trip to retrieve the replacement board from the shop.

At 5:00 P.M., the technician was back on the job at Ashley's home. The replacement procedure is somewhat complex, since a variety of tests must be performed once the board is installed. The job was completed at 6:00 P.M.

Ashley's repair bill showed the following:

Circuit board	$ 80
Labor charges	260
Total	$340

Ashley was surprised at the size of the bill and asked for some greater detail supporting the calculations. Reboot responded with the following explanations:

Cost of materials:	
Purchase price of circuit board	$65
Markup on purchase price to cover storage and handling	15
Total materials charge	$80

The labor charge per hour is detailed as follows:

2:00–3:00 P.M.	$ 65
3:00–4:00 P.M.	40
4:00–5:00 P.M.	95
5:00–6:00 P.M.	60
Total labor charge	$260

Further explanations in the differences in the hourly rates are as follows:

First hour:	
Base labor rate	$22
Fringe benefits	10
Overhead (other than storage and handling)	8
Total base labor rate	$40
Additional charge for first hour of any job to cover the cost of vehicle depreciation, fuel, and employee time in transit. A 30-minute transit time is assumed.	25
	$65

Third hour:

Base labor rate	$40
The trip back to the shop includes vehicle depreciation and fuel; therefore, a charge was added to the hourly rate to cover these costs. The round trip took an hour.	55
	$95

Fourth hour:

Base labor rate	$40
Overtime premium for time worked in excess of an eight-hour day (starting at 5:00 P.M.) is equal to the base rate.	20
	$60

1. If you were in Ashley's position, how would you respond to the bill? Are there parts of the bill that appear incorrect to you? If so, what argument would you employ to convince Reboot that the bill is too high?

2. Use the headings below to construct a table. Fill in the table by first listing the costs identified in the activity in the left-hand column. For each cost, place a check mark in the appropriate column identifying the correct cost classification. Assume that each service call is a job.

Cost	Direct Materials	Direct Labor	Overhead

Case 10-4   Managerial analysis

The controller of the plant of Martz Industries prepared a graph of the unit costs from the job cost reports for Product M908t. The graph appeared as follows:

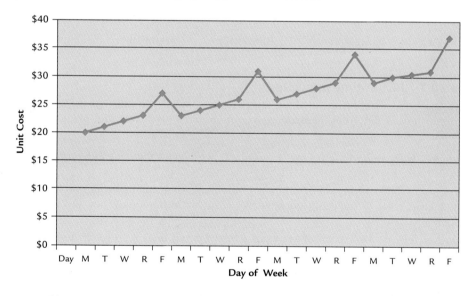

How would you interpret this information? What further information would you request?

Case 10-5   Factory overhead rate

Fabricator Inc., a specialized equipment manufacturer, uses a job order costing system. The overhead is allocated to jobs on the basis of direct labor hours. The overhead rate is now $3,000 per direct labor hour. The design engineer thinks that this is illogical. The design engineer has stated the following:

Our accounting system doesn't make any sense to me. It tells me that every labor hour carries an additional burden of $3,000. This means that while direct labor makes up only 5% of our total product cost, it drives all our costs. In addition, these rates give my design engineers incentives to "design out" direct labor by using machine technology. Yet, over the past years as we have had less and less direct labor, the overhead rate keeps going up and up. I won't be surprised if next year the rate is $4,000 per direct labor hour. I'm also concerned because small errors in our estimates of the direct labor content can have a large impact on our estimated costs. Just a 30-minute error in our estimate of assembly time is worth $1,500. Small mistakes in our direct labor time estimates really swing our bids around. I think this puts us at a disadvantage when we are going after business.

1. What is the engineer's concern about the overhead rate going "up and up"?
2. What did the engineer mean about the large overhead rate being a disadvantage when placing bids and seeking new business?
3. What do you think is a possible solution?

GROUP PROJECT

Case 10-6   Classifying costs

With a group of students, visit a local copy and graphics shop or a pizza restaurant. As you observe the operation, consider the costs associated with running the business. As a group, identify as many costs as you can and classify them according to the following table headings:

Cost	Direct Materials	Direct Labor	Overhead	Selling Expense

Case 10-7   Just-in-time principles

Warm Space Inc. manufactures electric space heaters. While the CEO, Gwen Willis, is visiting the production facility, the following conversation takes place with the plant manager, Tyra Chastain:

Gwen: As I walk around the facility, I can't help noticing all the materials inventories. What's going on?

Tyra: I have found our suppliers to be very unreliable in meeting their delivery commitments. Thus, I keep a lot of materials on hand so as to not risk running out and shutting down production.

Gwen: Not only do I see a lot of materials inventory, but there also seems to be a lot of finished goods inventory on hand. Why is this?

Tyra: As you know, I am evaluated on maintaining a low cost per unit. The one way that I am able to reduce my unit costs is by producing as many space heaters as possible. This allows me to spread my fixed costs over a larger base. When orders are down, the excess production builds up as inventory, as we are seeing now. But don't worry—I'm really keeping our unit costs down this way.

Gwen: I'm not so sure. It seems that this inventory must cost us something.

Tyra: Not really. I'll eventually use the materials and we'll eventually sell the finished goods. By keeping the plant busy, I'm using our plant assets wisely. This is reflected in the low unit costs that I'm able to maintain.

If you were Gwen Willis, how would you respond to Tyra Chastain? What recommendations would you provide Tyra Chastain?

Answers to Self-Examination Questions

1. **C**   Sales salaries (answer C) is a selling expense and is not considered a cost of manufacturing a product. Direct materials cost (answer A), factory overhead cost (answer B), and direct labor cost (answer D) are costs of manufacturing a product.

2. **B**   Depreciation of testing equipment (answer B) is included as part of the factory overhead costs of the computer manufacturer. The cost of memory chips (answer A) and the cost of disk drives (answer D) are both considered a part of direct materials cost. The wages of computer assemblers (answer C) are part of direct labor costs.

3. **B**

$$\text{Predetermined Factory} \atop \text{Overhead Rate} = \frac{\text{Estimated Total Factory Overhead Costs}}{\text{Estimated Activity Base}}$$

$$\text{Predetermined Factory} \atop \text{Overhead Rate} = \frac{\$420,000}{16,000 \text{ dlh}} = \$26.25$$

$$\text{Hours Applied} \atop \text{to the Job} = \frac{\$3,000}{\$15 \text{ per hour}} = 200 \text{ hours}$$

Factory overhead applied to the job:

$$200 \text{ hours} \times \$26.25 = \$5,250$$

4. **B**   If the amount of factory overhead applied during a particular period exceeds the actual overhead costs, the factory overhead account will have a negative balance and is said to be overapplied (answer B) or overabsorbed. If the amount applied is less than the actual costs, the account will have a positive balance and is said to be underapplied (answer A) or underabsorbed (answer C). Since an "estimated" predetermined overhead rate is used to apply overhead, a negative balance does not necessarily represent an error (answer D).

5. **B**   The just-in-time philosophy embraces a product-oriented layout (answer A), making lead times short (answer C), and reducing setup times (answer D). Pull manufacturing, the opposite of push manufacturing (answer B), is also a just-in-time principle.

CHAPTER 11

Cost Behavior and Cost-Volume-Profit Analysis

LEARNING OBJECTIVES

After studying this chapter, you should be able to:

Obj **1** Classify costs as variable costs, fixed costs, or mixed costs.

Obj **2** Compute the contribution margin, the contribution margin ratio, and the unit contribution margin.

Obj **3** Determine the break-even point and sales necessary to achieve a target profit.

Obj **4** Using a cost-volume-profit chart and a profit-volume chart, determine the break-even point and sales necessary to achieve a target profit.

Obj **5** Compute the break-even point for a company selling more than one product, the operating leverage, and the margin of safety.

How do you decide whether you are going to buy or rent a video game? It probably depends on how much you think you are going to use the game. If you are going to play the game a lot, you are probably better off buying the game than renting. The one-time cost of buying the game would be much less expensive than the cost of multiple rentals. If, on the other hand, you are uncertain about how frequently you are going to play the game, it may be less expensive to rent. The cost of an individual rental is much less than the cost of purchase. Understanding how the costs of rental and purchase behave affects your decision.

Understanding how costs behave is also important to companies like **Netflix**, an online DVD movie rental service. For a fee, Netflix customers can directly download movies directly to their computer. Alternatively, customers can select DVDs from their own computer and have the DVDs delivered to their home along with a prepaid return envelope. Customers can keep the DVDs as long as they want, but must return the DVDs before they rent additional movies. The number of DVDs that members can check out varies depending on their subscription plan.

In order to entice customers to subscribe, Netflix had to invest in a well-stocked library of DVD titles and build a warehouse to hold and distribute these titles. These costs do not change with the number of subscriptions. But how many subscriptions does Netflix need in order to make a profit? That depends on the price of each subscription, the costs incurred with each DVD rental, and the costs associated with maintaining the DVD library.

As with Netflix, understanding how costs behave and the relationship among costs, profits, and volume is important for all businesses. This chapter discusses commonly used methods for classifying costs according to how they change. Techniques that management can use to evaluate costs in order to make sound business decisions are also discussed.

Obj | 1

Classify costs as variable costs, fixed costs, or mixed costs.

Cost Behavior

Cost behavior is the manner in which a cost changes as a related activity changes. The behavior of costs is useful to managers for a variety of reasons. For example, knowing how costs behave allows managers to predict profits as sales and production volumes change. Knowing how costs behave is also useful for estimating costs, which affects a variety of decisions such as whether to replace a machine.

Understanding the behavior of a cost depends on:

1. Identifying the activities that cause the cost to change. These activities are called **activity bases** (or *activity drivers*).
2. Specifying the range of activity over which the changes in the cost are of interest. This range of activity is called the **relevant range**.

To illustrate, assume that a hospital is concerned about planning and controlling patient food costs. A good activity base is the number of patients who *stay* overnight in the hospital. The number of patients who are *treated* is not as good an activity base since some patients are outpatients and thus do not consume food. Once an activity base is identified, food costs can then be analyzed over the range of the number of patients who normally stay in the hospital (the relevant range).

Costs are normally classified as variable costs, fixed costs, or mixed costs.

Variable Costs

Variable costs are costs that vary in proportion to changes in the activity base. When the activity base is units produced, direct materials and direct labor costs are normally classified as variable costs.

To illustrate, assume that Dynamic Sound Inc. produces stereo systems. The parts for the stereo systems are purchased from suppliers for $10 per unit and are assembled by Dynamic Sound Inc. For Model DS-300, the direct materials costs for the relevant range of 5,000 to 30,000 units of production are shown below.

Number of Units of Model DS-300 Produced	Direct Materials Cost per Unit	Total Direct Materials Cost
5,000 units	$10	$ 50,000
10,000	10	100,000
15,000	10	150,000
20,000	10	200,000
25,000	10	250,000
30,000	10	300,000

As shown above, variable costs have the following characteristics:

1. *Cost per unit* remains the same regardless of changes in the activity base. For Model DS-300, the cost per unit is $10.
2. *Total cost* changes in proportion to changes in the activity base. For Model DS-300, the direct materials cost for 10,000 units ($100,000) is twice the direct materials cost for 5,000 units ($50,000).

Exhibit 1 illustrates how the variable costs for direct materials for Model DS-300 behave in total and on a per-unit basis as production changes.

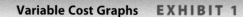

Variable Cost Graphs   EXHIBIT 1

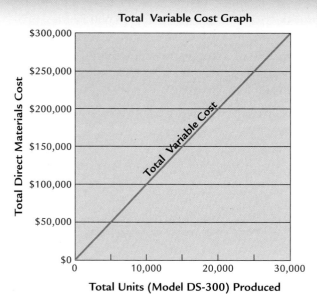

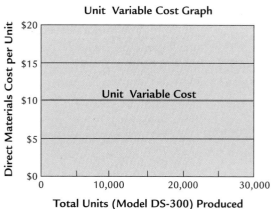

Some examples of variable costs and their related activity bases for various types of businesses are shown below.

Type of Business	Cost	Activity Base
University	Instructor salaries	Number of classes
Passenger airline	Fuel	Number of miles flown
Manufacturing	Direct materials	Number of units produced
Hospital	Nurse wages	Number of patients
Hotel	Maid wages	Number of guests
Bank	Teller wages	Number of banking transactions

Fixed Costs

Fixed costs are costs that remain the same in total dollar amount as the activity base changes. When the activity base is units produced, many factory overhead costs such as straight-line depreciation are classified as fixed costs.

To illustrate, assume that Hahn Inc. manufactures, bottles, and distributes perfume. The production supervisor is Molly Hahn, who is paid a salary of $75,000 per year. For the relevant range of 50,000 to 300,000 bottles of perfume, the total fixed cost of $75,000 does not vary as production increases. However, the fixed cost per bottle decreases as the units produced increase; thus, the fixed cost is spread over a larger number of bottles, as shown below.

Number of Bottles of Perfume Produced	Total Salary for Molly Hahn	Salary per Bottle of Perfume Produced
50,000 bottles	$75,000	$1.500
100,000	75,000	0.750
150,000	75,000	0.500
200,000	75,000	0.375
250,000	75,000	0.300
300,000	75,000	0.250

As shown on the preceding page, fixed costs have the following characteristics:

1. *Cost per unit* changes inversely to changes in the activity base. For Molly Hahn's salary, the cost per unit decreased from $1.50 for 50,000 bottles produced to $0.25 for 300,000 bottles produced.

2. *Total cost* remains the same regardless of changes in the activity base. Molly Hahn's salary of $75,000 remained the same regardless of whether 50,000 bottles or 300,000 bottles were produced.

Exhibit 2 illustrates how Molly Hahn's salary (fixed cost) behaves in total and on a per-unit basis as production changes.

EXHIBIT 2   Fixed Cost Graphs

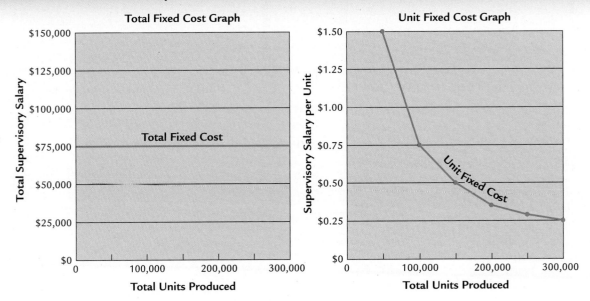

Some examples of fixed costs and their related activity bases for various types of businesses are shown below.

Type of Business	Fixed Cost	Activity Base
University	Building (straight-line) depreciation	Number of students
Passenger airline	Airplane (straight-line) depreciation	Number of miles flown
Manufacturing	Plant manager salary	Number of units produced
Hospital	Property insurance	Number of patients
Hotel	Property taxes	Number of guests
Bank	Branch manager salary	Number of customer accounts

A salesperson's compensation can be a mixed cost comprised of a salary (fixed portion) plus a commission as a percent of sales (variable portion).

Mixed Costs

Mixed costs are costs that have characteristics of both a variable and a fixed cost. Mixed costs are sometimes called *semivariable* or *semifixed* costs.

To illustrate, assume that Simpson Inc. manufactures sails, using rented machinery. The rental charges are as follows:

Rental Charge = $15,000 per year
                +$1 times each machine hour over 10,000 hours

The rental charges for various hours used within the relevant range of 8,000 hours to 40,000 hours are as follows:

Hours Used	Rental Charge
8,000 hours	$15,000
12,000	$17,000 {$15,000 + [(12,000 hrs. − 10,000 hrs.) × $1]}
20,000	$25,000 {$15,000 + [(20,000 hrs. − 10,000 hrs.) × $1]}
40,000	$45,000 {$15,000 + [(40,000 hrs. − 10,000 hrs.) × $1]}

Exhibit 3 illustrates the preceding mixed cost behavior.

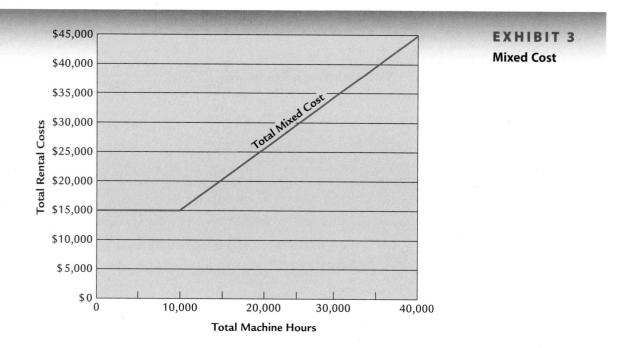

EXHIBIT 3

Mixed Cost

For purposes of analysis, mixed costs are usually separated into their fixed and variable components. The **high-low method** is a cost estimation method that may be used for this purpose.[1] The high-low method uses the highest and lowest activity levels and their related costs to estimate the variable cost per unit and the fixed cost.

To illustrate, assume that the Equipment Maintenance Department of Elgen Inc. incurred the following costs during the past five months:

	Production	Total Cost
June	1,000 units	$45,550
July	1,500	52,000
August	2,100	61,500
September	1,800	57,500
October	750	41,250

The number of units produced is the activity base, and the relevant range is the units produced between June and October. For Elgen Inc., the difference

---

1. Other methods of estimating costs, such as the scattergraph method and the least squares method, are discussed in cost accounting textbooks.

between the units produced and total costs at the highest and lowest levels of production are as follows:

	Production	Total Cost
Highest level	2,100 units	$61,500
Lowest level	750	41,250
Difference	1,350 units	$20,250

The total fixed cost does not change with changes in production. Thus, the $20,250 difference in the total cost is the change in the total variable cost. Dividing this difference of $20,250 by the difference in production is an estimate of the variable cost per unit. For Elgen Inc., this estimate is $15, as computed below.

$$\text{Variable Cost per Unit} = \frac{\text{Difference in Total Cost}}{\text{Difference in Production}}$$

$$= \frac{\$20,250}{1,350 \text{ units}} = \$15 \text{ per unit}$$

The fixed cost is estimated by subtracting the total variable costs from the total costs for the units produced as shown below.

Fixed Cost = Total Cost − (Variable Cost per Unit × Units Produced)

The fixed cost is the same at the highest and the lowest levels of production as shown below for Elgen Inc.

Highest level (2,100 units):

Fixed Cost = Total Cost − (Variable Cost per Unit × Units Produced)
= $61,500 − ($15 × 2,100 units)
= $61,500 − $31,500
= $30,000

Lowest level (750 units):

Fixed Cost = Total Cost − (Variable Cost per Unit × Units Produced)
= $41,250 − ($15 × 750 units)
= $41,250 − $11,250
= $30,000

Using the variable cost per unit and the fixed cost, the total equipment maintenance cost for Elgen Inc. can be computed for various levels of production as follows:

Total Cost = (Variable Cost per Unit × Units Produced) + Fixed Costs
= ($15 × Units Produced) + $30,000

To illustrate, the estimated total cost of 2,000 units of production is $60,000, as computed below.

Total Cost = ($15 × Units Produced) + $30,000
= ($15 × 2,000 units) + $30,000 = $30,000 + $30,000
= $60,000

Summary of Cost Behavior Concepts

The cost behavior of variable costs and fixed costs is summarized below.

Cost	Effect of Changing Activity Level	
	Total Amount	**Per-Unit Amount**
Variable	Increases and decreases proportionately with activity level.	Remains the same regardless of activity level.
Fixed	Remains the same regardless of activity level.	Increases and decreases inversely with activity level.

Mixed costs contain a fixed cost component that is incurred even if nothing is produced. For analysis, the fixed and variable cost components of mixed costs are separated using the high-low method.

Some examples of variable, fixed, and mixed costs for the activity base *units produced* are as follows:

Variable Cost	Fixed Cost	Mixed Cost
Direct materials	Straight-line depreciation	Quality Control Department salaries
Direct labor	Property taxes	Purchasing Department salaries
Electricity expense	Production supervisor salaries	Maintenance expenses
Supplies	Insurance expense	Warehouse expenses

One method of reporting variable and fixed costs is called **variable costing** or *direct costing*. Under variable costing, only the variable manufacturing costs (direct materials, direct labor, and variable factory overhead) are included in the product cost. The fixed factory overhead is treated as an expense of the period in which it is incurred. Variable costing is described and illustrated in advanced accounting courses.

Cost-Volume-Profit Relationships

Cost-volume-profit analysis is the examination of the relationships among selling prices, sales and production volume, costs, expenses, and profits. Cost-volume-profit analysis is useful for managerial decision making. Some of the ways cost-volume-profit analysis may be used include:

1. Analyzing the effects of changes in selling prices on profits
2. Analyzing the effects of changes in costs on profits
3. Analyzing the effects of changes in volume on profits
4. Setting selling prices
5. Selecting the mix of products to sell
6. Choosing among marketing strategies

Obj **2**

Compute the contribution margin, the contribution margin ratio, and the unit contribution margin.

Contribution Margin

Contribution margin is especially useful because it provides insight into the profit potential of a company. **Contribution margin** is the excess of sales over variable costs, as shown below.

$$\text{Contribution Margin} = \text{Sales} - \text{Variable Costs}$$

To illustrate, assume the following data for Waddell Inc.:

Sales	50,000 units
Sales price per unit	$20 per unit
Variable cost per unit	$12 per unit
Fixed costs	$300,000

Exhibit 4 illustrates an income statement for Waddell Inc. prepared in a contribution margin format.

EXHIBIT 4

Contribution Margin Income Statement

Sales (50,000 units × $20)...	$1,000,000
Variable costs (50,000 units × $12)......................................	600,000
Contribution margin (50,000 units × $8).................................	$ 400,000
Fixed costs...	300,000
Income from operations...	$ 100,000

Waddell's contribution margin of $400,000 is available to cover the fixed costs of $300,000. Once the fixed costs are covered, any additional contribution margin increases income from operations.

The graphic to the left illustrates the contribution margin and its effect on profits. The fixed costs are a bucket, and the contribution margin is water filling the bucket. Once the bucket is filled, the overflow represents income from operations. Up until the point of overflow, the contribution margin contributes to fixed costs (filling the bucket).

Contribution Margin Ratio

The contribution margin can also be expressed as a percentage. The **contribution margin ratio**, sometimes called the *profit-volume ratio*, indicates the percentage of each sales dollar available to cover fixed costs and to provide income from operations. The contribution margin ratio is computed as follows:

$$\text{Contribution Margin Ratio} = \frac{\text{Contribution Margin}}{\text{Sales}}$$

The contribution margin ratio is 40% for Waddell Inc., as computed below.

$$\text{Contribution Margin Ratio} = \frac{\text{Contribution Margin}}{\text{Sales}}$$

$$= \frac{\$400,000}{\$1,000,000} = 40\%$$

The contribution margin ratio is most useful when the increase or decrease in sales volume is measured in sales *dollars*. In this case, the change in sales dollars multiplied by the contribution margin ratio equals the change in income from operations, as shown below.

$$\text{Change in Income from Operations} = \text{Change in Sales Dollars} \\ \times \text{Contribution Margin Ratio}$$

To illustrate, if Waddell Inc. adds $80,000 in sales orders, its income from operations will increase by $32,000, as computed below.

$$\text{Change in Income from Operations} = \text{Change in Sales Dollars} \\ \times \text{Contribution Margin Ratio}$$

$$= \$80,000 \times 40\% = \$32,000$$

The preceding analysis is confirmed by the following contribution margin income statement of Waddell Inc.:

Sales...	$1,080,000
Variable costs ($1,080,000 × 60%)	648,000
Contribution margin ($1,080,000 × 40%)..................................	$ 432,000
Fixed costs...	300,000
Income from operations...	$ 132,000

Income from operations increased from $100,000 to $132,000 when sales increased from $1,000,000 to $1,080,000. Variable costs as a percentage of sales are equal to 100% minus the contribution margin ratio. Thus, in the above income statement, the variable costs are 60% (100% − 40%) of sales, or $648,000 ($1,080,000 × 60%). The total contribution margin, $432,000, can also be computed directly by multiplying the total sales by the contribution margin ratio ($1,080,000 × 40%).

In the preceding analysis, factors other than sales volume, such as variable cost per unit and sales price, are assumed to remain constant. If such factors change, their effect must also be considered.

The contribution margin ratio is also useful in developing business strategies. For example, assume that a company has a high contribution margin ratio and is producing below 100% of capacity. In this case, a large increase in income from operations can be expected from an increase in sales volume. Therefore, the company might consider implementing a special sales campaign to increase sales. In contrast, a company with a small contribution margin ratio will probably want to give more attention to reducing costs before attempting to promote sales.

Unit Contribution Margin

The unit contribution margin is also useful for analyzing the profit potential of proposed decisions. The **unit contribution margin** is computed as follows:

$$\text{Unit Contribution Margin} = \text{Sales Price per Unit} - \text{Variable Cost per Unit}$$

To illustrate, if Waddell Inc.'s unit selling price is $20 and its variable cost per unit is $12, the unit contribution margin is $8 as shown below.

$$\text{Unit Contribution Margin} = \text{Sales Price per Unit} - \text{Variable Cost per Unit}$$

$$= \$20 - \$12 = \$8$$

The unit contribution margin is most useful when the increase or decrease in sales volume is measured in sales *units* (quantities). In this case, the change in sales volume (units) multiplied by the unit contribution margin equals the change in income from operations, as shown below.

$$\text{Change in Income from Operations} = \text{Change in Sales Units} \times \text{Unit Contribution Margin}$$

To illustrate, assume that Waddell Inc.'s sales could be increased by 15,000 units, from 50,000 units to 65,000 units. Waddell's income from operations would increase by $120,000 (15,000 units × $8), as shown below.

$$\text{Change in Income from Operations} = \text{Change in Sales Units} \times \text{Unit Contribution Margin}$$
$$= 15{,}000 \text{ units} \times \$8 = \$120{,}000$$

The preceding analysis is confirmed by the following contribution margin income statement of Waddell Inc., which shows that income increased to $220,000 when 65,000 units are sold.

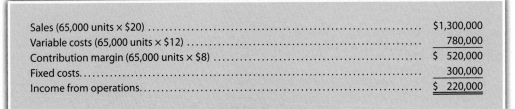

A room night at **Hilton Hotels** has a high contribution margin. The high contribution margin per room night is necessary to cover the high fixed costs for the hotel.

Sales (65,000 units × $20)	$1,300,000
Variable costs (65,000 units × $12)	780,000
Contribution margin (65,000 units × $8)	$ 520,000
Fixed costs	300,000
Income from operations	$ 220,000

The prior income statement in Exhibit 4 on page 438 indicates income of $100,000 when 50,000 units are sold. Thus, selling an additional 15,000 units increases income by $120,000 ($220,000 − $100,000).

Unit contribution margin analysis is useful information for managers. For example, in the preceding illustration, Waddell Inc. could spend up to $120,000 for special advertising or other product promotions to increase sales by 15,000 units. For example, if Waddell Inc. spent $90,000 to increase sales by 15,000, then income would increase by $30,000 ($120,000 − $90,000).

Obj | 3

Determine the break-even point and sales necessary to achieve a target profit.

Mathematical Approach to Cost-Volume-Profit Analysis

The mathematical approach to cost-volume-profit analysis uses equations to determine the following:

1. Sales necessary to break even
2. Sales necessary to make a target or desired profit

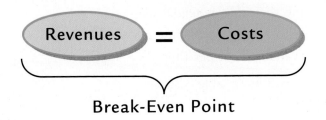

Break-Even Point

The **break-even point** is the level of operations at which a company's revenues and expenses are equal. At break-even, a company reports neither an income nor a loss from operations. The break-even point in *sales units* is computed as follows:

$$\text{Break-Even Sales (units)} = \frac{\text{Fixed Costs}}{\text{Unit Contribution Margin}}$$

To illustrate, assume the following data for Baker Corporation:

Fixed costs	$90,000
Unit selling price	$25
Unit variable cost	15
Unit contribution margin	$10

The break-even point is 9,000 units, as shown below.

$$\text{Break-Even Sales (units)} = \frac{\text{Fixed Costs}}{\text{Unit Contribution Margin}}$$

$$= \frac{\$90,000}{\$10} = 9,000 \text{ units}$$

The following income statement verifies the break-even point of 9,000 units:

Sales (9,000 units × $25)	$225,000
Variable costs (9,000 units × $15)	135,000
Contribution margin	$ 90,000
Fixed costs	90,000
Income from operations	$ 0

When the owner of a shopping center was asked how he was doing, he said, "My properties are *almost* fully rented." The questioner commented, "That must be pretty good." The shopping center owner responded, "Maybe so. But as you know, the profit is in the *almost*." This exchange reveals an important business principle: Income from operations is earned only after the break-even point is reached.

As shown in the preceding income statement, the break-even point is $225,000 (9,000 units × $25) of sales. The break-even point in *sales dollars* can be determined directly as follows:

$$\text{Break-Even Sales (dollars)} = \frac{\text{Fixed Costs}}{\text{Contribution Margin Ratio}}$$

The contribution margin ratio can be computed using the unit contribution margin and unit selling price as follows:

$$\text{Contribution Margin Ratio} = \frac{\text{Unit Contribution Margin}}{\text{Unit Selling Price}}$$

The contribution margin ratio for Baker Corporation is 40%, as shown below.

$$\text{Contribution Margin Ratio} = \frac{\text{Unit Contribution Margin}}{\text{Unit Selling Price}} = \frac{\$10}{\$25} = 40\%$$

Thus, the break-even sales dollars for Baker Corporation of $225,000 can be computed directly as follows:

$$\text{Break-Even Sales (dollars)} = \frac{\text{Fixed Costs}}{\text{Contribution Margin Ratio}} = \frac{\$90,000}{40\%} = \$225,000$$

The break-even point is affected by changes in the fixed costs, unit variable costs, and the unit selling price.

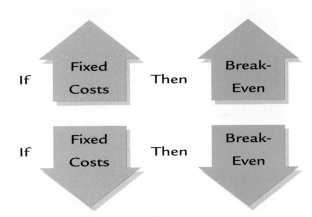

Effect of Changes in Fixed Costs Fixed costs do not change in total with changes in the level of activity. However, fixed costs may change because of other factors such as changes in property tax rates or factory supervisors' salaries. Changes in fixed costs affect the break-even point as follows:

1. Increases in fixed costs increase the break-even point.
2. Decreases in fixed costs decrease the break-even point.

To illustrate, assume that Steiner Co. is evaluating a proposal to budget an additional $100,000 for advertising. The data for Steiner Co. are as follows:

	Current	Proposed
Unit selling price	$90	$90
Unit variable cost	70	70
Unit contribution margin	$20	$20
Fixed costs	$600,000	$700,000

Steiner Co.'s break-even point *before* the additional advertising expense of $100,000 is 30,000 units, as shown below.

$$\text{Break-Even Sales (units)} = \frac{\text{Fixed Costs}}{\text{Unit Contribution Margin}}$$

$$= \frac{\$600,000}{\$20} = 30,000 \text{ units}$$

Steiner Co.'s break-even point *after* the additional advertising expense of $100,000 is 35,000 units, as shown below.

$$\text{Break-Even Sales (units)} = \frac{\text{Fixed Costs}}{\text{Unit Contribution Margin}}$$

$$= \frac{\$700,000}{\$20} = 35,000 \text{ units}$$

As shown above, the $100,000 increase in advertising (fixed costs) requires an additional 5,000 units (35,000 − 30,000) of sales to break even.[2] In other words, an increase in sales of 5,000 units is required in order to generate an additional $100,000 of total contribution margin (5,000 units × $20) to cover the increased fixed costs.

Effect of Changes in Unit Variable Costs Unit variable costs do not change with changes in the level of activity. However, unit variable costs may be affected by other factors such as changes in the cost per unit of direct materials.

Changes in unit variable costs affect the break-even point as follows:

1. Increases in unit variable costs increase the break-even point.
2. Decreases in unit variable costs decrease the break-even point.

---

2. The increase of 5,000 units can also be computed by dividing the increase in fixed costs of $100,000 by the unit contribution margin, $20, as follows: 5,000 units = $100,000/$20.

To illustrate, assume that Nagel Co. is evaluating a proposal to pay an additional 2% commission on sales to its salespeople as an incentive to increase sales. The data for Nagel Co. are as follows:

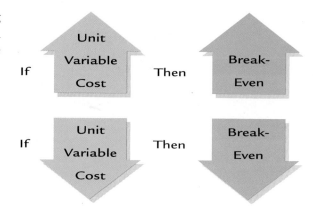

	Current	Proposed
Unit selling price	$250	$250
Unit variable cost	145	150
Unit contribution margin	$105	$100
Fixed costs	$840,000	$840,000

Nagel Co.'s break-even point *before* the additional 2% commission is 8,000 units, as shown below.

$$\text{Break-Even Sales (units)} = \frac{\text{Fixed Costs}}{\text{Unit Contribution Margin}}$$

$$= \frac{\$840,000}{\$105} = 8,000 \text{ units}$$

Increases in fuel prices increase the break-even freight load for the **Union Pacific** railroad.

If the 2% sales commission proposal is adopted, unit variable costs will increase by $5 ($250 × 2%) from $145 to $150 per unit. This increase in unit variable costs will decrease the unit contribution margin from $105 to $100 ($250 − $150). Thus, Nagel Co.'s break-even point *after* the additional 2% commission is 8,400 units, as shown below.

$$\text{Break-Even Sales (units)} = \frac{\text{Fixed Costs}}{\text{Unit Contribution Margin}}$$

$$= \frac{\$840,000}{\$100} = 8,400 \text{ units}$$

As shown above, an additional 400 units of sales will be required in order to break even. This is because if 8,000 units are sold, the new unit contribution margin of $100 provides only $800,000 (8,000 units × $100) of contribution margin. Thus, $40,000 more contribution margin is necessary to cover the total fixed costs of $840,000. This additional $40,000 of contribution margin is provided by selling 400 more units (400 units × $100).

Effect of Changes in Unit Selling Price Changes in the unit selling price affect the unit contribution margin and thus the break-even point. Specifically, changes in the unit selling price affect the break-even point as follows:

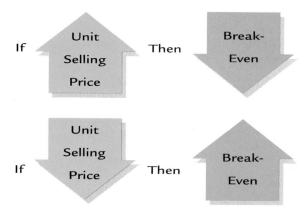

1. Increases in the unit selling price decrease the break-even point.
2. Decreases in the unit selling price increase the break-even point.

To illustrate, assume that Fraser Co. is evaluating a proposal to increase the unit selling price of its product from $50 to $60. The data for Fraser Co. are as follows:

	Current	Proposed
Unit selling price	$50	$60
Unit variable cost	30	30
Unit contribution margin	$20	$30
Fixed costs	$600,000	$600,000

Fraser Co.'s break-even point *before* the price increase is 30,000 units, as shown below.

$$\text{Break-Even Sales (units)} = \frac{\text{Fixed Costs}}{\text{Unit Contribution Margin}}$$

$$= \frac{\$600,000}{\$20} = 30,000 \text{ units}$$

The increase of $10 per unit in the selling price increases the unit contribution margin by $10. Thus, Fraser Co.'s break-even point *after the* price increase is 20,000 units, as shown below.

$$\text{Break-Even Sales (units)} = \frac{\text{Fixed Costs}}{\text{Unit Contribution Margin}}$$

$$= \frac{\$600,000}{\$30} = 20,000 \text{ units}$$

As shown above, the price increase of $10 increased the unit contribution margin by $10, which decreased the break-even point by 10,000 units (30,000 units − 20,000 units).

The **Golf Channel** went from a premium cable service price of per month to a much lower basic cable price, causing its subscriber break-even point to increase. The price change was successful, however, since the subscriber numbers exceeded the new break-even point.

Summary of Effects of Changes on Break-Even Point The break-even point in sales changes in the same direction as changes in the variable cost per unit and fixed costs. In contrast, the break-even point in sales changes in the opposite direction as changes in the unit selling price. These changes on the break-even point in sales are summarized below.

Type of Change	Direction of Change	Effect of Change on Break-Even Sales
Fixed cost	Increase	Increase
	Decrease	Decrease
Unit variable cost	Increase	Increase
	Decrease	Decrease
Unit selling price	Increase	Decrease
	Decrease	Increase

Target Profit

At the break-even point, sales and costs are exactly equal. However, the goal of most companies is to make a profit.

By modifying the break-even equation, the sales required to earn a target or desired amount of profit may be computed. For this purpose, target profit is added to the break-even equation as shown below.

$$\text{Sales (units)} = \frac{\text{Fixed Costs} + \text{Target Proft}}{\text{Unit Contribution Margin}}$$

To illustrate, assume the following data for Waltham Co.:

Fixed costs	$200,000
Target profit	100,000
Unit selling price	$75
Unit variable cost	45
Unit contribution margin	$30

The sales necessary to earn the target profit of $100,000 would be 10,000 units, computed as follows:

$$\text{Sales (units)} = \frac{\text{Fixed Costs} + \text{Target Proft}}{\text{Unit Contribution Margin}}$$

$$= \frac{\$200,000 + \$100,000}{\$30} = 10,000 \text{ units}$$

The following income statement verifies this computation:

Sales (10,000 units × $75)..	$750,000
Variable costs (10,000 units × $45)...................................	450,000
Contribution margin (10,000 units × $30)	$300,000
Fixed costs...	200,000
Income from operations..	$100,000

←— Target profit

HOW BUSINESSES MAKE MONEY

BREAKING EVEN ON HOWARD STERN

Satellite radio is one of the growing forms of entertainment. Customers are able to choose from a variety of types of music and talk radio and listen from just about anywhere in the country with limited commercials. The satellite radio market is dominated by Sirius XM Radio Inc. Prior to its merger with XM Radio, Sirius tripled its customer base by diversifying its product line and signing high-profile talk personalities. As part of this strategy, Sirius signed a five-year $500 million contract with radio "shock jock" Howard Stern. But how did Sirius determine that adding the self-proclaimed "King of All Media" to its play list was worth such a large amount of money? It used break-even analysis. Prior to signing with Sirius, 12 million listeners tuned in to Stern's show on Infinity Broadcasting Corporation. At the time the contract was signed, Sirius had about 600,000 subscribers. The company estimated that it would need 1 million of Stern's fans to subscribe to Sirius in order to break even on the $500 million fixed cost of the contract. Initial projections estimated that Stern's show would attract as many as 10 million listeners. It appears that the company's strategy worked as Sirius's subscriber base had grown to 20.2 million customers.

As shown in the preceding income statement, sales of $750,000 (10,000 units × $75) are necessary to earn the target profit of $100,000. The sales of $750,000 needed to earn the target profit of $100,000 can be computed directly using the contribution margin ratio, as shown below.

$$\text{Contribution Margin Ratio} = \frac{\text{Unit Contribution Margin}}{\text{Unit Selling Price}} = \frac{\$30}{\$75} = 40\%$$

$$\text{Sales (dollars)} = \frac{\text{Fixed Costs + Target Profit}}{\text{Contribution Margin Ratio}}$$

$$= \frac{\$200,000 + \$100,000}{40\%} = \frac{\$300,000}{40\%} = \$750,000$$

Integrity, Objectivity, and Ethics in Business

ORPHAN DRUGS

Each year, pharmaceutical companies develop new drugs that cure a variety of physical conditions. In order to be profitable, drug companies must sell enough of a product to exceed break even for a reasonable selling price. Break-even points, however, create a problem for drugs targeted at rare diseases, called "orphan drugs." These drugs are typically expensive to develop and have low sales volumes, making it impossible to achieve break even. To ensure that orphan drugs are not overlooked, Congress passed the Orphan Drug Act, which provides incentives for pharmaceutical companies to develop drugs for rare diseases that might not generate enough sales to reach break even. The program has been a great success. Since 1982, over 200 orphan drugs have come to market, including **Jacobus Pharmaceuticals Company, Inc.**'s drug for the treatment of tuberculosis and **Novartis AG**'s drug for the treatment of Paget's disease.

Obj 4

Using a cost-volume-profit chart and a profit-volume chart, determine the break-even point and sales necessary to achieve a target profit.

Graphic Approach to Cost-Volume-Profit Analysis

Cost-volume-profit analysis can be presented graphically as well as in equation form. Many managers prefer the graphic form because the operating profit or loss for different levels of sales can readily be seen.

Cost-Volume-Profit (Break-Even) Chart

A **cost-volume-profit chart**, sometimes called a *break-even chart*, graphically shows sales, costs, and the related profit or loss for various levels of units sold. It assists in understanding the relationship among sales, costs, and operating profit or loss.

To illustrate, the cost-volume-profit chart in Exhibit 5 is based on the following data:

Total fixed costs	$100,000
Unit selling price	$50
Unit variable cost	30
Unit contribution margin	$20

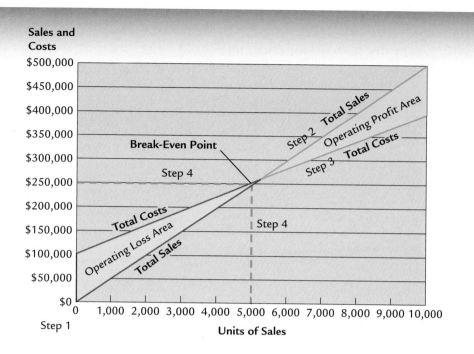

EXHIBIT 5

Cost-Volume-Profit Chart

The cost-volume-profit chart in Exhibit 5 is constructed using the following steps:

Step 1. Volume in units of sales is indicated along the horizontal axis. The range of volume shown is the relevant range in which the company expects to operate. Dollar amounts of total sales and costs are indicated along the vertical axis.

Step 2. A sales line is plotted by beginning at zero on the left corner of the graph. A second point is determined by multiplying any units of sales on the horizontal axis by the unit sales price of $50. For example, for 10,000 units of sales, the total sales would be $500,000 (10,000 units × $50). The sales line is drawn upward to the right from zero through the $500,000 point.

Step 3. A cost line is plotted by beginning with total fixed costs, $100,000, on the vertical axis. A second point is determined by multiplying any units of sales on the horizontal axis by the unit variable costs and adding the fixed costs. For example, for 10,000 units of sales, the total estimated costs would be $400,000 [(10,000 units × $30) + $100,000]. The cost line is drawn upward to the right from $100,000 on the vertical axis through the $400,000 point.

Step 4. The break-even point is the intersection point of the total sales and total cost lines. A vertical dotted line drawn downward at the intersection point indicates the units of sales at the break-even point. A horizontal dotted line drawn to the left at the intersection point indicates the sales dollars and costs at the break-even point.

In Exhibit 5, the break-even point is $250,000 of sales, which represents sales of 5,000 units. Operating profits will be earned when sales levels are to the right of the break-even point (*operating profit area*). Operating losses will be incurred when sales levels are to the left of the break-even point *(operating loss area)*.

Changes in the unit selling price, total fixed costs, and unit variable costs can be analyzed by using a cost-volume-profit chart. Using the data in Exhibit 5, assume that a proposal to reduce fixed costs by $20,000 is to be evaluated. In this case, the total fixed costs would be $80,000 ($100,000 − $20,000).

As shown in Exhibit 6, the total cost line is redrawn, starting at the $80,000 point (total fixed costs) on the vertical axis. A second point is determined by multiplying any units of sales on the horizontal axis by the unit variable costs and adding the fixed costs. For example, for 10,000 units of sales, the total estimated costs would be $380,000 [(10,000 units × $30) + $80,000]. The cost line is drawn upward to the right from $80,000 on the vertical axis through the $380,000 point. The revised cost-volume-profit chart in Exhibit 6 indicates that the break-even point decreases to $200,000 and 4,000 units of sales.

EXHIBIT 6

Revised Cost-Volume-Profit Chart

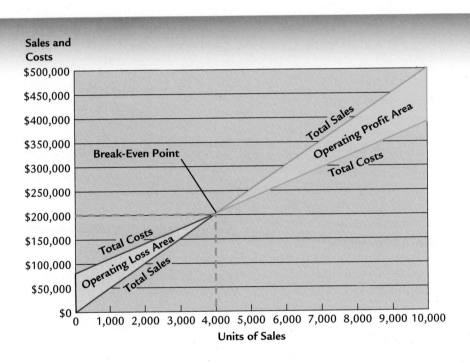

Profit-Volume Chart

Another graphic approach to cost-volume-profit analysis is the profit-volume chart. The **profit-volume chart** plots only the difference between total sales and total costs (or profits). In this way, the profit-volume chart allows managers to determine the operating profit (or loss) for various levels of units sold.

To illustrate, the profit-volume chart in Exhibit 7 is based on the same data as used in Exhibit 5. These data are as follows:

Total fixed costs	$100,000
Unit selling price	$50
Unit variable cost	30
Unit contribution margin	$20

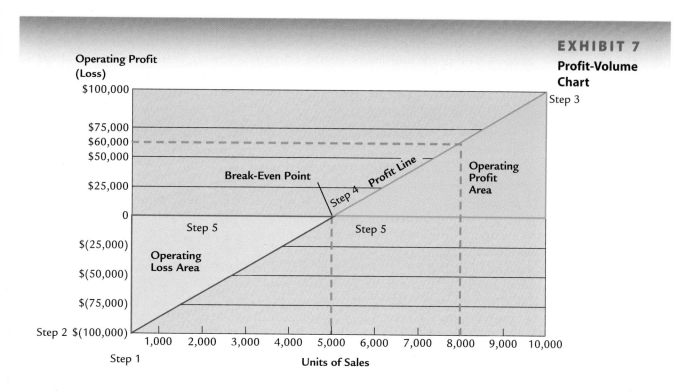

EXHIBIT 7

Profit-Volume Chart

The maximum operating loss is equal to the fixed costs of $100,000. Assuming that the maximum units that can be sold within the relevant range is 10,000 units, the maximum operating profit is $100,000, as shown below.

Sales (10,000 units × $50)...	$500,000
Variable costs (10,000 units × $30)..	300,000
Contribution margin (10,000 units × $20)	$200,000
Fixed costs..	100,000
Operating profit...	$100,000

← Maximum profit

The profit-volume chart in Exhibit 7 is constructed using the following steps:

Step 1. Volume in units of sales is indicated along the horizontal axis. The range of volume shown is the relevant range in which the company expects to operate. In Exhibit 7, the maximum units of sales is 10,000 units. Dollar amounts indicating operating profits and losses are shown along the vertical axis.

Step 2. A point representing the maximum operating loss is plotted on the vertical axis at the left. This loss is equal to the total fixed costs at the zero level of sales. Thus, the maximum operating loss is equal to the fixed costs of $100,000.

Step 3. A point representing the maximum operating profit within the relevant range is plotted on the right. Assuming that the maximum unit sales within the relevant range is 10,000 units, the maximum operating profit is $100,000.

Step 4. A diagonal profit line is drawn connecting the maximum operating loss point with the maximum operating profit point.

Step 5. The profit line intersects the horizontal zero operating profit line at the break-even point in units of sales. The area indicating an operating profit is identified to the right of the intersection, and the area indicating an operating loss is identified to the left of the intersection.

Many NBA franchises, such as the **Los Angeles Lakers,** state that their financial goal is to break even during the regular season and to make their profit during the playoffs, or basketball's so called "second season." The deeper the team goes into the playoffs, the greater the operating profit earned above break even from additional ticket sales and TV revenues.

In Exhibit 7, the break-even point is 5,000 units of sales, which is equal to total sales of $250,000 (5,000 units × $50). Operating profit will be earned when sales levels are to the right of the break-even point *(operating profit area)*. Operating losses will be incurred when sales levels are to the left of the break-even point *(operating loss area)*. For example, at sales of 8,000 units, an operating profit of $60,000 will be earned, as shown in Exhibit 7.

Changes in the unit selling price, total fixed costs, and unit variable costs on profit can be analyzed using a profit-volume chart. Using the data in Exhibit 7, assume the effect on profit of an increase of $20,000 in fixed costs is to be evaluated. In this case, the total fixed costs would be $120,000 ($100,000 + $20,000), and the maximum operating loss would also be $120,000. At the maximum sales of 10,000 units, the maximum operating profit would be $80,000, as shown below.

Sales (10,000 units × $50)...	$500,000
Variable costs (10,000 units × $30).................................	300,000
Contribution margin (10,000 units × $20)	$200,000
Fixed costs...	120,000
Operating profit..	$ 80,000

A revised profit-volume chart is constructed by plotting the maximum operating loss and maximum operating profit points and drawing the revised profit line. The original and the revised profit-volume charts are shown in Exhibit 8.

The revised profit-volume chart indicates that the break-even point is 6,000 units of sales. This is equal to total sales of $300,000 (6,000 units × $50). The operating loss area of the chart has increased, while the operating profit area has decreased.

Use of Computers in Cost-Volume-Profit Analysis

With computers, the graphic approach and the mathematical approach to cost-volume-profit analysis are easy to use. Managers can vary assumptions regarding selling prices, costs, and volume and can observe the effects of each change on the break-even point and profit. Such an analysis is called a *"what if" analysis* or *sensitivity analysis.*

Assumptions of Cost-Volume-Profit Analysis

Cost-volume-profit analysis depends on several assumptions. These assumptions simplify cost-volume-profit analysis. Since they are often valid for the relevant range of operations, cost-volume-profit analysis is useful for decision making.[3]

---

3. The impact of violating these assumptions is discussed in advanced accounting texts.

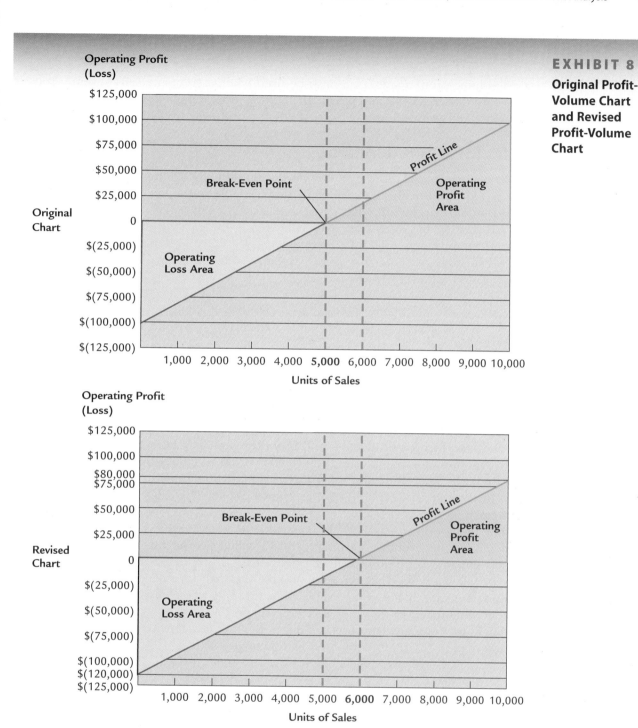

EXHIBIT 8

Original Profit-Volume Chart and Revised Profit-Volume Chart

The primary assumptions of cost-volume-profit analysis are listed below.

1. Total sales and total costs can be represented by straight lines.
2. Within the relevant range of operating activity, the efficiency of operations does not change.
3. Costs can be divided into fixed and variable components.
4. The sales mix is constant.
5. There is no change in the inventory quantities during the period.

Obj | **5**

Compute the break-even point for a company selling more than one product, the operating leverage, and the margin of safety.

Special Cost-Volume-Profit Relationships

Cost-volume-profit analysis can also be used when a company sells several products with different costs and prices. In addition, operating leverage and the margin of safety are useful in analyzing cost-volume-profit relationships.

Sales Mix Considerations

Many companies sell more than one product at different selling prices. In addition, the products normally have different unit variable costs and thus different unit contribution margins. In such cases, break-even analysis can still be performed by considering the sales mix. The **sales mix** is the relative distribution of sales among the products sold by a company.

To illustrate, assume that Burr Company sold Products A and B during the past year as follows:

Sales Mix

		Product A	Product B
Total fixed costs	$200,000		
Unit selling price		$90	$140
Unit variable cost		70	95
Unit contribution margin		$20	$ 45
Units sold		8,000	2,000
Sales mix		80%	20%

The sales mix for Products A and B is expressed as a percentage of total units sold. For Burr Company, a total of 10,000 (8,000 + 2,000) units were sold during the year. Therefore, the sales mix is 80% (8,000/10,000) for Product A and 20% for Product B (2,000/10,000) as shown above. The sales mix could also be expressed as the ratio 80:20.

For break-even analysis, it is useful to think of Products A and B as components of one overall enterprise product called E. The unit selling price of E equals the sum of the unit selling prices of each product multiplied by its sales mix percentage. Likewise, the unit variable cost and unit contribution margin of E equal the sum of the unit variable costs and unit contribution margins of each product multiplied by its sales mix percentage.

For Burr Company, the unit selling price, unit variable cost, and unit contribution margin for E are computed as follows:

Product E			Product A		Product B
Unit selling price of E	$100	=	($90 × 0.8)	+	($140 × 0.2)
Unit variable cost of E	75	=	($70 × 0.8)	+	($95 × 0.2)
Unit contribution margin of E	$ 25	=	($20 × 0.8)	+	($45 × 0.2)

The break-even point of 8,000 units of E can be determined in the normal manner as shown below.

$$\text{Break-Even Sales (units) for E} = \frac{\text{Fixed Costs}}{\text{Unit Contribution Margin}}$$

$$= \frac{\$200,000}{\$25} = 8,000 \text{ units}$$

Since the sales mix for Products A and B is 80% and 20% respectively, the break-even quantity of A is 6,400 units (8,000 units × 80%) and B is 1,600 units (8,000 units × 20%).

The preceding break-even analysis is verified by the following income statement:

	Product A	Product B	Total
Sales:			
6,400 units × $90	$576,000		$576,000
1,600 units × $140		$224,000	224,000
Total sales	$576,000	$224,000	$800,000
Variable costs:			
6,400 units × $70	$448,000		$448,000
1,600 units × $95		$152,000	152,000
Total variable costs	$448,000	$152,000	$600,000
Contribution margin	$128,000	$ 72,000	$200,000
Fixed costs			200,000
Income from operations			$ 0 ←— Break-even point

The daily break-even attendance at Universal Studios theme areas depends on how many tickets were sold at an *advance purchase discount rate* vs. the full gate rate. Likewise, the break-even point for an overseas flight of Delta Air Lines will be influenced by the number of first class, business class, and economy class tickets sold for the flight.

The effects of changes in the sales mix on the break-even point can be determined by assuming a different sales mix. The break-even point of E can then be recomputed.

Operating Leverage

The relationship of a company's contribution margin to income from operations is measured by **operating leverage**. A company's operating leverage is computed as follows:

$$\text{Operating Leverage} = \frac{\text{Contribution Margin}}{\text{Income from Operations}}$$

One type of business that has high operating leverage is what is called a "network" business—one in which service is provided over a network that moves either goods or information. Examples of network businesses include American Airlines, Verizon Communications, Yahoo!, and Google.

The difference between contribution margin and income from operations is fixed costs. Thus, companies with high fixed costs will normally have a high operating leverage. Examples of such companies include airline and automotive companies. Low operating leverage is normal for companies that are labor intensive, such as professional service companies, which have low fixed costs.

To illustrate operating leverage, assume the following data for Lund Inc. and Yates Inc.:

	Lund Inc.	Yates Inc.
Sales	$400,000	$400,000
Variable costs	300,000	300,000
Contribution margin	$100,000	$100,000
Fixed costs	80,000	50,000
Income from operations	$ 20,000	$ 50,000

As shown above, Lund Inc. and Yates Inc. have the same sales, the same variable costs, and the same contribution margin. However, Lund Inc. has larger fixed costs than Yates Inc. and thus a higher operating leverage. The operating leverage for each company is computed as follows:

$$\text{Operating Leverage} \atop \text{for Lund Inc.} = \frac{\text{Contribution Margin}}{\text{Income from Operations}} = \frac{\$100,000}{\$20,000} = 5$$

$$\frac{\text{Operating Leverage}}{\text{for Yates Inc.}} = \frac{\text{Contribution Margin}}{\text{Income from Operations}} = \frac{\$100,000}{\$50,000} = 2$$

Operating leverage can be used to measure the impact of changes in sales on income from operations. Using operating leverage, the effect of changes in sales on income from operations is computed as follows:

$$\frac{\text{Percent Change in}}{\text{Income from Operations}} = \frac{\text{Percent Change}}{\text{in Sales}} \times \frac{\text{Operating}}{\text{Leverage}}$$

To illustrate, assume that sales increased by 10%, or $40,000 ($400,000 × 10%), for Lund Inc. and Yates Inc. The percent increase in income from operations for Lund Inc. and Yates Inc. is computed below.

$$\frac{\text{Percent Change in}}{\text{Income from Operations}} = \frac{\text{Percent Change}}{\text{in Sales}} \times \frac{\text{Operating}}{\text{Leverage}}$$
for Lund Inc.

$$= 10\% \times 5 = 50\%$$

$$\frac{\text{Percent Change in}}{\text{Income from Operations}} = \frac{\text{Percent Change}}{\text{in Sales}} \times \frac{\text{Operating}}{\text{Leverage}}$$
for Yates Inc.

$$= 10\% \times 2 = 20\%$$

As shown above, Lund Inc.'s income from operations increases by 50%, while Yates Inc.'s income from operations increases by only 20%. The validity of this analysis is shown in the following income statements for Lund Inc. and Yates Inc. based on the 10% increase in sales:

	Lund Inc.	Yates Inc.
Sales	$440,000	$440,000
Variable costs	330,000	330,000
Contribution margin	$110,000	$110,000
Fixed costs	80,000	50,000
Income from operations	$ 30,000	$ 60,000

The preceding income statements indicate that Lund Inc.'s income from operations increased from $20,000 to $30,000, a 50% increase ($10,000 ÷ $20,000). In contrast, Yates Inc.'s income from operations increased from $50,000 to $60,000, a 20% increase ($10,000 ÷ $50,000).

Because even a small increase in sales will generate a large percentage increase in income from operations, Lund Inc. might consider ways to increase sales. Such actions could include special advertising or sales promotions. In contrast, Yates Inc. might consider ways to increase operating leverage by reducing variable costs.

The impact of a change in sales on income from operations for companies with high and low operating leverage can be summarized as follows:

Operating Leverage	Percentage Impact on Income from Operations from a Change in Sales
High	Large
Low	Small

Margin of Safety

The **margin of safety** indicates the possible decrease in sales that may occur before an operating loss results. Thus, if the margin of safety is low, even a small decline in sales revenue may result in an operating loss. The margin of safety may be expressed in the following ways:

1. Dollars of sales
2. Units of sales
3. Percent of current sales

To illustrate, assume the following data:

Sales	$250,000
Sales at the break-even point	200,000
Unit selling price	25

The margin of safety in dollars of sales is $50,000 ($250,000 − $200,000). The margin of safety in units is 2,000 units ($50,000/$25). The margin of safety expressed as a percent of current sales is 20%, as computed below.

$$\text{Margin of Safety} = \frac{\text{Sales} - \text{Sales at Break-Even Point}}{\text{Sales}}$$

$$= \frac{\$250,000 - \$200,000}{\$250,000} = \frac{\$50,000}{\$250,000} = 20\%$$

Therefore, the current sales may decline $50,000, 2,000 units, or 20% before an operating loss occurs.

Key Points

1. Classify costs as variable costs, fixed costs, or mixed costs.

Cost behavior refers to the manner in which a cost changes as a related activity changes. Variable costs are costs that vary in total in proportion to changes in the level of activity. Fixed costs are costs that remain the same in total dollar amount as the level of activity changes. A mixed cost has attributes of both a variable and a fixed cost.

2. Compute the contribution margin, the contribution margin ratio, and the unit contribution margin.

The contribution margin concept is useful in business planning because it gives insight into the profit potential of a firm. The contribution margin is the excess of sales revenues over variable costs. The contribution margin ratio is computed as follows:

$$\frac{\text{Contribution}}{\text{Margin Ratio}} = \frac{\text{Salels} - \text{Variable Costs}}{\text{Sales}}$$

The unit contribution margin is the excess of the unit selling price over the unit variable cost.

3. Determine the break-even point and sales necessary to achieve a target profit.

The mathematical approach to cost-volume-profit analysis uses the unit contribution margin concept and equations to determine the break-even point and the volume necessary to achieve a target profit for a business.

4. **Using a cost-volume-profit chart and a profit-volume chart, determine the break-even point and sales necessary to achieve a target profit.**

A cost-volume-profit chart focuses on the relationships among costs, sales, and operating profit or loss. Preparing and using a cost-volume-profit chart to determine the break-even point and the volume necessary to achieve a target profit are illustrated in this chapter.

The profit-volume chart focuses on profits rather than on revenues and costs. Preparing and using a profit-volume chart to determine the break-even point and the volume necessary to achieve a target profit are illustrated in this chapter.

5. **Compute the break-even point for a company selling more than one product, the operating leverage, and the margin of safety.**

Computing the break-even point for a business selling two or more products is based on a specified sales mix.

Given the sales mix, the break-even point can be computed, using the methods illustrated in this chapter.

Operating leverage is useful in measuring the impact of changes in sales on income from operations without preparing formal income statements. It is computed as follows:

$$\text{Operating Leverage} = \frac{\text{Contribution Margin}}{\text{Income from Operations}}$$

The margin of safety is useful in evaluating past operations and in planning future operations.

The margin of safety as a percentage of current sales is computed as follows:

$$\text{Margin of Safety} = \frac{\text{Sales} - \text{Sales at Break-Even Point}}{\text{Sales}}$$

Key Terms

Activity base (driver) (432)
Break-even point (440)
Contribution margin (437)
Contribution margin ratio (438)

Cost behavior (432)
Cost-volume-profit analysis (437)
Cost-volume-profit chart (446)
Fixed costs (433)
High-low method (435)

Margin of safety (455)
Mixed costs (434)
Operating leverage (453)
Profit-volume chart (448)
Relevant range (432)
Sales mix (452)

Unit contribution margin (439)
Variable costing (437)
Variable costs (432)

Illustrative Problem

Jackson Inc. expects to maintain the same inventories at the end of the year as at the beginning of the year. The estimated fixed costs for the year are $288,000, and the estimated variable costs per unit are $14. It is expected that 60,000 units will be sold at a price of $20 per unit. Maximum sales within the relevant range are 70,000 units.

Instructions

1. What is (a) the contribution margin ratio and (b) the unit contribution margin?
2. Determine the break-even point in units.
3. Construct a cost-volume-profit chart, indicating the break-even point.
4. Construct a profit-volume chart, indicating the break-even point.
5. What is the margin of safety?

Solution

1. a.   Contribution Margin Ratio $= \dfrac{\text{Sales} - \text{Variable Costs}}{\text{Sales}}$

$$= \dfrac{(60{,}000 \text{ units} \times \$20) - (60{,}000 \text{ units} \times \$14)}{(60{,}000 \text{ units} \times \$20)}$$

$$= \dfrac{\$1{,}200{,}000 - \$840{,}000}{\$1{,}200{,}000} = \dfrac{\$360{,}000}{\$1{,}200{,}000}$$

$$= 30\%$$

   b.   Unit Contribution Margin $=$ Unit Selling Price $-$ Unit Variable Costs
$$= \$20 - \$14 = \$6$$

2.   Break-Even Sales (units) $= \dfrac{\text{Fixed Costs}}{\text{Unit Contribution Margin}}$

$$= \dfrac{\$288{,}000}{\$6} = 48{,}000 \text{ units}$$

3.   **Sales and Costs**

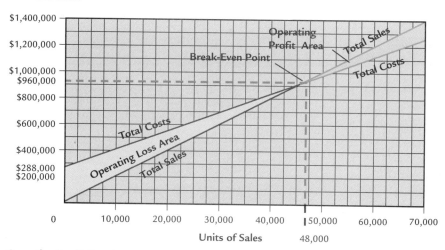

4.   **Operating Profit (Loss)**

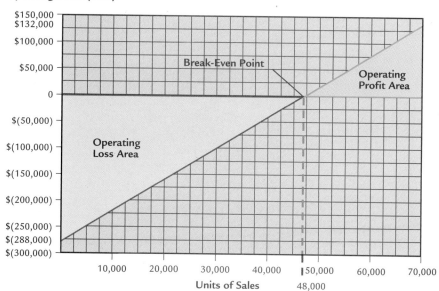

5.   **Margin of Safety:**

Expected sales (60,000 units × $20)	$1,200,000
Break-even point (48,000 units × $20)	960,000
Margin of safety	$ 240,000

or

$$\text{Margin of Safety (units)} = \frac{\text{Margin of Safety (dollars)}}{\text{Unit Contribution Margin}}$$

or

12,000 units ($240,000/$20)

or

$$\text{Margin of Safety} = \frac{\text{Sales} - \text{Sales at Break-Even Point}}{\text{Sales}}$$

$$= \frac{\$240,000}{\$1,200,000} = 20\%$$

Self-Examination Questions *(Answers appear at the end of chapter)*

1. Which of the following statements describes variable costs?

   A. Costs that vary on a per-unit basis as the level of activity changes.

   B. Costs that vary in total in direct proportion to changes in the level of activity.

   C. Costs that remain the same in total dollar amount as the level of activity changes.

   D. Costs that vary on a per-unit basis, but remain the same in total as the level of activity changes.

2. If sales are $500,000, variable costs are $200,000, and fixed costs are $240,000, what is the contribution margin ratio?

   A. 40%

   B. 48%

   C. 52%

   D. 60%

3. If the unit selling price is $16, the unit variable cost is $12, and fixed costs are $160,000, what are the break-even sales (units)?

   A. 5,714 units

   B. 10,000 units

   C. 13,333 units

   D. 40,000 units

4. Based on the data presented in Question 3, how many units of sales would be required to realize income from operations of $20,000?

   A. 11,250 units

   B. 35,000 units

   C. 40,000 units

   D. 45,000 units

5. Based on the following operating data, what is the operating leverage?

Sales	$600,000
Variable costs	240,000
Contribution margin	$360,000
Fixed costs	160,000
Income from operations	$200,000

   A. 0.8

   B. 1.2

   C. 1.8

   D. 4.0

Class Discussion Questions

1. Describe how total variable costs and unit variable costs behave with changes in the level of activity.

2. How would each of the following costs be classified if units produced is the activity base?
   a. Direct materials costs
   b. Direct labor costs
   c. Electricity costs of $0.09 per kilowatt-hour

3. Describe the behavior of (a) total fixed costs and (b) unit fixed costs as the level of activity increases.

4. How would each of the following costs be classified if units produced is the activity base?
   a. Salary of factory supervisor ($120,000 per year)
   b. Straight-line depreciation of plant and equipment
   c. Property rent of $11,500 per month on plant and equipment

5. In cost analyses, how are mixed costs treated?

6. Which of the following graphs illustrates how total fixed costs behave with changes in total units produced?

(a)
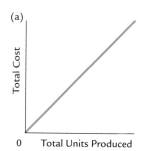

(b)
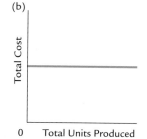

7. Which of the following graphs illustrates how unit variable costs behave with changes in total units produced?

(a)
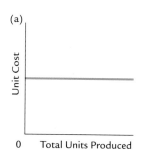

(b)
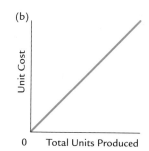

8. Which of the following graphs best illustrates fixed costs per unit as the activity base changes?

(a)
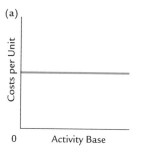

(b)
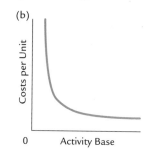

9. In applying the high-low method of cost estimation, how is the total fixed cost estimated?

10. If fixed costs increase, what would be the impact on the (a) contribution margin? (b) income from operations?

11. An examination of the accounting records of Larredo Company disclosed a high contribution margin ratio and production at a level below maximum capacity. Based on this information, suggest a likely means of improving income from operations. Explain.

12. If the unit cost of direct materials is decreased, what effect will this change have on the break-even point?

13. If insurance rates are increased, what effect will this change in fixed costs have on the break-even point?

14. Both Gouda Company and Cheddar Company had the same sales, total costs, and income from operations for the current fiscal year; yet Gouda Company had a lower break-even point than Cheddar Company. Explain the reason for this difference in break-even points.

15. The reliability of cost-volume-profit (CVP) analysis depends on several key assumptions. What are those primary assumptions?

16. How does the sales mix affect the calculation of the break-even point?

17. What does operating leverage measure, and how is it computed?

Exercises

Obj 1

E11-1 Classify costs

Following is a list of various costs incurred in producing computer monitors. With respect to the production and sale of these monitors, classify each cost as either variable, fixed, or mixed.

1. Computer chip (purchased from a vendor)
2. Electricity costs, $0.23 per kilowatt-hour
3. Hourly wages of inspectors
4. Hourly wages of machine operators
5. Janitorial costs, $4,000 per month
6. Metal
7. Packaging
8. Pension cost, $0.90 per employee hour on the job
9. Plastic
10. Property insurance premiums, $1,500 per month plus $0.04 for each dollar of property over $1,000,000
11. Property taxes, $375,000 per year on factory building and equipment
12. Oil used in manufacturing equipment
13. Rent on warehouse, $12,800 per month plus $2.50 per square foot of storage used
14. Salary of plant manager
15. Straight-line depreciation on the production equipment

Obj 1

E11-2 Identify cost graphs

The following cost graphs illustrate various types of cost behavior:

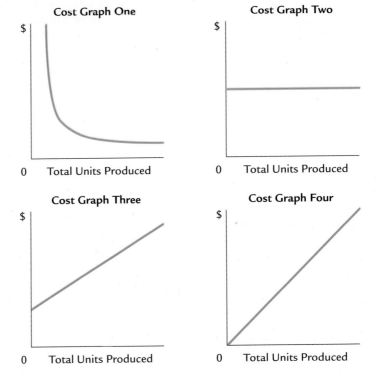

For each of the following costs, identify the cost graph that best illustrates its cost behavior as the number of units produced increases.

a. Electricity costs of $2,000 per month plus $0.09 per kilowatt-hour

b. Per-unit cost of straight-line depreciation on factory equipment

c. Per-unit direct labor cost

d. Salary of quality control supervisor, $10,000 per month

e. Total direct materials cost

E11-3   Identify activity bases

Obj 1

For a major university, match each cost in the following table with the activity base most appropriate to it. An activity base may be used more than once, or not used at all.

Cost	Activity Base
1. Admissions office salaries	a. Number of enrollment applications
2. Financial aid office salaries	b. Number of financial aid applications
3. Housing personnel wages	c. Number of student/athletes
4. Instructor salaries	d. Number of enrolled students and alumni
5. School supplies	e. Number of students living on campus
6. Student records office salaries	f. Student credit hours

E11-4   Identify activity bases

Obj 1

From the following list of activity bases for an automobile dealership, select the base that would be most appropriate for each of these costs: (1) preparation costs (cleaning, oil, and gasoline costs) for each car received, (2) salespersons' commission of 6% of the sales price for each car sold, and (3) administrative costs for ordering cars.

a. Dollar amount of cars on hand

b. Dollar amount of cars ordered

c. Dollar amount of cars received

d. Dollar amount of cars sold

e. Number of cars on hand

f. Number of cars ordered

g. Number of cars received

h. Number of cars sold

E11-5   Identify fixed and variable costs

Obj 1

Intuit Inc. develops and sells software products for the personal finance market, including popular titles such as Quicken® and TurboTax®. Classify each of the following costs and expenses for this company as either variable or fixed to the number of units produced and sold:

a. Shipping expenses

b. Property taxes on general offices

c. Straight-line depreciation of computer equipment

d. Salaries of human resources personnel

e. President's salary

f. Advertising

g. Sales commissions

h. CDs

i. Packaging costs

j. Salaries of software developers

k. Wages of telephone order assistants

l. User's guides

E11-6 Relevant range and fixed and variable costs

Digital Gamer Inc. manufactures components for computer games within a relevant range of 500,000 to 800,000 disks per year. Within this range, the following partially completed manufacturing cost schedule has been prepared:

Components produced	500,000	650,000	800,000
Total costs:			
Total variable costs	$ 900,000	(d)	(j)
Total fixed costs	1,560,000	(e)	(k)
Total costs	$2,460,000	(f)	(l)
Cost per unit:			
Variable cost per unit	(a)	(g)	(m)
Fixed cost per unit	(b)	(h)	(n)
Total cost per unit	(c)	(i)	(o)

Complete the cost schedule, identifying each cost by the appropriate letter (a) through (o).

E11-7 High-low method

Zeta Inc. has decided to use the high-low method to estimate the total cost and the fixed and variable cost components of the total cost. The data for various levels of production are as follows:

Units Produced	Total Costs
45,000	$1,535,000
50,000	1,650,000
70,000	2,110,000

a. Determine the variable cost per unit and the fixed cost.

b. Based on part (a), estimate the total cost for 60,000 units of production.

E11-8 High-low method for service company

Missoula Railroad decided to use the high-low method and operating data from the past six months to estimate the fixed and variable components of transportation costs. The activity base used by Missoula Railroad is a measure of railroad operating activity, termed "gross-ton miles," which is the total number of tons multiplied by the miles moved.

	Transportation Costs	Gross-Ton Miles
January	$1,575,000	125,000
February	2,095,800	180,000
March	1,675,000	136,000
April	1,800,000	150,000
May	1,426,600	110,000
June	2,050,000	175,000

Determine the variable cost per gross-ton mile and the fixed cost.

E11-9 Contribution margin ratio

a. Gloucester Company budgets sales of $11,750,000, fixed costs of $2,115,000, and variable costs of $6,815,000. What is the contribution margin ratio for Gloucester Company?

b. If the contribution margin ratio for Eatontown Company is 35%, sales were $6,440,000, and fixed costs were $1,300,000, what was the income from operations?

E11-10   Contribution margin and contribution margin ratio

For a recent year, McDonald's company-owned restaurants had the following sales and expenses (in millions):

Sales	$27,006
Food and packaging	$ 6,167
Payroll	4,606
Occupancy (rent, depreciation, etc.)	4,064
General, selling, and administrative expenses	2,394
Other expense (income)	1,245
	$18,476
Income from operations	$ 8,530

Assume that the variable costs consist of food and packaging, payroll, and 80% of the general, selling, and administrative expenses.

a. What is McDonald's contribution margin? Round to the nearest million.

b. What is McDonald's contribution margin ratio? Round to one decimal place.

c. How much would income from operations increase if same-store sales increased by $800 million for the coming year, with no change in the contribution margin ratio or fixed costs?

E11-11   Break-even sales and sales to realize income from operations

For the current year ending December 31, Rotisserie Industries expects fixed costs of $1,750,000, a unit variable cost of $6.25, and a unit selling price of $8.00.

a. Compute the anticipated break-even sales (units).

b. Compute the sales (units) required to realize income from operations of $612,500.

E11-12   Break-even sales

Molson-Coors Brewing Company reported the following operating information for a recent year (in millions):

Net sales	$3,516
Cost of goods sold	$2,049
Marketing, general, and admin. expenses	1,019
	$3,068
Income from operations	$ 448*

"Before special items

Assume that Molson-Coors sold 35 million barrels of beer during the year, variable costs were 80% of the cost of goods sold and 45% of marketing, general, and administrative expenses, and that the remaining costs are fixed. For the following year, assume that Molson-Coors expects pricing, variable costs per barrel, and fixed costs to remain constant, except that new distribution and general office facilities are expected to increase fixed costs by $75 million.
   Rounding to the nearest cent:

a. Compute the break-even sales (barrels) for the current year.

b. Compute the anticipated break-even sales (barrels) for the following year.

E11-13   Break-even sales

Currently, the unit selling price of a product is $300, the unit variable cost is $195, and the total fixed costs are $840,000. A proposal is being evaluated to increase the unit selling price to $315.

a. Compute the current break-even sales (units).

b. Compute the anticipated break-even sales (units), assuming that the unit selling price is increased and all costs remain constant.

Obj 3

E11-14 Break-even analysis

The Garden Club of Palm Springs, California, collected recipes from members and published a cookbook entitled *Desert Dishes*. The book will sell for $40 per copy. The chairperson of the cookbook development committee estimated that the club needed to sell 8,000 books to break even on its $40,000 investment. What is the variable cost per unit assumed in the Garden Club's analysis?

Obj 3

E11-15 Break-even analysis

Media outlets such as ESPN and Fox Sports often have Web sites that provide in-depth coverage of news and events. Portions of these Web sites are restricted to members who pay a monthly subscription to gain access to exclusive news and commentary. These Web sites typically offer a free trial period to introduce viewers to the Web site. Assume that during a recent fiscal year, ESPN.com spent $20,900,000 on a promotional campaign for its Web site, offering two free months of service for new subscribers. In addition, assume the following information:

Number of months an average new customer stays with the service (including the two free months)	18 months
Revenue per month per customer subscription	$9.95
Variable cost per month per customer subscription	$4.20

Determine the number of new customer accounts needed to break even on the cost of the promotional campaign. In forming your answer, (1) treat the cost of the promotional campaign as a fixed cost, and (2) treat the revenue less variable cost per account for the subscription period as the unit contribution margin.

Obj 3

E11-16 Break-even analysis

Sprint Nextel Corporation is one of the largest digital wireless service providers in the United States. In a recent year, it had approximately 46.6 million direct subscribers (accounts) that generated revenue of $33,679 million. Costs and expenses for the year were as follows (in millions):

Cost of revenue	$19,015
Selling, general, and administrative expenses	9,592
Depreciation, amortization, and other expenses	4,964

Assume that 75% of the cost of revenue and 35% of the selling, general, and administrative expenses are variable to the number of direct subscribers (accounts).

a. What is Sprint Nextel's break-even number of accounts, using the data and assumptions above? Round units to one decimal place (in millions).

b. How much revenue per account would be sufficient for Sprint Nextel to break even if the number of accounts remained constant?

Obj 4

✔ b. $200,000

E11-17 Cost-volume-profit chart

For the coming year, Cabinet Inc. anticipates fixed costs of $60,000, a unit variable cost of $70, and a unit selling price of $100. The maximum sales within the relevant range are $500,000.

a. Construct a cost-volume-profit chart.

b. Estimate the break-even sales (dollars) by using the cost-volume-profit chart constructed in part (a).

c. What is the main advantage of presenting the cost-volume-profit analysis in graphic form rather than equation form?

E11-18   Profit-volume chart

Using the data for Cabinet Inc. in Exercise 11-17, (a) determine the maximum possible operating loss, (b) compute the maximum possible income from operations, (c) construct a profit-volume chart, and (d) estimate the break-even sales (units) by using the profit-volume chart constructed in part (c).

E11-19   Break-even chart

Name the following chart, and identify the items represented by the letters (a) through (f).

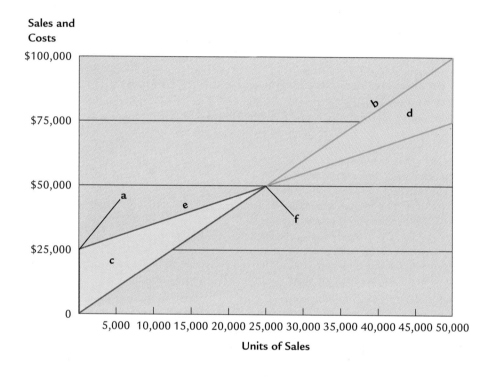

E11-20   Break-even chart

Name the following chart, and identify the items represented by the letters (a) through (f).

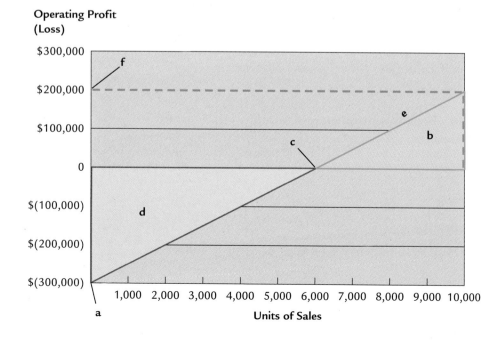

Obj | **5**

✔ a. 160,000 units

E11-21   Sales mix and break-even sales

Dontics Technology Inc. manufactures and sells two products, digital game players and computer tablets. The fixed costs are $6,640,000, and the sales mix is 65% game players and 35% computer tablets. The unit selling price and the unit variable cost for each product are as follows:

Products	Unit Selling Price	Unit Variable Cost
Game players	$ 30.00	$ 20.00
Tablets	250.00	150.00

a. Compute the break-even sales (units) for the overall product, E.

b. How many units of each product, game players and tablets, would be sold at the break-even point?

Obj | **5**

✔ a. 80 seats

E11-22   Break-even sales and sales mix for a service company

Yellow Dove Airways provides air transportation services between Portland and Minneapolis. A single Portland to Minneapolis round-trip flight has the following operating statistics:

Fuel and landing fees	$19,400
Flight crew salaries	3,760
Airplane depreciation	2,600
Variable cost per passenger—business class	50
Variable cost per passenger—economy class	20
Round-trip ticket price—business class	750
Round-trip ticket price—economy class	300

It is assumed that the fuel and landing fees, crew salaries, and airplane depreciation are fixed, regardless of the number of seats sold for the round-trip flight.

a. Compute the break-even number of seats sold on a single round-trip flight for the overall product. Assume that the overall product is 10% business class and 90% economy class tickets.

b. How many business class and economy class seats would be sold at the break-even point?

Obj | **5**

✔ a. (2) 20%

E11-23   Margin of safety

a. If Dunne Buggies Company, with a break-even point at $3,500,000 of sales, has actual sales of $4,375,000, what is the margin of safety expressed (1) in dollars and (2) as a percentage of sales?

b. If the margin of safety for Tri-City Company was 30%, fixed costs were $2,800,000 and variable costs were 75% of sales, what was the amount of actual sales (dollars)? (*Hint:* Determine the break-even in sales dollars first.)

Obj | **5**

E11-24   Break-even and margin of safety relationships

At a recent staff meeting, the management of Black Hat Technologies Inc. was considering discontinuing the Battle Royale line of electronic games from the product line. The chief financial analyst reported the following current monthly data for the Battle Royale:

Units of sales	190,000
Break-even units	215,000
Margin of safety in units	8,000

For what reason would you question the validity of these data?

E11-25 Operating leverage

Socket Inc. and Wrench Inc. have the following operating data:

	Socket Inc.	Wrench Inc.
Sales	$1,200,000	$1,400,000
Variable costs	750,000	600,000
Contribution margin	$ 450,000	$ 800,000
Fixed costs	300,000	480,000
Income from operations	$ 150,000	$ 320,000

a. Compute the operating leverage for Socket Inc. and Wrench Inc.

b. How much would income from operations increase for each company if the sales of each increased by 30%?

c. Why is there a difference in the increase in income from operations for the two companies? Explain.

Problems

P11-1 Classify costs

Mystique Apparel Co. manufactures a variety of clothing types for distribution to several major retail chains. The following costs are incurred in the production and sale of blue jeans:

a. Brass buttons

b. Consulting fee of $250,000 paid to industry specialist for marketing advice

c. Dye

d. Fabric

e. Electricity costs of $0.05 per kilowatt-hour

f. Hourly wages of machine operators

g. Insurance premiums on property, plant, and equipment, $85,000 per year plus $6 per $50,000 of insured value over $15,000,000

h. Janitorial supplies, $3,500 per month

i. Leather for patches identifying the brand on individual pieces of apparel

j. Legal fees paid to attorneys in defense of the company in a patent infringement suit, $50,000 plus $500 per hour

k. Property taxes on property, plant, and equipment

l. Rental costs of warehouse, $7,000 per month plus $2 per square foot of storage used

m. Rent on experimental equipment, $18,000 per year

n. Salary of designers

o. Salary of production vice president

p. Salesperson's salary, $45,000 plus 3% of the total sales

q. Shipping boxes used to ship orders

r. Straight-line depreciation on sewing machines

s. Supplies

t. Thread

Instructions

Classify the preceding costs as either fixed, variable, or mixed. Use the following tabular headings and place an "X" in the appropriate column. Identify each cost by letter in the cost column.

Cost	Fixed Cost	Variable Cost	Mixed Cost

Obj **2, 3**

✔ 2. a. $96.60

P11-2   Break-even sales under present and proposed conditions

Kearney Company, operating at full capacity, sold 400,000 units at a price of $246.60 per unit during 20Y5. Its income statement for 20Y5 is as follows:

Sales		$98,640,000
Cost of goods sold		44,500,000
Gross profit		$54,140,000
Expenses:		
Selling expenses	$8,000,000	
Administrative expenses	3,000,000	
Total expenses		11,000,000
Income from operations		$43,140,000

The division of costs between fixed and variable is as follows:

	Fixed	Variable
Cost of goods sold	28%	72%
Selling expenses	25%	75%
Administrative expenses	80%	20%

Management is considering a plant expansion program that will permit an increase of $8,631,000 (35,000 units at $246.60) in yearly sales. The expansion will increase fixed costs by $3,600,000, but will not affect the relationship between sales and variable costs.

Instructions

1. Determine for 20Y5 the total fixed costs and the total variable costs.
2. Determine for 20Y5 (a) the unit variable cost and (b) the unit contribution margin.
3. Compute the break-even sales (units) for 20Y5.
4. Compute the break-even sales (units) under the proposed program.
5. Determine the amount of sales (units) that would be necessary under the proposed program to realize the $43,140,000 of income from operations that was earned in 20Y5.
6. Determine the maximum income from operations possible with the expanded plant.
7. If the proposal is accepted and sales remain at the 20Y5 level, what will the income or loss from operations be for 20Y6?
8. Based on the data given, would you recommend accepting the proposal? Explain.

Obj **3, 4**

✔ 1. 6,000 units

P11-3   Break-even sales and cost-volume-profit chart

For the coming year, Bernardino Company anticipates a unit selling price of $85, a unit variable cost of $15, and fixed costs of $420,000.

Instructions

1. Compute the anticipated break-even sales (units).
2. Compute the sales (units) required to realize income from operations of $70,000.
3. Construct a cost-volume-profit chart, assuming maximum sales of 10,000 units within the relevant range.
4. Determine the probable income (loss) from operations if sales total 8,000 units.

P11-4   Break-even sales and cost-volume-profit chart

Obj 3, 4

✔ 1. 6,800 units

Last year, Ridgecrest Inc. had sales of $3,200,000, based on a unit selling price of $400. The variable cost per unit was $240, and fixed costs were $1,088,000. The maximum sales within Ridgecrest Inc.'s relevant range are 10,000 units. Ridgecrest Inc. is considering a proposal to spend an additional $160,000 on billboard advertising during the current year in an attempt to increase sales and utilize unused capacity.

Instructions

1. Construct a cost-volume-profit chart indicating the break-even sales for last year. Verify your answer, using the break-even equation.

2. Using the cost-volume-profit chart prepared in part (1), determine (a) the income from operations for last year and (b) the maximum income from operations that could have been realized during the year. Verify your answers arithmetically.

3. Construct a cost-volume-profit chart indicating the break-even sales for the current year, assuming that a noncancelable contract is signed for the additional billboard advertising. No changes are expected in the unit selling price or other costs. Verify your answer, using the break-even equation.

4. Using the cost-volume-profit chart prepared in part (3), determine (a) the income from operations if sales total 8,000 units and (b) the maximum income from operations that could be realized during the year. Verify your answers arithmetically.

P11-5   Sales mix and break-even sales

Obj 5

✔ 1. 7,500 units

Data related to the expected sales of kayaks and canoes for River Sports Inc. for the current year, which is typical of recent years, are as follows:

Products	Unit Selling Price	Unit Variable Cost	Sales Mix
Kayaks	$400	$240	80%
Canoes	800	480	20%

The estimated fixed costs for the current year are $1,440,000.

Instructions

1. Determine the estimated units of sales of the overall product necessary to reach the break-even point for the current year.

2. Based on the break-even sales (units) in part (1), determine the unit sales of kayaks and canoes for the current year.

3. Assume that the sales mix was 20% kayaks and 80% canoes. Determine the estimated units of sales of overall product necessary to reach the break-even point for the current year.

4. Based upon the break-even sales (units) in part (3), determine the unit sales of kayaks and canoes for the current year.

5. Why is the overall enterprise break-even point so different in (1) and (3)?

Obj | **2, 3, 4, 5**

✔ 2. 40%

P11-6 Contribution margin, break-even sales, cost-volume-profit chart, margin of safety, and operating leverage

Organic Health Care Products Inc. expects to maintain the same inventories at the end of 20Y8 as at the beginning of the year. The total of all production costs for the year is therefore assumed to be equal to the cost of goods sold. With this in mind, the various department heads were asked to submit estimates of the costs for their departments during 20Y8. A summary report of these estimates is as follows:

	Estimated Fixed Cost	Estimated Variable Cost (per unit sold)
Production costs:		
Direct materials	—	$ 8.00
Direct labor	—	3.00
Factory overhead	$ 200,000	1.50
Selling expenses:		
Advertising	1,450,000	—
Sales salaries and commissions	93,000	1.85
Travel	340,000	—
Miscellaneous selling expense	2,000	0.10
Administrative expenses:		
Office and officers' salaries	300,000	—
Supplies	10,000	0.50
Miscellaneous administrative expense	5,000	0.05
Total	$2,400,000	$15.00

It is expected that 400,000 units will be sold at a price of $25 a unit. Maximum sales within the relevant range are 500,000 units.

Instructions

1. Prepare an estimated income statement for 20Y8.
2. What is the expected contribution margin ratio?
3. Determine the break-even sales in units.
4. Construct a cost-volume-profit chart indicating the break-even sales.
5. What is the expected margin of safety in dollars and as a percentage of sales?
6. Determine the operating leverage.

Cases

Case 11-1   Ethics and professional conduct in business

Phil Fritz is a financial consultant to Magna Properties Inc., a real estate syndicate. Magna Properties Inc. finances and develops commercial real estate (office buildings). The completed projects are then sold as limited partnership interests to individual investors. The syndicate makes a profit on the sale of these partnership interests. Phil provides financial information for the offering prospectus, which is a document that provides the financial and legal details of the limited partnership offerings. In one of the projects, the bank has financed the construction of a commercial office building at a rate of 7% for the first four years, after which time the rate jumps to 9% for the remaining 21 years of the mortgage. The interest costs are one of the major ongoing costs of a real estate project. Phil has reported prominently in the prospectus that the break-even occupancy for the first four years is 48%. This is the amount of office space that must be leased to cover the interest and general upkeep costs over the first four years. The 48% break even is very low and thus communicates a low risk to potential investors. Phil uses the 48% break-even rate as a major marketing tool in selling the limited partnership interests. Buried in the fine print of the prospectus is additional information that would allow an astute investor to determine that the break-even occupancy will jump to 92% after the fourth year because of the contracted increase in the mortgage interest rate. Phil believes prospective investors are adequately informed as to the risk of the investment.

Comment on the ethical considerations of this situation.

Case 11-2 Break-even sales, contribution margin

"Every airline has what is called a break-even load factor. That is, the percentage of seats the airline . . . (flies) . . . that it must sell . . . to cover its costs. Since revenue and costs vary from one airline to another, so does the break-even factor. . . . Overall, the break-even load factor for the (airline) industry in recent years has been approximately 66 percent."

The airline industry is notorious for boom and bust cycles. Why is airline profitability very sensitive to these cycles? Do you think that during a down cycle the strategy to consolidate routes and raise ticket prices is reasonable? What would make this strategy succeed or fail? Why? **Source:** http://www.avjobs.com/history/airline-economics.asp.

Case 11-3 Break-even analysis

Aquarius Games Inc. has finished a new video game, *Triathlon Challenge*. Management is now considering its marketing strategies. The following information is available:

Anticipated sales price per unit	$75
Variable cost per unit*	$45
Anticipated volume	800,000
Production costs	$9,000,000
Anticipated advertising	$15,000,000

*The cost of the video game, packaging, and copying costs.

Two managers, Haley Chipana and Dan Gillespie, had the following discussion of ways to increase the profitability of this new offering:

Haley: I think we need to think of some way to increase our profitability. Do you have any ideas?

Dan: Well, I think the best strategy would be to become aggressive on price.

Haley: How aggressive?

Dan: If we drop the price to $60 per unit and maintain our advertising budget at $15,000,000, I think we will generate sales of 2,000,000 units.

Haley: I think that's the wrong way to go. You're giving too much up on price. Instead, I think we need to follow an aggressive advertising strategy.

Dan: How aggressive?

Haley: If we increase our advertising to a total of $20,000,000, we should be able to increase sales volume to 1,200,000 units without any change in price.

Dan: I don't think that's reasonable. We'll never cover the increased advertising costs.

Which strategy is best: Do nothing? Follow the advice of Dan Gillespie? Or follow Haley Chipana's strategy?

Case 11-4   Variable costs and activity bases in decision making

The owner of Dawg Prints, a printing company, is planning direct labor needs for the upcoming year. The owner has provided you with the following information for next year's plans:

	One Color	Two Color	Three Color	Four Color	Total
Number of banners	198	250	352	400	1,200

Each color on the banner must be printed one at a time. Thus, for example, a four-color banner will need to be run through the printing operation four separate times. The total production volume last year was 600 banners, as shown below.

	One Color	Two Color	Three Color	Total
Number of banners	152	206	242	600

The four-color banner is a new product offering for the upcoming year. The owner believes that the expected 600-unit increase in volume from last year means that direct labor expenses should increase by 100% (600 ÷ 600). What do you think?

Case 11-5   Variable costs and activity bases in decision making

Sales volume has been dropping at Pinnacle Publishing Company. During this time, however, the Shipping Department manager has been under severe financial constraints. The manager knows that most of the Shipping Department's effort is related to pulling inventory from the warehouse for each order and performing the paperwork. The paperwork involves preparing shipping documents for each order. Thus, the pulling and paperwork effort associated with each sales order is essentially the same, regardless of the size of the order. The Shipping Department manager has discussed the financial situation with senior management. Senior management has responded by pointing out that sales volume has been dropping, so that the amount of work in the Shipping Department should be dropping. Thus, senior management told the Shipping Department manager that costs should be decreasing in the department.

The Shipping Department manager prepared the following information:

Month	Sales Volume	Number of Customer Orders	Sales Volume per Order
January	$500,000	1,400	250
February	460,000	1,440	230
March	440,000	1,460	220
April	400,000	1,500	200
May	380,000	1,570	190
June	370,000	1,650	185
July	360,000	1,700	180
August	350,000	1,750	175

Given this information, how would you respond to senior management?

GROUP PROJECT ## Case 11-6   Break-even analysis

Break-even analysis is one of the most fundamental tools for managing any kind of business unit. Consider the management of your school. In a group, brainstorm some applications of break-even analysis at your school. Identify three areas where break-even analysis might be used. For each area, identify the revenues, variable costs, and fixed costs that would be used in the calculation.

Answers to Self-Examination Questions

1. **B** Variable costs vary in total in direct proportion to changes in the level of activity (answer B). Costs that vary on a per-unit basis as the level of activity changes (answer A) or remain constant in total dollar amount as the level of activity changes (answer C), or both (answer D), are fixed costs.

2. **D** The contribution margin ratio indicates the percentage of each sales dollar available to cover the fixed costs and provide income from operations and is determined as follows:

$$\text{Contribution Margin Ratio} = \frac{\text{Sales} - \text{Variable Costs}}{\text{Sales}}$$

$$= \frac{\$500,000 - \$200,000}{\$500,000}$$

$$= 60\%$$

3. **D** The break-even sales of 40,000 units (answer D) is computed as follows:

$$\text{Break-Even Sales (units)} = \frac{\text{Fixed Costs}}{\text{Unit Contribution Margin}}$$

$$= \frac{\$160,000}{\$4} = 40,000 \text{ units}$$

4. **D** Sales of 45,000 units are required to realize income from operations of $20,000, computed as follows:

$$\text{Sales (units)} = \frac{\text{Fixed Costs} + \text{Target Profit}}{\text{Unit Contribution Margin}}$$

$$= \frac{\$160,000 + \$20,000}{\$4}$$

$$= 45,000 \text{ units}$$

5. **C** The operating leverage is 1.8, computed as follows:

$$\text{Operating Leverage} = \frac{\text{Contribution Margin}}{\text{Income from Operations}}$$

$$= \frac{\$360,000}{\$200,000} = 1.8$$

CHAPTER 12

Differential Analysis and Product Pricing

LEARNING OBJECTIVES

After studying this chapter, you should be able to:

Obj **1** Prepare differential analysis reports for a variety of managerial decisions.

Obj **2** Determine the selling price of a product, using the total cost, product cost, and variable cost concepts.

Obj **3** Compute the relative profitability of products in bottleneck production processes.

Many of the decisions that you make depend on comparing the estimated costs of alternatives. The payoff from such comparisons is described in the following report from a University of Michigan study.

Richard Nisbett and two colleagues quizzed Michigan faculty members and university seniors on such questions as how often they walk out on a bad movie, refuse to finish a bad meal, or abandon a research project. They believe that people who cut their losses this way are following sound economic rules: calculating the net benefits of alternative courses of action, writing off past costs that can't be recovered, and weighing the opportunity to use future time and effort more profitably elsewhere.

Dr. Nisbett concedes that for many Americans, cost-benefit rules often appear to conflict with such traditional principles as "never give up" and "waste not, want not."

Managers must also apply cost-benefit rules in making decisions affecting their business. **RealNetworks, Inc.,** the Internet-based music and game company, like most companies must choose between alternatives. Examples of decisions faced by RealNetworks include whether it should expand or discontinue services, such as its recent decision to Mac-enable its digital music service, Rhapsody®, and whether to accept business at special prices, such as special pricing on its Helix Media Delivery System®.

In this chapter, differential analysis, which reports the effects of decisions on total revenues and costs, is discussed. Practical approaches to setting product prices are also described and illustrated. Finally, how production bottlenecks influence product mix and pricing decisions is discussed.

Source: Alan L. Otten, "Economic Perspective Produces Steady Yields," from People Patterns, *The Wall Street Journal*, March 31, 1992, p. B1.

Differential Analysis

Managerial decision making involves choosing between alternative courses of action. Although the managerial decision-making process varies by the type of decision, it normally involves the following steps:

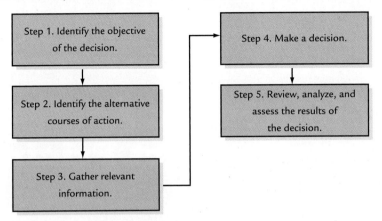

Step 1. Identify the objective of the decision.

Step 2. Identify the alternative courses of action.

Step 3. Gather relevant information.

Step 4. Make a decision.

Step 5. Review, analyze, and assess the results of the decision.

The management
of **Delta Air Lines**
decided to discontinue
its low-fare **Song
Airline** subsidiary after
assessing its profitability.

The objective (Step 1) for most decisions is to maximize the company's profits. The alternative courses of action (Step 2) could include actions such as discontinuing an unprofitable segment, replacing equipment, or offering a product at a special price to an exporter. The relevant information (Step 3) varies by decision, but oftentimes includes estimates and data that are not available in the accounting records. Making decisions (Step 4) is the most important function of managers. Once the decision is made, the results of the decision (Step 5) should be reviewed, analyzed, and assessed in terms of the initial objective of the decision.

Accounting facilitates the preceding process by:

1. Gathering relevant information for managerial decisions
2. Reporting this information to management
3. Providing management feedback on the results of the decisions

Have you ever walked
out on a bad movie?
The cost of the ticket is
a sunk cost and, thus,
irrelevant to the decision
to walk out early.

For managerial decisions, estimated future revenues and costs are relevant. Costs that have been incurred in the past are not relevant to the decision. These costs are called **sunk costs**.

Differential revenue is the amount of increase or decrease in revenue that is expected from a course of action as compared to an alternative. To illustrate, assume that equipment can be used to manufacture digital clocks or calculators. The differential revenue from making and selling digital clocks is $25,000, determined as follows:

Product	Estimated Revenue
Digital clocks	$175,000
Calculators	150,000
Differential revenue	$ 25,000

Differential cost is the amount of increase or decrease in cost that is expected from a course of action as compared to an alternative. For example, if increasing advertising expenses from $100,000 to $150,000 is being considered, the differential cost is $50,000.

Differential income (or loss) is the difference between the differential revenue and the differential costs. Differential income indicates that a decision is expected to be profitable, while a differential loss indicates the opposite.

Differential analysis, sometimes called *incremental analysis,* focuses on the effect of alternative courses of action on revenues and costs. An example of a reporting format for differential analysis is shown in Exhibit 1.

Differential revenue from alternatives:		
Revenue from alternative A.......................................	$XXX	
Revenue from alternative B......................................	XXX	
Differential revenue		$XXX
Differential cost of alternatives:		
Cost of alternative A	$XXX	
Cost of alternative B	XXX	
Differential cost		XXX
Net differential income or loss from alternatives...................		**$XXX**

EXHIBIT 1
Differential Analysis

In this chapter, differential analysis is illustrated for the following decisions:

1. Leasing or selling equipment
2. Discontinuing an unprofitable segment
3. Manufacturing or purchasing a needed part
4. Replacing fixed assets
5. Processing further or selling a product
6. Accepting additional business at a special price

Lease or Sell

Management may lease or sell a piece of equipment that is no longer needed. This may occur when a company changes its manufacturing process and can no longer use the equipment in the manufacturing process. In making a decision, differential analysis can be used.

To illustrate, assume that Karnes Company is considering leasing or disposing of the following equipment:

Cost of equipment	$200,000
Less accumulated depreciation	120,000
Book value	$ 80,000
Lease Option:	
Total revenue for five-year lease	$160,000
Total estimated repair, insurance, and property tax expenses during life of lease	35,000
Residual value at end of fifth year of lease	0
Sell Option:	
Sales price	$100,000
Commission on sales	6%

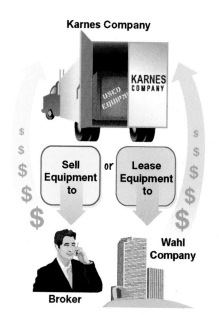

Exhibit 2 shows the differential analysis of whether to lease or sell the equipment.

EXHIBIT 2

Differential Analysis Report—Lease or Sell

Proposal to Lease or Sell Equipment		
Differential revenue from alternatives:		
Revenue from lease	$160,000	
Revenue from sale	100,000	
Differential revenue from lease......................................		$ 60,000
Differential cost of alternatives:		
Repair, insurance, and property tax expenses from lease	$ 35,000	
Commission expense on sale ($100,000 × 6%)	6,000	
Differential cost of lease...		29,000
Net differential income from the lease alternative		**$31,000**

Exhibit 2 includes only the differential revenues and differential costs associated with the lease or sell decision. The $80,000 book value ($200,000 − $120,000) of the equipment is a *sunk* cost and is not considered in the differential analysis shown in Exhibit 2. In other words, the $80,000 does not affect the decision to lease or sell the equipment.

The differential analysis shown in Exhibit 2 is verified by the more traditional analysis shown in Exhibit 3.

EXHIBIT 3

Traditional Analysis

Lease or Sell			
Lease alternative:			
Revenue from lease		$160,000	
Depreciation expense for remaining five years	$80,000		
Repair, insurance, and property tax expenses	35,000	115,000	
Net gain...			$ 45,000
Sell alternative:			
Sales price..		$100,000	
Book value of equipment..............................	$80,000		
Commission expense..................................	6,000	86,000	
Net gain...			14,000
Net differential income from the lease alternative			**$31,000**

Many companies that manufacture expensive equipment give customers the choice of leasing the equipment. For example, construction equipment from **Caterpillar** can either be purchased outright or leased through Caterpillar's financial services subsidiary.

To simplify, the following factors were not considered in Exhibits 2 and 3:

1. Differential revenue from investing funds
2. Differential income tax

Differential revenue (interest) could arise from investing the cash created by the two alternatives. Differential income tax could arise from differences in the timing of the income from the two alternatives and differences in the amount that is taxed. These factors are discussed in Chapter 15.

Discontinue a Segment or Product

A product, department, branch, territory, or other segment of a business may be generating losses. As a result, management may consider discontinuing (eliminating) the product or segment. In such cases, it may be erroneously assumed that the total company income will increase by eliminating the operating loss.

Discontinuing the product or segment usually eliminates all of the product's or segment's variable costs. Such costs include direct materials, direct labor, variable factory overhead, and sales commissions. However, fixed costs such as depreciation, insurance, and property taxes may not be eliminated. Thus, it is possible for total company income to decrease rather than increase if the unprofitable product or segment is discontinued.

To illustrate, the income statement for Montana Wheat Cereal Co. is shown in Exhibit 4.

EXHIBIT 4

Income (Loss) by Product

Montana Wheat Cereal Co. Condensed Income Statement				
	Corn Flakes	Toasted Oats	Bran Flakes	Total Company
Sales.........................	$500,000	$400,000	$100,000	$1,000,000
Cost of goods sold:				
Variable costs....................	$220,000	$200,000	$ 60,000	$ 480,000
Fixed costs	120,000	80,000	20,000	220,000
Total cost of goods sold	$340,000	$280,000	$ 80,000	$ 700,000
Gross profit........................	$160,000	$120,000	$ 20,000	$ 300,000
Operating expenses:				
Variable expenses.................	$ 95,000	$ 60,000	$ 25,000	$ 180,000
Fixed expenses	25,000	20,000	6,000	51,000
Total operating expenses..........	$120,000	$ 80,000	$ 31,000	$ 231,000
Income (loss) from operations	$ 40,000	$ 40,000	$ (11,000)	$ 69,000

As shown in Exhibit 4, Bran Flakes incurred an operating loss of $11,000. Because Bran Flakes has incurred annual losses for several years, management is considering discontinuing it.

If Bran Flakes is discontinued, what would be the total annual operating income of Montana Wheat Cereal? The first impression is that total annual operating income would be $80,000, as shown below.

	Corn Flakes	Toasted Oats	Total Company
Income from operations	$40,000	$40,000	$80,000

However, the differential analysis report in Exhibit 5 indicates that discontinuing Bran Flakes actually decreases operating income by $15,000. This is because discontinuing Bran Flakes has no effect on fixed costs and expenses.

Proposal to Discontinue Bran Flakes		
Differential revenue from annual sales of Bran Flakes:		
Revenue from sales		$100,000
Differential cost of annual sales of Bran Flakes:		
Variable cost of goods sold	$60,000	
Variable operating expenses.......................................	25,000	85,000
Annual differential income from sales of Bran Flakes............		**$15,000**

The differential analysis in Exhibit 5 is supported by the traditional analysis in Exhibit 6, which indicates that income from operations would decrease from $69,000 to $54,000.

Proposal to Discontinue Bran Flakes			
	Bran Flakes, Toasted Oats, and Corn Flakes	Discontinue Bran Flakes*	Toasted Oats and Corn Flakes
Sales	$1,000,000	$100,000	$900,000
Cost of goods sold:			
Variable costs	$ 480,000	$ 60,000	$420,000
Fixed costs..........................	220,000	—	220,000
Total cost of goods sold	$ 700,000	$ 60,000	$640,000
Gross profit.............................	$ 300,000	$ 40,000	$260,000
Operating expenses:			
Variable expenses	$ 180,000	$ 25,000	$155,000
Fixed expenses......................	51,000	—	51,000
Total operating expenses.........	$ 231,000	$ 25,000	$206,000
Income (loss) from operations	**$ 69,000**	**$ 15,000**	**$ 54,000**

*Fixed costs are assumed to remain unchanged with the discontinuance of Bran Flakes.

Exhibits 5 and 6 consider only the short-term (one-year) effects of discontinuing Bran Flakes. When discontinuing a product or segment, long-term effects should also be considered. For example, discontinuing Bran Flakes could decrease sales of other products. This might be the case if customers upset with the discontinuance of Bran Flakes quit buying other products from the company. Finally, employee morale and productivity might suffer if employees have to be laid off or relocated.

Make or Buy

Ford Motor Co.
purchases spark plugs,
GPS units, nuts, and bolts
from suppliers.

Companies often manufacture products made up of components that are assembled into a final product. For example, an automobile manufacturer assembles tires, radios, motors, interior seats, transmissions, and other parts into a finished automobile. In such cases, the manufacturer must decide whether to make a part or purchase it from a supplier.

Differential analysis can be used to decide whether to make or buy a part. The analysis is similar whether management is considering making a part that is currently being purchased or purchasing a part that is currently being made.

Integrity, Objectivity, and Ethics in Business

RELATED-PARTY DEALS

The make-or-buy decision can be complicated if the purchase (buy) is being made by a related party. A related party is one in which there is direct or indirect control of one party over another or the presence of a family member in a transaction. Such dependence or familiarity may interfere with the appropriateness of the business transaction. One investor has said, "Related parties are akin to steroids used by athletes. If you're an athlete and you can cut the mustard, you don't need steroids to make yourself stronger or faster. By the same token, if you're a good company, you don't need related parties or deals that don't make sense." While related-party transactions are legal, GAAP (FASB Statement No. 56) and the Sarbanes-Oxley Act require that they must be disclosed under the presumption that such transactions are less than arm's length.

Source: Herb Greenberg, "Poor Relations: The Problem with Related-Party Transactions," *Fortune Advisor* (February 5, 2001), p. 198.

To illustrate, assume that an automobile manufacturer has been purchasing instrument panels for $240 a unit. The factory is currently operating at 80% of capacity, and no major increase in production is expected in the near future. The cost per unit of manufacturing an instrument panel internally is estimated as follows:

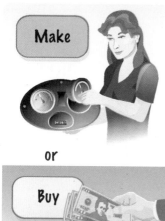

Direct materials	$ 80
Direct labor	80
Variable factory overhead	52
Fixed factory overhead	68
Total cost per unit	$280

If the make price of $280 is simply compared with the buy price of $240, the decision is to buy the instrument panel. However, if unused capacity could be used in manufacturing the part, there would be no increase in the total fixed factory overhead costs. Thus, only the variable factory overhead costs would be incurred.

The differential report for this make-or-buy decision is shown in Exhibit 7.

EXHIBIT 7

Differential Analysis Report—Make or Buy

Proposal to Manufacture Instrument Panels		
Purchase price of an instrument panel...................................		$240
Differential cost to manufacture:		
Direct materials...	$80	
Direct labor..	80	
Variable factory overhead	52	212
Cost savings from manufacturing an instrument panel..............		**$ 28**

As shown in Exhibit 7, there is a cost savings from manufacturing the instrument panel of $28 per panel. However, other factors should also be considered. For example, productive capacity used to make the instrument panel would not be available for other production. The decision may also affect the future business relationship with the instrument panel supplier. For example, if the supplier provides other parts, the company's decision to make instrument panels might jeopardize the timely delivery of other parts.

Replace Equipment

The usefulness of a fixed asset may decrease before it is worn out. For example, old equipment may no longer be as efficient as new equipment.

Differential analysis can be used for decisions to replace fixed assets such as equipment and machinery. The analysis normally focuses on the costs of continuing to use the old equipment versus replacing the equipment. The book value of the old equipment is a sunk cost and, thus, is irrelevant.

To illustrate, assume that a business is considering replacing the following machine:

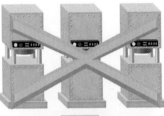

Estimated annual reduction of costs of $75,000

Old Machine	
Book value	$100,000
Estimated annual variable manufacturing costs	225,000
Estimated selling price	25,000
Estimated remaining useful life	5 years
New Machine	
Cost of new machine	$250,000
Estimated annual variable manufacturing costs	150,000
Estimated residual value	0
Estimated useful life	5 years

The differential report for the decision to replace the old machine is shown in Exhibit 8.

EXHIBIT 8

Differential Analysis Report—Replace Machine

Proposal to Replace Machine		
Annual variable costs—present machine..........................	$225,000	
Annual variable costs—new machine.............................	150,000	
Annual differential decrease in cost................................	$ 75,000	
Number of years applicable......................................	× 5	
Total differential decrease in cost................................	$375,000	
Proceeds from sale of present machine	25,000	$400,000
Cost of new machine..		250,000
Net differential decrease in cost, five-year total		$150,000
Annual net differential decrease in cost—new machine		
($150,000 ÷ 5 years).......................................		**$ 30,000**

As shown in Exhibit 8, there is an annual decrease in cost of $30,000 ($150,000 ÷ 5 years) from replacing the old machine. Thus, the decision should be to purchase the new machine and sell the old machine.

Other factors are often important in equipment replacement decisions. For example, differences between the remaining useful life of the old equipment and the estimated life of the new equipment could exist. In addition, the new equipment might improve the overall quality of the product and, thus, increase sales.

The time value of money and other uses for the cash needed to purchase the new equipment could also affect the decision to replace equipment.[1] The revenue that is forgone from an alternative use of an asset, such as cash, is called an **opportunity cost**. Although the opportunity cost is not recorded in the accounting records, it is useful in analyzing alternative courses of action.

To illustrate, assume that in the preceding illustration the cash outlay of $250,000 for the new machine, less the $25,000 proceeds from the sale of the old machine, could be invested to yield a 15% return. Thus, the annual opportunity cost related to the purchase of the new machine is $33,750 (15% × $225,000). Since the opportunity cost of $33,750 exceeds the annual cost savings of $30,000, the old machine should not be replaced.

Process or Sell

During manufacturing, a product normally progresses through various stages or processes. In some cases, a product can be sold at an intermediate stage of production, or it can be processed further and then sold.

Differential analysis can be used to decide whether to sell a product at an intermediate stage or to process it further. In doing so, the differential revenues and costs from further processing are compared. The costs of producing the intermediate product do not change, regardless of whether the intermediate product is sold or processed further. These costs are sunk costs and are irrelevant to the decision.

To illustrate, assume that a business produces kerosene as follows:

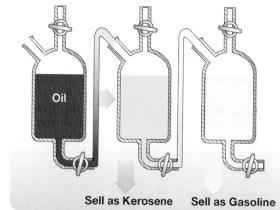

Kerosene:

Batch size	4,000 gallons
Cost of producing kerosene	$2,400 per batch
Selling price	$2.50 per gallon

The kerosene can be processed further to yield gasoline as follows:

Gasoline:

Input batch size	4,000 gallons
Less evaporation (20%)	800 (4,000 × 20%)
Output batch size	3,200 gallons
Additional processing costs	$650 per batch
Selling price	$3.50 per gallon

The differential report for the decision to process the kerosene further is shown in Exhibit 9.

---

1. The time value of money in purchasing equipment (capital assets) is discussed in Chapter 15.

EXHIBIT 9

Differential Analysis Report—Process or Sell

Proposal to Process Kerosene Further		
Differential revenue from further processing per batch:		
Revenue from sale of gasoline [(4,000 gallons − 800 gallons evaporation) × $3.50]	$11,200	
Revenue from sale of kerosene (4,000 gallons × $2.50)	10,000	
Differential revenue		$1,200
Differential cost per batch:		
Additional cost of producing gasoline		650
Differential income from further processing gasoline per batch		$ 550

The initial cost of producing the kerosene of $2,400 is not considered in deciding whether to process kerosene further. This initial cost will be incurred, regardless of whether gasoline is produced and, thus, is a sunk cost.

As shown in Exhibit 9, there is additional income from further processing the kerosene into gasoline of $550 per batch. Therefore, the decision should be to process the kerosene further.

Accept Business at a Special Price

A company may be offered the opportunity to sell its products at prices other than normal prices. For example, an exporter may offer to sell a company's products overseas at special discount prices.

Differential analysis can be used to decide whether to accept additional business at a special price. The differential revenue from accepting the additional business is compared to the differential costs of producing and delivering the product to the customer.

The differential costs of accepting additional business depend on whether the company is operating at full capacity.

1. If the company is *operating at full capacity,* any additional production increases fixed and variable manufacturing costs. Selling and administrative expenses may also increase because of the additional business.

2. If the company is *operating below full capacity,* any additional production does not increase fixed manufacturing costs. In this case, the differential costs of the additional production are the variable manufacturing costs. Selling and administrative expenses may also increase because of the additional business.

The Internet is forcing many companies to respond to "dynamic" pricing. For example, in **Priceline.com Inc.'s** "name your price" format, customers tell the company what they are willing to pay and then the company must decide if it is willing to sell at that price.

To illustrate, assume that Game Ball Inc. manufactures basketballs as follows:

Monthly productive capacity	12,500 basketballs
Current monthly sales	10,000 basketballs
Normal (domestic) selling price	$30.00 per basketball
Manufacturing costs:	
Variable costs	$12.50 per basketball
Fixed costs	7.50
Total	$20.00 per basketball

Order for 5,000 basketballs at $18 each

Game Ball Inc. has received an offer from an exporter for 5,000 basketballs at $18 each. Production can be spread over three months without interfering with normal production or incurring overtime costs. Pricing policies in the domestic market will not be affected.

Comparing the special offer sales price of $18 with the manufacturing cost of $20 per basketball indicates that the offer should be rejected. However, as shown in Exhibit 10, differential analysis indicates that the offer should be accepted.

Proposal to Sell Basketballs to Exporter	
Differential revenue from accepting offer:	
Revenue from sale of 5,000 additional units at $18..	$ 90,000
Differential cost of accepting offer:	
Variable costs of 5,000 additional units at $12.50......................................	62,500
Differential income from accepting offer...	**$27,500**

EXHIBIT 10

Differential Analysis Report—Sell at Special Price

Proposals to sell products at special prices often require additional considerations. For example, special prices in one geographic area may result in price reductions in other areas with the result that total company sales decrease. Manufacturers must also conform to the Robinson-Patman Act, which prohibits price discrimination within the United States unless price differences can be justified by different costs.

Setting Normal Product Selling Prices

Obj **2**

Determine the selling price of a product, using the total cost, product cost, and variable cost concepts.

The *normal* selling price is the target selling price to be achieved in the long term. The normal selling price must be set high enough to cover all costs and expenses (fixed and variable) and provide a reasonable profit. Otherwise, the business will not survive.

In contrast, in deciding whether to accept additional business at a special price, only differential costs are considered. Any price above the differential costs will increase profits in the short term. However, in the long term, products are sold at normal prices rather than special prices.

Managers can use one of two *market methods* to determine selling price:

1. Demand-based concept
2. Competition-based concept

The demand-based concept sets the price according to the demand for the product. If there is high demand for the product, then the price is set high. Likewise, if there is a low demand for the product, then the price is set low.

The competition-based concept sets the price according to the price offered by competitors. For example, if a competitor reduces the price, then management adjusts the price to meet the competition. The market-based pricing approaches are discussed in greater detail in marketing courses.

Hotels and motels use the demand-based concept in setting room rates. Room rates are set low during off-season travel periods (low demand) and high for peak-season travel periods (high demand) such as holidays.

Electronic stores such as **Best Buy** use the competition-based concept. If a buyer demonstrates that a lower price is available from **Target** or another competitor, Best Buy will often match the price.

Managers can also use one of three cost-plus methods to determine the selling price:

1. Total cost concept
2. Product cost concept
3. Variable cost concept

Cost-plus methods determine the normal selling price by estimating a cost amount per unit and adding a markup, as shown below.

$$\text{Normal Selling Price} = \text{Cost Amount per Unit} + \text{Markup}$$

The cost amount per unit depends on the cost concept used. Management determines the **markup** based on the desired profit for the product. The markup should be sufficient to earn the desired profit plus cover any costs and expenses that are not included in the cost amount.

Total Cost Concept

Under the **total cost concept,** manufacturing cost plus the selling and administrative expenses are included in the total cost per unit. The markup per unit is then computed and added to total cost per unit to determine the normal selling price.

The total cost concept is applied using the following steps:

Step 1. Estimate the total manufacturing cost as shown below.

Manufacturing costs:	
Direct materials	$XXX
Direct labor	XXX
Factory overhead	XXX
Total manufacturing cost	$XXX

Step 2. Estimate the total selling and administrative expenses.

Step 3. Estimate the total cost as shown below.

Total manufacturing costs	$XXX
Selling and administrative expenses	XXX
Total cost	$XXX

Step 4. Divide the total cost by the number of units expected to be produced and sold to determine the total cost per unit, as shown below.

$$\text{Total Cost per Unit} = \frac{\text{Total Cost}}{\text{Estimated Units Produced and Sold}}$$

Step 5. Compute the markup percentage as follows:

$$\text{Markup Percentage} = \frac{\text{Desired Profit}}{\text{Total Cost}}$$

The desired profit is normally computed based on a rate of return on assets as follows:

$$\text{Desired Profit} = \text{Desired Rate of Return} \times \text{Total Assets}$$

Step 6. Determine the markup per unit by multiplying the markup percentage times the total cost per unit as follows:

$$\text{Markup per Unit} = \text{Markup Percentage} \times \text{Total Cost per Unit}$$

Step 7. Determine the normal selling price by adding the markup per unit to the total cost per unit as follows:

Total cost per unit	$XXX
Markup per unit	XXX
Normal selling price per unit	$XXX

TOTAL COST CONCEPT

Desired Selling Price

Markup: Desired Profit

Total Cost:
Manufacturing Cost
Administrative Expense
Selling Expense

To illustrate, assume the following data for 100,000 digital projection clocks that Nebular Inc. expects to produce and sell during the current year:

Manufacturing costs:		
Direct materials ($3.00 × 100,000)		$ 300,000
Direct labor ($10.00 × 100,000)		1,000,000
Factory overhead:		
Variable costs ($1.50 × 100,000)	$150,000	
Fixed costs	50,000	200,000
Total manufacturing cost		$1,500,000
Selling and administrative expenses:		
Variable expenses ($1.50 × 100,000)	$150,000	
Fixed costs	20,000	
Total selling and administrative expenses		170,000
Total cost		$1,670,000
Desired rate of return		20%
Total assets		$ 800,000

Using the total cost concept, the normal selling price of $18.30 is determined as follows:

Step 1. Total manufacturing cost: $1,500,000

Step 2. Total selling and administrative expenses: $170,000

Step 3. Total cost: $1,670,000

Step 4. Total cost per unit: $16.70

$$\text{Total Cost per Unit} = \frac{\text{Total Cost}}{\text{Estimated Units Produced and Sold}}$$

$$= \frac{\$1,670,000}{100,000 \text{ units}} = \$16.70 \text{ per unit}$$

Step 5. Markup percentage: 9.6% (rounded)

$$\text{Desired Profit} = \text{Desired Rate of Return} \times \text{Total Assets}$$
$$= 20\% \times \$800,000 = \$160,000$$

$$\text{Markup Percentage} = \frac{\text{Desired Profit}}{\text{Total Cost}} = \frac{\$160,000}{\$1,670,000} = 9.6\% \text{ (rounded)}$$

Step 6. Markup per unit: $1.60

$$\text{Markup per Unit} = \text{Markup Percentage} \times \text{Total Cost per Unit}$$
$$= 9.6\% \times \$16.70 = \$1.60 \text{ per unit}$$

Step 7. Normal selling price: $18.30

Total cost per unit	$16.70
Markup per unit	1.60
Normal selling price per unit	$18.30

The ability of the selling price of $18.30 to generate the desired profit of $160,000 is illustrated by the income statement shown below.

Nebula Inc.
Income Statement

Sales (100,000 units × $18.30)		$1,830,000
Expenses:		
Variable (100,000 units × $16.00)	$1,600,000	
Fixed ($50,000 + $20,000)	70,000	1,670,000
Income from operations		$ 160,000

The total cost concept is often used by contractors who sell products to government agencies. This is because in many cases government contractors are required by law to be reimbursed for their products on a total-cost-plus-profit basis.

PRODUCT COST CONCEPT

Markup:
Administrative Expense
Selling Expense
Desired Profit

Product Cost:
Manufacturing Cost

Desired Selling Price

Product Cost Concept

Under the **product cost concept**, only the costs of manufacturing the product, termed the *product costs,* are included in the cost amount per unit to which the markup is added. Estimated selling expenses, administrative expenses, and desired profit are included in the markup. The markup per unit is then computed and added to the product cost per unit to determine the normal selling price.

The product cost concept is applied using the following steps:

Step 1. Estimate the total product costs as follows:

Product costs:	
Direct materials	$XXX
Direct labor	XXX
Factory overhead	XXX
Total product cost	$XXX

Step 2. Estimate the total selling and administrative expenses.

Integrity, Objectivity, and Ethics in Business

PRICE FIXING

Federal law prevents companies competing in similar markets from sharing cost and price information, or what is commonly termed "price fixing." For example, the Federal Trade Commission brought a suit against the major record labels and music retailers for conspiring to set CD prices at a minimum level, or MAP (minimum advertised price). In settling the suit, the major labels ceased their MAP policies and provided $143 million in cash and CDs for consumers.

Step 3. Divide the total product cost by the number of units expected to be produced and sold to determine the total product cost per unit, as shown below.

$$\text{Product Cost per Unit} = \frac{\text{Total Product Cost}}{\text{Estimated Units Produced and Sold}}$$

Step 4. Compute the markup percentage as follows:

$$\text{Markup Percentage} = \frac{\text{Desired Profit} + \text{Total Selling and Administrative Expenses}}{\text{Total Product Cost}}$$

The numerator of the markup percentage is the desired profit plus the total selling and administrative expenses. These expenses must be included in the markup percentage, since they are not included in the cost amount to which the markup is added.

As illustrated for the total cost concept, the desired profit is normally computed based on a rate of return on assets as follows:

$$\text{Desired Profit} = \text{Desired Rate of Return} \times \text{Total Assets}$$

Step 5. Determine the markup per unit by multiplying the markup percentage times the product cost per unit as follows:

$$\text{Markup per Unit} = \text{Markup Percentage} \times \text{Product Cost per Unit}$$

Step 6. Determine the normal selling price by adding the markup per unit to the product cost per unit as follows:

Product cost per unit	$XXX
Markup per unit	XXX
Normal selling price per unit	$XXX

To illustrate, assume the same data for the production and sale of 100,000 digital projection clocks by Nebula Inc. as in the preceding example. The normal selling price of $18.30 is determined under the product cost concept as follows:

Step 1. Total product cost: $1,500,000
Step 2. Total selling and administrative expenses: $170,000
Step 3. Total product cost per unit: $15.00

$$\text{Total Cost per Unit} = \frac{\text{Total Product Cost}}{\text{Estimated Units Produced and Sold}}$$

$$= \frac{\$1,500,000}{100,000 \text{ units}} = \$15.00 \text{ per unit}$$

Step 4. Markup percentage: 22%

$$\text{Desired Profit} = \text{Desired Rate of Return} \times \text{Total Assets}$$

$$= 20\% \times \$800,000 = \$160,000$$

$$\text{Markup Percentage} = \frac{\text{Desired Profit} + \text{Total Selling and Administrative Expenses}}{\text{Total Product Cost}}$$

$$= \frac{\$160,000 + \$170,000}{\$1,500,000} = \frac{\$330,000}{\$1,500,000} = 22\%$$

Step 5. Markup per unit: $3.30

$$\text{Markup per Unit} = \text{Markup Percentage} \times \text{Product Cost per Unit}$$
$$= 22\% \times \$15.00 = \$3.30 \text{ per unit}$$

Step 6. Normal selling price: $18.30

Total product cost per unit	$15.00
Markup per unit	3.30
Normal selling price per unit	$18.30

Variable Cost Concept

Under the **variable cost concept**, only variable costs are included in the cost amount per unit to which the markup is added. All variable manufacturing costs, as well as variable selling and administrative expenses, are included in the cost amount. Fixed manufacturing costs, fixed selling and administrative expenses, and desired profit are included in the markup. The markup per unit is then added to the variable cost per unit to determine the normal selling price.

The variable cost concept is applied using the following steps:

Step 1. Estimate the total variable product cost as follows:

Variable product costs:	
Direct materials	$XXX
Direct labor	XXX
Variable factory overhead	XXX
Total variable product cost	$XXX

Step 2. Estimate the total variable selling and administrative expenses.

Step 3. Determine the total variable cost as follows:

Total variable product cost	$XXX
Total variable selling and administrative expenses	XXX
Total variable cost	$XXX

Step 4. Compute the variable cost per unit as follows:

$$\text{Variable Cost per Unit} = \frac{\text{Total Variable Cost}}{\text{Estimated Units Produced and Sold}}$$

Step 5. Compute the markup percentage as follows:

$$\text{Markup Percentage} = \frac{\text{Desired Profit} + \text{Total Fixed Costs and Expenses}}{\text{Total Variable Cost}}$$

The numerator of the markup percentage is the desired profit plus the total fixed costs (fixed factory overhead) and expenses (selling and administrative). These fixed costs and expenses must be included in the markup percentage, since they are not included in the cost amount to which the markup is added.

As illustrated for the total and product cost concepts, the desired profit is normally computed based on a rate of return on assets as follows:

$$\text{Desired Profit} = \text{Desired Rate of Return} \times \text{Total Assets}$$

Step 6. Determine the markup per unit by multiplying the markup percentage times the variable cost per unit as follows:

$$\text{Markup per Unit} = \text{Markup Percentage} \times \text{Variable Cost per Unit}$$

Step 7. Determine the normal selling price by adding the markup per unit to the variable cost per unit as follows:

VARIABLE COST CONCEPT

Variable cost per unit	$XXX
Markup per unit	XXX
Normal selling price per unit	$XXX

To illustrate, assume the same data for the production and sale of 100,000 digital projection clocks by Nebula Inc. as in the preceding example. The normal selling price of $18.30 is determined under the variable cost concept as follows:

Step 1. Total variable product cost: $1,450,000

Variable product costs:	
Direct materials ($3 × 100,000)	$ 300,000
Direct labor ($10 × 100,000)	1,000,000
Variable factory overhead ($1.50 × 100,000)	150,000
Total variable product cost	$1,450,000

Step 2. Total variable selling and administrative expenses: $150,000 ($1.50 × 100,000)

Step 3. Total variable cost: $1,600,000 ($1,450,000 + $150,000)

Step 4. Variable cost per unit: $16.00

$$\text{Variable Cost per Unit} = \frac{\text{Total Variable Cost}}{\text{Estimated Units Produced and Sold}}$$

$$= \frac{\$1,600,000}{100,000 \text{ units}} = \$16.00 \text{ per unit}$$

Step 5. Markup percentage: 14.4% (rounded)

$$\text{Desired Profit} = \text{Desired Rate of Return} \times \text{Total Assets}$$
$$= 20\% \times \$800,000 = \$160,000$$

$$\text{Markup Percentage} = \frac{\text{Desired Profit} + \text{Total Fixed Costs and Expenses}}{\text{Total Variable Cost}}$$

$$= \frac{\$160,000 + \$50,000 + \$20,000}{\$1,600,000} = \frac{\$230,000}{\$1,600,000}$$

$$= 14.4\% \text{ (rounded)}$$

Step 6. Markup per unit: $2.30

$$\text{Markup per Unit} = \text{Markup Percentage} \times \text{Variable Cost per Unit}$$
$$= 14.4\% \times \$16.00 = \$2.30 \text{ per unit}$$

Step 7. Normal selling price: $18.30

Total variable cost per unit	$16.00
Markup per unit	2.30
Normal selling price per unit	$18.30

Choosing a Cost-Plus Approach Cost Concept

All three cost-plus concepts produced the same selling price ($18.30) for Nebula Inc. The three cost-plus concepts are summarized in Exhibit 11.

EXHIBIT 11   Cost-Plus Approach to Setting Normal Selling Prices

Normal Selling Price = Cost Amount per Unit + Markup

$$\text{Cost Amount per Unit} = \frac{\text{Cost Amount}}{\text{Estimated Units Produced and Sold}}$$

Markup = Cost Amount per Unit × Markup Percentage

Cost-Plus Concept	Cost Amount	Markup Percentages
Total cost	Manufacturing (product) costs: 　Direct materials 　Direct labor 　Factory overhead Selling and administrative expenses	$\dfrac{\text{Desired Profit}}{\text{Total Cost}}$
Product cost	Manufacturing (product) costs: 　Direct materials 　Direct labor 　Factory overhead	$\dfrac{\text{Desired Profit} + \text{Total Selling and Administrative Expenses}}{\text{Total Product Cost}}$
Variable cost	Variable manufacturing (product) costs: 　Direct materials 　Direct labor 　Variable factory overhead Variable selling and administrative expenses	$\dfrac{\text{Desired Profit} + \text{Total Fixed Costs and Expenses}}{\text{Total Variable Cost}}$

Estimated, rather than actual, costs and expenses may be used with any of the three cost-plus concepts. Management should be careful, however, when using estimated or standard costs in applying the cost-plus approach. Specifically, estimates should be based on normal (attainable) operating levels and not theoretical (ideal) levels of performance. In product pricing, the use of estimates based on ideal or maximum-capacity operating levels could lead to setting product prices too low. In such cases, the costs of such factors as normal spoilage or normal periods of idle time might not be considered.

The decision-making needs of management are also an important factor in selecting a cost concept for product pricing. For example, managers who often make special pricing decisions are more likely to use the variable cost concept. In contrast, a government defense contractor would be more likely to use the total cost concept.

Activity-Based Costing

As illustrated, costs are important in setting product prices and decision making. Inaccurate costs may lead to incorrect decisions and prices. To more accurately measure the costs and expenses, some companies use activity-based costing. **Activity-based costing (ABC)** identifies and traces costs and expenses to activities and then to specific products.

Activity-based costing is particularly useful when manufacturing operations involve large amounts of factory overhead. In such cases, traditional overhead allocation bases such as units produced, direct labor hours, direct labor costs, or machine hours may yield inaccurate cost allocations. This, in turn, may result in distorted product costs and product prices.[2]

Target Costing

Target costing is a method of setting prices that combines market-based pricing with a cost-reduction emphasis. Under target costing, a future selling price is anticipated, using the demand-based or the competition-based concepts. The target cost is then determined by subtracting a desired profit from the expected selling price, as shown below.

Target Cost = Expected Selling Price − Desired Profit

Target costing tries to reduce costs as shown in Exhibit 12. The bar at the left in Exhibit 12 shows the actual cost and profit that can be earned during the current period. The bar at the right shows that the market price is expected to decline in the future. The target cost is estimated as the difference between the expected market price and the desired profit.

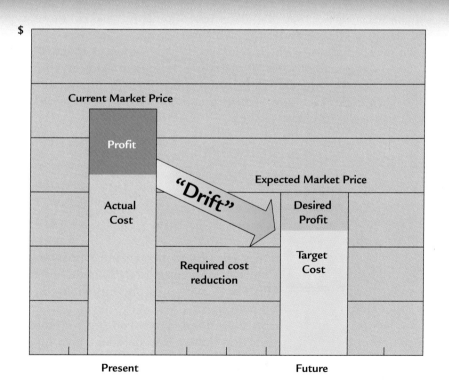

EXHIBIT 12

Target Cost Concept

The target cost is normally less than the current cost. Thus, managers must try to reduce costs from the design and manufacture of the product.

2. Activity-based costing for a service business is discussed and illustrated in Chapter 10.

The planned cost reduction is sometimes referred to as the cost "drift." Costs can be reduced in a variety of ways such as the following:

1. Simplifying the design
2. Reducing the cost of direct materials
3. Reducing the direct labor costs
4. Eliminating waste

Target costing is especially useful in highly competitive markets such as automobiles and the market for smartphones and computer tablets. Such markets require continual product cost reductions to remain competitive.

Production Bottlenecks, Pricing, and Profits

Obj 3

Compute the relative profitability of products in bottleneck production processes.

A production **bottleneck** (or *constraint*) is a point in the manufacturing process where the demand for the company's product exceeds the ability to produce the product. The **theory of constraints (TOC)** is a manufacturing strategy that focuses on reducing the influence of bottlenecks on production processes.

Production Bottlenecks and Profits

When a company has a production bottleneck in its production process, it should attempt to maximize its profits, subject to the production bottleneck. In doing so, the unit contribution margin of each product per production bottleneck constraint is used.

To illustrate, assume that Rapidan Tool Company makes three types of wrenches: small, medium, and large. All three products are processed through a heat treatment operation, which hardens the steel tools. Rapidan Tool's heat treatment process is operating at full capacity and is a production bottleneck. The product unit contribution margin and the number of hours of heat treatment used by each type of wrench are as follows:

The sand in the hourglass can pass only as fast as the narrowest point in the glass will allow.

Bottleneck

	Small Wrench	Medium Wrench	Large Wrench
Unit selling price	$130	$140	$160
Unit variable cost	40	40	40
Unit contribution margin	$ 90	$100	$120
Heat treatment hours per unit	1 hr.	4 hrs.	8 hrs.

The large wrench appears to be the most profitable product because its unit contribution margin of $120 is the greatest. However, the unit contribution margin can be misleading in a production bottleneck operation.

In a production bottleneck operation, the best measure of profitability is the unit contribution margin per production bottleneck constraint. For Rapidan Tool, the production bottleneck constraint is heat treatment process hours. Therefore, the unit contribution margin per bottleneck constraint is expressed as follows:

$$\text{Unit Contribution Margin per Production Bottleneck Hour} = \frac{\text{Unit Contribution Margin}}{\text{Heat Treatment Hours per Unit}}$$

The unit contribution per production bottleneck hour for each of the wrenches produced by Rapidan Tool is computed below.

Small Wrenches

$$\text{Unit Contribution Margin per Production Bottleneck Hour} = \frac{\$90}{1 \text{ hr.}} = \$90 \text{ per hr.}$$

Medium Wrenches

$$\text{Unit Contribution Margin per Production Bottleneck Hour} = \frac{\$100}{4 \text{ hrs.}} = \$25 \text{ per hr.}$$

Large Wrenches

$$\text{Unit Contribution Margin per Production Bottleneck Hour} = \frac{\$120}{8 \text{ hrs.}} = \$15 \text{ per hr.}$$

The small wrench produces the highest unit contribution margin per production bottleneck hour (heat treatment) of $90 per hour. In contrast, the large wrench has the largest contribution margin per unit of $120, but has the smallest unit contribution margin per production bottleneck hour of $15 per hour. Thus, the small wrench is the most profitable product per production bottleneck hour.

Production Bottlenecks and Pricing

When a company has a production bottleneck, the unit contribution margin per bottleneck hour is a measure of each product's profitability. This measure can be used to adjust product prices to reflect the product's use of the bottleneck.

To illustrate, the large wrench produced by Rapidan Tool Company uses eight bottleneck hours, but produces a contribution margin per unit of only $120. As a result, the large wrench is the least profitable of the wrenches per bottleneck hour ($15 per hour).

Rapidan Tool Company can improve the profitability of producing large wrenches by any combination of the following:

1. Increase the selling price of the large wrenches.
2. Decrease the variable cost per unit of the large wrenches.
3. Decrease the heat treatment hours required for the large wrenches.

Assume that the variable cost per unit and the heat treatment hours for the large wrench cannot be decreased. In this case, Rapidan Tool might be able to increase the selling price of the large wrenches.

The price of the large wrench that would make it as profitable as the small wrench is determined as follows:[3]

$$\text{Unit Contribution Margin per Bottleneck Hour for Small Wrench} = \frac{\text{Revised Price of Large Wrench} - \text{Unit Variable Cost for Large Wrench}}{\text{Bottleneck Hours per Unit for Large Wrench}}$$

---

3. Assuming that the selling price of the large wrench cannot be increased, the same approach (equation) could be used to determine the decrease in variable cost per unit or decrease in bottleneck hours that is required to make the large wrench as profitable as the small wrench.

$$\$90 = \frac{\text{Revised Price of Large Wrench} - \$40}{8}$$

$$\$720 = \text{Revised Price of Large Wrench} - \$40$$

$$\$760 = \text{Revised Price of Large Wrench}$$

If the large wrench's price is increased to $760, it would provide the same unit contribution margin per bottleneck hour as the small wrench, as shown below.

$$\text{Unit Contribution Margin per Bottleneck Hour} = \frac{\text{Unit Contribution Margin}}{\text{Heat Treatment Hours per Unit}}$$

$$= \frac{\$760 - \$40}{8 \text{ hrs.}} = \$90 \text{ per hr.}$$

At a price of $760, Rapidan Tool Company would be indifferent between producing and selling the small wrench or the large wrench. This assumes that there is unlimited demand for the products. If the market were unwilling to purchase the large wrench at a price of $760, then the company should produce and sell the small wrenches.

HOW BUSINESSES MAKE MONEY

WHAT IS A PRODUCT?

A product is often thought of in terms beyond just its physical attributes. For example, why a customer buys a product usually impacts how a business markets the product. Other considerations, such as warranty needs, servicing needs, and perceived quality, also affect business strategies.

Consider the four different types of products listed below. For these products, the frequency of purchase, the profit per unit, and the number of retailers differ. As a result, the sales and marketing approach for each product differs.

Product	Type of Product	Frequency of Purchase	Profit per Unit	Number of Retailers	Sales/Marketing Approach
Snickers®	Convenience	Often	Low	Many	Mass advertising
Sony® TV	Shopping	Occasional	Moderate	Many	Mass advertising; personal selling
Diamond ring	Specialty	Seldom	High	Few	Personal selling
Prearranged funeral	Unsought	Rare	High	Few	Aggressive selling

Key Points

1. Prepare differential analysis reports for a variety of managerial decisions.

Differential analysis reports for leasing or selling, discontinuing a segment or product, making or buying, replacing equipment, processing or selling, and accepting business at a special price are illustrated in the text. Each analysis focuses on the differential revenues and/or costs of the alternative courses of action.

2. Determine the selling price of a product, using the total cost, product cost, and variable cost concepts.

The three cost concepts commonly used in applying the cost-plus approach to product pricing are summarized in Exhibit 11.

Activity-based costing can be used to provide more accurate cost information in applying cost-plus concepts when indirect costs are insignificant. Target costing combines market-based methods with a cost-reduction emphasis.

3. Compute the relative profitability of products in bottleneck production processes.

The profitability of a product in a bottleneck production environment may not be accurately shown in the contribution margin product report. Instead, the best measure of profitability is determined by dividing the contribution margin per unit by the bottleneck hours per unit. The resulting measure indicates the product's profitability per hour of bottleneck use. This information can be used to support product pricing decisions.

Key Terms

Activity-based costing (ABC) (493)
Bottleneck (494)
Differential analysis (477)
Differential cost (476)

Differential income (or loss) (477)
Differential revenue (476)
Markup (486)
Opportunity cost (483)

Product cost concept (488)
Sunk cost (476)
Target costing (493)
Theory of constraints (TOC) (494)

Total cost concept (486)
Variable cost concept (490)

Illustrative Problem

Hillard Company recently began production of a new product, SR10, which required the investment of $1,600,000 in assets. The costs of producing and selling 80,000 units of Product SR10 are estimated as follows:

Variable costs:	
Direct materials	$10.00 per unit
Direct labor	6.00
Factory overhead	4.00
Selling and administrative expenses	5.00
Total	$25.00 per unit
Fixed costs:	
Factory overhead	$800,000
Selling and administrative expenses	400,000

Hillard Company is currently considering establishing a selling price for Product SR10. The president of Hillard Company has decided to use the cost-plus approach to product pricing and has indicated that Product SR10 must earn a 10% rate of return on invested assets.

Instructions

1. Determine the amount of desired profit from the production and sale of Product SR10.
2. Assuming that the total cost concept is used, determine (a) the cost amount per unit, (b) the markup percentage, and (c) the selling price of Product SR10.
3. Assuming that the product cost concept is used, determine (a) the cost amount per unit, (b) the markup percentage, and (c) the selling price of Product SR10.
4. Assuming that the variable cost concept is used, determine (a) the cost amount per unit, (b) the markup percentage, and (c) the selling price of Product SR10.
5. Assume that for the current year, the selling price of Product SR10 was $42 per unit. To date, 60,000 units have been produced and sold, and analysis of the domestic market indicates that 15,000 additional units are expected to be sold during the remainder of the year. Recently, Hillard Company received an offer from Ming Inc. for 4,000 units of Product SR10 at $28 each. Ming Inc. will market the units in China under its own brand name, and no additional selling and administrative expenses associated with the sale will be incurred by Hillard Company. The additional business is not expected to affect the domestic sales of

Product SR10, and the additional units could be produced during the current year, using existing capacity. (a) Prepare a differential analysis report of the proposed sale to Ming Inc. (b) Based on the differential analysis report in (a), should the proposal be accepted?

Solution

1. $160,000 ($1,600,000 × 10%)

2. a. Total costs:

Variable ($25 × 80,000 units)	$2,000,000
Fixed ($800,000 + $400,000)	1,200,000
Total	$3,200,000

Cost amount per unit: $3,200,000 ÷ 80,000 units = $40.00

b. $\text{Markup Percentage} = \dfrac{\text{Desired Profit}}{\text{Total Costs}}$

$= \dfrac{\$160,000}{\$3,200,000} = 5\%$

c.
Cost amount per unit	$40.00
Markup ($40 × 5%)	2.00
Selling price	$42.00

3. a. Total manufacturing costs:

Variable ($20 × 80,000 units)	$1,600,000
Fixed factory overhead	800,000
Total	$2,400,000

Cost amount per unit: $2,400,000 ÷ 80,000 units = $30.00

b. $\text{Markup Percentage} = \dfrac{\text{Desired Profit} + \text{Total Selling and Administrative Expenses}}{\text{Total Manufacturing Costs}}$

$= \dfrac{\$160,000 + \$400,000 + (\$5 \times 80,000 \text{ units})}{\$2,400,000}$

$= \dfrac{\$160,000 + \$400,000 + \$400,000}{\$2,400,000}$

$= \dfrac{\$960,000}{\$2,400,000} = 40\%$

c.
Cost amount per unit	$30.00
Markup ($30 × 40%)	12.00
Selling price	$42.00

4. a. Variable cost amount per unit: $25

Total variable costs: $25 × 80,000 units = $2,000,000

b. $\text{Markup Percentage} = \dfrac{\text{Desired Profit} + \text{Total Fixed Costs}}{\text{Total Variable Costs}}$

$$= \frac{\$160{,}000 + \$800{,}000 + \$400{,}000}{\$2{,}000{,}000}$$

$$= \frac{\$1{,}360{,}000}{\$2{,}000{,}000} = 68\%$$

c.
Cost amount per unit	$25.00
Markup ($25 × 68%)	17.00
Selling price	$42.00

5. a. **Proposal to Sell to Ming Inc.**

Differential revenue from accepting offer:	
Revenue from sale of 4,000 additional units at $28	$112,000
Differential cost from accepting offer:	
Variable production costs of 4,000 additional units at $20	80,000
Differential income from accepting offer	$ 32,000

b. The proposal should be accepted.

Self-Examination Questions (Answers appear at the end of chapter)

1. Marlo Company is considering discontinuing a product. The costs of the product consist of $20,000 fixed costs and $15,000 variable costs. The variable operating expenses related to the product total $4,000. What is the differential cost?

   A. $19,000

   B. $15,000

   C. $35,000

   D. $39,000

2. Victor Company is considering disposing of equipment that was originally purchased for $200,000 and has $150,000 of accumulated depreciation to date. The same equipment would cost $310,000 to replace. What is the sunk cost?

   A. $50,000

   B. $150,000

   C. $200,000

   D. $310,000

3. Henry Company is considering spending $100,000 for a new grinding machine. This amount could be invested to yield a 12% return. What is the opportunity cost?

   A. $112,000

   B. $88,000

   C. $12,000

   D. $100,000

4. For which cost concept used in applying the cost-plus approach to product pricing are fixed manufacturing costs, fixed selling and administrative expenses, and desired profit allowed for in determining the markup?

   A. Total cost

   B. Product cost

   C. Variable cost

   D. Standard cost

5. Mendosa Company produces three products. All the products use a furnace operation, which is a production bottleneck. The following information is available:

	Product 1	Product 2	Product 3
Unit volume—March	1,000	1,500	1,000
Per-unit information:			
Sales price	$35	$33	$29
Variable cost	15	15	15
Unit contribution margin	$20	$18	$14
Furnace hours	4	3	2

   From a profitability perspective, which product should be emphasized in April's advertising campaign?

   A. Product 1

   B. Product 2

   C. Product 3

   D. All three

Class Discussion Questions

1. Explain the meaning of (a) differential revenue, (b) differential cost, and (c) differential income.

2. It was reported that **Exabyte Corporation**, a fast growing Colorado marketer of computer devices has decided to purchase key components of its product from others. For example, **Sony Corporation of America** and **Solectron Corporation** provide components to Exabyte. A former chief executive officer of Exabyte stated, "If we'd tried to build our own plants, we could never have grown that fast or maybe survived." The decision to purchase key product components is an example of what type of decision illustrated in this chapter?

3. A company could sell a building for $650,000 or lease it for $5,000 per month. What would need to be considered in determining if the lease option would be preferred?

4. A chemical company has a commodity-grade and premium-grade product. Why might the company elect to process the commodity-grade product further to the premium-grade product?

5. A company accepts incremental business at a special price that exceeds the variable cost. What other issues must the company consider in deciding whether to accept the business?

6. A company fabricates a component at a cost of $7.75. A supplier offers to supply the same component for $6.15. Under what circumstances is it reasonable to purchase from the supplier?

7. Many fast-food restaurant chains, such as **McDonald's**, will occasionally discontinue restaurants in their system. What are some financial considerations in deciding to eliminate a store?

8. In the long run, the normal selling price must be set high enough to cover what factors?

9. Why might the use of ideal standards in applying the cost-plus approach to product pricing lead to setting product prices that are too low?

10. Although the cost-plus approach to product pricing may be used by management as a general guideline, what are some examples of other factors that managers should also consider in setting product prices?

11. What method of determining product cost may be appropriate in settings where the manufacturing process is complex?

12. How does the target cost concept differ from cost-plus approaches?

13. Under what circumstances is it appropriate to use the target cost concept?

14. What is a production bottleneck?

15. What is the appropriate measure of a product's value when a firm is operating under production bottlenecks?

Exercises

Obj | 1

✔ a. Differential revenue from lease, $90,000

E12-1   Lease or sell decision

Yamada Industries is considering selling excess machinery with a book value of $220,000 (original cost of $600,000 less accumulated depreciation of $380,000) for $200,000, less a 6% brokerage commission. Alternatively, the machinery can be leased for a total of $290,000 for five years, after which it is expected to have no residual value. During the period of the lease, Yamada Industries' costs of repairs, insurance, and property tax expenses are expected to be $71,000.

a. Prepare a differential analysis report for the lease or sell decision.

b. On the basis of the data presented, would it be advisable to lease or sell the machinery? Explain.

Note: The spreadsheet icon indicates an Excel template is available on the student companion site.

E12-2   Differential analysis report for a discontinued product

Obj 1

✔ a. Total differential variable costs, $2,675,000

A condensed income statement by product line for Cola Beverages Inc. indicated the following for Kiwi Cola for the past year:

Sales	$4,000,000
Cost of goods sold	3,175,000
Gross profit	$ 825,000
Operating expenses	1,100,000
Loss from operations	$ (275,000)

It is estimated that 40% of the cost of goods sold represents fixed factory overhead costs and that 30% of the operating expenses are fixed. Since Kiwi Cola is only one of many products, the fixed costs will not be significantly affected if the product is discontinued.

a. Prepare a differential analysis report for the proposed discontinuance of Kiwi Cola.

b. Should Kiwi Cola be retained? Explain.

E12-3   Differential analysis report for a discontinued product

Obj 1

The condensed product-line income statement for Dinner Ware Company is as follows:

✔ a. Differential income: bowls, $738,600

Dinner Ware Company
Product-Line Income Statement

	Bowls	Plates	Cups
Sales	$1,500,000	$2,350,000	$ 975,000
Cost of goods sold	900,000	1,400,000	780,000
Gross profit	$ 600,000	$ 950,000	$ 195,000
Selling and administrative expenses	270,000	700,000	300,000
Income (loss) from operations	$ 330,000	$ 250,000	$(105,000)

Fixed costs are 40% of the cost of goods sold and 18% of the selling and administrative expenses. Dinner Ware assumes that fixed costs would not be significantly affected if the Cups line were discontinued.

a. Prepare a differential analysis report for all three products.

b. Should the Cups line be retained? Explain.

E12-4   Segment analysis

Obj 1

Charles Schwab Corporation is one of the more innovative brokerage and financial service companies in the United States. The company provided information about its major business segments as follows (in millions) for a recent year.

	Individual Investor	Institutional Investor
Revenues	$3,189	$1,502
Income from operations before taxes	928	463
Depreciation and amortization	108	47

a. How do you believe Schwab defines the difference between the "Individual Investor" and "Institutional Investor" segments?

b. Provide a specific example of a variable and fixed cost in the "Individual Investor" segment.

c. Estimate the contribution margin for each segment.

d. If Schwab decided to sell its "Institutional Investor" accounts to another company, estimate how much operating income would decline.

Obj 1

E12-5   Decision to discontinue a product

On the basis of the following data, the general manager of Sandals Industries Inc. decided to discontinue Children's Sandals because it reduced income from operations by $65,000. What is the flaw in this decision?

Sandals Industries Inc.
Product-Line Income Statement

	Children's Sandals	Women's Sandals	Men's Sandals	Total
Sales	$400,000	$1,200,000	$1,100,000	$2,700,000
Costs of goods sold:				
Variable costs	$240,000	$ 620,000	$ 580,000	$1,440,000
Fixed costs	100,000	300,000	300,000	700,000
Total cost of goods sold	$340,000	$ 920,000	$ 880,000	$2,140,000
Gross profit	$ 60,000	$ 280,000	$ 220,000	$ 560,000
Selling and administrative expenses:				
Variable selling and admin. expenses	$ 75,000	$ 120,000	$ 100,000	$ 295,000
Fixed selling and admin. expenses	50,000	100,000	80,000	230,000
Total selling and admin. expenses	$125,000	$ 220,000	$ 180,000	$ 525,000
Income (loss) from operations	$ (65,000)	$ 60,000	$ 40,000	$ 35,000

Obj 1

E12-6   Make-or-buy decision

Balboa Technologies Company has been purchasing carrying cases for its portable computers at a delivered cost of $20 per unit. The company, which is currently operating below full capacity, charges factory overhead to production at the rate of 60% of direct labor cost. The fully absorbed unit costs to produce comparable carrying cases are expected to be as follows:

✔ a. Cost savings
from making,
$2.00 per case

Direct materials	$ 9.00
Direct labor	7.50
Factory overhead (60% of direct labor)	4.50
Total cost per unit	$21.00

If Balboa Technologies Company manufactures the carrying cases, fixed factory overhead costs will not increase and variable factory overhead costs associated with the cases are expected to be 20% of the direct labor costs.

a. Prepare a differential analysis report for the make-or-buy decision.

b. On the basis of the data presented, would it be advisable to make the carrying cases or to continue buying them? Explain.

Obj 1

E12-7   Make-or-buy decision

Wisconsin Arts of Milwaukee employs five people in its Publication Department. These people lay out pages for pamphlets, brochures, and other publications for the productions. The pages are delivered to an outside company for printing. The company is considering an outside publication service for the layout work. The outside service is quoting a price of $12.50 per layout page. The budget for the Publication Department is as follows:

Salaries	$185,000
Benefits	50,000
Supplies	30,000
Office expenses	25,000
Office depreciation	70,000
Computer depreciation	18,000
Total	$378,000

The department expects to lay out 30,000 pages. The computers used by the department have an estimated residual value of $6,500. The Publication Department office space would be used for future administrative needs, if the department's function were purchased from the outside.

a. Prepare a differential analysis report for the make-or-buy decision, considering the differential revenues and costs.

b. On the basis of your analysis in part (a), should the page layout work be purchased from an outside company?

c. What additional considerations might factor into the decision making?

E12-8   Machine replacement decision

Obj 1

Torrey Products Inc. is considering replacing an old piece of machinery, which cost $350,000 and has $115,000 of accumulated depreciation to date, with a new machine that costs $420,000. The old equipment could be sold for $90,000. The annual variable production costs associated with the old machine are estimated to be $75,000 for ten years. The annual variable production costs for the new machine are estimated to be $39,000 for ten years.

a. Determine the total and annualized differential income or loss anticipated from replacing the old machine.

b. What is the sunk cost in this situation?

E12-9   Differential analysis report for machine replacement

Obj 1

Sidney Technologies Inc. assembles circuit boards by using a manually operated machine to insert electronic components. The original cost of the machine is $60,000, the accumulated depreciation is $24,000, its remaining useful life is five years, and its residual value is negligible. A proposal was made to replace the present manufacturing procedure with a fully automatic machine that will cost $225,000. The automatic machine has an estimated useful life of five years and no significant residual value. For use in evaluating the proposal, the accountant accumulated the following annual data on present and proposed operations:

✔ a. Annual differential increase in costs and expenses, $5,000

	Present Operations	Proposed Operations
Sales	$400,000	$400,000
Direct materials	$100,000	$100,000
Direct labor	65,000	—
Power and maintenance	8,000	23,000
Taxes, insurance, etc.	4,000	14,000
Selling and administrative expenses	90,000	90,000
Total expenses	$267,000	$227,000

a. Prepare a differential analysis report for the proposal to replace the machine. Include in the analysis both the net differential change in costs anticipated over the five years and the net annual differential change in costs anticipated.

b. Based only on the data presented, should the proposal be accepted?

c. What are some of the other factors that should be considered before a final decision is made?

E12-10   Sell or process further

Obj 1

✔ a. Differential revenue, $120

Bitterroot Lumber Company incurs a cost of $275 per hundred board feet in processing certain "rough-cut" lumber, which it sells for $400 per hundred board feet. An alternative is to produce a "finished cut" at a total processing cost of $360 per hundred board feet, which can be sold for $520 per hundred board feet. What is the amount of (a) the differential revenue, (b) differential cost, and (c) differential income for processing rough-cut lumber into finished cut?

E12-11 Sell or process further

Spokane Coffee Company produces Columbian coffee in batches of 5,000 pounds. The standard quantity of materials required in the process is 5,000 pounds, which cost $4.00 per pound. Columbian coffee can be sold without further processing for $9.00 per pound. Columbian coffee can also be processed further to yield Decaf Columbian, which can be sold for $12.50 per pound. The processing into Decaf Columbian requires additional processing costs of $14,110 per batch. The additional processing will also cause an 8% loss of product due to evaporation.

a. Prepare a differential analysis report for the decision to sell or process further.

b. Should Spokane Coffee sell Columbian coffee or process further and sell Decaf Columbian?

c. Determine the price of Decaf Columbian that would cause neither an advantage nor a disadvantage for processing further and selling Decaf Columbian.

E12-12 Decision on accepting additional business

Tosca Industries Inc. has an annual plant capacity of 400,000 units, and current production is 320,000 units. Monthly fixed costs are $680,000, and variable costs are $29 per unit. The present selling price is $45 per unit. The company received an offer from DynaX Company for 50,000 units of the product at $32 each. DynaX Company will market the units in a foreign country under its own brand name. The additional business is not expected to affect the domestic selling price or quantity of sales of Tosca Industries Inc.

a. Prepare a differential analysis report for the proposed sale to DynaX Company.

b. Briefly explain the reason why accepting this additional business will increase operating income.

c. What is the minimum price per unit that would produce a contribution margin?

E12-13 Accepting business at a special price

Palomar Battery Company expects to operate at 75% of productive capacity during April. The total manufacturing costs for April for the production of 60,000 batteries are budgeted as follows:

Direct materials	$ 75,000
Direct labor	960,000
Variable factory overhead	111,000
Fixed factory overhead	288,000
Total manufacturing costs	$1,434,000

The company has an opportunity to submit a bid for 17,500 batteries to be delivered by April 30 to a government agency. If the contract is obtained, it is anticipated that the additional activity will not interfere with normal production during April or increase the selling or administrative expenses.

a. What is the April budgeted cost per battery for the production of 60,000 batteries?'

b. What is the unit cost below which Palomar Battery Company should not go in bidding on the government contract?

E12-14 Decision on accepting additional business

Miramar Tire and Rubber Company has capacity to produce 250,000 tires. Miramar presently produces and sells 200,000 tires for the North American market at a price of $40 per tire. Miramar is evaluating a special order from a South American automobile company, Rio Motors. Rio Motors is offering to buy 40,000 tires for $20 per tire. Miramar's accounting system indicates that the total cost per tire is as follows:

Direct materials	$10.00
Direct labor	5.00
Factory overhead (45% variable)	4.00
Selling and administrative expenses (75% variable)	3.00
Total	$22.00

Miramar pays a selling commission equal to 4% of the selling price on North American orders, which is included in the variable portion of the selling and administrative expenses. However, this special order would not have a sales commission. If the order was accepted, the tires would be shipped overseas for an additional shipping cost of $1.50 per tire. In addition, Rio has made the order conditional on Miramar Tire and Rubber Company receiving a Brazilian safety certification. Rio estimates that this certification would cost Miramar Tire $20,000.

a. Prepare a differential analysis report for the proposed sale to Rio Motors.

b. What is the minimum price per unit that would be financially acceptable to Miramar?

E12-15   Total cost concept of product costing

StarMed Products Inc. uses the total cost concept of applying the cost-plus approach to product pricing. The costs of producing and selling 100,000 units of medical tablets are as follows:

Obj **2**

✔ d. Selling price, $530.00

Variable costs:		Fixed costs:	
Direct materials	$270 per unit	Factory overhead	$2,400,000
Direct labor	60	Selling and admin. exp.	1,100,000
Factory overhead	90		
Selling and admin. exp.	45		
Total	$465 per unit		

StarMed Products desires a profit equal to a 20% rate of return on invested assets of $15,000,000.

a. Determine the amount of desired profit from the production and sale of 100,000 units.

b. Determine the total costs and the cost amount per unit for the production and sale of 100,000 units.

c. Determine the total cost markup percentage per unit.

d. Determine the selling price per unit.

E12-16   Product cost concept of product pricing

Based on the data presented in Exercise 12-15, assume that StarMed Products Inc. uses the product cost concept of applying the cost-plus approach to product pricing.

Obj **2**

✔ b. Markup percentage, 19.37%

a. Determine the total manufacturing costs and the cost amount per unit for the production and sale of 100,000 units.

b. Determine the product cost markup percentage per unit. Round to two decimal place.

c. Determine the selling price per unit. Round to the nearest dollar.

E12-17   Variable cost concept of product pricing

Based on the data presented in Exercise 12-15, assume that StarMed Products Inc. uses the variable cost concept of applying the cost-plus approach to product pricing.

Obj **2**

✔ b. Markup percentage, 13.98%

a. Determine the variable costs and the cost amount per unit for the production and sale of 100,000 units of medical tablets.

b. Determine the variable cost markup percentage per unit. Round to two decimal place.

c. Determine the selling price per unit. Round to the nearest dollar.

E12-18   Target costing

Obj **2**

Toyota Motor Corporation uses target costing. Assume that Toyota marketing personnel estimate that the competitive, average selling price for the Rav4 in the upcoming model year will need to be $24,000. Assume further that the Rav4's total unit cost for the upcoming model year is estimated to be $20,500 and that Toyota requires a 20% profit margin on selling price (which is equivalent to a 25% markup on total cost).

a. What price will Toyota establish for the Rav4 for the upcoming model year?

b. What impact will target costing have on Toyota, given the assumed information?

Obj 2

✔ b. $14.40

E12-19 Target costing

Millennium Printers Inc. manufactures color laser printers. Model L-1819 presently sells for $200 and has a total product cost of $160, as follows:

Direct materials	$ 40
Direct labor	80
Factory overhead	40
Total	$160

It is estimated that the competitive selling price for color laser printers of this type will drop to $182 next year. Millennium Printers wants to establish a target cost to maintain its historical markup percentage on product cost. Engineers have provided the following cost reduction ideas:

1. Purchase a plastic printer cover with snap-on assembly. This will reduce the amount of direct labor by six minutes per unit.

2. Add an inspection step that will add nine minutes per unit of direct labor but reduce the materials cost by $7.25 per unit.

3. Decrease the cycle time of the injection molding machine from four minutes to three minutes per part. Thirty percent of the direct labor and 28% of the factory overhead is related to running injection molding machines.

The direct labor rate is $20 per hour.

a. Determine the target cost for Model L-1819 assuming that the historical markup on product cost is maintained.

b. Determine the required cost reduction.

c. Evaluate the three engineering improvements to determine if the required cost reduction (drift) can be achieved.

Obj 3

E12-20 Product decisions under bottlenecked operations

Yumin Metals Inc. has three grades of metal product, Type A1, Type B3, and Type E6. Financial data for the three grades are as follows:

	Type A1	Type B3	Type E6
Revenue	$400,000	$578,000	$300,000
Variable cost	$250,000	$380,000	$270,000
Fixed cost	105,000	118,800	20,000
Total cost	$355,000	$498,800	$290,000
Income from operations	$ 45,000	$ 79,200	$ 10,000
Number of units	÷ 15,000	÷ 16,500	÷ 5,000
Income from operations per unit	$ 3.00	$ 4.80	$ 2.00

Yumin Metals' operations require all three grades to be melted in a furnace before being formed. The furnace runs 24 hours a day, 7 days a week, and is a production bottleneck. The furnace hours required per unit of each product are as follows:

Type A1:	8 hours
Type B3:	10 hours
Type E6:	6 hours

The Marketing Department is considering a new marketing and sales campaign. Which product should be emphasized in the marketing and sales campaign in order to maximize profitability?

E12-21   Product decisions under bottlenecked operations

Madero Glass Company manufactures three types of safety plate glass: large, medium, and small. All three products have high demand. Thus, Madero Glass is able to sell all the safety glass that it can make. The production process includes an autoclave operation, which is a pressurized heat treatment. The autoclave is a production bottleneck. Total fixed costs are $125,000. In addition, the following information is available about the three products:

	Large	Medium	Small
Unit selling price	$180	$150	$135
Unit variable cost	144	130	110
Unit contribution margin	$ 36	$ 20	$ 25
Autoclave hours per unit	10	8	4
Total process hours per unit	16	14	10
Budgeted units of production	5,000	5,000	5,000

Obj 3
✔ a. Total income from operations, $280,000

a. Determine the contribution margin by glass type and the total company income from operations for the budgeted units of production.

b. Prepare an analysis showing which product is the most profitable per bottleneck hour.

E12-22   Product pricing under bottlenecked operations

Based on the data presented in Exercise 12-21, assume that Madero Glass wanted to price all products so that they produced the same profit potential as the highest profit product. Thus, determine the prices for each of the products so that they would produce a profit equal to the highest profit product.

Obj 3
✔ Revised price of medium glass, $180

Problems

P12-1   Differential analysis report involving opportunity costs

Five Star is considering leasing a building and buying the necessary equipment to operate a public warehouse. Alternatively, the company could use the funds to invest in $900,000 of 4% U.S. Treasury bonds that mature in 15 years. The bonds could be purchased at face value. The following data have been assembled:

Obj 1

Cost of equipment	$900,000
Life of equipment	15 years
Estimated residual value of equipment	$100,000
Yearly costs to operate the warehouse, excluding depreciation of equipment	$175,000
Yearly expected revenues—years 1–7	$400,000
Yearly expected revenues—years 8–15	$250,000

Instructions

1. Prepare a differential analysis report of the proposed operation of the warehouse for the 15 years as compared with present conditions.

2. Based on the results disclosed by the differential analysis, should the proposal be accepted?

3. If the proposal is accepted, what is the total estimated income from operations of the warehouse for the 15 years?

Obj | 1

P12-2 Differential analysis report for machine replacement proposal

Catalina Tooling Company is considering replacing a machine that has been used in its factory for two years. Relevant data associated with the operations of the old machine and the new machine, neither of which has any estimated residual value, are as follows:

Old Machine

Cost of machine, 10-year life	$75,000
Annual depreciation (straight-line)	7,500
Annual manufacturing costs, excluding depreciation	33,150
Annual nonmanufacturing operating expenses	10,000
Annual revenue	60,000
Current estimated selling price of the machine	24,000

New Machine

Cost of machine, eight-year life	$90,000
Annual depreciation (straight-line)	11,250
Estimated annual manufacturing costs, exclusive of depreciation	18,200
Annual nonmanufacturing operating expenses	10,000

Annual nonmanufacturing operating expenses and revenue are not expected to be affected by purchase of the new machine.

Instructions

1. Prepare a differential analysis report comparing operations utilizing the new machine with operations using the present equipment. The analysis should indicate the differential income that would result over the eight-year period if the new machine is acquired.

2. List other factors that should be considered before a final decision is reached.

Obj | 1

✔ Differential income, cross-trainer shoe, $450,000

P12-3 Differential analysis report for sales promotion proposal

Rocket Shoe Company is planning a one-month campaign for August to promote sales of one of its two shoe products. A total of $500,000 has been budgeted for advertising, contests, redeemable coupons, and other promotional activities. The following data have been assembled for their possible usefulness in deciding which of the products to select for the campaign.

	Cross-Trainer Shoe	Running Shoe
Unit selling price	$90	$112
Unit production costs:		
Direct materials	$24	$ 30
Direct labor	10	8
Variable factory overhead	6	6
Fixed factory overhead	8	16
Total unit production costs	$48	$ 60
Unit variable selling expenses	12	12
Unit fixed selling expenses	4	16
Total unit costs	$64	$ 88
Operating income per unit	$26	$ 24

No increase in facilities would be necessary to produce and sell the increased output. It is anticipated that 25,000 additional units of cross-trainer shoes or 18,000 additional units of running shoes could be sold without changing the unit selling price of either product.

Instructions

1. Prepare a differential analysis report presenting the additional revenue and additional costs anticipated from the promotion of cross-trainer shoes and running shoes.

2. The sales manager had tentatively decided to promote cross-trainer shoes, estimating that operating income would be increased by $150,000 ($26 operating income per unit for 25,000

units, less promotion expenses of $500,000). The manager also believed that the selection of running shoes would decrease operating income by $68,000 ($24 operating income per unit for 18,000 units, less promotion expenses of $500,000). State briefly your reasons for supporting or opposing the tentative decision.

P12-4   Differential analysis report for further processing

Obj **1**

The management of Dorsch Aluminum Co. is considering whether to process aluminum ingot further into rolled aluminum. Rolled aluminum can be sold for $4,100 per ton, and ingot can be sold without further processing for $2,400 per ton. Ingot is produced in batches of 80 tons by smelting 400 tons of bauxite, which costs $500 per ton. Rolled aluminum will require additional processing costs of $750 per ton of ingot, and 1.25 tons of ingot will produce 1 ton of rolled aluminum (due to trim losses).

✔ 1. Differential revenue, $70,400

Instructions

1. Prepare a report presenting a differential analysis associated with the further processing of aluminum ingot to produce rolled aluminum.

2. Briefly report your recommendations.

P12-5   Product pricing using the cost-plus approach concepts; differential analysis report for accepting additional business

Obj **1, 2**

Twilight Lumina Company recently began production of a new product, the halogen light, which required the investment of $1,200,000 in assets. The costs of producing and selling 20,000 halogen lights are estimated as follows:

✔ 2. b. Markup percentage, 16%

Variable costs:		Fixed costs:	
Direct materials	$30 per unit	Factory overhead	$340,000
Direct labor	10	Selling and admin. exp.	160,000
Factory overhead	6		
Selling and admin. exp.	4		
Total	$50 per unit		

Twilight Lumina Company is currently considering establishing a selling price for the halogen light. The president of Twilight Lumina Company has decided to use the cost-plus approach to product pricing and has indicated that the halogen light must earn a 20% rate of return on invested assets.

Instructions

1. Determine the amount of desired profit from the production and sale of the halogen light.

2. Assuming that the total cost concept is used, determine (a) the cost amount per unit, (b) the markup percentage, and (c) the selling price of the halogen light.

3. Assuming that the product cost concept is used, determine (a) the cost amount per unit, (b) the markup percentage (round to the nearest two decimal places), and (c) the selling price of the halogen light (round to the nearest cent).

4. Assuming that the variable cost concept is used, determine (a) the cost amount per unit, (b) the markup percentage, and (c) the selling price of the halogen light.

5. Comment on any additional considerations that could influence establishing the selling price for the halogen light.

6. Assume that 15,000 units of halogen light have been produced and sold during the current year. Analysis of the domestic market indicates that 2,000 additional units of the halogen light are expected to be sold during the remainder of the year at the normal product price determined under the total cost concept. Twilight Lumina Company received an offer from Contech Inc. for 3,000 units of the halogen light at $52 each. Contech Inc. will market the units in Southeast Asia under its own brand name, and no selling and administrative expenses associated with the sale will be incurred by Twilight Lumina Company. The

additional business is not expected to affect the domestic sales of the halogen light, and the additional units could be produced using existing capacity.

a. Prepare a differential analysis report of the proposed sale to Contech Inc.

b. Based on the differential analysis report in part (a), should the proposal be accepted?

Obj | 1, 3

✔ 1. Ethylene contribution margin per unit, $100

P12-6   Product pricing and profit analysis with bottleneck operations

Chavez Chemical Company produces three products: ethylene, butane, and ester. Each of these products has high demand in the market, and Chavez Chemical is able to sell as much as it can produce of all three. The reaction operation is a bottleneck in the process and is running at 100% of capacity. Chavez Chemical wants to improve chemical operation profitability. The variable conversion cost is $20 per process hour. The fixed cost is $550,000. In addition, the cost analyst was able to determine the following information about the three products:

	Ethylene	Butane	Ester
Budgeted units produced	15,000	15,000	15,000
Total process hours per unit	6	6	4
Reactor hours per unit	1.0	0.8	0.5
Unit selling price	$400	$350	$250
Direct materials cost per unit	$180	$130	$90

The reaction operation is part of the total process for each of these three products. Thus, for example, 1.0 of the 6 hours required to process ethylene is associated with the reactor.

Instructions

1. Determine the unit contribution margin for each of the three products.

2. Provide an analysis to determine the relative product profitabilities, assuming that the reactor is a bottleneck.

3. Assume that management wishes to improve profitability by increasing prices on selected products. At what price would ethylene and butane need to be offered in order to produce the same relative profitability as ester?

Cases

Case 12-1   Product pricing

Bev Frazier is a cost accountant for Ocean Atlantic Apparel Inc. Jeff Rangel, vice president of marketing, has asked Bev to meet with representatives of Ocean Atlantic Apparel's major competitor to discuss product cost data. Jeff indicates that the sharing of these data will enable Ocean Atlantic to determine a fair and equitable price for its products.

Would it be ethical for Bev to attend the meeting and share the relevant cost data?

Case 12-2   Decision on accepting additional business

A manager of Coastal Sporting Goods Company is considering accepting an order from an overseas customer. This customer has requested an order for 50,000 dozen golf balls at a price of $12 per dozen. The variable cost to manufacture a dozen golf balls is $9 per dozen. The full cost is $14 per dozen. Coastal Sporting Goods has a normal selling price of $24 per dozen. Coastal's plant has just enough excess capacity on the second shift to make the overseas order.

What are some considerations in accepting or rejecting this order?

Case 12-3   Accept business at a special price

If you are not familiar with Priceline.com Inc., go to its Web site. Assume that an individual "names a price" of $90 on Priceline.com for a room in Miami, Florida, on September 3. Assume that September 3 is a Saturday, with low expected room demand in Miami at a **Marriott**

International, Inc., hotel, so there is excess room capacity. The fully allocated cost per room per day is assumed from hotel records as follows:

Housekeeping labor cost*	$ 30
Hotel depreciation expense	50
Cost of room supplies (soap, paper, etc.)	2
Laundry labor and material cost*	6
Cost of desk staff	8
Utility cost (mostly air conditioning)	4
Total cost per room per day	$100

*Both housekeeping and laundry staff include many part-time workers, so that the workload is variable to demand.

Should Marriott accept the customer bid for a night in Miami on September 3 at a price of $90?

Case 12-4 Cost-plus and target costing concepts

The following conversation took place between Dean Lancaster, vice president of marketing, and Dina Conaway, controller of Redwood Computer Company:

Dean: I am really excited about our new computer coming out. I think it will be a real market success.

Dina: I'm really glad you think so. I know that our success will be determined by our price. If our price is too high, our competitors will be the ones with the market success.

Dean: Don't worry about it. We'll just mark our product cost up by 25% and it will all work out. I know we'll make money at those markups. By the way, what does the estimated product cost look like?

Dina: Well, there's the rub. The product cost looks as if it's going to come in at around $1,000. With a 25% markup, that will give us a selling price of $1,250.

Dean: I see your concern. That's a little high. Our research indicates that computer prices are dropping and that this type of computer should be selling for around $900 when we release it to the market.

Dina: I'm not sure what to do.

Dean: Let me see if I can help. How much of the $1,000 is fixed cost?

Dina: About $300.

Dean: There you go. The fixed cost is sunk. We don't need to consider it in our pricing decision. If we reduce the product cost by $300, the new price with a 25% markup would be right at $875. Boy, I was really worried for a minute there. I knew something wasn't right.

1. If you were Dina, how would you respond to Dean's solution to the pricing problem?

2. How might target costing be used to help solve this pricing dilemma?

Case 12-5 Pricing decisions and markup on variable costs

GROUP PROJECT

Many businesses are offering their products and services over the Internet. Some of these companies and their Internet addresses are listed below.

Company Name	Internet Address (URL)	Product
Delta Air Lines	http://www.delta.com	Airline tickets
Amazon.com	http://www.amazon.com	Books
Dell Inc.	http://www.dell.com	Personal computers

1. In groups of three, assign each person in your group to one of the Internet sites listed above. For each site, determine the following:
   a. A product (or service) description.
   b. A product price.

      c. A list of costs that are required to produce and sell the product selected in part (1) as listed in the annual report on SEC Form 10-K.

      d. Whether the costs identified in part (3) are fixed costs or variable costs.

  2. Which of the three products do you believe has the largest markup on variable cost?

Answers to Self-Examination Questions

1. **A** Differential cost is the amount of increase or decrease in cost that is expected from a particular course of action compared with an alternative. For Marlo Company, the differential cost is $19,000 (answer A). This is the total of the variable product costs ($15,000) and the variable operating expenses ($4,000), which would not be incurred if the product is discontinued.

2. **A** A sunk cost is not affected by later decisions. For Victor Company, the sunk cost is the $50,000 (answer A) book value of the equipment, which is equal to the original cost of $200,000 (answer C) less the accumulated depreciation of $150,000 (answer B).

3. **C** The amount of income that could have been earned from the best available alternative to a proposed use of cash is the opportunity cost. For Henry Company, the opportunity cost is 12% of $100,000, or $12,000 (answer C).

4. **C** Under the variable cost concept of product pricing (answer C), fixed manufacturing costs, fixed administrative and selling expenses, and desired profit are allowed for in determining the markup. Only desired profit is allowed for in the markup under the total cost concept (answer A). Under the product cost concept (answer B), total selling and administrative expenses and desired profit are allowed for in determining the markup. Standard cost (answer D) can be used under any of the cost-plus approaches to product pricing.

5. **C** Product 3 has the highest unit contribution margin per bottleneck hour ($14 ÷ 2 = $7). Product 1 (answer A) has the largest unit contribution margin, but the lowest unit contribution per bottleneck hour ($20 ÷ 4 = $5), so it is the least profitable product in the constrained environment. Product 2 (answer B) has the highest total profitability in March (1,500 units × $18), but this does not suggest that it has the highest profit potential. Product 2's unit contribution per bottleneck hour ($18 ÷ 3 = $6) is between Products 1 and 3. Answer D is not true, since the products all have different profit potential in terms of unit contribution margin per bottleneck hour.

CHAPTER 13

Budgeting and Standard Cost Systems

LEARNING OBJECTIVES
After studying this chapter, you should be able to:

Obj **1** Describe budgeting, its objectives, its impact on human behavior, and types of budget systems.

Obj **2** Describe the master budget for a manufacturing company.

Obj **3** Describe the types of standards and how they are established.

Obj **4** Describe and illustrate how standards are used in budgeting.

Obj **5** Compute and interpret direct materials and direct labor variances.

Obj **6** Describe and provide examples of nonfinancial performance measures.

You may have financial goals for your life. To achieve these goals, it is necessary to plan for future expenses. For example, you may consider taking a part-time job to save money for school expenses for the coming school year. How much money would you need to earn and save in order to pay these expenses? One way to find an answer to this question would be to prepare a budget. A budget would show an estimate of your expenses associated with school, such as tuition, fees, and books. In addition, you would have expenses for day-to-day living, such as rent, food, and clothing. You might also have expenses for travel and entertainment. Once the school year begins, you can use the budget as a tool for guiding your spending priorities during the year.

The budget is used in businesses in much the same way as it can be used in personal life. For example, **The North**

Face sponsors mountain-climbing expeditions throughout the year for professional and amateur climbers. These events require budgeting to plan trip expenses, much like you might use a budget to plan a vacation.

Budgeting is also used by The North Face to plan the manufacturing costs associated with its outdoor clothing and equipment production. For example, budgets would be used to determine the number of coats to be produced, number of people to be employed, and amount of material to be purchased. The budget provides the company with a "game plan" for the year. In this chapter, you will see how budgets can be used for financial planning and control. This chapter concludes by describing and illustrating standard cost accounting systems.

Nature and Objectives of Budgeting

Budgets play an important role for organizations of all sizes and forms. For example, budgets are used in managing the operations of government agencies, churches, hospitals, and other nonprofit organizations. Individuals and families also use budgeting in managing their financial affairs. This chapter describes and illustrates budgeting for a manufacturing company.

Objectives of Budgeting

Budgeting involves (1) establishing specific goals, (2) executing plans to achieve the goals, and (3) periodically comparing actual results with the goals. In doing so, budgeting affects the following managerial functions:

1. Planning
2. Directing
3. Controlling

The relationships of these activities are illustrated in Exhibit 1.

EXHIBIT 1 **Planning, Directing, and Controlling**

Planning involves setting goals as a guide for making decisions. Budgeting supports the planning process by requiring all departments and other organizational units to establish their goals for the future. These goals help motivate employees. In addition, the budgeting process often identifies areas where operations can be improved or inefficiencies eliminated.

Directing involves decisions and actions to achieve budgeted goals. Budgeting aids in coordinating management's decisions and actions to achieve the company's budgeted goals. A budgetary unit of a company is called a **responsibility center**. Each responsibility center is led by a manager who has the authority and responsibility for achieving the center's budgeted goals.

Controlling involves comparing actual performance against the budgeted goals. Such comparisons provide feedback to managers and employees about their

A budget is like a road map. It charts a future course for a company in financial terms and thus aids the company in navigating through the year to reach its destination.

performance. If necessary, responsibility centers can use such feedback to adjust their activities in the future.

Human Behavior and Budgeting

Human behavior problems can arise in the budgeting process in the following situations:

1. Budgeted goals are set too tight, which are very hard or impossible to achieve.
2. Budgeted goals are set too loose, which are very easy to achieve.
3. Budgeted goals conflict with the objectives of the company and employees.

These behavior problems are illustrated in Exhibit 2.

EXHIBIT 2

Human Behavior Problems in Budgeting

Budget Goals Too Tight   Budget Goals Too Loose   Conflicting Budget Goals

Setting Budget Goals Too Tightly Employees and managers may become discouraged if budgeted goals are set too high. That is, if budgeted goals are viewed as unrealistic or unachievable, the budget may have a negative effect on the ability of the company to achieve its goals.

Reasonable, attainable goals are more likely to motivate employees and managers. For this reason, it is important that employees and managers be involved in the budgeting process. Involving employees in the budgeting process provides employees with a sense of control and thus more of a commitment in meeting budgeted goals. Finally, involving employees and managers also encourages cooperation across departments and responsibility centers. Such cooperation increases awareness of each department's importance to the overall goals of the company.

Setting Budget Goals Too Loosely Although it is desirable to establish attainable goals, it is undesirable to plan lower goals than may be possible. Such budget "padding" is termed **budgetary slack**. Managers may plan slack in the budget in order to provide a "cushion" for unexpected events or improve the appearance of operations. Budgetary slack can be reduced by properly training employees and managers in the importance of realistic, attainable budgets.

Slack budgets may cause a "spend it or lose it" mentality. This often occurs at the end of the budget period when actual spending is less than the budget.

Employees and managers may spend the remaining budget on unnecessary purchases in order to avoid having their budget reduced for the next period.

Setting Conflicting Budget Goals Goal conflict occurs when the employees' or managers' self-interest differs from the company's objectives or goals. Goal conflict may also occur among responsibility centers such as departments.

To illustrate, assume that the sales department manager is given an increased sales goal and as a result accepts customers who are poor credit risks. This, in turn, causes bad debt expense to increase and profitability to decline. Likewise, a manufacturing department manager may be told to reduce costs. As a result, the manufacturing department manager might use lower-cost direct materials, which are also of lower quality. As a result, customer complaints and returns might increase significantly, which would adversely affect the company's profitability.

Integrity, Objectivity, and Ethics in Business

BUDGET GAMES

The budgeting system is designed to plan and control a business. However, it is common for the budget to be "gamed" by its participants. For example, managers may pad their budgets with excess resources. In this way, the managers have additional resources for unexpected events during the period. If the budget is being used to establish the incentive plan, then sales managers have incentives to understate the sales potential of a territory in order to ensure hitting their quotas. Other times, managers engage in "land grabbing,"

which occurs when they overstate the sales potential of a territory in order to guarantee access to resources. If managers believe that unspent resources will not roll over to future periods, then they may be encouraged to "spend it or lose it," causing wasteful expenditures. These types of problems can be partially overcome by separating the budget into planning and incentive components. This is why many organizations have two budget processes, one for resource planning and another, more challenging budget, for motivating managers.

Western Digital Corporation, a computer hard drive manufacturer, introduced a new Web-based B&P (budget and planning) system to perform a continuous rolling budget. According to the financial executives at the company, "We're never [again] comparing results to old operating plans that were set months ago."

Budgeting Systems

Budgeting systems vary among companies and industries. For example, the budget system used by Ford Motor Company differs from that used by Delta Air Lines. However, the basic budgeting concepts discussed in this section apply to all types of businesses and organizations.

The budgetary period for operating activities normally includes the fiscal year of a company. A year is short enough that future operations can be estimated fairly accurately, yet long enough that the future can be viewed in a broad context. However, for control purposes, annual budgets are usually subdivided into shorter time periods, such as quarters of the year, months, or weeks.

A variation of fiscal year budgeting, called **continuous budgeting**, maintains a 12-month projection into the future. The 12-month budget is continually revised by replacing the data for the month just ended with the budget data for the same month in the next year. A continuous budget is illustrated in Exhibit 3.

Continuous Budgeting **EXHIBIT 3**

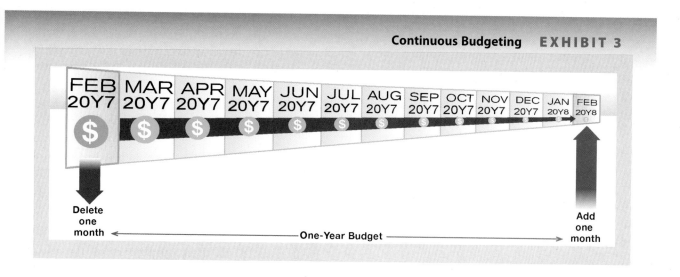

Developing an annual budget usually begins several months prior to the end of the current year. This responsibility is normally assigned to a budget committee. Such a committee often consists of the budget director, the controller, the treasurer, the production manager, and the sales manager. The budget process is monitored and summarized by the Accounting Department, which reports to the committee.

There are several methods of developing budget estimates. One method, termed **zero-based budgeting**, requires managers to estimate sales, production, and other operating data as though operations are being started for the first time. This approach has the benefit of taking a fresh view of operations each year. A more common approach is to start with last year's budget and revise it for actual results and expected changes for the coming year. Two major budgets using this approach are the static budget and the flexible budget.

Static Budget A **static budget** shows the expected results of a responsibility center for only one activity level. Once the budget has been determined, it is not changed, even if the activity changes. Static budgeting is used by many service companies and for some functions of manufacturing companies, such as purchasing, engineering, and accounting.

To illustrate, the static budget for the Assembly Department of Jewett Manufacturing Company is shown in Exhibit 4.

EXHIBIT 4

Static Budget

	A	B
1	Jewett Manufacturing Company	
2	Assembly Department Budget	
3	For the Year Ending July 31, 20Y7	
4	Direct labor	$40,000
5	Electric power	5,000
6	Supervisor salaries	15,000
7	Total department costs	$60,000
8		

A disadvantage of static budgets is that they do not adjust for changes in activity levels. For example, assume that the Assembly Department of Jewett Manufacturing spent $70,800 for the year ended July 31, 20Y7. Thus, the Assembly Department spent $10,800 ($70,800 − $60,000), or 18% ($10,800/$60,000) more than budgeted. Is this good news or bad news?

The first reaction is that this is bad news and the Assembly Department was inefficient in spending more than budgeted. However, assume that the Assembly Department's budget was based on plans to assemble 8,000 units during the year. If 10,000 units were actually assembled, the additional $10,800 spent in excess of budget might be good news. That is, the Assembly Department assembled 25% (2,000 units/8,000 units) more than planned for only 18% more cost.

Flexible Budget Unlike static budgets, **flexible budgets** show the expected results of a responsibility center for several activity levels. A flexible budget is, in effect, a series of static budgets for different levels of activity.

To illustrate, a flexible budget for the Assembly Department of Jewett Manufacturing Company is shown in Exhibit 5.

EXHIBIT 5

Flexible Budget

	A	B	C	D
1	Jewett Manufacturing Company			
2	Assembly Department Budget			
3	For the Year Ending July 31, 20Y7			
4				
5	Units of production	8,000	9,000	10,000	← Step 1
6	Variable cost:			
7	Direct labor ($5 per unit)	$40,000	$45,000	$50,000
8	Electric power ($0.50 per unit)	4,000	4,500	5,000
9	Total variable cost	$44,000	$49,500	$55,000
10	Fixed cost:			
11	Electric power	$ 1,000	$ 1,000	$ 1,000
12	Supervisor salaries	15,000	15,000	15,000
13	Total fixed cost	$16,000	$16,000	$16,000
14	Total department costs	$60,000	$65,500	$71,000

Step 2 brackets rows 6–12. Step 3 points to row 14.

A flexible budget is constructed as follows:

Step 1. Identify the relevant activity levels. The relevant levels of activity could be expressed in units, machine hours, direct labor hours, or some other activity base. In Exhibit 5, the levels of activity are 8,000, 9,000, and 10,000 units of production.

Step 2. Identify the fixed and variable cost components of the costs being budgeted. In Exhibit 5, the electric power cost is separated into its fixed cost ($1,000 per year) and variable cost ($0.50 per unit). The direct labor is a variable cost, and the supervisor salaries are all fixed costs.

Step 3. Prepare the budget for each activity level by multiplying the variable cost per unit by the activity level and then adding the monthly fixed cost.

With a flexible budget, actual costs can be compared to the budgeted costs for actual activity. To illustrate, assume that the Assembly Department spent $70,800 to produce 10,000 units. Exhibit 5 indicates that the Assembly Department was *under* budget by $200 ($71,000 − $70,800).

Under the static budget in Exhibit 4, the Assembly Department was $10,800 *over* budget. This comparison is illustrated in Exhibit 6.

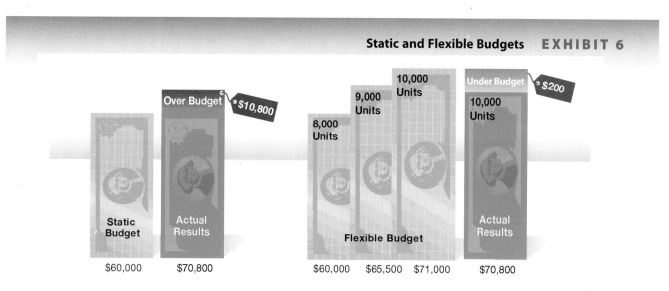

Static and Flexible Budgets   **EXHIBIT 6**

The flexible budget for the Assembly Department is much more accurate and useful than the static budget. This is because the flexible budget adjusts for changes in the level of activity.

Computerized Budgeting Systems

In developing budgets, companies use a variety of computerized approaches. Two of the most popular computerized approaches use:

1. Spreadsheet software such as Microsoft Excel
2. Integrated budget and planning (B&P) software systems

Integrated computerized budget and planning systems speed up and reduce the cost of preparing the budget. This is especially true when large quantities of data need to be processed.

B&P software systems are also useful in continuous budgeting. For example, the latest B&P systems use the Web to link thousands of employees together during the budget process. Employees can input budget data onto Web pages that are integrated and summarized throughout the company. In this way, a company can quickly and consistently integrate top-level strategies and goals to lower-level operational goals. These latest B&P software systems are moving companies closer to the real-time budget, wherein the budget is being "rolled" every day.[1]

Many hospitals use flexible budgeting to plan the number of nurses for patient floors. These budgets use a measure termed "relative value units," which is a measure of nursing effort. The more patients and the more severe their illnesses, the higher the total relative value units, and thus the higher the staffing budget.

One survey reported that 67% of the companies relied on spreadsheets for budgeting and planning.

Source: Tim Reason, "Budgeting in the Real World," *CFO Magazine*, July 1, 2005.

1. Janet Kersnar, "Rolling Along," *CFO Europe*, September 14, 2004.

HOW BUSINESSES MAKE MONEY

BUILD VERSUS HARVEST

Budgeting systems are not "one-size-fits-all" solutions but must adapt to the underlying business conditions. For example, a business can adopt either a build strategy or a harvest strategy. A *build* strategy is one where the business is designing, launching, and growing new products and markets. Build strategies often require short-term profit sacrifice in order to grow market share. **Apple Inc.**'s iPhone® is an example of a product managed under a build strategy. A *harvest* strategy is often employed for business units with mature products enjoying high market share in low-growth industries. **H.J. Heinz Company**'s Ketchup® and **P&G**'s *Ivory* soap are examples of such products. A build strategy often has greater uncertainty, unpredictability, and change than a harvest strategy. The difference between these strategies implies different budgeting approaches.

© NEIL FRASER/ALAMY

The build strategy should employ a budget approach that is flexible to the uncertainty of the business. Thus, budgets should adapt to changing conditions by allowing periodic revisions and flexible targets. The budget serves as a short-term planning tool to guide management in executing an uncertain and evolving product market strategy.

In a harvest strategy, the business is often much more stable and is managed to maximize profitability and cash flow. Because cost control is much more important in this strategy, the budget is used to restrict the actions of managers.

Fujitsu, a Japanese technology company, used B&P to reduce its budgeting process from 6–8 weeks down to 10–15 days.

Companies may also use computer simulation models to analyze the impact of various assumptions and operating alternatives on the budget. For example, the budget can be revised to show the impact of a proposed change in indirect labor wage rates. Likewise, the budgetary effect of a proposed product line can be determined.

Obj 2

Describe the master budget for a manufacturing company.

Master Budget

The **master budget** is an integrated set of operating, investing, and financing budgets for a period of time. Most companies prepare the master budget on a yearly basis.

For a manufacturing company, the master budget consists of the following integrated budgets:

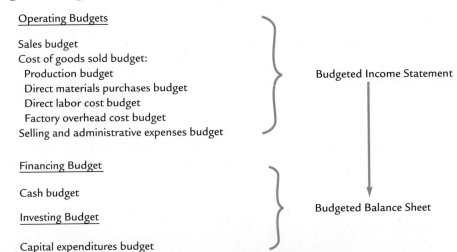

Operating Budgets

Sales budget
Cost of goods sold budget:
  Production budget
  Direct materials purchases budget
  Direct labor cost budget
  Factory overhead cost budget
Selling and administrative expenses budget

} Budgeted Income Statement

Financing Budget

Cash budget

Investing Budget

Capital expenditures budget

} Budgeted Balance Sheet

As shown on the previous page, the master budget is an integrated set of budgets that tie together a company's operating, financing, and investing activities into an integrated plan for the coming year.

The master budget begins with preparing the operating budgets, which form the budgeted income statement. The income statement budgets are normally prepared in the following order beginning with the sales budget:

1. Sales budget
2. Production budget
3. Direct materials purchases budget
4. Direct labor cost budget
5. Factory overhead cost budget
6. Cost of goods sold budget
7. Selling and administrative expenses budget
8. Budgeted income statement

After the budgeted income statement is prepared, the budgeted balance sheet is prepared. Two major budgets comprising the budgeted balance sheet are the cash budget and the capital expenditures budget.

Exhibit 7 shows the relationships among the income statement budgets.

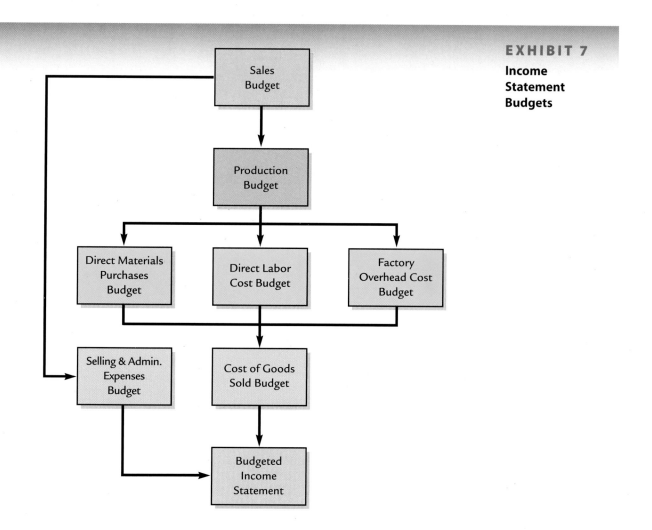

EXHIBIT 7

Income Statement Budgets

Income Statement Budgets

The integrated budgets that support the income statement budget are described and illustrated in this section. Cobbler Inc., a small manufacturing company, is used as a basis for illustration.

Sales Budget The **sales budget** begins by estimating the quantity of sales. As a starting point, the prior year's sales quantities are often used. These sales quantities are then revised for such factors as the following:

1. Backlog of unfilled sales orders from the prior period
2. Planned advertising and promotion
3. Productive capacity
4. Projected pricing changes
5. Findings of market research studies
6. Expected industry and general economic conditions

Once sales quantities are estimated, the expected sales revenue can be determined by multiplying the volume by the expected unit sales price.

To illustrate, Cobbler Inc. manufactures shoes and boots that are sold in two regions, the East and West Regions. Cobbler estimates the following sales quantities and prices for 20Y5:

	East Region	West Region	Unit Selling Price
Shoes	287,000	241,000	$12
Boots	156,400	123,600	25

Exhibit 8 illustrates the sales budget for Cobbler based on the preceding data.

EXHIBIT 8

Sales Budget

	A	B	C	D
1		Cobbler Inc.		
2		Sales Budget		
3		For the Year Ending December 31, 20Y5		
4		Unit Sales	Unit Selling	
5	Product and Region	Volume	Price	Total Sales
6	Shoes:			
7	East	287,000	$12.00	$ 3,444,000
8	West	241,000	12.00	2,892,000
9	Total	528,000		$ 6,336,000
10				
11	Boots:			
12	East	156,400	$25.00	$ 3,910,000
13	West	123,600	25.00	3,090,000
14	Total	280,000		$ 7,000,000
15				
16	Total revenue from sales			$13,336,000

Production Budget The production budget should be integrated with the sales budget to ensure that production and sales are kept in balance during the year. The **production budget** estimates the number of units to be manufactured to meet budgeted sales and desired inventory levels.

The budgeted units to be produced are determined as follows:

Expected units to be sold	XXX units
Plus desired units in ending inventory	+ XXX
Less estimated units in beginning inventory	− XXX
Total units to be produced	XXX units

Cobbler Inc. expects the following inventories of shoes and boots:

	Estimated Inventory, January 1, 20Y5	Desired Inventory, December 31, 20Y5
Shoes	88,000	80,000
Boots	48,000	60,000

Exhibit 9 illustrates the production budget for Cobbler Inc.

EXHIBIT 9
Production Budget

	A	B	C
1	Cobbler Inc.		
2	Production Budget		
3	For the Year Ending December 31, 20Y5		
4		Units	
5		Shoes	Boots
6	Expected units to be sold (from Exhibit 8)	528,000	280,000
7	Plus desired ending inventory, December 31, 20Y5	80,000	60,000
8	Total	608,000	340,000
9	Less estimated beginning inventory, January 1, 20Y5	88,000	48,000
10	Total units to be produced	520,000	292,000

Direct Materials Purchases Budget The direct materials purchases budget should be integrated with the production budget to ensure that production is not interrupted during the year. The **direct materials purchases budget** estimates the quantities of direct materials to be purchased to support budgeted production and desired inventory levels.

The direct materials to be purchased are determined as follows:

Materials required for production	XXX
Plus desired ending materials inventory	+ XXX
Less estimated beginning materials inventory	− XXX
Direct materials to be purchased	XXX

Cobbler Inc. uses leather and lining in producing shoes and boots. The quantity of direct materials expected to be used for each unit of product is as follows:

Shoes	Boots
Leather: 0.30 sq. yd. per unit	Leather: 1.25 sq. yds. per unit
Lining: 0.10 sq. yd. per unit	Lining: 0.50 sq. yd. per unit

Cobbler Inc. expects the following direct materials inventories of leather and lining:

	Estimated Direct Materials Inventory, January 1, 20Y5	Desired Direct Materials Inventory, December 31, 20Y5
Leather	18,000 sq. yds.	20,000 sq. yds.
Lining	15,000 sq. yds.	12,000 sq. yds.

The estimated price per square yard of leather and lining during 20Y5 is shown below.

	Price per Square Yard
Leather	$4.50
Lining	1.20

Exhibit 10 illustrates the direct materials purchases budget for Cobbler Inc.

EXHIBIT 10

Direct Materials Purchases Budget

	A	B	C	D	E
1		Cobbler Inc.			
2		Direct Materials Purchases Budget			
3		For the Year Ending December 31, 20Y5			
4			Direct Materials		
5			Leather	Lining	Total
6	Square yards required for production:				
7	Shoes (Note A)		156,000	52,000	
8	Boots (Note B)		365,000	146,000	
9	Plus desired inventory, December 31, 20Y5		20,000	12,000	
10	Total		541,000	210,000	
11	Less estimated inventory, January 1, 20Y5		18,000	15,000	
12	Total square yards to be purchased		523,000	195,000	
13	Unit price (per square yard)		× $4.50	× $1.20	
14	Total direct materials to be purchased		$2,353,500	$234,000	$2,587,500
15					
16	Note A:	Leather: 520,000 units × 0.30 sq. yd. per unit = 156,000 sq. yds.			
17		Lining: 520,000 units × 0.10 sq. yd. per unit = 52,000 sq. yds.			
18					
19	Note B:	Leather: 292,000 units × 1.25 sq. yds. per unit = 365,000 sq. yds.			
20		Lining: 292,000 units × 0.50 sq. yd. per unit = 146,000 sq. yds.			

The timing of the direct materials purchases should be coordinated between the Purchasing and Production departments so that production is not interrupted.

Direct Labor Cost Budget The **direct labor cost budget** estimates the direct labor hours and related cost needed to support budgeted production.

Cobbler Inc. estimates that the following direct labor hours are needed to produce shoes and boots:

Shoes	Boots
Cutting Department: 0.10 hr. per unit	Cutting Department: 0.15 hr. per unit
Sewing Department: 0.25 hr. per unit	Sewing Department: 0.40 hr. per unit

The estimated direct labor hourly rates for the Cutting and Sewing departments during 20Y5 are shown below.

	Hourly Rate
Cutting Department	$12.00
Sewing Department	15.00

Exhibit 11 illustrates the direct labor cost budget for Cobbler Inc.

EXHIBIT 11

Direct Labor Cost Budget

	A	B	C	D	E
1		Cobbler Inc.			
2		Direct Labor Cost Budget			
3		For the Year Ending December 31, 20Y5			
4			Cutting	Sewing	Total
5	Hours required for production:				
6	Shoes (Note A)		52,000	130,000	
7	Boots (Note B)		43,800	116,800	
8	Total		95,800	246,800	
9	Hourly rate		× $12.00	× $15.00	
10	Total direct labor cost		$1,149,600	$3,702,000	$4,851,600
11					
12	Note A: Cutting Department: 520,000 units × 0.10 hr. per unit = 52,000 hrs.				
13	Sewing Department: 520,000 units × 0.25 hr. per unit = 130,000 hrs.				
14					
15	Note B: Cutting Department: 292,000 units × 0.15 hr. per unit = 43,800 hrs.				
16	Sewing Department: 292,000 units × 0.40 hr. per unit = 116,800 hrs.				

As shown in Exhibit 11, for Cobbler Inc. to produce 520,000 shoes, 52,000 hours (520,000 units × 0.10 hr. per unit) of labor are required in the Cutting Department. Likewise, to produce 292,000 boots, 43,800 hours (292,000 units × 0.15 hour per unit) of labor are required in the Cutting Department. Thus, the estimated total direct labor cost for the Cutting Department is $1,149,600 [(52,000 hrs. + 43,800 hrs.) × $12.00 per hr.)]. In a similar manner, the direct labor hours and cost for the Sewing Department are determined.

The direct labor needs should be coordinated between the Production and Personnel departments so that there will be enough labor available for production.

Factory Overhead Cost Budget The **factory overhead cost budget** estimates the cost for each item of factory overhead needed to support budgeted production. Exhibit 12 illustrates the factory overhead cost budget for Cobbler Inc.

EXHIBIT 12

Factory Overhead Cost Budget

	A	B
1	Cobbler Inc.	
2	Factory Overhead Cost Budget	
3	For the Year Ending December 31, 20Y5	
4	Indirect factory wages	$ 732,800
5	Supervisor salaries	360,000
6	Power and light	306,000
7	Depreciation of plant and equipment	288,000
8	Indirect materials	182,800
9	Maintenance	140,280
10	Insurance and property taxes	79,200
11	Total factory overhead cost	$2,089,080

The factory overhead cost budget shown in Exhibit 12 may be supported by departmental schedules. Such schedules normally separate factory overhead costs into fixed and variable costs to better enable department managers to monitor and evaluate costs during the year.

The factory overhead cost budget should be integrated with the production budget to ensure that production is not interrupted during the year.

Cost of Goods Sold Budget The **cost of goods sold budget** is prepared by integrating the following budgets:

1. Direct materials purchases budget (Exhibit 10)
2. Direct labor cost budget (Exhibit 11)
3. Factory overhead cost budget (Exhibit 12)

In addition, the estimated and desired inventories for direct materials, work in process, and finished goods must be integrated into the cost of goods sold budget.

Cobbler Inc. expects the following direct materials, work in process, and finished goods inventories:

	Estimated Inventory, January 1, 20Y5	Desired Inventory, December 31, 20Y5
Direct materials:		
Leather	$ 81,000 (18,000 sq. yds. × $4.50)	$ 90,000 (20,000 sq. yds. × $4.50)
Lining	18,000 (15,000 sq. yds. × $1.20)	14,400 (12,000 sq. yds. × $1.20)
Total direct materials	$ 99,000	$ 104,400
Work in process:	$ 214,400	$ 220,000
Finished goods:	$1,095,600	$1,565,000

Exhibit 13 illustrates the cost of goods sold budget for Cobbler Inc. It indicates that total manufacturing costs of $9,522,780 are budgeted to be incurred in 20Y5. Of this total, $2,582,100 is budgeted for direct materials, $4,851,600 is budgeted for direct labor, and $2,089,080 is budgeted for factory overhead. After considering work in process inventories, the total budgeted cost of goods manufactured and transferred to finished goods during 20Y5 is $9,517,180. Based on expected sales, the budgeted cost of goods sold is $9,047,780.

Cost of Goods Sold Budget   EXHIBIT 13

	A	B	C	D	E	F	
1		Cobbler Inc.					
2		Cost of Goods Sold Budget					
3		For the Year Ending December 31, 20Y5					
4	Finished goods inventory, January 1, 20Y5					$ 1,095,600	
5	Work in process inventory, January 1, 20Y5				$ 214,400		
6	Direct materials:						
7	Direct materials inventory,						
8	January 1, 20Y5			$ 99,000			
9	Direct materials purchases (from Exhibit 10)			2,587,500			Direct materials
10	Cost of direct materials available for use			$2,686,500			purchases
11	Less direct materials inventory,						budget
12	December 31, 20Y5			104,400			
13	Cost of direct materials placed in production			$2,582,100			Direct labor
14	Direct labor (from Exhibit 11)			4,851,600			cost budget
15	Factory overhead (from Exhibit 12)			2,089,080			Factory overhead
16	Total manufacturing costs				9,522,780		cost budget
17	Total work in process during period				$9,737,180		
18	Less work in process inventory,						
19	December 31, 20Y5				220,000		
20	Cost of goods manufactured					9,517,180	
21	Cost of finished goods available for sale					$10,612,780	
22	Less finished goods inventory,						
23	December 31, 20Y5					1,565,000	
24	Cost of goods sold					$ 9,047,780	
25							

Selling and Administrative Expenses Budget The sales budget is often used as the starting point for the selling and administrative expenses budget. For example, a budgeted increase in sales may require more advertising expenses.

Exhibit 14 illustrates the selling and administrative expenses budget for Cobbler Inc. The selling and administrative expenses budget shown in Exhibit 14 is normally supported by departmental schedules. For example, an advertising expense schedule for the Marketing Department could include the advertising media to be used (newspaper, direct mail, television), quantities (column inches, number of pieces, minutes), the cost per unit, and related costs per unit.

EXHIBIT 14

Selling and Administrative Expenses Budget

	A	B	C
1	Cobbler Inc.		
2	Selling and Administrative Expenses Budget		
3	For the Year Ending December 31, 20Y5		
4	Selling expenses:		
5	Sales salaries expense	$715,000	
6	Advertising expense	360,000	
7	Travel expense	115,000	
8	Total selling expenses		$1,190,000
9	Administrative expenses:		
10	Officers' salaries expense	$360,000	
11	Office salaries expense	258,000	
12	Office rent expense	34,500	
13	Office supplies expense	17,500	
14	Miscellaneous administrative expenses	25,000	
15	Total administrative expenses		695,000
16	Total selling and administrative expenses		$1,885,000

Budgeted Income Statement

The budgeted income statement is shown in Exhibit 15.

EXHIBIT 15   Budgeted Income Statement

	A	B	C	
1	Cobbler Inc.			
2	Budgeted Income Statement			
3	For the Year Ending December 31, 20Y5			
4	Revenue from sales (from Exhibit 8)		$13,336,000	← Sales budget
5	Cost of goods sold (from Exhibit 13)		9,047,780	← Cost of goods sold budget
6				
7	Gross profit		$ 4,288,220	
8	Selling and administrative expenses:			
9	Selling expenses (from Exhibit 14)	$1,190,000		← Selling and administrative expenses budget
10	Administrative expenses (from Exhibit 14)	695,000		
11	Total selling and administrative expenses		1,885,000	
12	Income from operations		$ 2,403,220	
13	Other income:			
14	Interest revenue	$ 98,000		
15	Other expenses:			
16	Interest expense	90,000	8,000	
17	Income before income tax		$ 2,411,220	
18	Income tax		600,000	
19	Net income		$ 1,811,220	
20				

The budgeted income statement is prepared by integrating the following budgets:

1. Sales budget (Exhibit 8)
2. Cost of goods sold budget (Exhibit 13)
3. Selling and administrative expenses budget (Exhibit 14)

In addition, estimates of other income, other expense, and income tax are also integrated into the budgeted income statement.

Exhibit 15 illustrates the budgeted income statement for Cobbler Inc. This budget summarizes the budgeted operating activities of the company. In doing so, the budgeted income statement allows management to assess the effects of estimated sales, costs, and expenses on profits for the year.

Balance Sheet Budgets

While the income statement budgets reflect the operating activities of the company, the balance sheet budgets reflect the financing and investing activities. In this section, the following balance sheet budgets are described and illustrated:

1. Cash budget (financing activity)
2. Capital expenditures budget (investing activity)

Cash Budget The **cash budget** estimates the expected receipts (inflows) and payments (outflows) of cash for a period of time. The cash budget is integrated with the various operating budgets. In addition, the capital expenditures budget, dividends, and equity or long-term debt financing plans of the company affect the cash budget.

To illustrate, a monthly cash budget for January, February, and March 20Y5 for Cobbler Inc. is prepared. The preparation of the cash budget begins by estimating cash receipts.

Estimated Cash Receipts The primary source of estimated cash receipts is from cash sales and collections on account. In addition, cash receipts may be obtained from plans to issue equity or debt financing as well as other sources such as interest revenue.

To estimate cash receipts from cash sales and collections on account, a *schedule of collections from sales* is prepared. To illustrate, the following data for Cobbler Inc. are used:

	January	February	March
Sales:			
Budgeted sales	$1,080,000	$1,240,000	$970,000
Percent of cash sales	10%	10%	10%
Accounts receivable, January 1, 20Y5	$ 370,000		
Receipts from sales on account:			
From prior month's sales on account	40%		
From current month's sales on account	60		
	100%		

Using the preceding data, the schedule of collections from sales is prepared, as shown in Exhibit 16. Cash sales are determined by multiplying the percent of cash sales by the monthly budgeted sales. The cash receipts from sales on account are determined by adding the cash received from the prior month's sales on account (40%) and the cash received from the current month's sales

EXHIBIT 16

Schedule of Collections from Sales

	A	B	C	D	E
1		Cobbler Inc.			
2		Schedule of Collections from Sales			
3		For the Three Months Ending March 31, 20Y5			
4			January	February	March
5	Receipts from cash sales:				
6		Cash sales (10% × current month's sales—			
7		Note A)	$108,000	$ 124,000	$ 97,000
8					
9	Receipts from sales on account:				
10		Collections from prior month's sales (40% of			
11		previous month's credit sales—Note B)	$370,000	$ 388,800	$446,400
12		Collections from current month's sales (60%			
13		of current month's credit sales—Note C)	583,200	669,600	523,800
14	Total receipts from sales on account		$953,200	$1,058,400	$970,200
15					
16	Note A:	$108,000 = $1,080,000 × 10%			
17		$124,000 = $1,240,000 × 10%			
18		$ 97,000 = $ 970,000 × 10%			
19					
20	Note B:	$370,000, given as January 1, 20Y5, Accounts Receivable balance			
21		$388,800 = $1,080,000 × 90% × 40%			
22		$446,400 = $1,240,000 × 90% × 40%			
23					
24	Note C:	$583,200 = $1,080,000 × 90% × 60%			
25		$669,600 = $1,240,000 × 90% × 60%			
26		$523,800 = $ 970,000 × 90% × 60%			

on account (60%). To simplify, it is assumed that all accounts receivable are collected.

Estimated Cash Payments Estimated cash payments must be budgeted for operating costs and expenses such as manufacturing costs, selling expenses, and administrative expenses. In addition, estimated cash payments may be planned for capital expenditures, dividends, interest payments, or long-term debt payments.

To estimate cash payments for manufacturing costs, a *schedule of payments for manufacturing costs* is prepared. To illustrate, the following data for Cobbler Inc. are used:

	January	February	March
Manufacturing Costs:			
Budgeted manufacturing costs	$840,000	$780,000	$812,000
Depreciation on machines included in manufacturing costs	24,000	24,000	24,000
Accounts Payable:			
Accounts payable, January 1, 20Y5	$190,000		
Payments of manufacturing costs on account:			
From prior month's manufacturing costs	25%		
From current month's manufacturing costs	75		
	100%		

Using the preceding data, the schedule of payments for manufacturing costs is prepared, as shown in Exhibit 17. The cash payments are determined by adding the cash paid on costs incurred from the prior month (25%) to the cash paid on costs incurred in the current month (75%). The $24,000 of depreciation is excluded from all computations, since depreciation does not require a cash payment.

EXHIBIT 17

Schedule of Payments for Manufacturing Costs

	A	B	C	D	E
1		Cobbler Inc.			
2		Schedule of Payments for Manufacturing Costs			
3		For the Three Months Ending March 31, 20Y5			
4			January	February	March
5	Payments of prior month's manufacturing costs				
6	{[25% × previous month's manufacturing costs				
7	(less depreciation)]—Note A}		$190,000	$204,000	$189,000
8	Payments of current month's manufacturing costs				
9	{[75% × current month's manufacturing costs				
10	(less depreciation)]—Note B}		612,000	567,000	591,000
11	Total payments		$802,000	$771,000	$780,000
12					
13	Note A: $190,000, given as January 1, 20Y5, Accounts Payable balance				
14	$204,000 = ($840,000 − $24,000) × 25%				
15	$189,000 = ($780,000 − $24,000) × 25%				
16					
17	Note B: $612,000 = ($840,000 − $24,000) × 75%				
18	$567,000 = ($780,000 − $24,000) × 75%				
19	$591,000 = ($812,000 − $24,000) × 75%				

Completing the Cash Budget Assume the additional data for Cobbler Inc. shown below.

Cash balance on January 1, 20Y5	$280,000
Quarterly taxes paid on March 31, 20Y5	150,000
Quarterly interest expense paid on January 10, 20Y5	22,500
Quarterly interest revenue received on March 21, 20Y5	24,500
Sewing equipment purchased in February 20Y5	274,000

Selling and administrative expenses (paid in month incurred):

January	February	March
$160,000	$165,000	$145,000

Using the preceding data, the *cash budget* is prepared, as shown in Exhibit 18. Cobbler Inc. has estimated that a *minimum cash balance* of $340,000 is required at the end of each month to support its operations. This minimum cash balance is compared to the estimated ending cash balance for each month. In this way, any expected cash excess or deficiency is determined.

Exhibit 18 indicates that Cobbler expects a cash excess at the end of January of $16,700. This excess could be invested in temporary income-producing securities such as U.S. Treasury bills or notes. In contrast, the estimated cash

EXHIBIT 18 Cash Budget

	A	B	C	D	
1	Cobbler Inc.				
2	Cash Budget				
3	For the Three Months Ending March 31, 20Y5				
4		January	February	March	
5	Estimated cash receipts from:				
6	Cash sales (from Exhibit 16)	$ 108,000	$ 124,000	$ 97,000	→ Schedule of
7	Collections of accounts receivable				collections
8	(from Exhibit 16)	953,200	1,058,400	970,200	from sales
9	Interest revenue			24,500	
10	Total cash receipts	$1,061,200	$1,182,400	$1,091,700	
11	Estimated cash payments for:				
12	Manufacturing costs (from Exhibit 17)	$ 802,000	$ 771,000	$ 780,000	← Schedule of cash
13	Selling and administrative expenses	160,000	165,000	145,000	payments for
14	Capital additions		274,000		manufacturing
15	Interest expense	22,500			costs
16	Income taxes			150,000	
17	Total cash payments	$ 984,500	$1,210,000	$1,075,000	
18	Cash increase (decrease)	$ 76,700	$ (27,600)	$ 16,700	
19	Cash balance at beginning of month	280,000	356,700	329,100	
20	Cash balance at end of month	$ 356,700	$ 329,100	$ 345,800	
21	Minimum cash balance	340,000	340,000	340,000	
22	Excess (deficiency)	$ 16,700	$ (10,900)	$ 5,800	

deficiency at the end of February of $10,900 might require Cobbler Inc. to borrow cash from its bank.

Capital Expenditures Budget The **capital expenditures budget** summarizes plans for acquiring fixed assets. Such expenditures are necessary as machinery and other fixed assets wear out or become obsolete. In addition, purchasing additional fixed assets may be necessary to meet increasing demand for the company's product.

To illustrate, a five-year capital expenditures budget for Cobbler Inc. is shown in Exhibit 19.

EXHIBIT 19

Capital Expenditures Budget

	A	B	C	D	E	F
1	Cobbler Inc.					
2	Capital Expenditures Budget					
3	For the Five Years Ending December 31, 20Y9					
4	Item	20Y5	20Y6	20Y7	20Y8	20Y9
5	Machinery—Cutting Department	$400,000			$280,000	$360,000
6	Machinery—Sewing Department	274,000	$260,000	$560,000	200,000	
7	Office equipment		90,000			60,000
8	Total	$674,000	$350,000	$560,000	$480,000	$420,000

As shown in Exhibit 19, capital expenditures budgets are often prepared for five to ten years into the future. This is necessary since fixed assets often must be ordered years in advance. Likewise, it could take years to construct new buildings or other production facilities.

The capital expenditures budget should be integrated with the operating and financing budgets. For example, depreciation of new manufacturing equipment affects the factory overhead cost budget. The plans for financing the capital expenditures also affect the cash budget.

Budgeted Balance Sheet

The budgeted balance sheet is prepared based on the operating, financing, and investing budgets of the master budget. The budgeted balance sheet is dated as of the end of the budget period and is similar to a normal balance sheet except that estimated amounts are used. For this reason, a budgeted balance sheet for Cobbler Inc. is not illustrated.

Standards

Obj 3

Describe the types of standards and how they are established.

Standards are performance goals. Manufacturing companies normally use **standard cost** for each of the three following product costs:

1. Direct materials
2. Direct labor
3. Factory overhead

Accounting systems that use standards for product costs are called **standard cost systems**. Standard cost systems enable management to determine the following:

1. How much a product *should* cost (standard cost)
2. How much it does cost (actual cost)

When actual costs are compared with standard costs, the exceptions or cost variances are reported. This reporting by the *principle of exceptions* allows management to focus on correcting the cost variances.

Drivers for **United Parcel Service (UPS)** are expected to drive a standard distance per day. Salespersons for **The Limited** are expected to meet sales standards.

Setting Standards

The standard-setting process normally requires the joint efforts of accountants, engineers, and other management personnel. The accountant converts the results of judgments and process studies into dollars and cents. Engineers with the aid of operation managers identify the materials, labor, and machine requirements needed to produce a product. For example, engineers estimate direct materials by studying the product specifications and estimating normal spoilage. Time and motion studies may be used to determine the direct labor required for each manufacturing operation. Engineering studies may also be used to determine standards for factory overhead, such as the amount of power needed to operate machinery.

Setting standards often begins with analyzing past operations. However, caution must be used when relying on past cost data. For example, inefficiencies may be contained within past costs. In addition, changes in technology, machinery, or production methods may make past costs irrelevant for future operations.

Standards may be integrated into computerized manufacturing operations so that variances are automatically detected and reported and operations are adjusted during manufacturing.

Types of Standards

Kaizen costing uses ideal standards to motivate changes and improvement. *Kaizen* is a Japanese term meaning "continuous improvement."

Standards imply an acceptable level of production efficiency. One of the major objectives in setting standards is to motivate employees to achieve efficient operations.

Tight, unrealistic standards may have a negative impact on performance. This is because employees may become frustrated with an inability to meet the standards and may give up trying to do their best. Standards that can be achieved only under perfect operating conditions, such as no idle time, no machine breakdowns, and no materials spoilage, are called **ideal standards** or **theoretical standards**.

Standards that are too loose might not motivate employees to perform at their best. This is because the standard level of performance can be reached too easily. As a result, operating performance may be lower than what could be achieved.

Currently attainable standards, sometimes called *normal standards,* are standards that can be attained with reasonable effort. Such standards, which are used by most companies, allow for normal production difficulties and mistakes. For example, currently attainable standards allow for normal materials spoilage and machine breakdowns. When reasonable standards are used, employees focus more on cost and are more likely to put forth their best efforts.

An example from the game of golf illustrates the distinction between ideal and normal standards. In golf, "par" is an ideal standard for most players. Each player's USGA (United States Golf Association) handicap is the player's normal standard. The motivation of average players is to beat their handicaps because beating par is unrealistic for most players.

The difference between currently attainable and ideal standards is illustrated below.

Currently attainable (personal best)

Ideal (world record)

Reviewing and Revising Standards

Standard costs should be periodically reviewed to ensure that they reflect current operating conditions. Standards should not be revised, however, just because they differ from actual costs. For example, the direct labor standard would not be revised just because employees are unable to meet properly set standards. On the other hand, standards should be revised when prices, product designs, labor rates, or manufacturing methods change.

Criticisms of Standard Costs

Some criticisms of using standard costs for performance evaluation include the following:

1. Standards limit operating improvements by discouraging improvement beyond the standard.
2. Standards are too difficult to maintain in a dynamic manufacturing environment, resulting in "stale standards."
3. Standards can cause employees to lose sight of the larger objectives of the organization by focusing only on efficiency improvement.
4. Standards can cause employees to unduly focus on their own operations to the possible harm of other operations that rely on them.

Regardless of these criticisms, standards are widely used. In addition, standard costs are only one part of the performance evaluation system used by most companies. As discussed in this chapter, other nonfinancial performance measures are often used to supplement standard costs, with the result that many of the preceding criticisms are overcome.

Aluminum beverage cans were redesigned to taper slightly at the top of the can, which reduces the amount of aluminum required per can. As a result, beverage can manufacturers reduced the standard amount of aluminum per can.

Integrity, Objectivity, and Ethics in Business

COMPANY REPUTATION: THE BEST OF THE BEST

Harris Interactive annually ranks American corporations in terms of reputation. The ranking is based on how respondents rate corporations on 20 attributes in six major areas. The six areas are emotional appeal, products and services, financial performance, workplace environment, social responsibility, and vision and leadership. What are the five highest ranked companies in its 2011 survey? The five highest (best) ranked companies were Google, Johnson & Johnson, 3M, Berkshire Hathaway, and Apple.

Source: Harris Interactive, April 2011.

Budgetary Performance Evaluation

Obj | 4

Describe and illustrate how standards are used in budgeting.

As discussed earlier in this chapter, the master budget assists a company in planning, directing, and controlling performance. The control function, or budgetary performance evaluation, compares the actual performance against the budget.

To illustrate, Cowpoke Inc., a manufacturer of blue jeans, uses standard costs in its budgets. The standards for direct materials, direct labor, and factory overhead are separated into the following two components.

1. Standard price
2. Standard quantity

The standard cost per unit for direct materials, direct labor, and factory overhead is computed as follows:

$$\text{Standard Cost per Unit} = \text{Standard Price} \times \text{Standard Quantity}$$

Cowpoke's standard costs per unit for its XL jeans are shown in Exhibit 20.

EXHIBIT 20

Standards Cost for XL Jeans

Manufacturing Costs	Standard Price	×	Standard Quantity per Pair	=	Standard Cost per Pair of XL Jeans
Direct materials	$5.00 per sq. yd.		1.5 sq. yds.		$ 7.50
Direct labor	$9.00 per hr.		0.80 hr. per pair		7.20
Factory overhead	$6.00 per hr.		0.80 hr. per pair		4.80
Total standard cost per pair					$19.50

As shown in Exhibit 20, the standard cost per pair of XL jeans is $19.50, which consists of $7.50 for direct materials, $7.20 for direct labor, and $4.80 for factory overhead.

The standard price and standard quantity are separated for each product cost. For example, Exhibit 20 indicates that for each pair of XL jeans, the standard price for direct materials is $5.00 per square yard and the standard quantity is 1.5 square yards. The standard price and quantity are separated because the department responsible for their control is normally different. For example, the direct materials price per square yard is controlled by the Purchasing Department, and the direct materials quantity per pair is controlled by the Production Department.

As illustrated earlier in this chapter, the master budget is prepared based on planned sales and production. The budgeted costs for materials purchases, direct labor, and factory overhead are determined by multiplying their standard costs per unit by the planned level of production. Budgeted (standard) costs are then compared to actual costs during the year for control purposes.

Budget Performance Report

The report that summarizes actual costs, standard costs, and the differences for the units produced is called a **budget performance report**. To illustrate, assume that Cowpoke Inc. produced the following pairs of jeans during June 20Y8:

XL jeans produced and sold	5,000 pairs
Actual costs incurred in June:	
Direct materials	$ 40,150
Direct labor	38,500
Factory overhead	22,400
Total costs incurred	$101,050

Exhibit 21 illustrates the budget performance report for June for Cowpoke Inc. The report summarizes the actual costs, standard costs, and the differences for each product cost. The differences between actual and standard costs are called **cost variances**. A **favorable cost variance** occurs when the actual cost is less than the standard cost. An **unfavorable cost variance** occurs when the actual cost exceeds the standard cost.

The budget performance report shown in Exhibit 21 is based on the actual units produced in June of 5,000 XL jeans. Even though 6,000 XL jeans might have been *planned* for production, the budget performance report is based on *actual* production.

EXHIBIT 21

Budget Performance Report

Cowpoke Inc.
Budget Performance Report
For the Month Ended June 30, 20Y8

Manufacturing Costs	Actual Costs	Standard Cost at Actual Volume (5,000 pairs of XL Jeans)*	Cost Variance— (Favorable) Unfavorable
Direct materials	$ 40,150	$37,500	$ 2,650
Direct labor	38,500	36,000	2,500
Factory overhead	22,400	24,000	(1,600)
Total manufacturing costs	$101,050	$97,500	$ 3,550

*5,000 pairs × $7.50 per pair = $37,500
5,000 pairs × $7.20 per pair = $36,000
5,000 pairs × $4.80 per pair = $24,000

Manufacturing Cost Variances

The **total manufacturing cost variance** is the difference between total standard costs and total actual cost for the units produced. As shown in Exhibit 21, the total manufacturing cost unfavorable variance and the variance for each product cost are as follows:

	Cost Variance (Favorable) Unfavorable
Direct materials	$ 2,650
Direct labor	2,500
Factory overhead	(1,600)
Total manufacturing variance	$ 3,550

For control purposes, each product cost variance is separated into two additional variances as shown in Exhibit 22. The total direct materials variance is separated into a *price* and *quantity* variance. This is because standard and actual direct materials costs are computed as follows:

Cost		Price		Quantity
Actual Direct Materials Cost	=	Actual Price	×	Actual Quantity
− Standard Direct Materials Cost	=	− Standard Price	×	− Standard Quantity
Direct Materials Cost Variance	=	Price Difference	×	Quantity Difference

Thus, the actual and standard direct materials costs may differ because of either a price difference (variance) or a quantity difference (variance).

Likewise, the total direct labor variance is separated into a *rate* and a *time* variance. This is because standard and actual direct labor costs are computed as follows:

Cost		Rate		Time
Actual Direct Labor Cost	=	Actual Rate	×	Actual Time
− Standard Direct Labor Cost	=	− Standard Rate	×	− Standard Time
Direct Labor Cost Variance	=	Rate Difference	×	Time Difference

EXHIBIT 22 **Manufacturing Cost Variances**

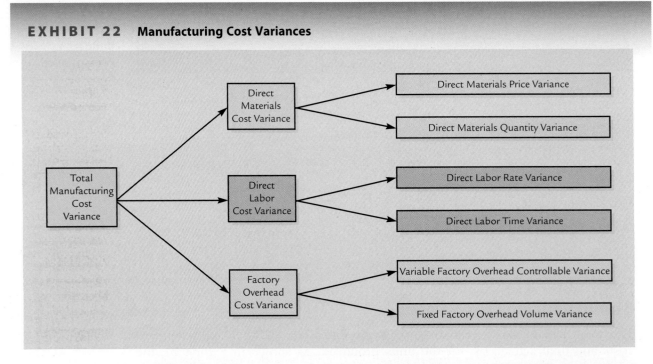

Therefore, the actual and standard direct labor costs may differ because of either a rate difference (variance) or a time difference (variance).

The total factory overhead variance is separated into a *controllable* and *volume* variance. Because factory overhead has fixed and variable cost elements, it is more complex to analyze than direct materials and direct labor, which are variable costs. The controllable variance is similar to a price or rate variance, and the volume variance is similar to the quantity or time variance.

In the next section, the price and quantity variances for direct materials and the rate and time variances for direct labor are described and illustrated. The controllable and volume variances for factory overhead are described and illustrated in the appendix to this chapter.

Obj | 5

Compute and interpret direct materials and direct labor variances.

Direct Materials and Direct Labor Variances

As indicated in the prior section, the total direct materials and direct labor variances are separated into the following variances for analysis and control purposes:

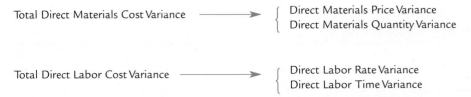

As a basis for illustration, the variances for Cowpoke Inc.'s June operations shown in Exhibit 21 are used.

Direct Materials Variances

During June, Cowpoke Inc. reported an unfavorable total direct materials cost variance of $2,650 for the production of 5,000 XL style jeans, as shown in Exhibit 21. This variance was based on the following actual and standard costs:

Actual costs	$40,150
Standard costs	37,500
Total direct materials cost variance	$ 2,650

The actual costs incurred of $40,150 consist of the following:

$$\text{Actual Direct Materials Cost} = \text{Actual Price} \times \text{Actual Quantity}$$
$$= (\$5.50 \text{ per sq. yd.}) \times (7,300 \text{ sq. yds.})$$
$$= \$40,150$$

The standard costs of $37,500 consist of the following:

$$\text{Standard Direct Materials Cost} = \text{Standard Price} \times \text{Standard Quantity}$$
$$= (\$5.00 \text{ per sq. yd.}) \times (7,500 \text{ sq. yds.})$$
$$= \$37,500$$

The standard price of $5.00 per square yard is taken from Exhibit 20. In addition, Exhibit 20 indicates that 1.5 square yards is the standard for producing one pair of XL jeans. Thus, 7,500 (5,000 × 1.5) square yards is the standard for producing 5,000 pairs of XL jeans.

Comparing the actual and standard cost computations shown above indicates that the total direct materials unfavorable cost variance of $2,650 is caused by the following:

1. A price per square yard of $0.50 ($5.50 − $5.00) more than standard
2. A quantity usage of 200 square yards (7,300 sq. yds. − 7,500 sq. yds.) less than standard

The impact of these differences from standard is reported and analyzed as a direct materials *price* variance and direct materials *quantity* variance.

Direct Materials Price Variance   The **direct materials price variance** is computed as follows:

$$\text{Direct Materials Price Variance} = (\text{Actual Price} - \text{Standard Price})$$
$$\times \text{Actual Quantity}$$

If the actual price per unit exceeds the standard price per unit, the variance is unfavorable. This positive amount (unfavorable variance) can be thought of as increasing costs. If the actual price per unit is less than the standard price per unit, the variance is favorable. This negative amount (favorable variance) can be thought of as decreasing costs.

To illustrate, the direct materials price variance for Cowpoke Inc. is computed as follows:[2]

$$\text{Direct Materials Price Variance} = (\text{Actual Price} - \text{Standard Price})$$
$$\times \text{Actual Quantity}$$
$$= (\$5.50 - \$5.00) \times 7,300 \text{ sq. yds.}$$
$$= \$3,650 \text{ Unfavorable Variance}$$

Most restaurants use standards to control the amount of food served to customers. For example, **Darden Restaurants, Inc.**, operator of the **Red Lobster** chain, establishes standards for the number of shrimp, scallops, or clams on a seafood plate.

---

2. To simplify, it is assumed that there is no change in the beginning and ending materials inventories. Thus, the amount of materials budgeted for production equals the amount purchased.

As shown on the previous page, Cowpoke Inc. has an unfavorable direct materials price variance of $3,650 for June.

Direct Materials Quantity Variance The **direct materials quantity variance** is computed as follows:

Direct Materials Quantity Variance = (Actual Quantity − Standard Quantity) × Standard Price

If the actual quantity for the units produced exceeds the standard quantity, the variance is unfavorable. This positive amount (unfavorable variance) can be thought of as increasing costs. If the actual quantity for the units produced is less than the standard quantity, the variance is favorable. This negative amount (favorable variance) can be thought of as decreasing costs.

To illustrate, the direct materials quantity variance for Cowpoke Inc. is computed as follows:

Direct Materials Quantity Variance = (Actual Quantity − Standard Quantity) × Standard Price
= (7,300 sq. yds. − 7,500 sq. yds.) × $5.00
= $1,000 Favorable Variance

As shown above, Cowpoke Inc. has a favorable direct materials quantity variance of $1,000 for June.

Direct Materials Variance Relationships The relationship among the *total* direct materials cost variance, the direct materials *price* variance, and the direct materials *quantity* variance is shown in Exhibit 23.

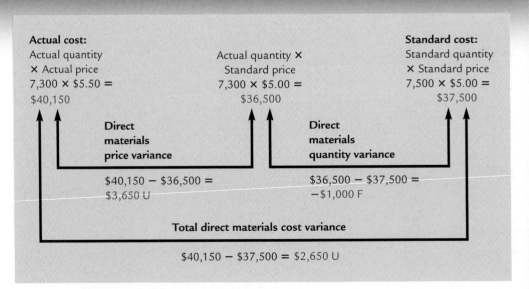

EXHIBIT 23
Direct Materials Variance Relationships

Actual cost:
Actual quantity
× Actual price
7,300 × $5.50 =
$40,150

Actual quantity ×
Standard price
7,300 × $5.00 =
$36,500

Standard cost:
Standard quantity
× Standard price
7,500 × $5.00 =
$37,500

Direct materials price variance

Direct materials quantity variance

$40,150 − $36,500 =
$3,650 U

$36,500 − $37,500 =
−$1,000 F

Total direct materials cost variance

$40,150 − $37,500 = $2,650 U

Reporting Direct Materials Variances The direct materials quantity variances should be reported to the manager responsible for the variance. For example, an unfavorable quantity variance might be caused by either of the following:

1. Equipment that has not been properly maintained
2. Low-quality (inferior) direct materials

In the first case, the operating department responsible for maintaining the equipment should be held responsible for the variance. In the second case, the Purchasing Department should be held responsible.

The price of a pound of copper has risen rapidly since the mid-2000s.

Not all variances are controllable. For example, an unfavorable materials price variance might be due to market-wide price increases. In this case, there is nothing the Purchasing Department might have done to avoid the unfavorable variance. On the other hand, if materials of the same quality could have been purchased from another supplier at the standard price, the variance was controllable.

Direct Labor Variances

During June, Cowpoke Inc. reported an unfavorable total direct labor cost variance of $2,500 for the production of 5,000 XL style jeans, as shown in Exhibit 21. This variance was based on the following actual and standard costs:

The **Internal Revenue Service** publishes a time standard for completing a tax return. The average 1040EZ return is expected to require 8.3 hours to prepare.

Actual costs	$38,500
Standard costs	36,000
Total direct labor cost variance	$ 2,500

The actual costs incurred of $38,500 consist of the following:

$$\text{Actual Direct Labor Cost} = \text{Actual Rate per Hour} \times \text{Actual Time}$$

$$= (\$10.00 \text{ per hr.}) \times (3,850 \text{ hrs.})$$

$$= \$38,500$$

The standard costs of $36,000 consist of the following:

$$\text{Standard Direct Labor Cost} = \text{Standard Rate per Hour} \times \text{Standard Time}$$

$$= (\$9.00 \text{ per hr.}) \times (4,000 \text{ hrs.})$$

$$= \$36,000$$

The standard rate of $9.00 per direct labor hour is taken from Exhibit 20. In addition, Exhibit 20 indicates that 0.80 hour is the standard time required for producing one pair of XL jeans. Thus, 4,000 (5,000 × 0.80) direct labor hours is the standard for producing 5,000 pairs of XL jeans.

Comparing the actual and standard cost computations shown above indicates that the total direct labor unfavorable cost variance of $2,500 is caused by the following:

1. A rate of $1.00 per hour ($10.00 − $9.00) more than standard
2. A quantity of 150 hours (3,850 hrs. − 4,000 hrs.) less than standard

The impact of these differences from standard is reported and analyzed as a direct labor *rate* variance and a direct labor *time* variance.

Direct Labor Rate Variance The **direct labor rate variance** is computed as follows:

Direct Labor Rate Variance = (Actual Rate per Hour − Standard Rate per Hour) × Actual Hours

If the actual rate per hour exeeds the standard rate per hour, the variance is unfavorable. This positive amount (unfavorable variance) can be thought of as increasing costs. If the actual rate per hour is less than the standard rate per hour, the variance is favorable. This negative amount (favorable variance) can be thought of as decreasing costs.

To illustrate, the direct labor rate variance for Cowpoke Inc. is computed as follows:

Direct Labor Rate Variance = (Actual Rate per Hour − Standard Rate per Hour) × Actual Hours

= ($10.00 − $9.00) × 3,850 hours

= $3,850 Unfavorable Variance

As shown above, Cowpoke Inc. has an unfavorable direct labor rate variance of $3,850 for June.

Direct Labor Time Variance The **direct labor time variance** is computed as follows:

Direct Labor Time Variance = (Actual Direct Labor Hours − Standard Direct Labor Hours) × Standard Rate per Hour

If the actual direct labor hours for the units produced exceeds the standard direct labor hours, the variance is unfavorable. This positive amount (unfavorable variance) can be thought of as increasing costs. If the actual direct labor hours for the units produced is less than the standard direct labor hours, the variance is favorable. This negative amount (favorable variance) can be thought of as decreasing costs.

To illustrate, the direct labor time variance for Cowpoke Inc. is computed as follows:

Direct Labor Time Variance = (Actual Direct Labor Hours − Standard Direct Labor Hours) × Standard Rate per Hour

= (3,850 hours − 4,000 direct labor hours) × $9.00

= −$1,350 Favorable Variance

As shown above, Cowpoke Inc. has a favorable direct labor time variance of $1,350 for June.

Direct Labor Variance Relationships The relationship among the *total* direct labor cost variance, the direct labor *rate* variance, and the direct labor *time* variance is shown in Exhibit 24.

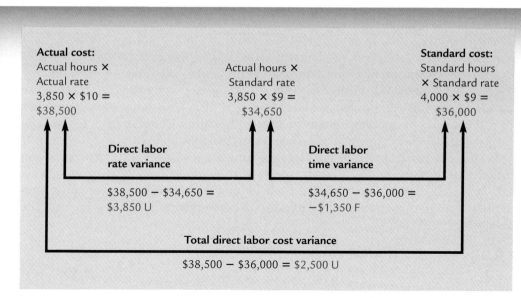

EXHIBIT 24

Direct Labor Variance Relationships

Reporting Direct Labor Variances Production supervisors are normally responsible for controlling direct labor cost. For example, an investigation could reveal the following causes for unfavorable rate and time variances:

1. An unfavorable rate variance may be caused by the improper scheduling and use of employees. In such cases, skilled, highly paid employees may be used in jobs that are normally performed by unskilled, lower-paid employees. In this case, the unfavorable rate variance should be reported to the managers who schedule work assignments.

2. An unfavorable time variance may be caused by a shortage of skilled employees. In such cases, there may be an abnormally high turnover rate among skilled employees. In this case, production supervisors with high turnover rates should be questioned as to why their employees are quitting.

Direct Labor Standards for Nonmanufacturing Activities Direct labor time standards can also be developed for use in administrative, selling, and service activities. This is most appropriate when the activity involves a repetitive task that produces a common output. In these cases, the use of standards is similar to that for a manufactured product.

To illustrate, standards could be developed for customer service personnel who process sales orders. A standard time for processing a sales order (the output) could be developed. The variance between the actual and the standard time could then be used to control sales order processing costs. Similar standards could be developed for computer help desk operators, nurses, and insurance application processors.

When labor-related activities are not repetitive, direct labor time standards are less commonly used. This often occurs when the time spent to perform the activity is not directly related to a unit of output. For example, the time spent by a senior executive or the work of a research and development scientist is not easily related to a measurable output. In these cases, the costs and expenses are normally controlled using static budgets.

Hospitals use time standards, termed *standard treatment protocols*, to evaluate the efficiency of performing hospital procedures.

Nonfinancial Performance Measures

In one company, machine operators were evaluated by a labor time standard (how fast they worked). This resulted in poor-quality products, which led the company to supplement its labor time standard with a product quality standard.

Many companies supplement standard costs and variances from standards with nonfinancial performance measures. A **nonfinancial performance measure** expresses performance in a measure other than dollars. For example, airlines use on-time performance, percent of bags lost, and number of customer complaints as nonfinancial performance measures. Such measures are often used to evaluate the time, quality, or quantity of a business activity.

Using financial and nonfinancial performance measures aids managers and employees in considering multiple performance objectives. Such measures often bring additional perspectives, such as quality of work, to evaluating performance. Some examples of nonfinancial performance measures include the following:

Nonfinancial Performance Measures

Inventory turnover
Percent on-time delivery
Elapsed time between a customer order and product delivery
Customer preference rankings compared to competitors
Response time to a service call
Time to develop new products
Employee satisfaction
Number of customer complaints

Nonfinancial measures are often linked to either the inputs or outputs of an activity or a process. A **process** is a sequence of activities for performing a task. The relationship between an activity or a process and its inputs and outputs is shown below.

To illustrate, the counter service activity of a fast-food restaurant is used. The following inputs/outputs could be identified for providing customer service:

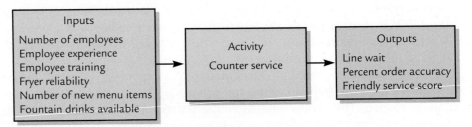

The customer service outputs of the counter service activity include the following:

1. Line wait for the customer
2. Percent order accuracy in serving the customer
3. Friendly service experience for the customer

Some of the inputs that impact the customer service outputs include the following:

1. Number of employees
2. Employee experience
3. Employee training
4. Fryer (and other cooking equipment) reliability
5. Number of new menu items
6. Fountain drink availability

A fast-food restaurant can develop a set of linked nonfinancial performance measures across inputs and outputs. The output measures tell management how the activity is performing, such as keeping the line wait to a minimum. The input measures are used to improve the output measures. For example, if the customer line wait is too long, then improving employee training or hiring more employees could improve the output (decrease customer line wait).

Appendix

Factory Overhead Variances

Factory overhead costs are analyzed differently from direct labor and direct materials costs. This is because factory overhead costs have fixed and variable cost elements. For example, indirect materials and factory supplies normally behave as a variable cost as units produced changes. In contrast, straight-line plant depreciation on factory machinery is a fixed cost.

Factory overhead costs are budgeted and controlled by separating factory overhead into fixed and variable costs. Doing so allows the preparation of flexible budgets and analysis of factory overhead controllable and volume variances.

The Factory Overhead Flexible Budget

The preparation of a flexible budget was described and illustrated earlier in this chapter. Exhibit 25 illustrates a flexible factory overhead budget for Cowpoke Inc. for June 20Y8.

Exhibit 25 indicates that the budgeted factory overhead rate for Cowpoke Inc. is $6.00, as computed below.

$$\text{Factory Overhead Rate} = \frac{\text{Budgeted Factory Overhead at Normal Capacity}}{\text{Normal Productive Capacity}}$$

$$= \frac{\$30,000}{5,000 \text{ direct labor hrs.}} = \$6.00 \text{ per direct labor hr.}$$

The normal productive capacity is expressed in terms of an activity base such as direct labor hours, direct labor cost, or machine hours. For Cowpoke Inc., 100% of normal capacity is 5,000 direct labor hours. The budgeted factory overhead cost at 100% of normal capacity is $30,000, which consists of variable overhead of $18,000 and fixed overhead of $12,000.

EXHIBIT 25

**Factory
Overhead Cost
Budget
Indicating
Standard
Factory
Overhead Rate**

	A	B	C	D	E
1	Cowpoke Inc.				
2	Factory Overhead Cost Budget				
3	For the Month Ending June 30, 20Y8				
4	Percent of normal capacity	80%	90%	100%	110%
5	Units produced	5,000	5,625	6,250	6,875
6	Direct labor hours (0.80 hr. per unit)	4,000	4,500	5,000	5,500
7	Budgeted factory overhead:				
8	Variable costs:				
9	Indirect factory wages	$ 8,000	$ 9,000	$10,000	$11,000
10	Power and light	4,000	4,500	5,000	5,500
11	Indirect materials	2,400	2,700	3,000	3,300
12	Total variable cost	$14,400	$16,200	$18,000	$19,800
13	Fixed costs:				
14	Supervisory salaries	$ 5,500	$ 5,500	$ 5,500	$ 5,500
15	Depreciation of plant				
16	and equipment	4,500	4,500	4,500	4,500
17	Insurance and property taxes	2,000	2,000	2,000	2,000
18	Total fixed cost	$12,000	$12,000	$12,000	$12,000
19	Total factory overhead cost	$26,400	$28,200	$30,000	$31,800
20					
21	Factory overhead rate per direct labor hour, $30,000/5,000 hours = $6.00				
22					

For analysis purposes, the budgeted factory overhead rate is subdivided into a variable factory overhead rate and a fixed factory overhead rate. For Cowpoke Inc., the variable overhead rate is $3.60 per direct labor hour, and the fixed overhead rate is $2.40 per direct labor hour, as computed below.

$$\text{Variable Factory Overhead} = \frac{\text{Budgeted Fixed Overhead at Normal Capacity}}{\text{Normal Productive Capacity}}$$

$$= \frac{\$18,000}{5,000 \text{ direct labor hrs.}} = \$3.60 \text{ per direct labor hr.}$$

$$\text{Fixed Factory Overhead Rate} = \frac{\text{Budgeted Variable Overhead at Normal Capacity}}{\text{Normal Productive Capacity}}$$

$$= \frac{\$12,000}{5,000 \text{ direct labor hrs.}} = \$2.40 \text{ per direct labor hr.}$$

To summarize, the budgeted factory overhead rates for Cowpoke Inc. are as follows:

Variable factory overhead rate	$3.60
Fixed factory overhead rate	2.40
Total factory overhead rate	$6.00

As mentioned earlier, factory overhead variances can be separated into a controllable variance and a volume variance as discussed in the next sections.

Variable Factory Overhead Controllable Variance

The variable factory overhead **controllable variance** is the difference between the actual variable overhead costs and the budgeted variable overhead for actual production. It is computed as shown below.

$$\text{Variable Factory Overhead Controllable Variance} = \text{Actual Variable Factory Overhead} - \text{Budgeted Variable Factory Overhead}$$

If the actual variable overhead is less than the budgeted variable overhead, the variance is favorable. If the actual variable overhead exceeds the budgeted variable overhead, the variance is unfavorable.

The **budgeted variable factory overhead** is the standard variable overhead for the *actual* units produced. It is computed as follows:

$$\text{Budgeted Variable Factory Overhead} = \text{Standard Hours for Actual Units Produced} \times \text{Variable Factory Overhead Rate}$$

To illustrate, the budgeted variable overhead for Cowpoke Inc. for June is $14,400, as computed below.

$$\text{Budgeted Variable Factory Overhead} = \text{Standard Hours for Actual Units Produced} \times \text{Variable Factory Overhead Rate}$$

$$= \text{4,000 direct labor hrs.} \times \$3.60$$
$$= \$14,400$$

The preceding computation is based on the fact that Cowpoke Inc. produced 5,000 XL jeans, which requires a standard of 4,000 (5,000 × 0.8 hr.) direct labor hours. The variable factory overhead rate of $3.60 was computed earlier. Thus, the budgeted variable factory overhead is $14,400 (4,000 direct labor hrs. × $3.60).

During June, assume that Cowpoke Inc. incurred the following actual factory overhead costs:

	Actual Costs in June
Variable factory overhead	$10,400
Fixed factory overhead	12,000
Total actual factory overhead	$22,400

Based on the actual variable factory overhead incurred in June, the variable factory overhead controllable variance is a $4,000 favorable variance, as computed below.

$$\text{Variable Factory Overhead Controllable Variance} = \text{Actual Variable Factory Overhead} - \text{Budgeted Variable Factory Overhead}$$

$$= \$10,400 - \$14,400$$
$$= -\$4,000 \text{ Favorable Variance}$$

The variable factory overhead controllable variance indicates the ability to keep the factory overhead costs within the budget limits. Since variable factory overhead costs are normally controllable at the department level, responsibility for controlling this variance usually rests with department supervisors.

Fixed Factory Overhead Volume Variance

Cowpoke Inc.'s budgeted factory overhead is based on a 100% normal capacity of 5,000 direct labor hours, as shown in Exhibit 25. This is the expected capacity that management believes will be used under normal business conditions. Exhibit 25 indicates that the 5,000 direct labor hours is less than the total available capacity of 110%, which is 5,500 direct labor hours.

The fixed factory overhead **volume variance** is the difference between the budgeted fixed overhead at 100% of normal capacity and the standard fixed overhead for the actual units produced. It is computed as follows:

$$
\begin{array}{c}
\text{Fixed Factory} \\
\text{Overhead} \\
\text{Volume Variance}
\end{array}
=
\left(
\begin{array}{c}
\text{Standard Hours} \\
\text{for 100\% of} \\
\text{Normal Capacity}
\end{array}
-
\begin{array}{c}
\text{Standard Hours} \\
\text{for Actual} \\
\text{Units Produced}
\end{array}
\right)
\times
\begin{array}{c}
\text{Fixed Factory} \\
\text{Overhead Rate}
\end{array}
$$

The volume variance measures the use of fixed overhead resources (plant and equipment). The interpretation of an unfavorable and a favorable fixed factory overhead volume variance is as follows:

1. *Unfavorable* fixed factory overhead variance. The actual units produced is *less than* 100% of normal capacity; thus, the company used its fixed overhead resources (plant and equipment) less than would be expected under normal operating conditions.
2. *Favorable* fixed factory overhead variance. The actual units produced is *more than* 100% of normal capacity; thus, the company used its fixed overhead resources (plant and equipment) more than would be expected under normal operating conditions.

To illustrate, the volume variance for Cowpoke Inc. is a $2,400 unfavorable variance, as computed below.

$$
\begin{array}{c}
\text{Fixed Factory} \\
\text{Overhead} \\
\text{Volume Variance}
\end{array}
=
\left(
\begin{array}{c}
\text{Standard Hours} \\
\text{for 100\% of} \\
\text{Normal Capacity}
\end{array}
-
\begin{array}{c}
\text{Standard Hours} \\
\text{for Actual} \\
\text{Units Produced}
\end{array}
\right)
\times
\begin{array}{c}
\text{Fixed Factory} \\
\text{Overhead Rate}
\end{array}
$$

$$
=
\left(
\begin{array}{c}
\text{5,000 direct} \\
\text{labor hrs.}
\end{array}
-
\begin{array}{c}
\text{4,000 direct} \\
\text{labor hrs.}
\end{array}
\right)
\times \$2.40
$$

$$
= \$2,400 \text{ Unfavorable Variance}
$$

Since Cowpoke Inc. produced 5,000 XL jeans during June, the standard for the actual units produced is 4,000 (5,000 × 0.80) direct labor hours. This is 1,000 hours less than the 5,000 standard hours of normal capacity. The fixed overhead rate of $2.40 was computed earlier. Thus, the unfavorable fixed factory overhead volume variance is $2,400 (1,000 direct labor hrs. × $2.40).

Exhibit 26 illustrates graphically the fixed factory overhead volume variance for Cowpoke Inc. The budgeted fixed overhead does not change and is $12,000 at all levels of production. At 100% of normal capacity (5,000 direct labor hours), the standard fixed overhead line intersects the budgeted fixed costs line. For production levels *more than* 100% of normal capacity (5,000 direct labor hours), the volume variance is *favorable*. For production levels *less than* 100% of normal capacity (5,000 direct labor hours), the volume variance is *unfavorable*.

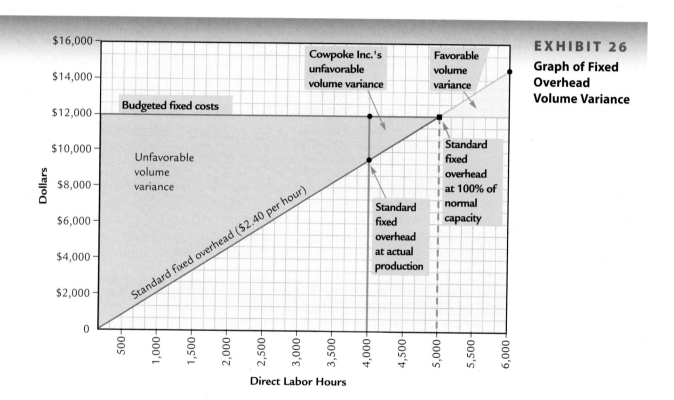

EXHIBIT 26

Graph of Fixed Overhead Volume Variance

Exhibit 26 indicates that Cowpoke Inc.'s volume variance is unfavorable in June because the actual production is 4,000 direct labor hours, or 80% of normal volume. The unfavorable volume variance of $2,400 can be viewed as the cost of the unused capacity (1,000 direct labor hours).

An unfavorable volume variance may be due to factors such as the following:

1. Failure to maintain an even flow of work
2. Machine breakdowns
3. Work stoppages caused by lack of materials or skilled labor
4. Lack of enough sales orders to keep the factory operating at normal capacity

Management should determine the causes of the unfavorable variance and consider taking corrective action. For example, a volume variance caused by an uneven flow of work could be remedied by changing operating procedures. Lack of sales orders may be corrected through increased advertising.

Favorable volume variances may not always be desirable. For example, in an attempt to create a favorable volume variance, manufacturing managers might run the factory above the normal capacity. This is favorable when the additional production can be sold. However, if the additional production cannot be sold, it must be stored as inventory, which would incur storage costs. In this case, a favorable volume variance may actually reduce company profits.

Reporting Factory Overhead Variances

The total factory overhead cost variance can also be determined as the sum of the factory overhead controllable and volume variances, as shown below for Cowpoke Inc.

Variable factory overhead controllable variance	−$4,000	Favorable Variance
Fixed factory overhead volume variance	2,400	Unfavorable Variance
Total factory overhead cost variance	−$1,600	Favorable Variance

A **factory overhead cost variance report** is useful to management in controlling factory overhead costs. Budgeted and actual costs for variable and fixed factory overhead along with the related controllable and volume variances are reported by each cost element.

Exhibit 27 illustrates a factory overhead cost variance report for Cowpoke Inc. for June.

Factory Overhead Account

The total actual factory overhead for Cowpoke Inc. as shown in Exhibit 27 is $22,400. Thus, the total factory overhead cost variance for Cowpoke Inc. for June is a $1,600 favorable variance.

At the end of the period, the factory overhead account normally has a balance. A positive balance in Factory Overhead represents underapplied overhead. Underapplied overhead occurs when actual factory overhead costs exceed the applied factory overhead. A negative balance in Factory Overhead represents overapplied overhead. Overapplied overhead occurs when actual factory overhead costs are less than the applied factory overhead.

To illustrate, the applied factory overhead for Cowpoke Inc. for the 5,000 XL jeans produced in June is $24,000, as computed below.

$$\text{Applied Factory Overhead} = \frac{\text{Standard Hours for}}{\text{Actual Units Produced}} \times \frac{\text{Total Factory}}{\text{Overhead Rate}}$$

$$= \left(\frac{5,000}{\text{jeans}} \times \frac{0.80 \text{ direct labor hr.}}{\text{per pair of jeans}} \right) \times \$6.00$$

$$= 4,000 \text{ direct labor hrs.} \times \$6.00 = \$24,000$$

EXHIBIT 27

**Factory
Overhead Cost
Variance Report**

	A	B	C	D	E
1	Cowpoke Inc.				
2	Factory Overhead Cost Variance Report				
3	For the Month Ending June 30, 20Y8				
4	Productive capacity for the month (100% of normal)	5,000 hours			
5	Actual production for the month	4,000 hours			
6					
7		**Budget**			
8		**(at Actual**		**Variances**	
9		**Production)**	**Actual**	**Favorable**	**Unfavorable**
10	Variable factory overhead costs:				
11	Indirect factory wages	$ 8,000	$ 5,100	$2,900	
12	Power and light	4,000	4,200		$ 200
13	Indirect materials	2,400	1,100	1,300	
14	Total variable factory				
15	overhead cost	$14,400	$10,400		
16	Fixed factory overhead costs:				
17	Supervisory salaries	$ 5,500	$ 5,500		
18	Depreciation of plant and				
19	equipment	4,500	4,500		
20	Insurance and property taxes	2,000	2,000		
21	Total fixed factory				
22	overhead cost	$12,000	$12,000		
23	Total factory overhead cost	$26,400	$22,400		
24	Total controllable variances			$4,200	$ 200
25					
26					
27	Net controllable variance—favorable				$4,000
28	Volume variance—unfavorable:				
29	Capacity not used at the standard rate for fixed				
30	factory overhead—1,000 × $2.40				2,400
31	Total factory overhead cost variance—favorable				$1,600
32					

The difference between the actual factory overhead and the applied factory overhead is the total factory overhead cost variance. Thus, underapplied and overapplied factory overhead account balances represent the following total factory overhead cost variances:

1. *Underapplied* Factory Overhead = *Unfavorable* Total Factory Overhead Cost Variance

2. *Overapplied* Factory Overhead = *Favorable* Total Factory Overhead Cost Variance

The factory overhead account for Cowpoke Inc. for the month ending June 30, 20Y8, is shown below.

Factory Overhead Account

Actual factory overhead ($10,400 + $12,000)	$22,400
Less applied factory overhead (4,000 hours × 6.00 per hour)	24,000
Balance, overapplied factory overhead, June 30	$ 1,600

The $1,600 overapplied factory overhead account balance shown above and the total factory cost variance shown in Exhibit 27 are the same.

The variable factory overhead controllable variance and the volume variance can be computed by comparing the factory overhead account with the budgeted total overhead for the actual level produced, as shown below.

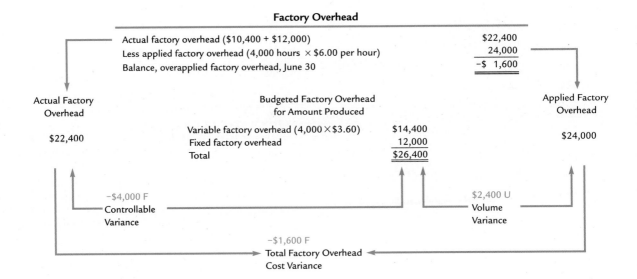

The controllable and volume variances are determined as follows:

1. The difference between the actual overhead incurred and the budgeted overhead is the *controllable* variance.

2. The difference between the applied overhead and the budgeted overhead is the *volume* variance.

If the actual factory overhead exceeds (is less than) the budgeted factory overhead, the controllable variance is unfavorable (favorable). In contrast, if the applied factory overhead is less than (exceeds) the budgeted factory overhead, the volume variance is unfavorable (favorable).

For many of the individual factory overhead costs, quantity and price variances can be computed similar to that for direct materials and direct labor. For example, the indirect factory labor cost variance may include both time and rate variances. Likewise, the indirect materials cost variance may include both a quantity variance and a price variance. Such variances are illustrated in advanced textbooks.

Key Points

1. Describe budgeting, its objectives, its impact on human behavior, and types of budget systems.

Budgeting involves (1) establishing specific goals, (2) executing plans to achieve the goals, and (3) periodically comparing actual results with these goals. In addition, budget goals should be established to avoid problems in human behavior. Thus, budgets should not be set too tightly, too loosely, or to cause goal conflict. Budgeting systems can use fiscal-year budgeting, continuous budgeting, or zero-based budgeting. Two major types of budgets are the static budget and the flexible budget. The static budget does not adjust with changes in activity while the flexible budget does adjust with changes in activity. Computers can be useful in speeding the budgetary process and in preparing timely budget performance reports. In addition, simulation models can be used to determine the impact of operating alternatives on various budgets.

2. Describe the master budget for a manufacturing company.

The master budget consists of the budgeted income statement and budgeted balance sheet. These two budgets are developed from detailed supporting budgets. The income statement supporting budgets are the sales budget, production budget, direct materials purchases budget, direct labor cost budget, factory overhead cost budget, cost of goods sold budget, and selling and administrative expenses budget. Both the cash budget and the capital expenditures budget support the budgeted balance sheet. The cash budget consists of budgeted cash receipts and budgeted cash payments. The capital expenditures budget is an important tool for planning expenditures for fixed assets.

3. Describe the types of standards and how they are established.

Standards represent performance benchmarks that can be compared to actual results in evaluating performance. Standards are developed, reviewed, and revised by accountants and engineers based on studies of operations. Standards are established so that they are neither too high nor too low but are attainable.

4. Describe and illustrate how standards are used in budgeting.

Budgets are prepared by multiplying the standard cost per unit by the planned production. To measure performance, the standard cost per unit is multiplied by the actual number of units produced, and the actual results are compared with the standard cost at actual volumes (cost variance).

5. Compute and interpret direct materials and direct labor variances.

The direct materials cost variance can be separated into a direct materials price and a quantity variance. The direct materials price variance is calculated by multiplying the actual quantity by the difference between the actual and standard price. The direct materials quantity variance is calculated by multiplying the standard price by the difference between the actual materials used and the standard materials at actual volumes.

The direct labor cost variance can be separated into a direct labor rate and time variance. The direct labor rate variance is calculated by multiplying the actual hours worked by the difference between the actual labor rate and the standard labor rate. The direct labor time variance is calculated by multiplying the standard labor rate by the difference between the actual labor hours worked and the standard labor hours at actual volumes.

6. Describe and provide examples of nonfinancial performance measures.

Many companies use a combination of financial and nonfinancial measures in order for multiple perspectives to be incorporated in evaluating performance. Combining financial and nonfinancial measures helps employees balance cost efficiency with quality and customer service performance. Nonfinancial measures are often used in conjunction with the inputs or outputs of a process or activity.

Key Terms

Budget (514)
Budget performance report (536)
Budgetary slack (515)
Budgeted variable factory overhead (547)
Capital expenditures budget (532)
Cash budget (529)
Continuous budgeting (516)
Controllable variance (547)
Cost of goods sold budget (526)
Cost variance (536)

Currently attainable standards (534)
Direct labor cost budget (525)
Direct labor rate variance (542)
Direct labor time variance (542)
Direct materials price variance (539)
Direct materials purchases budget (523)
Direct materials quantity variance (540)
Factory overhead cost budget (526)

Factory overhead cost variance report (550)
Favorable cost variance (536)
Flexible budget (518)
Goal conflict (516)
Ideal standards (534)
Master budget (520)
Nonfinancial performance measure (544)
Process (544)
Production budget (523)
Responsibility center (514)
Sales budget (522)
Standard cost (533)

Standard cost systems (533)
Standards (533)
Static budget (517)
Theoretical standards (534)
Total manufacturing cost variance (537)
Unfavorable cost variance (536)
Volume variance (548)
Zero-based budgeting (517)

Illustrative Problem

Mountain Art Inc. manufactures woven baskets for national distribution. The standard costs for the manufacture of Folk Art style baskets were as follows:

	Standard Costs	Actual Costs
Direct materials	1,500 lbs. at $35	1,600 lbs. at $32
Direct labor	4,800 hrs. at $11	4,500 hrs. at $11.80
Factory overhead	Rates per labor hour, based on 100% of normal capacity of 5,500 labor hrs.:	
	Variable cost, $2.40	$12,300 variable cost
	Fixed cost, $3.50	$19,250 fixed cost

Instructions

1. Determine the quantity variance, price variance, and total direct materials cost variance for the Folk Art style baskets.

2. Determine the time variance, rate variance, and total direct labor cost variance for the Folk Art style baskets.

3. Appendix: Determine the controllable variance, volume variance, and total factory overhead cost variance for the Folk Art style baskets.

Solution

1. **Direct Materials Cost Variance**

Quantity variance:
Direct Materials Quantity Variance = (Actual Quantity − Standard Quantity) × Standard Price
= (1,600 lbs. − 1,500 lbs.) × $35 per lb.
= $3,500 Unfavorable Variance

Price variance:
Direct Materials Price Variance = (Actual Price − Standard Price) × Actual Quantity
= ($32 per lb. − $35 per lb.) × 1,600 lbs.
= −$4,800 Favorable Variance

Total direct materials cost variance:

Direct Materials Cost Variance = Direct Materials Quantity Variance + Direct Materials Price Variance

$$= \$3,500 - \$4,800$$

$$= -\$1,300 \text{ Favorable Variance}$$

2.   **Direct Labor Cost Variance**

Time variance:

Direct Labor Time Variance = (Actual Direct Labor Hours − Standard Direct Labor Hours)
        × Standard Rate per Hour

$$= (4,500 \text{ hrs.} - 4,800 \text{ hrs.}) \times \$11 \text{ per hour}$$

$$= -\$3,300 \text{ Favorable Variance}$$

Rate variance:

Direct Labor Rate Variance = (Actual Rate per Hour − Standard Rate per Hour)
        × Actual Hours

$$= (\$11.80 - \$11.00) \times 4,500 \text{ hrs.}$$

$$= \$3,600 \text{ Unfavorable Variance}$$

Total direct labor cost variance:

Direct Labor Cost Variance = Direct Labor Time Variance + Direct Labor Rate Variance

$$= -\$3,300 + \$3,600$$

$$= \$300 \text{ Unfavorable Variance}$$

3. Appendix   **Factory Overhead Cost Variance**

Variable factory overhead—controllable variance:

$$\text{Variable Factory Overhead Controllable Variance} = \text{Actual Variable Factory Overhead} - \text{Budgeted Variable Factory Overhead}$$

$$= \$12,300 - \$11,520^*$$

$$= \$780 \text{ Unfavorable Variance}$$

* 4,800 hrs. × $2.40 per hour

Fixed factory overhead volume variance:

$$\text{Fixed Factory Overhead Volume Variance} = \left(\begin{array}{c} \text{Standard Hours for 100\%} \\ \text{of Normal Capacity} \end{array} - \begin{array}{c} \text{Standard Hours for} \\ \text{Actual Units Produced} \end{array} \right) \times \begin{array}{c} \text{Fixed Factory} \\ \text{Overhead Rate} \end{array}$$

$$= (5,500 \text{ hrs.} - 4,800 \text{ hrs.}) \times \$3.50 \text{ per hr.}$$

$$= \$2,450 \text{ Unfavorable Variance}$$

Total factory overhead cost variance:

$$\text{Factory Overhead Cost Variance} = \text{Variable Factory Overhead Controllable Variance} + \text{Fixed Factory Overhead Volume Variance}$$

$$= \$780 + \$2,450$$

$$= \$3,230 \text{ Unfavorable Variance}$$

Self-Examination Questions *(Answers appear at the end of chapter)*

1. Static budgets are often used by:
   A. production departments
   B. administrative departments
   C. responsibility centers
   D. capital projects

2. The total estimated sales for the coming year is 250,000 units. The estimated inventory at the beginning of the year is 22,500 units, and the desired inventory at the end of the year is 30,000 units. The total production indicated in the production budget is:
   A. 242,500 units
   B. 257,500 units
   C. 280,000 units
   D. 302,500 units

3. Dixon Company expects $650,000 of credit sales in March and $800,000 of credit sales in April. Dixon historically collects 70% of its sales in the month of sale and 30% in the following month. How much cash does Dixon expect to collect in April?

   A. $800,000

   B. $560,000

   C. $755,000

   D. $1,015,000

4. The actual and standard direct materials costs for producing a specified quantity of product are as follows:

Actual:	51,000 pounds at $5.05	$257,550
Standard:	50,000 pounds at $5.00	$250,000

The direct materials price variance is:

   A. $50 unfavorable

   B. $2,500 unfavorable

   C. $2,550 unfavorable

   D. $7,550 unfavorable

5. Bower Company produced 4,000 units of product. Each unit requires 0.5 standard hour. The standard labor rate is $12 per hour. Actual direct labor for the period was $22,000 (2,200 hours × $10 per hour). The direct labor time variance is:

   A. 200 hours unfavorable

   B. $2,000 unfavorable

   C. $4,000 favorable

   D. $2,400 unfavorable

Class Discussion Questions

1. What are the three major objectives of budgeting?

2. What is the manager's role in a responsibility center?

3. Briefly describe the type of human behavior problems that might arise if budget goals are set too tightly.

4. Give an example of budgetary slack.

5. What behavioral problems are associated with setting a budget too loosely?

6. What behavioral problems are associated with establishing conflicting goals within the budget?

7. When would a company use zero-based budgeting?

8. Under what circumstances would a static budget be appropriate?

9. How do computerized budgeting systems aid firms in the budgeting process?

10. What is the first step in preparing a master budget?

11. Why should the production requirements set forth in the production budget be carefully coordinated with the sales budget?

12. Why should the timing of direct materials purchases be closely coordinated with the production budget?

13. In preparing the budget for the cost of goods sold, what are the three budgets from which data on relevant estimates of quantities and costs are combined with data on estimated inventories?

14. a. Discuss the purpose of the cash budget.

    b. If the cash for the first quarter of the fiscal year indicates excess cash at the end of each of the first two months, how might the excess cash be used?

15. How does a schedule of collections from sales assist in preparing the cash budget?

16. Give an example of how the capital expenditures budget affects other operating budgets.

17. What are the basic objectives in the use of standard costs?

18. How can standards be used by management to help control costs?

19. What is meant by reporting by the "principle of exceptions," as the term is used in reference to cost control?

20. How often should standards be revised?

21. How are standards used in budgetary performance evaluation?

22. a. What are the two variances between the actual cost and the standard cost for direct materials?

    b. Discuss some possible causes of these variances.

23. The materials cost variance report for Nickols Inc. indicates a large favorable materials price variance and a significant unfavorable materials quantity variance. What might have caused these offsetting variances?

24. a. What are the two variances between the actual cost and the standard cost for direct labor?

    b. Who generally has control over the direct labor cost?

25. A new assistant controller recently was heard to remark: "All the assembly workers in this plant are covered by union contracts, so there should be no labor variances." Was the controller's remark correct? Discuss.

26. Would the use of standards be appropriate in a non-manufacturing setting, such as a fast-food restaurant?

27. Briefly explain why firms might use nonfinancial performance measures.

Exercises

E13-1 Flexible budget for selling and administrative expenses

Obj **1**

Homeport uses flexible budgets that are based on the following data:

Sales commissions	4% of sales
Advertising expense	12% of sales
Miscellaneous selling expense	$3,000 plus 2% of sales
Office salaries expense	$40,000 per month
Office supplies expense	1.5% of sales
Miscellaneous administrative expense	$1,500 per month plus 1% of sales

✔ Total selling and administrative expenses at $400,000 sales, $126,500

Prepare a flexible selling and administrative expenses budget for March for sales volumes of $400,000, $600,000, and $800,000. (Use Exhibit 5 as a model.)

E13-2 Static budget vs. flexible budget

Obj **1**

The production supervisor of the Machining Department for Paulk Company agreed to the following monthly static budget for the upcoming year:

PAULK COMPANY
Machining Department
Monthly Production Budget

Wages	$2,688,000
Utilities	196,000
Depreciation	45,000
Total	$2,929,000

✔ b. Excess of actual over budget for March, $49,250

The actual amount spent and the actual units produced in the first three months in the Machining Department were as follows:

	Amount Spent	Units Produced
January	$1,854,000	50,000
February	2,236,800	60,000
March	2,798,000	75,000

The Machining Department supervisor has been very pleased with this performance, since actual expenditures have been less than the monthly budget. However, the plant manager believes that the budget should not remain fixed for every month but should "flex" or adjust

Note: The spreadsheet icon indicates an Excel template is available on the student companion site.

to the volume of work that is produced in the Machining Department. Additional budget information for the Machining Department is as follows:

Wages per hour	$24.00
Utility cost per direct labor hour	$1.75
Direct labor hours per unit	1.4
Planned unit production	80,000

a. Prepare a flexible budget for the actual units produced for January, February, and March in the Machining Department. Assume depreciation is a fixed cost.

b. Compare the flexible budget with the actual expenditures for the first three months. What does this comparison suggest?

Obj 1

✔ Total
department cost
at 20,000 units,
$631,000

E13-3 Flexible budget for Fabrication Department

Steelcase Inc. is one of the largest manufacturers of office furniture in the United States. In Grand Rapids, Michigan, it produces filing cabinets in two departments: Fabrication and Trim Assembly. Assume the following information for the Fabrication Department:

Steel per filing cabinet	12 pounds
Direct labor per filing cabinet	45 minutes
Supervisor salaries	$175,000 per month
Depreciation	$18,000 per month
Direct labor rate	$22 per hour
Steel cost	$0.45 per pound

Prepare a flexible budget for 20,000, 25,000, and 30,000 filing cabinets for the month of May, similar to Exhibit 5, assuming that inventories are not significant.

Obj 2

✔ b. Model SJ30
total production,
16,250 units

E13-4 Sales and production budgets

Surround Audio Company manufactures two models of speakers, SJ30 and SX99. Based on the following production and sales data for April, prepare (a) a sales budget and (b) a production budget.

	SJ30	SX99
Estimated inventory (units), April 1	550	250
Desired inventory (units), April 30	800	350
Expected sales volume (units):		
East Region	7,000	3,000
West Region	9,000	4,000
Unit sales price	$80	$200

Obj 2

✔ Total professional
fees earned,
$16,005,000

E13-5 Professional fees earned budget

Salazar & Crenshaw, CPAs, offer three types of services to clients: auditing, tax, and small business accounting. Based on experience and projected growth, the following billable hours have been estimated for the year ending July 31, 20Y6:

	Billable Hours
Audit Department:	
Staff	40,000
Partners	6,000
Tax Department:	
Staff	30,000
Partners	4,500
Small Business Accounting Department:	
Staff	8,000
Partners	1,800

The average billing rate for staff is $150 per hour, and the average billing rate for partners is $350 per hour. Prepare a professional fees earned budget for Salazar & Crenshaw, CPAs, for the year ending July 31, 20Y6, using the following column headings and showing the estimated professional fees by type of service rendered:

Billable Hours	Hourly Rate	Total Revenue

E13-6   Professional labor cost budget

Based on the data in Exercise 13-5 and assuming that the average compensation per hour for staff is $50 and for partners is $200, prepare a professional labor cost budget for Salazar & Crenshaw, CPAs, for the year ending July 31, 20Y6. Use the following column headings:

Staff	Partners

Obj **2**

✔ Staff total labor cost, $3,900,000

E13-7   Direct materials purchases budget

Gino's Frozen Pizza Inc. has determined from its production budget the following estimated production volumes for 12" and 16" frozen pizzas for June:

	Units	
	12" Pizza	16" Pizza
Budgeted production volume	18,000	30,000

Obj **2**

✔ Total cheese purchases, $133,200

There are three direct materials used in producing the two types of pizza. The quantities of direct materials expected to be used for each pizza are as follows:

	12" Pizza	16" Pizza
Direct materials:		
Dough	0.75 lb. per unit	1.00 lb. per unit
Tomato	0.40	0.80
Cheese	0.60	1.10

In addition, Gino's has determined the following information about each material:

	Dough	Tomato	Cheese
Estimated inventory, June 1	4,000 lbs.	3,000 lbs.	3,400 lbs.
Desired inventory, June 30	5,500 lbs.	3,500 lbs.	4,000 lbs.
Price per pound	$0.90	$1.20	$3.00

Prepare June's direct materials purchases budget for Gino's Frozen Pizza Inc.

E13-8   Direct materials purchases budget

Coca-Cola Enterprises is the largest bottler of Coca-Cola® in North America. The company purchases Coke® and Sprite® concentrate from **The Coca-Cola Company**, dilutes and mixes the concentrate with carbonated water, and then fills the blended beverage into cans or plastic two-liter bottles. Assume that the estimated production for Coke and Sprite two-liter bottles at the Dallas, Texas, bottling plant are as follows for the month of October:

Obj **2**

✔ Concentrate budgeted purchases, $630,000

Coke	1,500,000 two-liter bottles
Sprite	800,000 two-liter bottles

In addition, assume that the concentrate costs $75 per pound for Coke and Sprite and is used at a rate of 0.20 pound per 100 liters of carbonated water in blending Coke and 0.15 pound per 100 liters of carbonated water in blending Sprite. Assume that two-liter bottles cost $0.04 per bottle and carbonated water costs $0.03 per liter.

Prepare a direct materials purchases budget for October, assuming no changes between beginning and ending inventories for all three materials.

E13-9 Direct labor cost budget

Isner Racket Company manufactures two types of tennis rackets, the Ace and Pro Tour models. The production budget for August for the two rackets is as follows:

	Ace	Pro Tour
Production budget	12,000 units	5,000 units

Both rackets are produced in two departments, Forming and Assembly. The direct labor hours required for each racket are estimated as follows:

	Forming Department	Assembly Department
Ace	0.25 hour per unit	0.40 hour per unit
Pro Tour	0.30 hour per unit	0.70 hour per unit

The direct labor rate for each department is as follows:

Forming Department	$20 per hour
Assembly Department	$14 per hour

Prepare the direct labor cost budget for August.

E13-10 Production and direct labor cost budgets

Levi Strauss & Co. manufactures slacks and jeans under a variety of brand names, such as Dockers® and 501 Jeans®. Slacks and jeans are assembled by a variety of different sewing operations. Assume that the sales budget for Dockers and 501 Jeans shows estimated sales of 62,500 and 48,000 pairs, respectively, for February. The finished goods inventory is assumed as follows:

	Dockers	501 Jeans
February 1 estimated inventory	4,500	2,000
February 28 desired inventory	5,000	2,500

Assume the following direct labor data per 10 pairs of Dockers and 501 Jeans for four different sewing operations:

	Direct Labor per 10 Pairs	
	Dockers	501 Jeans
Inseam	10 minutes	12 minutes
Outerseam	12	9
Pockets	6	6
Zipper	8	3
Total	36 minutes	30 minutes

a. Prepare a production budget for February. Prepare the budget in two columns: Dockers™ and 501 Jeans™.

b. Prepare the February direct labor cost budget for the four sewing operations, assuming a $14 wage per hour for the inseam and outerseam sewing operations and an $18 wage per hour for the pocket and zipper sewing operations. Prepare the direct labor cost budget in four columns: inseam, outerseam, pockets, and zipper.

E13-11   Factory overhead cost budget

Mickey's Candy Company budgeted the following costs for anticipated production for November:

Advertising expenses	$180,000	Production supervisor wages	$145,000
Manufacturing supplies	8,000	Production control salaries	40,000
Power and light	36,000	Executive officer salaries	300,000
Sales commissions	225,000	Materials management salaries	25,000
Factory insurance	42,000	Factory depreciation	88,000

Obj 2

✔ Total variable factory overhead costs, $254,000

Prepare a factory overhead cost budget, separating variable and fixed costs. Assume that factory insurance and depreciation are the only factory fixed costs.

E13-12   Cost of goods sold budget

The controller of Pueblo Ceramics Inc. wishes to prepare a cost of goods sold budget for April. The controller assembled the following information for constructing the cost of goods sold budget:

Obj 2

✔ Cost of goods sold, $491,900

Direct materials:	Enamel	Paint	Porcelain	Total
Total direct materials purchases budgeted for April	$35,000	$6,000	$140,000	$181,000
Estimated inventory, April 1	3,000	750	9,250	13,000
Desired inventory, April 30	3,200	1,000	10,800	15,000

Direct labor cost:	Kiln Department	Decorating Department	Total
Total direct labor cost budgeted for April	$38,000	$162,000	$200,000

Finished goods inventories:	Dish	Bowl	Figurine	Total
Estimated inventory, April 1	$4,500	$3,000	$2,500	$10,000
Desired inventory, April 30	4,000	750	1,250	6,000

Work in process inventories:	
Estimated inventory, April 1	$ 11,400
Desired inventory, April 30	9,500
Budgeted factory overhead costs for April:	
Indirect factory wages	$ 71,500
Depreciation of plant and equipment	19,000
Power and light	12,300
Indirect materials	4,200
Total	$107,000

Use the preceding information to prepare a cost of goods sold budget for April.

E13-13   Schedule of cash collections of accounts receivable

Fido & Lucy Wholesale Inc., a pet wholesale supplier, was organized on March 1. Projected sales for each of the first three months of operations are as follows:

Obj 2

March	$ 750,000
April	900,000
May	1,200,000

✔ Total cash collected in March, $390,000

The company expects to sell 20% of its merchandise for cash. Of sales on account, 40% are expected to be collected in the month of the sale, 55% in the month following the sale, and the remainder in the second month following the sale.

Prepare a schedule indicating cash collections from sales for March, April, and May.

E13-14 Schedule of cash collections of accounts receivable

Innovative Office Inc. has "cash and carry" customers and credit customers. Innovative Office estimates that 30% of monthly sales are to cash customers, while the remaining sales are to credit customers. Of the credit customers, 75% pay their accounts in the month of sale, while the remaining 25% pay their accounts in the month following the month of sale. Projected sales for the first three months of 20Y4 are as follows:

January	$1,200,000
February	1,450,000
March	1,600,000

The Accounts Receivable balance on December 31, 20Y3, was $180,000.

Prepare a schedule of cash collections from sales for January, February, and March.

E13-15 Schedule of cash payments

Peanut Learning Systems Inc. was organized on July 31, 20Y7. Projected selling and administrative expenses for each of the first three months of operations are as follows:

August	$137,000
September	165,000
October	140,000

Depreciation, insurance, and property taxes represent $30,000 of the estimated monthly expenses. The annual insurance premium was paid on July 31, and property taxes for the year will be paid in December. Sixty percent of the remainder of the expenses are expected to be paid in the month in which they are incurred, with the balance to be paid in the following month.

Prepare a schedule indicating cash payments for selling and administrative expenses for August, September, and October.

E13-16 Schedule of cash payments

Rehab Physical Therapy Inc. is planning its cash payments for operations for the second quarter (March–May). The Accrued Expenses Payable balance on March 1 is $36,000. The budgeted expenses for the next three months are as follows:

	March	April	May
Salaries	$100,000	$105,000	$110,000
Utilities	18,000	20,000	25,000
Other operating expenses	22,000	40,500	38,000
Total	$140,000	$165,500	$173,000

Other operating expenses include $7,500 of monthly depreciation expense and $1,000 of monthly insurance expense that was prepaid for the year on January 1 of the current year. Of the remaining expenses, 80% are paid in the month in which they are incurred, with the remainder paid in the following month. The Accrued Expenses Payable balance on March 1 relates to the expenses incurred in February.

Prepare a schedule of cash payments for operations for March, April, and May.

E13-17   Capital expenditures budget

Obj 2

On August 1, 20Y4, the controller of Handy Dan Tools Inc. is planning capital expenditures for the years 20Y5–20Y8. The controller interviewed several Handy Dan executives to collect the necessary information for the capital expenditures budget. Excerpts of the interviews are shown below.

✔ Total capital expenditures in 20Y5, $5,000,000

Director of Facilities: A construction contract was signed in May 20Y4 for the construction of a new factory building at a contract cost of $9,000,000. The construction is scheduled to begin in 20Y5 and be completed in 20Y6.

Vice President of Manufacturing: Once the new factory building is finished, we plan to purchase $3.6 million in equipment in late 20Y6. I expect that an additional $500,000 will be needed early in the following year (20Y7) to test and install the equipment before we can begin production. If sales continue to grow, I expect we'll need to invest another half million in equipment in 20Y8.

Vice President of Marketing: We have really been growing lately. I wouldn't be surprised if we need to expand the size of our new factory building in 20Y8 by at least 25%. Fortunately, we expect inflation to have minimal impact on construction costs over the next four years. Additionally, I would expect the cost of the expansion to be proportional to the size of the expansion.

Director of Information Systems: We need to upgrade our information systems to wireless network technology. It doesn't make sense to do this until after the new factory building is completed and producing product. During 20Y7, once the factory is up and running, we should equip the whole facility with wireless technology. I think it would cost us $400,000 today to install the technology. However, prices have been dropping by 10% per year, so it should be less expensive at a later date.

President: I am excited about our long-term prospects. My only short-term concern is financing the $5,000,000 of construction costs on the portion of the new factory building scheduled to be completed in 20Y5.

Use the interview information above to prepare a capital expenditures budget for Handy Dan Tools Inc. for the years 20Y5–20Y8.

E13-18   Standard product cost

Obj 4

Sorrento Furniture Company manufactures unfinished oak furniture. Sorrento uses a standard cost system. The direct labor, direct materials, and factory overhead standards for an unfinished dining room table are as follows:

Direct labor:	Standard rate	$21 per hr.
	Standard time per unit	2 hrs.
Direct materials (oak):	Standard price	$9.25 per bd. ft.
	Standard quantity	20 bd. ft.
Variable factory overhead:	Standard rate	$3.80 per direct labor hr.
Fixed factory overhead:	Standard rate	$4.25 per direct labor hr.

Determine the standard cost per dining room table.

Obj 4

✔ b. Direct labor cost variance, $475 U

E13-19 Budget performance report

McAlisters Bottle Company manufactures plastic two-liter bottles for the beverage industry. The cost standards per 100 two-liter bottles are as follows:

Cost Category	Standard Cost per 100 Two-Liter Bottles
Direct labor	$2.75
Direct materials	1.20
Factory overhead	0.35
Total	$4.30

At the beginning of May, McAlisters Bottle's management planned to produce 800,000 bottles. The actual number of bottles produced for May was 750,000 bottles. The actual costs for May of the current year were as follows:

Cost Category	Actual Cost for the Month Ended May 31
Direct labor	$21,100
Direct materials	9,200
Factory overhead	2,700
Total	$33,000

a. Prepare the May manufacturing standard cost budget (direct labor, direct materials, and factory overhead) for McAlisters Bottle Company, assuming planned production.

b. Prepare a budget performance report for manufacturing costs, showing the total cost variances for direct materials, direct labor, and factory overhead for May.

c. Interpret the budget performance report.

Obj 5

✔ a. Price variance, $150,000 F

E13-20 Direct materials variances

The following data relate to the direct materials cost for the production of 15,000 automobile tires:

Actual:	600,000 lbs. at $3.60	$2,160,000
Standard:	580,000 lbs. at $3.85	$2,233,000

a. Determine the price variance, quantity variance, and total direct materials cost variance.

b. To whom should the variances be reported for analysis and control?

Obj 5

E13-21 Standard direct materials cost per unit from variance data

The following data relating to direct materials cost for August of the current year are taken from the records of Happy Tots Inc., a manufacturer of plastic toys:

Quantity of direct materials used	12,000 lbs.
Actual unit price of direct materials	$2.30 per lb.
Units of finished product manufactured	5,900 units
Standard direct materials per unit of finished product	2 lbs.
Direct materials quantity variance—unfavorable	$410
Direct materials price variance—favorable	$3,000

Determine the standard direct materials cost per unit of finished product, assuming that there was no inventory of work in process at either the beginning or the end of the month.

E13-22   Standard product cost, direct materials variance

Obj 5

H.J. Heinz Company uses standards to control its materials costs. Assume that a batch of ketchup (6,000 pounds) has the following standards:

	Standard Quantity	Standard Price
Whole tomatoes	7,500 lbs.	$0.40 per lb.
Vinegar	600 gal.	1.75 per gal.
Corn syrup	50 gal.	8.00 per gal.
Salt	500 lbs.	0.70 per lb.

The actual materials in a batch may vary from the standard due to tomato characteristics. Assume that the actual quantities of materials for batch H3001 were as follows:

7,850 lbs. of tomatoes
575 gal. of vinegar
63 gal. of corn syrup
480 lbs. of salt

a. Determine the standard unit materials cost per pound for a standard batch.

b. Determine the total direct materials quantity variance for batch H3001.

E13-23   Direct labor variances

Obj 5

The following data relate to labor cost for production of smart telephones:

Actual:	4,200 hrs. at $17.20	$72,240
Standard:	4,260 hrs. at $16.75	$71,355

✔ a. Rate variance, $1,890 U

a. Determine the rate variance, time variance, and total direct labor cost variance.

b. Discuss what might have caused these variances.

E13-24   Direct labor variances

Obj 5

Death Valley Bicycle Company manufactures mountain bikes. The following data for October of the current year are available:

Quantity of direct labor used	1,100 hrs.
Actual rate for direct labor	$18.50 per hr.
Bicycles completed in October	350
Standard direct labor per bicycle	3 hrs.
Standard rate for direct labor	$19.00 per hr.
Planned bicycles for October	375

✔ Rate variance, −$550 F

Determine the direct labor rate and time variances.

E13-25   Direct materials and direct labor variances

Obj 5

At the beginning of August, Havasu Printers Company budgeted 30,000 books to be printed in August at standard direct materials and direct labor costs as follows:

Direct materials	$15,000
Direct labor	72,000
Total	$87,000

✔ Direct materials quantity variance, $1,070 U

The standard materials price is $0.40 per pound. The standard direct labor rate is $12 per hour. At the end of August, the actual direct materials and direct labor costs were as follows:

Actual direct materials	$13,320
Actual direct labor	60,000
Total	$73,320

There were no direct materials price or direct labor rate variances for August. In addition, assume no changes in the direct materials inventory balances in August. Havasu Printers Company actually produced 24,500 units during August.

Determine the direct materials quantity, direct labor time variances, and the total variance.

Obj 5

✔ a. $1,512

E13-26 Direct labor standards for nonmanufacturing expenses

Southwest Iowa Hospital began using standards to evaluate its Admissions Department. The standards were broken into two types of admissions as follows:

Type of Admission	Standard Time to Complete Admission Record
Unscheduled admission	30 min.
Scheduled admission	15 min.

The unscheduled admission took longer, since name, address, and insurance information needed to be determined at the time of admission. Information was collected on scheduled admissions prior to the admissions, which was less time consuming.

The Admissions Department employs two full-time people (36 hours per week, with no overtime) at $21 per hour. For the most recent week, the department handled 55 unscheduled and 210 scheduled admissions.

a. How much was actually spent on labor for the week?

b. What are the standard hours for the actual volume for the week?

c. Compute a time variance. How well did the department perform for the week?

Obj 6

E13-27 Nonfinancial performance measures

Indio Palms College wishes to monitor the efficiency and quality of its course registration process.

a. List three input and three output measures for this process.

b. Why would Indio Palms College use nonfinancial measures for monitoring this process?

Obj 6

E13-28 Nonfinancial performance measures

Par, Birdie, Eagle, Inc., is an Internet retailer of golf equipment. Customers order golf equipment from the company, using an online catalog. The company processes these orders and delivers the requested product from its warehouse. The company wants to provide customers with an excellent purchase experience in order to expand the business through favorable word-of-mouth advertising and to drive repeat business. To help monitor performance, the company developed a set of performance measures for its order placement and delivery process.

Average computer response time to customer "clicks"
Dollar amount of returned goods
Elapsed time between customer order and product delivery
Maintenance dollars divided by hardware investment
Number of customer complaints divided by the number of orders
Number of misfilled orders divided by the number of orders
Number of orders per warehouse employee
Number of page faults or errors due to software programming errors
Number of software fixes per week
Server (computer) downtime
Training dollars per programmer

a. For each performance measure, identify it as either an input or output measure related to the "order placement and delivery" process.

b. Provide an explanation for each performance measure.

E13-29 Factory overhead cost variances

The following data relate to factory overhead cost for the production of 8,000 computers:

Actual:	Variable factory overhead	$101,750
	Fixed factory overhead	180,000
Standard:	8,000 hrs. at $31	248,000

✔ Volume variance, $36,000 U

app

If productive capacity of 100% was 10,000 hours and the factory overhead cost budgeted at the level of 8,000 standard hours was $284,000, determine the variable factory overhead controllable variance, fixed factory overhead volume variance, and total factory overhead cost variance. The fixed factory overhead rate was $18 per hour.

E13-30 Factory overhead cost variances

Osceola Textiles Corporation began May with a budget for 45,000 hours of production in the Weaving Department. The department has a full capacity of 60,000 hours under normal business conditions. The budgeted overhead at the planned volumes at the beginning of May was as follows:

Variable overhead	$ 990,000
Fixed overhead	300,000
Total	$1,290,000

✔ a. −$16,000 F

app

The actual factory overhead was $1,428,000 for May. The actual fixed factory overhead was as budgeted. During May, the Weaving Department had standard hours at actual production volume of 52,000 hours.

a. Determine the variable factory overhead controllable variance.

b. Determine the fixed factory overhead volume variance.

E13-31 Factory overhead variance corrections

app

The data related to Danville Sporting Goods Company's factory overhead cost for the production of 40,000 units of product are as follows:

Actual:	Variable factory overhead	$269,000
	Fixed factory overhead	325,000
Standard:	105,000 hrs. at $9.00	945,000
	($5.75 for variable factory overhead)	

Productive capacity at 100% of normal was 100,000 hours, and the factory overhead cost budgeted at the level of 105,000 standard hours was $720,000. Based on these data, the chief cost accountant prepared the following variance analysis:

Variable factory overhead controllable variance:		
Actual variable factory overhead cost incurred	$600,000	
Budgeted variable factory overhead for 105,000 hours	603,750	
Variance—favorable		−$ 3,750
Fixed factory overhead volume variance:		
Normal productive capacity at 100%	100,000 hrs.	
Standard for amount produced	105,000	
Productive capacity not used	5,000 hrs.	
Standard variable factory overhead rate	× $9.00	
Variance—unfavorable		45,000
Total factory overhead cost variance—unfavorable		$41,250

Identify the errors in the factory overhead cost variance analysis.

E13-32   Factory overhead cost variance report

Topeka Plastics Inc. prepared the following factory overhead cost budget for the Trim Department for July, during which it expected to use 25,000 hours for production:

Variable overhead cost:		
Indirect factory labor	$20,000	
Power and light	18,000	
Indirect materials	9,000	
Total variable cost		$ 47,000
Fixed overhead cost:		
Supervisory salaries	$50,000	
Depreciation of plant and equipment	33,100	
Insurance and property taxes	11,400	
Total fixed cost		94,500
Total factory overhead cost		$141,500

Topeka Plastics has available 30,000 hours of monthly productive capacity in the Trim Department under normal business conditions. During July, the Trim Department actually used 28,000 hours for production. The actual fixed costs were as budgeted. The actual variable overhead for July was as follows:

Actual variable factory overhead cost:	
Indirect factory labor	$23,250
Power and light	20,000
Indirect materials	11,100
Total variable cost	$54,350

Construct a factory overhead cost variance report for the Trim Department for July.

Problems

P13-1   Sales, production, direct materials purchases, and direct labor cost

The budget director of Royal British Furniture Company requests estimates of sales, production, and other operating data from the various administrative units every month. Selected information concerning sales and production for March is summarized as follows:

a. Estimated sales of William and Kate chairs for March by sales territory:

Eastern Domestic:
  William   7,500 units at $800 per unit
  Kate   6,000 units at $650 per unit
Western Domestic:
  William   6,000 units at $700 per unit
  Kate   5,000 units at $550 per unit
International:
  William   2,500 units at $600 per unit
  Kate   1,000 units at $350 per unit

b. Estimated inventories at March 1:

Direct materials:		Finished products:	
Fabric	5,500 sq. yds.	William	1,500 units
Wood	13,700 lineal ft.	Kate	300 units
Filler	3,800 cu. ft.		
Springs	3,500 units		

c. Desired inventories at March 31:

Direct materials:
Fabric	9,000 sq. yds.
Wood	20,000 lineal ft.
Filler	5,000 cu. ft.
Springs	7,500 units

Finished products:
| William | 2,000 units |
| Kate | 900 units |

d. Direct materials used in production:

In manufacture of William:
Fabric	4.0 sq. yds. per unit of product
Wood	16 lineal ft. per unit of product
Filler	3.8 cu. ft. per unit of product
Springs	14 units per unit of product

In manufacture of Kate:
Fabric	2.5 sq. yds. per unit of product
Wood	12 lineal ft. per unit of product
Filler	3.2 cu. ft. per unit of product
Springs	10 units per unit of product

e. Anticipated purchase price for direct materials:

| Fabric | $9.00 per sq. yd. | Filler | $1.50 per cu. ft. |
| Wood | 5.00 per lineal ft. | Springs | 2.00 per unit |

f. Direct labor requirements:

William:
Framing Department	2.5 hrs. at $15 per hr.
Cutting Department	1.0 hr. at $12 per hr.
Upholstery Department	3.0 hrs. at $16 per hr.

Kate:
Framing Department	1.5 hrs. at $15 per hr.
Cutting Department	0.5 hr. at $12 per hr.
Upholstery Department	2.0 hrs. at $16 per hr.

Instructions

1. Prepare a sales budget for March.
2. Prepare a production budget for March.
3. Prepare a direct materials purchases budget for March.
4. Prepare a direct labor cost budget for March.

P13-2 Budgeted income statement and supporting budgets

Obj **2**

The budget director of Jupiter Helmets Inc., with the assistance of the controller, treasurer, production manager, and sales manager, has gathered the following data for use in developing the budgeted income statement for May:

a. Estimated sales for May:

| Bicycle helmet | 7,500 units at $24 per unit |
| Motorcycle helmet | 5,000 units at $175 per unit |

✔ 4. Total direct labor cost in Assembly Dept., $39,900

b. Estimated inventories at May 1:

Direct materials:
| Plastic | 1,480 lbs. |
| Foam lining | 520 lbs. |

Finished products:
| Bicycle helmet | 200 units at $15 per unit |
| Motorcycle helmet | 100 units at $90 per unit |

c. Desired inventories at May 31:

Direct materials:		Finished products:	
Plastic	2,000 lbs.	Bicycle helmet	400 units at $15 per unit
Foam lining	800 lbs.	Motorcycle helmet	300 units at $100 per unit

d. Direct materials used in production:

In manufacture of bicycle helmet:

Plastic	0.90 lb. per unit of product
Foam lining	0.20 lb. per unit of product

In manufacture of motorcycle helmet:

Plastic	3.50 lbs. per unit of product
Foam lining	1.40 lbs. per unit of product

e. Anticipated cost of purchases and beginning and ending inventory of direct materials:

Plastic	$4.40 per lb.
Foam lining	$0.90 per lb.

f. Direct labor requirements:

Bicycle helmet:

Molding Department	0.30 hr. at $15 per hr.
Assembly Department	0.10 hr. at $14 per hr.

Motorcycle helmet:

Molding Department	0.50 hr. at $15 per hr.
Assembly Department	0.40 hr. at $14 per hr.

g. Estimated factory overhead costs for May:

Indirect factory wages	$125,000	Power and light	$23,000
Depreciation of plant and equipment	45,000	Insurance and property tax	11,000

h. Estimated operating expenses for May:

Sales salaries expense	$175,000
Advertising expense	120,000
Office salaries expense	92,000
Depreciation expense—office equipment	6,000
Miscellaneous expense—selling	5,000
Utilities expense—administrative	3,000
Travel expense—selling	50,000
Office supplies expense	2,500
Miscellaneous administrative expense	1,500

i. Estimated other income and expense for May:

Interest revenue	$14,560
Interest expense	3,000

j. Estimated tax rate: 25%

Instructions

1. Prepare a sales budget for May.
2. Prepare a production budget for May.
3. Prepare a direct materials purchases budget for May.
4. Prepare a direct labor cost budget for May.

5. Prepare a factory overhead cost budget for May.

6. Prepare a cost of goods sold budget for May. Work in process at the beginning of May is estimated to be $4,200, and work in process at the end of May is desired to be $3,800.

7. Prepare a selling and administrative expenses budget for May.

8. Prepare a budgeted income statement for May.

P13-3 Cash budget

The controller of Shoe Mart Inc. asks you to prepare a monthly cash budget for the next three months. You are presented with the following budget information:

Obj 2

✔ 1. March
deficiency, $26,000

	January	February	March
Sales	$450,000	$550,000	$700,000
Manufacturing costs	260,000	330,000	420,000
Selling and administrative expenses	100,000	140,000	150,000
Capital expenditures	—	—	45,000

The company expects to sell about 20% of its merchandise for cash. Of sales on account, 75% are expected to be collected in full in the month following the sale and the remainder the following month. Depreciation, insurance, and property tax expense represent $40,000 of the estimated monthly manufacturing costs. The annual insurance premium is paid in June, and the annual property taxes are paid in October. Of the remainder of the manufacturing costs, 90% are expected to be paid in the month in which they are incurred and the balance in the following month. All sales and administrative expenses are paid in the month incurred.

Current assets as of January 1 include cash of $45,000, marketable securities of $65,000, and accounts receivable of $290,000 ($240,000 from December sales and $50,000 from November sales). Sales on account in November and December were $200,000 and $240,000, respectively. Current liabilities as of January 1 include a $50,000, 8%, 90-day note payable due March 20 and $18,000 of accounts payable incurred in December for manufacturing costs. All selling and administrative expenses are paid in cash in the period they are incurred. It is expected that $20,000 in dividends will be received in January. An estimated income tax payment of $15,000 will be made in February. Shoe Mart's regular quarterly dividend of $5,000 is expected to be declared in February and paid in March. Management desires to maintain a minimum cash balance of $35,000.

Instructions

1. Prepare a monthly cash budget and supporting schedules for January, February, and March.

2. On the basis of the cash budget prepared in part (1), what recommendation should be made to the controller?

P13-4 Direct materials and direct labor variance analysis

Faucet Industries Inc. manufactures faucets in a small manufacturing facility. The faucets are made from zinc. Manufacturing has 60 employees. Each employee presently provides 36 hours of labor per week. Information about a production week is as follows:

Obj 5

✔ c. Direct labor time
variance, $4,320 F

Standard wage per hr.	$18.00
Standard labor time per faucet	12 min.
Standard number of lbs. of zinc	0.80 lb.
Standard price per lb. of zinc	$1.25
Actual price per lb. of zinc	$1.40
Actual lbs. of zinc used during the week	10,200 lbs.
Number of faucets produced during the week	12,000
Actual wage per hr.	$18.75
Actual hrs. per week	2,160 hrs.

Instructions

Determine (a) the standard cost per unit for direct materials and direct labor; (b) the price variance, quantity variance, and total direct materials cost variance; and (c) the rate variance, time variance, and total direct labor cost variance.

P13-5 Direct materials and direct labor, variance analysis; factory overhead cost variance analysis

Route 66 Tire Co. manufactures automobile tires. Standard costs and actual costs for direct materials, direct labor, and factory overhead incurred for the manufacture of 10,000 tires were as follows:

	Standard Costs	Actual Costs
Direct materials	85,000 lbs. at $6.25	83,800 lbs. at $6.17
Direct labor	4,000 hrs. at $20.80	4,450 hrs. at $21.00
Factory overhead	Rates per direct labor hr., based on 100% of normal capacity of 5,000 direct labor hrs.:	
	Variable cost, $2.90	$11,375 variable cost
	Fixed cost, $11.40	$57,000 fixed cost

Each tire requires 0.40 hour of direct labor.

Instructions

Determine (a) the price variance, quantity variance, and total direct materials cost variance; (b) the rate variance, time variance, and total direct labor cost variance; and (c) Appendix: variable factory overhead controllable variance, the fixed factory overhead volume variance, and total factory overhead cost variance.

P13-6 Standards for nonmanufacturing expenses

The Radiology Department provides imaging services for Northeast Washington Medical Center. One important activity in the Radiology Department is transcribing digitally recorded analyses of images into a written report. The manager of the Radiology Department determined that the average transcriptionist could type 800 lines of a report in an hour. The plan for the first week in July called for 64,000 typed lines to be written. The Radiology Department has two transcriptionists. Each transcriptionist is hired from an employment firm that requires temporary employees to be hired for a minimum of a 40-hour week. Transcriptionists are paid $18.00 per hour. The manager offered a bonus if the department could type more than 70,000 lines for the week, without overtime. Due to high service demands, the transcriptionists typed more lines in the first week of July than planned. The actual amount of lines typed in the first week of July was 70,400 lines, without overtime. As a result, the bonus caused the average transcriptionist hourly rate to increase to $20.00 per hour during the first week in July.

Instructions

1. If the department typed 64,000 lines according to the original plan, what would have been the labor time variance?

2. What was the labor time variance as a result of typing 70,400 lines?

3. What was the labor rate variance as a result of the bonus?

4. The manager is trying to determine if a better decision would have been to hire a temporary transcriptionist to meet the higher typing demands in the first week of July, rather than paying out the bonus. If another employee was hired from the employment firm, what would have been the labor time variance in the first week?

5. Which decision is better, paying the bonus or hiring another transcriptionist?

6. Are there any performance-related issues that the labor time and rate variances fail to consider? Explain.

P13-7   Standard factory overhead variance report

Seabury, Inc., a manufacturer of disposable medical supplies, prepared the following factory overhead cost budget for the Assembly Department for October. The company expected to operate the department at 100% of normal capacity of 25,000 hours.

✔ Controllable variance, −$390 F

app

Variable costs:		
Indirect factory wages	$150,000	
Power and light	29,500	
Indirect materials	17,000	
Total variable cost		$196,500
Fixed costs:		
Supervisory salaries	$125,000	
Depreciation of plant and equipment	49,000	
Insurance and property taxes	29,750	
Total fixed cost		203,750
Total factory overhead cost		$400,250

During October, the department operated at 23,500 hours, and the factory overhead costs incurred were indirect factory wages, $140,500; power and light, $28,600; indirect materials, $15,220; supervisory salaries, $125,000; depreciation of plant and equipment, $49,000; and insurance and property taxes, $29,750.

Instructions

Prepare a factory overhead cost variance report for October. To be useful for cost control, the budgeted amounts should be based on 23,500 hours.

Cases

Case 13-1   Ethics and professional conduct in business

The director of marketing for Truss Industries Inc., Ellen Knutson, had the following discussion with the company controller, Bud Wyckoff, on February 26 of the current year:

Ellen: Bud, it looks like I'm going to spend much less than indicated on my February budget.

Bud: I'm glad to hear it.

Ellen: Well, I'm not so sure it's good news. I'm concerned that the president will see that I'm under budget and reduce my budget in the future. The only reason that I look good is that we've delayed an advertising campaign. Once the campaign hits in May, I'm sure my actual expenditures will go up. You see, we are also having our sales convention in May. Having the advertising campaign and the convention at the same time is going to kill my May numbers.

Bud: I don't think that's anything to worry about. We all expect some variation in actual spending month to month. What's really important is staying within the budgeted targets for the year. Does that look as if it's going to be a problem?

Ellen: I don't think so, but just the same, I'd like to be on the safe side.

Bud: What do you mean?

Ellen: Well, this is what I'd like to do. I want to pay the convention-related costs in advance this month. I'll pay the hotel for room and convention space and purchase the airline tickets in advance. In this way, I can charge all these expenditures to February's budget. This would cause my actual expenses to come close to budget for February. Moreover, when the big advertising campaign hits in May, I won't have to worry about expenditures for the convention on my May budget as well. The convention costs will already be paid. Thus, my May expenses should be pretty close to budget.

Bud: I can't tell you when to make your convention purchases, but I'm not too sure that it should be expensed on February's budget.

Ellen: What's the problem? It looks like "no harm, no foul" to me. I can't see that there's anything wrong with this—it's just smart management.

How should Bud Wyckoff respond to Ellen Knutson's request to expense the advanced payments for convention-related costs against February's budget?

Case 13-2 Evaluating budgeting systems

Children's Hospital of the King's Daughters Health System in Norfolk, Virginia, introduced a new budgeting method that allowed the hospital's annual plan to be updated for changes in operating plans. For example, if the budget was based on 1,000 patient-days (number of patients × number of days in the hospital) and the actual count rose to 1,200 patient-days, the variable costs of staffing, lab work, and medication costs could be adjusted to reflect this change. The budget manager stated, "I work with hospital directors to turn data into meaningful information and effect change before the month ends."

1. What budgeting methods are being used under the new approach?
2. Why are these methods superior to the former approaches?

Case 13-3 Service company static decision making

A bank manager of Oxford First Bank Inc. uses the managerial accounting system to track the costs of operating the various departments within the bank. The departments include Cash Management, Trust, Commercial Loans, Mortgage Loans, Operations, Credit Card, and Branch Services. The budget and actual results for the Operations Department are as follows:

Resources	Budget	Actual
Salaries	$300,000	$300,000
Benefits	40,000	40,000
Supplies	27,000	22,000
Travel	15,000	43,000
Training	13,000	15,000
Overtime	20,000	15,000
Total	$415,000	$435,000
Excess of actual over budget	$20,000	

1. What information is provided by the budget? Specifically, what questions can the bank manager ask of the Operations Department manager?
2. What information does the budget fail to provide? Specifically, could the budget information be presented differently to provide even more insight for the bank manager?

Case 13-4 Objectives of the master budget

Domino's Pizza LLC operates pizza delivery and carryout restaurants. The annual report describes its business as follows:

We offer a focused menu of high-quality, value priced pizza with three types of crust (Hand-Tossed, Thin Crust, and Deep Dish), along with buffalo wings, bread sticks, cheesy bread, CinnaStix®, and Coca Cola® products. Our hand-tossed pizza is made from fresh dough produced in our regional distribution centers. We prepare every pizza using real cheese, pizza sauce made from fresh tomatoes, and a choice of high-quality meat and vegetable toppings in generous portions. Our focused menu and use of premium ingredients enable us to consistently and efficiently produce the highest-quality pizza.

Over the 41 years since our founding, we have developed a simple, cost-efficient model. We offer a limited menu, our stores are designed for delivery and carry-out, and we do not generally offer dine-in service. As a result, our stores require relatively small, lower-rent locations and limited capital expenditures.

How would a master budget support planning, directing, and control for Domino's?

Case 13-5 Integrity and evaluating budgeting systems

The city of Rosebud has an annual budget cycle that begins on July 1 and ends on June 30. At the beginning of each budget year, an annual budget is established for each department. The annual budget is divided by 12 months to provide a constant monthly static budget. On

June 30, all unspent budgeted monies for the budget year from the various city departments must be "returned" to the General Fund. Thus, if department heads fail to use their budget by year-end, they will lose it. A budget analyst prepared a chart of the difference between the monthly actual and budgeted amounts for the recent fiscal year. The chart was as follows:

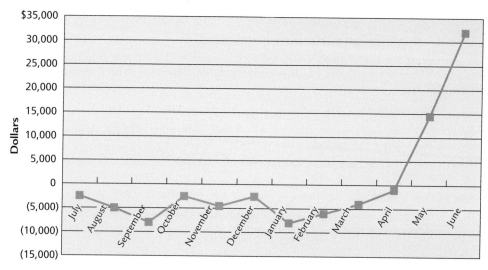

1. Interpret the chart.
2. Suggest an improvement in the budget system.

Case 13-6 Ethics and professional conduct in business using nonmanufacturing standards

Christy Eisenbeis is a cost analyst with Nations Insurance Company. Nations Insurance is applying standards to its claims payment operation. Claims payment is a repetitive operation that could be evaluated with standards. Christy used time and motion studies to identify an ideal standard of 24 claims processed per hour. The Claims Processing Department manager, Everett Boyle, has rejected this standard and has argued that the standard should be 18 claims processed per hour. Everett and Christy were unable to agree, so they decided to discuss this matter openly at a joint meeting with the vice president of operations, who would arbitrate a final decision. Prior to the meeting, Christy wrote the following memo to the VP.

To: Megan Wilkins, Vice President of Operations
From: Christy Eisenbeis
Re: Standards in the Claims Processing Department

As you know, Everett and I are scheduled to meet with you to discuss our disagreement with respect to the appropriate standards for the Claims Processing Department. I have conducted time and motion studies and have determined that the ideal standard is 24 claims processed per hour. Everett argues that 18 claims processed per hour would be more appropriate. I believe he is trying to "pad" the budget with some slack. I'm not sure what he is trying to get away with, but I believe a tight standard will drive efficiency up in his area. I hope you will agree when we meet with you next week.

Discuss the ethical and professional issues in this situation.

Case 13-7 Nonfinancial performance measures

The senior management of Trinity Industries Inc. has proposed the following three performance measures for the company:

1. Net income as a percent of stockholders' equity
2. Revenue growth
3. Employee satisfaction

Management believes these three measures combine both financial and nonfinancial measures and are thus superior to using just financial measures.

What advice would you give Trinity Industries Inc. for improving its performance measurement system?

Case 13-8 Nonfinancial performance measures

The controller of a manufacturing company used a number of measures to provide managers information about the performance of its manufacturing operation. Three measures used by the company are:

- Scrap Index: The sales dollar value of scrap for the period.
- Orders Past Due: Sales dollar value of orders that were scheduled for shipment, but were not shipped during the period.
- Buyer's Misery Index: Number of different customers that have orders that are late (scheduled for shipment, but not shipped).

1. Why do you think the scrap index is measured at sales dollar value, rather than at cost?
2. How is the "orders past due" measure different from the "buyer's misery index," or are the two measures just measuring the same thing?

Case 13-9 Variance interpretation

Harmony Industries Inc. is a small manufacturer of electronic musical instruments. The plant manager received the following variable factory overhead report for the period:

	Actual	Budgeted Variable Factory Overhead at Actual Production	Controllable Variance
Indirect factory wages	$100,800	$ 72,000	$28,800 U
Power and light	38,000	40,000	2,000 F
Supplies	21,000	18,000	3,000 U
Total	$159,800	$130,000	$29,800 U

Actual units produced: 15,000 (75% of practical capacity)

The plant manager is not pleased with the $29,800 unfavorable variable factory overhead controllable variance and has come to discuss the matter with the controller. The following discussion occurred:

Plant Manager: I just received this factory report for the latest month of operation. I'm not very pleased with these figures. Before these numbers go to headquarters, you and I will need to reach an understanding.

Controller: Go ahead, what's the problem?

Plant Manager: What's the problem? Well, everything. Look at the variance. It's too large. If I understand the accounting approach being used here, you are assuming that my costs are variable to the units produced. Thus, as the production volume declines, so should these costs. Well, I don't believe that these costs are variable at all. I think they are fixed costs. As a result, when we operate below capacity, the costs really don't go down at all. I'm being penalized for costs I have no control over at all. I need this report to be redone to reflect this fact. If anything, the difference between actual and budget is essentially a volume variance. Listen, I know that you're a team player. You really need to reconsider your assumptions on this one.

If you were in the controller's position, how would you respond to the plant manager?

Answers to Self-Examination Questions

1. **B** Administrative departments (answer B), such as Purchasing or Human Resources, will often use static budgeting. Production departments (answer A) frequently use flexible budgets. Responsibility centers (answer C) can use either static or flexible budgeting. Capital expenditure budgets are used to plan capital projects (answer D).

2. **B** The total production indicated in the production budget is 257,500 units (answer B), which is computed as follows:

Sales	250,000 units
Plus desired ending inventory	30,000 units
Total	280,000 units
Less estimated beginning inventory	22,500 units
Total production	257,500 units

3. **C** Dixon expects to collect 70% of April sales ($560,000) plus 30% of the March sales ($195,000) in April, for a total of $755,000 (answer C). Answer A is 100% of April sales. Answer B is 70% of April sales. Answer D adds 70% of both March and April sales.

4. **C** The unfavorable direct materials price variance of $2,550 is determined as follows:

Actual price	$5.05 per pound
Standard price	5.00
Price variance—unfavorable	$0.05 per pound

Direct materials price variance: $2,550 = $0.05 × 51,000 actual pounds

5. **D** The unfavorable direct labor time variance of $2,400 is determined as follows:

Actual direct labor time	2,200 hours
Standard direct labor time	2,000
Direct labor time variance	200 hours

Direct labor time variance: Unfavorable $2,400 = 200 × $12 standard rate

CHAPTER 14

Performance Evaluation for Decentralized Operations

LEARNING OBJECTIVES

After studying this chapter, you should be able to:

Obj 1 Describe the advantages and disadvantages of decentralized operations.

Obj 2 Prepare a responsibility accounting report for a cost center.

Obj 3 Prepare a responsibility accounting report for a profit center.

Obj 4 Compute and interpret the rate of return on investment, the residual income, and the balanced scorecard for an investment center.

Obj 5 Describe and illustrate how the market price, negotiated price, and cost price approaches to transfer pricing may be used by decentralized segments of a business.

Have you ever wondered why large retail stores like **Wal-mart**, **The Home Depot**, and **Sports Authority** are divided into departments? Dividing into departments allows retailers to provide products and expertise in specialized areas, while offering a broad line of products. Departments also allow companies to assign responsibility for financial performance. This information can be used to make product decisions, evaluate operations, and guide company strategy. Strong performance in a department might be attributed to a good department manager, who might be rewarded with a promotion. Poor departmental performance might lead to a change in the mix of products that the department sells.

Like retailers, most businesses organize into operational units, such as divisions and departments. For example,

K2 Sports, a leading maker of athletic and outdoor equipment, manages its business across four primary business segments: Marine and Outdoor, Action Sports, Team Sports, and Footwear and Apparel. These segments are further divided into product lines, such as K2 skis, Rawlings athletic equipment, Marmot outdoor products, and WGP Paintball.

Managers are responsible for running the operations of their segment of the business. Each segment is evaluated based on operating profit, and this information is used to plan and control K2's operations.

In this chapter, the role of accounting in assisting managers in planning and controlling operational units, such as departments, divisions, and stores, is described and illustrated.

Obj | **1**

Describe the advantages and disadvantages of decentralized operations.

Centralized and Decentralized Operations

In a *centralized* company, all major planning and operating decisions are made by top management. For example, a one-person, owner-manager-operated company is centralized because all plans and decisions are made by one person. In a small owner-manager-operated business, centralization may be desirable. This is because the owner-manager's close supervision ensures that the business will be operated in the way the owner-manager wishes.

In a *decentralized* company, managers of separate divisions or units are delegated operating responsibility. The division (unit) managers are responsible for planning and controlling the operations of their divisions. Divisions are often structured around products, customers, or regions.

The proper amount of decentralization for a company depends on the company's unique circumstances. For example, in some companies, division managers have authority over all operations, including fixed asset purchases. In other companies, division managers have authority over profits but not fixed asset purchases.

Procter & Gamble is organized around products such as Tide (laundry soap), Braun (home appliance), Charmin (bath tissue), CoverGirl (cosmetics), and Crest (toothpaste).

Advantages of Decentralization

For large companies, it is difficult for top management to do the following:

1. Maintain daily contact with all operations
2. Maintain operating expertise in all product lines and services

In such cases, delegating authority to managers closest to the operations usually results in better decisions. These managers often anticipate and react to operating data more quickly than could top management. These managers also can focus their attention on becoming "experts" in their area of operation.

Decentralized operations provide excellent training for managers. Delegating responsibility allows managers to develop managerial experience early in their careers. This helps a company retain managers, some of whom may be later promoted to top management positions.

Managers of decentralized operations often work closely with customers. As a result, they tend to identify with customers and thus are often more creative in suggesting operating and product improvements. This helps create good customer relations.

Wachovia Corporation, a national bank, decentralized decisions about how the bank does business over the Internet. Each business unit independently decides how it will conduct business over the Internet. For example, the Mortgage Loan Division allows customers to check current mortgage rates and apply for mortgages online.

Disadvantages of Decentralization

A primary disadvantage of decentralized operations is that decisions made by one manager may negatively affect the profits of the company. For example, managers of divisions whose products compete with each other might start a price war that decreases the profits of both divisions and thus the overall company.

Another disadvantage of decentralized operations is that they may result in duplicate assets and expenses. For example, each manager of a product line might have a separate sales force and office support staff.

The advantages and disadvantages of decentralization are summarized in Exhibit 1.

When the **Pizza Hut** chain added chicken to its menu, **Kentucky Fried Chicken (KFC)** retaliated with an advertising campaign against Pizza Hut. However, Pizza Hut and KFC are owned by the same company, **Yum! Brands, Inc.**

EXHIBIT 1

Advantages and Disadvantages of Decentralized Operations

Advantages of Decentralization
- Allows managers closest to the operations to make decisions
- Provides excellent training for managers
- Allows managers to become experts in their area of operation
- Helps retain managers
- Improves creativity and customer relations

Disadvantages of Decentralization
- Decisions made by managers may negatively affect the profits of the company
- Duplicates assets and expenses

Responsibility Accounting

In a decentralized business, accounting assists managers in evaluating and controlling their areas of responsibility, called *responsibility centers*. **Responsibility accounting** is the process of measuring and reporting operating data by responsibility center.

Three types of responsibility centers are:

1. Cost centers, which have responsibility over costs.
2. Profit centers, which have responsibility over revenues and costs.
3. Investment centers, which have responsibility over revenue, costs, and investment in assets.

Responsibility Accounting for Cost Centers

Obj **2**

Prepare a responsibility accounting report for a cost center.

A **cost center** manager has responsibility for controlling costs. For example, the supervisor of the Power Department has responsibility for the costs of providing power. A cost center manager does not make decisions concerning sales or the amount of fixed assets invested in the center.

Cost centers may vary in size from a small department to an entire manufacturing plant. In addition, cost centers may exist within other cost centers. For example, an entire university or college could be viewed as a cost center, and each college and department within the university also could be a cost center, as shown in Exhibit 2.

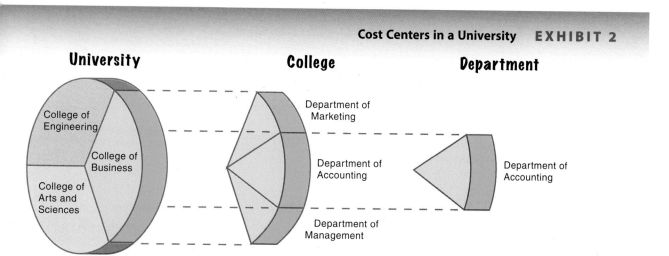

Cost Centers in a University   **EXHIBIT 2**

University — College of Engineering, College of Business, College of Arts and Sciences

College — Department of Marketing, Department of Accounting, Department of Management

Department — Department of Accounting

Responsibility accounting for cost centers focuses on controlling and reporting of costs. Budget performance reports that report budgeted and actual costs are normally prepared for each cost center.

Exhibit 3 illustrates budget performance reports for the following cost centers:

1. Vice President, Production
2. Manager, Plant A
3. Supervisor, Department 1—Plant A

EXHIBIT 3   **Responsibility Accounting Reports for Cost Centers**

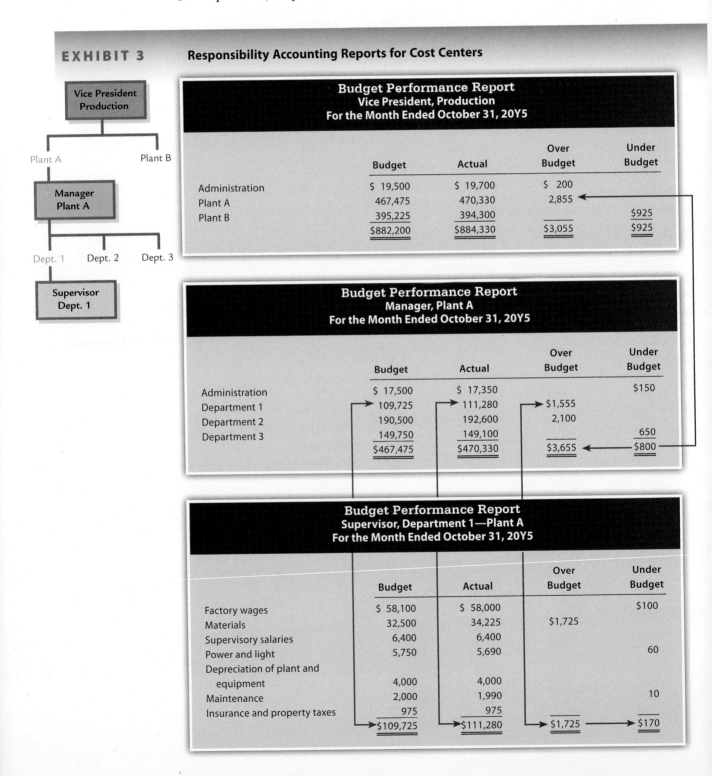

Budget Performance Report
Vice President, Production
For the Month Ended October 31, 20Y5

	Budget	Actual	Over Budget	Under Budget
Administration	$ 19,500	$ 19,700	$ 200	
Plant A	467,475	470,330	2,855	
Plant B	395,225	394,300		$925
	$882,200	$884,330	$3,055	$925

Budget Performance Report
Manager, Plant A
For the Month Ended October 31, 20Y5

	Budget	Actual	Over Budget	Under Budget
Administration	$ 17,500	$ 17,350		$150
Department 1	109,725	111,280	$1,555	
Department 2	190,500	192,600	2,100	
Department 3	149,750	149,100		650
	$467,475	$470,330	$3,655	$800

Budget Performance Report
Supervisor, Department 1—Plant A
For the Month Ended October 31, 20Y5

	Budget	Actual	Over Budget	Under Budget
Factory wages	$ 58,100	$ 58,000		$100
Materials	32,500	34,225	$1,725	
Supervisory salaries	6,400	6,400		
Power and light	5,750	5,690		60
Depreciation of plant and equipment	4,000	4,000		
Maintenance	2,000	1,990		10
Insurance and property taxes	975	975		
	$109,725	$111,280	$1,725	$170

Exhibit 3 shows how cost centers are often linked together within a company. For example, the budget performance report for Department 1—Plant A supports the report for Plant A, which supports the report for the vice president of production.

The reports in Exhibit 3 show the budgeted costs and actual costs along with the differences. Each difference is classified as either *over* budget or *under* budget. Such reports allow cost center managers to focus on areas of significant differences.

For example, the supervisor for Department 1 of Plant A can focus on why the materials cost was over budget. The supervisor might discover that excess materials were scrapped. This could be due to such factors as machine malfunctions, improperly trained employees, or low quality materials.

As shown in Exhibit 3, responsibility accounting reports are usually more summarized for higher levels of management. For example, the budget performance report for the manager of Plant A shows only administration and departmental data. This report enables the plant manager to identify the departments responsible for major differences. Likewise, the report for the vice president of production summarizes the cost data for each plant.

Responsibility Accounting for Profit Centers

Obj **3**

Prepare a responsibility accounting report for a profit center.

Lester B. Korn of **Korn/ Ferry International** offered the following strategy for young executives en route to top management positions: "Get profit-center responsibility."

A **profit center** manager has the responsibility and authority for making decisions that affect revenues and costs and, thus, profits. Profit centers may be divisions, departments, or products.

The manager of a profit center does not make decisions concerning the fixed assets invested in the center. However, profit centers provide excellent training for new managers.

Responsibility accounting for profit centers focuses on reporting revenues, expenses, and income from operations. Thus, responsibility accounting reports for profit centers take the form of income statements.

The profit center income statement should include only revenues and expenses that are controlled by the manager. **Controllable revenues** are revenues earned by the profit center. **Controllable expenses** are costs that can be influenced (controlled) by the decisions of profit center managers.

Service Department Charges

The controllable expenses of profit centers include *direct operating expenses* such as sales salaries and utility expenses. In addition, a profit center may incur expenses provided by internal centralized *service departments*. Examples of such service departments include the following:

1. Research and Development
2. Legal
3. Telecommunications
4. Information and Computer Systems
5. Facilities Management
6. Purchasing
7. Publications and Graphics

8. Payroll Accounting

9. Transportation

10. Personnel Administration

Service department charges are *indirect* expenses to a profit center. They are similar to the expenses that would be incurred if the profit center purchased the services from outside the company. A profit center manager has control over service department expenses if the manager is free to choose how much service is used. In such cases, **service department charges** are allocated to profit centers based on the usage of the service by each profit center.

To illustrate, Tadpole Inc., a diversified entertainment company shown in Exhibit 4, is used. Tadpole Inc. has the following two operating divisions organized as profit centers:

1. Theme Park Division

2. Photography Division

EXHIBIT 4

Payroll Accounting Department Charges to Tadpole Inc.'s Theme Park and Photography Divisions

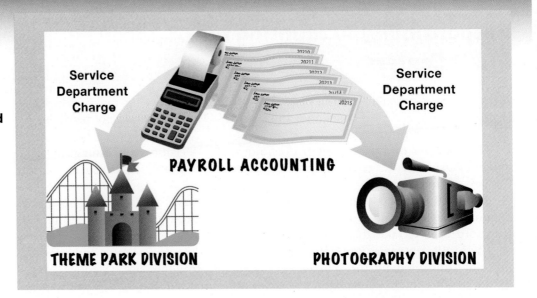

Employees of **IBM** speak of "green money" and "blue money." Green money comes from customers. Blue money comes from providing services to other IBM departments via service department charges. IBM employees note that blue money is easier to earn than green money; yet from the stockholders' perspective, green money is the only money that counts.

The revenues and direct operating expenses for Tadpole's two divisions are shown below. The operating expenses consist of direct expenses, such as the wages and salaries of a division's employees.

	Theme Park Division	Photography Division
Revenues	$6,000,000	$2,500,000
Operating expenses	2,495,000	405,000

Tadpole Inc.'s service departments and the expenses they incurred for the year ended December 31, 20Y7, are shown at the top of the next page.

Purchasing	$400,000
Payroll Accounting	255,000
Legal	250,000
Total	$905,000

An activity base for each service department is used to charge service department expenses to the Theme Park and Photography divisions. The activity base for each service department is a measure of the services performed. For Tadpole Inc., the service department activity bases are as follows:

Department	Activity Base
Purchasing	Number of purchase requisitions
Payroll Accounting	Number of payroll checks
Legal	Number of billed hours

The use of services by the Theme Park and Photography divisions is as follows:

	Service Usage		
Division	Purchasing	Payroll Accounting	Legal
Theme Park	25,000 purchase requisitions	12,000 payroll checks	100 billed hrs.
Photography	15,000	3,000	900
Total	40,000 purchase requisitions	15,000 payroll checks	1,000 billed hrs.

The rates at which services are charged to each division are called *service department charge rates*. These rates are computed as follows:

$$\text{Service Department Charge Rate} = \frac{\text{Service Department Expense}}{\text{Total Service Department Usage}}$$

Tadpole Inc.'s service department charge rates are computed as follows:

$$\frac{\text{Purchasing}}{\text{Charge Rate}} = \frac{\$400,000}{40,000 \text{ purchase requisitions}} = \$10 \text{ per purchase requisition}$$

$$\text{Payroll Charge Rate} = \frac{\$255,000}{15,000 \text{ payroll checks}} = \$17 \text{ per payroll check}$$

$$\text{Legal Charge Rate} = \frac{\$250,000}{1,000 \text{ billed hrs.}} = \$250 \text{ per hr.}$$

The services used by each division are multiplied by the service department charge rates to determine the service charges for each division, as shown below.

$$\text{Service Department Charge} = \text{Service Usage} \times \text{Service Department Charge Rate}$$

Exhibit 5 illustrates the service department charges and related computations for Tadpole Inc.'s Theme Park and Photography divisions.

EXHIBIT 5

Service Department Charges to Tadpole Inc. Divisions

Tadpole Inc.
Service Department Charges to Tadpole Inc.'s Divisions
For the Year Ended December 31, 20Y7

Service Department	Theme Park Division	Photography Division
Purchasing (Note A)	$250,000	$150,000
Payroll Accounting (Note B)	204,000	51,000
Legal (Note C)	25,000	225,000
Total service department charges	$479,000	$426,000

Note A:
25,000 purchase requisitions × $10 per purchase requisition = $250,000
15,000 purchase requisitions × $10 per purchase requisition = $150,000

Note B:
12,000 payroll checks × $17 per check = $204,000
3,000 payroll checks × $17 per check = $51,000

Note C:
100 hours × $250 per hour = $25,000
900 hours × $250 per hour = $225,000

The differences in the service department charges between the two divisions can be explained by the nature of their operations and, thus, usage of services. For example, the Theme Park Division employs many part-time employees who are paid weekly. As a result, the Theme Park Division requires 12,000 payroll checks and incurs a $204,000 payroll service department charge (12,000 × $17). In contrast, the Photography Division has more permanent employees who are paid monthly. Thus, the Photography Division requires only 3,000 payroll checks and incurs a payroll service department charge of $51,000 (3,000 × $17).

Profit Center Reporting

The divisional income statements for Tadpole Inc. are shown in Exhibit 6. In evaluating the profit center manager, the income from operations should be compared over time to a budget. However, it should not be compared across profit centers, since the profit centers are usually different in terms of size, products, and customers.

EXHIBIT 6

Divisional Income Statements— Tadpole Inc.

Tadpole Inc.
Divisional Income Statements
For the Year Ended December 31, 20Y7

	Theme Park Division	Photography Division
Revenues*	$6,000,000	$2,500,000
Operating expenses	2,495,000	405,000
Income from operations before service department charges	$3,505,000	$2,095,000
Less service department charges:		
Purchasing	$ 250,000	$ 150,000
Payroll Accounting	204,000	51,000
Legal	25,000	225,000
Total service department charges	$ 479,000	$ 426,000
Income from operations	$3,026,000	$1,669,000

*For a profit center that sells products, the income statement would show: Net sales − Cost of goods sold = Gross profit. The operating expenses would be deducted from the gross profit to arrive at the income from operations before service department charges.

Responsibility Accounting for Investment Centers

Obj | **4**

Compute and interpret the rate of return on investment, the residual income, and the balanced scorecard for an investment center.

An **investment center** manager has the responsibility and the authority to make decisions that affect not only costs and revenues but also the assets invested in the center. Investment centers are often used in diversified companies organized by divisions. In such cases, the divisional manager has authority similar to that of a chief operating officer or president of a company.

Since investment center managers have responsibility for revenues and expenses, *income from operations* is part of investment center reporting. In addition, because the manager has responsibility for the assets invested in the center, the following two additional measures of performance are used:

1. Rate of return on investment
2. Residual income

To illustrate, In-Touch Inc., a cellular phone company with three regional divisions, is used. Condensed divisional income statements for the Northern, Central, and Southern divisions of In-Touch are shown in Exhibit 7.

Using only income from operations, the Central Division is the most profitable division. However, income from operations does not reflect the amount of assets invested in each center. For example, the Central Division could have twice as many assets as the Northern Division. For this reason, performance measures that consider the amount of invested assets, such as the rate of return on investment and residual income, are used.

EXHIBIT 7

**Divisional
Income
Statements—
In-Touch Inc.**

In-Touch Inc. Divisional Income Statements For the Year Ended December 31, 20Y7			
	Northern Division	Central Division	Southern Division
Revenues	$560,000	$672,000	$750,000
Operating expenses	336,000	470,400	562,500
Income from operations before service department charges	$224,000	$201,600	$187,500
Service department charges	154,000	117,600	112,500
Income from operations	$ 70,000	$ 84,000	$ 75,000

Rate of Return on Investment

Since investment center managers control the amount of assets invested in their centers, they should be evaluated based on the use of these assets. One measure that considers the amount of assets invested is the **rate of return on investment (ROI)** or *rate of return on assets*. It is computed as follows:

$$\text{Rate of Return on Investment (ROI)} = \frac{\text{Income from Operations}}{\text{Invested Assets}}$$

The interest you earn on a savings account is *your* "rate of return on investment."

The rate of return on investment is useful because the three factors subject to control by divisional managers (revenues, expenses, and invested assets) are considered. The higher the rate of return on investment, the better the division is using its assets to generate income. In effect, the rate of return on investment measures the income (return) on each dollar invested. As a result, the rate of return on investment can be used as a common basis for comparing divisions with each other.

To illustrate, the invested assets of In-Touch's three divisions are as follows:

	Invested Assets
Northern Division	$350,000
Central Division	700,000
Southern Division	500,000

Using the income from operations for each division shown in Exhibit 7, the rate of return on investment for each division is computed below.

Northern Division:

$$\text{Rate of Return on Investment} = \frac{\text{Income from Operations}}{\text{Invested Assets}} = \frac{\$70,000}{\$350,000} = 20\%$$

Central Division:

$$\text{Rate of Return on Investment} = \frac{\text{Income from Operations}}{\text{Invested Assets}} = \frac{\$84,000}{\$700,000} = 12\%$$

Southern Division:

$$\text{Rate of Return on Investment} = \frac{\text{Income from Operations}}{\text{Invested Assets}} = \frac{\$75,000}{\$500,000} = 15\%$$

Although the Central Division generated the largest income from operations, its rate of return on investment (12%) is the lowest. Thus, relative to the assets invested, the Central Division is the least profitable division. In comparison, the rate of return on investment of the Northern Division is 20%, and the Southern Division is 15%.

To analyze differences in the rate of return on investment across divisions, the **DuPont formula** for the rate of return on investment is often used.[1] The DuPont formula views the rate of return on investment as the product of the following two factors:

1. **Profit margin**, which is the ratio of income from operations to sales.
2. **Investment turnover**, which is the ratio of sales to invested assets.

Using the DuPont formula, the rate of return on investment is expressed as follows:

$$\text{Rate of Return on Investment} = \text{Profit Margin} \times \text{Investment Turnover}$$

$$\text{Rate of Return on Investment} = \frac{\text{Income from Operations}}{\text{Sales}} \times \frac{\text{Sales}}{\text{Invested Assets}}$$

The DuPont formula is useful in evaluating divisions. This is because the profit margin and the investment turnover reflect the following underlying operating relationships of each division:

1. Profit margin indicates *operating profitability* by computing the rate of profit earned on each sales dollar.
2. Investment turnover indicates *operating efficiency* by computing the number of sales dollars generated by each dollar of invested assets.

If a division's profit margin increases, and all other factors remain the same, the division's rate of return on investment will increase. For example, a division might add more profitable products to its sales mix and thus increase its operating profit, profit margin, and rate of return on investment.

If a division's investment turnover increases, and all other factors remain the same, the division's rate of return on investment will increase. For example, a division might attempt to increase sales through special sales promotions and thus increase operating efficiency, investment turnover, and rate of return on investment.

The graphic below illustrates the relationship of the rate of return on investment, the profit margin, and investment turnover. Specifically, more income can be earned by either increasing the investment turnover (installing a bigger engine), by increasing the profit margin (pressing the gas pedal), or both.

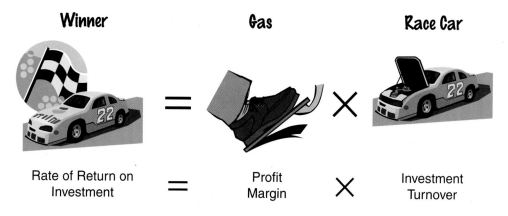

Winner		Gas		Race Car
Rate of Return on Investment	=	Profit Margin	×	Investment Turnover

1. The DuPont formula was created by a financial executive of E. I. du Pont Nemours and Company in 1919.

Using the DuPont formula yields the same rate of return on investment for each of In-Touch's divisions, as shown below.

$$\text{Rate of Return on Investment} = \frac{\text{Income from Operations}}{\text{Sales}} \times \frac{\text{Sales}}{\text{Invested Assets}}$$

Northern Division:

$$\text{Rate of Return on Investment} = \frac{\$70,000}{\$560,000} \times \frac{\$560,000}{\$350,000} = 12.5\% \times 1.6 = 20\%$$

Central Division:

$$\text{Rate of Return on Investment} = \frac{\$84,000}{\$672,000} \times \frac{\$672,000}{\$700,000} = 12.5\% \times 0.96 = 12\%$$

Southern Division:

$$\text{Rate of Return on Investment} = \frac{\$75,000}{\$750,000} \times \frac{\$750,000}{\$500,000} = 10\% \times 1.5 = 15\%$$

The Northern and Central divisions have the same profit margins of 12.5%. However, the Northern Division's investment turnover of 1.6 is larger than that of the Central Division's turnover of 0.96. By using its invested assets more efficiently, the Northern Division's rate of return on investment of 20% is 8 percentage points higher than the Central Division's rate of return of 12%.

The Southern Division's profit margin of 10% and investment turnover of 1.5 are lower than those of the Northern Division. The product of these factors results in a return on investment of 15% for the Southern Division, compared to 20% for the Northern Division.

Even though the Southern Division's profit margin is lower than the Central Division's, its higher turnover of 1.5 results in a rate of return of 15%, which is greater than the Central Division's rate of return of 12%.

To increase the rate of return on investment, the profit margin and investment turnover for a division may be analyzed. For example, assume that the Northern Division is in a highly competitive industry in which the profit margin cannot be easily increased. As a result, the division manager might focus on increasing the investment turnover.

To illustrate, assume that the revenues of the Northern Division could be increased by $56,000 through increasing operating expenses, such as advertising, to $385,000. The Northern Division's income from operations will increase from $70,000 to $77,000, as shown below.

Revenues ($560,000 + $56,000)	$616,000
Operating expenses	385,000
Income from operations before service department charges	$231,000
Service department charges	154,000
Income from operations	$ 77,000

The rate of return on investment for the Northern Division, using the DuPont formula, is recomputed as follows:

$$\text{Rate of Return on Investment} = \frac{\text{Income from Operations}}{\text{Sales}} \times \frac{\text{Sales}}{\text{Invested Assets}}$$

$$\text{Rate of Return on Investment} = \frac{\$77,000}{\$616,000} \times \frac{\$616,000}{\$350,000} = 12.5\% \times 1.76 = 22\%$$

Although the Northern Division's profit margin remains the same (12.5%), the investment turnover has increased from 1.6 to 1.76, an increase of 10% (0.16 ÷ 1.6). The 10% increase in investment turnover increases the rate of return on investment by 10% (from 20% to 22%).

The rate of return on investment is also useful in deciding where to invest additional assets or expand operations. For example, In-Touch should give priority to expanding operations in the Northern Division because it earns the highest rate of return on investment. In other words, an investment in the Northern Division will return 20 cents (20%) on each dollar invested. In contrast, investments in the Central and Southern divisions will earn only 12 cents and 15 cents, respectively, per dollar invested.

A disadvantage of the rate of return on investment as a performance measure is that it may lead divisional managers to reject new investments that could be profitable for the company as a whole. To illustrate, assume the following rates of return for the Northern Division of In-Touch:

The CFO of **Millennium Chemicals** stated: "We had too many divisional executives who failed to spend money on capital projects with more than satisfactory returns because those projects would have lowered the average return on assets of their particular business."

Current rate of return on investment	20%
Minimum acceptable rate of return on investment set by top management	10%
Expected rate of return on investment for new project	14%

If the manager of the Northern Division invests in the new project, the Northern Division's overall rate of return will decrease from 20% due to averaging. Thus, the division manager might decide to reject the project, even though the new project's expected rate of return of 14% exceeds In-Touch's minimum acceptable rate of return of 10%.

Residual Income

Residual income is useful in overcoming some of the disadvantages of the rate of return on investment. **Residual income** is the excess of income from operations over a minimum acceptable income from operations, as shown below.[2]

Income from operations	$XXX
Less minimum acceptable income from operations as a percent of invested assets	XXX
Residual income	$XXX

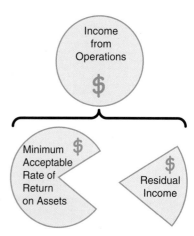

The minimum acceptable income from operations is computed by multiplying the company minimum rate of return by the invested assets. The minimum rate is set by top management, based on such factors as the cost of financing.

To illustrate, assume that In-Touch Inc. has established 10% as the minimum acceptable rate of return on divisional assets. The residual incomes for the three divisions are shown on the next page.

2. Another popular term for residual income is economic value added (EVA), which has been trademarked by the consulting firm Stern Stewart & Co.

	Northern Division	Central Division	Southern Division
Income from operations	$70,000	$84,000	$75,000
Less minimum acceptable income from operations as a percent of invested assets:			
$350,000 × 10%	35,000		
$700,000 × 10%		70,000	
$500,000 × 10%			50,000
Residual income	$35,000	$14,000	$25,000

The Northern Division has more residual income ($35,000) than the other divisions, even though it has the least amount of income from operations ($70,000). This is because the invested assets are less for the Northern Division than for the other divisions.

The major advantage of residual income as a performance measure is that it considers both the minimum acceptable rate of return, invested assets, and the income from operations for each division. In doing so, residual income encourages division managers to maximize income from operations in excess of the minimum. This provides an incentive to accept any project that is expected to have a rate of return in excess of the minimum.

HOW BUSINESSES MAKE MONEY

RETURN ON INVESTMENT

The annual reports of public companies must provide segment disclosure information identifying revenues, income from operations, and total assets. This information can be used to compute the return on investment for the segments of a company. For example, **The E.W. Scripps Company,** a media company, operates two major segments:

1. Newspapers: Owns and operates daily and community newspapers in markets throughout the United States.
2. Television: The Scripps television group reaches approximately 10% of U.S. households and includes stations in Detroit, Phoenix, Tampa, Cleveland, Baltimore, Kansas City, Cincinnati, and Tulsa.

The DuPont formulas for these segments, as derived from a recent annual report, are as follows:

	Segment Profit Margin	×	Investment Turnover	=	Return on Investment
Newspapers	16.6%		0.70		11.6%
Television	5.1%		1.40		7.1%

As can be seen from the data, Scripps' newspapers segment earns the highest rate of return on investment of 11.6% compared to 7.1% for the television segment. The higher rate of return by the newspapers segment is due to its higher profit margin of 16.6%, which is over three times that of the television segment of 5.1%. The television segment, however, has a higher investment turnover of 1.40 compared to only 0.70 for the newspapers segment. Although the television segment's turnover is twice that of the newspapers segment, it is not enough to offset the profit margin of the newspapers.

To illustrate, assume the following rates of return for the Northern Division of In-Touch:

Current rate of return on investment	20%
Minimum acceptable rate of return on investment, set by top management	10%
Expected rate of return on investment for new project	14%

If the manager of the Northern Division is evaluated using only return on investment, the division manager might decide to reject the new project. This is because investing in the new project will decrease Northern's current rate of return of 20%. Thus, the manager might reject the new project, even though its expected rate of return of 14% exceeds In-Touch's minimum acceptable rate of return of 10%.

In contrast, if the manager of the Northern Division is evaluated using residual income, the new project would probably be accepted because it will increase the Northern Division's residual income. In this way, residual income supports both divisional and overall company objectives.

The Balanced Scorecard[3]

The **balanced scorecard** is a set of multiple performance measures for a company. In addition to financial performance, a balanced scorecard normally includes performance measures for customer service, innovation and learning, and internal processes, as shown in Exhibit 8.

Performance measures for learning and innovation often revolve around a company's research and development efforts. For example, the number of new products developed during a year and the time it takes to bring new products to the market are performance measures for innovation. Performance measures for learning could include the number of employee training sessions and the number of employees who are cross-trained in several skills.

Performance measures for customer service include the number of customer complaints and the number of repeat customers. Customer surveys can also be used to gather measures of customer satisfaction with the company as compared to competitors.

Performance measures for internal processes include the length of time it takes to manufacture a product. The amount of scrap and waste is a measure of the efficiency of a company's manufacturing processes. The number of customer returns is a performance measure of both the manufacturing and sales ordering processes.

All companies will use financial performance measures. Some financial performance measures have been discussed earlier in this chapter and include income from operations, rate of return on investment, and residual income.

The balanced scorecard attempts to identify the underlying nonfinancial drivers, or causes, of financial performance related to innovation and learning, customer service, and internal processes. In this way, the financial performance may be improved. For example, customer satisfaction is often measured by the number

Merck & Co., Inc., measures the number of drugs in its FDA (Food and Drug Administration) approval pipeline and the length of time it takes to turn ideas into marketable products.

A survey by **Bain & Co.,** a consulting firm, indicated that 57% of large companies use the balanced scorecard.

3. The balanced scorecard was developed by R. S. Kaplan and D. P. Norton and explained in *The Balanced Scorecard: Translating Strategy into Action* (Cambridge: Harvard Business School Press, 1996).

EXHIBIT 8
The Balanced Scorecard

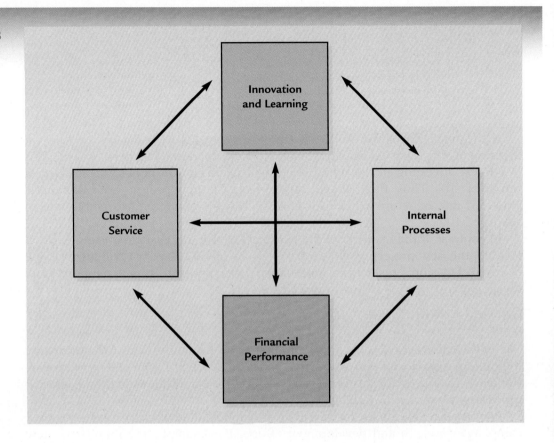

Hilton Hotels Corporation uses a balanced scorecard to measure employee satisfaction, customer loyalty, and financial performance.

of repeat customers. By increasing the number of repeat customers, sales and income from operations can be increased.

Some common performance measures used in the balanced scorecard approach are shown below.

Innovation and Learning

Number of new products
Number of new patents
Number of cross-trained employees
Number of training hours
Number of ethics violations
Employee turnover

Internal Processes

Waste and scrap
Time to manufacture products
Number of defects
Number of rejected sales orders
Number of stockouts
Labor utilization

Customer Service

Number of repeat customers
Customer brand recognition
Delivery time to customer
Customer satisfaction
Number of sales returns
Customer complaints

Financial

Sales
Income from operations
Return on investment
Profit margin and investment turnover
Residual income
Actual versus budgeted (standard) costs

Transfer Pricing

Obj | 5

Describe and illustrate how the market price, negotiated price, and cost price approaches to transfer pricing may be used by decentralized segments of a business.

When divisions transfer products or render services to each other, a **transfer price** is used to charge for the products or services.[4] Since transfer prices will affect a division's financial performance, setting a transfer price is a sensitive matter for the managers of both the selling and buying divisions.

Three common approaches to setting transfer prices are as follows:

1. Market price approach
2. Negotiated price approach
3. Cost approach

Transfer prices may be used for cost, profit, or investment centers. The objective of setting a transfer price is to motivate managers to behave in a manner that will increase the overall company income. As will be illustrated, however, transfer prices may be misused in such a way that overall company income suffers.

Transfer prices can be set as low as the variable cost per unit or as high as the market price. Often, transfer prices are negotiated at some point between variable cost per unit and market price. Exhibit 9 shows the possible range of transfer prices.

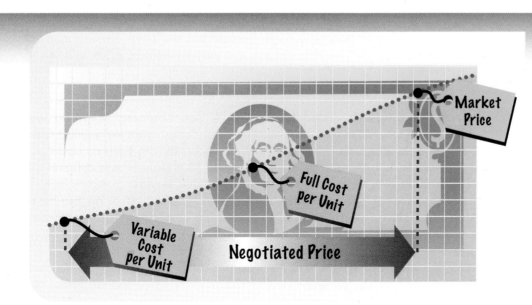

EXHIBIT 9

Commonly Used Transfer Prices

To illustrate, Wilson Company, a packaged snack food company with no service departments, is used. Wilson Company has two operating divisions (Eastern and Western) that are organized as investment centers. Condensed income statements for Wilson Company, assuming no transfers between divisions, are shown in Exhibit 10.

---

4. The discussion in this chapter highlights the essential concepts of transfer pricing. In-depth discussion of transfer pricing can be found in advanced texts.

EXHIBIT 10

Income Statements— No Transfers Between Divisions

Wilson Company
Income Statements
For the Year Ended December 31, 20Y8

	Eastern Division	Western Division	Total Company
Sales:			
50,000 units × $20 per unit	$1,000,000		$1,000,000
20,000 units × $40 per unit		$800,000	800,000
			$1,800,000
Expenses:			
Variable:			
50,000 units × $10 per unit	$ 500,000		$ 500,000
20,000 units × $30* per unit		$600,000	600,000
Fixed	300,000	100,000	400,000
Total expenses	$ 800,000	$700,000	$1,500,000
Income from operations	$ 200,000	$100,000	$ 300,000

*$20 of the $30 per unit represents materials costs, and the remaining $10 per unit represents other variable conversion expenses incurred within the Western Division.

Market Price Approach

Using the **market price approach**, the transfer price is the price at which the product or service transferred could be sold to outside buyers. If an outside market exists for the product or service transferred, the current market price may be a proper transfer price.

Transfer Price = Market Price

To illustrate, assume that materials used by Wilson Company in producing snack food in the Western Division are currently purchased from an outside supplier at $20 per unit. The same materials are produced by the Eastern Division. The Eastern Division is operating at full capacity of 50,000 units and can sell all it produces to either the Western Division or to outside buyers.

A transfer price of $20 per unit (the market price) has no effect on the Eastern Division's income or total company income. The Eastern Division will earn revenues of $20 per unit on all its production and sales, regardless of who buys its product.

Likewise, the Western Division will pay $20 per unit for materials (the market price). Thus, the use of the market price as the transfer price has no effect on the Eastern Division's income or total company income.

In this situation, the use of the market price as the transfer price is proper. The condensed divisional income statements for Wilson Company would be the same as shown in Exhibit 10.

Negotiated Price Approach

If unused or excess capacity exists in the supplying division (the Eastern Division), and the transfer price is equal to the market price, total company profit may not be maximized. This is because the manager of the Western Division will be indifferent toward purchasing materials from the Eastern Division or from outside suppliers. That is, in both cases the Western Division manager pays

$20 per unit (the market price). As a result, the Western Division may purchase the materials from outside suppliers.

If, however, the Western Division purchases the materials from the Eastern Division, the difference between the market price of $20 and the variable costs of the Eastern Division of $10 per unit (from Exhibit 10) can cover fixed costs and contribute to overall company profits. Thus, the Western Division manager should be encouraged to purchase the materials from the Eastern Division.

The **negotiated price approach** allows the managers to agree (negotiate) among themselves on a transfer price. The only constraint is that the transfer price be less than the market price, but greater than the supplying division's variable costs per unit, as shown below.

Variable Costs per Unit < Transfer Price < Market Price

To illustrate, assume that instead of a capacity of 50,000 units, the Eastern Division's capacity is 70,000 units. In addition, assume that the Eastern Division can continue to sell only 50,000 units to outside buyers.

A transfer price less than $20 would encourage the manager of the Western Division to purchase from the Eastern Division. This is because the Western Division is currently purchasing its materials from outside suppliers at a cost of $20 per unit. Thus, its materials cost would decrease, and its income from operations would increase.

At the same time, a transfer price above the Eastern Division's variable costs per unit of $10 (from Exhibit 10) would encourage the manager of the Eastern Division to supply materials to the Western Division. In doing so, the Eastern Division's income from operations would also increase.

Exhibit 11 illustrates the divisional and company income statements, assuming that the Eastern and Western division managers agree to a transfer price of $15.

EXHIBIT 11

Income Statements—Negotiated Transfer Price

Wilson Company
Income Statements
For the Year Ended December 31, 20Y8

	Eastern Division	Western Division	Total Company
Sales:			
50,000 units × $20 per unit	$1,000,000		$1,000,000
20,000 units × $15 per unit	300,000		300,000
20,000 units × $40 per unit		$800,000	800,000
	$1,300,000	$800,000	$2,100,000
Expenses:			
Variable:			
70,000 units × $10 per unit	$ 700,000		$ 700,000
20,000 units × $25* per unit		$500,000	500,000
Fixed	300,000	100,000	400,000
Total expenses	$1,000,000	$600,000	$1,600,000
Income from operations	$ 300,000	$200,000	$ 500,000

*$10 of the $25 represents variable conversion expenses incurred solely within the Western Division, and $15 per unit represents the transfer price per unit from the Eastern Division.

The Eastern Division increases its sales by $300,000 (20,000 units × $15 per unit) to $1,300,000. As a result, the Eastern Division's income from operations increases by $100,000 ($300,000 sales − $200,000 variable costs) to $300,000, as shown in Exhibit 11.

The increase of $100,000 in the Eastern Division's income can also be computed as follows:

$$\begin{array}{l}\text{Increase in Eastern} \\ \text{(Supplying) Division's} \\ \text{Income from Operations}\end{array} = \left(\begin{array}{cc}\text{Transfer} \\ \text{Price}\end{array} - \begin{array}{c}\text{Variable Cost} \\ \text{per Unit}\end{array}\right) \times \begin{array}{c}\text{Units} \\ \text{Transferred}\end{array}$$

$$\begin{array}{l}\text{Increase in Eastern} \\ \text{(Supplying) Division's} \\ \text{Income from Operations}\end{array} = (\$15 - \$10) \times 20,000 \text{ units} = \$100,000$$

The Western Division's materials cost decreases by $5 per unit ($20 − $15) for a total of $100,000 (20,000 units × $5 per unit). Thus, the Western Division's income from operations increases by $100,000 to $200,000, as shown in Exhibit 11.

The increase of $100,000 in the Western Division's income can also be computed as follows:

$$\begin{array}{l}\text{Increase in Western} \\ \text{(Purchasing) Division's} \\ \text{Income from Operations}\end{array} = (\text{Market Price} - \text{Transfer Price}) \times \begin{array}{c}\text{Units} \\ \text{Transferred}\end{array}$$

$$\begin{array}{l}\text{Increase in Western} \\ \text{(Purchasing) Division's} \\ \text{Income from Operations}\end{array} = (\$20 - \$15) \times 20,000 \text{ units} = \$100,000$$

Comparing Exhibits 10 and 11 shows that Wilson Company's income from operations increased by $200,000, as shown below.

	Income from Operations		
	No Units Transferred (Exhibit 10)	**20,000 Units Transferred at $15 per Unit (Exhibit 11)**	**Increase (Decrease)**
Eastern Division	$200,000	$300,000	$100,000
Western Division	100,000	200,000	100,000
Wilson Company	$300,000	$500,000	$200,000

In the preceding illustration, any negotiated transfer price between $10 and $20 is acceptable, as shown below.

$$\text{Variable Cost per Unit} < \text{Transfer Price} < \text{Market Price}$$

$$\$10 < \text{Transfer Price} < \$20$$

Any transfer price within this range will increase the overall income from operations for Wilson Company by $200,000. However, the increases in the Eastern and Western divisions' income from operations will vary depending on the transfer price.

To illustrate, a transfer price of $16 would increase the Eastern Division's income from operations by $120,000, as shown below.

$$\begin{matrix} \text{Increase in Eastern} \\ \text{(Supplying) Division's} \\ \text{Income from Operations} \end{matrix} = \left(\begin{matrix} \text{Transfer} \\ \text{Price} \end{matrix} - \begin{matrix} \text{Variable Cost} \\ \text{per Unit} \end{matrix} \right) \times \begin{matrix} \text{Units} \\ \text{Transferred} \end{matrix}$$

$$\begin{matrix} \text{Increase in Eastern} \\ \text{(Supplying) Division's} \\ \text{Income from Operations} \end{matrix} = (\$16 - \$10) \times 20{,}000 \text{ units} = \$120{,}000$$

A transfer price of $16 would increase the Western Division's income from operations by $80,000, as shown below.

$$\begin{matrix} \text{Increase in Western} \\ \text{(Purchasing) Division's} \\ \text{Income from Operations} \end{matrix} = (\text{Market Price} - \text{Transfer Price}) \times \begin{matrix} \text{Units} \\ \text{Transferred} \end{matrix}$$

$$\begin{matrix} \text{Increase in Western} \\ \text{(Purchasing) Division's} \\ \text{Income from Operations} \end{matrix} = (\$20 - \$16) \times 20{,}000 \text{ units} = \$80{,}000$$

With a transfer price of $16, Wilson Company's income from operations still increases by $200,000, which consists of the Eastern Division's increase of $120,000 plus the Western Division's increase of $80,000.

As shown above, the negotiated price provides each division manager with an incentive to negotiate the transfer of materials. At the same time, the overall company's income from operations will increase. However, the negotiated approach only applies when the supplying division has excess capacity. In other words, the supplying division cannot sell all its production to outside buyers at the market price.

Cost Price Approach

Under the **cost price approach**, cost is used to set transfer prices. A variety of costs may be used in this approach, including the following:

1. Total product cost per unit
2. Variable product per unit

If total product cost per unit is used, direct materials, direct labor, and factory overhead are included in the transfer price. If variable product cost per unit is used, the fixed factory overhead cost is excluded from the transfer price.

Actual costs or standard (budgeted) costs may be used in applying the cost price approach. If actual costs are used, inefficiencies of the producing (supplying) division are transferred to the purchasing division. Thus, there is little incentive for the producing (supplying) division to control costs. For this reason, most companies use standard costs in the cost price approach. In this way, differences between actual and standard costs remain with the producing (supplying) division for cost control purposes.

The cost price approach is most often used when the responsibility centers are organized as cost centers. When the responsibility centers are organized as profit or investment centers, the cost price approach is normally not used.

For example, using the cost price approach when the supplying division is organized as a profit center ignores the supplying division manager's responsibility for earning profits. In this case, using the cost price approach prevents the supplying division from reporting any profit (revenues – costs) on the units transferred. As a result, the division manager has little incentive to transfer units to another division, even though it may be in the best interests of the company.

Integrity, Objectivity, and Ethics in Business

SHIFTING INCOME THROUGH TRANSFER PRICES

Transfer prices allow companies to minimize taxes by shifting taxable income from countries with high tax rates to countries with low taxes. For example, GlaxoSmithKline, a British company and the second biggest drug maker in the world, had been in a dispute with the U.S. Internal Revenue Service (IRS) over international transfer prices since the early 1990s. The company pays U.S. taxes on income from its U.S. Division and British taxes on income from the British Division. The IRS, however, claimed that the transfer prices on sales from the British Division to the U.S. Division were too high, which reduced profits and taxes in the U.S. Division. The company received a new tax bill from the IRS in 2005 for almost $1.9 billion related to the transfer pricing issue, raising the total bill to almost $5 billion. In January 2006, the company agreed to settle this dispute with the IRS for $3.4 billion, the largest tax settlement in history.

Source: J. Whalen, "Glaxo Gets New IRS Bill Seeking Another $1.9 Billion in BackTax," *The Wall Street Journal*, January 27, 2005.

Key Points

1. Describe the advantages and disadvantages of decentralized operations.

The advantages of decentralization may include better decisions by the managers closest to the operations, more time for top management to focus on strategic planning, training for managers, improved ability to serve customers and respond to their needs, and improved manager morale. The disadvantages of decentralization may include failure of the company to maximize profits because decisions made by one manager may affect other managers in such a way that the profitability of the entire company may suffer.

2. Prepare a responsibility accounting report for a cost center.

Since managers of cost centers have responsibility and authority to make decisions regarding costs, responsibility accounting for cost centers focuses on costs. The primary accounting tools for planning and controlling costs for a cost center are budgets and budget performance reports. An example of a budget performance report is shown in Exhibit 3.

3. Prepare a responsibility accounting report for a profit center.

In preparing a profitability report for a profit center, operating expenses are subtracted from revenues in order to determine the income from operations before service department charges. Service department charges are then subtracted in order to determine the income from operations of the profit center. An example of a divisional income statement is shown in Exhibit 6.

4. Compute and interpret the rate of return on investment, the residual income, and the balanced scorecard for an investment center.

The rate of return on investment for an investment center is the income from operations divided by invested assets. The rate of return on investment may also be computed as the product of (1) the profit margin and (2) the investment turnover. Residual income for an investment center is the excess of income from operations over a minimum amount of desired income from operations. The balanced scorecard combines nonfinancial measures in order to help managers consider the underlying causes of financial performance and trade-offs between short- and long-term performance.

5. Describe and illustrate how the market price, negotiated price, and cost price approaches to transfer pricing may be used by decentralized segments of a business.

Under the market price approach, the transfer price is the price at which the product or service transferred could be sold to outside buyers. Market price should be used when the supplier division is able to sell to outsiders and is operating at capacity.

Under the negotiated price approach, the managers of decentralized units agree (negotiate) among themselves as to the transfer price. Negotiated prices should be used when the supplier division is operating below capacity.

Under the cost price approach, cost is used as the basis for setting transfer prices. A variety of cost concepts may be used, such as total product cost per unit or variable product cost per unit. In addition, actual costs or standard (budgeted) costs may be used. The cost price approach should be used for supplier divisions that are organized as cost centers.

Key Terms

Balanced scorecard (593)
Controllable expenses (583)
Controllable revenues (583)
Cost center (581)
Cost price approach (599)

DuPont formula (589)
Investment center (587)
Investment turnover (589)
Market price approach (596)

Negotiated price approach (597)
Profit center (583)
Profit margin (589)
Rate of return on investment (ROI) (588)
Residual income (591)

Responsibility accounting (581)
Service department charges (584)
Transfer price (595)

Illustrative Problem

Quinn Company has two divisions, Domestic and International. Invested assets and condensed income statement data for each division for the past year are as follows:

	Domestic Division	International Division
Revenues	$675,000	$480,000
Operating expenses	450,000	372,400
Service department charges	90,000	50,000
Invested assets	600,000	384,000

Instructions

1. Prepare condensed income statements for the past year for each division.
2. Using the DuPont formula, determine the profit margin, investment turnover, and rate of return on investment for each division.
3. If management's minimum acceptable rate of return is 10%, determine the residual income for each division.

Solution

1.
Quinn Company
Divisional Income Statements

	Domestic Division	International Division
Revenues	$675,000	$480,000
Operating expenses	450,000	372,400
Income from operations before service department charges	$225,000	$107,600
Service department charges	90,000	50,000
Income from operations	$135,000	$ 57,600

2. Rate of Return on Investment (ROI) = Profit Margin $\times$ Investment Turnover

$$\frac{\text{Rate of Return}}{\text{on Investment}} = \frac{\text{Income from Operations}}{\text{Sales}} \times \frac{\text{Sales}}{\text{Invested Assets}}$$

$$\text{Domestic Division: ROI} = \frac{\$135,000}{\$675,000} \times \frac{\$675,000}{\$600,000}$$

$$\text{ROI} = 20\% \times 1.125$$

$$\text{ROI} = 22.5\%$$

$$\text{International Division: ROI} = \frac{\$57,600}{\$480,000} \times \frac{\$480,000}{\$384,000}$$

$$\text{ROI} = 12\% \times 1.25$$

$$\text{ROI} = 15\%$$

3. Domestic Division: $75,000 [$135,000 − (10% × $600,000)]
   International Division: $19,200 [$57,600 − (10% × $384,000)]

Self-Examination Questions (Answers appear at the end of chapter)

1. When the manager has the responsibility and authority to make decisions that affect costs and revenues but no responsibility for or authority over assets invested in the department, the department is called:

   A. a cost center
   B. a profit center
   C. an investment center
   D. a service department

2. The Accounts Payable Department has expenses of $600,000 and makes 150,000 payments to the various vendors who provide products and services to the divisions. Division A has income from operations of $900,000, before service department charges, and requires 60,000 payments to vendors. If the Accounts Payable Department is treated as a service department, what is Division A's income from operations?

   A. $300,000
   B. $900,000
   C. $660,000
   D. $540,000

3. Division A of Kern Co. has sales of $350,000, cost of goods sold of $200,000, operating expenses of

$30,000, and invested assets of $600,000. What is the rate of return on investment for Division A?

   A. 20%
   B. 25%
   C. 33%
   D. 40%

4. Division L of Liddy Co. has a rate of return on investment of 24% and an investment turnover of 1.6. What is the profit margin?

   A. 6%
   B. 15%
   C. 24%
   D. 38%

5. Which approach to transfer pricing uses the price at which the product or service transferred could be sold to outside buyers?

   A. Cost price approach
   B. Negotiated price approach
   C. Market price approach
   D. Standard cost approach

Class Discussion Questions

1. Differentiate between a cost center and a profit center.

2. Differentiate between a profit center and an investment center.

3. In what major respect would budget performance reports prepared for the use of plant managers of a manufacturing business with cost centers differ from those prepared for the use of the various department supervisors who report to the plant managers?

4. For what decisions is the manager of a cost center *not* responsible?

5. **Weyerhaeuser** developed a system that assigns service department expenses to user divisions on the basis of actual services consumed by the division. Here are a number of Weyerhaeuser's activities in its central Financial Services Department:

   • Payroll

   • Accounts payable

   • Accounts receivable

   • Database administration—report preparation

   For each activity, identify an activity base that could be used to charge user divisions for service.

6. What is the major shortcoming of using income from operations as a performance measure for investment centers?

7. Why should the factors under the control of the investment center manager (revenues, expenses, and invested assets) be considered in computing the rate of return on investment?

8. In a decentralized company in which the divisions are organized as investment centers, how could a division be considered the least profitable, even though it earned the largest amount of income from operations?

9. How does using the rate of return on investment facilitate comparability between divisions of decentralized companies?

10. The rates of return on investment for Shear Co.'s three divisions, North, South, and Midwest are 38%, 30%, and 22%, respectively. In expanding operations, which of Shear Co.'s divisions should be given priority? Explain.

11. Why would a firm use a balanced scorecard in evaluating divisional performance?

12. What is the objective of transfer pricing?

13. When is the negotiated price approach preferred over the market price approach in setting transfer prices?

14. Why would standard cost be a more appropriate transfer cost between cost centers than actual cost?

15. When using the negotiated price approach to transfer pricing, within what range should the transfer price be established?

Exercises

E14-1 Budget performance reports for cost centers

Partially completed budget performance reports for Meridian Company, a manufacturer of air conditioners, are provided below.

Obj **2**

✔ a. (c) $10,750

Meridian Company
Budget Performance Report—Vice President, Production
For the Month Ended June 30, 20Y4

Plant	Budget	Actual	Over Budget	Under Budget
Orlando, Florida	$750,000	$752,000	$2,000	
Waco, Texas	400,000	398,200		$1,800
Peoria, Illinois	(g)	(h)	(i)	
	$ (j)	$ (k)	$ (l)	$1,800

Meridian Company
Budget Peformance Report—Plant Manager, Peoria, Illinois
For the Month Ended June 30, 20Y4

Department	Budget	Actual	Over Budget	Under Budget
Condenser Assembly	$ (a)	$ (b)	$ (c)	
Electronic Assembly	75,000	75,300	300	
Final Assembly	60,000	59,275		$725
	$ (d)	$ (e)	$ (f)	$725

Meridian Company
Budget Performance Report—Supervisor, Condenser Assembly
For the Month Ended June 30, 20Y4

Department	Budget	Actual	Over Budget	Under Budget
Factory wages	$ 30,000	$ 33,400	$ 3,400	
Materials	85,000	84,650		$350
Power and light	14,500	16,900	2,400	
Maintenance	10,500	15,800	5,300	
	$140,000	$150,750	$11,100	$350

a. Complete the budget performance reports by determining the correct amounts for the lettered spaces.

b. Compose a memo to Darla Pennington, president of Meridian Company, explaining the performance of the Production Division for June.

Obj 3

✔ Residential
Division income
from operations,
$575,000

E14-2   Divisional income statements

The following data were summarized from the accounting records for Statham Construction Company for the year ended November 30, 20Y3.

Cost of goods sold:		Service department charges:	
Residential Division	$1,450,000	Residential Division	$ 100,000
Industrial Division	3,450,000	Industrial Division	200,000
Administrative expenses:		Net sales:	
Residential Division	$ 175,000	Residential Division	$2,300,000
Industrial Division	480,000	Industrial Division	5,750,000

Prepare divisional income statements for Statham Construction Company.

Obj 3

E14-3   Service department charges and activity bases

For each of the following service departments, identify an activity base that could be used for charging the expense to the profit center.

a. Accounts Receivable
b. Central Purchasing
c. Duplication Services

d. Electronic Data Processing
e. Legal
f. Telecommunications

E14-4   Activity bases for service department charges

Obj **3**

For each of the following service departments, select the activity base listed that is most appropriate for charging service expenses to responsible units.

Service Department	Activity Base
a. Accounts Receivable	1. Number of computers
b. Central Purchasing	2. Number of trainees
c. Computer Support	3. Number of employees trained
d. Conferences	4. Number of payroll checks
e. Employee Travel	5. Number of purchase requisitions
f. Payroll Accounting	6. Number of sales invoices
g. Telecommunications	7. Number of telephone lines
h. Training	8. Number of travel claims

E14-5   Service department charges

Obj **3**

✔ b. Commercial
payroll, $15,390

In divisional income statements prepared for Iguana Construction Company, the Payroll Department costs are charged back to user divisions on the basis of the number of payroll checks, and the Purchasing Department costs are charged back on the basis of the number of purchase requisitions. The Payroll Department had expenses of $42,750, and the Purchasing Department had expenses of $87,600 for the year. The following annual data for the Residential, Commercial, and Government Contract divisions were obtained from corporate records:

	Residential	Commercial	Government Contract
Sales	$9,400,000	$6,800,000	$2,400,000
Number of employees:			
Weekly payroll (52 weeks per year)	80	60	25
Monthly payroll	20	10	5
Number of purchase requisitions per year	12,400	8,900	2,700

a. Determine the total amount of payroll checks and purchase requisitions processed per year by each division.

b. Using the activity base information in (a), determine the annual amount of payroll and purchasing costs charged back to the Residential, Commercial, and Government Contract divisions from payroll and purchasing services.

c. Why does the Residential Division have a larger service department charge than the other two divisions?

E14-6   Service department charges and activity bases

Obj **3**

✔ b. Help desk,
$14,580

Harris Corporation, a manufacturer of electronics and communications systems, uses a service department charge system to charge profit centers with Computing and Communications Services (CCS) service department costs. The following table identifies an abbreviated list of service categories and activity bases used by the CCS department. The table also includes some assumed cost and activity base quantity information for each service for February.

CCS Service Category	Activity Base	Assumed Cost	Assumed Activity Base Quantity
Help desk	Number of calls	$135,000	5,000
Network center	Number of devices monitored	363,000	7,500
Electronic mail	Number of user accounts	45,000	4,000
Local voice support	Number of phone extensions	39,000	3,000

One of the profit centers for Harris Corporation is the Electronics Systems sector. Assume the following information for the Electronics sector:

- The sector has 2,000 employees, of whom 60% are office employees.
- All the office employees have a phone, and all of them have a computer on the network.
- Ninety-five percent of the employees with a computer also have an e-mail account.
- The average number of help desk calls for February was 0.45 call per individual with a computer.
- There are 80 additional printers, servers, and peripherals on the network beyond the personal computers.

a. Determine the service charge rate for the four CCS service categories for February.

b. Determine the charges to the Electronics sector for the four CCS service categories for February.

Obj | 3

✔ **Retail income from operations, $4,624,000**

E14-7   Divisional income statements with service department charges

Power Sports Company has two divisions, Wholesale and Retail, and two corporate service departments, Tech Support and Accounts Payable. The corporate expenses for the year ended December 31, 20Y7, are as follows:

Tech Support Department	$ 855,000
Accounts Payable Department	390,000
Other corporate administrative expenses	355,000
Total corporate expense	$1,600,000

The other corporate administrative expenses include officers' salaries and other expenses required by the corporation. The Tech Support Department charges the divisions for services rendered, based on the number of computers in the department, and the Accounts Payable Department charges divisions for services, based on the number of checks issued. The usage of service by the two divisions is as follows:

	Tech Support	Accounts Payable
Wholesale Division	250 computers	18,000 checks
Retail Division	500	12,000
Total	750 computers	30,000 checks

The service department charges of the Tech Support Department and the Accounts Payable Department are considered controllable by the divisions. Corporate administrative expenses are not considered controllable by the divisions. The revenues, cost of goods sold, and operating expenses for the two divisions are as follows:

	Wholesale	Retail
Revenues	$24,600,000	$13,750,000
Cost of goods sold	14,500,000	8,000,000
Operating expenses	1,500,000	400,000

Prepare the divisional income statements for the two divisions.

Note: The spreadsheet icon indicates an Excel template is available on the student companion site.

E14-8   Corrections to service department charges

Panda Airlines Inc. has two divisions organized as profit centers, the Passenger Division and the Cargo Division. The following divisional income statements were prepared:

✔ b. Income from operations, Cargo Division, $2,105,000

Panda Airlines Inc.
Divisional Income Statements
For the Year Ended April 30, 20Y9

	Passenger Division		Cargo Division	
Revenues		$7,500,000		$5,000,000
Operating expenses		4,500,000		2,700,000
Income from operations before service department charges		$3,000,000		$2,300,000
Less service department charges:				
Training	$300,000		$200,000	
Flight scheduling	210,000		140,000	
Reservations	153,000	663,000	102,000	442,000
Income from operations		$2,337,000		$1,858,000

The service department charge rate for the service department costs was based on revenues. The following additional information is available:

	Passenger Division	Cargo Division	Total
Number of personnel trained	600	200	800
Number of flights	4,000	1,000	5,000
Number of reservations requested	750,000	0	750,000

a. Does the income from operations for the two divisions accurately measure performance?

b. Correct the divisional income statements, using the activity bases provided on the preceding page in revising the service department charges.

E14-9   Profit center responsibility reporting

On-Demand Sports Co. operates two divisions—the Action Sports Division and the Team Sports Division. The following income and expense accounts were provided as of November 30, 20Y1, the end of the current fiscal year, after all adjustments, including those for inventories, were recorded:

✔ Income from operations, Action Sports Division, $2,823,000

Sales—Action Sports (AS) Division	$18,500,000
Sales—Team Sports (TS) Division	30,600,000
Cost of Goods Sold—Action Sports (AS) Division	10,700,000
Cost of Goods Sold—Team Sports (TS) Division	19,200,000
Sales Expense—Action Sports (AS) Division	1,500,000
Sales Expense—Team Sports (TS) Division	2,100,000
Administrative Expense—Action Sports (AS) Division	1,250,000
Administrative Expense—Team Sports (TS) Division	1,450,000
Advertising Expense	3,000,000
Transportation Expense	654,900
Accounts Receivable Collection Expense	400,500
Warehouse Expense	800,000

The bases to be used in allocating expenses, together with other essential information, are as follows:

a. Advertising expense—incurred at headquarters, charged back to divisions on the basis of usage: Action Sports Division, $1,200,000; Team Sports Division, $1,800,000.

b. Transportation expense—charged back to divisions at a charge rate of $18.50 per bill of lading: Action Sports Division, 14,000 bills of lading; Team Sports Division, 21,400 bills of lading.

c. Accounts receivable collection expense—incurred at headquarters, charged back to divisions at a charge rate of $9.00 per invoice: Action Sports Division, 32,000 sales invoices; Team Sports Division, 12,500 sales invoices.

d. Warehouse expense—charged back to divisions on the basis of floor space used in storing division products: Action Sports Division, 120,000 square feet; Team Sports Division, 80,000 square feet.

Prepare divisional income statements with two column headings: Action Sports Division and Team Sports Division. Provide supporting schedules for determining service department charges.

Obj **4**

✔ a. Health Club Division, 19%

E14-10   Rate of return on investment

The income from operations and the amount of invested assets in each division of Gantt Industries are as follows:

	Income from Operations	Invested Assets
Sporting Goods Division	$540,000	$3,000,000
Health Club Division	418,000	2,200,000
School Division	455,000	3,500,000

a. Compute the rate of return on investment for each division.

b. Which division is the most profitable per dollar invested?

Obj **4**

✔ a. Sporting Goods Division, $180,000

E14-11   Residual income

Based on the data in Exercise 14-10, assume that management has established a 12% minimum acceptable rate of return for invested assets.

a. Determine the residual income for each division.

b. Which division has the most residual income?

Obj **4**

✔ d. 1.50

E14-12   Determining missing items in rate of return computation

One item is omitted from each of the following computations of the rate of return on investment:

Rate of Return on Investment	=	Profit Margin	×	Investment Turnover
12%	=	8%	×	(a)
(b)	=	16%	×	1.25
24%	=	(c)	×	1.20
15%	=	10%	×	(d)
(e)	=	10%	×	1.70

Determine the missing items, identifying each by the appropriate letter.

E14-13   Profit margin, investment turnover, and rate of return on investment

Obj 4
✔ a. ROI, 19.2%

The condensed income statement for the International Division of Valgenti Inc. is as follows (assuming no service department charges):

Sales	$24,000,000
Cost of goods sold	14,100,000
Gross profit	$ 9,900,000
Administrative expenses	6,060,000
Income from operations	$ 3,840,000

The manager of the International Division is considering ways to increase the rate of return on investment.

a. Using the DuPont formula for rate of return on investment, determine the profit margin, investment turnover, and rate of return on investment of the International Division, assuming that $20,000,000 of assets have been invested in the International Division.

b. If expenses could be reduced by $240,000 without decreasing sales, what would be the impact on the profit margin, investment turnover, and rate of return on investment for the International Division?

E14-14   Rate of return on investment

Obj 4
✔ a. Parks and Resorts ROI, 9.1%

The Walt Disney Company has four major sectors, described as follows:

- **Media Networks:** The ABC television and radio network, Disney channel, ESPN, A&E, E!, and Disney.com.
- **Parks and Resorts:** Walt Disney World Resort, Disneyland, Disney Cruise Line, and other resort properties.
- **Studio Entertainment:** Walt Disney Pictures, Touchstone Pictures, Hollywood Pictures, Miramax Films, and Buena Vista Theatrical Productions.
- **Consumer Products:** Character merchandising, Disney stores, books, and magazines.

Disney recently reported sector income from operations, revenue, and invested assets (in millions) as follows:

	Income from Operations	Revenue	Invested Assets
Media Networks	$6,619	$19,436	$28,660
Parks and Resorts	1,902	12,920	20,951
Studio Entertainment	722	5,825	12,928
Consumer Products	937	3,252	5,016

a. Use the DuPont formula to determine the rate of return on investment for the four Disney sectors. Round profit margin and rate of return on investment to one decimal place and investment turnover to two decimal places.

b. How do the four sectors differ in their profit margin, investment turnover, and return on investment?

E14-15   Determining missing items in rate of return and residual income computations

Obj 4
✔ c. $100,000

Data are presented in the following table of rates of return on investment and residual incomes:

Invested Assets	Income from Operations	Rate of Return on Investment	Minimum Rate of Return	Minimum Acceptable Income from Operations	Residual Income
$ 2,500,000	$ 400,000	(a)	12%	(b)	(c)
6,000,000	(d)	(e)	(f)	$600,000	$240,000
7,500,000	(g)	20%	(h)	900,000	(i)
14,000,000	2,380,000	(j)	13%	(k)	(l)

Determine the missing items, identifying each item by the appropriate letter.

Obj 4

✔ a. (e) $9,000,000

E14-16 Determining missing items from computations

Data for the California, Midwest, Northwest, and Texas divisions of Firefly Industries are as follows:

	Sales	Income from Operations	Invested Assets	Rate of Return on Investment	Profit Margin	Investment Turnover
California	$ 6,000,000	(a)	(b)	16%	20%	(c)
Midwest	(d)	$1,512,000	(e)	(f)	12%	1.4
Northwest	13,750,000	(g)	$11,000,000	17.5%	(h)	(i)
Texas	5,250,000	840,000	3,500,000	(j)	(k)	(l)

a. Determine the missing items, identifying each by the letters (a) through (l). Round profit margin to one decimal place and investment turnover to two decimal places.

b. Determine the residual income for each division, assuming that the minimum acceptable rate of return established by management is 10%.

c. Which division is the most profitable in terms of (1) return on investment and (2) residual income?

E14-17 Rate of return on investment, residual income

Obj 4

Marriott International, Inc., provides lodging services around the world. The company is organized into the following four segments:

- **North American—Full Service:** Marriott and Renaissance Hotels.
- **North American—Limited Service:** Courtyard, Fairfield, SpringHill Suites, and Residence Hotels.
- **International:** Hotels outside of North America.
- **Luxury:** The Ritz-Carlton, Bulgari, and Edition Hotels.

Financial information for each segment taken from a recent annual report is as follows (in millions):

	North American—Full Service	North American—Limited Service	International	Luxury
Revenues	$5,450	$2,358	$1,278	$1,673
Income from operations	351	382	175	74
Total assets	1,241	497	1,026	931

a. Use the DuPont formula to determine the return on investment for each of the Marriott business divisions. Round profit margin and rate of return on investment to one decimal place and investment turnover to two decimal places.

b. Determine the residual income for each division, assuming a minimum acceptable income of 10% of total assets. Round minimal acceptable return to the nearest million dollars.

c. Interpret your results.

E14-18 Balanced scorecard

Obj 4

American Express Company is a major financial services company, noted for its American Express® card. Below are some of the performance measures used by the company in its balanced scorecard.

Average cardmember spending
Cards in force
Earnings growth
Hours of credit consultant training
Investment in information technology
Number of Internet features

Number of merchant signings
Number of card choices
Number of new card launches
Return on equity
Revenue growth

For each measure, identify whether the measure best fits the innovation, customer, internal process, or financial dimension of the balanced scorecard.

E14-19 Balanced scorecard

Obj 4

Several years ago, **United Parcel Service (UPS)** believed that the Internet was going to change the parcel delivery market and would require UPS to become a more nimble and customer-focused organization. As a result, UPS replaced its old measurement system, which was 90% oriented toward financial performance, with a balanced scorecard. The scorecard emphasized four "point of arrival" measures, which were:

1. Customer satisfaction index—a measure of customer satisfaction.
2. Employee relations index—a measure of employee sentiment and morale.
3. Competitive position—delivery performance relative to competition.
4. Time in transit—the time from order entry to delivery.

   a. Why did UPS introduce a balanced scorecard and nonfinancial measures in its new performance measurement system?

   b. Why do you think UPS included a factor measuring employee sentiment?

E14-20 Decision on transfer pricing

Obj 5
✔ a. $225,000

Wiring used by the Aircraft Division of Retina Manufacturing is currently purchased from outside suppliers at a cost of $75 per unit. However, the same materials are available from the Electronic Division. The Electronic Division has unused capacity and can produce the materials needed by the Aircraft Division at a variable cost of $66 per unit.

a. If a transfer price of $70 per unit is established and 25,000 units of materials are transferred, with no reduction in the Electronic Division's current sales, how much would Retina Manufacturing's total income from operations increase?

b. How much would the Aircraft Division's income from operations increase?

c. How much would the Electronic Division's income from operations increase?

E14-21 Decision on transfer pricing

Obj 5
✔ b. $75,000

Based on Retina Manufacturing's data in Exercise 14-20, assume that a transfer price of $72 has been established and that 25,000 units of materials are transferred, with no reduction in the Electronic Division's current sales.

a. How much would Retina Manufacturing's total income from operations increase?

b. How much would the Aircraft Division's income from operations increase?

c. How much would the Electronic Division's income from operations increase?

d. If the negotiated price approach is used, what would be the range of acceptable transfer prices and why?

Problems

P14-1 Budget performance report for a cost center

Obj 2

Sneed Industries Company sells vehicle parts to manufacturers of heavy construction equipment. The Crane Division is organized as a cost center. The budget for the Crane Division for the month ended August 31, 20Y6, is as follows (in thousands):

Customer service salaries	$ 250,000
Insurance and property taxes	50,000
Distribution salaries	475,000
Marketing salaries	300,000
Engineer salaries	740,000
Warehouse wages	280,000
Equipment depreciation	155,000
Total	$2,250,000

During August, the costs incurred in the Crane Division were as follows:

Customer service salaries	$ 368,000
Insurance and property taxes	49,100
Distribution salaries	469,500
Marketing salaries	371,000
Engineer salaries	738,250
Warehouse wages	274,900
Equipment depreciation	155,000
Total	$2,425,750

Instructions

1. Prepare a budget performance report for the director of the Crane Division for the month of August.

2. For which costs might the director be expected to request supplemental reports?

Obj 3

✔ 1. Income
from operations,
Air Division,
$753,300

P14-2   Profit center responsibility reporting

A-One Freight Inc. has three regional divisions organized as profit centers. The chief executive officer (CEO) evaluates divisional performance, using income from operations as a percent of revenues. The following quarterly income and expense accounts were provided from the trial balance as of December 31, 20Y3.

Revenues—Air Division	$5,000,000
Revenues—Rail Division	6,000,000
Revenues—Truck Division	9,000,000
Operating Expenses—Air Division	4,100,000
Operating Expenses—Rail Division	4,900,000
Operating Expenses—Truck Division	7,555,000
Corporate Expenses—Shareholder Relations	220,000
Corporate Expenses—Customer Support	990,000
Corporate Expenses—Legal	880,000
General Corporate Officers' Salaries	500,000

The company operates three service departments: Shareholder Relations, Customer Support, and Legal. The Shareholder Relations Department conducts a variety of services for shareholders of the company. The Customer Support Department is the company's point of contact for new service, complaints, and requests for repair. The department believes that the number of customer contacts is an activity base for this work. The Legal Department provides legal services for division management. The department believes that the number of hours billed is an activity base for this work. The following additional information has been gathered:

	Air	Rail	Truck
Number of customer contacts	1,500	4,500	16,000
Number of hours billed	900	2,400	6,700

Instructions

1. Prepare quarterly income statements showing income from operations for the three divisions. Use three column headings: Air, Rail, and Truck.

2. Identify the most successful division according to the profit margin. Round to one decimal place.

3. Provide a recommendation to the CEO for a better method for evaluating the performance of the divisions. In your recommendation, identify the major weakness of the present method.

P14-3   Divisional income statements and rate of return on investment analysis

Pastry Inc. is a diversified food products company with three operating divisions organized as investment centers. Condensed data taken from the records of the three divisions for the year ended April 30, 20Y7, are as follows:

Obj 4

✔ 2. Breakfast Division, ROI, 17.6%

	Breakfast Division	Cookies Division	Frozen Desserts Division
Sales	$19,800,000	$8,550,000	$33,300,000
Cost of goods sold	14,850,000	6,400,000	25,100,000
Operating expenses	1,782,000	1,124,000	2,206,000
Invested assets	18,000,000	9,000,000	27,750,000

The management of Pastry Inc. is evaluating each division as a basis for planning a future expansion of operations.

Instructions

1. Prepare condensed divisional income statements for the three divisions, assuming that there were no service department charges.

2. Using the DuPont formula for rate of return on investment, compute the profit margin, investment turnover, and rate of return on investment for each division.

3. If available funds permit the expansion of operations of only one division, which of the divisions would you recommend for expansion, based on parts (1) and (2)? Explain.

P14-4   Effect of proposals on divisional performance

A condensed income statement for the Jet Ski Division of Amazing Rides Inc. for the year ended December 31, 20Y2, is as follows:

Obj 4

✔ 1. ROI, 11.2%

Sales	$12,000,000
Cost of goods sold	7,200,000
Gross profit	$ 4,800,000
Operating expenses	3,120,000
Income from operations	$ 1,680,000
Invested assets	$15,000,000

Assume that the Jet Ski Division received no charges from service departments. The president of Amazing Rides has indicated that the division's rate of return on a $15,000,000 investment must be increased to at least 12% by the end of the next year if operations are to continue. The division manager is considering the following three proposals:

Proposal 1: Transfer equipment with a book value of $3,000,000 to other divisions at no gain or loss and lease similar equipment. The annual lease payments would exceed the amount of depreciation expense on the old equipment by $264,000. This increase in expense would be included as part of the cost of goods sold. Sales would remain unchanged.

Proposal 2: Purchase new and more efficient machining equipment and thereby reduce the cost of goods sold by $480,000. Sales would remain unchanged, and the old equipment, which has no remaining book value, would be scrapped at no gain or loss. The new equipment would increase invested assets by an additional $1,000,000 for the year.

Proposal 3: Reduce invested assets by discontinuing the tandem jet ski line. This action would eliminate sales of $2,280,000, cost of goods sold of $1,400,000, and operating expenses of $463,600. Assets of $4,200,000 would be transferred to other divisions at no gain or loss.

Instructions

1. Using the DuPont formula for rate of return on investment, determine the profit margin, investment turnover, and rate of return on investment for the Jet Ski Division for the past year.

2. Prepare condensed estimated income statements and compute the invested assets for each proposal.

3. Using the DuPont formula for rate of return on investment, determine the profit margin, investment turnover, and rate of return on investment for each proposal.

4. Which of the three proposals would meet the required 12% rate of return on investment?

5. If the Jet Ski Division were in an industry where the profit margin could not be increased, how much would the investment turnover have to increase to meet the president's required 12% rate of return on investment?

Obj 4

✔ 2. On-Road Bike Division ROI, 16.8%

P14-5   Divisional performance analysis and evaluation

The vice president of operations of Montana Bike Company is evaluating the performance of two divisions organized as investment centers. Invested assets and condensed income statement data for the past year for each division are as follows:

	On-Road Bike Division	Off-Road Bike Division
Sales	$10,500,000	$8,000,000
Cost of goods sold	6,300,000	5,600,000
Operating expenses	2,940,000	1,560,000
Invested assets	7,500,000	5,000,000

Instructions

1. Prepare condensed divisional income statements for the year ended December 31, 20Y9, assuming that there were no service department charges.

2. Using the DuPont formula for rate of return on investment, determine the profit margin, investment turnover, and rate of return on investment for each division.

3. If management desires a minimum acceptable rate of return of 15%, determine the residual income for each division.

4. Discuss the evaluation of the two divisions, using the performance measures determined in parts (1), (2), and (3).

Obj 5

✔ 3. Total income from operations, $4,750,000

P14-6   Transfer pricing

Pendray Scientific Inc. manufactures electronic products, with two operating divisions, the GPS Systems and Communication Systems divisions. Condensed divisional income statements, which involve no intracompany transfers and which include a breakdown of expenses into variable and fixed components, are as follows:

Pendray Scientific Inc.
Divisional Income Statements
For the Year Ended December 31, 20Y5

	GPS Systems Division	Communication Systems Division	Total
Sales:			
75,000 units @ $60 per unit	$4,500,000		$ 4,500,000
140,000 units @ $115 per unit		$16,100,000	16,100,000
	$4,500,000	$16,100,000	$20,600,000
Expenses:			
Variable:			
75,000 units @ $40 per unit	$3,000,000		$ 3,000,000
140,000 units @ $90* per unit		$12,600,000	12,600,000
Fixed	250,000	500,000	750,000
Total expenses	$3,250,000	$13,100,000	$16,350,000
Income from operations	$1,250,000	$ 3,000,000	$ 4,250,000

*$60 of the $90 per unit represents materials costs, and the remaining $30 per unit represents other variable conversion expenses incurred within the Communication Systems Division.

The GPS Systems Division is presently producing 75,000 units out of a total capacity of 100,000 units. Materials used in producing the Communication Systems Division's product are currently purchased from outside suppliers at a price of $60 per unit. The GPS Systems Division is able to produce the materials used by the Communication Systems Division. Except for the possible transfer of materials between divisions, no changes are expected in sales and expenses.

Instructions

1. Would the market price of $60 per unit be an appropriate transfer price for Pendray Scientific Inc.? Explain.

2. If the Communication Systems Division purchases 25,000 units from the GPS Systems Division, rather than externally, at a negotiated transfer price of $52 per unit, how much would the income from operations of each division and the total company income from operations increase?

3. Prepare condensed divisional income statements for Pendray Scientific Inc. based on the data in part (2).

4. If a transfer price of $49 per unit is negotiated, how much would the income from operations of each division and the total company income from operations increase?

5. a. What is the range of possible negotiated transfer prices that would be acceptable for Pendray Scientific Inc.?

    b. Assuming that the managers of the two divisions cannot agree on a transfer price, what price would you suggest as the transfer price?

Cases

Case 14-1   Ethics and professional conduct in business

Sisel Company has two divisions, the Optic Lens Division and the Camera Division. The Camera Division may purchase lenses from the Optic Lens Division or from outside suppliers. The Optic Lens Division sells products both internally and externally. The market price for lenses is $2,500 per carton (100). Newt Watt is the controller of the Camera Division, and Tani Trudeau is the controller of the Optic Lens Division. The following conversation took place between Newt and Tani:

Newt: I hear you are having problems selling lenses out of your division. Maybe I can help.

Tani: You've got that right. We're producing and selling at about 75% of our capacity to outsiders. Last year we were selling at capacity. Would it be possible for your division to pick up some of our excess capacity? After all, we are part of the same company.

Newt: What kind of price could you give me?

Tani: Well, you know as well as I that we are under strict profit responsibility in our divisions, so I would expect to get market price, $2,500 per carton (100).

Newt: I'm not so sure we can swing that. I was expecting a price break from a "sister" division.

Tani: Hey, I can only take this "sister" stuff so far. If I give you a price break, our profits will fall from last year's levels. I don't think I could explain that. I'm sorry, but I must remain firm—market price. After all, it's only fair—that's what you would have to pay from an external supplier.

Newt: Fair or not, I think we'll pass. Sorry we couldn't have helped.

Was Newt behaving ethically by trying to force the Optic Lens Division into a price break? Comment on Tani's reactions.

Case 14-2   Service department charges

The Customer Service Department of Bragg Inc. asked the Publications Department to prepare a brochure for its training program. The Publications Department delivered the brochures and charged the Customer Service Department a rate that was 15% higher than could be obtained from an outside printing company. The policy of the company required the Customer Service Department to use the internal publications group for brochures. The Publications Department claimed that it had a drop in demand for its services during the fiscal year, so it had to charge higher prices in order to recover its payroll and fixed costs.

Should the cost of the brochure be transferred to the Customer Service Department in order to hold the department head accountable for the cost of the brochure? What changes in policy would you recommend?

Case 14-3   Evaluating divisional performance

The three divisions of Dixie Foods are Cereal, Produce, and Snacks. The divisions are structured as investment centers. The following responsibility reports were prepared for the three divisions for the prior year:

	Cereal	Produce	Snacks
Revenues	$5,400,000	$16,000,000	$9,000,000
Operating expenses	4,200,000	12,800,000	6,300,000
Income from operations before service department charges	$1,200,000	$ 3,200,000	$2,700,000
Service department charges:			
Promotion	$ 500,000	$ 1,500,000	$1,200,000
Legal	268,000	740,000	420,000
	$ 768,000	$ 2,240,000	$1,620,000
Income from operations	$ 432,000	$ 960,000	$1,080,000
Invested assets	$4,500,000	$ 8,000,000	$5,000,000

1. Which division is making the best use of invested assets and thus should be given priority for future capital investments?

2. Assuming that the minimum acceptable rate of return on new projects is 10%, would all investments that produce a return in excess of 10% be accepted by the divisions?

3. Determine the overall return on investment for Dixie Foods. Round to one decimal place.

4. Can you identify opportunities for improving Dixie Foods' financial performance?

Case 14-4   Evaluating division performance over time

The Laser Division of FOX Technologies Inc. has been experiencing revenue and profit growth during the years 20Y6–20Y8. The divisional income statements are provided below.

FOX Technologies Inc.
Divisional Income Statements, Laser Division
For the Years Ended December 31, 20Y6–20Y8

	20Y6	20Y7	20Y8
Sales	$3,000,000	$4,500,000	$7,000,000
Cost of goods sold	1,800,000	2,625,000	3,800,000
Gross profit	$1,200,000	$1,875,000	$3,200,000
Operating expenses	300,000	300,000	400,000
Income from operations	$ 900,000	$1,575,000	$2,800,000

Assume that there are no charges from service departments. The vice president of the division, Stacy Harper, is proud of her division's performance over the last three years. The president of FOX Technologies Inc., Hal Nelson, is discussing the division's performance with Stacy, as follows:

Stacy: As you can see, we've had a successful three years in the Laser Division.

Hal: I'm not too sure.

Stacy: What do you mean? Look at our results. Our income from operations has more than tripled, while our profit margins are improving.

Hal: I am looking at your results. However, your income statements fail to include one very important piece of information; namely, the invested assets. You have been investing a great deal of assets into the division. You had $2,000,000 in invested assets in 20Y6, $4,500,000 in 20Y7, and $10,000,000 in 20Y8.

Stacy: You are right. I've needed the assets in order to upgrade our technologies and expand our operations. The additional assets are one reason we have been able to grow and improve our profit margins. I don't see that this is a problem.

Hal: The problem is that we want to maintain a 30% rate of return on invested assets.

1. Determine the profit margins for the Laser Division for 20Y6–20Y8.
2. Compute the investment turnover for the Laser Division for 20Y6–20Y8.
3. Compute the rate of return on investment for the Laser Division for 20Y6–20Y8.
4. Evaluate the division's performance over the 20Y6–20Y8 time period. Why was Hal concerned about the performance?

Case 14-5 Evaluating division performance

Modern Living Inc. is a privately held diversified company with five separate divisions organized as investment centers. A condensed income statement for the Patio Division for the past year, assuming no service department charges, is as follows:

Modern Living Inc.— Patio Division
Income Statement
For the Year Ended December 31, 20Y4

Sales	$18,000,000
Cost of goods sold	13,000,000
Gross profit	$ 5,000,000
Operating expenses	1,400,000
Income from operations	$ 3,600,000
Invested assets	$15,000,000

The manager of the Patio Division was recently presented with the opportunity to add an outdoor fireplace product line, which would require invested assets of $4,500,000. A projected income statement for the new product line is as follows:

Outdoor Fireplace Line
Projected Income Statement
For the Year Ended December 31, 20Y5

Sales	$4,050,000
Cost of goods sold	2,340,000
Gross profit	$1,710,000
Operating expenses	900,000
Income from operations	$ 810,000

The Patio Division currently has $15,000,000 in invested assets, and Modern Living Inc.'s overall rate of return on investment, including all divisions, is 14%. Each division manager is evaluated on the basis of divisional rate of return on investment, and a bonus equal to $10,000 for each percentage point by which the division's rate of return on investment exceeds the company average is awarded each year.

The president is concerned that the manager of the Patio Division rejected the addition of the new product line, when all estimates indicated that the product line would be profitable and would increase overall company income. You have been asked to analyze the possible reasons why the Patio Division manager rejected the new product line.

1. Determine the rate of return on investment for the Patio Division for the past year.
2. Determine the Patio Division manager's bonus for the past year.
3. Determine the estimated rate of return on investment for the new product line.

4. Determine the rate of return for the Patio Division if the Outdoor Fireplace product line was added and the 20Y5 operating results were similar to those of 20Y4. Round to one decimal place.

5. Why might the manager of the Patio Division decide to reject the new product line?

6. Can you suggest an alternative performance measure for motivating division managers to accept new investment opportunities that would increase the overall company income and rate of return on investment?

GROUP PROJECT

Case 14-6   The balanced scorecard and EVA

Divide responsibilities between two groups, with one group going to the home page of **The Palladium Group** at http://www.thepalladiumgroup.com, and the second group going to the home page of **Stern Stewart & Co.** at http://www.eva.com. The Palladium Group is a consulting firm that helped develop the balanced scorecard concept. Stern Stewart & Co. is a consulting firm that developed the concept of economic value added (EVA), another method of measuring corporate and divisional performance, similar to residual income.

After reading about the balanced scorecard at the palladiumgroup.com site, prepare a brief report describing the balanced scorecard and its claimed advantages. In the Stern group, use links in the home page of Stern Stewart & Co. to learn about EVA. After reading about EVA, prepare a brief report describing EVA and its claimed advantages. After preparing these reports, both groups should discuss their research and prepare a brief analysis comparing and contrasting these two approaches to corporate and divisional performance measurement.

Answers to Self-Examination Questions

1. **B** The manager of a profit center (answer B) has responsibility for and authority over costs and revenues. If the manager has responsibility for only costs, the department is called a cost center (answer A). If the responsibility and authority extend to the investment in assets as well as costs and revenues, it is called an investment center (answer C). A service department (answer D) provides services to other departments. A service department could be a cost center, a profit center, or an investment center.

2. **C** $600,000/150,000 = $4 per payment. Division A anticipates 60,000 payments or $240,000 (60,000 × $4) in service department charges from the Accounts Payable Department. Income from operations is thus $900,000 − $240,000, or $660,000. Answer A assumes that all of the service department overhead is assigned to Division A, which would be incorrect, since Division A does not use all of the accounts payable service. Answer B incorrectly assumes that there are no service department charges from Accounts Payable. Answer D incorrectly determines the accounts payable transfer rate from Division A's income from operations.

3. **A** The rate of return on investment for Division A is 20% (answer A), computed as follows:

$$\text{Rate of Return on Investment (ROI)} = \frac{\text{Income from Operations}}{\text{Invested Assets}}$$

$$\text{ROI} = \frac{\$350,000 - \$200,000 - \$30,000}{\$600,000} = 20\%$$

4. **B** The profit margin for Division L of Liddy Co. is 15% (answer B), computed as follows:

$$\text{Rate of Return on Investment (ROI)} = \frac{\text{Profit}}{\text{Margin}} \times \frac{\text{Investment}}{\text{Turnover}}$$

$$24\% = \text{Profit Margin} \times 1.6$$

$$15\% = \text{Profit Margin}$$

5. **C** The market price approach (answer C) to transfer pricing uses the price at which the product or service transferred could be sold to outside buyers. The cost price approach (answer A) uses cost as the basis for setting transfer prices. The negotiated price approach (answer B) allows managers of decentralized units to agree (negotiate) among themselves as to the proper transfer price. The standard cost approach (answer D) is a version of the cost price approach that uses standard costs in setting transfer prices.

CHAPTER 15

Capital Investment Analysis

LEARNING OBJECTIVES
After studying this chapter, you should be able to:

Obj **1** Explain the nature and importance of capital investment analysis.

Obj **2** Evaluate capital investment proposals using the average rate of return and cash payback methods.

Obj **3** Evaluate capital investment proposals using the net present value and internal rate of return methods.

Obj **4** List and describe factors that complicate capital investment analysis.

Obj **5** Diagram the capital rationing process.

Why are you paying tuition, studying this text, and spending time and money on a higher education? Most people believe that the money and time spent now will return them more earnings in the future. In other words, the cost of higher education is an investment in your future earning ability. How would you know if this investment is worth it?

One method would be for you to compare the cost of a higher education against the estimated increase in your future earning power. The bigger the difference between your expected future earnings and the cost of your education, the better the investment. The same is true for the investments businesses make in fixed assets. Business organizations use a variety of methods to compare the cost of an investment to its future earnings and cash flows.

For example, **Carnival Corporation** is one of the the largest vacation cruise companies in the world, with over 98 cruise ships that sail to locations around the world. Carnival's

fleet required an investment of nearly $38 billion, with each new ship costing over $600 million. Carnival used capital investment analysis to compare this investment with the future earnings ability of the ships over their 30-year expected lives. Carnival must be satisfied with its investments, because it has signed agreements with shipyards to add additional cruise ships to its fleet.

In this chapter, the methods used to make investment decisions, which may involve thousands, millions, or even billions of dollars, are described and illustrated. The similarities and differences among the most commonly used methods of evaluating investment proposals, as well as the benefits of each method, are emphasized. Qualitative considerations affecting investment analyses, considerations complicating investment analyses, and the process of allocating available investment funds among competing proposals are also discussed.

Obj | **1**

Explain the nature and importance of capital investment analysis.

Nature of Capital Investment Analysis

Companies use capital investment analysis to evaluate long-term investments. **Capital investment analysis** (or *capital budgeting*) is the process by which management plans, evaluates, and controls investments in fixed assets. Capital investments use funds and affect operations for many years and must earn a reasonable rate of return. Thus, capital investment decisions are some of the most important decisions that management makes.

Capital investment evaluation methods can be grouped into the following categories:

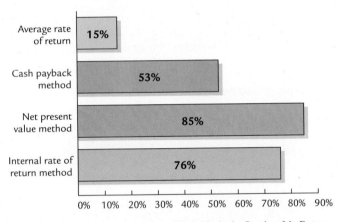

Percent of U.S. Companies Reporting Using These Methods "Always" or "Often"

- Average rate of return: 15%
- Cash payback method: 53%
- Net present value method: 85%
- Internal rate of return method: 76%

(0% 10% 20% 30% 40% 50% 60% 70% 80% 90%)

Source: Patricia A. Ryan and Glenn P. Ryan, "Capital Budgeting Practice of the Fortune 1000: How Have Things Changed?" *Journal of Business and Management* (Winter 2002).

Methods That Do Not Use Present Values

1. Average rate of return method
2. Cash payback method

Methods That Use Present Values

1. Net present value method
2. Internal rate of return method

The two methods that use present values consider the time value of money. The **time value of money concept** recognizes that an amount of cash invested today will earn income and thus has value over time.

Obj | **2**

Evaluate capital investment proposals using the average rate of return and cash payback methods.

Methods Not Using Present Values

The methods not using present values are often useful in evaluating capital investment proposals that have relatively short useful lives. In such cases, the timing of the cash flows (the time value of money) is less important.

Since the methods not using present values are easy to use, they are often used to screen proposals. Minimum standards for accepting proposals are set, and proposals not meeting these standards are dropped. If a proposal meets the minimum standards, it may be subject to further analysis using the present value methods.

Average Rate of Return Method

The **average rate of return**, sometimes called the *accounting rate of return*, measures the average income as a percent of the average investment. The average rate of return is computed as follows:

$$\text{Average Rate of Return} = \frac{\text{Estimated Average Annual Income}}{\text{Average Investment}}$$

In the preceding equation, the numerator is the average of the annual income expected to be earned from the investment over its life, after deducting

Dow Chemical Company reported over $2 billion in capital expenditures. The majority of these expenditures were related to adding capacity for new and existing products as well as for projects related to the environment, safety, and loss prevention.

depreciation. The denominator is the average investment (book value) over the life of the investment. Assuming straight-line depreciation, the average investment is computed as follows:

$$\text{Average Investment} = \frac{\text{Initial Cost} + \text{Residual Value}}{2}$$

To illustrate, assume that management is evaluating the purchase of a new machine as follows:

Cost of new machine	$500,000
Residual value	0
Estimated total income from machine	200,000
Expected useful life	4 years

The estimated average annual income from the machine is $50,000 ($200,000 ÷ 4 years). The average investment is $250,000, as computed below.

$$\text{Average Investment} = \frac{\text{Initial Cost} + \text{Residual Value}}{2}$$

$$= \frac{\$500,000 + \$0}{2} = \$250,000$$

The average rate of return on the average investment is 20%, as computed below.

$$\text{Average Rate of Return} = \frac{\text{Estimated Average Annual Income}}{\text{Average Investment}}$$

$$= \frac{\$50,000}{\$250,000} = 20\%$$

The average rate of return of 20% should be compared to the minimum rate of return required by management. If the average rate of return equals or exceeds the minimum rate, the machine should be purchased or considered for further analysis.

Several capital investment proposals can be ranked by their average rates of return. The higher the average rate of return, the more desirable the proposal. For example, assume that management is considering two capital investment proposals with the following average rates of return:

	Proposal A	Proposal B
Average rate of return	20%	25%

If only the average rate of return is considered, Proposal B, with an average rate of return of 25%, is preferred over Proposal A.

The average rate of return has the following advantages:

1. It is easy to compute.
2. It includes the entire amount of income earned over the life of the proposal.
3. It emphasizes accounting income, which is often used by investors and creditors in evaluating management performance.

The average rate of return has the following disadvantages:

1. It does not directly consider the expected cash flows from the proposal.
2. It does not directly consider the timing of the expected cash flows.

Cash Payback Method

A capital investment uses cash and must return cash in the future to be successful. The expected period of time between the date of an investment and the recovery in cash of the amount invested is the **cash payback period**.

When annual net cash inflows are equal, the cash payback period is computed as follows:

$$\text{Cash Payback Period} = \frac{\text{Initial Cost}}{\text{Annual Net Cash Inflow}}$$

To illustrate, assume that management is evaluating the purchase of the following new machine:

Cost of new machine	$200,000
Cash revenues from machine per year	50,000
Expenses of machine per year	30,000
Depreciation per year	20,000

To simplify, the revenues and expenses other than depreciation are assumed to be in cash. Hence, the net cash inflow per year from use of the machine is as follows:

Net cash inflow per year:		
Cash revenues from machine		$50,000
Less cash expenses of machine:		
Expenses of machine	$30,000	
Less depreciation	20,000	10,000
Net cash inflow per year		$40,000

The time required for the net cash flow to equal the cost of the new machine is the payback period. Thus, the estimated cash payback period for the investment is five years, as computed below.

$$\text{Cash Payback Period} = \frac{\text{Initial Cost}}{\text{Annual Net Cash Inflow}} = \frac{\$200,000}{\$40,000} = 5 \text{ years}$$

In the preceding illustration, the annual net cash inflows are equal ($40,000 per year). When the annual net cash inflows are not equal, the cash payback period is determined by adding the annual net cash inflows until the cumulative total equals the initial cost of the proposed investment.

To illustrate, assume that a proposed investment has an initial cost of $400,000. The annual and cumulative net cash inflows over the proposal's six-year life are as follows:

Year	Net Cash Flow	Cumulative Net Cash Flow
1	$ 60,000	$ 60,000
2	80,000	140,000
3	105,000	245,000
4	155,000	400,000
5	100,000	500,000
6	90,000	590,000

The cumulative net cash flow at the end of Year 4 equals the initial cost of the investment, $400,000. Thus, the payback period is four years, as shown in the graph on the following page.

If the initial cost of the proposed investment had been $450,000, the cash payback period would occur during Year 5. Since $100,000 of net cash flow is expected during Year 5, the additional $50,000 to increase the cumulative total to $450,000 occurs halfway through the year ($50,000/$100,000). Thus, the cash payback period would be 4½ years.[1]

1. Unless otherwise stated, net cash inflows are received uniformly throughout the year.

A short cash payback period is desirable. This is because the sooner cash is recovered, the sooner it can be reinvested in other projects. In addition, there is less chance of losses from changing economic conditions or other risks such as a decreasing customer demand when the payback period is short.

A short cash payback period is also desirable for repaying debt used to purchase the investment. The sooner the cash is recovered, the sooner the debt can be paid.

A disadvantage of the cash payback method is that it ignores cash flows occurring after the payback period. In addition, the cash payback method does not use present value concepts in valuing cash flows occurring in different periods.

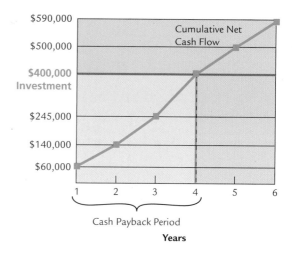

Methods Using Present Values

Obj **3**

Evaluate capital investment proposals using the net present value and internal rate of return methods.

An investment in fixed assets may be viewed as purchasing a series of net cash flows over a period of time. The timing of when the net cash flows will be received is important in determining the value of a proposed investment.

Present value methods use the amount and timing of the net cash flows in evaluating an investment. The two methods of evaluating capital investments using present values are as follows:

1. Net present value method
2. Internal rate of return method

Present Value Concepts

Both the net present value and the internal rate of return methods use the following two **present value concepts**:

1. Present value of an amount
2. Present value of an annuity

Present Value of an Amount If you were given the choice, would you prefer to receive $1 now or $1 three years from now? You should prefer to receive $1 now, because you could invest the $1 and earn interest for three years. As a result, the amount you would have after three years would be greater than $1.

To illustrate, assume that you have $1 to invest as follows:

Amount to be invested	$1
Period to be invested	3 years
Interest rate	12%

Present value concepts can also be used to evaluate personal finances. For example, you can determine house or car payments under various interest rate and term assumptions using present value concepts.

After one year, the $1 earns interest of $0.12 ($1 × 12%) and thus will grow to $1.12 ($1 × 1.12). In the second year, the $1.12 earns 12% interest of $0.134 ($1.12 × 12%) and thus will grow to $1.254 ($1.12 × 1.12) by the end of the second year. This process of interest earning interest is called *compounding*. By the end of the third year, your $1 investment will grow to $1.404 as shown on the next page.

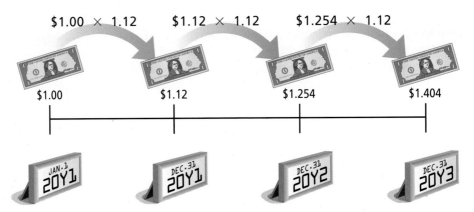

$1.00 × 1.12 $1.12 × 1.12 $1.254 × 1.12

$1.00 $1.12 $1.254 $1.404

JAN.1   DEC.31   DEC.31   DEC.31
20Y1   20Y1   20Y2   20Y3

On January 1, 20Y1, what is the present value of $1.404 to be received on December 31, 20Y3? This is a present value question. The answer can be determined with the aid of a present value of $1 table. For example, the partial table in Exhibit 1 indicates that the present value of $1 to be received in three years with earnings compounded at the rate of 12% a year is 0.712. Multiplying 0.712 by $1.404 yields $1 as follows:

	Present Value		Amount to Be Received in 3 Years		Present Value of $1 to Be Received in 3 Years (from Exhibit 1)
$1	=		$1.404	×	0.712

EXHIBIT 1

Partial Present Value of $1 Table

Present Value of $1 at Compound Interest					
Year	6%	10%	12%	15%	20%
1	0.943	0.909	0.893	0.870	0.833
2	0.890	0.826	0.797	0.756	0.694
3	0.840	0.751	0.712	0.658	0.579
4	0.792	0.683	0.636	0.572	0.482
5	0.747	0.621	0.567	0.497	0.402
6	0.705	0.564	0.507	0.432	0.335
7	0.665	0.513	0.452	0.376	0.279
8	0.627	0.467	0.404	0.327	0.233
9	0.592	0.424	0.361	0.284	0.194
10	0.558	0.386	0.322	0.247	0.162

In other words, the present value of $1.404 to be received in three years using a compound interest rate of 12% is $1, as shown below.

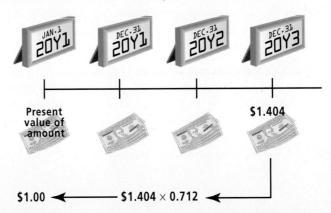

JAN.1   DEC.31   DEC.31   DEC.31
20Y1   20Y1   20Y2   20Y3

Present value of amount $1.404

$1.00 ◄——— $1.404 × 0.712 ◄———

Present Value of an Annuity An **annuity** is a series of equal net cash flows at fixed time intervals. Cash payments for monthly rent, salaries, and bond interest are all examples of annuities.

The present value of an annuity is the sum of the present values of each cash flow. That is, the **present value of an annuity** is the amount of cash needed today to yield a series of equal net cash flows at fixed time intervals in the future.

To illustrate, the present value of a $100 annuity for five periods at 12% could be determined by using the present value factors in Exhibit 1. Each $100 net cash flow could be multiplied by the present value of $1 at a 12% factor for the appropriate period and summed to determine a present value of $360.50, as shown below.

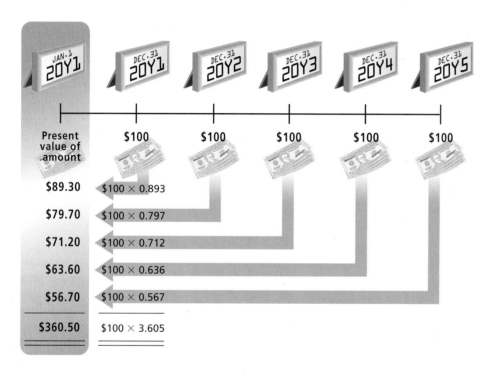

Using a present value of an annuity table is a simpler approach. Exhibit 2 is a partial table of present value of annuity factors.

Present Value of an Annuity of $1 at Compound Interest					
Year	6%	10%	12%	15%	20%
1	0.943	0.909	0.893	0.870	0.833
2	1.833	1.736	1.690	1.626	1.528
3	2.673	2.487	2.402	2.283	2.106
4	3.465	3.170	3.037	2.855	2.589
5	4.212	3.791	3.605	3.353	2.991
6	4.917	4.355	4.111	3.785	3.326
7	5.582	4.868	4.564	4.160	3.605
8	6.210	5.335	4.968	4.487	3.837
9	6.802	5.759	5.328	4.772	4.031
10	7.360	6.145	5.650	5.019	4.192

EXHIBIT 2

Partial Present Value of an Annuity Table

The present value factors in the table shown in Exhibit 2 are the sum of the present value of $1 factors in Exhibit 1 for the number of annuity periods. Thus, 3.605 in the annuity table (Exhibit 2) is the sum of the five present value of $1 factors at 12%, as shown below.

	Present Value of $1 (Exhibit 1)
Present value of $1 for 1 year @12%	0.893
Present value of $1 for 2 years @12%	0.797
Present value of $1 for 3 years @12%	0.712
Present value of $1 for 4 years @12%	0.636
Present value of $1 for 5 years @12%	0.567
Present value of an annuity of $1 for 5 years (from Exhibit 2)	3.605

Multiplying $100 by 3.605 yields the same amount ($360.50) as follows:

Present Value		Amount to Be Received Annually for 5 Years		Present Value of an Annuity of $1 to Be Received for 5 Years (Exhibit 2)
$360.50	=	$100	×	3.605

This amount ($360.50) is the same as what was determined in the preceding illustration by five successive multiplications.

Net Present Value Method

The **net present value method** compares the amount to be invested with the present value of the net cash inflows. It is sometimes called the *discounted cash flow method*.

The interest rate (return) used in net present value analysis is the company's minimum desired rate of return. This rate, sometimes termed the *hurdle rate,* is based on such factors as the purpose of the investment and the cost of obtaining funds for the investment. If the present value of the cash inflows equals or exceeds the amount to be invested, the proposal is desirable.

To illustrate, assume the following data for a proposed investment in new equipment:

Cost of new equipment	$200,000
Expected useful life	5 years
Minimum desired rate of return	10%
Expected cash flows to be received each year:	
Year 1	$ 70,000
Year 2	60,000
Year 3	50,000
Year 4	40,000
Year 5	40,000
Total expected cash flows	$260,000

A 55-year-old janitor won a $5 million lottery jackpot, payable in 21 annual installments of $240,245. Unfortunately, the janitor died after collecting only one payment. What happens to the remaining unclaimed payments? In this case, the lottery winnings were auctioned off for the benefit of the janitor's estate. The winning bid approximated the present value of the remaining cash flows, or about $2.1 million.

The present value of the net cash flow for each year is computed by multi-plying the net cash flow for the year by the present value factor of $1 for that year as shown below.

Year	Present Value of $1 at 10%	Net Cash Flow	Present Value of Net Cash Flow
1	0.909	$ 70,000	$ 63,630
2	0.826	60,000	49,560
3	0.751	50,000	37,550
4	0.683	40,000	27,320
5	0.621	40,000	24,840
Total		$260,000	$202,900
Amount to be invested			200,000
Net present value			$ 2,900

The preceding computations are also graphically illustrated as shown below.

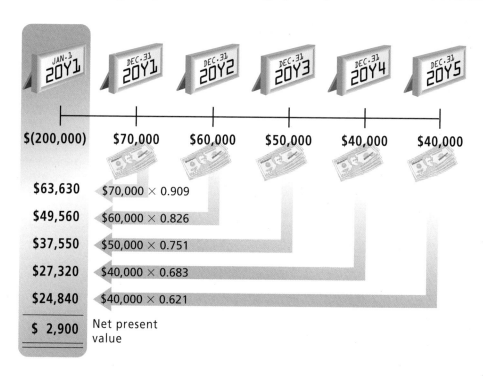

The net present value of $2,900 indicates that the purchase of the new equipment is expected to recover the investment and provide more than the minimum rate of return of 10%. Thus, the purchase of the new equipment is desirable.

When capital investment funds are limited and the proposals involve differ-ent investments, a ranking of the proposals can be prepared by using a present value index. The **present value index** is computed as follows:

$$\text{Present Value Index} = \frac{\text{Total Present Value of Net Cash Flow}}{\text{Amount to Be Invested}}$$

The present value index for the investment in the preceding illustration is 1.0145, as computed below.

$$\text{Present Value Index} = \frac{\text{Total Present Value of Net Cash Flow}}{\text{Amount to Be Invested}}$$

$$\text{Present Value Index} = \frac{\$202,900}{\$200,000} = 1.0145$$

To illustrate, assume that a company is considering three proposals. The net present value and the present value index for each proposal are as follows:

	Proposal A	Proposal B	Proposal C
Total present value of net cash flow	$107,000	$86,400	$86,400
Amount to be invested	100,000	80,000	90,000
Net present value	$ 7,000	$ 6,400	$ (3,600)
Present value index:			
Proposal A ($107,000/$100,000)	1.07		
Proposal B ($86,400/$80,000)		1.08	
Proposal C ($86,400/$90,000)			0.96

A project will have a present value index greater than 1 when the net present value is positive. This is the case for Proposals A and B. When the net present value is negative, the present value index will be less than 1, as is the case for Proposal C.

Although Proposal A has the largest net present value, the present value indices indicate that it is not as desirable as Proposal B. That is, Proposal B returns $1.08 present value per dollar invested, whereas Proposal A returns only $1.07. Proposal B requires an investment of $80,000, compared to an investment of $100,000 for Proposal A. The possible use of the $20,000 difference between Proposals A and B investments should also be considered before making a final decision.

An advantage of the net present value method is that it considers the time value of money. A disadvantage is that the computations are more complex than the average rate of return and cash payback methods. In addition, the net present value method assumes that the cash received from the proposal can be reinvested at the minimum desired rate of return. This assumption may not always be reasonable.

The use of spreadsheet software such as **Microsoft Excel** can simplify present value computations.

Internal Rate of Return Method The **internal rate of return (IRR) method** uses present value concepts to compute the rate of return from a capital investment proposal based on its expected net cash flows. This method, sometimes called the *time-adjusted rate of return method*, starts with the proposal's net cash flows and works backward to estimate the proposal's expected rate of return. To illustrate, assume that management is evaluating the following proposal to purchase new equipment:

Cost of new equipment	$33,530
Yearly expected cash flows to be received	10,000
Expected life	5 years
Minimum desired rate of return	12%

The present value of the net cash flows, using the present value of an annuity table in Exhibit 2, is $2,520, as shown in Exhibit 3.

Annual net cash flow (at the end of each of five years)	$10,000
Present value of an annuity of $1 at 12% for five years (Exhibit 2)	× 3.605
Present value of annual net cash flows	$36,050
Less amount to be invested	33,530
Net present value	$ 2,520

EXHIBIT 3

Net Present Value Analysis at 12%

In Exhibit 3, the $36,050 present value of the cash inflows, based on a 12% rate of return, is greater than the $33,530 to be invested. Thus, the internal rate of return must be greater than 12%. Through trial and error, the rate of return equating the $33,530 cost of the investment with the present value of the net cash flows can be determined to be 15%, as shown below.

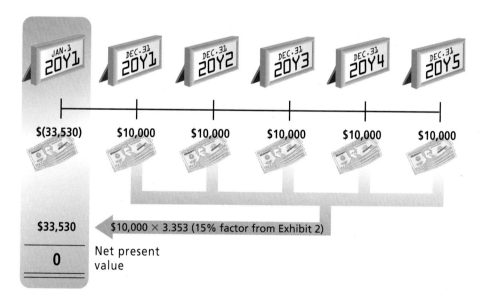

When equal annual net cash flows are expected from a proposal, as in the above example, the internal rate of return can be determined as follows:[2]

Step 1. Determine a present value factor for an annuity of $1 as follows:

$$\text{Present Value Factor for an Annuity of \$1} = \frac{\text{Amount to Be Invested}}{\text{Equal Annual Net Cash Flows}}$$

Step 2. Locate the present value factor determined in Step 1 in the present value of an annuity of $1 table (Exhibit 2) as follows:

   a. Locate the number of years of expected useful life of the investment in the Year column.

   b. Proceed horizontally across the table until you find the present value factor computed in Step 1.

2. To simplify, equal annual net cash flows are assumed. If the net cash flows are not equal, spreadsheet software can be used to determine the rate of return.

Step 3. Identify the internal rate of return by the heading of the column in which the present value factor in Step 2 is located.

To illustrate, assume that management is evaluating the following proposal to purchase new equipment:

Cost of new equipment	$97,360
Yearly expected cash flows to be received	20,000
Expected useful life	7 years

The present value factor for an annuity of $1 is 4.868, as shown below.

$$\text{Present Value Factor for an Annuity of } \$1 = \frac{\text{Amount to Be Invested}}{\text{Equal Annual Net Cash Flows}}$$

$$\text{Present Value Factor for an Annuity } \$1 = \frac{\$97,360}{\$20,000} = 4.868$$

Using the following partial present value of an annuity of $1 table and a period of seven years, the factor 4.868 is related to 10%. Thus, the internal rate of return for this proposal is 10%.

	Present Value of an Annuity of $1 at Compound Interest		
		Step 3	
Year	6%	10%	12%
1	0.943	0.909	0.893
2	1.833	1.736	1.690
3	2.673	2.487	2.402
4	3.465	3.170	3.037
5	4.212	3.791	3.605
6	4.917	Step 2(b) 4.355	4.111
Step 2(a) 7	5.582	4.868	4.564
8	6.210	5.335	4.968
9	6.802	5.759	5.328
10	7.360	6.145	5.650

Step 1: Determine present value factor for an annuity of $1 $= \dfrac{\$97,360}{\$20,000} = 4.868$

The minimum acceptable rate of return for **Owens Corning** is 18%; for **General Electric Company,** it is 20%. The CFO of Owens Corning once stated, "I'm here to challenge anyone—even the CEO—who gets emotionally attached to a project that doesn't reach our benchmark."

If the minimum acceptable rate of return is 10%, then the proposal is considered acceptable. Several proposals can be ranked by their internal rates of return. The proposal with the highest rate is the most desirable.

A primary advantage of the internal rate of return method is that the present values of the net cash flows over the entire useful life of the proposal are considered. In addition, all proposals can be compared based on their internal rates of return.

The primary disadvantage of the internal rate of return method is that the computations are more complex. Also, like the net present value method, it assumes that the cash received from a proposal can be reinvested at the internal rate of return. This assumption may not always be reasonable.

Factors That Complicate Capital Investment Analysis

Obj **4**

List and describe factors that complicate capital investment analysis.

Four widely used methods of evaluating capital investment proposals have been described and illustrated in this chapter. In practice, additional factors such as the following may impact capital investment decisions:

1. Income tax
2. Proposals with unequal lives
3. Leasing versus purchasing

4. Uncertainty
5. Changes in price levels
6. Qualitative factors

HOW BUSINESSES MAKE MONEY

PANERA BREAD STORE RATE OF RETURN

Panera Bread owns, operates, and franchises bakery-cafes throughout the United States. An annual report to the Securities and Exchange Commission (SEC Form 10-K) disclosed the following information about an average company-owned store:

Operating profit	$ 302,000
Depreciation	98,000
Investment	1,000,000

Assume that the operating profit and depreciation will remain unchanged for the next 10 years. Assume operating profit plus depreciation approximates annual net cash flows, and that the investment residual value will be zero. The average rate of return and internal rate of return can then be estimated. The average rate of return on a company-owned store is:

$$\frac{\$302,000}{\$1,000,000 \div 2} = 60.4\%$$

The internal rate of return is calculated by first determining the present value of an annuity of $1:

$$\text{Present value of an annuity of } \$1 = \frac{\$1,000,000}{\$302,000 + \$98,000} = 2.50$$

For a period of 10 years, this present value of an annuity of $1 implies an estimated internal rate of return of over 35%. Clearly, both the average rate of return and the internal rate of return methods indicate a highly successful business.

Income Tax

The impact of income taxes on capital investment decisions can be material. For example, in determining depreciation for federal income tax purposes, useful lives that are much shorter than the actual useful lives are often used. Also, depreciation for tax purposes often differs from depreciation for financial statement purposes. As a result, the timing of the cash flows for income taxes can have a significant impact on capital investment analysis.[3]

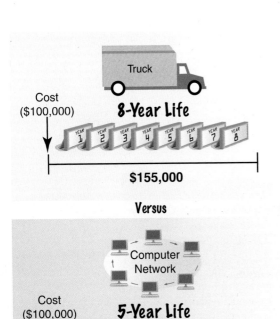

Unequal Proposal Lives

The prior capital investment illustrations assumed that the alternative proposals had the same useful lives. In practice, however, proposals often have different lives.

To illustrate, assume that a company is considering purchasing a new truck or a new computer network. The data for each proposal are shown below.

	Truck	Computer Network
Cost	$100,000	$100,000
Minimum desired rate of return	10%	10%
Expected useful life	8 years	5 years
Yearly expected cash flows to be received:		
Year 1	$ 30,000	$ 30,000
Year 2	30,000	30,000
Year 3	25,000	30,000
Year 4	20,000	30,000
Year 5	15,000	35,000
Year 6	15,000	0
Year 7	10,000	0
Year 8	10,000	0
Total	$155,000	$155,000

The expected cash flows and net present value for each proposal are shown in Exhibit 4. Because of the unequal useful lives, however, the net present values in Exhibit 4 are not comparable.

To make the proposals comparable, the useful lives are adjusted to end at the same time. In this illustration, this is done by assuming that the truck will be sold at the end of five years. The selling price (residual value) of the truck at the end of five years is estimated and included in the cash inflows. Both proposals will then cover five years; thus, the net present value analyses will be comparable.

To illustrate, assume that the truck's estimated selling price (residual value) at the end of Year 5 is $40,000. Exhibit 5 shows the truck's revised present value analysis assuming a five-year life.

As shown in Exhibit 5, the net present value for the truck exceeds the net present value for the computer network by $1,835 ($18,640 − $16,805). Thus, the truck is the more attractive of the two proposals.

3. The impact of taxes on capital investment analysis is covered in advanced accounting textbooks.

Net Present Value Analysis—Unequal Lives of Proposals   EXHIBIT 4

	A	B	C	D
1			Truck	
2		Present	Net	Present
3		Value of	Cash	Value of
4	Year	$1 at 10%	Flow	Net Cash Flow
5	1	0.909	$ 30,000	$ 27,270
6	2	0.826	30,000	24,780
7	3	0.751	25,000	18,775
8	4	0.683	20,000	13,660
9	5	0.621	15,000	9,315
10	6	0.564	15,000	8,460
11	7	0.513	10,000	5,130
12	8	0.467	10,000	4,670
13	Total		$155,000	$112,060
14				
15	Amount to be invested			100,000
16	Net present value			$ 12,060

	A	B	C	D
1			Computer Network	
2		Present	Net	Present
3		Value of	Cash	Value of
4	Year	$1 at 10%	Flow	Net Cash Flow
5	1	0.909	$ 30,000	$ 27,270
6	2	0.826	30,000	24,780
7	3	0.751	30,000	22,530
8	4	0.683	30,000	20,490
9	5	0.621	35,000	21,735
10	Total		$155,000	$116,805
11				
12	Amount to be invested			100,000
13	Net present value			$ 16,805

EXHIBIT 5

Net Present Value Analysis—Equalized Lives of Proposals

	A	B	C	D
1		Truck—Revised to 5-Year Life		
2		Present	Net	Present
3		Value of	Cash	Value of
4	Year	$1 at 10%	Flow	Net Cash Flow
5	1	0.909	$ 30,000	$ 27,270
6	2	0.826	30,000	24,780
7	3	0.751	25,000	18,775
8	4	0.683	20,000	13,660
9	5	0.621	15,000	9,315
10	5 (Residual			
11	value)	0.621	40,000	24,840
12	Total		$160,000	$118,640
13				
14	Amount to be invested			100,000
15	Net present value			$ 18,640

Truck Net Present Value Greater than Computer Network Net Present Value by $1,835

Lease Versus Capital Investment

Leasing fixed assets is common in many industries. For example, hospitals often lease medical equipment. Some advantages of leasing a fixed asset include the following:

1. The company has use of the fixed asset without spending large amounts of cash to purchase the asset.
2. The company eliminates the risk of owning an obsolete asset.
3. The company may deduct the annual lease payments for income tax purposes.

A disadvantage of leasing a fixed asset is that it is normally more costly than purchasing the asset. This is because the lessor (owner of the asset) includes in the rental price not only the costs of owning the asset, but also a profit.

The methods of evaluating capital investment proposals illustrated in this chapter also can be used to decide whether to lease or purchase a fixed asset.

Uncertainty

All capital investment analyses rely on factors that are uncertain. For example, estimates of revenues, expenses, and cash flows are uncertain. This is especially true for long-term capital investments. Errors in one or more of the estimates could lead to incorrect decisions. Methods that consider the impact of uncertainty on capital investment analysis are discussed in advanced accounting and finance textbooks.

Changes in Price Levels

Price levels normally change as the economy improves or deteriorates. General price levels often increase in a rapidly growing economy, which is called **inflation**. During such periods, the rate of return on an investment should exceed the rising price level. If this is not the case, the cash returned on the investment will be less than expected.

Price levels may also change for foreign investments. This occurs as currency exchange rates change. **Currency exchange rates** are the rates at which currency in another country can be exchanged for U.S. dollars.

If the amount of local dollars that can be exchanged for one U.S. dollar increases, then the local currency is said to be weakening to the dollar. When a company has an investment in another country where the local currency is weakening, the return on the investment, as expressed in U.S. dollars, is adversely impacted. This is because the expected amount of local currency returned on the investment would purchase fewer U.S. dollars.

Qualitative Considerations

Some benefits of capital investments are qualitative in nature and cannot be estimated in dollar terms. However, if a company does not consider qualitative considerations, an acceptable investment proposal could be rejected.

Some examples of qualitative considerations that may influence capital investment analysis include the impact of the investment proposal on the following:

1. Product quality
2. Manufacturing flexibility
3. Employee morale
4. Manufacturing productivity
5. Market (strategic) opportunities

Qualitative factors may be as important as, if not more important than, quantitative factors.

IBM decided to develop molecular and atomic-level nanotechnology based more on its strategic market potential than on an economic analysis of cash flows.

Capital Rationing

Capital rationing is the process by which management allocates funds among competing capital investment proposals. In this process, management often uses a combination of the methods described in this chapter, as shown in Exhibit 6.

Capital Rationing Decision Process   **EXHIBIT 6**

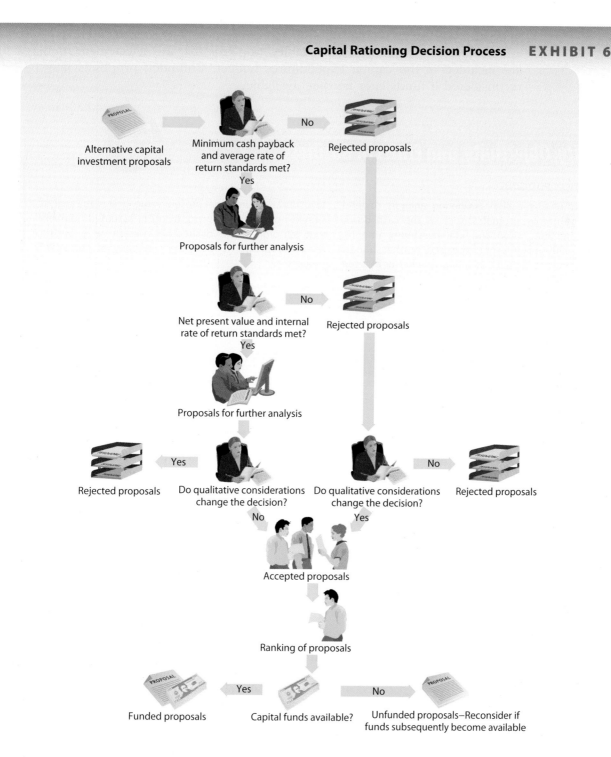

Exhibit 6 illustrates the capital rationing decision process. Alternative proposals are initially screened by establishing minimum standards using the cash payback and the average rate of return methods. The proposals that survive this screening are further analyzed, using the net present value and internal rate of return methods.

Qualitative factors related to each proposal also should be considered throughout the capital rationing process. For example, new equipment might improve the quality of the product and thus increase consumer satisfaction and sales.

At the end of the capital rationing process, accepted proposals are ranked and compared with the funds available. Proposals that are selected for funding are included in the capital expenditures budget. Unfunded proposals may be reconsidered if funds later become available.

Integrity, Objectivity, and Ethics in Business

ASSUMPTION FUDGING

The results of any capital budgeting analysis depend on many subjective estimates, such as the cash flows, discount rate, time period, and total investment amount. The results of the analysis should be used to either support or reject a project. Capital budgeting should not be used to justify an assumed net present value. That is, the analyst should not work backward, filling in assumed numbers that will produce the desired net present value. Such a reverse approach reduces the credibility of the entire process.

Key Points

1. Explain the nature and importance of capital investment analysis.

Capital investment analysis is the process by which management plans, evaluates, and controls investments involving fixed assets. Capital investment analysis is important to a business because such investments affect profitability for a long period of time.

2. Evaluate capital investment proposals using the average rate of return and cash payback methods.

The average rate of return method measures the expected profitability of an investment in fixed assets. It is calculated using the following formula:

$$\text{Average Rate of Return} = \frac{\text{Estimated Average Annual Income}}{\text{Average Investment}}$$

The expected period of time that will pass between the date of an investment and the complete recovery in cash (or equivalent) of the amount invested is the cash payback period. Investment proposals with the shortest cash payback are considered the most desirable.

3. Evaluate capital investment proposals using the net present value and internal rate of return methods.

The net present value method uses present values to compute the net present value of the cash flows expected from a proposal. The net present values of the cash flows are then compared across proposals. The present value of a cash flow is computed by using a table of present values and multiplying it by the amount of the future cash flows, as shown in the text.

The internal rate of return method uses present values to compute the rate of return from the net cash flows expected from capital investment proposals. When equal annual net cash flows are expected from a proposal, the computations are simplified by using a table of the present value of an annuity, as shown in the text.

4. **List and describe factors that complicate capital investment analysis.**

Factors that may complicate capital investment analysis include the impact of the federal income tax, unequal lives of alternative proposals, leasing, uncertainty, changes in price levels, and qualitative considerations. A brief description of the effect of each of these factors appears in the text.

5. **Diagram the capital rationing process.**

Capital rationing refers to the process by which management allocates available investment funds among competing capital investment proposals. A diagram of the capital rationing process appears in Exhibit 6.

Key Terms

Annuity (625)
Average rate of return (620)
Capital investment analysis (620)
Capital rationing (635)

Cash payback period (622)
Currency exchange rate (634)
Inflation (634)
Internal rate of return (IRR) method (628)

Net present value method (626)
Present value concept (623)
Present value index (627)

Present value of an annuity (625)
Time value of money concept (620)

Illustrative Problem

The capital investment committee of McEntyre Company is currently considering two projects. The estimated income from operations and net cash flows expected from each project are shown below.

	Project A		Project B	
Year	Income from Operations	Net Cash Flow	Income from Operations	Net Cash Flow
1	$ 6,000	$ 22,000	$13,000	$ 29,000
2	9,000	25,000	10,000	26,000
3	10,000	26,000	8,000	24,000
4	8,000	24,000	8,000	24,000
5	11,000	27,000	3,000	19,000
	$44,000	$124,000	$42,000	$122,000

Each project requires an investment of $80,000. Straight-line depreciation will be used, and no residual value is expected. The committee has selected a rate of 15% for purposes of the net present value analysis.

Instructions

1. Compute the following:

    a. The average rate of return for each project.

    b. The net present value for each project. Use the present value of $1 table appearing in this chapter.

2. Why is the net present value of Project B greater than Project A, even though its average rate of return is less?

3. Prepare a summary for the capital investment committee, advising it on the relative merits of the two projects.

Solution

1. a. Average rate of return for Project A:

$$\frac{\$44,000 \div 5}{(\$80,000 + \$0) \div 2} = 22\%$$

Average rate of return for Project B:

$$\frac{\$42,000 \div 5}{(\$80,000 + \$0) \div 2} = 21\%$$

b. Net present value analysis:

Year	Present Value of $1 at 15%	Net Cash Flow Project A	Net Cash Flow Project B	Present Value of Net Cash Flow Project A	Present Value of Net Cash Flow Project B
1	0.870	$ 22,000	$ 29,000	$19,140	$25,230
2	0.756	25,000	26,000	18,900	19,656
3	0.658	26,000	24,000	17,108	15,792
4	0.572	24,000	24,000	13,728	13,728
5	0.497	27,000	19,000	13,419	9,443
Total		$124,000	$122,000	$82,295	$83,849
Amount to be invested				80,000	80,000
Net present value				$ 2,295	$ 3,849

2. Project B has a lower average rate of return than Project A because Project B's total income from operations for the five years is $42,000, which is $2,000 less than Project A's. Even so, the net present value of Project B is greater than that of Project A, because Project B has higher cash flows in the early years.

3. Both projects exceed the selected rate established for the net present value analysis. Project A has a higher average rate of return, but Project B offers a larger net present value. Thus, if only one of the two projects can be accepted, Project B would be the more attractive.

Self-Examination Questions (Answers appear at the end of chapter)

1. Methods of evaluating capital investment proposals that ignore present value include:
    A. average rate of return
    B. cash payback
    C. both A and B
    D. neither A nor B

2. Management is considering a $100,000 investment in a project with a five-year life and no residual value. If the total income from the project is expected to be $60,000 and recognition is given to the effect of straight-line depreciation on the investment, the average rate of return is:
    A. 12%
    B. 24%
    C. 60%
    D. 75%

3. The expected period of time that will elapse between the date of a capital investment and the complete recovery of the amount of cash invested is called:
    A. the average rate of return period
    B. the cash payback period

C. the net present value period
D. the internal rate of return period

4. A project that will cost $120,000 is estimated to generate cash flows of $25,000 per year for eight years. What is the net present value of the project, assuming a 10% required rate of return? (Use the present value tables in this chapter.)
    A. $11,675
    B. $13,375
    C. $75,000
    D. $95,000

5. A project is estimated to generate cash flows of $40,000 per year for 10 years. The cost of the project is $226,000. What is the internal rate of return for this project?
    A. 8%
    B. 10%
    C. 12%
    D. 15%

Class Discussion Questions

1. What are the principal objections to the use of the average rate of return method in evaluating capital investment proposals?

2. Discuss the principal limitations of the cash payback method for evaluating capital investment proposals.

3. Why would the average rate of return differ from the internal rate of return on the same project?

4. What information does the cash payback period ignore that is included by the net present value method?

5. Your boss has suggested that a one-year payback period is the same as a 100% average rate of return. Do you agree?

6. Why would the cash payback method understate the value of a project with a large residual value?

7. Why might the use of the cash payback period for analyzing the financial performance of theatrical releases from a motion picture production studio be used over the net present value method?

8. A net present value analysis used to evaluate a proposed equipment acquisition indicated a $115,000 net present value. What is the meaning of the $115,000 as it relates to the desirability of the proposal?

9. Two projects have an identical net present value of $360,000. Are both projects equal in desirability?

10. What are the major disadvantages of the use of the net present value method of analyzing capital investment proposals?

11. What are the major disadvantages of the use of the internal rate of return method of analyzing capital investment proposals?

12. What provision of the Internal Revenue Code is especially important to consider in analyzing capital investment proposals?

13. What method can be used to place two capital investment proposals with unequal useful lives on a comparable basis?

14. What are the major advantages of leasing a fixed asset rather than purchasing it?

15. Give an example of a qualitative factor that should be considered in a capital investment analysis related to acquiring automated factory equipment.

16. **Monsanto Company**, a large chemical and fibers company, invested $37 million in state-of-the-art systems to improve process control, laboratory automation, and local area network (LAN) communications. The investment was not justified merely on cost savings but was also justified on the basis of qualitative considerations. Monsanto management viewed the investment as a critical element toward achieving its vision of the future. What qualitative and quantitative considerations do you believe Monsanto would have considered in its strategic evaluation of these investments?

Exercises

E15-1   Average rate of return

Obj 2

✔ Testing equipment, 15%

The following data are accumulated by Specialty Motors Inc. evaluating two competing capital investment proposals:

	Testing Equipment	Diagnostic Software
Amount of investment	$540,000	$170,000
Useful life	6 years	8 years
Estimated residual value	$0	$0
Estimated total income over the useful life	$243,000	$88,400

Determine the expected average rate of return for each proposal.

E15-2   Average rate of return—cost savings

Obj 2

Espinosa Industries is considering an investment in equipment that will replace direct labor. The equipment has a cost of $615,000 with a $75,000 residual value and a 10-year life. The equipment will replace one employee who has an average wage of $134,100 per year. In addition, the equipment will have operating and energy costs of $18,000 per year.

Determine the average rate of return on the equipment, giving effect to straight-line depreciation on the investment.

Obj 2

✔ Average
annual income,
$4,320,000

E15-3 Average rate of return—new product

Arrowhead Inc. is considering an investment in new equipment that will be used to manufacture a mobile communications product. The product is expected to generate additional annual sales of 24,000 units at $400 per unit. The equipment has a cost of $27,000,000, residual value of $1,800,000, and a 10-year life. The equipment only can be used to manufacture the product. The cost to manufacture the product is shown below.

Cost per unit:	
Direct labor	$ 40.00
Direct materials	60.00
Factory overhead (including depreciation)	120.00
Total cost per unit	$220.00

Determine the average rate of return on the equipment.

Obj 2

✔ Year 1:
$28,000

E15-4 Calculate cash flows

Daffodil Inc. is planning to invest in new manufacturing equipment to make a new garden tool. The new garden tool is expected to generate additional annual sales of 120,000 units at $9 each. The new manufacturing equipment will cost $320,000, have a 10-year life, have a residual value of $20,000, and will be depreciated using the straight-line method. Selling expenses related to the new product are expected to be 15% of sales revenue. The cost to manufacture the product includes the following on a per-unit basis:

Direct labor	$1.00
Direct materials	3.40
Fixed factory overhead—depreciation	1.25
Variable factory overhead	0.35
Total	$6.00

a. Determine the net cash flows for the first year of the project, Years 2–9, and for the last year of the project.

b. Assume that the operating cash flows occur evenly throughout the year and that the equipment is purchased on January 1, 20Y1. Determine when the cash payback will occur by year, month, and day.

Obj 2

✔ Location 1:
5 years

E15-5 Cash payback period

Platte Woodworks is evaluating two capital investment proposals for a retail outlet store, each requiring an investment of $350,000 and each with an eight-year life and expected total net cash flows of $560,000. Location 1 is expected to provide equal annual net cash flows of $70,000, and Location 2 is expected to have the following unequal annual net cash flows:

Year 1	$125,000
Year 2	85,000
Year 3	70,000
Year 4	70,000
Year 5	70,000
Year 6	60,000
Year 7	40,000
Year 8	40,000

Determine the cash payback period for both location proposals.

E15-6   Cash payback method

Obj **2**

Charisma Beauty Products is considering an investment in one of two new product lines. The investment required for either product line is $1,125,000. The net cash flows associated with each product are shown below.

Year	Shampoo/Conditioner	Body Wash
1	$ 450,000	$ 187,500
2	375,000	187,500
3	300,000	187,500
4	100,000	187,500
5	85,000	187,500
6	80,000	187,500
7	60,000	187,500
8	50,000	187,500
Total	$1,500,000	$1,500,000

✔ a. Shampoo/
Conditioner: 3 years

a. Recommend a product offering to Charisma Beauty Products, based on the cash payback period for each product line.

b. Why is one product line preferred over the other, even though they both have the same total net cash flows through eight periods?

c. Assume that instead of $300,000 of cash flows in Year 3 and $100,000 in Year 4, the Shampoo/Conditioner had cash flows of $250,000 in Year 3 and $150,000 in Year 4. What would be the cash payback period assuming that the cash flows occur uniformly throughout the year?

E15-7   Net present value method

Obj **3**

The following data are accumulated by California Hat Company in evaluating the purchase of $400,000 of equipment, having a four-year useful life:

✔ a. NPV $211,500

	Net Income	Net Cash Flows
Year 1	$200,000	$300,000
Year 2	150,000	250,000
Year 3	100,000	200,000
Year 4	50,000	150,000

a. Assuming that the desired rate of return is 20%, determine the net present value for the proposal. Use the table of the present value of $1 appearing in Exhibit 1 of this chapter.

b. Would management be likely to look with favor on the proposal? Explain.

E15-8   Net present value method

Obj **3**

Master Delivery Inc. is considering the purchase of an additional delivery truck for $90,000 on January 1, 20Y4. The truck is expected to have a five-year life with an expected residual value of $10,000 at the end of five years. The expected additional revenues from the added delivery capacity are anticipated to be $60,000 per year for each of the next five years. A driver will cost $30,000 in 20Y4, with an expected annual salary increase of $2,000 for each year thereafter. The insurance for the truck is estimated to cost $1,000 per year.

✔ a. 20Y4, $29,000

a. Determine the expected annual net cash flows from the delivery truck investment for 20Y4–20Y8.

b. Calculate the net present value of the investment, assuming that the minimum desired rate of return is 12%. Use the present value of $1 table appearing in Exhibit 1 of this chapter.

c. Is the additional truck a good investment based on your analysis?

Note: The spreadsheet icon   indicates an Excel template is available on the student companion site.

E15-9 Net present value method—annuity

Model 99 Hotels is considering the construction of a new hotel for $80 million. The expected life of the hotel is 20 years with no residual value. The hotel is expected to earn revenues of $15 million per year. Total expenses, including straight-line depreciation, are expected to be $6 million per year. Model 99 management has set a minimum acceptable rate of return of 10%.

a. Determine the equal annual net cash flows from operating the hotel.

b. Calculate the net present value of the new hotel, using the present value factor of an annuity of $1 at 10% for 20 periods of 8.5136. Round to the nearest million dollars.

c. Does your analysis support construction of the new hotel?

E15-10 Net present value method—annuity

Osborne Excavation Company is planning an investment of $315,000 for a bulldozer. The bulldozer is expected to operate for 1,850 hours per year for five years. Customers will be charged $140 per hour for bulldozer work. The bulldozer operator costs $37 per hour in wages and benefits. The bulldozer is expected to require annual maintenance costing $9,750. The bulldozer uses fuel that is expected to cost $48 per hour of bulldozer operation.

a. Determine the equal annual net cash flows from operating the bulldozer.

b. Determine the net present value of the investment, assuming that the desired rate of return is 10%. Use the table of present values of an annuity of $1 in the chapter. Round to the nearest dollar.

c. Should Osborne Excavation invest in the bulldozer, based on this analysis?

E15-11 Net present value method

Carnival Corporation has recently placed into service some of the largest cruise ships in the world. One of these ships, the *Carnival Dream,* can hold up to 3,600 passengers and cost $750 million to build. Assume the following additional information:

- There will be 300 cruise days per year operated at a full capacity of 3,600 passengers.
- The variable expenses per passenger are estimated to be $90 per cruise day.
- The revenue per passenger is expected to be $450 per cruise day.
- The fixed expenses for running the ship, other than depreciation, are estimated to be $100,000,000 per year.
- The ship has a service life of 10 years, with a residual value of $120,000,000 at the end of 10 years.

a. Determine the annual net cash flows from operating the cruise ship.

b. Determine the net present value of this investment, assuming a 12% minimum rate of return. Use the present value tables provided in the chapter in determining your answer.

E15-12 Present value index

Colorado Grill has computed the net present value for capital expenditures for the Denver and Boulder locations using the net present value method. Relevant data related to the computation are as follows:

	Denver	Boulder
Total present value of net cash flow	$2,061,879	$1,718,233
Amount to be invested	1,500,000	1,200,000
Net present value	$ 561,879	$ 518,233

Determine the present value index for each proposal. Round to two decimal places.

E15-13 Net present value method and present value index

Obj 3
✔ b. Stitching Machine, 1.25

Ball Sports Inc. is considering an investment in one of two machines. The stitching machine will increase productivity from sewing 300 baseballs per hour to stitching 360 per hour. The contribution margin is $0.30 per baseball. Assume that any increased production of baseballs can be sold. The second machine applies a synthetic balata cover to golf balls. The golf ball machine will reduce labor cost. The labor cost saved is equivalent to $40 per hour. The stitching machine will cost $484,600, have an eight-year life, and will operate for 7,500 hours per year. The golf ball machine will cost $897,400, have an eight-year life, and will operate for 6,000 hours per year. Ball Sports Inc. seeks a minimum rate of return of 15% on its investments.

a. Determine the net present value for the two machines. Use the table of present values of an annuity of $1 in the chapter. Round to the nearest dollar.

b. Determine the present value index for the two machines. Round to two decimal places.

c. If Ball Sports Inc. has sufficient funds for only one of the machines and qualitative factors are equal between the two machines, in which machine should it invest?

E15-14 Average rate of return, cash payback period, net present value method

Obj 2, 3
✔ b. 5 years

Glacier Transportation Inc. is considering a distribution facility at a cost of $8,000,000. The facility has an estimated life of 10 years and a $2,000,000 residual value. It is expected to provide yearly net cash flows of $1,600,000. The company's minimum desired rate of return for net present value analysis is 10%.

Compute the following:

a. The average rate of return, giving effect to straight-line depreciation on the investment.

b. The cash payback period.

c. The net present value. Use the table of the present value of an annuity of $1 appearing in this chapter. Round to the nearest dollar.

E15-15 Payback period, net present value analysis, and qualitative considerations

Obj 2, 3, 4
✔ a. 4.75 years

The plant manager of Jurassic Industries is considering the purchase of new automated assembly equipment. The new equipment will cost $2,375,000. The manager believes that the new investment will result in direct labor savings of $500,000 per year for 10 years.

a. What is the payback period on this project?

b. What is the net present value, assuming a 10% rate of return? Use the present value tables appearing in this chapter.

c. What else should the manager consider in the analysis?

E15-16 Internal rate of return method

Obj 3
✔ a. 3.326

The internal rate of return method is used by Premier Construction Co. in analyzing a capital expenditure proposal that involves an investment of $41,575 and annual net cash flows of $12,500 for each of the six years of its useful life.

a. Determine a present value factor for an annuity of $1 which can be used in determining the internal rate of return.

b. Using the factor determined in part (a) and the present value of an annuity of $1 table appearing in this chapter, determine the internal rate of return for the proposal.

E15-17 Internal rate of return method

Obj 3

The Canyons Resort, a Utah ski resort, announced a $400 million expansion of lodging properties, lifts, and terrain. Assume that this investment is estimated to produce $79.7 million in equal annual cash flows for each of the first 10 years of the project life.

Determine the expected internal rate of return of this project for 10 years, using the present value of an annuity of $1 table found in Exhibit 2.

Obj **3**

✔ a. Delivery
truck, 12%

E15-18   Internal rate of return method—two projects

Strahn Foods Inc. is considering two possible investments: a delivery truck or a bagging machine. The delivery truck would cost $65,970 and could be used to deliver an additional 90,000 bags of taquitos chips per year. Each bag of chips can be sold for a contribution margin of $0.35. The delivery truck operating expenses, excluding depreciation, are $0.55 per mile for 24,000 miles per year. The bagging machine would replace an old bagging machine, and its net investment cost would be $35,890. The new machine would require 2.5 fewer hours of direct labor per day. Direct labor is $20 per hour. There are 240 operating days in the year. Both the truck and the bagging machine are estimated to have five-year lives. The minimum rate of return is 14%. However, Strahn Foods has funds to invest in only one of the projects.

a. Compute the internal rate of return for each investment. Use the table of present values of an annuity of $1 in the chapter.

b. Provide a memo to management with a recommendation.

Obj **3**

✔ a. ($307,000)

E15-19   Net present value method and internal rate of return method

Wisconsin Healthcare Corp. is proposing to spend $3,810,000 on a project that has estimated net cash flows of $620,000 for each of the 10 years.

a. Compute the net present value, using a rate of return of 12%. Use the table of present values of an annuity of $1 in the chapter.

b. Based on the analysis prepared in part (a), is the rate of return (1) more than 12%, (2) 12%, or (3) less than 12%? Explain.

c. Determine the internal rate of return by computing a present value factor for an annuity of $1 and using the table of the present value of an annuity of $1 presented in the text.

Obj **3**

E15-20   Identify error in capital investment analysis calculations

Fireproofing Solutions Inc. is considering the purchase of automated machinery that is expected to have a useful life of eight years and no residual value. The average rate of return on the average investment has been computed to be 15%, and the cash payback period was computed to be 10 years.

Do you see any reason to question the validity of the data presented? Explain.

Obj **3, 4**

✔ Net present value,
Office Building,
$381,300

E15-21   Net present value—unequal lives

Healey Development Company has two competing projects: an office building and a condominium complex. Both projects have an initial investment of $2,000,000. The net cash flows estimated for the two projects are as follows:

	Net Cash Flow	
Year	Office Building	Condominium Complex
1	$950,000	$1,200,000
2	600,000	900,000
3	500,000	700,000
4	450,000	400,000
5	350,000	
6	350,000	
7	300,000	
8	300,000	

The estimated residual value of the office building at the end of Year 4 is $900,000.

Determine which project should be favored, comparing the net present values of the two projects and assuming a minimum rate of return of 15%. Use the table of present values in the chapter.

E15-22 Net present value—unequal lives

Obj 3, 4

Buscho Industries is considering one of two investment options. Option 1 is a $45,000 investment in new blending equipment that is expected to produce equal annual cash flows of $18,000 for each of eight years. Option 2 is a $17,000 investment in a new computer system that is expected to produce equal annual cash flows (savings) of $10,000 for each of four years. The residual value of the blending equipment at the end of the fourth year is estimated to be $5,000. The computer system has no expected residual value at the end of the fourth year.

Assume there is sufficient capital to fund only one of the projects. Determine which project should be selected, comparing the (a) net present values and (b) present value indices of the two projects, assuming a minimum rate of return of 12%. Round the present value index to two decimal places. Use the table of present values in the chapter.

Problems

P15-1 Average rate of return method, net present value method, and analysis

Obj 2, 3

The capital investment committee of Overnight Express Inc. is considering two investment projects. The estimated income from operations and net cash flows from each investment are as follows:

✔ 1. a. 16.5%

| | Distribution Center Expansion | | Internet Tracking Technology | |
Year	Income from Operations	Net Cash Flows	Income from Operations	Net Cash Flows
1	$ 66,000	$ 226,000	$200,000	$ 360,000
2	66,000	226,000	90,000	250,000
3	66,000	226,000	30,000	190,000
4	66,000	226,000	10,000	170,000
5	66,000	226,000	0	160,000
Total	$330,000	$1,130,000	$330,000	$1,130,000

Each project requires an investment of $800,000. Straight-line depreciation will be used, and no residual value is expected. The committee has selected a rate of 15% for purposes of the net present value analysis.

Instructions

1. Compute the following:

   a. The average rate of return for each investment.

   b. The net present value for each investment. Use the present value of $1 table appearing in this chapter.

2. Prepare a brief report for the capital investment committee, advising it on the relative merits of the two projects.

P15-2 Cash payback period, net present value method, and analysis

Obj 2, 3

McMorris Publications Inc. is considering two new magazine products. The estimated net cash flows from each product are as follows:

✔ 1. b. European Hiking, $189,674

Year	Canadian Cycling	European Hiking
1	$220,000	$188,000
2	180,000	212,000
3	158,000	150,000
4	131,000	110,000
5	61,000	90,000
Total	$750,000	$750,000

Each product requires an investment of $400,000. A rate of 10% has been selected for the net present value analysis.

Instructions

1. Compute the following for each product:

   a. Cash payback period.

   b. The net present value. Use the present value of $1 table appearing in this chapter.

2. Prepare a brief report advising management on the relative merits of each of the two products.

Obj 3

✔ 1. Product Line Expansion, net present value, $66,640

P15-3 Net present value method, present value index, and analysis

Soares Industries Inc. wishes to evaluate three capital investment projects by using the net present value method. Relevant data related to the projects are summarized as follows:

	Product Line Expansion	Computer System Upgrade	Internet Bill-Pay
Amount to be invested	$980,000	$665,000	$392,000
Annual net cash flows:			
Year 1	490,000	350,000	224,000
Year 2	455,000	315,000	154,000
Year 3	420,000	280,000	112,000

Instructions

1. Assuming that the desired rate of return is 15%, prepare a net present value analysis for each project. Use the present value of $1 table appearing in this chapter.

2. Determine a present value index for each project. Round to two decimal places.

3. Which project offers the largest amount of present value per dollar of investment? Explain.

Obj 3
✔ 1. a. Radio station, $176,400

P15-4 Net present value method, internal rate of return method, and analysis

The management of Heckel Communications Inc. is considering two capital investment projects. The estimated net cash flows from each project are as follows:

Year	Radio Station	TV Station
1	$560,000	$1,120,000
2	560,000	1,120,000
3	560,000	1,120,000
4	560,000	1,120,000

The radio station requires an investment of $1,598,800, while the TV station requires an investment of $3,401,440. No residual value is expected from either project.

Instructions

1. Compute the following for each project:

   a. The net present value. Use a rate of 10% and the present value of an annuity of $1 table appearing in this chapter.

   b. A present value index. Round to two decimal places.

2. Determine the internal rate of return for each project by (a) computing a present value factor for an annuity of $1 and (b) using the present value of an annuity of $1 table appearing in this chapter.

3. What advantage does the internal rate of return method have over the net present value method in comparing projects?

P15-5   Evaluate alternative capital investment decisions

The investment committee of Iron Skillet Restaurants Inc. is evaluating two restaurant sites. The sites have different useful lives, but each requires an investment of $1,000,000. The estimated net cash flows from each site are as follows:

	Net Cash Flows	
Year	Site A	Site B
1	$400,000	$500,000
2	400,000	500,000
3	400,000	500,000
4	400,000	500,000
5	400,000	
6	400,000	

The committee has selected a rate of 20% for purposes of net present value analysis. It also estimates that the residual value at the end of each restaurant's useful life is $0, but at the end of the fourth year, Site A's residual value would be $300,000.

Instructions

1. For each site, compute the net present value. Use the present value of an annuity of $1 table appearing in this chapter. (Ignore the unequal lives of the projects.)

2. For each site, compute the net present value, assuming that Site A is adjusted to a four-year life for purposes of analysis. Use the present value of $1 table appearing in this chapter.

3. Prepare a report to the investment committee, providing your advice on the relative merits of the two sites.

P15-6   Capital rationing decision involving four proposals

Kopecky Industries Inc. is considering allocating a limited amount of capital investment funds among four proposals. The amount of proposed investment, estimated income from operations, and net cash flow for each proposal are as follows:

	Investment	Year	Income from Operations	Net Cash Flows
Proposal Sierra:	$850,000	1	$ 80,000	$ 250,000
		2	80,000	250,000
		3	80,000	250,000
		4	30,000	200,000
		5	(70,000)	100,000
			$200,000	$1,050,000
Proposal Tango:	$1,200,000	1	$320,000	$ 560,000
		2	320,000	540,000
		3	160,000	400,000
		4	60,000	300,000
		5	(40,000)	220,000
			$820,000	$2,020,000
Proposal Uniform:	$550,000	1	$ 90,000	$ 200,000
		2	90,000	200,000
		3	90,000	200,000
		4	90,000	200,000
		5	70,000	180,000
			$430,000	$ 980,000
Proposal Victor:	$380,000	1	$44,000	$ 120,000
		2	44,000	120,000
		3	44,000	120,000
		4	4,000	80,000
		5	4,000	80,000
			$140,000	$ 520,000

The company's capital rationing policy requires a maximum cash payback period of three years. In addition, a minimum average rate of return of 12% is required on all projects. If the preceding standards are met, the net present value method and present value indexes are used to rank the remaining proposals.

Instructions

1. Compute the cash payback period for each of the four proposals. Assume that net cash flows are uniform throughout the year.

2. Giving effect to straight-line depreciation on the investments and assuming no estimated residual value, compute the average rate of return for each of the four proposals. Round to one decimal place.

3. Using the following format, summarize the results of your computations in parts (1) and (2). By placing the calculated amounts in the first two columns on the left and by placing a check mark in the appropriate column to the right, indicate which proposals should be accepted for further analysis and which should be rejected.

Proposal	Cash Payback Period	Average Rate of Return	Accept for Further Analysis	Reject
Sierra				
Tango				
Uniform				
Victor				

4. For the proposals accepted for further analysis in part (3), compute the net present value. Use a rate of 12% and the present value of $1 table appearing in this chapter. Round to the nearest dollar.

5. Compute the present value index for each of the proposals in part (4). Round to two decimal places.

6. Rank the proposals from most attractive to least attractive, based on the present values of net cash flows computed in part (4).

7. Rank the proposals from most attractive to least attractive, based on the present value indexes computed in part (5). Round to two decimal places.

8. Based on the analyses, comment on the relative attractiveness of the proposals ranked in parts (6) and (7).

Cases

Case 15-1   Ethics and professional conduct in business

Erin Haywood was recently hired as a cost analyst by Wind River Medical Supplies Inc. One of Erin's first assignments was to perform a net present value analysis for a new warehouse. Erin performed the analysis and calculated a present value index of 0.8. The plant manager, Zuhair Barbat, is very intent on purchasing the warehouse because he believes that more storage space is needed. Zuhair asks Erin into his office and the following conversation takes place:

Zuhair: Erin, you're new here, aren't you?

Erin: Yes, sir.

Zuhair: Well, Erin, let me tell you something. I'm not at all pleased with the capital investment analysis that you performed on this new warehouse. I need that warehouse for my production. If I don't get it, where am I going to place our output?

Erin: Hopefully with the customer, sir.

Zuhair: Now don't get smart with me.

Erin: No, really, I was being serious. My analysis does not support constructing a new warehouse. The numbers don't lie; the warehouse does not meet our investment return targets.

In fact, it seems to me that purchasing a warehouse does not add much value to the business. We need to be producing product to satisfy customer orders, not to fill a warehouse.

Zuhair: Listen, you need to understand something. The headquarters people will not allow me to build the warehouse if the numbers don't add up. You know as well as I that many assumptions go into your net present value analysis. Why don't you relax some of your assumptions so that the financial savings will offset the cost?

Erin: I'm willing to discuss my assumptions with you. Maybe I overlooked something.

Zuhair: Good. Here's what I want you to do. I see in your analysis that you don't project greater sales as a result of the warehouse. It seems to me, if we can store more goods, then we will have more to sell. Thus, logically, a larger warehouse translates into more sales. If you incorporate this into your analysis, I think you'll see that the numbers will work out. Why don't you work it through and come back with a new analysis? I'm really counting on you on this one. Let's get off to a good start together and see if we can get this project accepted.

What is your advice to Erin?

Case 15-2 Personal investment analysis

A Masters of Accountancy degree at Jalapeno University would cost $15,000 for an additional fifth year of education beyond the bachelor's degree. Assume that all tuition is paid at the beginning of the year. A student considering this investment must evaluate the present value of cash flows from possessing a graduate degree versus holding only the undergraduate degree. Assume that the average student with an undergraduate degree is expected to earn an annual salary of $50,000 per year (assumed to be paid at the end of the year) for 10 years. Assume that the average student with a graduate Masters of Accountancy degree is expected to earn an annual salary of $65,000 per year (assumed to be paid at the end of the year) for nine years after graduation. Assume a minimum rate of return of 10%.

1. Determine the net present value of cash flows from an undergraduate degree. Use the present value tables provided in this chapter. Round to nearest dollar.

2. Determine the net present value of cash flows from a Masters of Accountancy degree, assuming no salary is earned during the graduate year of schooling. Round to nearest dollar.

3. What is the net advantage or disadvantage of pursuing a graduate degree under these assumptions?

Case 15-3 Changing prices

World Electronics Inc. invested $16,000,000 to build a plant in a foreign country. The labor and materials used in production are purchased locally. The plant expansion was estimated to produce an internal rate of return of 20% in U.S. dollar terms. Due to a currency crisis, the currency exchange rate between the local currency and the U.S. dollar doubled from two local units per U.S. dollar to four local units per U.S. dollar.

1. Assume that the plant produced and sold product in the local economy. Explain what impact this change in the currency exchange rate would have on the project's internal rate of return.

2. Assume that the plant produced product in the local economy but exported the product back to the United States for sale. Explain what impact the change in the currency exchange rate would have on the project's internal rate of return under this assumption.

Case 15-4 Qualitative issues in investment analysis

The following are some selected quotes from senior executives:

> **CEO, Worthington Industries (a high technology steel company):** "We try to find the best technology, stay ahead of the competition, and serve the customer.... We'll make any investment that will pay back quickly ... but if it is something that we really see as a must down the road, payback is not going to be that important."
>
> **Chairman of Amgen Inc. (a biotech company):** "You cannot really run the numbers, do net present value calculations, because the uncertainties are really gigantic.... You decide on a project you want to run, and then you run the numbers [as a reality check on your assumptions]. Success in a business like this is much more dependent on tracking rather than on predicting, much more dependent on seeing results over time, tracking and adjusting and readjusting, much more dynamic, much more flexible."
>
> **Chief Financial Officer of Merck & Co., Inc. (a pharmaceutical company):** " ... at the individual product level—the development of a successful new product requires on the order of $230 million in R&D, spread over more than a decade—discounted cash flow style analysis does not become a factor until development is near the point of manufacturing scale-up effort. Prior to that point, given the uncertainties associated with new product development, it would be lunacy in our business to decide that we know exactly what's going to happen to a product once it gets out."

Explain the role of capital investment analysis for these companies.

Case 15-5 Net present value method

Metro-Goldwyn-Mayer Studios Inc. (MGM) is a major producer and distributor of theatrical and television filmed entertainment. Regarding theatrical films, MGM states, "Our feature films are exploited through a series of sequential domestic and international distribution channels, typically beginning with theatrical exhibition. Thereafter, feature films are first made available for home video generally six months after theatrical release; for pay television, one year after theatrical release; and for syndication, approximately three to five years after theatrical release."

Assume that MGM produces a film during early 20Y5 at a cost of $200 million, and releases it halfway through the year. During the last half of 20Y5, the film earns revenues of $240 million at the box office. The film requires $80 million of advertising during the release. One year later, by the end of 20Y6, the film is expected to earn MGM net cash flows from home video sales of $50 million. By the end of 20Y7, the film is expected to earn MGM $25 million from pay TV; and by the end of 20Y8, the film is expected to earn $10 million from syndication.

1. Determine the net present value of the film as of the beginning of 20Y5 if the desired rate of return is 20%. To simplify present value calculations, assume all annual net cash flows occur at the end of each year. Use the table of the present value of $1 appearing in Exhibit 1 of this chapter. Round to the nearest whole million dollars.

2. Under the assumptions provided here, is the film expected to be financially successful?

GROUP PROJECT

Case 15-6 Capital investment analysis

In one group, find a local business, such as a copy shop, that charges for printing, faxing, copying, and scanning documents. In the other group, determine the price of a mid-range printer/copier/scanner/fax machine. Combine this information from the two groups and perform a capital budgeting analysis. Assume that one student will use the machine for 1,000 documents per semester for the next three years. Also assume that the minimum rate of return is 10%. In performing your analysis, use the present value factor for 5% compounded for six semiannual periods of 5.08.

Does your analysis support the student purchasing the printer/copier/scanner/fax machine?

Answers to Self-Examination Questions

1. **C** Methods of evaluating capital investment proposals that ignore the time value of money are categorized as methods that ignore present value. This category includes the average rate of return method (answer A) and the cash payback method (answer B).

2. **B** The average rate of return is 24% (answer B), determined by dividing the expected average annual earnings by the average investment, as follows:

$$\frac{\$60{,}000 \div 5}{(\$100{,}000 + \$0) \div 2} = 24\%$$

3. **B** Of the four methods of analyzing proposals for capital investments, the cash payback period (answer B) refers to the expected period of time required to recover the amount of cash to be invested. The average rate of return (answer A) is a measure of the anticipated profitability of a proposal. The net present value method (answer C) reduces the expected future net cash flows originating from a proposal to their present values. The internal rate of return method (answer D) uses present value concepts to compute the rate of return from the net cash flows expected from the investment.

4. **B** The net present value is determined as follows:

Present value of $25,000 for 8 years	
at 10% ($25,000 × 5.335)	$133,375
Less: Project cost	120,000
Net present value	$ 13,375

5. **C** The internal rate of return for this project is determined by solving for the present value of an annuity factor that when multiplied by $40,000 will equal $226,000. By division, the factor is:

$$\frac{\$226{,}000}{\$40{,}000} = 5.65$$

In Exhibit 2, scan along the $n = 10$ years row until finding the 5.65 factor. The column for this factor is 12%.

APPENDIX A

Double-Entry Accounting Systems

Throughout this text, transactions are recorded and summarized by using the accounting equation and the integrated financial statement framework. Transactions were recorded as pluses or minuses for each item affected by a transaction. At the same time, the effects of the transaction on the financial statements were shown. The equality of the accounting equation aided in preventing and detecting errors. That is, total assets must always equal total liabilities plus stockholders' equity.

Double-entry accounting also uses the accounting equation. However, double-entry accounting uses debit and credit rules as an additional control on the accuracy of recording transactions. This appendix describes and illustrates the basic elements of double-entry accounting.

In a double-entry accounting system, transactions are recorded in accounts. An **account**, in its simplest form, has three parts.

1. A title, which identifies the accounting equation element recorded in the account.
2. A space for recording increases in the amount of the element.
3. A space for recording decreases in the amount of the element.

The account form presented below is called a **T account** because it resembles the letter T. The left side of the account is called the debit side, and the right side is called the credit side.[1]

Title

Left side	Right side
debit	*credit*

Amounts entered on the left side of an account, regardless of the account title, are called debits to the account. When debits are entered in an account, the account is said to be *debited*. Amounts entered on the right side of an account are called credits, and the account is said to be *credited*. Debits and credits are sometimes abbreviated as *Dr.* and *Cr.*

To illustrate, a T account for Cash is shown below.

Cash

Debit side of account	(a) 25,000 (d) 7,500	(b) 20,000 (e) 3,650 (f) 950 (h) 2,000	Credit side of account
	Balance 5,900		

Balance of account

1. The terms *debit* and *credit* are derived from the Latin *debere* and *credere*.

Recording transactions in accounts using double-entry accounting follows certain rules. For example, increases in assets are recorded on the debit (left) side of the account. Likewise, decreases in assets are recorded on the credit (right) side of the account. With an asset account, the excess of debits over its credits is the balance of the account.

To illustrate, the preceding cash account is used. The receipt of cash (increase in Cash) of $25,000 in transaction (a) is entered on the debit (left) side of the cash account. A reference notation (letter or date of the transaction) is also entered into the account. The reference notation provides a means of backtracking to the underlying transaction data, should any questions arise.

The payment of cash (decrease in Cash) of $20,000 in transaction (b) is entered on the credit (right) side of the account. The balance of the cash account of $5,900 is the excess of debits over credits, as shown below.

Debits ($25,000 + $7,500)	$32,500
Less credits ($20,000 + $3,650 + $950 + $2,000)	26,600
Balance of Cash	$ 5,900

The balance of the cash account is inserted in the account, in the Debit column. In this way, the balance is identified as a debit balance.

Rules of Debit and Credit

A standard method of recording debits and credits in accounts is essential to ensure that businesses record transactions in a similar manner. The rules of debit and credit are shown in Exhibit 1.

EXHIBIT 1   Rules of Debit and Credit; Normal Balances of Accounts

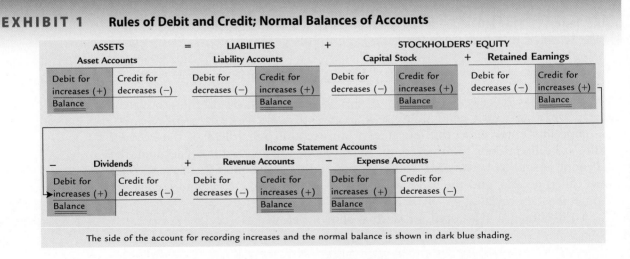

The side of the account for recording increases and the normal balance is shown in dark blue shading.

Exhibit 1 illustrates the following characteristics of the rules of debit and credit.

1. The normal balance of an account is the side of the account used to record increases. Thus, the normal balance of an asset account is a debit balance, while the normal balance of a liability account is a credit balance. This characteristic is often useful in detecting errors in the recording process. That

is, when an account normally having a debit balance actually has a credit balance, or vice versa, an error has occurred or an unusual situation exists.

2. Asset accounts (on the left side of the accounting equation) are increased by debits and have a normal debit balance. The only exception is that some asset accounts, called *contra asset accounts,* are increased by credits and have normal credit balances. As the words *contra asset* imply, these accounts offset the normal debit balances of asset accounts. For example, accumulated depreciation, an offset to plant assets, is increased by credits and has a normal credit balance. Thus, accumulated depreciation is a contra asset account.

3. Liability and stockholders' equity accounts (on the right side of the accounting equation) are increased by credits and have normal credit balances.

4. Dividend accounts appear on the right side of the accounting equation and decrease stockholders' equity (retained earnings). Thus, dividends accounts are increased by debits and have a normal debit balance. In this sense, the dividends accounts can be thought of as a type of contra account to retained earnings.

5. Revenue accounts appear on the right side of the accounting equation and increase stockholders' equity (retained earnings). Thus, revenue accounts are increased by credits and have normal credit balances.

6. Expense accounts appear on the right side of the accounting equation and decrease stockholders' equity (retained earnings). Thus, expense accounts are increased by debits and have a normal debit balance. Expense accounts can be thought of as a type of contra account. In this case, expense accounts can be thought of as contra accounts to revenues.

The rules of debit and credit require that for each transaction, the total debits equal the total credits. That is, each transaction must be recorded so that the total debits for the transaction equal the total credits.

To illustrate, assume that a company pays cash of $500 for supplies. The asset account Supplies is debited (increased) by $500 and Cash is credited (decreased) by $500. Likewise, if the company provides services and receives $2,000 from customers, Cash is debited (increased) and Fees Earned is credited (increased) by $2,000. This equality of debits and credits for each transaction provides a control over the recording of transactions.

To summarize, under double-entry accounting each transaction is recorded using the rules shown in Exhibit 1. In doing so, the total debits equal the total credits for each transaction.

The Journal

Under double-entry accounting, each transaction is initially entered in chronological order in a record called a **journal**. In this way, the journal documents the history of the company. The process of recording transactions in the journal is called **journalizing**. The specific transaction record entered in the journal is called a **journal entry**.

In practice, companies use a variety of formats for recording journal entries. A small company may use one all-purpose journal, sometimes called a **general journal**. Alternatively, another company may use **special journals** for recording different types of transactions. To simplify, a basic two-column general journal is used in this appendix.

Illustration of Double-Entry Accounting

Assume that on November 1, 20Y7, Lee Dunbar organizes a corporation that will be known as Web Solutions. The first phase of Lee's business plan is to operate Web Solutions as a service business providing assistance to individuals and small businesses by developing Web pages and configuring and installing application software. Lee expects this initial phase of the business to last one to two years. During this period, Web Solutions will gather information on the software and hardware needs of customers. During the second phase of the business plan, Web Solutions will expand into an Internet-based retailer of software and hardware to individuals and small business markets.

To start the business, Lee deposits $25,000 in a bank account in the name of Web Solutions in return for shares of stock in the corporation. This first transaction increases Cash and Capital Stock by $25,000. This transaction is recorded in the journal using the following steps:

Step 1. The date of the transaction is entered in the Date column.

Step 2. The title of the account to be debited is recorded at the left-hand margin under the Description column, and the amount to be debited is entered in the Debit column.

Step 3. The title of the account to be credited is listed below and to the right of the debited account title, and the amount to be credited is entered in the Credit column.

Using the preceding steps, the transaction is recorded in the journal as follows:

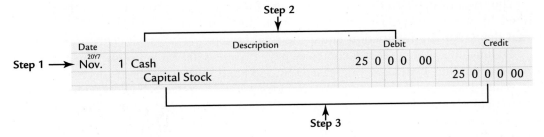

The increase in the asset is debited to the cash account. The increase in stockholders' equity (capital stock) is credited to the capital stock account. As other assets are acquired, the increases are also recorded as debits to asset accounts. Likewise, other increases in stockholders' equity will be recorded as credits to stockholders' equity accounts.

Web Solutions entered into the following additional transactions during the remainder of November:

Nov. 5 Purchased land for $20,000, paying cash. The land is located in a new business park with convenient access to transportation facilities. Web Solutions plans to rent office space and equipment during the first phase of its business plan. During the second phase, the company plans to build an office and a warehouse on the land.

10 Purchased supplies on account for $1,350.

18 Received $7,500 for services provided to customers for cash.

30 Paid expenses as follows: wages, $2,125; rent, $800; utilities, $450; and miscellaneous, $275.

Nov. 30 Paid creditors on account, $950.

   30 Paid stockholder (Lee Dunbar) dividends of $2,000.

The journal entries to record these transactions follow.

Nov.	5	Land	20 0 0 0 00		
		Cash		20 0 0 0 00
	10	Supplies	1 3 5 0 00	
		Accounts Payable		1 3 5 0 00
	18	Cash	7 5 0 0 00	
		Fees Earned		7 5 0 0 00
	30	Wages Expense	2 1 2 5 00	
		Rent Expense	8 0 0 00	
		Utilities Expense	4 5 0 00	
		Miscellaneous Expense	2 7 5 00	
		Cash		3 6 5 0 00
	30	Accounts Payable	9 5 0 00	
		Cash		9 5 0 00
	30	Dividends	2 0 0 0 00	
		Cash		2 0 0 0 00

Posting to the Ledger

The journal lists the chronological history of businesses' transactions. Periodically, the journal entries must be transferred to the accounts. The group of accounts for a business is called its **general ledger**. The list of accounts in the general ledger is called the **chart of accounts**. The accounts are normally listed in the order in which they appear in the financial statements, beginning with the balance sheet and concluding with the income statement.

The chart of accounts for Web Solutions is shown in Exhibit 2.

Balance Sheet Accounts	Income Statement Accounts
Assets	**Revenue**
Cash	Fees Earned
Accounts Receivable	Rent Revenue
Supplies	**Expenses**
Prepaid Insurance	Wages Expense
Office Equipment	Rent Expense
Accumulated Depreciation	Depreciation Expense
Land	Utilities Expense
Liabilities	Supplies Expense
Accounts Payable	Insurance Expense
Wages Payable	Miscellaneous Expense
Unearned Rent	
Stockholders' Equity	
Capital Stock	
Retained Earnings	
Dividends	

EXHIBIT 2

Chart of Accounts for Web Solutions

The process of transferring the journal entry debits and credits to the accounts in the ledger is called **posting**. To illustrate the posting process, Web Solutions' November 1 transaction, along with its posting to the cash and capital stock accounts, is shown in Exhibit 3.

EXHIBIT 3

Posting a Journal Entry

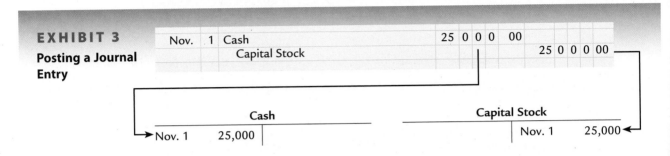

The debits and credits for each journal entry are posted to the accounts in the order in which they occur in the journal. In posting to the accounts, the date is entered followed by the amount of the entry. After the journal entries have been posted, the ledger becomes a chronological history of transactions by account. The posting of Web Solutions' remaining journal entries is shown in Exhibit 7 on page 662.

Trial Balance and Financial Statements

Errors may occur in posting debits and credits from the journal to the ledger. One way to detect such errors is by preparing a **trial balance**. Double-entry accounting requires that debits must always equal credits. The trial balance verifies this equality. The steps in preparing a trial balance are as follows:

Step 1. List the name of the company, the title of the trial balance, and the date the trial balance is prepared.
Step 2. List the accounts from the ledger and enter their debit or credit balance in the Debit or Credit column of the trial balance.
Step 3. Total the Debit and Credit columns of the trial balance.
Step 4. Verify that the total of the Debit column equals the total of the Credit column.

The trial balance for Web Solutions as of December 31, 20Y7, is shown in Exhibit 4. The account balances in Exhibit 4 are taken from the November 30 balances, which are shown in a darker green screen in the ledger shown in Exhibit 7.

The trial balance does not provide complete proof of the accuracy of the ledger. It indicates only that the debits and the credits are equal. However, this proof is still of value as errors often affect the equality of debits and credits.

If the two totals of a trial balance are not equal, an error has occurred. In such a case, the error must be located and corrected before financial statements are prepared. This ability to detect errors in recording when the trial balance totals are not equal is a primary control feature of the double-entry accounting system.

The trial balance can be used as the source of data for preparing financial statements. The financial statements prepared in a double-entry accounting system

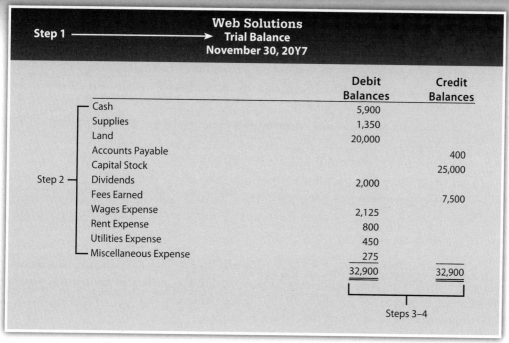

EXHIBIT 4

Trial Balance

are similar to those described and illustrated in the text. For this reason, the financial statements are not illustrated in this appendix.

Review of Double-Entry Accounting

As a review of the double-entry accounting financial reporting system, Web Solutions' transactions for December are used. The journal entries for the following December transactions are shown in Exhibit 5.

Dec. 1 Paid a premium of $2,400 for a comprehensive insurance policy covering liability, theft, and fire. The policy covers a two-year period.

1 Paid rent for December, $800. The company from which Web Solutions is renting its store space now requires the payment of rent on the first day of each month rather than at the end of the month.

1 Received an offer from a local retailer to rent the land purchased on November 5. The retailer plans to use the land as a parking lot for its employees and customers. Web Solutions agreed to rent the land to the retailer for three months with the rent payable in advance. Web Solutions received $360 for three months' rent beginning December 1.

4 Purchased office equipment on account from Executive Supply Co. for $1,800.

6 Paid $180 for a newspaper advertisement.

11 Paid creditors $400.

13 Paid a receptionist and a part-time assistant $950 for two weeks' wages.

Dec. 16 Received $3,100 from fees earned for the first half of December.

16 Earned fees on account totaling $1,750 for the first half of December.

20 Paid $1,800 to Executive Supply Co. on the debt owed from the December 4 transaction.

21 Received $650 from customers in payment of their accounts.

23 Purchased $1,450 of supplies by paying $550 cash and charging the remainder on account.

27 Paid the receptionist and the part-time assistant $1,200 for two weeks' wages.

31 Paid $310 telephone bill for the month.

31 Paid $225 electric bill for the month.

31 Received $2,870 from fees earned for the second half of December.

31 Earned fees on account totaling $1,120 for the second half of December.

31 Paid dividends of $2,000 to stockholders.

The posting of the journal entries to the ledger accounts is shown in Exhibit 7 on page 662. The trial balance shown in Exhibit 6 indicates that after posting December transactions to the general ledger, the total of the debit balances of accounts equals the total of the credit balances.

EXHIBIT 5

Journal Entries: December Transactions for Web Solutions

				Debit	Credit
Dec.	1	Prepaid Insurance		2 4 0 0 00	
		Cash			2 4 0 0 00
	1	Rent Expense		8 0 0 00	
		Cash			8 0 0 00
	1	Cash		3 6 0 00	
		Unearned Rent			3 6 0 00
	4	Office Equipment		1 8 0 0 00	
		Accounts Payable			1 8 0 0 00
	6	Miscellaneous Expense		1 8 0 00	
		Cash			1 8 0 00
	11	Accounts Payable		4 0 0 00	
		Cash			4 0 0 00
	13	Wages Expense		9 5 0 00	
		Cash			9 5 0 00
	16	Cash		3 1 0 0 00	
		Fees Earned			3 1 0 0 00
	16	Accounts Receivable		1 7 5 0 00	
		Fees Earned			1 7 5 0 00

Dec.	20	Accounts Payable	1 8 0 0 00	
		Cash		1 8 0 0 00
	21	Cash	6 5 0 00	
		Accounts Receivable		6 5 0 00
	23	Supplies	1 4 5 0 00	
		Cash		5 5 0 00
		Accounts Payable		9 0 0 00
	27	Wages Expense	1 2 0 0 00	
		Cash		1 2 0 0 00
	31	Utilities Expense	3 1 0 00	
		Cash		3 1 0 00
	31	Utilities Expense	2 2 5 00	
		Cash		2 2 5 00
	31	Cash	2 8 7 0 00	
		Fees Earned		2 8 7 0 00
	31	Accounts Receivable	1 1 2 0 00	
		Fees Earned		1 1 2 0 00
	31	Dividends	2 0 0 0 00	
		Cash		2 0 0 0 00

EXHIBIT 5
Continued

EXHIBIT 6
Trial Balance for Web Solutions

Web Solutions
Trial Balance
December 31, 20Y7

	Debit Balances	Credit Balances
Cash	2,065	
Accounts Receivable	2,220	
Supplies	2,800	
Prepaid Insurance	2,400	
Office Equipment	1,800	
Land	20,000	
Accounts Payable		900
Unearned Rent		360
Capital Stock		25,000
Dividends	4,000	
Fees Earned		16,340
Wages Expense	4,275	
Rent Expense	1,600	
Utilities Expense	985	
Miscellaneous Expense	455	
	42,600	42,600

EXHIBIT 7

Ledger for Web Solutions

Cash

Nov.	1	25,000	Nov.	5	20,000
	18	7,500		30	3,650
				30	950
				30	2,000
		32,500			26,600
Nov. 30	Bal.	5,900	Dec.	1	2,400
Dec.	1	360		1	800
	16	3,100		6	180
	21	650		11	400
	31	2,870		13	950
				20	1,800
				23	550
				27	1,200
				31	310
				31	225
				31	2,000
		12,880			10,815
Dec. 31	Bal.	2,065			

Accounts Receivable

Dec.	16	1,750	Dec. 21	650
	31	1,120		—
Dec. 31	Bal.	2,220		

Supplies

Nov.	10	1,350		
Dec.	23	1,450		
Dec. 31	Bal.	2,800		

Prepaid Insurance

Dec.	1	2,400		

Office Equipment

Dec.	4	1,800		

Land

Nov.	5	20,000		

Accounts Payable

Nov. 30		950	Nov. 10	1,350
			Nov. 30 Bal.	400
Dec.	11	400	Dec.	4	1,800
	20	1,800		23	900
		2,200			3,100
			Dec. 31 Bal.	900

Unearned Rent

			Dec.	1	360

Capital Stock

			Nov.	1	25,000

Dividends

Nov. 30	2,000		
Dec. 31	2,000		
Dec. 31	Bal.	4,000	

Fees Earned

			Nov.	18	7,500
			Dec.	16	3,100
				16	1,750
				31	2,870
				31	1,120
			Dec. 31	Bal.	16,340

Wages Expense

Nov.	30	2,125		
Dec.	13	950		
	27	1,200		
Dec. 31	Bal.	4,275		

Rent Expense

Nov.	30	800		
Dec.	1	800		
Dec. 31	Bal.	1,600		

Utilities Expense

Nov.	30	450		
Dec.	31	310		
	31	225		
Dec. 31	Bal.	985		

Miscellaneous Expense

Nov.	30	275		
Dec.	6	180		
Dec. 31	Bal.	455		

Exercises

E-1   Rules of debit and credit

The following table summarizes the rules of debit and credit. For each of the items (a) through (l), indicate whether the proper answer is a debit or a credit.

	Increase	Decrease	Normal Balance
Balance sheet accounts:			
Asset	Debit	(a)	(b)
Liability	Credit	(c)	(d)
Stockholders' equity:			
Capital stock	(e)	Debit	(f)
Retained earnings	(g)	Debit	Credit
Dividends	Debit	(h)	Debit
Income statement accounts:			
Revenue	(i)	(j)	(k)
Expense	(l)	Credit	Debit

E-2   Identifying transactions

Wild River Tours Co. is a travel agency. The nine transactions recorded by Wild River Tours during May 20Y5, its first month of operations, are indicated in the following T accounts:

Cash				Equipment		Dividends	
(1)	25,000	(2)	1,750	(3) 18,000		(9) 2,500	
(7)	10,000	(3)	3,600				
		(4)	2,700				
		(6)	7,500				
		(9)	2,500				

Accounts Receivable				Accounts Payable				Service Revenue			
(5)	13,500	(7)	10,000	(6)	7,500	(3)	14,400			(5)	13,500

Supplies				Capital Stock			Operating Expenses		
(2)	1,750	(8)	1,050		(1)	25,000	(4)	2,700	
							(8)	1,050	

Indicate for each debit and each credit: (a) whether an asset, liability, capital stock, dividend, revenue, or expense account was affected and (b) whether the account was increased (+) or decreased (−). Present your answers in the following form, with transaction (1) given as an example:

	Account Debited		Account Credited	
Transaction	Type	Effect	Type	Effect
(1)	asset	+	capital stock	+

E-3 Journal entries

Based upon the T accounts in Exercise 2, prepare the nine journal entries from which the postings were made.

E-4 Trial balance

Based upon the data presented in Exercise 2, prepare a trial balance, listing the accounts in their proper order.

✔ Total Debit
column: $45,400

E-5 Normal entries for accounts

During the month, Demko Labs Co. has a substantial number of transactions affecting each of the following accounts. State for each account whether it is likely to have (a) debit entries only, (b) credit entries only, or (c) both debit and credit entries.

1. Accounts Payable
2. Accounts Receivable
3. Cash
4. Fees Earned

5. Insurance Expense
6. Dividends
7. Supplies Expense

E-6 Normal balances of accounts

Identify each of the following accounts of Shredder Services Co. as an asset, liability, stockholders' equity, revenue, or expense, and state in each case whether the normal balance is a debit or a credit.

a. Accounts Payable
b. Accounts Receivable
c. Capital Stock
d. Cash
e. Dividends

f. Fees Earned
g. Office Equipment
h. Rent Expense
i. Supplies
j. Wages Expense

E-7 Cash account balance

During the month, Shogun Co. received $515,000 in cash and paid out $331,000 in cash.
a. Do the data indicate that Shogun Co. had net income of $184,000 during the month? Explain.
b. If the balance of the cash account is $222,350 at the end of the month, what was the cash balance at the beginning of the month?

✔ c. $283,600

E-8 Account balances

a. During October, $100,000 was paid to creditors on account, and purchases on account were $115,150. Assuming the October 31 balance of Accounts Payable was $39,000, determine the account balance on October 1.

b. On May 1, the accounts receivable account balance was $36,200. During May, $315,000 was collected from customers on account. Assuming the May 31 balance was $41,600, determine the fees billed to customers on account during May.

c. On June 1, the cash account balance was $20,000. During June, cash receipts totaled $279,100 and the June 30 balance was $15,500. Determine the cash payments made during June.

Note: The spreadsheet icon indicates an Excel template is available on the student companion site at www.cengagebrain.com.

E-9   Transactions

Off-Peak Co. has the following accounts in its ledger: Cash; Accounts Receivable; Supplies; Office Equipment; Accounts Payable; Capital Stock; Retained Earnings; Dividends; Fees Earned; Rent Expense; Advertising Expense; Utilities Expense; Miscellaneous Expense.

Journalize the following selected transactions for July 20Y9 in a two-column journal.

July   1   Paid rent for the month, $4,500.

        2   Paid advertising expense, $1,800.

        5   Paid cash for supplies, $900.

        6   Purchased office equipment on account, $12,300.

      10   Received cash from customers on account, $4,100.

      15   Paid creditor on account, $1,200.

      27   Paid cash for repairs to office equipment, $500.

      30   Paid telephone bill for the month, $180.

      31   Fees earned and billed to customers for the month, $26,800.

      31   Paid electricity bill for the month, $315.

      31   Paid dividends, $2,000.

E-10   Journalizing and posting

On November 2, 20Y3, Fibrosis Co. purchased $1,800 of supplies on account.

a. Journalize the November 2, 20Y3, transaction.

b. Prepare a T account for Supplies. Enter a debit balance of $1,050 as of November 1, 20Y3.

c. Prepare a T account for Accounts Payable. Enter a credit balance of $15,600 as of November 1, 20Y3.

d. Post the November 2, 20Y3, transaction to the accounts.

E-11   Transactions and T accounts

The following selected transactions were completed during January of the current year:

1. Billed customers for fees earned, $41,730.

2. Purchased supplies on account, $1,800.

3. Received cash from customers on account, $39,150.

4. Paid creditors on account, $1,100.

a. Journalize the above transactions in a two-column journal, using the appropriate number to identify the transactions.

b. Post the entries prepared in (a) to the following T accounts: Cash, Supplies, Accounts Receivable, Accounts Payable, Fees Earned. To the left of each amount posted in the accounts, place the appropriate number to identify the transactions.

E-12 Trial balance

The accounts in the ledger of Cupid Co. as of December 31, 20Y7, are listed in alphabetical order as follows. All accounts have normal balances. The balance of the cash account has been intentionally omitted.

✔ Total of Credit
column: $700,000

Accounts Payable	$ 28,000	Notes Payable	$ 60,000
Accounts Receivable	59,900	Prepaid Insurance	4,500
Capital Stock	50,000	Rent Expense	90,000
Cash	?	Retained Earnings	83,500
Dividends	30,000	Supplies	3,150
Fees Earned	465,000	Supplies Expense	11,850
Insurance Expense	9,000	Unearned Rent	13,500
Land	127,500	Utilities Expense	62,250
Miscellaneous Expense	13,350	Wages Expense	262,500

Prepare a trial balance, listing the accounts in their proper order and inserting the missing figure for cash.

Problems

P-1 Journal entries and trial balance

On March 1, 20Y1, Larry Kinyon established Valley Realty, which completed the following transactions during the month:

✔ 3. Total of credit
column: $32,650

a. Larry Kinyon transferred cash from a personal bank account to an account to be used for the business in exchange for capital stock, $20,000.

b. Purchased supplies on account, $1,000.

c. Earned sales commissions, receiving cash, $12,250.

d. Paid rent on office and equipment for the month, $3,800.

e. Paid creditor on account, $600.

f. Paid dividends, $3,000.

g. Paid automobile expenses (including rental charge) for month, $1,500, and miscellaneous expenses, $400.

h. Paid office salaries, $3,100.

i. Determined that the cost of supplies used was $725.

Instructions

1. Journalize entries for transactions (a) through (i), using the following account titles: Cash; Supplies; Accounts Payable; Capital Stock; Dividends; Sales Commissions; Rent Expense; Office Salaries Expense; Automobile Expense; Supplies Expense; Miscellaneous Expense. Journal entry explanations may be omitted.

2. Prepare T accounts, using the account titles in part (1). Post the journal entries to these accounts, placing the appropriate letter to the left of each amount to identify the transaction. Determine the account balances, after all posting is complete. Accounts containing only a single entry do not need a balance.

3. Prepare a trial balance as of March 31, 20Y1.

P-2   Journal entries and trial balance

Apple Realty acts as an agent in buying, selling, renting, and managing real estate. The trial balance on October 31, 20Y4, is shown below.

✔ 4. Total of Debit column: $573,350

APPLE REALTY
Trial Balance
October 31, 20Y4

	Debit Balances	Credit Balances
Cash	33,920	
Accounts Receivable	69,800	
Prepaid Insurance	7,200	
Office Supplies	1,600	
Land	—	
Accounts Payable		9,920
Unearned Rent		—
Notes Payable		—
Capital Stock		10,000
Retained Earnings		53,080
Dividends	25,600	
Fees Earned		352,000
Salary and Commission Expense	224,000	
Rent Expense	28,000	
Advertising Expense	22,880	
Automobile Expense	10,240	
Miscellaneous Expense	1,760	
	425,000	425,000

The following business transactions were completed by Apple Realty during November 20Y4:

Nov. 1 Purchased office supplies on account, $2,100.
   2 Paid rent on office for month, $4,000.
   3 Received cash from clients on account, $44,600.
   5 Paid annual insurance premiums, $5,700.
   9 Returned a portion of the office supplies purchased on November 1, receiving full credit for their cost, $400.
   17 Paid advertising expense, $5,500.
   23 Paid creditors on account, $4,950.
   29 Paid miscellaneous expenses, $500.
   30 Paid automobile expense (including rental charges for an automobile), $1,500.
   30 Discovered an error in computing a commission; received cash from the salesperson for the overpayment, $1,000.
   30 Paid salaries and commissions for the month, $27,800.
   30 Recorded revenue earned and billed to clients during the month, $83,000.
   30 Purchased land for a future building site for $75,000, paying $10,000 in cash and giving a note payable for the remainder.
   30 Paid dividends, $5,000.
   30 Rented land purchased on November 30 to a local university for use as a parking lot for athletic events; received advance payment of $3,600.

Instructions

1. Record the November 1, 20Y4, balance of each account in the appropriate balance column of a T account, and write Balance to identify the opening amounts.

2. Journalize the transactions for November in a two-column journal.

3. Post the journal entries to the T accounts, placing the date to the left of each amount to identify the transaction. Determine the balances for all accounts with more than one posting.

4. Prepare a trial balance of the ledger as of November 30, 20Y4.

APPENDIX B

Process Cost Systems

A **process manufacturer** produces products that are indistinguishable from each other, using a continuous production process. For example, an oil refinery processes crude oil through a series of steps to produce a barrel of gasoline. One barrel of gasoline, the product, cannot be distinguished from another barrel. Other examples of process manufacturers include paper producers, chemical processors, aluminum smelters, and food processors.

The cost accounting system used by process manufacturers is called the **process cost system**. A process cost system records product costs for each manufacturing department or process.

In contrast, a job order manufacturer produces custom products for customers or batches of similar products. For example, a custom printer produces wedding invitations, graduation announcements, or other special print items that are tailored to the specifications of each customer. Each item manufactured is unique to itself. Other examples of job order manufacturers include furniture manufacturers, shipbuilders, and home builders.

As described and illustrated in Chapter 10, the cost accounting system used by job order manufacturers is called the *job order cost system.* A job order cost system records product costs for each job using job cost sheets.

Some examples of process and job order manufacturers are shown below.

Process Manufacturers		Job Order Manufacturers	
Company	Product	Company	Product
Pepsi	soft drinks	Walt Disney	movies
Alcoa	aluminum	Nike, Inc.	athletic shoes
Intel	computer chips	Tiger Woods Design	golf courses
Apple	iPhone	Heritage Log Homes	log homes
Hershey Foods	chocolate bars	DDB Advertising Agency	advertising

Comparing Job Order and Process Cost Systems

Process and job order cost systems are similar in that each system:

1. Records and summarizes product costs.
2. Classifies product costs as direct materials, direct labor, and factory overhead.
3. Allocates factory overhead costs to products.
4. Uses a perpetual inventory system for materials, work in process, and finished goods.
5. Provides useful product cost information for decision making.

Process and job costing systems are different in several ways. As a basis for illustrating these differences, the cost systems for La Scoop and Quixote Guitars are used.

Exhibit 1 illustrates the process cost system for La Scoop, an ice cream manufacturer. As a basis for comparison, Exhibit 1 also illustrates the job order cost system for Quixote Guitars, a custom guitar manufacturer. Quixote Guitars was described and illustrated in Chapter 10.

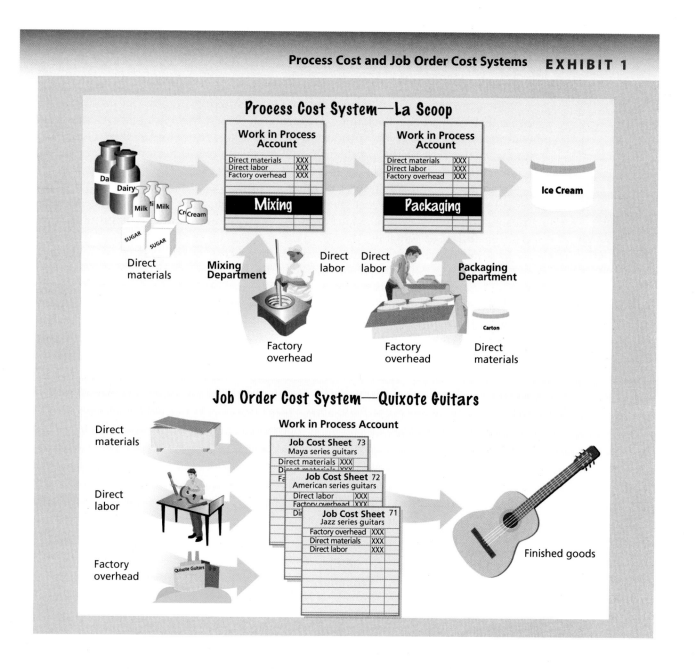

Process Cost and Job Order Cost Systems   **EXHIBIT 1**

Exhibit 1 indicates that La Scoop manufactures ice cream using two departments:

1. Mixing Department mixes the ingredients using large vats.
2. Packaging Department puts the ice cream into cartons for shipping to customers.

Since each gallon of ice cream is similar, product costs are recorded in each department's work-in-process account. As shown in Exhibit 1, La Scoop accumulates (records) the cost of making ice cream in *work-in-process accounts* for the Mixing and Packaging departments. The product costs of making a gallon of ice cream include:

1. *Direct materials cost,* which includes milk, cream, sugar, and packing cartons. All materials costs are added at the beginning of the process for both the Mixing Department and the Packaging Department.
2. *Direct labor cost,* which is incurred by employees in each department who run the equipment and load and unload product.
3. *Factory overhead costs,* which include the utility costs (power) and depreciation on the equipment.

When the Mixing Department completes the mixing process, its product costs are transferred to the Packaging Department. When the Packaging Department completes its process, the product costs are transferred to Finished Goods. In this way, the cost of the product (a gallon of ice cream) accumulates across the entire production process.

In contrast, Exhibit 1 shows that Quixote Guitars accumulates (records) product costs by jobs using a job cost sheet for each type of guitar. Thus, Quixote Guitars uses just one work-in-process account. As each job is completed, its product costs are transferred to Finished Goods.

Materials costs can be as high as 70% of the total product costs for many process manufacturers.

In a job order cost system, the work in process at the end of the period is the sum of the job cost sheets for partially completed jobs. In a process cost system, the work in process at the end of the period is determined by allocating costs between completed and partially completed units within each department.

Cost Flows for a Process Manufacturer

Exhibit 2 illustrates the *physical flow* of materials for La Scoop. Ice cream is made in a manufacturing plant in a similar way as you would at home, except on a larger scale.

EXHIBIT 2 **Physical Flows for a Process Manufacturer**

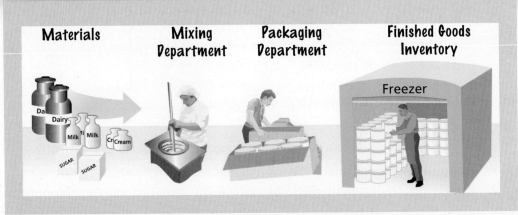

Materials | Mixing Department | Packaging Department | Finished Goods Inventory

Freezer

In the Mixing Department, direct materials in the form of milk, cream, and sugar are placed into a vat. An employee (direct labor) fills each vat, sets the cooling temperature, and sets the mix speed. The vat is cooled (refrigerated) as the direct materials are being mixed by agitators (paddles). Factory overhead is incurred in the form of power to run the vat (electricity) and vat (equipment) depreciation.

In the Packaging Department, the ice cream is received from the Mixing Department in a form ready for packaging. The Packaging Department uses direct labor and factory overhead (conversion costs) to package the ice cream into one-gallon containers (direct materials). The ice cream is then transferred to finished goods where it is frozen and stored in refrigerators prior to shipment to customers (stores).

The *cost flows* in a process cost accounting system are similar to the *physical flow* of materials described above. The cost flows for La Scoop are illustrated in Exhibit 3.

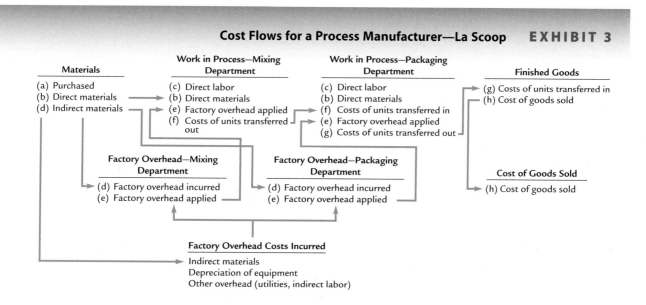

Cost Flows for a Process Manufacturer—La Scoop   EXHIBIT 3

Transactions (a) through (h) in Exhibit 3 are described and explained below.

a. The cost of materials purchased is recorded in the materials account.
b. The cost of direct materials used by the Mixing and Packaging departments is recorded in the work-in-process accounts for each department.
c. The cost of direct labor used by the Mixing and Packaging departments is recorded in work-in-process accounts for each department.
d. The cost of factory overhead incurred for indirect materials and other factory overhead such as depreciation is recorded in the factory overhead accounts for each department.
e. The factory overhead incurred in the Mixing and Packaging departments is applied to the work-in-process accounts for each department.

f. The cost of units completed in the Mixing Department is transferred to the Packaging Department.

g. The cost of units completed in the Packaging Department is transferred to Finished Goods.

h. The cost of units sold is transferred to Cost of Goods Sold.

As shown in Exhibit 3, the Mixing and Packaging departments have separate factory overhead accounts. The factory overhead costs incurred for indirect materials, depreciation, and other overhead are recorded as an increase to each department's factory overhead account. The overhead is applied to work in process by increasing each department's work-in-process account and decreasing the department's factory overhead account.

Exhibit 3 illustrates how the Mixing and Packaging departments have separate work-in-process accounts. Each work-in-process account is increased for the direct materials, direct labor, and applied factory overhead. In addition, the work-in-process account for the Packaging Department is increased for the cost of the units transferred in from the Mixing Department. Each work-in-process account is decreased for the cost of the units transferred to the next department.

Exhibit 3 also shows that the finished goods account is increased for the cost of the units transferred from the Packaging Department. The finished goods account is decreased for the cost of the units sold, which is recorded as an increase to the cost of goods sold account.

Weighted Average Cost Method

A cost flow assumption must be used as product costs flow through manufacturing processes. In this appendix, the weighted average cost flow method is illustrated for Granny's Ice Cream Company.[1]

Determining Costs Using the Weighted Average Cost Method

Granny's operations are similar to those of La Scoop. Like La Scoop, Granny's mixes direct materials (milk, cream, sugar) in refrigerated vessels and has two manufacturing departments, Mixing and Packaging.

The manufacturing data for the Mixing Department for July are as follows:

Work-in-process inventory, July 1, 5,000 gallons (70% completed)		$ 6,200
Direct materials cost incurred in July, 60,000 gallons	$66,000	
Direct labor cost incurred in July	10,500	
Factory overhead applied in July	6,405	82,905
Total production costs to account for		$89,105
Cost of goods transferred to Packaging in July (includes units in process on July 1), 62,000 gallons		?
Cost of work-in-process inventory, July 31, 3,000 gallons, 25% completed as to conversion costs		?

1. The first-in, first-out and last-in, first-out cost flow assumptions are described and illustrated in advanced cost accounting textbooks and courses.

Using the weighted average cost method, the objective is to allocate the total costs of production of $89,105 to the following:

1. The 62,000 gallons completed and transferred to the Packaging Department
2. The 3,000 gallons in the July 31 (ending) work-in-process inventory

The preceding costs show two question marks. These amounts are determined by preparing a cost of production report using the following four steps:

Step 1. Determine the units to be assigned costs.
Step 2. Compute equivalent units of production.
Step 3. Determine the cost per equivalent unit.
Step 4. Allocate costs to transferred out and partially completed units.

Under the weighted average cost method, all production costs (materials and conversion costs) are combined for determining equivalent units and cost per equivalent unit.

Step 1: Determine the Units to Be Assigned Costs

The first step is to determine the units to be assigned costs. A unit can be any measure of completed production, such as tons, gallons, pounds, barrels, or cases. For Granny's, a unit is a gallon of ice cream.

Granny's Mixing Department had 65,000 gallons of direct materials to account for during July, as shown here.

Total gallons to account for:	
Work in process, July	5,000 gallons
Received from materials storeroom	60,000
Total units to account for by the Packaging Department	65,000 gallons

There are two groups of units to be assigned costs for the period.

Group 1 Units completed and transferred out
Group 2 Units in the July 31 (ending) work-in-process inventory

During July, the Mixing Department completed and transferred 62,000 gallons to the Packaging Department. Of the 60,000 gallons started in July, 57,000 (60,000 − 3,000) gallons were completed and transferred to the Packaging Department. Thus, the ending work-in-process inventory consists of 3,000 gallons.

The total units (gallons) to be assigned costs for Granny's can be summarized as follows:

Group 1	Units transferred out to the Packaging Department in July	62,000 gallons
Group 2	Work-in-process inventory, July 31	3,000
	Total gallons to be assigned costs	65,000 gallons

The total units (gallons) to be assigned costs (65,000 gallons) equal the total units to account for (65,000 gallons).

Step 2: Compute Equivalent Units of Production

Granny's has 3,000 gallons of units in the work-in-process inventory for the Mixing Department on July 31. Since these units are 25% complete, the number of equivalent units in process in the Mixing Department on July 31 is 750 gallons (3,000 gallons × 25%). Since the units transferred to the Packaging Department have been completed, the units (62,000 gallons) transferred are the same as the equivalent units transferred.

The total equivalent units of production for the Mixing Department are determined by adding the equivalent units in the ending work-in-process inventory to the units transferred and completed during the period as shown below.

Equivalent units completed and transferred to the Packaging Department during July	62,000 gallons
Equivalent units in ending work in process, July 31	750
Total equivalent units	62,750 gallons

Step 3: Determine the Cost per Equivalent Unit

Materials and conversion costs are combined under the weighted average cost method. The cost per equivalent unit is determined by dividing the total production costs by the total equivalent units of production as follows:

$$\text{Cost per Equivalent Unit} = \frac{\text{Total Production Costs}}{\text{Total Equivalent Units}}$$

$$\text{Cost per Equivalent Unit} = \frac{\text{Total Production Costs}}{\text{Total Equivalent Units}} = \frac{\$89,105}{62,750 \text{ gallons}} = \$1.42$$

The cost per equivalent unit shown above is used in Step 4 to allocate the production costs to the completed and partially completed units.

Step 4: Allocate Costs to Transferred Out and Partially Completed Units

The cost of transferred and partially completed units is determined by multiplying the cost per equivalent unit times the equivalent units of production. For the Mixing Department, these costs are determined as follows:

Group 1	Transferred out to the Packaging Department (62,000 gallons × $1.42)	$88,040
Group 2	Work-in-process inventory, July 31 (3,000 gallons × 25% × $1.42)	1,065
	Total production costs assigned	$89,105

The Cost of Production Report

The July cost of production report for Granny's Mixing Department is shown in Exhibit 4. This cost of production report summarizes the following:

1. The units for which the department is accountable and the disposition of those units
2. The production costs incurred by the department and the allocation of those costs between completed and partially completed units

Cost Flows for a Process Cost System

Exhibit 5 on page 675 shows the flow of costs for each transaction. Note that the highlighted amounts in Exhibit 5 were determined from assigning the costs charged to production in the Mixing Department. These amounts were computed and are shown at the bottom of the cost of production report for the department in Exhibit 4.

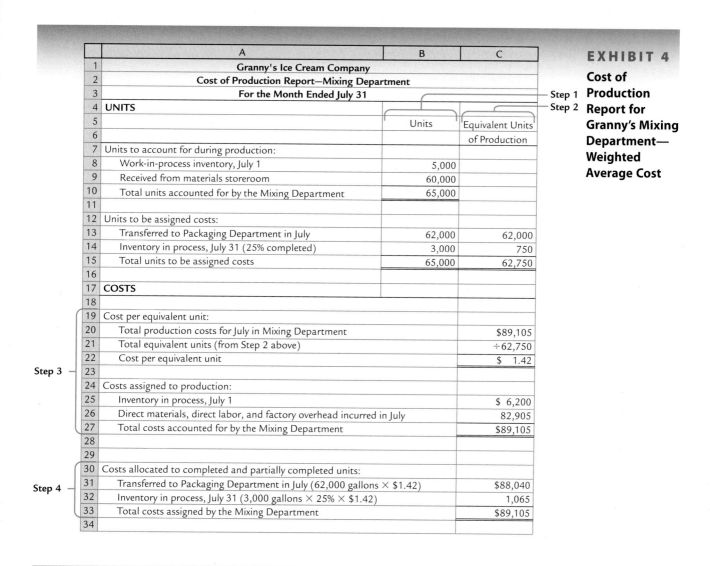

EXHIBIT 4

Cost of Production Report for Granny's Mixing Department— Weighted Average Cost

	A	B	C
1	Granny's Ice Cream Company		
2	Cost of Production Report—Mixing Department		
3	For the Month Ended July 31		
4	**UNITS**		
5		Units	Equivalent Units
6			of Production
7	Units to account for during production:		
8	Work-in-process inventory, July 1	5,000	
9	Received from materials storeroom	60,000	
10	Total units accounted for by the Mixing Department	65,000	
11			
12	Units to be assigned costs:		
13	Transferred to Packaging Department in July	62,000	62,000
14	Inventory in process, July 31 (25% completed)	3,000	750
15	Total units to be assigned costs	65,000	62,750
16			
17	**COSTS**		
18			
19	Cost per equivalent unit:		
20	Total production costs for July in Mixing Department		$89,105
21	Total equivalent units (from Step 2 above)		÷62,750
22	Cost per equivalent unit		$ 1.42
23			
24	Costs assigned to production:		
25	Inventory in process, July 1		$ 6,200
26	Direct materials, direct labor, and factory overhead incurred in July		82,905
27	Total costs accounted for by the Mixing Department		$89,105
28			
29			
30	Costs allocated to completed and partially completed units:		
31	Transferred to Packaging Department in July (62,000 gallons × $1.42)		$88,040
32	Inventory in process, July 31 (3,000 gallons × 25% × $1.42)		1,065
33	Total costs assigned by the Mixing Department		$89,105
34			

Step 1
Step 2
Step 3
Step 4

Granny's Cost Flows   EXHIBIT 5

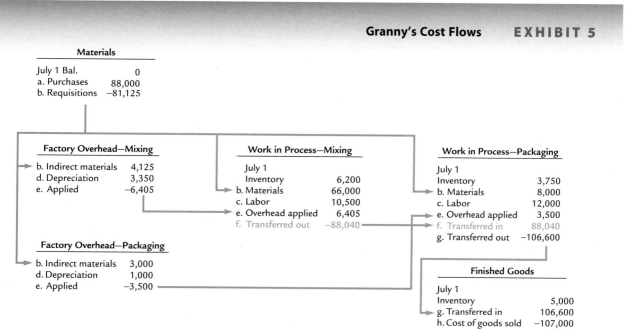

Materials

July 1 Bal.	0
a. Purchases	88,000
b. Requisitions	−81,125

Factory Overhead—Mixing

b. Indirect materials	4,125
d. Depreciation	3,350
e. Applied	−6,405

Factory Overhead—Packaging

b. Indirect materials	3,000
d. Depreciation	1,000
e. Applied	−3,500

Work in Process—Mixing

July 1	
Inventory	6,200
b. Materials	66,000
c. Labor	10,500
e. Overhead applied	6,405
f. Transferred out	−88,040

Work in Process—Packaging

July 1	
Inventory	3,750
b. Materials	8,000
c. Labor	12,000
e. Overhead applied	3,500
f. Transferred in	88,040
g. Transferred out	−106,600

Finished Goods

July 1	
Inventory	5,000
g. Transferred in	106,600
h. Cost of goods sold	−107,000

Likewise, the amount transferred out of the Packaging Department to Finished Goods also would have been determined from a cost of production report for the Packaging Department.

Using the Cost of Production Report for Decision Making

The cost of production report is often used by managers for decisions involving the control and improvement of operations. To illustrate, cost of production reports for Soda Butte Beverage Company are used. Finally, the computation and use of yield is discussed.

Soda Butte Beverage Company

A cost of production report may be prepared in greater detail than shown in Exhibit 4. This greater detail can help managers isolate problems and seek opportunities for improvement.

To illustrate, the Blending Department of Soda Butte Beverage Company prepared cost of production reports for April and May. To simplify, assume that the Blending Department had no beginning or ending work-in-process inventory in either month. In other words, all units started were completed in each month. The cost of production reports for April and May in the Blending Department are as follows:

	A	B	C
1	Cost of Production Reports		
2	Soda Butte Beverage Company—Blending Department		
3	For the Months Ended April 30 and May 31		
4		April	May
5	Direct materials	$ 20,000	$ 40,600
6	Direct labor	15,000	29,400
7	Energy	8,000	20,000
8	Repairs	4,000	8,000
9	Tank cleaning	3,000	8,000
10	Total	$ 50,000	$106,000
11	Units completed	÷100,000	÷200,000
12	Cost per unit	$ 0.50	$ 0.53
13			

The May results indicate that total unit costs have increased from $0.50 to $0.53, or 6% from April. To determine the possible causes for this increase, the cost of production report is restated in per-unit terms by dividing the costs by the number of units completed, as shown below.

	A	B	C	D
1	Blending Department			
2	Per-Unit Expense Comparisons			
3		April	May	% Change
4	Direct materials	$0.200	$0.203	1.50%
5	Direct labor	0.150	0.147	−2.00%
6	Energy	0.080	0.100	25.00%
7	Repairs	0.040	0.040	0.00%
8	Tank cleaning	0.030	0.040	33.33%
9	Total	$0.500	$0.530	6.00%
10				

Per-unit costs for energy (25% change) and tank cleaning (33.33% change) have increased significantly in May. These increases should be further investigated. For example, the increase in energy may be due to the machines losing fuel efficiency. This could lead management to repair the machines. The tank cleaning costs could be investigated in a similar fashion.

Yield

In addition to unit costs, managers of process manufacturers are also concerned about yield. The yield is computed as follows:

$$\text{Yield} = \frac{\text{Quantity of Material Output}}{\text{Quantity of Material Input}}$$

To illustrate, assume that 1,000 pounds of sugar entered the Packaging Department, and 980 pounds of sugar were packed. The yield is 98% as computed below.

$$\text{Yield} = \frac{\text{Quantity of Material Output}}{\text{Quantity of Material Input}} = \frac{980 \text{ pounds}}{1,000 \text{ pounds}} = 98\%$$

Thus, 2% (100% − 98%) or 20 pounds of sugar was lost or spilled during the packing process. Managers can investigate significant changes in yield over time or significant differences in yield from industry standards.

Exercises

E-1 Entries for materials cost flows in a process cost system

The Hershey Foods Company manufactures chocolate confectionery products. The three largest raw materials are cocoa beans, sugar, and dehydrated milk. These raw materials first go into the Blending Department. The blended product is then sent to the Molding Department, where the bars of candy are formed. The candy is then sent to the Packing Department, where the bars are wrapped and boxed. The boxed candy is then sent to the distribution center, where it is sold to food brokers and retailers.

Show the accounts increased and decreased for each of the following business events:

a. Materials used by the Blending Department

b. Transfer of blended product to the Molding Department

c. Transfer of chocolate to the Packing Department

d   Transfer of boxed chocolate to the distribution center

e. Sale of boxed chocolate

E-2 Flowchart of accounts related to service and processing departments

Alcoa Inc. is the world's largest producer of aluminum products. One product that Alcoa manufactures is aluminum sheet products for the aerospace industry. The entire output of the Smelting Department is transferred to the Rolling Department. Part of the fully processed goods from the Rolling Department are sold as rolled sheet, and the remainder of the goods are transferred to the Converting Department for further processing into sheared sheet.

Prepare a chart of the flow of costs from the processing department accounts into the finished goods accounts and then into the cost of goods sold account. The relevant accounts are as follows:

Cost of Goods Sold	Finished Goods—Rolled Sheet
Materials	Finished Goods—Sheared Sheet
Factory Overhead—Smelting Department	Work in Process—Smelting Department
Factory Overhead—Rolling Department	Work in Process—Rolling Department
Factory Overhead—Converting Department	Work in Process—Converting Department

✔ a. 28,400

E-3 Equivalent units of production

The Converting Department of Girders Company uses the weighted average cost method and had 3,500 units in work in process that were 60% complete at the beginning of the period. During the period, 24,900 units were started and 25,200 units were completed and transferred to the Packing Department. There were 3,200 units in process that were 30% complete at the end of the period.

a. Determine the number of units to be accounted for and to be assigned costs for the period.

b. Determine the number of equivalent units of production for the period.

✔ a. 94,000 units to be accounted for

E-4 Equivalent units of production

Units of production data for the two departments of Alaska Cable and Wire Company for May of the current fiscal year are as follows:

	Drawing Department	Winding Department
Work in process, May 1	3,000 units, 50% completed	2,000 units, 30% completed
Units started during May	91,000 units	90,000 units
Completed and transferred to next processing department during May	90,000 units	89,200 units
Work in process, May 31	4,000 units, 55% completed	2,800 units, 25% completed

Each department uses the weighted average cost method.

a. Determine the number of units to be accounted for and to be assigned costs and the equivalent units of production for the Drawing Department.

b. Determine the number of units to be accounted for and to be assigned costs and the equivalent units of production for the Winding Department.

✔ a. 21,500

E-5 Equivalent units of production

The following information concerns production in the Finishing Department for July. The Finishing Department uses the weighted average cost method.

ACCOUNT Work in Process—Finishing Department

Date		Item	
July	1	Bal., 20,000 units, 40% completed	24,600
	31	Direct materials, 144,000 units	345,000
	31	Direct labor	163,200
	31	Factory overhead	86,700
	31	Goods transferred, 142,500 units	−578,550
	31	Bal., ? units, 60% completed	40,950

a. Determine the number of units in work-in-process inventory at the end of the month.

b. Determine the number of units to be accounted for and to be assigned costs and the equivalent units of production for July.

E-6 Equivalent units of production and related costs

The charges to Work in Process—Baking Department for a period as well as information concerning production are as follows. The Baking Department uses the weighted average cost method, and all direct materials are placed in process during production.

✔ b. 84,600 units

Work in Process—Baking Department

Bal., 10,000 units, 70% completed	12,280
Direct materials, 82,300 units	161,000
Direct labor	91,800
Factory overhead	81,780
To Finished Goods, 81,300 units	?
Bal., 11,000 units, 30% completed	?

Determine the following:

a. The number of units to be accounted for and to be assigned costs
b. The number of equivalent units of production
c. The cost per equivalent unit
d. The cost of the units transferred to Finished Goods
e. The cost of units in the ending Work in Process

E-7 Cost per equivalent unit

✔ a. $11.50

The following information concerns production in the Forging Department for April. The Forging Department uses the weighted average cost method.

ACCOUNT Work in Process—Forging Department

Date	Item	
Apr. 1	Bal., 2,000 units, 40% completed	9,120
30	Direct materials, 46,200 units	324,800
30	Direct labor	137,045
30	Factory overhead	75,400
30	Goods transferred, 45,900 units	?
30	Bal., 2,300 units, 70% completed	?

a. Determine the cost per equivalent unit.
b. Determine the cost of the units transferred to Finished Goods.
c. Determine the cost of units in the ending Work in Process.

E-8 Cost of production report

The increases to Work in Process—Roasting Department for Colonel Dirks Coffee Company for August as well as information concerning production are as follows:

Work in process, August 1, 2,000 pounds, 40% completed	$ 8,130
Coffee beans added during August, 93,000 pounds	391,420
Conversion costs during August	187,900
Work in process, August 31, 1,250 pounds, 80% completed	—
Goods finished during August, 93,750 pounds	—

✔ Cost per equivalent unit, $6.20

Prepare a cost of production report, using the weighted average cost method.

E-9 Cost of production report

Prepare a cost of production report for the Cutting Department of Oriental Carpet Company for May. Use the weighted average cost method with the following data:

Work in process, May 1, 8,000 units, 75% completed		$ 75,000
Materials added during May from Weaving Department,		
105,000 units	$807,750	
Direct labor for May	275,200	
Factory overhead for May	100,850	1,183,800
Total production costs to account for		$1,258,800
Goods finished during May (includes goods in process,		
May 1), 104,000 units		—
Work in process, May 31, 9,000 units, 10% completed		—

E-10 Decision making

Ganges Bottling Company bottles popular beverages in the Bottling Department. The beverages are produced by blending concentrate with water and sugar. The concentrate is purchased from a concentrate producer. The concentrate producer sets higher prices for the more popular concentrate flavors. Below is a simplified Bottling Department cost of production report separating the costs of bottling the four flavors.

	A	B	C	D	E
1		Grape	Cola	Orange	Root Beer
2	Concentrate	$ 6,650	$135,000	$ 99,000	$ 3,600
3	Water	2,100	36,000	27,000	1,200
4	Sugar	3,500	60,000	45,000	2,000
5	Bottles	7,700	132,000	99,000	4,400
6	Flavor changeover	3,500	6,000	4,500	5,000
7	Conversion cost	2,625	24,000	18,000	1,500
8	Total cost transferred to Finished Goods	$26,075	$393,000	$292,500	$17,700
9	Number of cases	3,500	60,000	45,000	2,000
10					

Beginning and ending work-in-process inventories are negligible, so they are omitted from the cost of production report. The flavor changeover cost represents the cost of cleaning the bottling machines between production runs of different flavors.

Prepare a memo to the production manager analyzing this comparative cost information. In your memo, provide recommendations for further action, along with supporting schedules showing the total cost per case and the cost per case by cost element.

E-11 Decision making

Lasting Memories Inc. produces photographic paper for printing digital images. One of the processes for this operation is a coating (solvent spreading) operation, where chemicals are coated onto paper stock. There has been some concern about the cost performance of this operation. As a result, you have begun an investigation. You first discover that all materials and conversion prices have been stable for the last six months. Thus, increases in prices for inputs are not an explanation for increasing costs. However, you have discovered three possible problems from some of the operating personnel whose quotes follow:

Operator 1: "I've been keeping an eye on my operating room instruments. I feel as though our energy consumption is becoming less efficient."

Operator 2: "Every time the coating machine goes down, we produce waste on shutdown and subsequent startup. It seems like during the last half year we have had more unscheduled machine shutdowns than in the past. Thus, I feel as though our yields must be dropping."

Operator 3: "My sense is that our coating costs are going up. It seems to me like we are spreading a thicker coating than we should. Perhaps the coating machine needs to be recalibrated."

The Coating Department had no beginning or ending inventories for any month during the study period. The following data from the cost of production report are made available:

A	B	C	D	E	F	G
1	April	May	June	July	August	September
2 Paper stock	$72,960	$69,120	$76,800	$69,120	$65,280	$61,440
3 Coating	$16,416	$17,280	$21,120	$21,600	$21,216	$23,040
4 Conversion cost (incl. energy)	$36,480	$34,560	$38,400	$34,560	$32,640	$30,720
5 Pounds input to the process	95,000	90,000	100,000	90,000	85,000	80,000
6 Pounds transferred out	91,200	86,400	96,000	86,400	81,600	76,800
7						

a. Prepare a table showing the paper cost per output pound, coating cost per output pound, conversion cost per output pound, and yield for each month.

b. Interpret your table results.

Problems

P1 Equivalent units and related costs; cost of production report: weighted average cost method

Joshua Flour Company manufactures flour by a series of three processes, beginning in the Milling Department. From the Milling Department, the materials pass through the Sifting and Packaging departments, emerging as packaged refined flour.

The balance in the account Work in Process—Sifting Department was as follows on March 1:

Work in Process—Sifting Department (3,200 units, 75% completed) $3,500

The following costs were charged to Work in Process—Sifting Department during December:

Direct materials transferred from Milling Department: 14,500 units $51,400
Direct labor   13,325
Factory overhead   5,125

During March, 14,900 units of flour were completed. The balance of Work in Process—Sifting Department on March 31 was 2,800 units, 50% completed.

Instructions

Prepare a cost of production report for the Sifting Department for March, using the weighted average cost method.

✔ Transferred to Packaging Dept., $67,050

P2 Cost of production report: Weighted average cost method

Sergeant Wilkes Coffee Company roasts and packs coffee beans. The process begins in the Roasting Department. From the Roasting Department, the coffee beans are transferred to the Packaging Department.

On October 1, the balance of the account Work in Process—Roasting Department was as follows:

Work in Process—Roasting Department (7,500 units, 80% completed) $27,600

✔ Cost per equivalent unit, $5.00

The account Work in Process—Roasting Department was increased during October by the following costs:

Direct materials (64,500 units)	$135,600
Direct labor	118,900
Factory overhead	67,900

During October, 64,000 units were completed and transferred to the Packaging Department. As of October 31, there were 8,000 units, 75% complete in the Roasting Department.

Instructions

Prepare a cost of production report for the Roasting Department, using the weighted average cost method.

GLOSSARY

A

Accelerated depreciation method A depreciation method that provides for a higher depreciation amount in the first year of the asset's use, followed by a gradually declining amount of depreciation.

Account A record in which increases and decreases in a financial statement element are recorded.

Account form The form of balance sheet presented with assets on the left-hand side and the liabilities and stockholders' equity on the right-hand side.

Accounting An information system that provides reports to stakeholders about the economic activities and condition of a business.

Accounting cycle The process that begins with analzing transactions and ends with preparing the financial statements.

Accounting equation Assets = Liabilities + Stockholders' Equity

Accounting period concept An accounting concept in which accounting data are recorded and summarized in a period process.

Accounts payable Liabilities for amounts incurred from purchases of products or services in the normal operations of a business.

Accounts receivable Receivables created by selling merchandise or services on credit.

Accounts receivable analysis Analysis of a company's ability to collect its accounts receivable.

Accounts receivable turnover The relationship between net sales and accounts receivable computed by dividing the net sales by the average net accounts receivable; measures how frequently during the year the accounts receivable are being converted to cash.

Accrual basis of accounting A system of accounting in which revenue is recorded as it is earned and expenses are recorded and matched against the revenue they generate.

Accruals Recognition of revenue when earned or expenses when incurred regardless of when cash is received or disbursed.

Accrued assets Revenues that have been earned at the end of an accounting period but have not been recorded in the accounts; sometimes called *accrued revenues*.

Accrued expenses Expenses that have been incurred at the end of an accounting period but have not been recorded in the accounts; sometimes called *accrued liabilities*.

Accrued liabilities Expenses that have been incurred at the end of an accounting period but have not been recorded in the accounts; sometimes called *accrued expenses*.

Accrued revenues Revenues that have been earned at the end of an accounting period but have not been recorded in the accounts; sometimes called *accrued assets*.

Accumulated depreciation An offsetting or contra asset account used to record depreciation on a fixed asset.

Activity base (driver) A measure of activity that is related to changes in cost and is used in the denominator in calculating the predetermined factory overhead rate to assign factory overhead costs to cost objects.

Activity cost pools Cost accumulations that are associated with a given activity, such as machine usage, inspections, moving, and production setups.

Activity-based costing (ABC) An accounting framework based on determining the cost of activities and allocating these costs to products using activity rates.

Adequate disclosure concept An accounting concept that requires financial statements to include all relevant data a reader needs to understand the financial condition and performance of a business.

Adjustment process A process required by the accrual basis of accounting in which the accounts are updated prior to preparing financial statements.

Administrative expenses Expenses incurred in the administration or general operations of the business; costs not directly related to selling, such as officer salaries.

Aging the receivables The process of analyzing the accounts receivable and classifying them according to various age groupings, with the due date being the base point for determining age.

Allowance for doubtful accounts The contra asset account for accounts receivable.

Allowance method The method of accounting for uncollectible accounts that provides an expense for uncollectible receivables in advance of their write-off.

Amortization The periodic transfer of the cost of an intangible asset to expense.

Annuity A series of equal cash flows at fixed intervals.

Assets The resources owned by a business.

Average cost inventory cost flow method The method of inventory costing that is based upon the assumption that costs should be charged against revenue by using the weighted average unit cost of the items sold.

Average markup percent Gross profit divided by cost of merchandise sold.

Average rate of return A method of evaluating capital investment proposals that focuses on the expected profitability of the investment.

B

Bad debt expense The operating expense incurred because of the failure to collect receivables.

Balance sheet A list of the assets, liabilities, and owner's equity as of a specific date, usually at the close of the last day of a month or a year.

Balanced scorecard A performance evaluation approach that incorporates multiple performance dimensions by combining financial and nonfinancial measures.

Bank reconciliation The analysis that details the items responsible for the difference between the cash balance reported in the bank statement and the cash balance in the ledger.

Bank statement A summary of all transactions mailed to the depositor by the bank each month.

Bond A form of interest-bearing note used by corporations to borrow on a long-term basis.

Bond indenture The contract between a corporation issuing bonds and the bondholders.

Bonds payable A type of long-term debt financing with a face amount that is in the future with interest that is normally paid semiannually.

Book value The cost of a fixed asset minus accumulated depreciation on the asset.

Bottleneck A condition that occurs when product demand exceeds product capacity.

Break-even point The level of business operations at which revenues and expired costs are equal.

Budget An accounting device used to plan and control resources of operational departments and divisions.

Budget performance report A report comparing actual results with budget figures.

Budgetary slack Excess resources set within a budget to provide for uncertain events.

Budgeted variable factory overhead The standard variable overhead for the actual units produced.

Business An organization in which basic resources (inputs), such as materials and labor, are assembled and processed to provide goods and services (outputs) to customers.

Business entity concept An accounting concept that limits the economic data in the accounting system of a specific business or entity to data related directly to the activities of that business or entity.

Business stakeholder A person or entity that has an interest in the economic performance of a business.

C

Capital expenditures The costs of acquiring fixed assets, adding a component, or replacing a component of a fixed asset.

Capital expenditures budget The budget summarizing future plans for acquiring plant facilities and equipment.

Capital investment analysis The process by which management plans, evaluates, and controls long-term capital investments involving fixed assets.

Capital rationing The process by which management allocates available investment funds among competing capital investment proposals.

Capital stock The portion of a corporation's stockholders' equity contributed by investors (owners) in exchange for shares of stock.

Cash Coins, currency (paper money), checks, money orders, and money on deposit available for unrestricted withdrawal from banks and other financial institutions.

Cash basis of accounting A system of accounting in which only transactions involving increases or decreases of the entity's cash are recorded.

Cash budget A budget of estimated cash receipts and payments.

Cash dividend A cash distribution of earnings by a corporation to its shareholders.

Cash equivalents Highly liquid investments that are usually reported with cash on the balance sheet.

Cash payback period The expected period of time that will elapse between the date of a capital expenditure and the complete recovery in cash (or equivalent) of the amount invested.

Cash short and over The account used to record the difference between the amount of cash in a cash register and the amount of cash that should be on hand according to the records.

Classified balance sheet A balance sheet prepared with various sections, subsections, and captions that aid in its interpretation and analysis.

Common stock The basic type of stock issued to stockholders of a corporation when a corporation has issued only one class of stock.

Common-sized balance sheet A balance sheet where each amount is expressed as a percent of total assets or total liabilities plus stockholders' equity.

Common-sized financial statements Financial statements that express each amount as a percent of a base amount.

Common-sized income statement An income statement where each amount is expressed as a percent of sales.

Common-sized statement A financial statement in which all items are expressed only in relative terms.

Compensating balance A requirement by some banks that depositors maintain minimum cash balances in their bank accounts.

Contingent liabilities Potential liabilities if certain events occur in the future.

Continuous budgeting A method of budgeting that provides for maintaining a 12-month projection into the future.

Contract rate The periodic interest to be paid on the bonds that is identified in the bond indenture; expressed as a percentage of the face amount of the bond.

Contribution margin Sales less variable cost of goods sold and variable selling and administrative expenses.

Contribution margin ratio The percentage of each sales dollar that is available to cover the fixed costs and provide income from operations.

Controllable expenses Costs that can be influenced by the decisions of a manager of a cost, profit, or investment center.

Controllable revenues Revenues that can be influenced by the decisions of a manager of a profit or investment center.

Controllable variance The difference between the actual amount of variable factory overhead cost incurred and the amount of variable factory overhead budgeted for the standard product.

Controlling account The account in the general ledger that summarizes the balances of the accounts in the subsidiary ledger.

Conversion costs The combination of direct labor and factory overhead costs.

Copyright An exclusive right to publish and sell a literary, artistic, or musical composition.

Corporation A business organized under state or federal statutes as a separate legal entity.

Cost A payment of cash (or a commitment to pay cash in the future) for the purpose of generating revenues.

Cost accounting system A system used to accumulate manufacturing costs for decision-making and financial reporting purposes.

Cost allocation The process of assigning indirect costs to a cost object, such as a job.

Cost behavior The manner in which a cost changes in relation to its activity base (driver).

Cost center A decentralized unit in which the department or division manager has responsibility for the control of costs incurred and the authority to make decisions that affect these costs.

Cost concept An accounting concept that determines the amount initially entered into the accounting records for purchases.

Cost of goods sold The cost of products sold; also may be referred to as *cost of merchandise sold* or *cost of sales*.

Cost of goods sold budget A budget of the estimated direct materials, direct labor, and factory overhead consumed by sold products.

Cost of merchandise purchased The cost of merchandise purchased during a period, computed as purchases less purchases returns and allowances, less purchases discounts, plus freight in.

Cost of merchandise sold The cost of products sold; also may be referred to as cost of sales or cost of goods sold.

Cost of sales The cost of products sold; also may be referred to as *cost of merchandise sold* or *cost of goods sold*.

Cost price approach An approach to transfer pricing that uses cost as the basis for setting the transfer price.

Cost variance The difference between the actual cost and the standard cost at actual volumes.

Cost-volume-profit analysis The systematic examination of the relationships among costs, expenses, sales, and operating profit or loss.

Cost-volume-profit chart A chart used to assist management in understanding the relationships among costs, expenses, sales, and operating profit or loss.

Credit memorandum A form used by a seller to inform the buyer of the amount the seller proposes to decrease the account receivable due from the buyer.

Credit period The amount of time the buyer is allowed in which to pay the seller.

Credit terms Terms for payment on account by the buyer to the seller.

Currency exchange rate The rate at which currency in another country can be exchanged for local currency.

Current assets Cash and other assets that are expected to be converted to cash or sold or used up through the normal operations of the business within 1 year or less.

Current liabilities Liabilities that will be due within a short time (usually 1 year or less) and that are to be paid out of current assets.

Current position analysis Analysis of a company's ability to pay its current liabilities.

Current ratio A financial ratio that is computed by dividing current assets by current liabilities.

Currently attainable standards Standards that represent levels of operation that can be attained with reasonable effort.

D

Debit memorandum A form used by a buyer to inform the seller of the amount the buyer proposes to decrease the account payable due the seller.

Deferrals Delayed recordings of expenses or revenues.

Deferred expenses Items that are initially recorded as assets but are expected to become expenses over time or through the normal operations of the business; sometimes called *prepaid expenses*.

Deferred revenues Items that are initially recorded as liabilities but are expected to become revenues over time or through the normal operations of the business; sometimes called *unearned revenues*.

Depletion The process of transferring the cost of natural resources to an expense account.

Depreciation The systematic periodic transfer of the cost of a fixed asset to an expense account during its expected useful life.

Differential analysis The area of accounting concerned with the effect of alternative courses of action on revenues and costs.

Differential cost The amount of increase or decrease in cost expected from a particular course of action compared with an alternative.

Differential income (or loss) The difference between differential revenue and differential cost.

Differential revenue The amount of increase or decrease in revenue expected from a particular course of action as compared with an alternative.

Direct labor cost Wages of factory workers who are directly involved in converting materials into a finished product.

Direct labor cost budget A budget that estimates the direct labor hours and related costs needed to support budgeted production.

Direct labor rate variance The cost associated with the difference between the standard rate and the actual rate paid for direct labor used in producing a commodity.

Direct labor time variance The cost associated with the difference between the standard hours and the actual hours of direct labor spent producing a commodity.

Direct materials cost The cost of materials that are an integral part of the finished product.

Direct materials price variance The difference between the actual price and standard price times the actual quantity.

Direct materials purchases budget A budget that uses the production budget as a starting point.

Direct materials quantity variance The cost associated with the difference between the standard quantity and the actual quantity of direct materials used in producing a commodity.

Direct write-off method The method of accounting for uncollectible accounts that recognizes the expense only when accounts are judged to be worthless.

Discount on bonds payable The excess of the face amount of bonds over their issue price.

Dividend yield A ratio, computed by dividing the annual dividends paid per share of common stock by the market price per share at a specific date, which indicates the rate of return to stockholders in terms of cash dividend distributions.

Dividends Distributions of the earnings of a corporation to its stockholders.

Dividends per share Measures the extent to which earnings are being distributed to common shareholders.

Double-declining balance method A method of depreciation that provides periodic depreciation expense based on the declining book value of a fixed asset over its estimated life.

DuPont formula An expanded expression of return on investment determined by multiplying the profit margin by the investment turnover.

E

Earnings per share (EPS) A measure of profitability computed by dividing net income, reduced by preferred dividends, by the number of shares outstanding.

Earnings per share (EPS) on common stock Net income per share of common stock outstanding during a period.

Electronic data interchange (EDI) An information technology that allows different business organizations to use computers to communicate orders, relay information, and make or receive payments.

Electronic funds transfer (EFT) A system in which computers rather than paper (money, checks, etc.) are used to effect cash transactions.

Elements of internal control The control environment, risk assessment, control activities, information and communication, and monitoring.

Employee fraud The intentional act of deceiving an employer for personal gain.

Employee involvement A philosophy that grants employees the responsibility and authority to make their own decisions about their operations.

Enterprise resource planning A system used to plan and control internal and supply chain operations.

Expenses Costs used to earn (generate) revenues.

Extraordinary item An event or transaction reported on the income statement that is (1) unusual in nature and (2) infrequent in occurrence.

F

Factory overhead cost All of the costs of operating the factory except for direct materials and direct labor.

Factory overhead cost budget A budget that estimates the cost for each item of factory overhead needed to support budgeted production.

Factory overhead cost variance report Reports budgeted and actual costs for variable and fixed factory overhead for each cost element along with the related controllable and volume variances.

Favorable cost variance Actual cost is less than standard cost.

Fees earned Revenues received from providing services.

Financial accounting The area of accounting that focuses on recording transactions and events so that general-purpose financial statements can be prepared.

Financial Accounting Standards Board (FASB) The authoritative body that has the primary responsibility for developing accounting principles.

Financial accounting system A system that includes (1) a set of rules for determining what, when, and the amount that should be recorded for an economic event; (2) a framework for facilitating preparing financial statements; and (3) one or more controls to determine whether errors could have occurred in the recording process.

Financial statements Financial reports that summarize the effects of events on a business.

Financing activities Business activities that involve obtaining funds to begin and operate a business.

Finished goods inventory The cost of finished products on hand that have not been sold.

Finished goods ledger The subsidiary ledger that contains the individual accounts for each kind of commodity or product produced.

First-in, first-out (FIFO) inventory cost flow method A method of inventory costing based on the assumption that the costs of merchandise sold should be charged against revenue in the order in which the costs were incurred.

Fixed assets Long-lived or relatively permanent tangible assets that are used in the normal business operations; sometimes called *plant assets*.

Fixed asset turnover A ratio measuring the efficiency of a company's use of its fixed assets; computed by dividing net sales by average fixed assets.

Fixed costs Costs that tend to remain the same in amount, regardless of variations in the level of activity.

Flexible budget A budget that adjusts for varying rates of activity.

FOB (free on board) destination Freight terms in which the seller pays the transportation costs from the shipping point to the final destination.

FOB (free on board) shipping point Freight terms in which the buyer pays the transportation costs from the shipping point to the final destination.

Freight in Freight costs incurred in obtaining merchandise.

Fringe benefits Benefits provided to employees in addition to wages and salaries.

G

General expenses Expenses incurred in the administration or general operations of the business; sometimes called administrative expenses.

Generally accepted accounting principles (GAAP) Rules for the way financial statements should be prepared.

Goal conflict Situation when individual self-interest differs from business objectives.

Going concern concept An accounting concept that assumes a business will continue operating for an indefinite period of time.

Goodwill An intangible asset of a business that is created from favorable factors such as location, product quality, reputation, and managerial skill, as verified from a merger transaction.

Gross pay The total earnings of an employee for a payroll period.

Gross profit Sales minus the cost of merchandise sold.

Gross profit percent Gross profit divided by net sales.

H

High-low method A technique that uses the highest and lowest total cost as a basis for estimating the variable cost per unit and the fixed cost component of a mixed cost.

Horizontal analysis Financial analysis that compares an item in a current statement with the same item in prior statements.

I

Ideal standards Standards that can be achieved only under perfect operating conditions, such as no idle time, no machine breakdowns, and no materials spoilage; also called *theoretical standards*.

Income from operations The excess of gross profit over total operating expenses; sometimes called *operating income*.

Income statement A summary of the revenue and expenses for a specific period of time, such as a month or a year.

Indirect method A method of preparing the statement of cash flows that reconciles net income with net cash flows from operating activities.

Inflation A period when prices in general are rising and the purchasing power of money is declining.

Intangible assets Long-lived assets that are useful in the operations of a business, are not held for sale, and are without physical qualities.

Interest payable A liability to pay interest on a due date.

Internal control The policies and procedures used to safeguard assets, ensure accurate business information, and ensure compliance with laws and regulations.

Internal rate of return (IRR) method A method of analyzing proposed capital investments that focuses on using present value concepts to compute the rate of return from the net cash flows expected from the investment.

International Accounting Standards Board An authoritative body that establishes accounting principles and practices for companies outside of the United States.

Inventory analysis A company's ability to manage its inventory effectively.

Inventory shortage The amount by which the merchandise for sale, as indicated by the balance of the merchandise inventory account, is larger than the total amount of merchandise counted during the physical inventory; sometimes called *inventory shrinkage*.

Inventory shrinkage The amount by which the merchandise for sale, as indicated by the balance of the merchandise inventory account, is larger than the total amount of merchandise counted during the physical inventory; sometimes called *inventory shortage*.

Inventory turnover The relationship between the volume of goods sold and inventory, computed by dividing the cost of goods sold by the average inventory.

Investing activities Business activities that involve obtaining the necessary resources to start and operate the business.

Investment center A decentralized unit in which the manager has the responsibility and authority to make decisions that affect not only costs and revenues but also the fixed assets available to the center.

Investment turnover A component of the rate of return on investment computed as the ratio of sales to invested assets.

Invoice The bill that the seller sends to the buyer.

J

Job cost sheet An account in the work-in-process subsidiary ledger in which the costs charged to a particular job order are recorded.

Job order cost system A type of cost accounting system that provides for a separate record of the cost of each particular quantity of product that passes through the factory.

Just-in-time (JIT) processing A business philosophy that focuses on eliminating time, cost, and poor quality within manufacturing processes.

L

Last-in, first-out (LIFO) inventory cost flow method A method of inventory costing based on the assumption that the most recent merchandise inventory costs should be charged against revenue.

Lead time The elapsed time between starting a unit of product into the beginning of a process and its completion.

Liabilities The rights of creditors that represent a legal obligation to repay an amount borrowed according to terms of the borrowing agreement.

LIFO conformity rule A financial reporting rule requiring a firm that elects to use LIFO inventory valuation for tax purposes to also use LIFO for external financial reporting.

LIFO reserve A required disclosure for LIFO firms, showing the difference between inventory valued under FIFO and inventory valued under LIFO.

Limited liability company (LLC) A form of corporation that combines attributes of a partnership and a corporation.

Liquidity Refers to the ability to convert an asset to cash.

Long-term liabilities Liabilities due beyond one year or liabilities that will be paid out of noncurrent assets.

Low-cost strategy A strategy where a company designs and produces products or services at a lower cost than its competitors.

Lower-of-cost-or-market (LCM) method A method of valuing inventory that reports the inventory at the lower of its cost or current market value (replacement cost).

M

Management's Discussion and Analysis (MD&A) An annual report disclosure that provides management's analysis of the results of operations and financial condition.

Managerial accounting The branch of accounting that aids management in making financing, investing, and operating decisions for the company.

Manufacturing business A type of business that changes basic inputs into products that are sold to individual customers.

Margin of safety The difference between current sales revenue and the sales at the break-even point.

Market price approach An approach to transfer pricing that uses the price at which the product or service transferred could be sold to outside buyers as the transfer price.

Market rate of interest The effective rate of interest at the time the bonds were issued.

Markup An amount that is added to a "cost" amount to determine product price.

Master budget The comprehensive budget plan linking the individual budgets related to sales, cost of goods sold, operating expenses, capital expenditures, and cash.

Matching concept An accounting concept that requires expenses of a period to be matched with the revenue generated during that period.

Materials inventory The cost of materials that have not yet entered into the manufacturing process.

Materials ledger The subsidiary ledger containing the individual accounts for each type of material.

Materials requisition The form or electronic transmission used by a manufacturing department to authorize the issuance of materials from the storeroom.

Maturity value The amount that is due at the maturity or due date of a note.

Merchandise available for sale The cost of merchandise available for sale to customers.

Merchandise inventory Merchandise on hand (not sold) at the end of an accounting period.

Merchandising businesses Businesses that sell products they purchase from other businesses to customers.

Mixed costs Costs with both variable and fixed characteristics.

Monthly cash expenses Computed for companies with negative cash flows from operations as net cash flows from operations divided by 12.

Multiple-step income statement A form of income statement that contains several sections, subsections, and subtotals.

N

Negotiated price approach An approach to transfer pricing that allows managers of decentralized units to agree (negotiate) among themselves as to the transfer price.

Net income The excess of revenues over expenses.

Net loss The excess of expenses over revenues.

Net pay Gross pay less payroll deductions; the amount the employer is obligated to pay the employee.

Net present value method A method of analyzing proposed capital investments that focuses on the present value of the cash flows expected from the investments.

Net purchases Purchases less purchases returns and allowances and purchases discounts.

Net realizable value For a receivable, the amount of cash expected to be realized in the future. For inventory, the estimated selling price of an item of inventory less any direct costs of disposal, such as sales commissions.

Net sales Gross sales less sales returns and allowances and sales discounts.

Nonfinancial performance measure A performance measure expressed in other than dollars.

Non-value-added lead time The time that units wait in inventories, move unnecessarily, and wait during machine breakdowns.

Note payable A type of short- or long- term financing that requires payment of the amount borrowed plus interest.

Notes receivable Written claims against debtors who promise to pay the amount of the note plus interest at an agreed upon rate.

Number of days' sales in inventory The relationship between the volume of sales and inventory, computed by dividing the average inventory by the average daily cost of goods sold.

Number of days' sales in receivables The relationship between sales and accounts receivable, computed by dividing the average accounts receivable by the average daily sales.

Number of times interest charges are earned A ratio that measures creditor margin of safety for interest payments, calculated as income before interest and taxes divided by interest expense.

O

Objectivity concept An accounting concept that requires accounting records and data reported in financial statements be based on objective evidence.

Operating activities Business activities that involve using the business's resources to implement its business strategy.

Operating income The excess of gross profit over total operating expenses; sometimes called *income from operations*.

Operating leverage A measure of the relative mix of a business's variable costs and fixed costs, computed as contribution margin divided by income from operations.

Opportunity cost The amount of income forgone from an alternative to a proposed use of cash or its equivalent.

Other expense Expenses that cannot be traced directly to operations.

Other income Revenue from sources other than the primary operating activities of a business.

Outstanding stock The stock in the hands of stockholders.

Overapplied factory overhead The amount of factory overhead applied in excess of the actual factory overhead costs incurred for production during a period.

Owner's equity The financial rights of the owner.

P

Par The monetary amount printed on a stock certificate.

Partnership A business owned by two or more individuals.

Patents Exclusive rights to produce and sell goods with one or more unique features.

Payroll The total amount paid to employees for a certain period.

Period costs Those costs that are used up in generating revenue during the current period and that are not involved in the manufacturing process.

Periodic inventory system The inventory method in which the inventory records do not show the amount available for sale or sold during the period.

Permanent differences Differences between taxable income and income before income taxes that are created because some revenues are exempt from tax or some expenses are not deductible.

Perpetual inventory system The inventory system in which each purchase and sale of merchandise is recorded in an inventory account.

Petty cash fund A special-purpose cash fund to pay relatively small amounts.

Predetermined factory overhead rate The rate used to apply factory overhead costs to the goods manufactured. The rate is determined from budgeted overhead cost and estimated activity usage data at the beginning of the fiscal period.

Preferred stock A class of stock with preferential rights over common stock.

Premium on bonds payable The excess of the issue price of bonds over their face amount.

Premium on stock The excess of the issue price of a stock over its par value.

Premium-price strategy A strategy where a company tries to design and produce products or services that serve unique market needs, allowing it to charge premium prices.

Prepaid expenses Assets resulting from the prepayment of future expenses such as insurance or rent that are expected to become expenses over time or through the normal operations of the business; often called *deferred expenses*.

Present value concept Cash today is not the equivalent of the same amount of money to be received in the future.

Present value index An index computed by dividing the total present value of the next cash flow to be received from a proposed capital investment by the amount to be invested.

Present value of an annuity The sum of the present values of a series of equal cash flows to be received at fixed intervals.

Price-earnings (P/E) ratio The ratio of the market price per share of common stock, at a specific date, to the annual earnings per share.

Prime costs The combination of direct materials and direct labor costs.

Process A sequence of activities linked together for performing a particular task.

Process cost system A type of cost accounting system in which costs are accumulated by department or process within a factory.

Process-oriented layout Organizing work in a plant or administrative function around processes (tasks).

Product cost concept A concept used in applying the cost-plus approach to product pricing in which only the costs of manufacturing the product, termed the *product costs*, are included in the cost amount to which the markup is added.

Product costs The three components of manufacturing costs: direct materials, direct labor, and factory overhead costs.

Production budget A budget of estimated unit production.

Product-oriented layout Organizing work in a plant or administrative function around products; sometimes referred to as *product cells*.

Profit The excess of the amounts received from customers for goods or services and the amounts paid for the inputs used to provide the goods or services.

Profit center A decentralized unit in which the manager has the responsibility and the authority to make decisions that affect both costs and revenues (and thus profits).

Profit margin A component of the rate of return on investment computed as the ratio of income from operations to sales.

Profitability The ability of a firm to earn income.

Profit-volume chart A chart used to assist management in understanding the relationship between profit and volume.

Proprietorship A business owned by one individual.

Pull manufacturing A just-in-time method wherein customer orders trigger the release of finished goods, which triggers production, which triggers release of materials from suppliers.

Purchases discounts Discounts taken by the buyer for early payment of an invoice.

Purchases returns and allowances From the buyer's perspective, returned merchandise or an adjustment for defective merchandise.

Push manufacturing Materials are released into production and work in process is released into finished goods in anticipation of future sales.

Q

Quick assets Cash and other current assets that can be quickly converted to cash, such as marketable securities and receivables.

Quick ratio A financial ratio that measures the ability to pay current liabilities with quick assets (cash, marketable securities, accounts receivable).

R

Radio frequency identification devices Electronic tags (chips) placed on or embedded within products that can be read by radio waves and that allow instant monitoring of product location.

Rate earned on common stockholders' equity A measure of profitability computed by dividing net income less preferred dividends by average common stockholders' equity.

Rate earned on stockholders' equity A measure of profitability computed by dividing net income by average total stockholders' equity.

Rate earned on total assets A measure of the profitability of assets, without regard to the equity of creditors and stockholders in the assets.

Rate of return on assets A profitability measure that is computed by dividing net income before taxes and interest expense by average total assets.

Rate of return on investment (ROI) A measure of managerial efficiency in the use of investments in assets computed as income from operations divided by invested assets.

Ratio of cash to monthly cash expenses A ratio that is useful in assessing how a company with negative cash flows from operations can continue to operate. Computed as cash and cash equivalents divided by monthly cash expenses.

Ratio of fixed assets to long-term liabilities A leverage ratio that measures the margin of safety of long-term creditors, calculated as the net fixed assets divided by the long-term liabilities.

Ratio of liabilities to stockholders' equity A comprehensive leverage ratio that measures the relationship of the claims of creditors to stockholders' equity.

Ratio of liabilities to total assets Sometimes called the debt ratio, it indicates the percent of a company's total assets that are financed with debt.

Ratio of net sales to assets Ratio that measures how effectively a company uses its assets, computed as net sales divided by average total assets.

Ratio of sales to assets A ratio used to assess how efficient a company generates sales from its assets. Computed as net sales divided by average assets.

Ratio of stockholders' equity to total assets A ratio that indicates the percent of a company's total assets that are financed with equity; equals one minus the ratio of liabilities to total assets.

Receivables All money claims against other entities, including people, business firms, and other organizations.

Receiving report The form or electronic transmission used by the receiving personnel to indicate that materials have been received and inspected.

Relevant range The range of activity over which changes in cost are of interest to management.

Report form The form of balance sheet in which assets, liabilities, and stockholders' equity are reported in a downward sequence.

Residual income The excess of divisional income from operations over a "minimum" acceptable income from operations.

Residual value The estimated value of a fixed asset at the end of its useful life.

Responsibility accounting The process of measuring and reporting operating data by areas of responsibility.

Responsibility center A budgetary unit within a company for which a manager is assigned responsibility over costs, revenues, or assets.

Retained earnings Net income retained in a corporation.

Retained earnings statement A summary of the changes in the retained earnings of a corporation for a specific period of time, such as a month or a year.

Revenue The increase in assets from selling products or services to customers.

Revenue expenditures Costs that benefit only the current period or costs incurred for normal maintenance and repairs of fixed assets.

S

Sales Revenues received from selling products; the total amount charged to customers for merchandise sold, including cash sales and sales on account.

Sales budget A budget that indicates for each product (1) the quantity of estimated sales, and (2) the expected unit selling price.

Sales discounts From the seller's perspective, discounts that a seller can offer the buyer for early payment.

Sales mix The relative distribution of sales among the various products available for sale.

Sales returns and allowances From the seller's perspective, returned merchandise or an adjustment for damaged or defective merchandise.

Sarbanes-Oxley Act of 2002 An act passed by Congress to restore public confidence and trust in the financial statements of companies.

Securities and Exchange Commission An agency of the U.S. government that has authority over the accounting and financial disclosures for corporations whose stock is traded and sold to the public.

Selling expenses Costs directly related to the selling of a product or service such as sales salaries and advertising expenses.

Service business A type of business that provides services rather than products to customers.

Service department charges The costs of services provided by an internal service department and transferred to a responsibility center.

Setup The effort required to prepare an operation for a new production run.

Six Sigma A method of improving product quality and manufacturing processes developed by Motorola Corporation that consists of five steps: define, measure, analyze, improve, and control.

Solvency The ability of a firm to pay its debts as they come due.

Special-purpose fund A cash fund used for a special business need.

Specific identification inventory cost flow method An inventory cost flow method where the cost of each inventory unit is separately identified.

Standard cost A detailed estimate of what a product should cost.

Standard cost systems Accounting systems that use standards for each manufacturing cost entering into the finished product.

Standards Performance goals.

Stated value A value, similar to par value, approved by the board of directors of a corporation for no-par stock.

Statement of cash flows A summary of the cash receipts and cash payments for a specific period of time, such as a month or a year.

Statement of financial condition Reports the financial condition as of a point in time; often referred to as the *balance sheet*.

Static budget A budget that does not adjust to changes in activity levels.

Stock dividend A distribution of shares of stock to stockholders.

Stock split The reduction in the par or stated value of common stock and issuance of a proportionate number of additional shares.

Stockholders Investors who purchase stock in a corporation.

Stockholders' equity The stockholders' rights to the assets of a business.

Straight-line method A method of depreciation that provides for equal periodic depreciation expense over the estimated life of a fixed asset.

Subsidiary ledger A ledger containing individual accounts with a common characteristic.

Sunk cost A cost that is not affected by subsequent decisions.

Supply chain management The coordination and control of materials, services, information, and finances as they move in a process from the supplier, through the manufacturer, wholesaler, and retailer to the consumer.

T

Tangible assets Assets such as machinery, buildings, computers, office furnishings, trucks, and automobiles that have physical characteristics.

Target costing A concept used to design and manufacture a product at a cost that will deliver a target profit for a given market-determined price.

Taxable income The income of a corporation that is subject to taxes as determined according to the tax laws.

Temporary differences Differences between taxable income and income before income taxes that are created because items are recognized in one period for tax purposes and in another period for income statement purposes.

Theoretical standards Standards that can be achieved only under perfect operating conditions, such as no idle time, no machine breakdowns, and no materials spoilage; also called *ideal standards*.

Theory of constraints (TOC) A manufacturing strategy that attempts to remove the influence of bottlenecks (constraints) on a process.

Time tickets The form on which the amount of time spent by each employee and the labor costs incurred for each individual job, or for factory overhead, are recorded.

Time value of money concept The concept that an amount of money invested today will earn interest.

Total cost concept A concept used in applying the cost-plus approach to product pricing in which all the costs of manufacturing the product plus the selling and administrative expenses are included in the cost amount to which the markup is added.

Total manufacturing cost variance The difference between the total actual cost and the total standard cost for the units produced.

Trademark A name, term, or symbol used to identify a business and its products.

Transaction An economic event that under generally accepted accounting principles (GAAP), affects an element of the accounting equation and must be recorded.

Transfer price The price charged one decentralized unit by another for the goods or services provided.

Treasury stock Stock that a corporation has once issued and then reacquired.

U

Underapplied factory overhead The actual factory overhead costs incurred in excess of the amount of factory overhead applied for production during a period.

Unearned revenues Items that are initially recorded as liabilities but are expected to become revenues over time or through the normal operations of the business.

Unfavorable cost variance Actual cost exceeds standard cost.

Unit contribution margin The dollars available from each unit of sales to cover fixed costs and provide income from operations.

Unit of measure concept An accounting concept requiring that economic data be recorded in dollars.

V

Value-added lead time The time required to manufacture a unit of product or other output.

Variable cost concept Often referred to as *variable costing*, a method of reporting variable and fixed costs that includes only the variable manufacturing costs in the cost of the product.

Variable costing A method of reporting variable and fixed costs that includes only the variable manufacturing costs in the cost of the product.

Variable costs Costs that vary in total dollar amount as the level of activity changes.

Vertical analysis An analysis that compares each item in a current statement with a total amount within the same statement.

Volume variance The difference between the budgeted fixed overhead at 100% of normal capacity and the standard fixed overhead for the actual units produced.

Voucher Any document that serves as proof of authority to pay cash.

Voucher system A set of procedures for authorizing and recording liabilities and cash payments.

W

Working capital The excess of the current assets of a business over its current liabilities.

Work-in-process (WIP) inventory The direct materials costs, the direct labor costs, and the factory overhead costs that have entered into the manufacturing process but are associated with products that have not been finished.

Z

Zero-based budgeting A concept of budgeting that requires all levels of management to start from zero and estimate budget data as if there had been no previous activities in their units.

SUBJECT INDEX

COMPANY INDEX

699